AUTOMOTIVE ENGINES
Theory and Servicing

Third Edition

AUTOMOTIVE ENGINES
Theory and Servicing

Third Edition

James D. Halderman
Professor
Sinclair Community College

Herbert E. Ellinger
Professor Emeritus
Western Michigan University

Prentice Hall
Upper Saddle River, New Jersey   Columbus, Ohio

Library of Congress Cataloging-in-Publication Data

Halderman, James D.
    Automotive engines : theory and servicing / James D. Halderman,
  Herbert E. Ellinger.— 3rd ed.
        p.   cm.
    Includes bibliographical references and index.
    ISBN 0-13-505686-1
    1. Automobiles—Motors.   2. Automobiles—Motors—Maintenance and
repair.   I. Ellinger, Herbert E.   II. Title.
TL210.H29   1996
629.25—dc20   96-23414
                                                       CIP

Editor: Ed Francis
Production Supervision: Carlisle Publishers Services
Design Coordinator: Jill E. Bonar
Production Manager: Patricia A. Tonneman
Marketing Manager: Danny Hoyt

This book was set in Palatino by Carlisle Communications, Ltd., and was printed and bound by Courier/Kendallville, Inc. The cover was printed by Phoenix Color Corp.

 © 1997,1991,1981,1974 by Prentice-Hall, Inc.
Simon & Schuster/A Viacom Company
Upper Saddle River, New Jersey 07458

Printed in the United States of America

10   9   8   7   6   5   4   3   2

ISBN: 0-13-505686-1

Prentice-Hall International (UK) Limited, *London*
Prentice-Hall of Australia Pty. Limited, *Sydney*
Prentice-Hall of Canada, Inc., *Toronto*
Prentice-Hall Hispanoamericana, S. A., *Mexico*
Prentice-Hall of India Private Limited, *New Delhi*
Prentice-Hall of Japan, Inc., *Tokyo*
Simon & Schuster Asia Pte. Ltd., *Singapore*
Editora Prentice-Hall do Brasil, Ltda., *Rio de Janeiro*

Contents

■ 8
Engine Cleaning, Crack Detection, and Repair   127

■ 9
Intake and Exhaust Manifolds   138

■ 10
Cylinder Head and Guide Service   157

■ 11

Valve and Seat Service   180

■ 12

Camshaft and Valve Train Problem Diagnosis and Service   215

■ 13
Engine Block Design and Service   249

■ 14
Pistons, Rings, and Connecting Rods   270

■ 15
Crankshafts and Bearings   302

■ 18
Engine Installation and Break-In 378

Preface

This third edition of *Automotive Engines: Theory and Servicing* is designed for students or technicians wishing to know about engine rebuilding, as well as engine theory and in-the-vehicle servicing. This textbook can also be used in a general automotive course with an emphasis on engines. All areas are logically arranged with technical material presented first, then problem diagnosis, troubleshooting, and service procedures in the same chapter. This makes learning easier because theory and servicing are linked closely together.

The third edition has been updated to include more information on the all-aluminum V-8, V-6, and four-cylinder engines. Complete problem diagnosis, operation, and engine machining information is included for the technician wishing to take the Automotive Service Excellence (ASE) tests (issued by the National Institute of Automotive Service Excellence) for

- Engine repair technicians
- Engine performance technicians
- Cylinder head machinists
- Cylinder block machinists
- Engine assembly specialists

Tech tips and diagnostic stories are included throughout to help the technician with troubleshooting and with fixing it right the first time. Excellent illustrations bring the subject to life and make learning the technical material easier. Detailed captions provide greater understanding of the illustrations.

At the request of instructors from throughout the United States and Canada, other new features of the third edition include the following:

- Objectives at the beginning of each chapter
- Summary at the end of each chapter
- Both review (discussion) and multiple-choice questions at the end of each chapter
- Sample ASE certification-type test questions for engine repair technicians and engine machinists in the appendixes

The chapter layout has been streamlined to make learning easier and quicker. For example, all information on engine blocks or cylinder heads is grouped together.

Acknowledgments

A great number of individuals and organizations have cooperated in providing reference material and illustrations used in this text. The authors wish to express sincere thanks to the following organizations for their special contributions:

Auto Parts Distributors
Automotion, Inc.
Automotive Engine Rebuilders Association
B-H-J Products, Inc.
Camwerks Corporation
Castrol Incorporation
Champion Spark Plug Company
Chrysler Corporation
Clayton Manufacturing Company
Curtiss Wright Corporation
Dana Corporation
Defiance Engine Rebuilders Incorporated
Dow Chemical Company
Fel-Pro Incorporated
Ford Motor Company
General Motors Corporation:
  AC Delco Division
  Buick Motor Division
  Cadillac Motor Car Division
  Central Foundry Division
  Chevrolet Motor Division
  Oldsmobile Division

George Olcott Company
Goodson Auto Machine Shop Tools and Supplies
Greenlee Brothers and Company
Jasper Engines and Transmission
K-Line
Modine Manufacturing Company
Neway
Parsons and Meyers Racing Engines
Prestolite Company
Rottler Manufacturing
Sealed Power Corporation
Society of Automotive Engineers
Sunnen Products Company
TRW, Michigan Division

We also wish to thank the faculty, staff, and students at Sinclair Community College in Dayton, Ohio, for their comments and suggestions.

Most of all, we wish to thank Michelle Halderman for her assistance in all phases of manuscript preparation.

James D. Halderman
Herbert E. Ellinger

Tools, Fasteners, and Safety

1

OBJECTIVES

After studying Chapter 1, the reader will be able to

1. Explain the strength ratings of threaded fasteners.
2. Identify hazardous materials.
3. Describe how to safely hoist a vehicle.
4. Discuss how to safely use hand tools.

THREADED FASTENERS

Most of the threaded fasteners used on engines are cap screws. They are called **cap screws** when they are threaded into a casting. Automotive service technicians usually refer to these fasteners as bolts, regardless of how they are used. In this chapter, they are called bolts. Sometimes, studs are used for threaded fasteners. A **stud** is a short rod with threads on both ends. Often, a stud will have coarse threads on one end and fine threads on the other end. The end of the stud with coarse threads is screwed into the casting. A nut is used on the opposite end to hold the parts together. See Figure 1–1.

The fastener threads *must* match the threads in the casting or nut. The threads may be either measured in fractions of an inch (called fractional) or metric. The size is measured across the outside of the threads. This is called the **crest** of the thread.

Fractional threads are either coarse or fine. The coarse threads are called Unified National Coarse (UNC), and the fine threads are called Unified National Fine (UNF). Standard combinations of size of bolt and number of threads per inch (called **pitch**) are used.

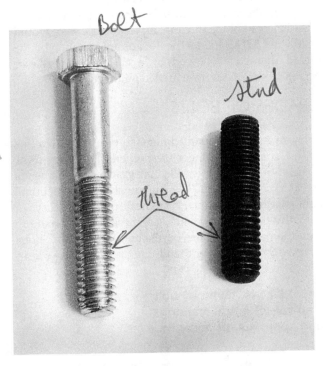

FIGURE 1–1 Typical bolt on the left and stud on the right. Note the different thread pitch on the top and bottom portions of the stud.

Pitch can be measured with a thread pitch gauge as shown in Figure 1–2. Bolts are identified by their diameter and length as measured from below the head as shown in Figure 1–3.

Fractional thread sizes are specified by the diameter in fractions of an inch and the number of threads per inch. Typical UNC thread sizes would be 5/16-18 and 1/2-13. Similar UNF thread sizes would be 5/16-24 and 1/2-20.

1

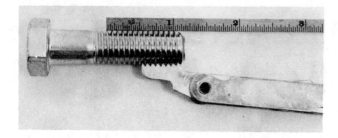

FIGURE 1–2 Thread pitch gauge used to measure the pitch of the thread. This is a ½-inch-diameter bolt with thirteen threads to the inch (½-13).

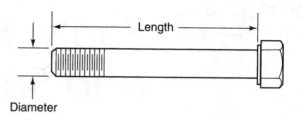

FIGURE 1–3 Bolt size identification.

METRIC BOLTS

The size of a metric bolt is specified by the letter *M* followed by the diameter in millimeters (mm) across the outside (crest) of the threads. Typical metric sizes would be M8 and M12. Fine metric threads are specified by the thread diameter followed by a × and the distance between the threads measured in millimeters (M8 × 1.5).

GRADES OF BOLTS

Bolts are made from many different types of steel. For this reason, some are stronger than others. The strength or classification of a bolt is called the **grade.** The bolt heads are marked to indicate their grade strength. Fractional bolts have lines on the head to indicate the grade as shown in Figure 1–4. The actual grade of these bolts is two more than the number of lines on the bolt head. Metric bolts have a decimal number to indicate the grade. More lines

or a higher grade number indicate a stronger bolt. In some cases, nuts and machine screws have similar grade markings. See Figure 1–4 for typical grade markings.

■ **CAUTION:** *Never* use hardware store (non-graded) bolts, studs or nuts on any vehicle steering, suspension or brake component. Always use the exact size and grade of hardware that is specified and used by the vehicle manufacturer. ■

NUTS

Most nuts used on cap screws have the same hex size as the cap screw head. Some inexpensive nuts use a hex size larger than the cap screw head. Metric nuts are often marked with dimples to show their strength. More dimples indicate stronger nuts. Some nuts and cap screws use interference fit threads to keep them from accidentally loosening. This means that the shape of the nut is slightly distorted or that a section of the threads is deformed. Nuts can also be kept from loosening with a nylon washer fastened in the nut, or with a nylon patch or strip on the threads. See Figure 1–5.

FIGURE 1–4 Typical bolt (cap screw) grade markings and approximate strength.

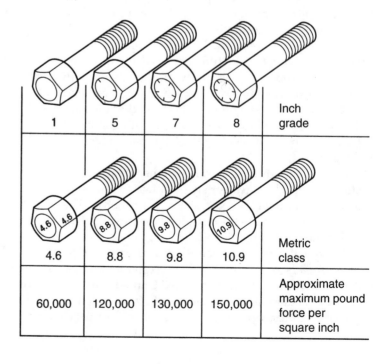

■ TECH TIP ■

A ½-INCH WRENCH DOES NOT FIT A ½-INCH BOLT

A common mistake made by persons new to the automotive field is to think that the size of a bolt or nut is the size of the head. The size of the bolt or nut (outside diameter of threads) is usually smaller than the size of the wrench or socket that fits the head of the bolt or nut. Examples are given in the following table:

Wrench size	Thread size
$\frac{7}{16}$ in	¼ in
½ in	$\frac{5}{16}$ in
$\frac{9}{16}$ in	⅜ in
⅝ in	$\frac{7}{16}$ in
¾ in	½ in
10 mm	6 mm
12 mm or 13 mm*	8 mm
14 mm or 17 mm*	10 mm

* European (Système international d'unités—SI) metric.

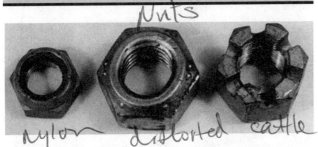

FIGURE 1–5 Types of lock nuts. On the left, a nylon ring; in the center, a distorted shape; and on the right, a castle for use with a cotter key.

NOTE: Most of these "locking nuts" are grouped together and are commonly referred to as **prevailing torque nuts**. This means that the nut will hold its tightness or torque and not loosen with movement or vibration. Most prevailing torque nuts should be replaced whenever removed to ensure that the nut will not loosen during service. Always follow manufacturers' recommendations. Anaerobic sealers, such as Loctite, are used on the threads where the nut or cap screw must be both locked and sealed.

WASHERS

Washers are often used under cap screw heads and under nuts. Plain flat washers are used to provide an even clamping load around the fastener. Lock washers are added to prevent accidental loosening. In some accessories, the washers are locked onto the nut to provide easy assembly.

BASIC TOOL LIST

Hand tools are used to turn fasteners (bolts, nuts, and screws). The following is a list of hand tools every automotive technician should possess. Specialty tools are not included. See Figures 1–6 through 1–41.

tool chest
¼-inch drive socket set
¼-inch drive ratchet
¼-inch drive 2-inch extension
¼-inch drive 6-inch extension
¼-inch drive handle
⅜-inch drive socket set
⅜-inch drive Torx set
⅜-inch drive $\frac{13}{16}$-inch plug socket
⅜-inch drive ⅝-inch plug socket
⅜-inch drive ratchet
⅜-inch drive 1½-inch extension
⅜-inch drive 3-inch extension
⅜-inch drive 6-inch extension
⅜-inch drive 18-inch extension
⅜-inch drive universal joint
½-inch drive socket set
½-inch drive ratchet
½-inch drive breaker bar
½-inch drive 5-inch extension
½-inch drive 10-inch extension
⅜-inch to ¼-inch adapter
½-inch to ⅜-inch adapter
⅜-inch to ½-inch adapter
⅜-inch through 1-inch combination wrench set
10 millimeters through 19 millimeters combination wrench set
$\frac{1}{16}$-inch through ¼-inch hex wrench set
2 millimeters through 12 millimeters hex wrench set
⅜-inch hex socket
13 millimeters-14 millimeters flare nut wrench
15 millimeters-17 millimeters flare nut wrench
$\frac{5}{16}$-inch-⅜-inch flare nut wrench
$\frac{7}{16}$-inch-½-inch flare nut wrench
½-inch-$\frac{9}{16}$-inch flare nut wrench
Diagonal pliers
Needle pliers
Adjustable-jaw pliers
Locking pliers
Snap-ring pliers
Stripping or crimping pliers
Ball-peen hammer
Rubber hammer
Dead-blow hammer

Five-piece standard screwdriver set
Four-piece Phillips screwdriver set
#15 Torx screwdriver
#20 Torx screwdriver
Crowfoot set (fractional inch)
Crowfoot set (metric)
Awl
Mill file
Center punch
Pin punches (assorted sizes)
Chisel
Utility knife

Valve core tool
Coolant tester
Filter wrench (large filters)
Filter wrench (smaller filters)
Safety glasses
Circuit tester
Feeler gauge
Scraper
Pinch bar
Sticker knife
Magnet

FIGURE 1–6 Combination wrench. The openings are the same size at both ends. Notice the angle of the open end to permit use in close spaces.

FIGURE 1–7 Three different qualities of open-end wrenches. The cheap wrench on the left is made from weaker steel and is thicker and less accurately machined than the standard in the center. The wrench on the right is of professional quality (and price).

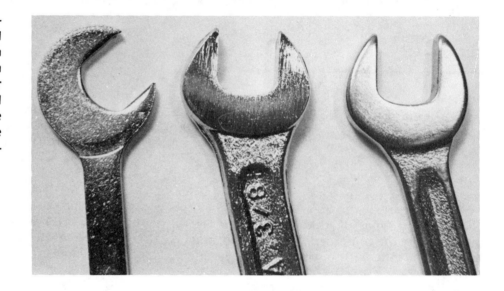

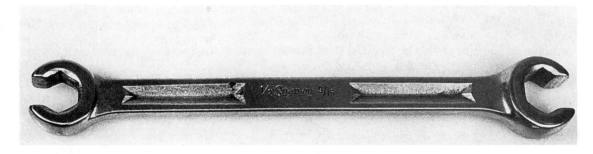

FIGURE 1–8 Flare-nut wrench. Also known as a line wrench, fitting wrench, or tube-nut wrench. This style of wrench is designed to grasp most of the flats of a six-sided (hex) tubing fitting to provide the most grip without damage to the fitting.

FIGURE 1–9 Box-end wrench. Recommended to loosen or tighten a bolt or nut where a socket will not fit. A box-end wrench has a different size at each end and is better to use than an open-end wrench because it touches the bolt or nut around the entire head instead of at just two places.

FIGURE 1–10 Open-end wrench. Each end has a different-sized opening and is recommended for general usage. Do not attempt to loosen or tighten bolts or nuts from or to full torque with an open-end wrench because it could round the flats of the fastener.

FIGURE 1–11 Adjustable wrench. The size (12 inches) is the length of the wrench, not how far the jaws open!

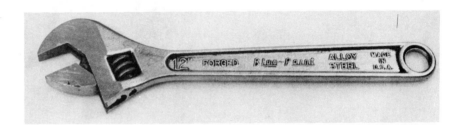

FIGURE 1–12 A flat-blade (or straight-blade) screwdriver (on the left) is specified by the length of the screwdriver and width of the blade. The width of the blade should match the width of the screw slot of the fastener. A Phillips-head screwdriver (in the middle) is specified by the length of the handle and the size of the point at the tip. A #1 is a sharp point, #2 is most common (as shown), and a #3 Phillips is blunt and is only used for larger sizes of Phillips-head fasteners. A clutch-head screwdriver is on the right.

FIGURE 1-13 A properly ground flat screwdriver blade (top) and a blade improperly ground to a chisel point (bottom).

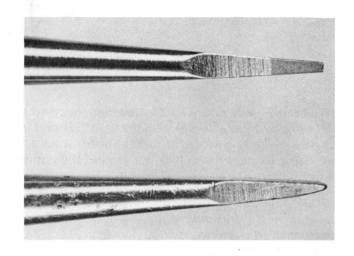

FIGURE 1-14 Assortment of pliers. Slip-joint pliers (far left) are often confused with water pump pliers (second from left).

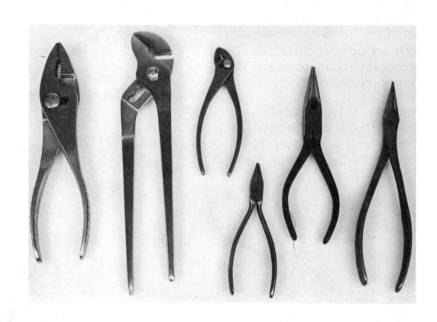

FIGURE 1-15 A ball-peen hammer (top) is purchased according to weight (usually in ounces) of the head of the hammer. At bottom is a soft-faced (plastic) hammer. Always use a hammer that is softer than the material being driven. Use a block of wood or similar material between a steel hammer and steel or iron engine parts to prevent damage to the engine parts.

6

FIGURE 1–16 Typical drive handles for sockets.

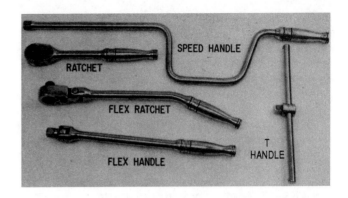

FIGURE 1–17 Various socket extensions. The universal joint (U-joint) in the center (bottom) is useful for gaining access in tight areas.

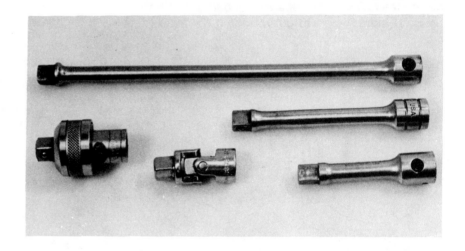

FIGURE 1–18 Socket drive adapters. These adapters permit the use of a ⅜-inch drive ratchet with ½-inch drive sockets, or other combinations as the various adapters permit. Adapters should not be used where a larger tool used with excessive force could break or damage a smaller-sized socket.

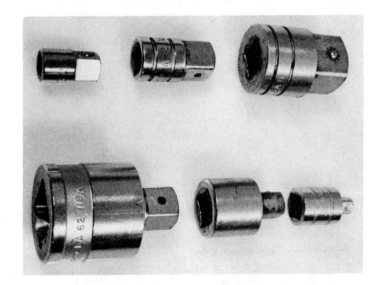

FIGURE 1–19 Twelve-point, six-point, and eight-point sockets. Six-point sockets are recommended because they contact all six sides of a typical bolt or nut and can exert more force without rounding the head.

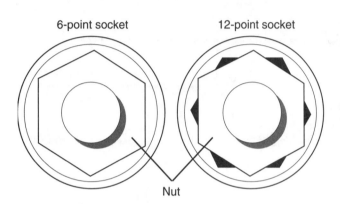

6-point socket   12-point socket

Nut

FIGURE 1–20 A six-point socket fits the head of the bolt or nut on all sides. A twelve-point socket can round off the head of a bolt or nut if a lot of force is applied.

FIGURE 1–21 Standard twelve-point short socket (left), universal-joint socket (center), and deep-well socket (right). Both the universal and deep well are six-point sockets.

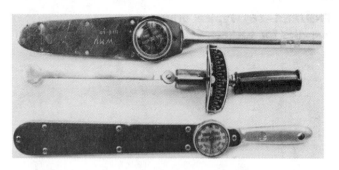

FIGURE 1–22 Typical torque wrenches. All of these give bolt-tightening torque in foot-pound units.

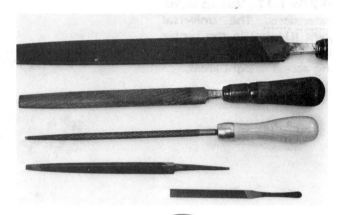

FIGURE 1–23 Typical files.

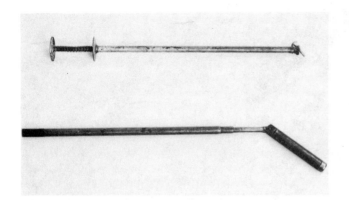

FIGURE 1–24 Mechanical pickup finger (top) and extendable magnet (bottom) are excellent tools to have when a nut drops down into a small area where fingers can never reach.

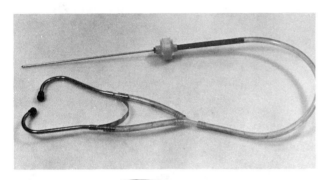

FIGURE 1–25 Stethoscope used by technicians to listen for the exact location of the problem noise.

FIGURE 1–26 Bench grinder. Note that proper eye shields, (though lacking here) should be provided over the stone and wire wheel, even though the technician should always wear safety glasses when using this or any other power equipment.

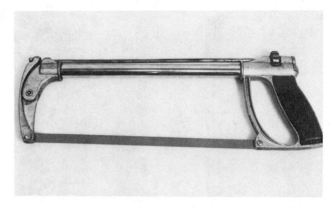

FIGURE 1–27 Hacksaw. The teeth of the blade should point away from the handle. The thinner the material being cut, the finer the blade teeth.

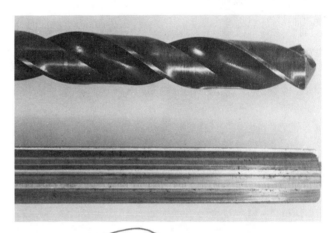

FIGURE 1–28 Drill bit (top) with twisted flutes (grooves) and a reamer (bottom) with straight flutes.

FIGURE 1–29 Cutting edge of a drill bit.

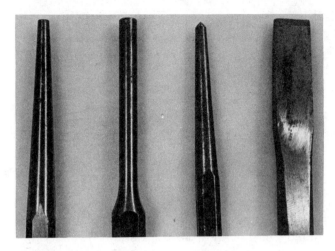

FIGURE 1–30 Various punches on the left and a **chisel** on the right.

FIGURE 1–32 A standard and a bottoming tap. These taps are commonly used to "chase" or clean existing threads in blocks.

FIGURE 1–31 Using a die to cut threads on a rod.

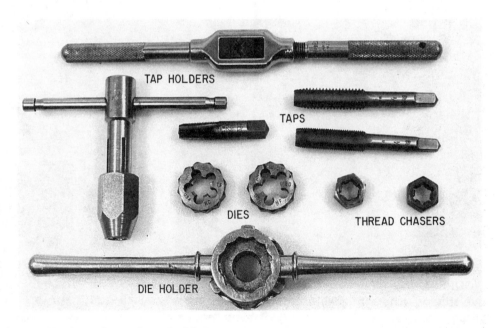

TAP HOLDERS

TAPS

DIES

THREAD CHASERS

DIE HOLDER

FIGURE 1–33 Dies are used to make threads on the outside of round stock. Taps are used to make threads inside holes.

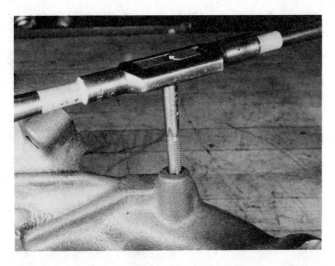

FIGURE 1-34 Starting a tap in a drilled hole. The hole diameter should be matched exactly to the tap size for proper thread clearance. The proper drill size to use is called the <u>tap drill size</u>.

FIGURE 1-35 A group of thickness gauges (also known as feeler gauges), used to measure between two parts. The long gauges on the bottom are used to measure the piston-to-cylinder wall clearance.

FIGURE 1-36 Typical micrometers used for dimensional inspection.

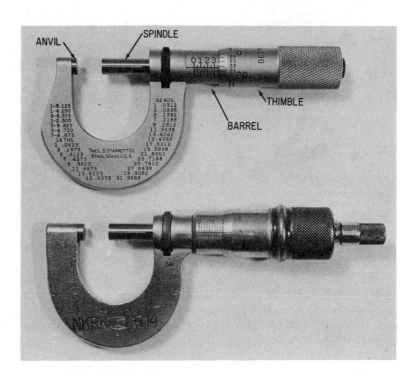

11

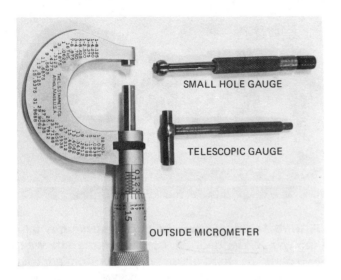

FIGURE 1-37 Small hole and telescopic gauges used with an outside micrometer to measure the inside diameter of a hole.

FIGURE 1-39 The outside of a hole gauge being measured with a micrometer.

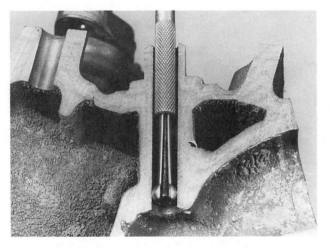

FIGURE 1-38 Cutaway of a valve guide with a hole gauge adjusted to the hole diameter.

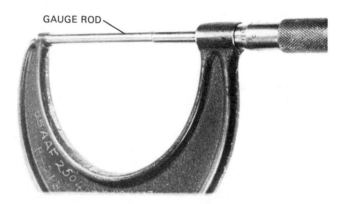

FIGURE 1-40 All micrometers should be checked and calibrated as needed using a gauge rod.

FIGURE 1-41 The dial gauge (or dial indicator) (top) and vernier caliper (bottom) are two other precision measuring instruments.

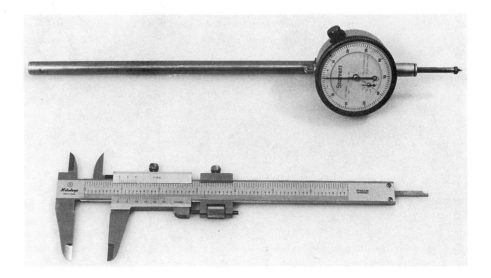

■ **TECH TIP** ■

THE VALVE GRINDING COMPOUND TRICK

Apply a small amount of valve grinding compound to a Phillips or Torx screw or bolt head. The gritty valve grinding compound "grips" the screwdriver or tool bit and prevents the tool from slipping up and out of the screw head. Valve grinding compound is available in a tube from most automotive parts stores.

BRAND NAME VERSUS PROPER TERM

Technicians often use slang or brand names of tools rather than the proper term. This results in some confusion for new technicians. Some examples are given in the following table.

Brand name	Proper term	Slang name
Crescent wrench	Adjustable wrench	Monkey wrench
Vise Grips	Locking pliers	—
Channel Locks	Water pump pliers, multigroove adjustable pliers	Pump pliers
—	Diagonal cutting pliers	Dikes or side cuts

SAFETY TIPS FOR USING HAND TOOLS

The following safety tips should be kept in mind whenever you are working with hand tools:

- Always *pull* a wrench toward you for best control and safety. Never push a wrench.
- Keep wrenches and all hand tools clean to help prevent rust and for a better, firmer grip.
- Always use a six-point socket or a box-end wrench to break loose a tight bolt or nut.
- Use a box-end wrench for torque and the open-end wrench for speed.
- Never use a pipe extension or other types of "cheater bars" on a wrench or ratchet handle. If more force is required, use a larger tool or use penetrating oil and/or heat on the frozen fastener. (If heat is used on a bolt or nut to remove it, always replace it with a new part.)
- Always use the proper tool for the job. If a specialized tool is required, use the proper tool and do not try to use another tool improperly.

■ **TECH TIP** ■

IT JUST TAKES A SECOND

Whenever removing any automotive component, it is wise to put the bolts back into the holes a couple of threads with your hand. This ensures that the right bolt will be used in its original location when the component or part is put back on the vehicle. Often the same diameter of fastener is used on a component, but the length of the bolt may vary. Spending just a couple of seconds to put the bolts and nuts back where they belong when the part is removed can save a lot of time when the part is being re-installed. Besides making certain that the right fastener is being installed in the right place, this method helps prevent bolts and nuts from being lost or kicked away. How much time have you wasted looking for that lost bolt or nut?

- Never expose any tool to excessive heat. High temperatures can reduce the strength ("draw the temper") of metal tools.
- Never use a hammer on any wrench or socket handle unless you are using a special "staking face" wrench designed to be used with a hammer.
- Replace any tools that are damaged or worn.

SAFETY TIPS FOR TECHNICIANS

Safety is not just a buzzword on a poster in the work area. Safe work habits can reduce accidents and injuries, ease the workload, and keep employees pain free. Suggested safety tips include the following:

- *Wear safety glasses at all times while servicing any vehicle.*
- Watch your toes—always keep your toes protected with steel-toed safety shoes. If safety shoes are not available, then leather-topped shoes offer more protection than canvas or cloth.
- Wear gloves to protect your hands from rough or sharp surfaces. Thin rubber gloves are recommended to be worn when working around automotive liquids such as engine oil, antifreeze, transmission fluid, or any other liquids that may be hazardous.
- Service technicians working under a vehicle should wear a **bump cap** to protect their head against under-vehicle objects and the pads of the lift.

- Remove jewelry that may get caught on something or act as a conductor to an exposed electrical circuit.
- Avoid loose or dangling clothing.
- When lifting any object, get a secure grip with solid footing. Keep the load close to your body to minimize the strain. Lift with your legs and arms, not your back.
- Do not twist your body when carrying a load. Instead, pivot your feet to help prevent strain on the spine.
- Ask for help when moving or lifting heavy objects.
- Push a heavy object rather than pulling it. (This is opposite to the way you should work with tools— never push a wrench! If you do and a bolt or nut loosens, your entire weight is used to propel your hand(s) forward. This usually results in cuts, bruises, or other painful injury.)
- When standing, keep objects, parts, and tools with which you are working between chest height and waist height. If seated, work at tasks that are at elbow height.

SAFETY IN LIFTING (HOISTING) A VEHICLE

Many chassis and underbody service procedures require that the vehicle be hoisted or lifted off the ground. The simplest methods involve the use of drive-on ramps or a floor jack and safety (jack) stands, whereas in-ground or surface-mounted lifts provide greater access.

Setting the pads is a critical part of this procedure. All automobile and light-truck service manuals include recommended locations to be used when hoisting (lifting) a vehicle. Newer vehicles have a triangle decal on the driver's door indicating the recommended lift points. The recommended standards for the lift points and lifting procedures are found in SAE Standard JRP-2184. These locations typically include the following:

1. The vehicle should be centered on the lift or hoist so as not to overload one side or put too much force either forward or rearward.
2. The pads of the lift should be spread as far apart as possible to provide a stable platform.
3. Each pad should be placed under a portion of the vehicle that is strong and capable of supporting the weight of the vehicle.
   a. Pinch welds at the bottom edge of the body are generally considered to be strong.

■ **CAUTION:** Even though pinch weld seams are the recommended location for hoisting many vehicles with unitized bodies (unit body), care should be taken not to place the pad(s) too far forward or rearward. Incorrect placement of the vehicle on the lift could cause the imbalance of the vehicle on the lift, and the vehicle could fall. This is exactly what happened to the vehicle in Figure 1–42. ■

   b. Boxed areas of the body are the best places to position the pads on a vehicle without a frame. Be careful to note whether the arms of the lift might come into contact with other parts of the vehicle before the pad touches the intended location. Commonly damaged areas include the following:
      i.   Rocker panel moldings
      ii. Exhaust system (including catalytic converter)
      iii. Tires, especially if the edges of the pads or arms are sharp

4. The vehicle should be raised about a foot (30 centimeters [cm]) off the floor, then stopped. The vehicle should be shaken to check for stability. If the vehicle seems to be stable when checked at a short distance from the floor, continue raising the vehicle and continue to view the vehicle until it has reached the desired height.

■ **CAUTION:** Do not look away from the vehicle while it is being raised (or lowered) on a hoist. Often one side or one end of the hoist can stop or fail, resulting in the vehicle being slanted enough to slip or fall, not only creating physical damage to the vehicle and/or hoist, but also to the technician or others that may be near. ■

HINT: *Most hoists can be safely placed at any desired height. For ease while working, the area on which you are working should be at chest level. When working on brakes or suspension components, it is not necessary to work on them down near the floor or over your head; raise the hoist so that the components are at chest level.*

5. Before lowering the hoist, the safety latch(es) must be released and the direction of the controls reversed to lower the hoist. The speed downward is often adjusted to be as slow as possible for additional safety.

FIGURE 1–42 This vehicle fell from the lift because the pads were not set correctly. A technician had just removed the left front strut assembly when the vehicle fell. No one was hurt, but the vehicle was a total loss.

HAZARDOUS MATERIALS

The Environmental Protection Agency (EPA) regulates the handling of hazardous materials in the United States. A material is considered hazardous if it meets one or more of the following conditions:

■ It contains over 1000 parts per million (PPM) of halogenated compounds (halogenated compounds are chemicals containing chlorine, fluorine, bromine, or iodine). Common items that contain these solvents include the following:
Carburetor cleaner
Silicone spray
Aerosols
Adhesives
Stoddard solvent
Trichloromethane
Gear oils
Brake cleaner
Air-conditioning (A/C) compressor oils
Floor cleaners
Anything else that contains a *chlor* or *fluor* in its ingredient name
■ It has a flash point below 140° F (60° C).
■ It is corrosive (has a pH level of 2 or lower or 12.5 or higher).
■ It contains toxic metals or organic compounds. Volatile organic compounds (VOCs) must also be limited and controlled. This classification greatly affects the painting and finishing aspects of the automobile industry.

Always follow recommended procedures for handling of any chemicals and dispose of all used engine oil and other waste products according to local, provincial, state, or federal laws.

To help safeguard workers and the environment, the following guidelines are recommended:

- A technician's hands should always be washed thoroughly after touching used engine oils, transmission fluids, and greases. Dispose of all waste oil according to established standards and laws in your area.

    NOTE: The Environmental Protection Agency current standard permits used engine oil to be recycled only if it contains less than 1000 parts per million of total halogens (chlorinated solvents). Oil containing greater amounts of halogens must be considered **hazardous waste.** See Figure 1–43.

- Asbestos and products that contain asbestos are known cancer-causing agents. Even though most brake linings and clutch facing materials are now being manufactured without asbestos, millions of vehicles are being serviced every day that *may* contain asbestos. The general procedure for handling asbestos is to put the used parts into a sealed plastic bag and

FIGURE 1–43 Waste products such as used engine oil, transmission oil, and antifreeze should be kept separated and disposed of or recycled according to established standards and laws.

EYE WASH

FIGURE 1–44   The eyewash station should be centrally located in the shop and next to the parts-cleaning stations, where solvents may be splashed.

return the parts as cores for rebuilding or dispose of them according to current laws and regulations.

■ Eyewash stations should be readily accessible near the work area or near where solvents or other contaminants could get into the eyes. See Figure 1–44.

MATERIAL SAFETY DATA SHEETS

Businesses and schools in the United States are required to provide a detailed data sheet on each of the chemicals or materials to which a person may be exposed in the area. These sheets of information on each of the materials that *may* be harmful are called **material safety data sheets (MSDs).**

■ **TECH TIP** ■

HIDE THOSE FROM THE BOSS

An apprentice technician started working for a dealership and put his top tool box on a workbench. Another technician observed that along with a complete set of good-quality tools, the box contained several adjustable wrenches. The more experienced technician said, "Hide those from the boss." If any adjustable wrench is used on a bolt or nut, the movable jaw often moves or loosens and starts to round the head of the fastener. If the head of the bolt or nut becomes rounded, it becomes that much more difficult to remove.

■ **TECH TIP** ■

POUND WITH SOMETHING SOFTER

If you *must* pound on something, be sure to use a tool that is softer than what you are about to pound on to avoid damage. Examples are given in the following table.

The material being pounded	What to pound with
Steel or cast iron	Brass or aluminum hammer or punch
Aluminum	Plastic or rawhide mallet or plastic-covered dead-blow hammer
Plastic	Rawhide mallet or plastic dead-blow hammer

If in doubt, always use a block of wood between the hammer and the component to help protect the part from damge.

SUMMARY

1. Bolts, studs, and nuts are commonly used as fasteners in the chassis. The sizes for fractional and metric threads are different and are not interchangeable. The grade is the rating of the strength of a fastener.
2. Whenever a vehicle is raised above the ground, it must be supported at a substantial section of the body or frame.
3. Hazardous materials include common automotive chemicals, liquids, and lubricants, especially those whose ingredients contain *chlor* or *fluor* in their name. Asbestos fibers should be avoided and removed according to current laws and regulations.

REVIEW QUESTIONS

1. List three precautions that must be taken whenever hoisting (lifting) a vehicle.
2. List five common automotive chemicals or products that may be considered hazardous materials.
3. List five precautions to which every technician should adhere when working with automotive products and chemicals.
4. Describe how to determine the grade of a fastener, including how the markings differ between customary and metric bolts.

MULTIPLE-CHOICE QUESTIONS

1. Two technicians are discussing the hoisting of a vehicle. Technician A says to put the pads of a lift under a notch at the pinch weld of a unit-body vehicle. Technician B says to place the pads on four corners of the frame of a full-frame vehicle. Which technician is correct?
   a. A only
   b. B only
   c. Both A and B
   d. Neither A nor B
2. The correct location for the pads when hoisting or jacking the vehicle can often be found in the _____ .
   a. Service manual
   b. Shop manual
   c. Owner's manual
   d. All of the above
3. Hazardous materials include all of the following *except* _____ .
   a. Engine oil
   b. Asbestos
   c. Water
   d. Brake cleaner

4. To determine if a product or substance being used is hazardous, consult _____ .
   a. A dictionary
   b. An MSDS
   c. SAE standards
   d. EPA guidelines

5. For the best working position, the work should be _____ .
   a. At neck or head level
   b. At knee or ankle level
   c. Overhead by about 1 foot
   d. At chest or elbow level

6. When working with hand tools, always _____ .
   a. Push the wrench—don't pull toward you
   b. Pull a wrench—don't push a wrench

7. A high-strength bolt is identified by _____ .
   a. A UNC symbol
   b. Lines on the head
   c. Strength letter codes
   d. The coarse threads

8. A fastener that uses threads on both ends is called a _____ .
   a. Cap screw
   b. Stud
   c. Machine screw
   d. Crest fastener

9. The proper term for Channel Locks is _____ .
   a. Vise Grips
   b. Crescent wrench
   c. Locking pliers
   d. Multigroove adjustable pliers

10. The proper term for Vise Grips is _____ .
    a. Locking pliers
    b. Slip-joint pliers
    c. Side cuts
    d. Multigroove adjustable pliers

2

Automobile Engine Operation and Specifications

OBJECTIVES

After studying Chapter 2, the reader will be able to

1. Explain how a four stroke–cycle gasoline engine operates.
2. List the various characteristics by which vehicle engines are classified.
3. Describe how engine power is measured and calculated.
4. Discuss how a compression ratio is calculated.
5. Explain how engine size is determined.

The engine converts part of the fuel energy to useful power. This power is used to move the vehicle.

ENERGY AND POWER

Energy is used to produce power. Chemical energy in fuel is converted to heat by the burning of the fuel at a controlled rate. This process is called combustion. If engine combustion occurs within the power chamber, the engine is called an **internal combustion engine.**

NOTE: An **external combustion engine** is an engine that burns fuel outside of the engine itself, such as a steam engine.

Engines used in automobiles are internal combustion heat engines. They convert the chemical energy of the gasoline into heat within a power chamber that is called a **combustion chamber.** Heat energy released in the combustion chamber raises the temperature of the combustion gases within the chamber. The increase in gas temperature causes the pressure of the gases to increase. The pressure developed within the combustion chamber is applied to the head of a piston or to a turbine wheel to produce a usable **mechanical force.** This force is converted into useful **mechanical power.**

FOUR STROKE–CYCLE OPERATION

Most automotive engines use the four-stroke cycle of events. The starter motor rotates the engine. The four-stroke cycle is repeated for each cylinder of the engine. See Figure 2–1.

- **Intake stroke**—The piston inside the cylinder travels *downward*, drawing a mixture of air-fuel into the cylinder through the open intake valve.
- **Compression stroke**—As the engine continues to rotate, the piston is forced *upward* in the cylinder, compressing the air-fuel mixture.
- **Power stroke**—When the piston gets near the top of the cylinder (called **top dead center [TDC]**), the spark at the spark plug ignites the air-fuel mixture. The piston is forced *downward*.
- **Exhaust stroke**—The engine continues to rotate, and the piston again moves *upward* in the cylinder. The exhaust valve opens, and the piston forces the residual burned gases out of the **exhaust valve** and into the exhaust manifold and exhaust system.

This sequence repeats as the engine rotates. To stop the engine, the electricity to the spark plugs is shut off by the ignition switch.

Figure 2–2 shows a cutaway section of a basic automotive engine. A piston that moves up and down, or reciprocates, in a **cylinder** can be seen in this illustration. The piston is attached to a **crankshaft** with a **connecting rod.** This arrangement allows the piston to

FIGURE 2–1 *Typical four-stroke cycle of a spark-ignited gasoline engine.*

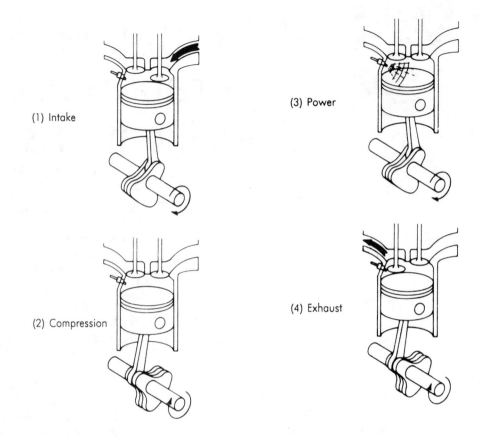

(1) Intake

(2) Compression

(3) Power

(4) Exhaust

reciprocate (move up and down) in the cylinder as the crankshaft rotates. The combustion pressure developed in the combustion chamber at the correct time will push the piston downward to rotate the crankshaft.

THE 720-DEGREE CYCLE

Each cycle of events requires that the engine crankshaft make two complete revolutions, or rotate 720 degrees (360° × 2 = 720°). The greater the number of cylinders, the closer together the power strokes occur. To find the angle between cylinders of an engine, divide the number of cylinders into 720 degrees.

$$\text{Angle with four cylinders} = \frac{720°}{4} = 180°$$

$$\text{Angle with six cylinders} = \frac{720°}{6} = 120°$$

$$\text{Angle with eight cylinders} = \frac{720°}{8} = 90°$$

This means that in a four-cylinder engine, a power stroke occurs at every 180 degrees of the crankshaft rotation (every ½ rotation). A V-8 is a much smoother operating engine because a power stroke occurs twice as often (every 90 degrees of crankshaft rotation).

Engine cycles are identified by the number of piston strokes required to complete the cycle. A **piston stroke** is a one-way piston movement between the top and bottom of the cylinder. During one stroke, the crankshaft revolves 180 degrees (½ revolution). A **cycle** is a complete series of events that continually repeat. Most automobile engines use a **four-stroke cycle**.

ENGINE CLASSIFICATION

Engines are classified by several characteristics, including the following:

■ **Number of strokes.** Most automotive engines use the four-stroke cycle.

■ **Cylinder arrangement.** An engine with more cylinders is smoother operating because the power pulses produced by the power strokes are more closely spaced. An inline engine places all cylinders in a straight line. Four-, five-, and six-cylinder engines are commonly manufactured inline engines. A V-type engine, such as a V-6 or V-8, has the number of cylinders split and built into a V shape. See Figure 2–3.

■ **Longitudinal or transverse mounting.** Engines may be mounted either parallel with the length of the vehicle (longitudinally) or crosswise

FIGURE 2–2 Cutaway of an overhead camshaft inline automotive engine.

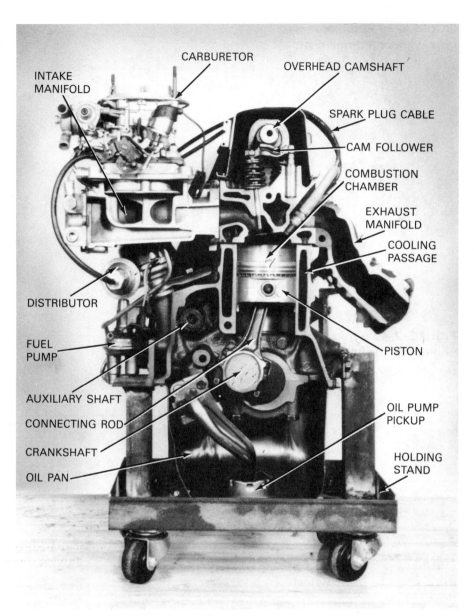

(transversely). See Figures 2–4 through 2–6. The same engine may be mounted in various vehicles in either direction.

NOTE: Although it might be possible to mount an engine in different vehicles, both longitudinally and transversely, the engine component parts may *not* be interchangeable. Differences can include different engine blocks and crankshafts, as well as different coolant pumps. ————————

■ **Valve and camshaft number and location.** The number of valves and the number and location of camshafts are a major factor in engine opera-

tion. A typical older-model engine uses one intake valve and one exhaust valve per cylinder. Many newer engines use two intake and two exhaust valves per cylinder. The valves are opened by a camshaft. For high-speed engine operation, the camshaft should be overhead (over the valves). Some engines use one camshaft for the intake valves and a separate camshaft for the exhaust valves. When the camshaft is located in the block, the valves are operated by lifters, pushrods, and rocker arms. See Figure 2–7. This type of engine is called a **pushrod engine.** An overhead camshaft engine has the camshaft above the valves in the cylinder head. When one

FIGURE 2–3 Automotive engine cylinder arrangements.

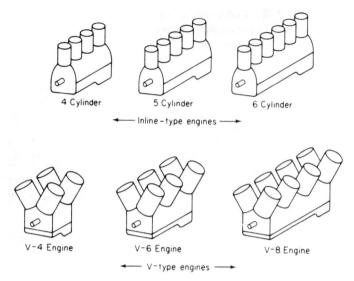

4 Cylinder   5 Cylinder   6 Cylinder

◄—— Inline-type engines ——►

V-4 Engine   V-6 Engine   V-8 Engine

◄—— V-type engines ——►

FIGURE 2–4 Typical front engine, rear wheel–drive.

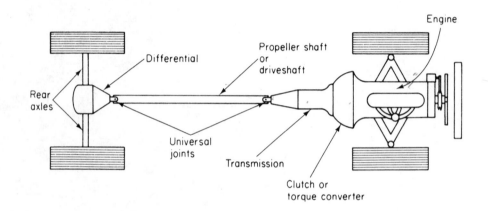

Engine

Propeller shaft
or
driveshaft

Differential

Rear
axles

Universal
joints

Transmission

Clutch or
torque converter

FIGURE 2–5 Two types of front engine, front wheel–drive.

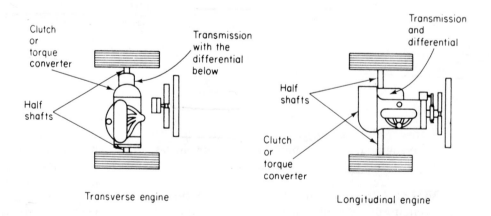

Clutch
or
torque
converter

Transmission
with the
differential
below

Half
shafts

Transverse engine

Transmission
and
differential

Half
shafts

Clutch
or
torque
converter

Longitudinal engine

overhead camshaft is used, it is called a **single overhead camshaft (SOHC)** design. See Figures 2–8 and 2–9. When two overhead camshafts are used, it is called a **double overhead camshaft (DOHC)** design.

NOTE: A V-type engine uses two banks or rows of cylinders. An SOHC design, therefore, uses two camshafts, but only one camshaft per bank (row) of cylinders. A DOHC V-6, therefore, has four camshafts, two for each bank.

FIGURE 2–6 Prototype transversely mounted inline six-cylinder engine. An inline six-cylinder engine is very smooth because there is a power pulse for every 120 degrees of crankshaft rotation. Note the long intake manifold runners that extend from the cylinder head almost back to the bulkhead (firewall).

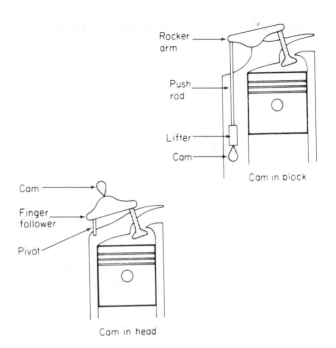

FIGURE 2–8   Camshaft locations.

FIGURE 2–7 Cutaway of an overhead valve engine showing the piston, valve, valve spring, rocker arm, and pushrod.

FIGURE 2–9 A double overhead camshaft V-6 engine with the cam covers and timing belt removed.

- **Type of fuel.** Most engines operate on gasoline, whereas some engines are designed to operate on methanol, natural gas, propane, or diesel fuel.
- **Cooling method.** Most engines are liquid cooled, but some older models were air cooled.
- **Type of induction pressure.** If normal air pressure is used to force the air-fuel mixture into the cylinders, the engine is called **normally aspirated.** Some engines use a **turbocharger** or **supercharger** to *force* the air-fuel mixture into the cylinder for even greater power.

ENGINE DESIGN CLASSIFICATIONS

Internal combustion engines are described by reference to a number of their different design features. These can be broken down into the following readily recognized features.

Two-Stroke Cycle Engine

Some small engines use a **two-stroke cycle.** This cycle starts with the piston at top center on the power stroke. As the piston nears the bottom of the power stroke, the exhaust valve or port opens to release the spent gases. A **port** is an opening in the side of the cylinder. The intake valve or port opens very shortly after the exhaust opens, and an intake charge is forced into the cylinder under pressure. This aids in pushing the exhaust gases from the cylinder. Both intake and exhaust valves or ports close as the piston starts up on the compression stroke. The two stroke–cycle engine has a power stroke for *each* crankshaft revolution. See Figure 2–10 for an example of a two-stroke engine wherein the fuel charge, with oil added, flows through and lubricates the bottom parts of the engine before entering the combustion chamber. Newer two-stroke engines use fuel injectors that spray fuel directly into the combustion chamber. The

air is forced into the combustion chamber by an air pump type of device called a supercharger. With a direct injection–type two-stroke engine, the crankcase is filled with engine oil for lubrication, as in a four stroke–cycle engine.

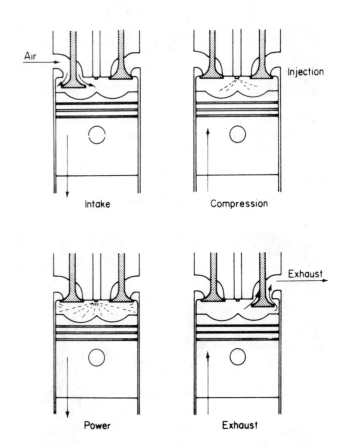

FIGURE 2–11   Four stroke–cycle diesel engine.

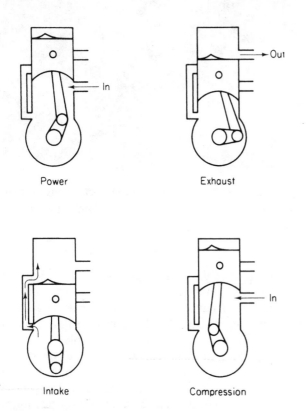

FIGURE 2–10   Two-stroke cycle of a spark-ignited gasoline engine.

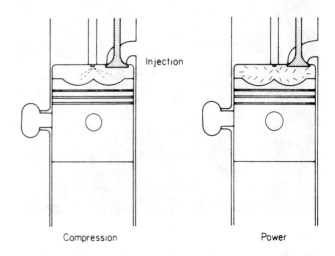

FIGURE 2–12   Two stroke–cycle diesel engine.

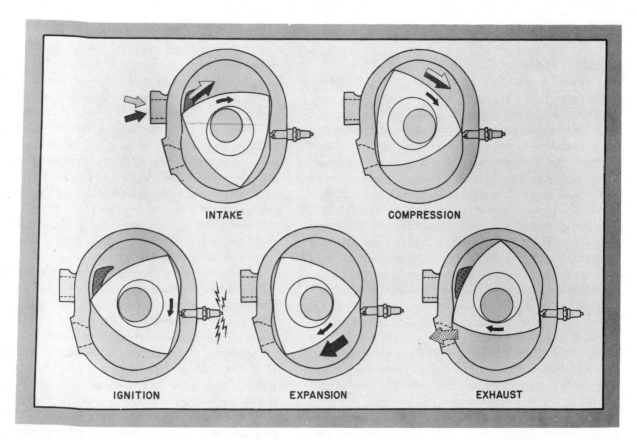

INTAKE   COMPRESSION

IGNITION   EXPANSION   EXHAUST

FIGURE 2–13   Rotating (rotary) combustion chamber engine. (Courtesy of Curtiss-Wright Corporation)

FIGURE 2–15   With the rotor removed, the housing shape (called epitrochoid) can be seen. The smoothness of the housing is a tribute to the manufacturing process.

FIGURE 2–14   Disassembled Mazda rotary engine.

Diesel Engine

The diesel engine has been commonly used in heavy vehicles and on stationary machinery that generally operates at constant speeds. The diesel engine has high thermal efficiency, so it provides good fuel economy. The diesel engine produces exhaust emissions that are low in hydrocarbons and carbon monoxide. These characteristics make it a good alternative to the reciprocating gasoline engine for use in automobiles. Mechanically, the two engines are very much alike. The diesel engine is somewhat heavier, and it is more expensive. The greatest difference is in their fuel and ignition systems. A diesel engine draws just air into the combustion. This air is compressed by the piston on the compression stroke. The compression is high enough to heat the air to about 1000° F (540° C). When the piston is near top dead center, fuel under pressure is squirted from a fuel-injection nozzle. The fuel is ignited by the hot air. The resulting burning fuel forces the piston downward on the power stroke. The crankshaft rotates and the piston is moved upward forcing the exhaust out of the exhaust valve. Two factors limit the application of the diesel engine in passenger vehicles. First is the high price, and second is the fact that it is difficult for the diesel engine to meet the very low nitrogen oxide emission standards. See Figures 2–11 and 2–12.

Rotating Combustion Chamber Engine

A second successful alternative engine is the **rotary engine,** also called the **Wankel engine** after its inventor. The Mazda RX-7 represents the only long-term use of the rotary engine. It has some advantages over a piston engine. The rotating combustion chamber engine runs very smoothly, and it produces high power for its size and weight. It operates on low-octane gasoline as a result of the large cooling surface around the combustion chamber. The basic rotating combustion chamber engine has a triangular-shaped rotor turning in a housing. The housing is in the shape of a geometric figure called a **two-lobed epitrochoid.** A seal on each corner, or apex, of the rotor is in constant contact with the housing, so the rotor must turn with an eccentric motion. This means that the center of the rotor moves around the center of the engine. The eccentric motion can be seen in Figure 2–13. This eccentric movement makes expanding and contracting chambers between the flat portions of the rotor and the housing. As a chamber expands, or increases in volume, an air-fuel intake charge is drawn in through an intake port. In Figure 2–14 the port is shown in the housing. When the chamber reaches its largest volume, the port is closed as the apex seal moves past it. Continued rotor rotation re-

duces the volume, compressing the charge. Spark plugs ignite the charge. The high-pressure gases developed during combustion force the volume to expand. This pulse of power provides the engine-rotating force. When the chamber again reaches its largest volume, one of the apex seals moves past an exhaust port, allowing the spent high-pressure gases to escape from the engine. Continued rotation reduces the combustion chamber volume to force the remaining exhaust gases from the engine. This completes a cycle similar to the four-stroke cycle of the reciprocating engine. Continued rotation of the rotor starts the next cycle with the next intake charge.

While the one chamber is going through its cycle, the other two chambers formed between the rotor and housing also go through similar cycles. This produces three power pulses each time the rotor makes one revolution. Power produced by the rotor forces an eccentric shaft—or simply, eccentric—to turn. The action is similar to that of the connecting rod and crankshaft. The eccentric shaft makes three revolutions for each revolution of the rotor. This places the eccentric in the correct position to be pushed or rotated by each power pulse. An internal gear within the rotor meshes with an external tooth gear on one of the side housings. The purpose of the gear is to keep the rotor correctly indexed to the eccentric and housing. The gears do not carry any of the torque load.

Intake and exhaust ports are located in the rotor housing on some engines and in the side housings on others. A depression in the rotor forms the combustion chamber. Because the combustion chamber is relatively long, some engines use two spark plugs to ignite the charge for rapid, complete combustion. Two complete ignition systems are required when two spark plugs are used. See Figures 2–15 and 2–16.

ENGINE ROTATION DIRECTION

The SAE standard for automotive engine rotation counterclockwise (CCW) as viewed from the flywheel end (clockwise as viewed from the front of the engine). The flywheel end of the engine is the end from which the power is taken to drive the vehicle. This is the **principal end** of the engine. The **nonprincipal** of the engine is opposite the principal end and generally referred to as the front of the engine, where accessory belts are used. See Figure 2–17.

Therefore, in most rear wheel–drive vehicles engine is mounted longitudinally with the end at the rear of the engine. Most front-mounted engines also adhere to the same direction of rotation. Honda and some manufacturers may differ from this standard.

BORE

The diameter of a cylinder is called the **bore**. The larger the bore, the greater the area on which the gases have to work. Pressure is measured in units, such as pounds per square inch (psi). The greater the area (in square inches), the higher the force exerted by the pistons to rotate the crankshaft. See Figure 2–18.

STROKE

The distance the piston travels down in the cylinder is called the **stroke**. The longer this distance, the greater the amount of air-fuel mixture that can be drawn into the cylinder. The more air-fuel mixture inside the cylinder, the more force will result when the mixture is ignited.

FIGURE 2–16   Rotor with apex seal removed.

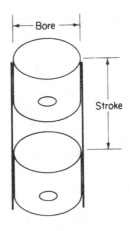

FIGURE 2–18   Dimensions used to determine the displacement of one cylinder.

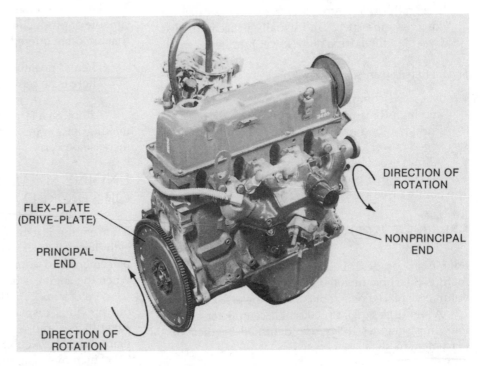

FIGURE 2–17   Inline four-cylinder engine showing principal and non-principal ends. Normal direction of rotation is clockwise (CW) as viewed from the front or accessory belt end (nonprincipal end).

OVER SQUARE AND UNDER SQUARE

An engine with a bore larger in dimension than its stroke is called **over square**.

An engine with a bore smaller in dimension than its stroke is called **under square**.

An engine with equal-size bore and stroke is called a **square** engine.

Engine operating characteristics differ as a result of many variables, including bore-stroke relationship; however, some general operating features include the following:

Over Square Engine (bore larger than stroke)

- Usually is fast revving; reaches higher engine speeds (in revolutions per minute [RPM])
- Is responsive at higher engine speeds
- Tends to lack low-speed torque
- Usually is used with a lower final drive ratio (higher number) to take advantage of faster engine speed characteristic

Under Square Engine (bore smaller than stroke)

- Usually is slow to rev because of longer stroke
- Has good low–engine speed torque
- Is basically a low-RPM engine
- Generally gives good fuel economy because of lower engine speed and usually is accompanied by a high final drive ratio (lower number)

Square Engine (bore same as stroke)

- Is a good compromise between low-RPM torque and high-RPM power
- Provides good low-speed torque with good high-speed power
- Allows use of higher final drive ratios (lower numbers) for fuel economy, yet still maintains driveability in slow city driving

ENGINE DISPLACEMENT

Engine size is described as displacement. **Displacement** is the cubic inch (cu in) or cubic centimeter (cc) volume displaced or swept by all of the pistons.

A liter (L) is equal to 1000 cubic centimeters; therefore, most engines today are identified by their displacement in liters.

$$1 \text{ Liter} = 1000 \text{ cc}$$
$$1 \text{ Liter} = 61 \text{ cu in}$$
$$1 \text{ cu in} = 16.4 \text{ cc}$$

The formula to calculate the displacement of an engine is basically the formula for determining the volume of a cylinder multiplied by the number of cylinders. However, it seems somewhat confusing because the formula has been publicized in many different forms. Regardless of the method used, the results will be the same. The easiest and most commonly used formula is

$$\text{Bore} \times \text{Bore} \times \text{Stroke} \times 0.7854 \times \text{Number of cylinders}$$

For example, take a six-cylinder engine where

Bore = 4.000 in
Stroke = 3.000 in

Applying the formula,

$$4.000 \text{ in} \times 4.000 \text{ in} \times 3.000 \text{ in} \times 0.7854 \times 6 = 226 \text{ cu in}$$

Because 1 cubic inch equals 16.4 cubic centimeters, this engine's displacement equals 3706 cubic centimeters; rounded to 3700 cubic centimeters, this becomes 3.7 liters.

ENGINE SIZE VERSUS HORSEPOWER

The larger the engine, the more easily the engine is capable of producing power. There are several sayings that are often quoted about engine size, including

There is no substitute for cubic inches.
There is no replacement for displacement.

Although a large engine generally uses more fuel, making an engine larger is often the easiest way to increase power.

ENGINE SIZE IF BORED OR STROKED

If an engine is bored, material is removed from the cylinder walls and a larger piston is installed. The displacement and compression ratio are both increased when the engine is bored.

A stock six-cylinder engine (like the one used in the previous displacement example) with a bore of 4.000 inches and a stroke of 3.000 inches has a displacement of 226 cubic inches. If the engine is bored to 0.060 inch oversize, the size of the bore now becomes 4.060 inches.

The formula for displacement in cubic inches remains the same except that 4.060 is substituted for 4.000.

Cubic inch
displacement $=$ Bore $\times$ Bore $\times$ Stroke $\times$ 0.7854 $\times$
Number of cylinders
$=$ 4.060 in $\times$ 4.060 in $\times$ 3.000 in $\times$
0.7854 $\times$ 6
$=$ 233 cu in
$=$ 33818 cc

If the bore remains the same and the stroke is increased by changing the crankshaft, the cubic inch displacement will increase and the compression ratio will also increase. If the stroke is increased ⅛ inch (0.125 inch), keeping the same stock bore, the new displacement will be calculated as follows:

Cubic inch
displacement $=$ Bore $\times$ Bore $\times$ Stroke $\times$ 0.7854 $\times$
Number of cylinders
$=$ 4.000 in $\times$ 4.000 in $\times$ 3.125 in $\times$
0.7854 $\times$ 6
$=$ 236 cu in
$=$ 3867 cc

If the engine is both bored and stroked (bored 0.060 inches, stroked 0.125 inches), the resultant displacement will be

4.060 in $\times$ 4.060 in $\times$ 3.125 in $\times$ 0.7854 $\times$ 6 = 243 cu in
$=$ 3982 cc

COMPRESSION RATIO

The compression ratio of an engine is an important consideration when rebuilding or repairing an engine.

The **compression ratio** (CR) is the ratio of the volume in the cylinder above the piston when the piston is at the bottom of the stroke to the volume in the cylinder above the piston when the piston is at the top of the stroke. See Figure 2–19.

■ **TECH TIP** ■

ALL 3.8-LITER ENGINES ARE NOT THE SAME!

Most engine sizes are currently identified by displacement in liters. However, not all 3.8-liter engines are the same. For example, see the following table.

Engine	Displacement
Chevrolet-built 3.8-L V-6	229 cu in
Buick-built 3.8-L V-6	
(also called 3800-cc)	231 cu in
Ford-built 3.8-L V-6	232 cu in

The *exact* conversion from liters (or cubic centimeters) to cubic inches figures to 231.9 cubic inches. However, due to rounding of exact cubic inch displacement *and* rounding of the exact cubic centimeter volume, several entirely different engines can be marketed with the exact same liter designation. To reduce confusion and reduce the possibility of ordering incorrect parts, the vehicle identification number (VIN) should be noted for the vehicle being serviced. The VIN should be visible through the windshield on all vehicles. Since 1980, the *engine* identification number or letter is usually the eighth digit or letter from the left.

A 5.0-liter V-8 can also be confusing to many owners *and* technicians. For example, some rear wheel–drive General Motors vehicles may use a 5.0-L V-8 (305–cubic inch) engine made by Chevrolet. The same model of vehicle may also use a 5.0-L V-8 (307–cubic inch) engine made by Oldsmobile. The two GM 5.0-L V-8s are not the same engine and no engine parts will interchange! Ford also sells a 5.0-L V-8—of 302 cubic inches. Ford 5.0-L V-8s also differ from year to year in such major characteristics as firing order.

Smaller, four-cylinder engines can also cause confusion because many vehicle manufacturers use both engines from overseas and domestically produced engines. Always refer to service manual information to be assured of correct engine identification.

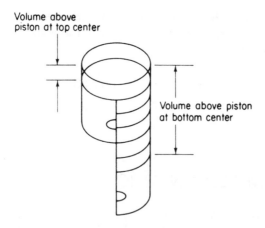

FIGURE 2–19   Dimensions used to determine the compression ratio of one cylinder.

If compression is lower	If compression is higher
Lower power	Higher power possible
Poorer fuel economy	Better fuel economy
Easier engine cranking	Harder to crank engine, especially when hot
More advanced ignition timing possible without spark knock (detonation)	Less ignition timing required to prevent spark knock (detonation)

$$CR = \frac{\text{Volume in cylinder with piston at bottom center}}{\text{Volume in cylinder with piston at top center}}$$

For example: What is the compression ratio of an engine with 50.3–cubic inch displacement in one cylinder having a combustion chamber volume of 6.7 cubic inches?

$$CR = \frac{50.3 + 6.7 \text{ cu in}}{6.7 \text{ cu in}} = \frac{57.0}{6.7} = 8.5$$

COMPRESSION AFTER MACHINING

During routine engine remanufacturing, the following machining operations are performed:

1. Cylinders are bored oversize and larger-diameter pistons are installed. Boring the cylinder increases displacement and compression ratio because the cylinder volume is increased and combustion chamber volume remains the same, resulting in more air being squeezed into the same volume.

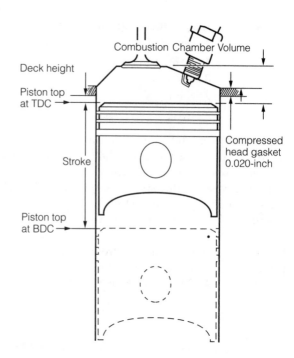

FIGURE 2–20   Combustion chamber volume is the volume above the piston, with the piston at top dead center.

2. Block top surfaces are refinished. This machining operation is called "decking the block" and increases the compression ratio because it results in the cylinder heads being down closer to the tops of the pistons.
3. Cylinder head(s) are resurfaced, which also increases the compression ratio.

   NOTE: To avoid raising the compression ratio beyond stock rating, most remanufacturers use replacement pistons that are 0.015 to 0.020 inch *shorter* than usual.

To calculate the exact compression ratio of the engine, exact measurements must be made of the bore, stroke, and combustion chamber volume. See Figure 2–20.

$$\text{Compression ratio} = \frac{(PV + DV + GV + CV)}{(DV + GV + CV)}$$

where

PV = Piston volume
DV = Deck clearance volume (volume in cylinder above piston at TDC)
GV = Head gasket volume = Bore × Bore × 0.7854 × Thickness of gasket

CV = Combustion chamber volume (if measured in cubic centimeters, divide by 16.386 to convert to cubic inches)

For example: What is the compression ratio of a 350–cubic inch Chevrolet V-8 if the only change was to install 62–cubic centimeter instead of 74–cubic centimeter cylinder heads?

Bore = 4.000 in
Stroke = 3.480 in
Number of cylinders = 8

CV = 74 cc = 4.52 cu in
CV = 62 cc = 3.78 cu in
GV = Bore × Bore × 0.7854 × Thickness of compressed gasket
    = 4.000 in × 4.000 in × 0.7854 × 0.020 in
    = 0.87 cu in

To keep the math easier and to illustrate just the effect of changing combustion chamber volume, it is assumed that flat-top pistons are being used with zero deck clearance volume.

NOTE: This is almost never the situation, but is assumed here to simplify the calculation. ——————

PV = Bore × Bore × Stroke × 0.7854
    = 4.000 in × 4.000 in × 3.48 in × 0.7854
    = 43.78 cu in

With 74–cubic centimeter (4.52–cubic inch) heads,

$$CR = \frac{(PV + DV + GV + CV)}{(DV + GV + CV)}$$
$$= \frac{(43.73 + 0 + 0.87 + 4.52)}{(0 + 0.87 + 4.52)}$$
$$= \frac{49.12}{5.39} = 9.1{:}1$$

With 62–cubic centimeter (3.78–cubic inch) heads,

$$CR = \frac{(PV + DV + GV + CV)}{(DV + GV + CV)}$$
$$= \frac{(43.73 + 0 + 0.87 + 3.78)}{(0 + 0.87 + 3.78)}$$
$$= \frac{48.38}{4.65} = 10.4{:}1$$

The compression ratio was increased from 9.1:1 to 10.4:1 by just changing cylinder heads from 74 cubic

centimeters to 62 cubic centimeters. Because 10.4:1 compression is usually *not* recommended for use with today's gasoline, this change should only be done for racing purposes where expensive fuel or fuel additives will be used.

THE CRANKSHAFT DETERMINES THE STROKE

The stroke of an engine is the distance the piston travels from top dead center (TDC) to bottom dead center (BDC). This distance is determined by the throw of the crankshaft. The throw is the distance from the centerline of the crankshaft to the centerline of the crankshaft rod journal. The throw is one-half of the stroke.

If the crankshaft is replaced with one with a greater stroke, the pistons will be pushed up over the height of the top of the block (deck). The solution to this problem is to install replacement pistons with the piston pin relocated higher on the piston. Another alternative is to replace the connecting rod with a shorter one to prevent the piston from traveling too far up in the cylinder.

Changing the connecting rod length does *not* change the stroke of an engine. Changing the connecting rod only changes the position of the piston in the cylinder.

HORSEPOWER

The power an engine produces is called horsepower (hp). One horsepower is the power required to move 550 pounds 1 foot in 1 second or 33,000 pounds 1 foot in 1 minute (550 lb × 60 sec = 33,000 lb). This is expressed as 500 foot-pounds (ft lb) per second or 33,000 foot-pounds per minute.

The actual horsepower produced by an engine is measured with a dynamometer. See Figure 2–21.

A dynamometer (often abbreviated as **dyno** or **dyn**) places a load on the engine and measures the amount of twisting force the engine crankshaft places against the load. The load holds the engine speed, so it is called a **brake.** The horsepower derived from a dynamometer is called **brake horsepower** (bhp). The dynamometer actually measures the **torque** output of the engine. Torque is a rotating force that may or may not cause movement. The horsepower is calculated from the torque readings at various engine speeds (in revolutions per minute or RPM). **Horsepower is torque times RPM divided by 5252.**

$$Horsepower = \frac{Torque \times RPM}{5252}$$

See Figure 2–22.

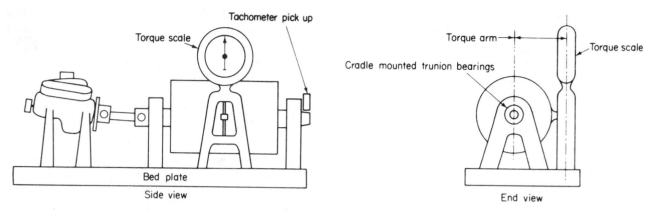

FIGURE 2–21   Line drawing of an engine dynamometer.

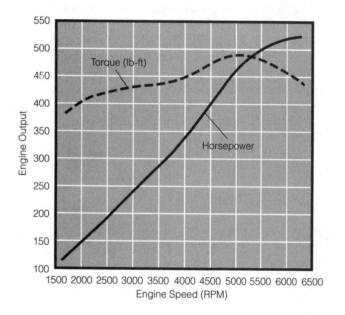

FIGURE 2–22 Typical torque and horsepower curves. Note that the torque and horsepower are the same (curves cross) at exactly 5252 RPM.

Torque is what the driver "feels" as the vehicle is being accelerated. A small engine operating at a high RPM may have the same horsepower as a large engine operating at a low RPM.

NOTE: As can be seen by the formula for horsepower, the higher the engine speed for a given amount of torque, the greater the horsepower. Many engines are high revving. To help prevent catastrophic damage due to excessive engine speed, most manufacturers limit the maximum RPM by programming fuel injectors to shut off if the engine speed increases past a certain level. Sometimes this cutoff speed can be as low as 3000 RPM if the transmission is in neutral or park. Complaints of high-speed "miss" or "cutting out" may be normal if the engine is approaching the "rev limiter." _____

BRAKE-SPECIFIC FUEL CONSUMPTION

Brake-specific fuel consumption (BSFC) is another factor calculated by a dynamometer from engine test readings.

$$\text{BSFC} = \frac{\text{Pounds of fuel per hour}}{\text{Brake horsepower}} = \frac{\text{lb}}{\text{bhp-hr}}$$

The brake-specific fuel consumption is a measure of the amount of fuel an engine needs to create horsepower. The lower the number for BSFC, the more efficient the engine. Most engines require about 0.5 pound of fuel per hour to produce 1 horsepower.

WHERE THE ENERGY GOES

In a spark-ignited gasoline engine, only 25% of the energy in the fuel is changed to useful work as engine power at the crankshaft. In a diesel engine, this percentage may be as high as 35%. The rest of the fuel energy is wasted as heat. About half of the wasted heat energy goes out of the engine with the exhaust gas. The other half leaves the engine through the cooling system. In this way, the friction heat is removed from the engine.

Unfortunately, all of the power produced at the crankshaft, called **gross horsepower**, is not usable to drive the vehicle. A number of power-absorbing accessories are mounted on the engine. These include a coolant pump, cooling fan, electrical charging system, fuel pump, air-injection pump, air-conditioner compressor, power steering, and air cleaner. Some power is also required to pull the intake charge into the combustion chamber and to push the exhaust out through a catalytic converter and muffler. When all the power-absorbing accessories are being fully used, they will absorb about 25% of the power being produced by the crankshaft. The remaining 75% of the power at the crankshaft is usable power, and it is called **net horsepower.** This remaining useful power is further reduced as it goes through the driveline of the vehicle.

WATTS AND HORSEPOWER

James Watt (1736–1819) first determined the power of a typical horse while measuring the amount of coal being lifted out of a mine. For over 200 years, the power of a horse has been defined as 33,000 foot-pounds per minute. In Europe, power is commonly expressed in watts (W). It takes 746 watts to equal 1 horsepower. One kilowatt (kW—1000 watts) times 1.341 equals 1 horsepower.

TAXABLE HORSEPOWER

Taxable horsepower was developed as a means of taxation of motor vehicles based on engine size and number of cylinders.

Taxable hp = Bore × Bore × Number of cylinders × 0.4

For example, take a six-cylinder engine with a 4-inch bore:

Taxable hp = 4 × 4 × 6 × 0.4 = 38.4

Notice that the stroke dimension is not used. When taxable horsepower was first used, the bore and the number of cylinders generally determined the price range or value of the vehicle.

Taxable horsepower is still used by some state and local governments for tax or licensing purposes. The National Automotive Dealers Association (NADA) vehicle guides routinely list taxable horsepower in their listings of specifications.

SAE GROSS VERSUS NET HORSEPOWER

SAE standards for measuring horsepower include gross and net horsepower ratings. Gross horsepower is the maximum power an engine develops without some accessories in operation. SAE net horsepower is the

power an engine develops as installed in the vehicle. A summary of the differences is given in the following table.

SAE gross horsepower	SAE net horsepower
No air cleaner or filter	Stock air cleaner or filter
No cooling fan	Stock cooling fan
No alternator	Stock alternator
No mufflers	Stock exhaust system
No emission controls	Full emission and noise control

Ratings are about 20% lower for the net rating method. Before 1971, most manufacturers used gross horsepower rating (the higher method) for advertising purposes. After 1971, the manufacturers started advertising only SAE net-rated horsepower.

METRIC VERSUS BRAKE HORSEPOWER

Engine power is usually expressed in watts or kilowatts (1000 watts equals 1 kilowatt). Metric horsepower differs slightly from brake horsepower because of slight differences in units and test procedures. The difference is very minor, the measurements being within 99% of each other. Metric horsepower may be labeled as **pferoestarke** (PS) or **Cheval-Vapeur** (CV). To convert metric horsepower (PS or CV) to brake horsepower, multiply by 0.986.

For example:

150 metric hp × 0.986 = 147.9 bhp

To convert from kilowatts to SAE net horsepower, multiply by 1.341.

For example:

150 kW × 1.341 = 201.15 SAE net hp

DEUTSCHE INDUSTRIE NORM HORSEPOWER VERSUS SAE HORSEPOWER

Deutsche Industrie Norm (DIN), or German Industrial Norm, is similar to SAE. The DIN testing standards for net horsepower vary slightly from the SAE testing parameters. All DIN horsepower ratings are *net*. To convert from DIN horsepower to SAE net horsepower, multiply by 0.963 to compensate for the slight differences in test conditions. For example:

$$150 \text{ DIN hp} \times 0.963 = 144.45 \text{ SAE net hp}$$

JAPAN INDUSTRY STANDARD VERSUS SAE HORSEPOWER

Japan Industry Standard is the standardization organization in Japan. After 1985, all JIS horsepower ratings are the same as SAE ratings because JIS converted to SAE test conditions. For JIS net horsepower readings before 1985, multiply the reading by 0.984 to get SAE net horsepower. In other words, after April 1, 1985,

$$\text{JIS net hp} = \text{SAE net hp}$$

whereas before April 1, 1985,

$$\text{JIS net hp} \times 0.984 = \text{SAE net hp}$$

HORSEPOWER AND ALTITUDE

Because the density of the air is lower at high altitude, the power that a normal engine can develop is greatly reduced at high altitude. According to SAE conversion factors, a nonsupercharged or nonturbocharged engine loses about 3% of its power for every 1000 feet (300 meters [m]) of altitude.

Therefore, an engine that develops 150 brake horsepower at sea level will only produce about 85 brake horsepower at the top of Pikes Peak in Colorado at 14,110 feet (4300 meters). Supercharged and turbocharged engines are not as greatly affected by altitude as normally aspirated engines. Normally aspirated refers to engines that breathe air at normal atmospheric pressure.

SUMMARY

1. The four strokes of the four-stroke cycle are intake, compression, power, and exhaust.
2. Engines are classified by number and arrangement of cylinders and by number and location of valves and camshafts, as well as by type of fuel used, cooling method, and induction pressure.
3. Most engines rotate clockwise as viewed from the front (accessory) end of the engine. The SAE standard is counterclockwise as viewed from the principal (flywheel) end of the engine.
4. Engine size is called displacement and represents the volume displaced or swept by all of the pistons.
5. Engine power is expressed in horsepower, which is a calculated value based on the amount of torque or twisting force the engine produces.

REVIEW QUESTIONS

1. Name the strokes of a four-stroke cycle.
2. Describe the operation of the rotary engine.
3. What does a dynamometer actually measure?
4. Define volumetric efficiency.
5. What is the difference between SAE net and SAE gross horsepower?
6. If an engine at sea level produces 100 horsepower, how many horsepower would it develop at 6000 feet of altitude?

MULTIPLE-CHOICE QUESTIONS

1. All overhead valve engines _____.
   a. Use an overhead camshaft
   b. Have the overhead valves in the head
   c. Operate by the two-stroke cycle
   d. Use the camshaft to *close* the valves

■ TECH TIP ■

QUICK AND EASY EFFICIENCY CHECK

A good, efficient engine is able to produce a lot of power from little displacement. A common rule of thumb is that an engine is efficient if it can produce *1 horsepower per cubic inch* of displacement. Many engines today are capable of this feat, such as the following:

Ford	4.6-L V-8 (281 cu in)	—305 hp
Chevrolet	3.4-L V-6 (207 cu in)	—210 hp
Chrysler	3.5-L V-6 (214 cu in)	—214 hp
Acura	3.2-L V-6 (195 cu in)	—230 hp

An engine is very powerful for its size if it can produce *100 horsepower per liter*. This efficiency goal is harder to accomplish. Most factory stock engines that can achieve this feat are supercharged or turbocharged. For example:

Toyota	2.0-L four-cylinder (turbocharged)	—200 hp

2. An SOHC V-8 engine has how many camshafts?
   a. One
   b. Two
   c. Three
   d. Four

3. Brake horsepower is calculated by which of the following?
   a. Torque times RPM
   b. 2 pi times stroke
   c. Torque times RPM divided by 5252
   d. Stroke times bore times 3300

4. Torque is expressed in units of _____ .
   a. Pound-feet
   b. Foot-pounds
   c. Foot-pounds per minute
   d. Pound-feet per second

5. Horsepower is expressed in units of _____ .
   a. Pound-feet
   b. Foot-pounds
   c. Foot-pounds per minute
   d. Pound-feet per second

6. A normally aspirated automobile engine loses about _____ power per 1000 feet of altitude.
   a. 1%
   b. 3%
   c. 5%
   d. 6%

7. One cylinder of an automotive four stroke–cycle engine completes a cycle every _____ .
   a. 90 degrees
   b. 180 degrees
   c. 360 degrees
   d. 720 degrees

8. How many rotations of the crankshaft are required to complete each *stroke* of a four stroke–cycle engine?
   a. One-fourth
   b. One-half
   c. One
   d. Two

9. A *rotating force* is called _____ .
   a. Horsepower
   b. Torque
   c. Combustion pressure
   d. Eccentric movement

10. When gasoline and air in any engine burn, about how much of the total energy in the fuel (gasoline) is available at the crankshaft of the engine?
    a. About 15% to 18%
    b. About 25%
    c. About 50%
    d. About 75% to 80%

3 Engine Operating Systems

OBJECTIVES

After studying Chapter 3, the reader will be able to

1. List the various engine operating systems.
2. Describe how to test the battery and starting system.
3. Discuss how the ignition system works.
4. Explain how turbochargers and superchargers can increase engine power output.

Two systems are necessary to allow the engine to run. These are the **fuel delivery system** and the **ignition system.** A **cranking or starting system** is required to rotate the crankshaft to get the engine started. A **battery** is needed to store energy so that it is available for the starter and ignition. A **charging system** is required to provide electricity for the electrical running load and to recharge the battery after the engine starts.

There are only three basic things necessary for the engine to run as it is cranked for starting. First, the **air-fuel intake charge** inducted into the engine must be a combustible mixture. Second, the engine must be mechanically sound so that the intake charge will be compressed. Third, the ignition system must flash an **arc across the spark plug** at the correct instant in the cycle. The arc must have enough energy to ignite the compressed charge. The pressure that builds up in the combustion gases forces the piston down. The up-and-down motion of the piston is converted to rotary motion through a connecting rod and crankshaft. All other parts within the engine support these basic functions.

36

STARTING SYSTEM

Before any engine can perform useful work, it must start. To start, every engine must have the following:

1. Spark or other source of ignition
2. Fuel delivery to the engine cylinders
3. Compression
4. Rotational speed high enough to ensure continuous operation (generally between 80 and 250 engine RPM)

The cranking electrical circuit must be able to provide the proper amount of current to a cranking motor to start the engine. The components of the cranking circuit include the battery and the starter.

BATTERY

The condition of the battery is critical for proper operation of the cranking circuit. Because a battery must produce electricity from a chemical reaction, as the temperature decreases, the amount of current available from the battery decreases. A good battery can only produce about 40% of the amount of current at $0° F(-18° C)$ that the same battery can produce at $80° F(27° C)$. However, the starter motor requires more current to crank a cold engine. Even SAE 5W-30 engine oil becomes thicker at cold temperatures, and the starter motor has to overcome this increased drag. The life of most automotive batteries is 3 to 5 years. The life and performance of any battery depend on proper maintenance and service , including the following:

■ All automotive and truck batteries must be bolted down to prevent vibration damage to the plates in the battery.

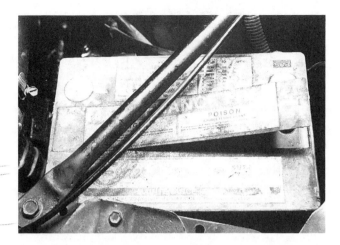

FIGURE 3–1 Many batteries can have their electrolyte level checked. This maintenance-free battery was easily opened, and clean (distilled) water could be added if needed. The battery also needs to be cleaned to help prevent self-discharge.

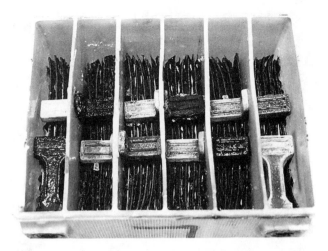

FIGURE 3–2 This battery suffered from overcharging, which blew the cover off the top of the battery case. Note the warped plates as a result of the overcharging.

■ The charging system should be adequate to provide for proper recharging of the battery. Charging voltage higher than 15.0 volts (V) can damage the battery. The alternator belt should be checked regularly and replaced whenever the alternator can be rotated by hand (engine off) even though the belt is tight. Most drive belts use a slight interference angle between the angle(s) on the pulley and the angle(s) of the belt.

■ Battery electrolyte level should be checked regularly and distilled water added as necessary to bring the electrolyte up to the proper level. See Figure 3–1.

NOTE: Some maintenance-free batteries are sealed so that adding water is not possible. ____

If distilled water is not available, clean drinkable water can be used. Avoid adding water with high mineral content.

■ Before testing the starter or alternator, make certain that the battery is at least 75% charged and known to be in good condition. If the battery is weak, the starter motor test and alternator output test will not give accurate results. The starter and alternator can test as being bad if the battery is weak or defective. See Figure 3–2.

BATTERY TESTING

One of the easiest ways to test the state of charge of a battery is to measure its voltage. Most batteries have a "surface charge" that increases the voltage reading of

the battery to higher than its true state of charge. Therefore, the surface charge should be removed before testing to get accurate voltage readings.

Step #1. Connect the leads of a voltmeter to the positive (+) and negative (−) terminals of the battery.

Step #2. Remove the surface charge by turning on the headlights for 1 minute on high beam. Turn off the headlights and let the battery "recover" for 1 minute.

Step #3. Connect the voltmeter to the battery as follows:
  a. Select a 20 or 30 scale labeled DC volts on the voltmeter.
  b. Connect the red meter lead to the positive terminal of the battery.
  c. Connect the black meter lead to the negative terminal of the battery.

Step #4. Read the voltmeter (at 70° to 80° F [21° to 27° C]). The reading can be interpreted according to the following table.

Voltage (V)	State of charge
12.6 or higher	100% charged
12.4	75% charged
12.2	50% charged
12.0	25% charged
11.9 or lower	Discharged

The best battery-testing method is to load the battery with a known amount of electrical load and

FIGURE 3–3 Typical starting and charging tester with cover removed. Note the carbon pile used to provide an electrical load while testing the battery, starter, and charging systems.

measure its voltage at the end of 15 seconds while it is still under load. The test is frequently called a **battery load test**.

To load test a battery requires the use of a carbon pile to provide the electrical load for the battery. See Figure 3–3.

Step #1. Determine the cold cranking ampere (CCA) rating of the battery being tested.

Step #2. Load the test battery to one-half of the CCA rating for a full 15 seconds.

Step #3. With the carbon pile still providing the electrical load, observe the voltmeter at the end of the 15-second test.

Step #4. A good, serviceable battery at room temperature should be able to maintain a battery voltage higher than 9.6 volts. The

■ **TECH TIP** ■

BATTERY VOLTAGE AND ENGINE OPERATION

Proper battery voltage is important not only to start an engine, but also for its proper operation. Most ignition systems, for example, require at least 9 volts for starting. After the engine starts, battery voltage also affects the operation of most electronic fuel-injection systems. If battery voltage is lower than normal due to an old, defective, or discharged battery, the engine computer increases the fuel injectors' "on time." This additional "on time" (called pulse width) is calculated by the computer to compensate for lower fuel pump pressure from the electric fuel pump.

Therefore, one of the first items that should be checked when diagnosing flooding, poor fuel economy, or rich mixture problems, is the battery condition and operating voltage.

NOTE: A vehicle could even fail an exhaust emissions test because of a defective or discharged battery. The extra fuel that the vehicle computer supplies increases carbon monoxide (CO) emissions. In severe cases, both hydrocarbon (HC) and CO levels may exceed allowable limits.

higher the voltage at the end of the test, the stronger the battery.

NOTE: Due to the surface charge that most batteries have as a result of being operated in a vehicle or from being charged, it is wise to perform the battery load test twice. The first test removes the surface charge, and the second test will more accurately determine the true condition of the battery under load.

STARTER

The starter is designed to crank the engine fast enough (80 to 250 RPM) to permit starting. If the starter fails to crank, or if it cranks too slowly for the engine to start, the cause could be one of the following:

1. Weak or defective battery
2. Loose or corroded battery cables and/or connections
3. High starter motor and/or solenoid temperatures (high temperatures cause high electrical

resistance and a decrease in current flow; the decrease in current flow decreases the power and speed of the starter motor)

4. Worn or defective starter motor and/or solenoid
5. Tight engine caused by excessive heat or too-close tolerances of bearings, or piston- to-cylinder or engine mechanical failure.

STARTER TESTING USING A VOLTMETER

The first and easiest test for the starter and the electrical cranking circuit is a voltmeter check of the battery voltage during cranking.

Step #1. Prevent the engine from starting by removing the secondary coil wire from the center of the distributor cap, and ground the wire to prevent damaging the ignition coil. (High voltage trying to jump a disconnected wire can cause a high-voltage track or hole to be burned through the windings of the coil.) Disconnect the power feed wire to the ignition system using integral coils such as those of the GM high energy ignition (HEI) system.

HINT: *On most fuel-injected engines, the engine can be made to crank without starting by depressing the throttle until it is wide open. The engine will crank so that a voltage reading can be observed, but the engine will not start because most or all of the fuel is shut off (a feature designed to help in starting if the engine becomes flooded).*

Step #2. Take the voltmeter reading. If the battery has tested as being good, a good starting (cranking) circuit should maintain *above* 9.6 volts battery voltage. If the battery voltage is below or close to 9.6 volts, the starter motor could be defective *or* an engine mechanical problem could be causing a drag on the starter.

STARTER TESTING USING A CARBON PILE TESTER

The starter motor circuit can also be tested using an ammeter. An ammeter large enough to read hundreds of amperes (A) is usually combined with a carbon pile part of a starting and charging tester unit. If exact starter amperage draw specifications are not available for on-the-vehicle testing, the following may be used:

FIGURE 3–4 If the starter motor must be disassembled for service or repair, be certain to mark the location of the through-bolts to be assured of proper reassembly.

Four- or six-cylinder engines:	150 A maximum
V-8 and V-6 engines	
(except GM V-8):	200 A maximum
GM V-8 engines:	250 A maximum

If the starting circuit current exceeds these values, the starter motor should be checked. If the starter motor is okay, the problem of excessive current draw could be due to excessive tightness in the engine. See Figure 3–4.

With the ignition system disconnected and the ignition off, use a socket and ratchet to attempt to rotate the engine. It should be possible to rotate the engine by hand if all internal clearances are correct and everything is properly lubricated. Also see the tech tip Check the Alternator—Then the Engine.

IGNITION SYSTEM OPERATION

All ignition systems use electromagnetic induction to produce a high-voltage spark from the ignition coil. Electromagnetic induction is the creation of a current in a conductor (coil winding) by a moving magnetic field. The magnetic field in an ignition coil is produced by

■ TECH TIP ■

CHECK THE ALTERNATOR— THEN THE ENGINE

Many alternators are driven by a long, serpentine drive belt. If an alternator is damaged and "locks up," the force on the drive belt is enough to stop the engine from rotating. Even when a long breaker bar is used on the engine crankshaft pulley, the engine will not move.

Many technicians have assumed from this test that the engine must be damaged internally and has locked up. Engines have even been replaced for this reason!

Therefore, whenever an engine does not rotate, remove the serpentine drive belt and try again before removing the engine.

current flowing through the primary windings of the coil. The current for the primary windings is supplied through the ignition switch to the positive terminal of the ignition coil. The negative terminal is connected to the ground return through the use of movable mechanical ignition points or through an electronic ignition module.

If the primary circuit is completed, current (approximately 2 to 6 amperes) can flow through the primary coil windings. This creates a strong magnetic field inside the coil. When the primary coil winding ground return path connection is "opened," the magnetic field *collapses* and induces a high-voltage (20,000- to 40,000- volts), low-amperage (20- to 80- milliampere [mA]) current in the secondary coil windings. This high-voltage pulse flows through the coil wire, through the distributor cap and rotor (if the vehicle is so equipped), and through the spark plug wires to the spark plugs. For each spark that occurs, the coil must be charged with a magnetic field and then discharged. The ignition components, which regulate the current in the coil primary winding by turning it "on" and "off," are known collectively as the **primary ignition circuit.** All of the components necessary to create and distribute the high voltage produced in the secondary windings of the coil are called the **secondary ignition circuit.** The components of each circuit include the following:

Primary Ignition Circuit

1. Battery
2. Ignition switch
3. Primary windings of the coil
4. Pickup coil (crank sensor)
5. Ignition module (igniter)

Secondary Ignition Circuit

1. Secondary windings of coil
2. Distributor cap and rotor (if the vehicle is so equipped)
3. Spark plug wires
4. Spark plugs

In many cases the computer does not operate the ignition coils directly, but instead controls when the ignition module should trigger the ignition coil(s) for optimum performance and fuel economy with lowest possible exhaust emissions. Many engines equipped with a distributor use a pickup coil to trigger the module. The generic name for a pickup coil is a **pulse generator** because it creates a voltage pulse to the electronic ignition module. See Figure 3–5.

ELECTRONIC IGNITION PRINCIPLES OF OPERATION

All inductive ignition systems use ignition coils to store electromagnetic energy. When the power to the coil is interrupted (opened), the stored energy in the coil discharges a high-voltage pulse from the secondary windings. This high-voltage, low-amperage electrical spark is conducted to the spark plug, and the electrical arc provides the ignition energy to ignite the air-fuel mixture.

With most electronic ignition systems, the positive side of the ignition coil is connected to full battery voltage through the ignition switch. The negative side of the coil is connected to the ignition module. It is the module that controls the current through the ignition coil (turns on and off the primary current). See Figure 3–6.

The module must, itself, be triggered as to when to trigger (turn on and off) the coil primary current path. The trigger for the module is the pickup coil in the distributor or crankshaft sensor. To summarize:

■ The pickup coil or crankshaft sensor triggers the module.
■ The module triggers the coil.
■ The coil being turned on and off produces a high-voltage spark.

Since the early 1980s, most electronic ignition systems have also been controlled by the engine management computer. The computer controls ignition timing. Ignition timing is a matter of when the spark occurs in relation to the piston position. The computer receives a pulsing signal from the ignition module that corresponds to the engine speed (in RPM) and piston position (as de-

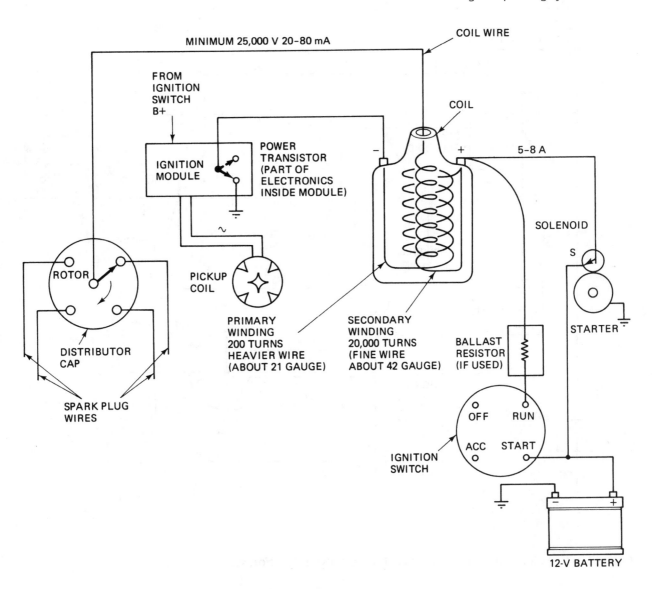

FIGURE 3–5   Typical primary and secondary electronic ignition using a ballast resistor and a distributor. Many electronic ignitions do not use a ballast resistor to protect the ignition coil from overheating at lower engine speeds, but use electronic circuits within the module.

termined by the pickup coil or crankshaft sensor). The computer calculates the best ignition timing based on information and values from all of its sensors and returns a pulse signal to the ignition module. This computer pulse is used by the module to trigger the ignition coil.

PULSE GENERATORS

A pulse generator consists of

1. A permanent magnet (stationary)
2. A pole piece (stationary)
3. A reluctor (rotating)

All three units occupy the area in the distributor below the rotor.

The various component names of a pulse generator differ among various manufacturers. The terms commonly used include those in the following table.

Manufacturer	Stationary pickup coil	Rotating trigger wheel
Chrysler	Pickup coil	Reluctor
Ford	Stator	Armature
General Motors	Pole piece and magnetic pickup	Timer core

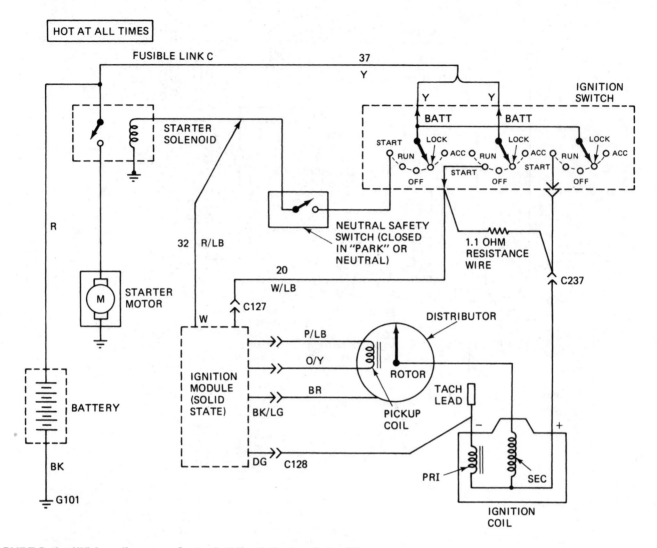

FIGURE 3–6   *Wiring diagram of a typical Ford electronic ignition system.*

Surrounding the pickup coil is a magnetic field formed by the permanent magnet (PM). When a conductor comes close to the magnetic lines of force, the **reluctance** (resistance) to the magnetic lines of force decreases. Therefore, the movable armature is often called a **reluctor** because it decreases the reluctance of the magnetic field surrounding the pickup coil. See Figures 3–7 and 3–8.

As the armature tooth approaches the center of the stator, a strong magnetic field begins to build around the magnetic pickup, permitting the primary coil current to flow across the emitter-base circuit through the magnetic pickup to ground. This allows the ignition coil to build up a strong magnetic field. When the reluctor tooth passes the center of the magnetic pickup and starts away from it, it reverses the induced voltage and

turns off the base of the switching transistor. This, in turn, switches off the emitter-collector circuit of the transistor and turns off the primary ignition coil current. The very rapid cutoff of primary current collapses the magnetic field in the ignition coil to produce the high secondary voltage required to fire the spark plug.

HALL-EFFECT SENSORS

The **Hall effect** was discovered by Edwin H. Hall (1855–1938) in 1879. He found that when a thin rectangular gold conductor, carrying a current, was crossed at right angles by a magnetic field, a difference of potential was produced at the edges of the gold conductor. Modern Hall-effect units use semiconductor material (usually silicon) instead of gold. See Figure 3–9.

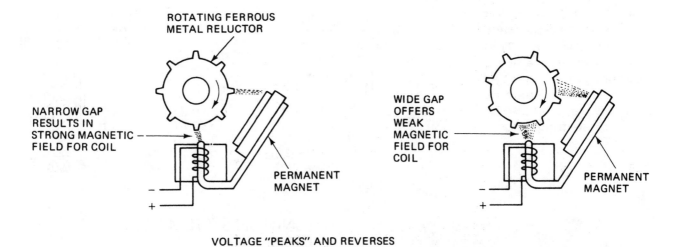

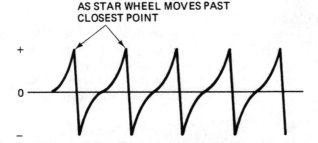

FIGURE 3–7 Operation of a typical pulse generator (pickup coil). At the bottom is a line drawing of a typical scope pattern of the output voltage of a pickup coil. The module receives this voltage from the pickup coil and opens the ground circuit to the ignition coil when the voltage starts down from its peak (just as the reluctor teeth start moving away from the pickup coil).

FIGURE 3–8 Photo of a typical pickup coil assembly from an older-style Ford electronic ignition.

The Hall effect can be used as a very accurate electronic switch when a moving metallic shutter blocks the magnetic field from striking the semiconductor. Whenever the opening of the shutter allows the magnetic field to strike the sensor, a small voltage is produced and is sent to the electronic control unit. As the distributor rotates, a blocking shutter blocks the magnetic field and the current stops flowing from the sensor. The electronic control unit can be designed to either turn on or turn off the ignition coil primary current when the shutter blades are blocking. See Figure 3–10. Hall-effect ignition is used by many manufacturers, including Ford, GM, Chrysler, and many import brand vehicles. The advantage of the Hall effect over the magnetic pulse generator is in its accuracy. The Hall effect can easily trigger the ignition to within ±¼ degree of distributor rotation.

Not all Hall-effect sensors use a shutter vane to shunt the magnetic lines of force. Some Hall-effect sensors that trigger off of notches or slots are used by Chrysler Corporation.

DISTRIBUTORLESS IGNITION

The operation of distributorless (direct-fire) ignition is similar to that of any other ignition system. Generally, two ignition coils are used for a four-cylinder engine, three for a six-cylinder engine, and four for an

FIGURE   3–9 Hall-effect switches use metallic shutters to shunt magnetic lines of force away from a silicon chip and related circuits. All Hall-effect switches produce a square wave output for very accurate triggering.

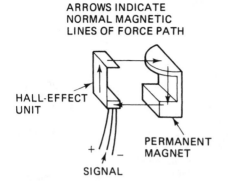

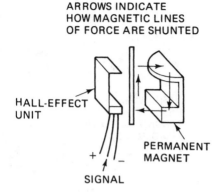

ARROWS INDICATE
NORMAL MAGNETIC
LINES OF FORCE PATH

HALL-EFFECT
UNIT

PERMANENT
MAGNET

SIGNAL

ARROWS INDICATE
HOW MAGNETIC LINES
OF FORCE ARE SHUNTED

HALL-EFFECT
UNIT

PERMANENT
MAGNET

SIGNAL

FIGURE 3–10 Photo of shutter blade of a rotor as it passes between the sensing silicon chip and the permanent magnet.

eight-cylinder engine. Each coil fires two cylinders at the same time. One cylinder is fired on the compression stroke and the other, paired cylinder is fired on the exhaust stroke. The spark occurring on the exhaust stroke is called a **wasted spark**, requiring a voltage of only 3000 to 4000 volts (3 to 4 kilovolts). The remaining coil energy is available to fire the cylinder on the compression stroke. Like any other electronic ignition, the distributorless ignition uses a pulse from a triggering device to signal when the spark is to occur. The electronic ignition module pulses the correct ignition coil at just the right time to ignite the spark plugs.

Distributorless ignition systems vary ignition timing through the use of the engine computer system. Various engine sensors are used by the computer to provide input, and the computer calculates the best ignition timing and controls the firing of each coil through a signal from the computer to the ignition module. The ignition module triggers the firing of the coil and, therefore, the spark plugs. See Figure 3–11.

IGNITION SYSTEM PROBLEM DIAGNOSIS

If the engine is running rough, use a water spray bottle to spray the spark plug wires, distributor (if the vehicle is so equipped), and coils(s). Defective secondary circuit insulation will cause a spark to occur where the water provides a path to ground. See Figures 3–12 and 3–13.

HINT: *To make the water more conductive, add a small amount of salt or liquid soap to it. Salt or soapy water is a better conductor of electricity than pure water.*

To determine which cylinder is causing the rough engine operation, connect 2-inch (5-centimeter) lengths of 5⁄32-inch (4-millimeter) I.D. vacuum hose to each spark plug or coil tower as shown in Figure 3–14. Connect the spark plug wire to the other end of the rubber hose. The resistance of most rubber hoses is less than 1000 ohms (Ω) because of the carbon in the rubber. The carbon is what makes the rubber electrically conductive.

With the engine running, touch a *grounded* jumper wire or test light to the rubber hose. The high-voltage electricity will flow through the test light (without damaging the bulb) to ground.

This stops the spark plug from firing, and the engine should stumble and slow slightly. If there is no effect on the engine operation, remove the spark plug wire and check for spark. *Always check for spark using a spark tester.* See Figures 3–15 and 3–16.

SPARK PLUG WIRE TESTING

Most spark plug wire is made from carbon-impregnated thread surrounded by insulation. A good spark plug wire should measure 10,000 ohms of resistance or less for each foot of length. Another easy-to-remember specification is that no spark plug wire should have more than 30,000 ohms of resistance. See Figure 3–17.

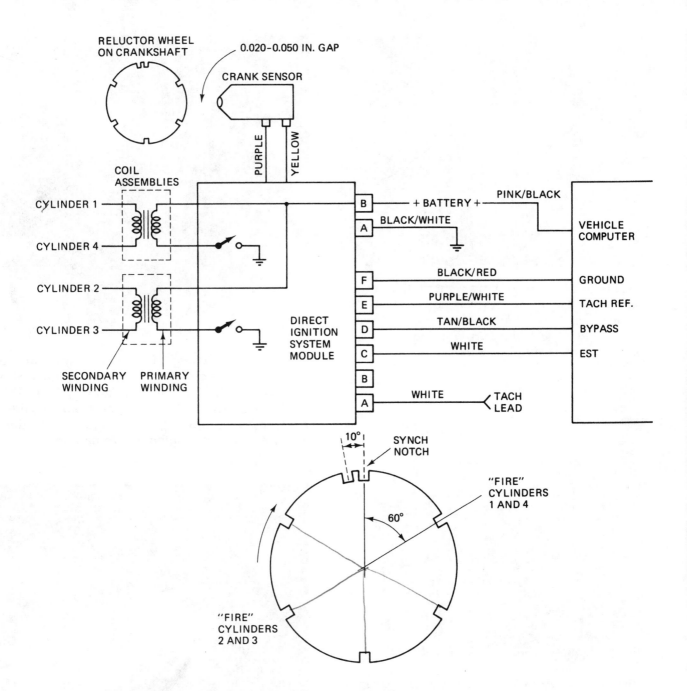

FIGURE 3–11 Wiring diagram of a typical four-cylinder direct-fire ignition system. Note that the computer receives and sends signals from and to the ignition module, but the module is the unit that actually turns on and off the primary coil circuit.

FIGURE 3–12 This coil was shorting out and caused the engine to miss on acceleration. The problem was intermittent and the cause was difficult to find. One technician was convinced that the engine required a valve job!

FIGURE 3–14 Using a vacuum hose and a grounded test light to ground one cylinder at a time on a distributorless ignition system. This works on all types of ignition systems and provides a method for grounding out one cylinder at a time without fear of damaging any component.

FIGURE 3–13 An HEI GM distributor being tested on a bench. Note how the high-voltage spark can travel quite a distance to reach the ground of the coil laminations located under the plastic coil cap.

FIGURE 3–15 Typical spark tester for conventional electronic ignition. Notice that the center electrode is visible. Required voltage to fire the tester is about 20,000 volts.

FIGURE 3–16   High-energy electronic ignition spark tester with recessed center electrode. Required voltage to fire this tester is about 25,000 volts.

FIGURE 3–17   Checking the resistance of a spark plug wire using a digital multimeter set to the ohms (Ω) position. A good spark plug wire should measure less than 10,000 ohms per foot of length.

NOTE: If a defective distributor cap or rotor is found, look further at all of the spark plug wires. When a spark plug wire fails, the voltage from the ignition coil increases. The increased voltage from the coil can penetrate through the plastic of the distributor and rotor. See Figure 3–18.

FIGURE 3–18   A carbon track in a distributor cap. These faults are sometimes difficult to spot and can cause intermittent engine missing. The usual cause of a tracked distributor cap (or coil, if the ignition is distributorless) is a defective (open) spark plug wire.

Spark plug wire can also be checked by using an oscilloscope (scope) to view the firing lines.

SPARK PLUG INSPECTION

The spark plugs should be removed and inspected whenever there is any engine operating problem. As can be seen by the photo in Figure 3–19, the condition of the spark plug indicates the condition inside the cylinder. Many technicians remove and inspect the spark plugs whenever any engine driveability problem exists to get a better understanding of what is actually occurring inside the engine. See Figures 3–20 through 3–25.

IGNITION TIMING

Ignition timing is when the spark occurs in a cylinder in relation to piston position. For maximum power and fuel economy, the spark timing must be varied according to engine RPM and engine loads to produce the peak combustion pressures in the cylinder, yet be able to perform knock free. See Figure 3–26.

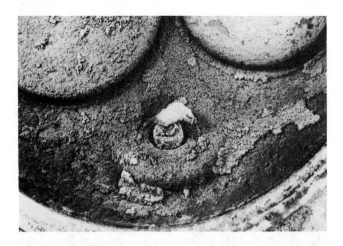

FIGURE 3–19 The engine deposits in this engine are typical of an engine run at idle or at a constant speed and load for many hours. Notice that if the spark plug is removed, the condition of the combustion chamber can be viewed without removing the cylinder head.

FIGURE 3–21 New spark plug that was fouled by a too-rich air-fuel mixture.

FIGURE 3–22 Spark plug showing heat shock damage. Abnormal combustion is the most likely cause of this condition.

FIGURE 3–20 Typical worn spark plug showing gasoline- or oil-additive deposits.

FIGURE 3–23 Severely eroded center electrode indicates excessive heat. This spark plug burned up because it was not tightened in the cylinder head, where it gets rid of its heat.

FIGURE 3–24   Note the heat blisters on the center porcelain of this spark plug. Preignition (abnormal combustion) is the most likely cause of the severe damage to this spark plug. The piston in the cylinder also suffered from the heat and started to melt.

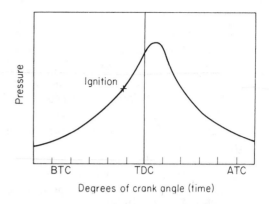

FIGURE 3–26   Pressure crank-angle graph showing normal combustion. Note how the peak pressure in the cylinder lags behind the spark and occurs slightly after the piston reaches top dead center (TDC).

FIGURE 3–25   This cracked spark plug caused the engine to miss, but not all the time. The spark plug wire was also found to be defective (too much resistance) on the same cylinder.

■ TECH TIP ■

WHAT ARE PAIRED CYLINDERS?

To help adjust valves, set cam timing, and so forth, it is helpful to know which cylinders of an engine are paired. <u>Paired cylinders are cylinders in the engine that are on exactly opposite strokes</u>. See the following examples.

Stroke	Opposite stroke
Intake	Power
Compression	Exhaust
Power	Intake
Exhaust	Compression

Paired cylinders are easily determined by writing out the firing order, then taking the last half of the firing order and placing it under the first half. Each number is paired with the number directly above or below it. For example:

1. Six–cylinder engine firing order: 165432
2. Divide in half: 165, 432
3. Place second half under first: $\dfrac{165}{432}$
4. Paired cylinders: 1 and 4, 6 and 3, 5 and 2

Most distributorless (direct-fire) ignitions fire paired cylinders at the same time.

Retarded Ignition Timing

Retarded timing means that the spark occurs *after* it should. For example, retarded timing means that the timing is set at 4 degrees before top dead center (BTDC) instead of 10 degrees BTDC.

Characteristics of excessively retarded timing include the following:

1. Long cranking period before starting
2. Poor or reduced performance and gas mileage
3. Possible slow, rough idle

Advanced Ignition Timing

Advanced timing means that a spark occurs *before* it should. For example, advanced timing means that the timing is set at 10 degrees BTDC instead of 4 degrees BTDC.

Characteristics of excessively advanced timing include the following:

1. Pings (spark knock, detonation) on acceleration
2. Possible slow, jerky engine cranking when engine is warm

METHODS OF IGNITION TIMING

Before computer-controlled ignition timing, two methods were used , either individually or combined.

Mechanical Advance

(Centrifugal Advance). The mechanical advance mechanism includes weights that are able to pivot outward with increasing engine speed. The weights are controlled and brought back by return springs. As the weights move outward, their action advances ignition timing up to a certain point determined by a "stop" in the distributor. The mechanical advance affects the performance of the engine. If the mechanical advance is working correctly, the rotor should "snap back" when turned and released while the distributor is in the engine.

Vacuum Advance

The distributor vacuum advance unit contains a rubber diaphragm that moves according to changes in engine vacuum. When engine load is light, engine vacuum is high and the vacuum advance is close to its maximum for best fuel economy. When engine load is high, engine vacuum is lower and the vacuum advance provides less spark advance to prevent spark knock. Ignition timing is set or adjusted by turning the distributor after loosening the hold-down bracket. A timing light or magnetic timing probe is used to set or adjust the base or initial timing. See Figure 3–27.

Computer-Controlled Ignition Timing

Since the early 1980s, most vehicle engines have used computer-controlled ignition timing. The computer uses

FIGURE 3–27 Typical timing marks as found on this four-cylinder display engine. Note the hole in the timing mark plate for use of a magnetic timing probe.

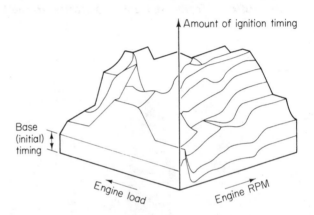

FIGURE 3–28 Typical ignition timing map developed from testing and used by the engine computer to provide the optimum ignition timing for all engine speed and load combinations.

the throttle position (TP) sensor, engine coolant temperature (ECT) sensor, engine RPM, and engine intake manifold absolute pressure (MAP) as inputs and then calculates the optimum ignition timing for maximum power and fuel economy with lowest emission. The computer program that determines what the timing should be at various values of the sensors is called a mapping, or cartographic program. The ignition timing "map" is determined by engineers by operating the engine on a dynamometer while only one variable at a time is changed; the data is then plotted on a graph that becomes the map. See Figure 3–28.

FUEL SYSTEM OPERATION

The fuel delivery system is designed to supply the carburetor(s) or fuel-injection system with clean fuel under pressure. Typical pressures include the following:

- Carburetor-equipped engine (usually uses a mechanical engine-driven fuel pump): 4 to 8 psi (28 to 55 kilopascals (kPa), 0.3 to 0.5 bar) (one bar is equal to 14.7 psi)
- Low-pressure throttle body type of fuel injector (usually uses an electric pump in the fuel tank): 9 to 13 psi (62 to 90 kilopascals (kPa), 0.6 to 0.9 bar)
- Port fuel injection (uses an electric pump in the fuel tank): 35 to 45 psi (240 to 310 kilopascals (kPa), 2.4 to 3.0 bar)

Fuel pressure alone is not enough for proper engine operation. Sufficient fuel capacity (flow) must be present. This should be at least 2 pints (1 liter) per minute (½ pint in 15 seconds).

All fuel must be filtered to prevent dirt and impurities from damaging the fuel system and/or engine. The first filter is inside the gas tank. This filter, commonly called the **fuel sock filter,** is usually not replaceable separately, but is attached to the fuel pump (if the pump is electric) and/or fuel gauge sending unit.

The replaceable fuel filter is usually located between the fuel tank and the inlet to the carburetor or fuel-injection system. For long engine and fuel system life and optimum performance, the fuel filter should be replaced every year or every 12,000 miles (19,000 kilometers [km]). (Consult vehicle manufacturers' recommendations for exact time and mileage intervals.)

If the fuel filter becomes partially clogged, the following are likely to occur:

1. There will be low power at higher engine speeds. The vehicle usually will not go faster than a certain speed (engine acts as if it has a built-in speed limit governor).
2. The engine will cut out or miss on acceleration, especially when climbing hills or during heavy-load acceleration.

A weak or defective fuel pump can also be the cause of the symptoms just listed. If an electric fuel pump for a fuel-injected engine becomes weak, additional problems include the following:

1. The engine may be hard to start.
2. There may be a rough idle and stalling.
3. Erratic shifting of the automatic transmission may be noticed as a result of engine missing due to lack of fuel pump pressure and/or volume.

■ **CAUTION:** Be certain to consult the vehicle manufacturer's recommended service and testing procedures before attempting to test or replace any component of a high-pressure electronic fuel-injection system. ■

AIR FILTERS

Every engine uses 10,000 cubic feet (cu ft) of air for every gallon of gasoline burned (or 9,000 gallons of air for every gallon of gasoline)! This air contains dirt, and dirt is an abrasive. No engine, especially a fuel-injected engine, should ever be run with dirty or partially clogged air filters. Some very poorly running engines have been "repaired" by having the air filter replaced.

NOTE: Many fuel-injected engines use air filters wherein the air enters the *inside* of the air filter and exists through to the outside of the air filter. If observed from the outside, the air filter looks clean. Always carefully inspect the inside *and* outside of all air filters.

TURBOCHARGING

A turbocharged (exhaust-driven) system is designed to provide a pressure greater than atmospheric pressure in the intake manifold. This increased pressure forces additional amounts of air and fuel into the combustion chamber over what would normally be forced in by atmospheric pressure. This increased charge increases engine power. The amount of "boost" (or pressure in the intake manifold) is measured in psi, in inches of mercury (in Hg), in bars, or in atmospheres.

1 atmosphere = 14.7 psi
1 atmosphere = 30 in Hg
1 atmosphere = 1.0 bar
1 bar = 14.7 psi

The higher the level of boost (pressure), the greater the horsepower *potential.*

However, other factors must be considered when increasing boost pressure:

1. As boost pressure increases, the temperature of the air also increases.
2. As the temperature of the air increases, combustion temperatures also increase, which increases the possibility of detonation.
3. Power can be increased by cooling the compressed air after it leaves the turbocharger. *The power can be increased about 1% per 10° F by which the air is cooled.* A typical cooling device is called an **intercooler** and is similar to a radiator, wherein outside air can pass through, cooling the pressurized heated air.

FIGURE 3–29 Typical turbocharger operation.

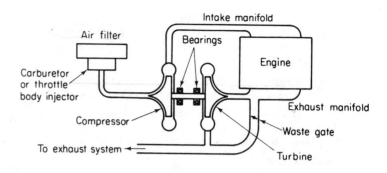

4. As boost pressure increases, combustion temperature and pressures increase, which if not limited, can do severe engine damage. The maximum exhaust gas temperature must be 1550° F (840° C). Higher temperatures decrease the durability of the turbocharger *and* the engine. See Figure 3–29.

WASTEGATE OPERATION

To prevent severe engine damage, most turbocharger systems use a wastegate. A wastegate is a valve similar to a door that can open and close. If the valve is closed, all of the exhaust travels to the turbocharger. When a predetermined amount of boost pressure develops in the intake manifold, the wastegate valve is opened. As the valve opens, the exhaust flows directly out the exhaust system, bypassing the turbocharger. With less exhaust flowing across the vanes of the turbocharger, the turbocharger decreases in speed and boost pressure is reduced. When the boost pressure drops, the wastegate valve can then close to direct the exhaust over the turbocharger vanes and again allow the boost pressure to rise. This is a continuous process of wastegate operation to control boost pressure.

The wastegate is the pressure control valve of a turbocharger system. The wastegate is usually controlled by the on-board computer. The **manifold absolute pressure (MAP) sensor** is the most important sensor used by the computer to control the wastegate. The computer usually controls a vacuum valve, which operates the wastegate valve. See Figures 3–30 and 3–31.

TURBOCHARGER FAILURES

When turbochargers fail to function correctly, a drop in power is noticed. To restore proper operation, the turbocharger must be rebuilt, repaired, or replaced. It is not possible to simply remove the turbocharger and seal any openings—and still maintain decent driveability. Bearing failure is a common cause of turbocharger failure, and replacement bearings are usually only available to rebuilders. Another common turbocharger problem

FIGURE 3–30 Turbocharger cutaway showing internal parts. The vacuum-operated wastegate is usually computer controlled.

is excessive and continuous oil consumption resulting in blue exhaust smoke. Turbochargers use small rings similar to piston rings on the shaft to prevent exhaust (combustion gases) from entering the central bearing. Because there are no seals to keep oil in, usual causes of excessive oil consumption include the following:

1. A plugged **positive crankcase ventilation (PCV)** system resulting in excessive crankcase pressures forcing oil into the air inlet. This failure is not related to the turbocharger, but the turbocharger is often blamed.
2. A clogged air filter, which causes a low-pressure area in the inlet, which can draw oil past the turbo shaft rings and into the intake manifold.
3. A clogged oil return (drain) line from the turbocharger to the oil pan (sump), which can cause the engine oil pressure to force oil past the turbocharger's shaft rings and into the intake *and* exhaust manifolds. Obviously, oil being forced into both the intake and exhaust would create lots of smoke.

FIGURE 3–31 Typical turbocharger installation. The wastegate is computer controlled based on input signals regarding engine RPM, coolant temperature, MAP, and other variables.

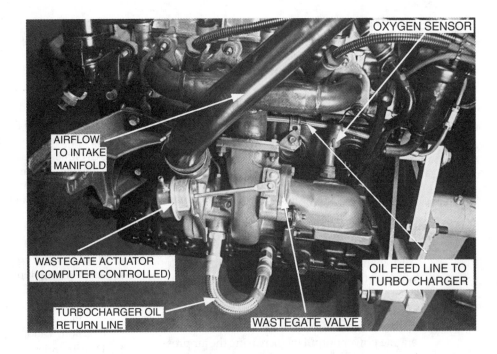

SUPERCHARGING

A supercharging system is an engine-driven system designed to provide pressure greater than atmospheric pressure in the intake manifold. See Figure 3–32. Supercharging has some advantages and some disadvantages as compared to turbocharging.

Advantages	Disadvantages
1. Gives instantaneous throttle response (no lag)	1. Takes power from the engine
2. Involves less plumbing (no connections to the exhaust system)	2. Drains power from the engine all the time

BOOST IS THE RESULT OF RESTRICTION

Boost pressure of a turbocharger (or supercharger) is commonly measured in pounds per square inch. If a cylinder head is restricted because of small valves and ports, the turbocharger will quickly provide boost. Boost results when the air being forced into the cylinder heads cannot flow into the cylinders fast enough and "piles up" in the intake manifold, increasing boost pressure. If an engine had large valves and ports, the turbocharger could provide a much greater *amount* of air into the engine at the same boost pressure as an identical engine with smaller valves and ports.

FIGURE 3–32 Cutaway of a Roots-type, positive displacement–type supercharger. The air is drawn from the top and flows outward and down between the rotors and the housing, where the air is trapped and compressed.

SUMMARY

1. The engine operating system includes those systems that support the purpose and function of the engine.
2. The engine operating system includes the fuel delivery system, the ignition system, and the battery, plus the starter and charging circuits.
3. A battery must be fully charged to be able to supply the current (amperes) necessary for

cranking, especially when the engine is cold and the engine oil is thick.

4. A fully charged 12-volt battery should give a reading of 12.6 volts or higher on a voltmeter.

5. A starter motor can be tested for current draw.

6. The ignition system functions by supplying battery voltage to the positive terminal of an ignition coil and pulsing the negative terminal to ground. A spark occurs when the ground is removed by the ignition module.

7. A pickup coil or crankshaft sensor signals the ignition module as to when to fire the spark plugs.

8. Spark plugs are the window to the inside of the engine and should be thoroughly inspected during engine trouble diagnosis.

9. Ignition timing is a matter of when the spark occurs to the spark plug in relation to piston position.

10. Turbochargers and superchargers both increase engine power output by increasing the air pressure in the intake manifold to above the atmospheric pressure level, thereby increasing the amount of air and fuel drawn into the engine.

REVIEW QUESTIONS

1. Explain why a battery loses much of its current-producing capability at low temperatures.

2. Explain why all batteries must be bolted down to the vehicle.

3. Explain how to test a battery using a voltmeter.

4. Describe the procedure for load testing a battery.

5. Describe starter motor testing using a voltmeter and an ammeter.

6. Describe the operation of an electronic ignition.

7. Why does an engine require that the ignition timing be changed according to engine speed and load?

8. List three reasons why a turbocharged engine might burn oil.

MULTIPLE-CHOICE QUESTIONS

1. Technician A says that a fully charged 12-volt battery should have 12.6 volts or higher. Technician B says that a battery should be loaded to one-half of its CCA rating for 15 seconds during a load test. Which technician is correct?
   a. A only
   b. B only
   c. Both A and B
   d. Neither A nor B

2. Technician A says that a slowly cranking engine could be caused by a weak battery or worn starter motor. Technician B says that a mechanical engine problem could be the cause of slow cranking. Which technician is correct?
   a. A only
   b. B only
   c. Both A and B
   d. Neithe.r A nor B

3. A voltmeter reads 11.1 volts while an engine is being cranked. Technician A says that the starter is okay. Technician B says that the battery may be discharged. Which technician is correct?
   a. A only
   b. B only
   c. Both A and B
   d. Neither a nor b

4. Electronic ignition works by means of a _____ .
   a. Pickup coil triggering a module
   b. Module triggering an ignition coil
   c. Pickup coil triggering an ignition coil
   d. Both a and b

5. Distributorless ignition systems _____ .
   a. Fire two cylinders at the same time
   b. Fire paired cylinders
   c. Use the computer to control ignition timing
   d. All of the above

6. Ignition timing that is too far advanced can cause _____ .
   a. A long cranking period before starting
   b. Poor performance
   c. Reduced fuel economy
   d. Pinging on acceleration

7. Ignition timing that is too far retarded can cause _____ .
   a. Pinging on acceleration
   b. Possible slow, jerky cranking
   c. A long cranking period before starting
   d. None of the above

8. Technician A says that spark plugs should be checked using a spark tester. Technician B says that spark plugs should be tested using an old spark plug. Which technician is correct?
   a. A only
   b. B only
   c. Both A and B
   d. Neither A nor B

9. Typical port fuel-injection fuel pump pressure is _____ .
   a. 4 to 8 psi
   b. 9 to 13 psi
   c. 10 to 20 psi
   d. 35 to 45 psi

10. The wastegate of a turbocharger controls _____ .
   a. The air inlet to the turbo
   b. The air outlet from the turbo
   c. The exhaust flow to the turbo
   d. The intercooler temperature

Engine Fuels and Driveability Diagnosis

OBJECTIVES

After studying Chapter 4, the reader will be able to

1. Discuss the properties of gasoline.
2. Describe how to select the proper grade of gasoline.
3. List gasoline purchasing hints.
4. Explain how volatility affects driveability.
5. Explain how oxygenated fuels can reduce CO exhaust emissions.

The quality of the fuel any engine uses is very important to its proper operation and long life. If the fuel is not right for the air temperature or if the tendency of the fuel to evaporate is incorrect, severe driveability problems can result. An engine burns about 10,000 cubic feet of air (a box 10 feet × 10 feet × 100 feet) for every cubic foot of gasoline (about 7.5 gallons).

GASOLINE

Gasoline is a term used to describe a complex mixture of various hydrocarbons refined from crude petroleum oil for use as a fuel in engines. The word **petroleum** means rock oil. The refinery where gasoline is produced removes undesirable ingredients such as paraffins and puts in additives such as octane improvers. Most gasoline is "blended" to meet the needs of the local climates and altitudes.

VOLATILITY

Volatility describes how easily the gasoline evaporates (forms a vapor). The definition of volatility assumes that the vapors will remain in the fuel tank or fuel line and will cause a certain pressure based on the temperature of the fuel.

Winter Blend

Reid vapor pressure (RVP) is the pressure of the vapor above the fuel when the fuel is at 100° F (38° C). Increased vapor pressure permits the engine to start in cold weather. Gasoline without air will not burn. Gasoline must be vaporized (mixed with air) to burn in an engine. Cold temperatures reduce the normal vaporization of gasoline; therefore, winter-blended gasoline is specially formulated to vaporize at lower temperatures for proper starting and driveability at low ambient temperatures. The **American Society for Testing and Materials (ASTM)** standards for winter-blend gasoline allow volatility of up to 15 psi RVP.

Summer Blend

At warm ambient temperatures, gasoline vaporizes easily. However, the fuel system (fuel pump, carburetor, fuel-injector nozzles, etc.) is designed to operate with *liquid* gasoline. The volatility of summer-grade gasoline should be about 7.0 psi RVP. According to ASTM standards, the maximum RVP should be 10.5 psi for summer-blend gasoline.

VOLATILITY PROBLEMS

At higher temperatures, liquid gasoline can easily vaporize and this can cause **vapor lock**. Vapor lock is a *lean* condition caused by vaporized fuel in the fuel system. This vaporized fuel takes up space normally occupied by liquid fuel and prevents normal fuel pump operation.

Vapor lock is caused by bubbles that form in the fuel, preventing proper operation of the fuel pump, carburetor, or fuel-injection system.

■ TECH TIP ■

THE SNIFF TEST

Problems can occur with stale gasoline from which the lighter parts of the gasoline have evaporated. Stale gasoline usually results in a "no start" situation. If stale gasoline is suspected, smell the gasoline. If it is rancid smelling, replace the gasoline with fresh gasoline.

NOTE: If storing a vehicle, boat, or lawn mower over the winter, put some gasoline stabilizer into the gasoline to reduce the evaporation and separation that can occur during storage. Gasoline stabilizer is frequently found at lawn mower repair shops or marinas.

Bubbles in the fuel can be caused by heat or by sharp bends in the fuel system. Heat causes some of the fuel to evaporate, thereby causing bubbles. Sharp bends cause the fuel to be restricted at the bend. When the fuel flows past the bend, the fuel can expand to fill the space after the bend. This expansion drops the pressure, and bubbles form in the fuel lines. When the fuel is full of bubbles, the engine is not being supplied with enough fuel and the engine runs lean. A lean engine will stumble during acceleration, will run rough, and may stall. Warm weather and alcohol-blended fuels both tend to increase vapor lock and engine performance problems.

If winter-blend gasoline (or high-RVP fuel) is used in an engine during warm weather, the following problems may occur:

- Rough idle
- Stalling
- Hesitation on acceleration
- Surging

NORMAL AND ABNORMAL COMBUSTION

The octane rating of gasoline is the measure of its antiknock properties. **Engine knock** (also called **detonation, spark knock,** or **ping**) is a metallic noise an engine makes, usually during acceleration, resulting from abnormal or uncontrolled combustion inside the cylinder.

Normal combustion occurs smoothly and progresses across the combustion chamber from the point of ignition. See Figure 4–1.

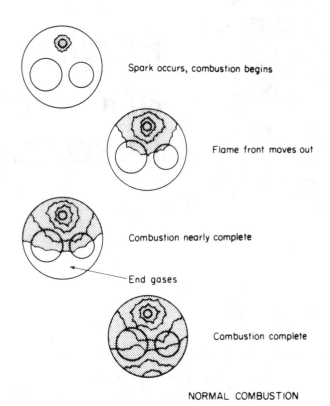

Spark occurs, combustion begins

Flame front moves out

Combustion nearly complete

End gases

Combustion complete

NORMAL COMBUSTION

FIGURE 4–1 Flame front movement during normal combustion.

Normal combustion propagation is between 45 and 90 miles per hour (mph) (72 and 145 kilometers per hour [km/ph]). The speed of the flame front depends on air-fuel ratio, combustion chamber design (determining amount of turbulence), and temperature.

During periods of spark knock (detonation), the combustion speed increases by up to 10 times to near the speed of sound. The increased combustion speed also causes increased temperatures and pressures, which can damage pistons, gaskets, and cylinder heads. See Figures 4–2 and 4–3.

One of the first additives used in gasoline was **tetraethyl lead** (TEL). Tetraethyl lead was added to gasoline in the early 1920s to reduce the tendency to knock. It was often called "ethyl" or "high test" gasoline.

Shortly after the introduction of tetraethyl lead as a fuel additive, the Society of Automotive Engineers established standards for the antiknock rating of gasoline. With standardized fuel, the automobile manufacturers could produce engines that would operate knock free based on the quality of the available fuel.

The antiknock "standard" or basis of comparison was the knock-resistant hydrocarbon **isooctane**, chemically called trimethylpentane (C_8H_{18}), also known as 2-2-4 trimethylpentane. If a gasoline tested had the exact same antiknock characteristics as isooctane, it

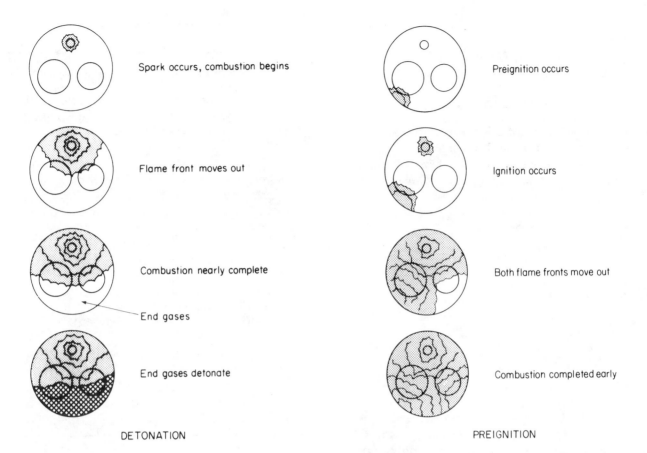

DETONATION

PREIGNITION

FIGURE 4–2   Flame front movement and end gas reaction during knock or detonation.

FIGURE 4–3   Flame front movement during preignition.

was rated as 100-octane gasoline. If the gasoline tested had only 85% of the antiknock properties of isooctane, it was rated as 85 octane. Remember, octane rating is only a *comparison* test.

In actual testing, a special single-cylinder engine called a **cooperative fuel research (CFR) engine** is used. A test fuel is compared in this engine with a known combination of isooctane (with an octane rating of 100) and another hydrocarbon called N-heptane (C_7H_{16}) (with an octane rating of zero). For example, if the knock resistance of a fuel is the same as that of a test fuel with a ratio of 9 parts isooctane to 1 part N-heptane, the unknown fuel has a rating of 90 octane.

RESEARCH AND MOTOR METHODS OF OCTANE RATING

There are two basic methods used to rate gasoline for antiknock properties (octane rating): the "research method" and the "motor method." Each uses a model of the special CFR single-cylinder engine. The research method and the motor method vary as to temperature of air, spark advance, and other parameters.

The research method typically results in readings that are 6 to 10 "points" higher than those of the motor method. For example, a fuel with a research octane number (RON) of 93 might have a motor octane number (MON) of 85.

The octane rating posted on pumps in the United States is the average of the two methods and is referred to as $(R + M)/2$, meaning that, for the fuel used in the previous example, the rating posted on the pumps would be

$$\frac{RON + MON}{2} = \frac{93 + 85}{2} = 89$$

See Figures 4–4 and 4–5.

GASOLINE GRADES AND OCTANE NUMBERS

The posted octane ratings on gasoline pumps are the ratings achieved by the average of the research and the motor methods. Except in high-altitude areas, the grades and octane ratings are as follows:

Grades	Octane ratings
Regular	87
Mid-grade (also called Plus)	89
Premium	91 or higher

OCTANE IMPROVERS

When the gasoline companies, under federal EPA regulations, removed tetraethyl lead from gasoline, other methods were developed to help maintain the antiknock properties of gasoline. Octane improvers (enhancers) can be grouped into three broad categories:

Knock Test

Condition	Research	Motor
* Engine speed	600	900
Oil temperature	135	135
Coolant temperature	212	212
Intake humidity 9r/lb air	25–50	25–50
* Intake air temperature	125	100
* Mixture temperature	—	300
* Spark advance	13	varies with CR
Fuel/air ratio	adj for max knock	adj for max knock

FIGURE 4–4   Test parameters for research and motor methods. Notice that the research method results in less knock (higher-octane reading) because the ignition timing is fixed, whereas the motor method varies the timing and has a higher engine speed than the speed used during the research test.

FIGURE 4–5   Engine and instruments used to check the octane rating of gasoline. The large meter in the center top of the console is called the knockmeter.

HORSEPOWER AND FUEL FLOW

To produce 1 horsepower, the engine must be supplied ½ pound of fuel per hour. Fuel injectors are rated in pounds per hour. For example, a V-8 engine equipped with 25 lb/hr fuel injectors could produce 50 horsepower per cylinder (per injector) or 400 horsepower. Even if the cylinder heads or block are modified to produce more horsepower, the limiting factor may be the injector flow rate.

The following are flow rates and resulting horsepower for a V-8 engine:

30 lb/hr: 60 hp per cylinder or 480 hp
35 lb/hr: 70 hp per cylinder or 560 hp
40 lb/hr: 80 hp per cylinder or 640 hp

Of course, injector flow rate is just one of many variables that affect power output. Installing larger injectors without other major engine modification could decrease engine output and drastically increase exhaust emissions.

1. Aromatic hydrocarbons (hydrocarbons containing the benzene ring) such as xylene and toluene
2. Alcohols such as ethanol (ethyl alcohol), methanol (methyl alcohol), and tertiary butyl alcohol (TBA)
3. Metallic compounds such as tetraethyl lead and methylcyclopentadienyl manganese tricarbonyl (MMT)

NOTE: Both TEL and MMT have been proven to be harmful to catalytic converters and are no longer being used as octane improvers in pump gasoline. However, MMT is currently one of the active ingredients commonly found in octane improvers available to the public.

Propane and butane, which are volatile by-products of the refinery process, are also often added to gasoline as octane improvers. The increase in volatility caused by the added propane and butane often leads to hot weather driveability problems.

OXYGENATED FUELS

Oxygenated fuels contain oxygen in the molecule of the fuel itself. Examples of oxygenated fuels include methanol, ethanol, methyl tertiary butyl ether (MTBE), and ethyl tertiary butyl ether (ETBE).

Oxygenated fuels are commonly used in high-altitude areas to reduce carbon monoxide (CO) emissions. The extra oxygen in the fuel itself is used to convert harmful CO into CO_2 (carbon dioxide). The extra oxygen in the fuel helps ensure that there is enough oxygen to convert all the CO into CO_2 during the combustion process in the engine or catalytic converter.

MTBE

Methyl tertiary butyl ether is manufactured by means of the chemical reaction of methanol and isobutylene. Unlike methanol, MTBE does not increase the volatility of the fuel, and it is not as sensitive to water as are other alcohols. The maximum allowable volume level, according to the EPA, is 15%.

ETBE

Ethyl tertiary butyl ether is derived from ethanol. The maximum allowable volume level is 17.2%. The use of ETBE is the cause of much of the odor from the exhaust of vehicles using reformulated gasoline.

Ethanol

Ethyl alcohol is drinkable alcohol made from grain. Adding 10% ethanol (ethyl alcohol or grain alcohol) increases the (R + M)/2 octane rating by 3 points. The alcohol added to the base gasoline, however, also raises the volatility of the fuel about ½ psi. Most automobile manufacturers permit up to 10% ethanol if driveability problems are not experienced. The oxygen content of a 10% blend of ethanol in gasoline is 3.5% oxygen by weight. See Figure 4–6.

Methanol

Methyl alcohol is made from wood (wood alcohol), natural gas, or coal. Methanol is poisonous if drunk and tends to be more harmful to the materials in the fuel system, and it tends to separate when combined with gasoline unless used with a cosolvent. A cosolvent is another substance (usually another alcohol) that is soluble in both methanol and gasoline and is used to reduce the tendency of the liquids to separate. Methanol can damage fuel system parts. Methanol is corrosive to lead (used as a coating of fuel tanks), aluminum, magnesium, and some plastics and rubber. Methanol can also cause rubber products (elastomers) to swell and soften. Methanol itself is 50% oxygen. Gasoline containing 5% methanol would have an oxygen content of 2.5% by weight.

FIGURE 4–6   Note that the midgrade contains 10% ethanol, whereas the regular and the premium grade are listed as containing 100% pure gasoline.

■ **CAUTION:**   All alcohols can absorb water, and the alcohol-water mixture can separate from the gasoline and sink to the bottom of the fuel tank. This is called **phase separation.** To help avoid engine performance problems, try to keep at least a quarter tank of fuel at all times, especially during seasons in which there is a wide temperature span between daytime highs and nighttime lows. These conditions can cause moisture to accumulate in the fuel tank as a result of condensation of the moisture in the air. ■

ALCOHOL ADDITIVES—ADVANTAGES AND DISADVANTAGES

The advantages and disadvantages of using alcohol as an additive to gasoline can be summarized as follows:

Advantages

1. Alcohol absorbs moisture in the fuel tank.
2. Ten percent alcohol added to gasoline raises the octane rating—(R + M)/2—by 3 points.
3. Alcohol cleans the fuel system.
4. The addition of alcohol reduces carbon monoxide (CO) emissions because alcohol contains oxygen.

Disadvantages

1. The use of alcohol can result in the clogging of fuel filters with dirt and so forth cleaned from fuel tank, pump, and lines.
2. Alcohol raises the volatility of fuel about ½ psi; this can cause hot weather driveability problems.
3. Addition of alcohol reduces the heat content of the resulting fuel mixture (alcohol has about

one-half of the energy content of gasoline)—compare 60,000 to 75,000 British thermal units (BTUs) per gallon for alcohol versus about 130,000 BTUs per gallon for gasoline.

4. Alcohol absorbs water and then separates from the gasoline, especially as temperature drops. Separated alcohol and water on the bottom of the tank can cause hard starting during cold weather. Alcohol does not vaporize easily at low temperatures.

COMBUSTION CHEMISTRY

Internal combustion engines burn an organic fuel to produce power. The term **organic** refers to a product (gasoline) from a source that originally was alive. Because crude oil originally came from living plants and animals, all products of petroleum are considered organic fuels and are composed primarily of hydrogen (H) and carbon (C).

The combustion process involves the chemical combination of oxygen (O_2) from the air (about 21% of the atmosphere) with the hydrogen and carbon from the fuel. In a gasoline engine, a spark starts the combustion process, which takes about 3 milliseconds (ms) (0.003 seconds) to be completed inside the cylinder of an engine. The chemical reaction that takes place can be summarized as follows: hydrogen (H) plus carbon (C) plus oxygen (O_2) plus nitrogen plus spark equals heat plus water (H_2O) plus carbon monoxide (CO) plus carbon dioxide (CO_2) plus hydrocarbons (HC) plus oxides of nitrogen (NO_X) plus many other chemicals.

If the combustion process is complete, all of the gasoline (hydrocarbons [HC]) will be completely combined with all of the available oxygen (O_2). This total combination of all components of the fuel is called **stoichiometric.** The stoichiometric quantities for gasoline are 14.7 parts air for 1 part gasoline by weight. Different fuels have different stoichiometric proportions.

The heat produced by the combustion process is measured in BTUs. One BTU is the amount of heat required to raise 1 pound of water 1 Fahrenheit degree. The metric unit of heat is the calorie (cal). One calorie is the amount of heat required to raise the temperature of 1 gram (g) of water 1 Celsius degree.

Fuel	Heat energy (BTUs/gal)	Stoichiometric ratio
Gasoline	About 130,000	14.7:1
Ethanol alcohol	About 76,000	9.0:1
Methanol alcohol	About 60,000	6.4:1

HIGH-ALTITUDE OCTANE REQUIREMENTS

As the altitude increases, atmospheric pressure drops. The air is less dense because a pound of air takes more volume. The octane rating of fuel does not need to be as high because the engine cannot intake as much air. This will reduce the combustion (compression) pressures inside the engine. In mountainous areas, gasoline (R + M)/2 octane ratings are two or more numbers lower than normal (according to SAE, about one octane number lower per 1000 feet [300 meters] in altitude). See Figure 4–7. A secondary reason for the lowered octane requirement of engines running at higher altitudes is the normal enrichment of the air-fuel ratio and lower engine vacuum with the decreased air density. Some problems, therefore, may occur when driving out of high-altitude areas into lower-altitude areas where octane rating needs to be higher. Most computerized engine control systems can compensate for changes in altitude and modify air-fuel ratio and ignition timing for best operation.

FIGURE 4–7 *Photo of gasoline pump taken in a high-altitude area. Note the lower than normal octane ratings. The "Ethanol" sticker reads that all grades contain 10% ethanol from November 1 through February 28 each year to help reduce carbon monoxide (CO) exhaust emissions.*

Because the combustion burn rate slows down at high altitude, the ignition (spark) timing can be advanced to improve power. The amount of timing advance can be about 1 degree per 1000 feet over 5000 feet. Therefore, if driving at 8000 feet of altitude, the ignition timing can be advanced 3 degrees.

High altitude also allows fuel to evaporate more easily. The volatility of fuel should be reduced at higher altitudes to prevent vapor from forming in sections of the fuel system, which can cause driveability and stalling problems. The extra heat generated in climbing to higher altitudes plus the lower atmospheric pressure at higher altitudes combine to cause vapor lock problems as the vehicle is going to higher altitudes.

VALVE RECESSION AND UNLEADED FUEL

Unleaded fuel has been available since the early 1970s, and ever since that time there has been concern about valve problems related to using unleaded fuel. However, back in the 1920s when "leaded" gasoline was first introduced, the main problem then was with the valves. In the 1920s, the lead deposits in the engine prevented the valves from fully seating. This resulted in overheated valves because the major place where valves get rid of their heat is through the valve face or seat area. The solution to valve burning in the 1920s with leaded fuel was to increase the valve spring tension. This increased pressure smashed the lead deposits into a thin lubricating film, allowing the valve to fully close and thereby transfer heat to the seat area.

Without lead, the valve movement against the seat tears away tiny iron oxide particles during engine operation. The valve movement causes these particles of iron oxide to act like valve grinding compound, cutting into the valve seat surface. As the valve seat is eroded, the valve recedes further into the cylinder head. See Figure 4–8.

Vehicle engines produced after 1971 for sale in the United States had to be able to operate on unleaded fuel. Most engine manufacturers started induction hardening of valve seats to help prevent valve recession. A summary of factors regarding unleaded fuel is as follows:

1. All vehicle engines built after the mid-1970s should have hardened valve seats (usually, just the exhaust seats). (Some light-duty and medium-duty truck engines may not have hardened seats if unleaded fuel was not required when the truck was manufactured.)

2. Many heavy-duty engines were manufactured using hardened valve seats *prior* to the mid-1970s.

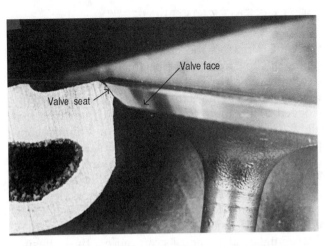

FIGURE 4–8 Using unleaded gasoline in an engine without hardened valve seats can cause valve seat erosion (wear). This wear may require years of driving before the valves will have to be ground and the seat restored or replaced.

3. Valve seat erosion is most likely to occur, or to be substantially increased, because of high engine speeds (RPMs) and/or high engine loads, both of which create higher combustion chamber temperatures and pressures.

4. Generally a level of only 0.1 gram of tetraethyl lead per gallon is required to prevent valve seat recession.

5. Additives containing tetraethyl lead are generally not economically feasible because the amount of lead that can be sold cannot exceed 4.2 grams per gallon. Therefore, it would require an entire quart of additive per 10 gallons of unleaded fuel to bring the level to 0.1 gram per gallon.

6. Older-model and antique vehicles would probably not suffer valve damage from using unleaded fuel for many years if the engines were not used for long periods at high RPM or under high loads. If and when the engine needed to be overhauled, hardened exhaust valve seats could be installed to prevent any future valve problems.

7. Engines with the highest risk of valve damage (recession) are engines that are continuously operated at high engine speeds (RPM) and/or high engine loads. Typical examples of such engines would be those used in farm equipment, irrigation pumps, generators, or similar industry or mining applications. Whenever repairing or overhauling an engine used in continuous service, hardened valve seats should be installed.

DETERGENT GASOLINE

Since the mid-1980s most gasoline refiners have added detergents to gasoline. The original reason for adding detergents was to clean fuel-injection nozzles and keep them clean. The injector nozzles become partially clogged as a result of heat and short-trip driving that allow the olefins (a classification of organic compounds) in the gasoline to accumulate and form deposits on the critical surfaces of the injector nozzle. The added detergents (usually **polyether amine**) did help dissolve the deposits and keep injectors clean; but while removing deposits on the fuel-injector nozzles, they also tend to *create* deposits on the intake valves. These intake valve deposits can cause a **tip-in hesitation** (a hesitation that occurs as soon as the driver's foot is tipped into the accelerator). The hesitation occurs because these deposits tend to be porous like a sponge and can absorb fuel, especially when the engine is cold, keeping some of the fuel from reaching the combustion chamber. These deposits are often called "cauliflower" deposits because they resemble that vegetable in appearance. This type of valve deposit can also reduce power output by restricting the flow of the intake charge going into the engine and by reducing the swirl of the charge that is normally designed to be part of the induction system. According to several manufacturers, the only recommended method for removing these intake valve deposits without removing the cylinder head(s) or valves, is to blast the back of the closed valves with walnut shells, then vacuum them out. The walnut shells are angular and hard enough to dislodge the deposits without damaging aluminum heads.

REFORMULATED GASOLINE

To help reduce emissions, the gasoline refiners reformulate gasoline in the following manner:

1. **Reduce light compounds.** They eliminate butane, pentane, and propane, which have a low boiling point and evaporate easily. These unburned hydrocarbons (HC) are released into the atmosphere during refueling and through the fuel tank vent system, contributing to smog formation.
2. **Reduce heavy compounds.** They eliminate heavy compounds with high boiling points such as aromatics and olefins. The purpose of this reduction is to reduce the amount of unburned hydrocarbons (HC) that goes to the catalytic converter. Increased use of oxygen-containing MTBE (methyl tertiary butyl ether) helps the combustion process to reduce emissions.

GOVERNMENT TEST FUEL

Because of the variation of commercially available fuel, the federal government uses a standardized fuel for testing engines for emission and fuel economy. This standard fuel is **indolene,** and it is used as a standard replacement for regular unleaded gasoline during these tests.

DIESEL FUEL

Diesel fuel must meet an entirely different set of standards than gasoline. The fuel in a diesel engine is not ignited with a spark, but is ignited by the heat generated by high compression. The pressure of compression (400 to 700 psi or 2800 to 4800 kilopascals) generates temperatures of 1200° to 1600° F (700° to 900° C), which speeds the preflame reaction to start the ignition of fuel injected into the cylinder.

All diesel fuel must be clean, be able to flow at low temperatures, and be of the proper cetane rating.

- **Cleanliness.** It is imperative that the fuel used in a diesel engine be clean and free from water. Unlike the case with gasoline engines, the fuel is the lubricant and coolant for the diesel injector pump and injectors. Good-quality diesel fuel contains additives such as oxidation inhibitors, detergents, dispersants, rust preventives, and metal deactivators.
- **Low-temperature fluidity.** Diesel fuel must be able to flow freely at all expected ambient temperatures. One specification for diesel fuel is its "pour point," which is the temperature below which the fuel would stop flowing. **Cloud point** is another concern with diesel fuel at lower temperatures. Cloud point is the low-temperature point at which the waxes present in most diesel fuel tend to form wax crystals that clog the fuel filter. Most diesel fuel suppliers distribute fuel with the proper pour point and cloud point for the climate conditions of the area.
- **Cetane number.** The cetane number for diesel fuel is the opposite of the octane number for gasoline. The cetane number is a measure of the ease with which the fuel can be ignited. The cetane rating of the fuel determines, to a great extent, its ability to start the engine at low temperatures and to provide smooth warm-up and even combustion. The cetane rating of diesel fuel should be between 45 and 50. The higher the cetane rating, the more easily the fuel is ignited, whereas the higher the octane rating, the more slowly the fuel is ignited.

Other diesel fuel specifications include its flash point, sulfur content, and classification. The **flash point** is the temperature at which the vapors on the surface of the fuel will ignite if exposed to an open flame. The flash point does *not* affect diesel engine operation. However, a lower than normal flash point could indicate contamination of the diesel fuel with gasoline or a similar substance.

The sulfur content of diesel fuel is very important to the life of the engine. Most engine manufacturers specify that only fuel containing less than about 0.3% sulfur be used. The current limit as set by the American Society for Testing and Materials (ASTM) is 0.5% maximum. Sulfur in the fuel creates sulfuric acid during the combustion process, which can damage engine components and cause piston ring wear.

ASTM also classifies diesel fuel by volatility (boiling range) into the following grades:

Grade #1. This grade of diesel fuel has the lowest boiling point and the lowest cloud and pour points. As a result, grade #1 is suitable for use during low-temperature operation. Grade #1 may be specified for use in diesel engines involved in frequent changes in load and speed, such as those found in city buses and delivery trucks.

Grade #2. This grade has a higher boiling range, cloud point, and pour point as compared with grade #1. It is usually specified where constant speed and high loads are encountered, such as in long-haul trucking and automotive diesel applications.

Grade #4. This very high boiling range fuel is designed for use in low-speed engines running under a constant load. Grade #4, therefore, is used in stationary power plants and ships.

GENERAL GASOLINE RECOMMENDATIONS

The fuel used by an engine is a major expense in the operation cost of the vehicle. The proper operation of the engine depends on clean fuel of the proper octane rating and vapor pressure for the atmospheric conditions.

To help ensure proper engine operation and keep fuel costs to a minimum, follow these guidelines:

■ Purchase fuel from a busy station. This helps ensure that the fuel is fresh and less likely to be contaminated with water or moisture.

■ Keep the fuel tank above one-quarter full, especially during seasons in which the temperature rises and falls by more than 20 degrees between daytime highs and nighttime lows. This helps to reduce condensed moisture in the fuel tank and could prevent gas line freeze-up in freezing weather.

NOTE: Gasline freeze-up occurs when the *water in the gasoline freezes and forms an ice blockage in the fuel line.*

■ Do not purchase fuel with a higher-octane rating than is necessary. Try using premium high-octane fuel to check for operating differences. Most newer engines are equipped with a detonation (knock) sensor that signals the vehicle

■ TECH TIP ■

CAN WATER INJECTION INCREASE HORSEPOWER AND FUEL ECONOMY?

Water-injection systems are often sold as a method for increasing power and fuel economy and reducing spark knock (ping). Most of these "kits" incorporate a vacuum (engine load) sensor and an electric water pump that supplies a stream of water into the air intake of the engine while the engine is under load. The water (or water and alcohol mixture to prevent freezing in cold weather) reduces the temperature of the combustion process inside the cylinders. The water does not burn, but rather, occupies space and mass. The water droplets must absorb heat while being turned into steam inside the combustion chamber. A lot of heat is required to turn this water to steam (heat of vaporization), and therefore, the water takes heat from the combustion process. Because the combustion process is cooled, the rate of preflame reactions is slowed, which allows the flame front to sweep through the charge to reduce spark knock (ping) and permits controlled, normal combustion to occur.

Because the combustion process is cooled by the water, it may be possible to advance the ignition timing to provide more power without spark knock. It is the advancement of the ignition timing that *could* improve the performance and fuel economy, and not the water injection itself directly.

NOTE: Using water injection can be harmful to the engine. Excessive water can cause rust and create acids when combined with engine oil.

computer to retard the ignition timing when spark knock occurs. Therefore, an operating difference may not be noticeable to the driver when using a low-octane fuel, except for a decrease in power and fuel economy. In other words, the engine with a knock sensor will tend to operate knock free on regular fuel, even if premium, higher-octane fuel is specified. Using premium fuel may result in more power and greater fuel economy. The increase in fuel economy, however, would have to be substantial to justify the increased cost of high-octane premium fuel. Some drivers find a good compromise by using midgrade fuel to benefit from the engine power and fuel economy gains without the cost of using premium fuel all the time.

■ Avoid using gasoline with alcohol in warm weather, even though many alcohol blends do not affect engine driveability. If warm-engine stumble, stalling, or rough idle occurs, change brands of gasoline.

■ Do not purchase fuel from a retail outlet when a tanker truck is filling the underground tanks. During the refilling procedure, dirt, rust, and water may be stirred up in the underground tanks. This undesirable material may be pumped into your vehicle's fuel tank.

■ Do not overfill the gas tank. After the nozzle "clicks off," add just enough fuel to round up to the next dime. Adding additional gasoline will cause the excess to be drawn into the charcoal canister. This can lead to engine flooding and excessive exhaust emissions.

SUMMARY

1. Gasoline is a complex blend of hydrocarbons. Gasoline is blended for seasonal usage for the correct volatility for easy starting and maximum fuel economy under all driving conditions.
2. Winter-blend fuel used in a vehicle during warm weather can cause a rough idle and stalling because of the higher RVP or Reid vapor pressure of winter-grade fuel.
3. Abnormal combustion (also called detonation or spark knock) increases both the temperature and the pressure inside the combustion chamber.
4. Most regular-grade gasoline today (using the [R + M]/2 rating method) is 87 octane, midgrade (plus) is 89, and premium grade is 91 or higher.

5. Oxygenated fuels usually contain alcohol or MTBE that includes oxygen in its content to lower CO exhaust emissions.
6. Gasoline should always be purchased from a busy station, and the tank should not be overfilled.

REVIEW QUESTIONS

1. Describe the difference between summer-blend and winter-blend gasoline.
2. Define Reid vapor pressure.
3. Define vapor lock.
4. Describe the (R + M)/2 gasoline pump octane rating.
5. Name five octane improvers that may be used during the refinery process.
6. Define *stoichiometric*.
7. Describe how valves can recede into the head on engines using unleaded gasoline without hardened valve seats.
8. What are cauliflower deposits?
9. Compare the cetane rating for diesel fuel with the octane rating for gasoline.

MULTIPLE-CHOICE QUESTIONS

1. Winter-blend gasoline _____ .
   a. Vaporizes more easily than summer-blend gasoline
   b. Has a higher RVP
   c. Can cause engine driveability problems if used during warm weather
   d. All of the above
2. Vapor lock _____ .
   a. Can occur as a result of excessive heat near fuel lines
   b. Can occur if a fuel line is restricted
   c. Both A and B
   d. Neither A nor B
3. Technician A says that spark knock, ping, and detonation are different names for abnormal combustion. Technician B says that any abnormal combustion raises the temperature and pressure inside the combustion chamber and can cause severe engine damage. Which technician is correct?
   a. A only
   b. B only
   c. Both A and B
   d. Neither A nor B
4. Technician A says that the research octane number is higher than the motor octane number. Technician B says that the octane rating posted on fuel pumps is an average of the two ratings. Which technician is correct?
   a. A only
   b. B only
   c. Both A and B
   d. Neither A nor B

5. Technician A says that in going to high altitudes, a non-computer-controlled engine becomes richer and lower on power. Technician B says that most computerized engine control systems can compensate for changes in altitude. Which technician is correct?
   a.   A only
   b.   B only
   c.   Both A and B
   d.   Neither A nor B

6. Valve seat recession is most likely to occur with older engines *not* equipped with hardened valve seats if _____ .
   a.   Driven at high speeds and with heavy loads
   b.   Driven at slow speeds and with light loads
   c.   Used at idle most or all of the time
   d.   Both a and c

7. Where would a technician use walnut shells while servicing an engine?
   a.   Added to gasoline to reduce valve recession
   b.   Added to gasoline to dissolve cauliflower deposits
   c.   Used to blast the deposits from intake valves only
   d.   Both a and c

8. To avoid problems with the variation of gasoline, all government testing uses_____ as a fuel during testing procedures.
   a.   MTBE (methyl tertiary butyl ether)
   b.   Indolene
   c.   Xylene
   d.   TBA (tertiary butyl alcohol)

5 Cooling System Operation and Problem Diagnosis

OBJECTIVES

After studying Chapter 5, the reader will be able to

1. Describe how coolant flows through an engine.
2. Discuss the operation of the thermostat.
3. Explain the radiator pressure cap purpose and function.
4. Describe the various types of antifreezes and how to recycle and discard used coolant.
5. Discuss how to diagnose cooling system problems.

Satisfactory cooling system operation depends on the design and operating conditions of the system. The design is based on heat output of the engine, radiator size, type of coolant, size of coolant pump, type of fan, thermostat, and system pressure. Unfortunately, the cooling system is usually neglected until there is a problem. Proper routine maintenance can prevent problems.

COOLING SYSTEM PURPOSE AND FUNCTION

The cooling system must allow the engine to warm up to the required operating temperature as rapidly as possible and then maintain that temperature. It must be able to do this when the outside air temperature is as low as $-30°$ F ($-35°$ C) or as high as $110°$ F ($45°$ C).

Peak combustion temperatures in the engine cycle run from $4000°$ to $6000°$ F ($2200°$ to $3300°$ C). The combustion temperatures will average between $1200°$ and $1700°$ F ($650°$ and $925°$ C). Continued temperatures as

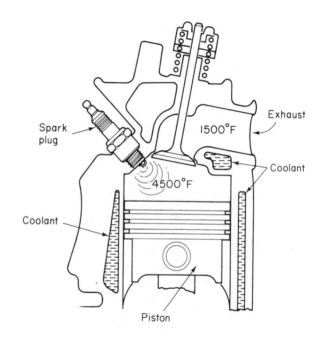

FIGURE 5–1 Typical combustion and exhaust temperatures.

high as this would weaken engine parts, so heat must be removed from the engine. The cooling system keeps the head and cylinder walls at a temperature that is within the range for maximum efficiency. See Figure 5–1.

LOW-TEMPERATURE ENGINE PROBLEMS

Engine operating temperatures must be above a minimum temperature for proper engine operation. When the temperature is too low, there is not enough heat to properly vaporize the fuel in the intake charge. As a

66

■ TECH TIP ■

OVERHEATING CAN BE EXPENSIVE

A faulty cooling system seems to be a major cause of engine failure. Engine rebuilders often have nightmares about seeing their rebuilt engine placed back in service in a vehicle with a clogged radiator. Most engine technicians routinely replace the coolant pump and all hoses after an engine overhaul or repair. The radiator should also be checked for leaks and proper flow whenever the engine is repaired or replaced. Overheating is one of the most common causes of engine failure.

(a)

(b)

FIGURE 5–2 (a) Loosening the screw that tightens the block heater element into the core plug opening in the side of the block. (b) Block heater element removed from block. The heater warms the coolant around the element, and the warm coolant rises, drawing cooler coolant up. As a result of this thermal circulation, all of the coolant surrounding the entire engine is warmed.

result, extra fuel must be added to supply more volatile fuel to make a combustible mixture. The heavy, less volatile part of the gasoline does not vaporize, and so it remains as unburned liquid fuel. In addition, cool engine surfaces quench part of the combustion gases, leaving partially burned fuel as soot.

Gasoline combustion is a rapid oxidation process that releases heat as the hydrocarbon fuel chemically combines with oxygen from the air. *For each gallon of fuel used, moisture equal to a gallon of water is produced.* It is a part of this moisture that condenses and gets into the oil pan, along with unburned fuel and soot, and causes **sludge** formation. The condensed moisture combines with unburned hydrocarbons and additives to form carbonic acid, sulfuric acid, nitric acid, hydrobromic acid, and hydrochloric acid. These acids are responsible for engine wear by causing corrosion and rust within the engine. Rust occurs rapidly when the coolant temperature is below 130° F (55° C). Below 110° F (45° C), water from the combustion process will actually accumulate in the oil. High cylinder wall wear rates occur whenever the coolant temperature is below 150° F (65° C).

To reduce cold-engine problems and to help start engines in cold climates, most manufacturers offer block heaters as an option. These block heaters are plugged into household current (110 V AC) and the heating element warms the coolant. See Figure 5–2.

HIGH-TEMPERATURE ENGINE PROBLEMS

Maximum temperature limits are required to protect the engine. High temperatures will oxidize the engine oil. This breaks the oil down, producing hard carbon and varnish. If high temperatures are allowed to con-

tinue, the carbon that is produced will plug piston rings. The varnish will cause the hydraulic valve lifter plungers to stick. High temperatures always thin the oil. Metal-to-metal contact within the engine will occur when the oil is too thin. This will cause high friction, loss of power, and rapid wear of the parts. Thinned oil will also get into the combustion chamber by going past the piston rings and through valve guides to cause excessive oil consumption.

The combustion process is very sensitive to temperature. High coolant temperatures raise the combustion temperatures to a point that may cause detonation and preignition to occur. These are common forms of abnormal combustion. If they are allowed to continue for any period of time, the engine will be damaged.

■ *TECH TIP* ■

ENGINE TEMPERATURE AND EXHAUST EMISSIONS

Many areas of the United States and Canada have exhaust emission testing. Hydrocarbon (HC) emissions are simply unburned gasoline. To help reduce HC emissions and be able to pass emission tests, be sure that the engine is at normal operating temperature. Vehicle manufacturers' definition of "normal operating temperature" includes the following:

■ Upper radiator hose is hot and pressurized.
■ Electric cooling fan(s) cycle twice.

Be sure that the engine is operating at normal operating temperature before testing for exhaust emissions. For best results, the vehicle should be driven about *20 miles* (32 kilometers) to be certain that the catalytic converter and engine oil, as well as the coolant, are at normal temperature. This is particularly important in cold weather. Most drivers think that their vehicle will "warm up" if allowed to idle until heat starts flowing from the heater. The heat from the heater comes from the coolant. Most manufacturers recommend that idling be limited to a maximum of 5 minutes and that the vehicle should be warmed up by driving slowly after just a minute or two to allow the oil pressure to build.

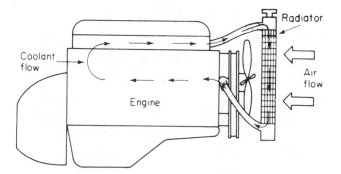

FIGURE 5–3 Coolant flow through an engine cooling system.

FIGURE 5–4 This block with the deck cut away shows the coolant passages surrounding the cylinders. Notice that coolant flows completely around and between the cylinders.

COOLING SYSTEM DESIGN

Coolant flows through the engine, where it picks up heat. It then flows to the radiator, where the heat is given up to the outside air. The coolant continually recirculates through the cooling system, as illustrated in Figures 5–3 and 5–4. Its temperature rises as much as 15° F (8° C) as it goes through the engine; then it cools back down as it goes through the radiator. *The coolant flow rate may be as high as 1 gallon (4 liters) per minute for each horsepower the engine produces.*

Hot coolant comes out of the thermostat housing on the top of the engine. The engine coolant outlet is connected to the top of the radiator by the upper hose and clamps. The coolant in the radiator is cooled by air flowing through the radiator. As it cools, it moves from the top to the bottom of the radiator. Cool coolant leaves the lower radiator area through an outlet and lower hose, going into the inlet side of the coolant pump, where it is recirculated through the engine.

Much of the cooling capacity of the cooling system is based on the functioning of the radiator. Radiators are designed for the maximum rate of heat transfer using minimum space. Cooling airflow through the radiator is aided by a belt- or electric motor–driven cooling fan.

THERMOSTAT TEMPERATURE CONTROL

There is a normal operating temperature range between low-temperature and high-temperature extremes. The thermostat controls the minimum normal temperature. The thermostat is a temperature-controlled valve placed at the engine coolant outlet. See Figure 5–5. An encapsulated wax-based plastic pellet heat sensor is located on the engine side of the thermostatic valve. As the engine warms, heat swells the heat sensor. A mechanical link, connected to the heat sensor, opens the thermostat

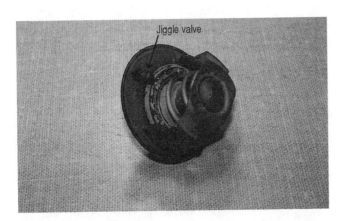

FIGURE 5–5 A typical automotive engine thermostat. This style of thermostat includes a small hole with a movable stopper called a _jiggle valve_. The jiggle valve moves and breaks up air pockets and allows air to escape the engine block and flow to the radiator. This helps prevent air from getting trapped in the engine, which could lead to overheating. The thermostat is usually installed with the jiggle valve up.

FIGURE 5–6 Typical coolant flow in a V-type engine.

FIGURE 5–7 One type of cooling system internal bypass.

valve. As the thermostat begins to open, it allows some coolant to flow to the radiator, where it is cooled. The remaining part of the coolant continues to flow through the bypass, thereby bypassing the thermostat and flowing back through the engine. See Figure 5–6. The rated temperature of the thermostat indicates the temperature at which the thermostat _starts_ to open. The thermostat is fully open at about 20° higher than its opening temperature. See the following examples.

Thermostat opening temperature	Starts to open	Fully open
180°	180°	200°
195°	195°	215°

If the radiator, coolant pump, and coolant passages are functioning correctly, the engine should always be operating within the opening and fully open temperature range of the thermostat.

NOTE: A **bypass** around the closed thermostat allows a small part of the coolant to circulate within the engine during warm-up. It is a small passage that leads from the engine side of the thermostat to the inlet side of the coolant pump. It allows some coolant to bypass the thermostat even when the thermostat is open. The bypass may be cast or drilled into the engine and pump parts. See Figures 5–7 and 5–8. The bypass aids in uniform engine warm-up. Its operation eliminates hot spots and prevents the building of excessive coolant pressure in the engine when the thermostat is closed. _____

TESTING THE THERMOSTAT

There are several methods that can be used to check the operation of the thermostat.

■ **Hot water method.** If the thermostat is removed from the vehicle and is closed, insert a 0.015-inch (0.4-millimeter) feeler gauge in the opening so that the thermostat will hang on the feeler gauge. The thermostat should then be suspended by the feeler gauge in a bath along with a thermometer. See Figure 5–9. The bath should be heated until the thermostat opens enough to release and fall from

FIGURE 5–8   One type of cooling system external bypass.

the feeler gauge. The temperature of the bath when the thermostat falls is the opening temperature of the thermostat. If it is within 5° F (4° C) of the temperature stamped on the thermostat, the thermostat is satisfactory for use. If the temperature difference is greater, the thermostat should be replaced.

■ **Infrared pyrometer method.** An infrared pyrometer can be used to measure the temperature of the coolant near the thermostat. The area on the engine side of the thermostat should be at the highest temperature that exists in the engine. A properly operating cooling system should cause the pyrometer to read as follows:

1.   As the engine warms up: temperature reaches near thermostat opening temperature
2.   As the thermostat opens: temperature drops just as the thermostat opens, sending coolant to the radiator
3.   As the thermostat cycles: temperature should range between the opening temperature of the thermostat and 20° F (11° C) above the opening temperature

NOTE: If the temperature rises higher than 20° F (11° C) above the opening temperature of the thermostat, inspect the cooling system for a restriction or low coolant flow. A clogged radiator could also cause the excessive temperature rise.

■ TECH TIP ■

DO NOT TAKE OUT THE THERMOSTAT!

Some vehicle owners and technicians remove the thermostat in the cooling system to "cure" an overheating problem. In some cases, removing the thermostat can *cause* overheating—not stop overheating. This is true for three reasons:

1.   Without a thermostat the coolant can flow more quickly through the radiator. The thermostat adds some restriction to the coolant flow, and therefore, keeps the coolant in the radiator longer. Therefore, the presence of the thermostat ensures a greater reduction in the coolant temperature before it returns to the engine.
2.   Heat transfer is greater with a greater difference between the coolant temperature and air temperature. Therefore, when coolant flow rate is increased (no thermostat), the temperature difference is reduced.
3.   Without the restriction of the thermostat, much of the coolant flow often bypasses the radiator entirely and returns directly to the engine.

If overheating is a problem, removing the thermostat will usually not solve the problem. Remember, the thermostat controls the temperature of the engine coolant by opening at a certain temperature and closing when the temperature falls below the minimum rated temperature of the thermostat. If overheating occurs, two basic problems could be the cause:

1.   The engine is producing too much heat for the cooling system to handle. For example, if the engine is running too lean or if the ignition timing is either excessively advanced or excessively retarded, overheating of the engine can result.
2.   The cooling system has a malfunction or defect that prevents it from getting rid of its heat.

■ **Scan tool method.** A scan tool can be used on many vehicles to read the actual temperature of the coolant as detected by the engine coolant temperature (ECT) sensor. Although the sensor, or the

FIGURE 5–9 Setup used to check the opening temperature of a thermostat.

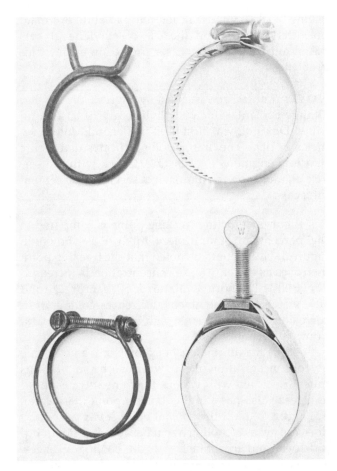

FIGURE 5–10 Types of hose clamps used on coolant hoses. Most replacement clamps are of the screw type. Hose clamps are sold by number. The higher the clamp number, the larger the clamp. Typical sizes include #10 or #12 for heater hoses and #24 to #30 for radiator hoses.

wiring to and from the sensor, may be defective, at least the scan tool can indicate what the computer "thinks" the coolant temperature is.

THERMOSTAT REPLACEMENT

An overheating engine may result from a faulty thermostat. An engine that does not get warm enough always indicates a faulty thermostat.

To replace the thermostat, coolant will have to be drained from the radiator drain petcock to lower the coolant level below the thermostat. It is not necessary to completely drain the system. The upper hose should be removed from the thermostat housing neck; then the housing must be removed to expose the thermostat.

The gasket flanges of the engine and thermostat housing should be cleaned, and the gasket surface of the housing must be flat. One of the flanges may be coated with gasket sealer. The thermostat should be placed in the engine with the sensing pellet *toward* the engine. Make sure that the thermostat position is correct, and install the thermostat housing with a new gasket.

■ **CAUTION:** Failure to set the thermostat into the recessed groove will cause the housing to become tilted when tightened. If this happens, and the housing bolts are tightened, the housing will usually crack, creating a leak. ■

The bolt threads should be coated with sealer and tightened in place. Then the upper hose should be installed and the system refilled. Install the proper size of radiator hose clamp. See Figure 5–10.

ANTIFREEZE

Water is able to absorb more heat per gallon than any other liquid coolant. Under standard conditions, water boils at 212° F (100° C) and freezes at 32° F (0° C). *When water freezes, it increases in volume by about 9%.* The expansion of the freezing water can easily crack engine blocks, cylinder heads, and radiators. All manufacturers recommend the use of **ethylene glycol–based antifreeze** mixtures for protection against this problem.

NOTE: Antifreeze is usually *green* or *orange*. Orange coolant, which is ethylene glycol based and called **Dexcool,** was first used in General Motors vehicles in 1996. The orange color indicates that its life in a *new* engine is long lasting. Check with the service manual for recommended service replacement intervals. ───────────────

A curve depicting freezing point as compared to the percentage of antifreeze mixture is shown in Figure 5–11. It should be noted that the freezing point increases as the antifreeze concentration is increased above 60%. The normal mixture is 50% antifreeze and 50% water. Ethylene glycol antifreezes contain anticorrosion additives, rust inhibitors, and coolant pump lubricants.

At the maximum level of protection, an ethylene glycol concentration of 60% will absorb about 85% as much heat as will water. Ethylene glycol–based antifreeze also has a higher boiling point than water. See Figure 5–12. If the coolant boils, it vaporizes and does not act as a cooling agent because it is not in liquid form and in contact with the cooling surfaces. The use of antifreeze will allow the cooling system to run at a higher-temperature level, so that a smaller radiator may be used on the vehicle.

PROPYLENE GLYCOL ANTIFREEZE

Propylene glycol antifreeze is advertised as being safer and less toxic than ethylene glycol. Although propylene glycol is less poisonous to humans and animals, it can still be harmful if ingested.

NOTE: Because ethylene glycol is sweet, animals are attracted to it and drink any coolant that is within reach. Ethylene glycol is often fatal if ingested. ───────

Propylene glycol has freezing and boiling temperatures similar to those of ethylene glycol. It is when the two types of antifreeze are mixed that heat transfer reduction may occur. This is the reason that most vehicle manufacturers warn against using propylene glycol unless all of the existing coolant is thoroughly flushed from the system. Always check the vehicle manufacturer's recommendation before using propylene glycol antifreeze.

PHOSPHATE-FREE ANTIFREEZE

Volkswagen specifies phosphate-free antifreeze for use in any of their liquid-cooled engines. Volkswagen testing revealed that the phosphate additive tended to settle out of the coolant when it was used with high–mineral content (hard) water.

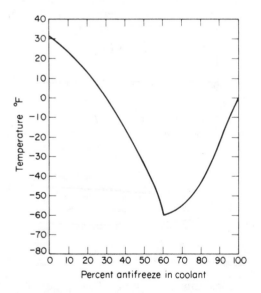

FIGURE 5–11 **Graph showing the relationship of the freezing point of the coolant to the percentage of antifreeze used in the coolant.**

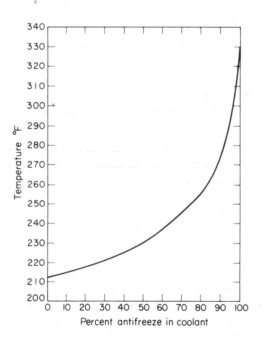

FIGURE 5–12 **Graph showing how the boiling point of the coolant increases as the percentage of antifreeze in the coolant increases.**

The phosphate antifreeze *does* tend to produce white chalky deposits. Although these do not cause any cooling system problems, it is not recommended by Volkswagen. However, there is a compromise: using any good-quality antifreeze containing phosphate with *distilled water* should reduce the problems associated with phosphate use, without requiring the purchase of the expensive phosphate-free formula.

ANTIFREEZE CAN FREEZE

The term **eutectic** means the physical properties of a material composed of more than one substance is different from the physical properties of any of the individual ingredients. Antifreeze and water mixture is an example wherein the freezing point differs from the freezing point of either pure antifreeze or pure water.

	Freezing point	
Pure water	32° F	(0° C)
Pure antifreeze*	0° F	(−18° C)
50/50 mixture	−34° F	(−37° C)
70% antifreeze/30% water	−84° F	(−64° C)

*Pure antifreeze is usually 95% ethylene glycol, 2%–3% water, and 2%–3% additives (usually silicon

■ **DIAGNOSTIC STORY** ■

IF 50% IS GOOD, 100% MUST BE BETTER

A vehicle owner said that the cooling system of his vehicle would never freeze or rust. He said that he used 100% antifreeze (ethylene glycol) instead of a 50/50 mixture with water.

However, after the temperature dropped to −20° F (−29° C), the radiator froze and cracked. (Pure antifreeze freezes at about 0° F [−18° C].) After thawing, the radiator had to be repaired. The owner was lucky that the engine block did not also crack.

For best freeze protection with good heat transfer, use a 50/50 mixture of antifreeze and water. A 50/50 mixture of antifreeze and water is the best compromise between temperature protection and the heat transfer that is necessary for cooling system operation. Do not exceed 70% antifreeze (30% water). As the percentage of antifreeze increases, the boiling temperature increases, and freezing protection increases (up to 70% antifreeze), but the heat transfer performance of the mixture *decreases*.

or silicates). Depending on the exact percentage of water used, antifreeze as sold in containers freezes between −8° and +8° F (−13° and −22° C). Therefore, it is easiest just to remember that most antifreeze freezes at about 0° F (−18° C).

The boiling point of antifreeze and water is also a factor of mixture concentrations.

	Boiling point at sea level	Boiling point with 15-psi pressure cap
Pure water	212° F (100° C)	257° F (125° C)
50/50 mixture	218° F (103° C)	265° F (130° C)
70/30 mixture	225° F (107° C)	276° F (136° C)

HYDROMETER TESTING

Coolant can be checked using a coolant hydrometer. The hydrometer measures the *density* of the coolant. The higher the density, the more concentration of antifreeze in the water. Most coolant hydrometers read the *freezing point* and *boiling point* of the coolant. See Figure 5–13. If the engine is overheating and the hydrometer reading is near −50° F (−60° C), suspect that pure 100% antifreeze is present. For best results, the coolant should have a freezing point lower than −20° F and a boiling point above 234° F.

FIGURE 5–13 Checking the freezing and boiling protection levels of the coolant using a hydrometer.

■ TECH TIP ■

IGNORE THE WINDCHILL FACTOR

The windchill factor is a temperature that combines the actual temperature and the wind speed to determine the overall heat loss effect on open skin. Because it is the heat loss factor for open skin, the windchill temperature is *not* to be considered when determining antifreeze protection levels.

Although moving air does make it feel colder, the actual temperature is not changed by the wind and the engine coolant will not be affected by the windchill. Not convinced? Try this. Place a thermometer in a room and wait until a stable reading is obtained. Now turn on a fan and have the air blow across the thermometer. The temperature will not change.

TESTING ANTIFREEZE WITH A VOLTMETER

A quick and easy method for determining the condition of the antifreeze and the extent of cooling system deterioration is to use a digital voltmeter. Insert one voltmeter test lead into the coolant and attach the other lead to a good engine ground or to the negative terminal of the battery (disregarding polarity) as shown in Figure 5–14. The reading should be interpreted as follows:

> Lower than 0.2 volts—acceptable
> 0.5 volts—borderline
> 0.7 volts or higher—unacceptable

The cooling system should be flushed and refilled with new antifreeze-water mixture. The voltage reading is caused by the chemical reaction between engine metals and the coolant. Old, weak antifreeze with depleted additives can become a weak acid. The entire cooling system then becomes a weak battery.

RECYCLING COOLANT

Coolant (antifreeze and water) should be recycled. Used coolant may contain heavy metals, such as lead, aluminum, and iron that are absorbed by the coolant during its use in the engine.

Recycle machines filter out these metals and dirt and reinstall the depleted additives. The recycled coolant, restored to be like new, can be reinstalled into the vehicle.

FIGURE 5–14 Testing for coolant contamination with a voltmeter. The meter reading is in millivolts (mV—$\frac{1}{1000}$ of a volt) and is well below the ½ volt considered harmful. A reading higher than ½ volt indicates old, contaminated coolant. If relatively new coolant measures ½ volt or higher, this often means a blown head gasket or similar failure. Combustion gases can turn coolant acidic and increase its voltage reading.

■ **CAUTION:** Most vehicle manufacturers warn that antifreeze coolant should not be reused unless it is recycled and the additives restored. ■

DISPOSING OF USED COOLANT

Used coolant drained from vehicles can usually be disposed of by combining it with the used engine oil. The equipment used for recycling the used engine oil can easily separate the coolant from the waste oil. Check with recycling companies authorized by local or state government for the exact method recommended for disposal in your area.

RADIATOR

Two types of radiator cores are in common use in domestic vehicles—the **serpentine fin core** and the **plate fin core.** In each of these types the coolant flows through oval-shaped **core tubes.** Heat is transferred through the tube wall and soldered joint to **fins.** The fins are exposed to airflow, which removes heat from the radiator and carries it away. See Figures 5–15 through 5–18.

Most automobile radiators are made from yellow brass or aluminum. These materials are corrosion resistant, have good heat-transferring ability, and are easily formed.

FIGURE 5–15 *Typical down-flow radiator. (Courtesy of Dow Chemical Company)*

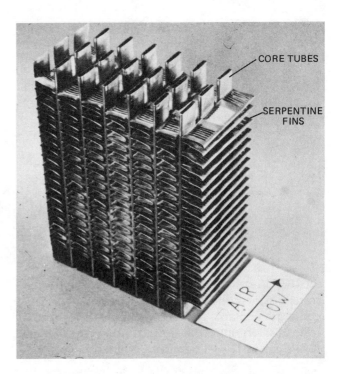

FIGURE 5–17 *Section from a serpentine core radiator. (Courtesy of Modine Manufacturing Company)*

FIGURE 5–16 *Typical cross-flow radiator. (Courtesy of Modine Manufacturing Company)*

FIGURE 5–18 *Cutaway of a typical radiator showing restriction of tubes. Changing antifreeze frequently helps prevent this type of problem.*

Core tubes are made from 0.0045- to 0.012-inch (0.1- to 0.3-millimeter) sheet brass or aluminum, using the thinnest possible materials for each application. The metal is rolled into round tubes, and the joints are sealed with a locking seam.

The main limitation of heat transfer in a cooling system is in the transfer from the radiator to the air. Heat transfers from the water to the fins as much as 7 times faster than heat transfers from the fins to the air, assuming equal surface exposure. The radiator must be capable of removing an amount of heat energy approximately equal to the heat energy of the power produced by the engine. *Each horsepower is equivalent to 42 BTU (10,800 calories) per minute.* As the engine power is increased, the heat-removing requirement of the cooling system is also increased.

Coolant tubes are straight, free-flowing tubes. The fins are given a pattern to break up any smooth, laminar airflow (flow staying in layers) that would keep the air from contacting the surface of the fin. With a given frontal area, radiator capacity may be increased by increasing the core thickness, packing more material into the same volume, or both. The radiator capacity may also be increased by placing a shroud around the fan so that more air will be pulled through the radiator.

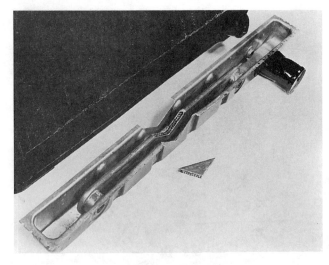

FIGURE 5–19 Cutaway showing an automatic transmission cooler passage inside the radiator. Air cools the coolant, which then cools the automatic transmission fluid that flows through the radiator. (Courtesy of Dow Chemical Company)

■ TECH TIP ■

WORKING BETTER UNDER PRESSURE

A problem that sometimes occurs with a high-pressure cooling system involves the coolant pump. For the pump to function, the inlet side of the pump must have a lower pressure than its outlet side. If inlet pressure is lowered too much, the coolant at the pump inlet can boil, producing vapor. The pump will then spin the coolant vapors and not pump coolant. This condition is called **pump cavitation.** Therefore, a radiator cap could be the cause of an overheating problem. A pump will not pump enough coolant if not kept under the proper pressure for preventing vaporization of the coolant.

Radiator headers and tanks that close off the ends of the core are made of sheet brass 0.020 to 0.050 inch (0.5 to 1.25 millimeters) thick or of molded plastic. When a transmission oil cooler is used in the radiator, it is placed in the outlet tank, where the coolant has the lowest temperature (Figure 5–19).

PRESSURE CAP

The filler neck is fitted with a pressure cap. The cap has a spring-loaded valve that closes the cooling system vent. This causes cooling pressure to build up to the

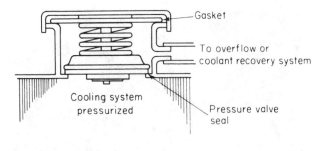

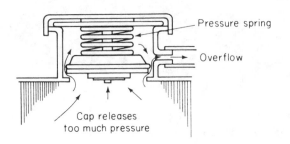

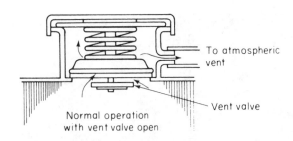

FIGURE 5–20   **The operation of a typical pressure cap.**

pressure setting of the cap. At this point, the valve will release the excess pressure to prevent system damage. See Figure 5–20.

Engine cooling systems are pressurized to raise the boiling temperature of the coolant. *The boiling temperature will increase by approximately 3° F (1.6° C) for each pound of increase in pressure.* At standard atmospheric pressure, water will boil at 212° F (100° C). With a 15-psi (100-kPa) pressure cap, water will boil at 257° F (125° C), which is a maximum operating temperature for an engine.

The high coolant system temperature serves two functions. First, it allows the engine to run at an efficient temperature, close to 200° F (93° C), with no danger of boiling the coolant. Second, the higher the coolant temperature, the more heat the cooling system can transfer. The heat transferred by the cooling system is proportional to the temperature difference between the coolant and the outside air. This characteristic has led to the design of small, high-pressure radiators that are capable of handling large quantities of heat. For proper cooling, the system must have the right pressure cap correctly installed.

NOTE: The proper operation of the pressure cap is especially important at high altitudes. The boiling point of water is lowered by about 1° F for every 550-foot increase in altitude. Therefore in Denver, Colorado (altitude 5280 feet), the boiling point of water is about 202° F, and at the top of Pikes Peak in Colorado (14,110 feet), water boils at 186° F.

METRIC RADIATOR CAPS

According to the *SAE Handbook,* all radiator caps must indicate their nominal (normal) pressure rating. Most original equipment radiator caps are rated at about 14 to 16 psi (97 to 110 kPa).

However, many vehicles manufactured in Japan or Europe have the radiator pressure indicated in a unit called a **bar.** One bar is the pressure of the atmosphere at sea level, or about 14.7 psi. The following conversion table can be used when replacing a radiator cap to make certain it matches the pressure rating of the original.

Bar or atmospheres	Pounds per square inch (psi)
1.1	16
1.0	15
0.9	13
0.8	12
0.7	10
0.6	9
0.5	7

NOTE: Many radiator repair shops use a 7-psi (0.5-bar) radiator cap on a repaired radiator. A 7-psi cap can still provide boil protection of 21° ($3° \times 7$ psi = 21°) above the boiling point of the coolant. For example, if the boiling point of the antifreeze coolant is 223°, 21° is added for the pressure cap, and boil over will not occur until about 244° (223° + 21° = 244°). Even though this lower-pressure radiator cap does provide some protection and will also help protect the radiator repair, the coolant can still boil *before* the "hot" dash warning light comes on.

COOLANT RECOVERY SYSTEM

Excess pressure usually forces some coolant from the system through an overflow. Most cooling systems connect the overflow to a plastic reservoir to hold excess coolant while the system is hot. See Figure 5–21. When the system cools, the pressure in the cooling system is reduced and a partial vacuum forms. This pulls the coolant from the plastic container back into the cooling system, keeping the system full. Because of this action, this system is called a **coolant recovery system.**

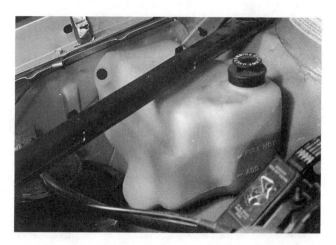

FIGURE 5–21   Typical coolant recovery container.

NOTE: If the upper radiator hose collapses after the engine is turned off, the radiator cap (not the hose) is at fault!

PRESSURE TESTING

Pressure testing using a hand-operated pressure tester is a quick and easy cooling system test. The radiator cap is removed (engine cold!) and the tester attached in the place of the radiator cap. By operating the plunger on the pump, the entire cooling system is pressurized. See Figure 5–22.

■ **CAUTION:** Do not pump up the pressure beyond that specified by the vehicle manufacturer. Most systems should not be pressurized beyond 14 psi (100 kPa). If a greater pressure is used, it may cause the coolant pump, radiator, heater core, or hoses to fail. ■

If the cooling system is free from leaks, the pressure should stay and not drop. If the pressure drops, look for evidence of leaks anywhere in the cooling system including

- Heater hoses
- Radiator hoses
- Radiator
- Heat core
- Cylinder head
- Core plugs in the side of the block or cylinder head

Pressure testing should be performed whenever there is a leak or suspected leak. The pressure tester can also be used to test the radiator cap. An adapter is used to connect the pressure tester to the radiator cap. Replace any cap that will not hold pressure.

FIGURE 5–22 Pressure testing the cooling system. A typical hand-operated pressure tester applies pressure equal to the radiator cap pressure. The pressure should hold; if it drops, this indicates a leak somewhere in the cooling system. An adapter is used to attach the pump to the cap to determine if the radiator cap can hold pressure, and release when pressure rises above its maximum rated pressure setting. (Courtesy of Dow Chemical Company)

COOLANT DYE LEAK TESTING

One of the best methods for checking for a coolant leak is to use a fluorescent dye in the coolant. Use a dye designed for coolant. Operate the vehicle with the dye in the coolant until the engine reaches normal operating temperature. Use a black light to inspect all areas of the cooling system. When there is a leak, it will be easy to spot because the dye in the coolant will be seen as a bright green.

COOLANT PUMP OPERATION

The coolant pump is driven by a belt from the crankshaft or driven by the camshaft. Coolant recirculates from the radiator to the engine and back to the radiator. Low-temperature coolant leaves the radiator by the bottom outlet. It is pumped into the warm engine block, where it picks up some heat. From the block, the warm coolant flows to the hot cylinder head, where it picks up more heat.

NOTE: Some engines today use **reverse cooling**. This means that the coolant flows from the radiator to the cylinder head(s) before flowing to the engine block. This results in cooling of the cylinder heads and allows for a high compression ratio and more advanced ignition timing without engine-damaging detonation (spark knock). _____

FIGURE 5–23 Coolant flow through the impeller and scroll of a coolant pump for a V-type engine.

Coolant pumps are not positive displacement pumps. The coolant pump is a **centrifugal pump** that can move a large volume of coolant without increasing the pressure of the coolant. The pump pulls coolant in at the center of the **impeller**. Centrifugal force throws the coolant outward so that it is discharged at the impeller tips. This can be seen in Figure 5–23.

As engine speeds increase, more heat is produced by the engine and more cooling capacity is required.

■ TECH TIP ■

USE DISTILLED WATER IN THE COOLING SYSTEM

Two technicians are discussing refilling the radiator after changing antifreeze. One technician says that distilled water is best to use because it does not contain minerals that can coat the passages of the cooling system. The other technician says that any water that is suitable to drink can be used in a cooling system. Both technicians are correct. If water contains minerals, however, it can leave deposits in the cooling system that could prevent proper heat transfer. Because the mineral content of most water is unknown, distilled water, which has no minerals, is better to use. Although the cost of distilled water must be considered, the amount of water required (usually about 2 gallons [8 liters] or less of water) makes the expense minor in comparison with the cost of radiator or cooling system failure.

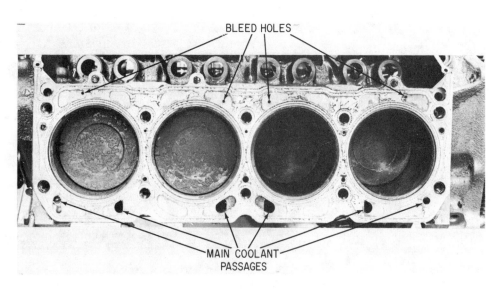

BLEED HOLES

MAIN COOLANT PASSAGES

FIGURE 5–24 *Gasket openings for a cooling system with a parallel type of flow.*

The pump impeller speed increases as the engine speed increases to provide extra coolant flow at the very time it is needed.

Coolant leaving the pump impeller is fed through a **scroll.** The scroll is a smoothly curved passage that changes the fluid flow direction with minimum loss in velocity. The scroll is connected to the front of the engine so as to direct the coolant into the engine block. On V-type engines, two outlets are used, one for each cylinder bank. Occasionally, diverters are necessary in the coolant pump scroll to equalize coolant flow between the cylinder banks of a V-type engine to equalize the cooling.

HOW MUCH COOLANT CAN A COOLANT PUMP PUMP?

A typical coolant pump (also called a water pump) can move a maximum of about 7500 gallons (28,000 liters) of coolant per hour, or recirculate the coolant in the engine over 20 times per minute. This means that a coolant pump could be used to empty a typical private swimming pool in an hour! The slower the engine speed, the less power is consumed by the coolant pump. However, even at 35 miles per hour (56 kilometers per hour), the typical coolant pump still moves about 2000 gallons (7500 liters) per hour or ½ gallon (2 liters) per second!

COOLANT FLOW IN THE ENGINE

Coolant flows through the engine in one of two ways—in parallel or series. In the **parallel flow system,** coolant flows into the block under pressure and then crosses the gasket to the head through main coolant passages beside *each* cylinder. The gasket openings of a parallel system are shown in Figure 5–24. In the **series flow system,** the coolant flows around all the cylinders on each bank. All the coolant flows to the *rear* of the block, where large main coolant passages allow the coolant to flow across the gasket. Figure 5–25 shows the main coolant passages. The coolant then enters the rear of the heads. In the heads, the coolant flows forward to an outlet at the *highest point* in the engine cooling passage. This is usually located at the front of the engine. The outlet is either on the heads or in the intake manifold. Some engines use a combination of these two coolant flow systems and call it a **series-parallel coolant flow.**

Any steam that develops will go directly to the top of the radiator. In series flow systems, **bleed holes** or **steam slits** in the gasket, block, and head perform the function of letting out the steam.

COOLANT PUMP SERVICE

A worn impeller on a coolant pump can reduce the amount of coolant flow through the engine. See Figure 5–26. If the seal of the coolant pump fails, coolant will leak out of the hole as seen in Figure 5–27. The hole allows coolant to escape without getting trapped and forced into the coolant pump bearing assembly.

If the bearing is defective, the pump will usually be noisy and will have to be replaced. Before replacing a coolant pump that has failed because of a loose or noisy bearing, be sure to do all of the following:

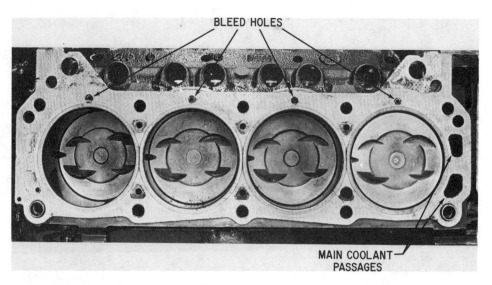

FIGURE 5–25 *Gasket openings for a series-type cooling system.*

FIGURE 5–26 This severely corroded coolant pump could not circulate enough coolant to keep the engine cool. As a result, the engine overheated and blew a head gasket.

FIGURE 5–27 The bleed hole in the coolant pump allows coolant to leak out of the pump and not be forced into the bearing. If the bearing failed, more serious damage could result.

■ Check belt tension.
■ Check for bent fan.
■ Check fan for balance.

If the coolant pump drive belt is too tight, excessive force may be exerted against the pump bearing. If the cooling fan is bent or out of balance, the resulting vibration can damage the coolant pump bearing.

COOLING FANS

Air is forced across the radiator core by a cooling fan. On older engines used in rear wheel–drive vehicles, it is attached to a fan hub that is pressed on the coolant pump shaft. See Figure 5–28. Most installations with rear-wheel drive and transverse engines drive the fan with an electric motor. See Figure 5–29.

NOTE: Most electric cooling fans are computer controlled. To save energy, most cooling fans are turned off whenever the vehicle is traveling faster than 35 mph (55 km/h). The ram air from the vehicle's traveling at that speed should be enough to keep the radiator cool. Of course, if the computer senses that the temperature is still too high, the computer will turn on the cooling fan, to "high," if possible, in an attempt to cool the engine to avoid severe engine damage.

■ DIAGNOSTIC STORY ■

THE HEAVY-DUTY COOLANT PUMP STORY

A rear wheel–drive Chevrolet was returned to the dealer for a replacement coolant (water) pump that was defective. Even though it was not covered by warranty, the owner wanted to be certain that a heavy-duty (HD) coolant pump was used as a replacement. The owner had purchased the vehicle new and had ordered a heavy-duty cooling system including a larger (thicker) radiator and an HD coolant pump.

When the technician went to the parts department to get an HD coolant pump, the parts person did not even look up the part number, but brought out a typical small-block Chevrolet V-8 coolant pump. The technician repeated the request for a "heavy-duty" pump as specified by the customer. Just to satisfy the technician, the parts manager showed the technician that the part number was the same for standard *and* HD pump.

The technician said, "Then what did the customer get when the vehicle was purchased equipped with an HD coolant pump? The parts manager said, "An HD coolant pump is driven by a slightly *smaller* pulley to turn the pump faster, and the drive pulley is not part of the pump."

NOTE: This is one of the reasons why replacement drive belts are not always exactly the same length as the original. Replacement drive belts are designed to fit several applications and therefore may be slightly longer or shorter than the original.

FIGURE 5–28   Typical coolant pump shaft and fan hub with the fan removed.

THERMOSTATIC FANS

Since the early 1980s, most cooling fans have been computer-controlled electric motor units. On some rear wheel–drive vehicles, a thermostatic cooling fan is driven by a belt from the crankshaft. It turns faster as the engine turns faster. Generally, the engine is required to produce more power at higher speeds. Therefore, the cooling system will also transfer more heat. Increased fan speed aids in the required cooling. Engine heat also becomes critical at low engine speeds in traffic where the vehicle moves slowly.

The thermal fan is designed so that it uses little power at high engine speeds and minimizes noise. The thermal fan has a **silicone coupling** fan drive mounted between the drive pulley and the fan.

HINT: *Whenever diagnosing an overheating problem, look carefully at the cooling fan. If silicone is leaking, then*

The fan is designed to move enough air at the lowest fan speed to cool the engine when it is at its highest coolant temperature. The fan shroud is used to increase the cooling system efficiency. The horsepower required to drive the fan increases at a much faster rate than the increase in fan speed. Higher fan speeds also increase fan noise. Fans with flexible plastic or flexible steel blades have been used. These fans have high blade angles that pull a high volume of air when turning at low speeds. As the fan speed increases, the fan blade angle flattens, reducing the horsepower required to rotate the blade at high speeds. See Figures 5–30 and 5–31.

FIGURE 5–29 Typical electric cooling fan.

the fan may not be able to function correctly and should be replaced.

A second type of thermal fan has a **thermostatic spring** added to the silicone coupling fan drive. The thermostatic spring operates a valve that allows the fan to freewheel when the radiator is cold. As the radiator warms to about 150° F (65° C), the air hitting the thermostatic spring will cause the spring to change its shape. The new shape of the spring opens a valve that allows the drive to operate like the silicone coupling drive. When the engine is very cold, the fan may operate at high speeds for a short time until the drive fluid warms slightly. The silicone fluid will then flow into a reservoir to let the fan speed drop to idle. See Figures 5–32 through 5–34.

HEATER CORE

Most of the heat absorbed from the engine by the cooling system is wasted. Some of this heat, however, is recovered by the vehicle heater. Heated coolant is passed through tubes in the small core of the heater. Air

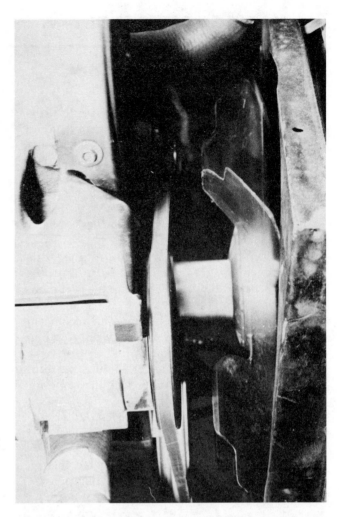

FIGURE 5–30 Photo taken with high-speed flash showing the shape of flexible fan blades at low speed. Compare with figure 5–31.

is passed across the heater fins; then it is sent to the passenger compartment. In some vehicles, the heater and air conditioning work in series to maintain vehicle compartment temperature.

HEATER PROBLEM DIAGNOSIS

When the vehicle's heater does not produce the desired amount of heat, many owners and technicians replace the thermostat before doing any other troubleshooting. It is true that a defective thermostat is the reason for the engine not to reach normal operating temperature. Many other causes besides a defective thermostat can result in lack of heat from the heater. To determine the exact cause, follow this procedure:

Step #1. After the engine has been operated, feel the upper radiator hose. If the engine is

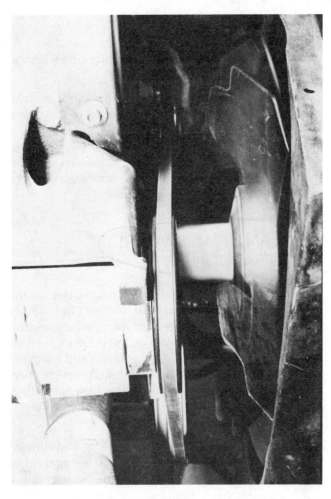

FIGURE 5-31 Same fan as shown in figure 5-30, except at higher engine speed. Note the decrease in pitch of the fan blades.

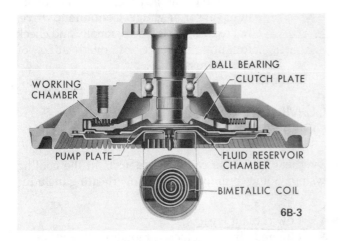

FIGURE 5-32 Sectional view of a thermostatic fan drive. (Courtesy of Buick Motor Division, GMC)

WORKING CHAMBER
BALL BEARING
CLUTCH PLATE
PUMP PLATE
FLUID RESERVOIR CHAMBER
BIMETALLIC COIL
6B-3

FIGURE 5-33 Thermoregulating and viscous fan drives. A silicone drive coupling is on the left, with thermostatic spring valves in the center, and the drive couplings on the right.

FAN SHROUD
FAN CLUTCH
FAN

FIGURE 5-34 Note the relationship of the fan and fan shroud. At least 50% of the fan should be within the shroud to prevent overheating caused by under-the-hood air being drawn by the fan instead of outside air being drawn through the radiator.

■ TECH TIP ■

CAUSE AND EFFECT

A common cause of overheating is an inoperative cooling fan. Most front wheel–drive vehicles and many rear wheel–drive vehicles use electric motor–driven cooling fans. A fault in the cooling fan circuit often causes overheating during slow city-type driving.

Even slight overheating can soften or destroy rubber vacuum hoses and gaskets. The gaskets most prone to overheating damage are rocker cover (valve cover) and intake manifold gaskets. Gasket and/or vacuum hose failure often results in an air (vacuum) leak that leans the air-fuel mixture. The resulting lean mixture burns hotter in the cylinders and contributes to the overheating problem.

The vehicle computer can often compensate for a minor air leak (vacuum leak), but more severe leaks can lead to driveability problems; especially idle quality problems. If the leak is severe enough, a lean computer trouble code may be present. If a lean code is not set, the vehicle's computer may indicate a defective or out-of-range MAP sensor code in diagnostics.

Therefore, a typical severe engine problem can often be traced back to a simple, easily repaired, cooling system–related problem.

up to proper operating temperature, the upper radiator hose should be too hot for you to keep your hand on it. The hose should also be pressurized.

  a. If the hose is not hot enough, replace the thermostat.
  b. If the hose is not pressurized, test it. Replace the radiator pressure cap if it will not hold the specified pressure.
  c. If okay, see step #2.

Step #2. With the engine running, feel both heater hoses. (The heater should be set to the maximum heat position.) Both hoses should be too hot to hold. If both hoses are warm (not hot) or cool, check the heater control valve for proper operation. If one hose is hot and the other (return) is just warm or cool, remove both hoses from the heater core or

engine and flush the heater core with water from a garden hose.

HINT: *Heat from the heater that "comes and goes" is most likely the result of low coolant level. Usually with the engine at idle, there is enough coolant flow through the heater; but at higher engine speeds the circulation of coolant through the heads and block prevents sufficient flow through the heater.*

COOLANT TEMPERATURE WARNING LIGHT

Most vehicles are equipped with a heat sensor for the engine operating temperature. If the "hot" light comes on during driving (or the temperature gauge goes into the red danger zone), the coolant temperature is about 250° to 258° F (120° to 126° C), which is still *below* the boiling point of the coolant (assuming a properly operating pressure cap and system). If this happens, follow these steps:

Step #1. Shut off the air conditioning and turn on the heater. The heater will help get rid of extra heat from the engine. Set the blower speed to high.

Step #2. If possible, shut the engine off and let it cool. (This may take over an hour.)

Step #3. Never remove the radiator cap when the engine is hot.

Step #4. Do *not* continue to drive with the hot light on, or serious damage to your engine could result.

Step #5. If the engine does not feel or smell hot, it is possible that the problem is a faulty hot light sensor or gauge. Continue to drive, but to be safe, stop occasionally and check for any evidence of overheating or coolant loss.

COMMON CAUSES OF OVERHEATING

Overheating can be caused by defects in the cooling system. Some common causes of overheating include

■ Low coolant level
■ Plugged, dirty, or blocked radiator
■ Defective fan clutch or electric fan
■ Incorrect ignition timing

- Low engine oil level
- Broken fan belt
- Defective radiator cap
- Dragging brakes
- Frozen coolant (in freezing weather)
- Defective thermostat
- Defective coolant pump (the impeller slipping on the shaft internally)

COOLING SYSTEM MAINTENANCE

The cooling system is one of the most maintenance-free systems in the engine. Normal maintenance involves an occasional check on the coolant level. It should also include a visual inspection for signs of coolant system leaks and for the condition of the coolant hoses and fan drive belts.

■ DIAGNOSTIC STORY ■

HIGHWAY OVERHEATING

A vehicle owner complained of an overheating vehicle, but the problem occurred only while driving at highway speeds. The vehicle, equipped with a General Motors *QUAD* 4, would run in a perfectly normal manner in city driving situations.

The technician flushed the cooling system and replaced the radiator cap and the coolant pump, thinking that restricted coolant flow was the cause of the problem. Further testing revealed coolant spray out of one cylinder when the engine was turned over by the starter with the spark plugs removed.

A new head gasket solved the problem. Obviously, the head gasket leak was not great enough to cause any problems until the engine speed and load created enough flow and heat to cause the coolant temperature to soar.

The technician also replaced the oxygen (O_2) sensor, because coolant contains silicone and silicates that often contaminate the sensor. The deteriorated oxygen sensor could have contributed to the problem. When contaminated, the oxygen sensor sends a higher-voltage signal to the computer that is interpreted to mean a rich exhaust. The computer then reduces fuel delivery, causing a leaner mixture. A lean mixture burns hotter than a rich mixture. The hotter-burning lean mixture could have added to the problem of the already hot-running engine.

■ **CAUTION:** The coolant level should only be checked when the engine is cool. Removing the pressure cap from a hot engine will release the cooling system pressure while the coolant temperature is above its atmospheric boiling temperature. When the cap is removed, the pressure will instantly drop to atmospheric pressure level, causing the coolant to boil immediately. Vapors from the boiling liquid will blow coolant from the system. Coolant will be lost, and someone may be injured or burned by the high-temperature coolant that is blown out of the filler opening. ■

The coolant-antifreeze mixture is renewed at periodic intervals. When the coolant system is empty, during the coolant change, it is a good time to replace hoses and to check the thermostat.

Cooling system problems are indicated by leaks, excessive engine temperature, and low engine temperature. The cause of a cooling problem is primarily determined through knowledge of the system's operation and by a good visual inspection. This is supplemented by tests to determine the coolant temperature and coolant pressure. Drive belt condition and proper installation are important for the proper operation of the cooling system. See Figures 5–35 through 5–37.

FLUSH AND REFILL

Manufacturers recommend that a cooling system be flushed and that the antifreeze be replaced at specified intervals. Some recommendations specify yearly antifreeze replacement. Others recommend replacement every 2 years or every 24,000 miles (36,000 km). Draining coolant when the engine is cool eliminates the danger of being injured by hot coolant. The radiator is drained by opening a petcock in the bottom tank, and the block is drained by opening plugs located in the lower part of the cooling passage—one on an inline engine and two on V-type engines, one on each side. See Figure 5–38.

A commercially available flushing "T" fitting can also be used to flush a cooling system. A heater hose is cut, and the T fitting is inserted in the heater hose. A garden hose is then connected to the T fitting, and clean water is forced through the cooling system and out of the top of the radiator.

Water should be run into the filler opening while the drains remain open. Flushing should be continued until only clear water comes from the system.

The volume of the cooling system must be determined. It is specified in the owner's handbook and in the engine service manual. The antifreeze quantity needed for the protection desired is shown on a chart

FIGURE 5–35 In the mid-1980s, many manufacturers started using serpentine belts. Older-model pumps will bolt onto the engine, but the direction of rotation may be opposite. This could lead to overheating after the new pump is installed. If the wrong application of fan is installed, the blades of the fan will not be angled correctly to provide adequate airflow through the radiator.

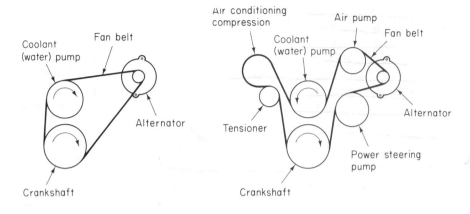

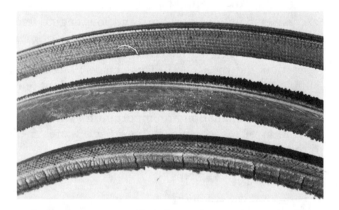

FIGURE 5–36 Selection of V-type belts. The top belt shows normal wear. The middle belt is glazed, which can cause slippage and squealing noise. The bottom belt is cracked.

that comes with the antifreeze. See Figure 5–39. The correct amount of antifreeze is put into the radiator, followed by enough water to completely fill the system. The coolant recovery reservoir should be filled to the "level-cold" mark with the correct antifreeze mixture.

BURPING THE SYSTEM

In most systems, small air pockets can occur. The engine must be thoroughly warmed to open the thermostat. This allows full coolant flow to remove the air pockets. The heater must also be turned to full heat.

HINT: *The cooling system will not function correctly if air is not released (burped) from the system after a refill. An easy method involves replacing the radiator cap after the refill, but only to the first locked position. Drive the vehicle for several minutes and check the radiator level. Without the radiator*

FIGURE 5–37 Drive belt tension is critical for the proper operation of the coolant pump, as well as the alternator, air-conditioning compressor, and other belt-driven accessories. A belt tension gauge should be used to make certain that accurate belt tension is achieved when replacing or retensioning any belt.

cap tightly sealed, no pressure will build in the cooling system, and driving the vehicle helps circulate the coolant enough to force all air pockets up and out of the radiator filler. Top off the radiator after burping and replace the radiator cap to the fully locked position. Failure to burp the cooling system to remove all the air will often result in lack of heat from the heater and may result in engine overheating.

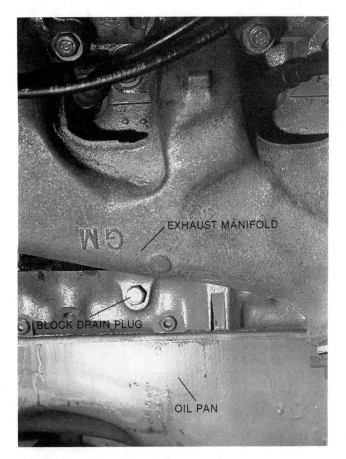

FIGURE 5–38 To thoroughly clean the cooling passages on the block, many technicians remove the block drain plugs and flush the block assembly separately from the rest of the cooling system.

HOSES

Coolant system hoses are critical to engine cooling. As the hoses get old, they become either soft or brittle and sometimes swell in diameter. Their condition depends on the material from which they are made and on the engine service conditions. If a hose breaks while the engine is running, all coolant will be lost. A hose should be replaced anytime it appears to be abnormal or every 2 years as a preventive maintenance item.

When hoses require replacement, the coolant must be drained. If the same coolant is to be reinstalled in the engine, it will have to be caught in a drain pan. It is only necessary to drain coolant from the petcock located at the bottom of the radiator for hose removal. Hose clamps are loosened and slipped off the part of the hose that is on the hose neck.

HINT: *To make hose removal easier and to avoid possible damage to the radiator, use a utility knife and slit the hose lengthwise. Then simply peel the hose off.*

Care should be taken to avoid bending the soft metal hose neck on the radiator. The hose neck should be cleaned before a new hose is slipped in place. The clamp is placed on the hose; then the hose is pushed fully over the neck. The hose should be cut so that the clamp is close to the bead on the neck. This is especially important on aluminum hose necks to avoid corrosion. When the hoses are in place and the drain petcock is closed, the cooling system can be refilled with the correct coolant mixture.

BACK FLUSHING A RADIATOR

Overheating problems may be caused by deposits that restrict coolant flow. These can often be loosened by **back flushing.** Back flushing requires the use of a special gun that mixes air with water. Low-pressure air is used so that it will not damage the cooling system. See Figure 5–40. Deposits will come out of the filler opening and out of the hose connected to the upper hose neck.

If, after flushing, some deposits still plug the radiator core, the radiator will have to be removed and sent to a radiator repair shop for cleaning.

CLEANING THE RADIATOR EXTERIOR

Overheating can result from exterior radiator plugging as well as internal plugging. External plugging is caused by dirt and insects. This type of plugging can be seen if you look straight through the radiator while a light is held behind it. It is most likely to occur on off-road vehicles. The plugged exterior of the radiator core can usually be cleaned with water pressure from a hose. The water is aimed at the *engine side* of the radiator. The water should flow freely through the core at all locations. If this does not clean the core, the radiator should be removed for cleaning at a radiator shop.

■ **TECH TIP** ■

QUICK AND EASY COOLING SYSTEM PROBLEM DIAGNOSIS

If overheating occurs in slow stop-and-go traffic, the usual cause is low airflow through the radiator. Check for airflow blockages or cooling fan malfunction. If overheating occurs at highway speeds, the cause is usually a radiator or coolant circulation problem. Check for a restricted or clogged radiator.

COOLING SYSTEM CAPACITY CHART

Cooling system Capacity (QTS.)	\multicolumn{9}{c}{Quarts of antifreeze required}

Cooling system Capacity (QTS.)	3	4	5	6	7	8	9	10	11
6	−34°								(10 liters)
7	−17								
8	−7	−34°							
9	0	−21							
(9.5 liters) 10	4	−12	−34°						
11	8	−6	−23						
12	10	0	−15	−34°					
13		3	−9	−25					
14		6	−5	−17	−34°				
15		8	0	−12	−26				
16		10	2	−7	−19	−34°			
17			5	−4	−14	−27			
18			7	0	−10	−21	−34°		
19			9	2	−7	−16	−28		
(19 liters) 20			10	4	−3	−12	−22	−34°	

For best year–round operation under all driving conditions, install a 50/50 mix of antifreeze and water. Protects against freeze-ups down to −34°F (−37°C)

FIGURE 5–39　Typical cooling system capacity chart. To use, determine the capacity of the cooling system as listed on the left side of the chart. The numbers along the top indicate the number of quarts of antifreeze required to give the freezing temperature protection listed. Remember, 4 quarts equals 1 gallon.

FIGURE 5–40　Setup to back flush a radiator.

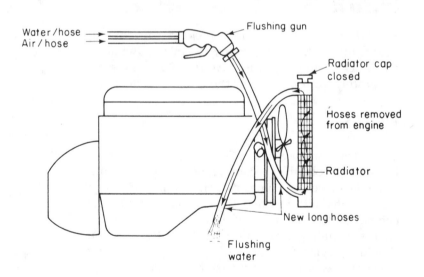

Water/hose →
Air/hose →
Flushing gun
Radiator cap closed
Hoses removed from engine
Radiator
New long hoses
Flushing water

SUMMARY

1. The purpose and function of the cooling system is to maintain proper engine operating temperature.
2. The thermostat controls engine coolant temperature by opening at its rated opening temperature to allow coolant to flow through the radiator.
3. Antifreeze coolant is usually ethylene glycol based. Other coolants include propylene glycol and phosphate-free coolants.
4. Used coolant should be recycled whenever possible. Antifreeze coolant can usually be disposed of mixed with used engine oil.
5. Coolant fans are designed to draw air through the radiator to aid in the heat transfer process,

drawing the heat from the coolant and transferring it to the outside air through the radiator.

6. The cooling system should be tested for leaks using a hand-operated pressure pump.

7. The freezing and boiling temperature of the coolant can be tested using a hydrometer.

8. Proper cooling system maintenance usually calls for replacing the antifreeze coolant every 2 years or every 24,000 miles (36,000 kilometers).

REVIEW QUESTIONS

1. Explain why the normal operating coolant temperature is about 200° to 220° F (93° to 104° C).

2. Explain why a 50/50 mixture of antifreeze and water is commonly used as a coolant.

3. Explain the flow of coolant through the engine and radiator.

4. Why is a cooling system pressurized?

5. Describe the difference between a series and a parallel coolant flow system.

6. Explain the purpose of the coolant system bypass.

7. Describe how to perform a drain, flush, and refill procedure on a cooling system.

8. Explain the operation of a thermostatic cooling fan.

9. Describe how to diagnose a heater problem.

10. List ten common causes of overheating.

MULTIPLE-CHOICE QUESTIONS

1. Permanent antifreeze is mostly _____ .
   a. Methanol
   b. Glycerine
   c. Kerosene
   d. Ethylene glycol

2. As the percentage of antifreeze in the coolant increases, _____ .
   a. The freeze point decreases (up to a point)
   b. The boiling point decreases
   c. The heat transfer increases
   d. All of the above

3. Heat transfer from the coolant to the air is improved when _____ .
   a. The temperature difference is great
   b. The temperature difference is small
   c. The coolant is 95% antifreeze
   d. Both a and c

4. The term eutectic point means _____ .
   a. Dissimilar metal used in engine construction
   b. Dissimilar materials together do not share physical properties
   c. Similar materials share physical properties
   d. Freeze point of coolant depends on pressure

5. Coolant pumps _____ .
   a. Only work at idle and low speeds; the pump is disengaged at higher speeds
   b. Use engine oil as a lubricant and coolant
   c. Rotate at about the same speed as the engine
   d. Disengage during freezing weather to prevent radiator failure

6 . The procedure that should be used when refilling an empty cooling system includes the following: _____ .
   a. Determine capacity, then fill the cooling system halfway with antifreeze and the rest of the way with water
   b. Fill completely with antifreeze, but mix a 50/50 solution for the overflow bottle
   c. Fill the block and one-half of the radiator with 100% pure antifreeze and fill the rest of the radiator with water
   d. Fill the radiator with antifreeze, start the engine, drain the radiator, and refill with a 50/50 mixture of antifreeze and water

7. Which statement is *true* about thermostats?
   a. The temperature marked on the thermostat is the temperature at which the thermostat should be fully open.
   b. Thermostats often cause overheating.
   c. The temperature marked on the thermostat is the temperature at which the thermostat should start to open.
   d. Both a and b

8. Technician A says that the radiator should always be inspected for leaks and proper flow before installing a rebuilt engine. Technician B says that overheating during slow city driving can only be due to a defective electric cooling fan. Which technician is correct?
   a. A only
   b. B only
   c. Both A and B
   d. Neither A nor B

6

Engine Condition Diagnosis

OBJECTIVES

After studying Chapter 6, the reader will be able to

1. List the visual checks to determine engine condition.
2. Discuss engine noise and its relation to engine condition.
3. Describe how to perform a dry and a wet compression test.
4. Explain how to perform a cylinder leakage test.
5. Discuss how to measure the amount of timing chain slack.
6. Describe how an oil sample analysis can be used to determine engine condition.

If there is an engine operation problem, the cause could be any one of many items including the engine itself. The condition of the engine should be tested anytime the operation of the engine is not satisfactory.

TYPICAL ENGINE-RELATED COMPLAINTS

Many driveability problems are *not* caused by mechanical engine problems. A thorough inspection and testing of the ignition and fuel systems should be performed before testing for mechanical engine problems.

Typical engine problem complaints include the following:

- Excessive oil consumption
- Engine misfiring
- Loss of power

■ TECH TIP ■

THE BINDER CLIP TRICK

It is important to always use fender covers whenever working on an engine. The problem is, few covers remain in place and they often become more of a hindrance than a help. A binder clip, available at most office supply stores, can be easily used to hold fender covers to the lip of the fender of most vehicles. See Figure 6–1. When clipped over the lip, the cover is securely attached and cannot even be pulled loose. This method works with cloth, as well as vinyl, covers.

- Smoke from the engine or exhaust
- Engine noise

DRIVER IS YOUR BEST RESOURCE

The driver of the vehicle knows a lot about the vehicle and how it is driven. *Before* diagnosis is started, always ask the following questions:

- When did the problem first occur?
- Under what conditions does it occur?
  1. Cold or hot?
  2. Acceleration, cruise, or deceleration?
  3. At what distance?

After the nature and scope of the problem are determined, the complaint should be verified before further diagnostic tests are performed.

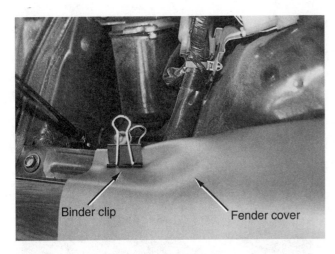

FIGURE 6–1 It is very important to use fender covers to protect the paint of the vehicle. Use a binder clip, available at local office supply stores, to clip the fender cover to the lip of the fender, preventing the fender cover from slipping.

Binder clip   Fender cover

VISUAL CHECKS

The first and most important "test" that can be performed is a careful visual inspection.

Oil Level and Condition

The first area for visual inspection is oil level and condition.

1. Oil level—oil should be to the proper level
2. Oil condition
   a. Using a match or lighter, try to light the oil on the dipstick; if the oil flames up, gasoline is present in the engine oil.
   b. Drip some of the engine oil from the dipstick onto the hot exhaust manifold. If the oil bubbles or boils, there is coolant (water) in the oil.
   c. Check for grittiness by rubbing the oil between your fingers.

Coolant Level and Condition

Most mechanical engine problems are caused by overheating. The proper operation of the cooling system is critical to the life of any engine.

NOTE: Check the coolant level in the radiator only if the radiator is cool. If the radiator is hot and the radiator cap is removed, the drop in pressure above the coolant will cause the coolant to boil immediately and can cause severe burns when the coolant explosively expands upward and outward from the radiator opening. _____

1. The coolant level in the coolant recovery container should be within the limits indicated on the overflow bottle. If this level is too low or the coolant recovery container is empty, then check the level of coolant in the radiator (only when cool) and also check the operation of the pressure cap.
2. The coolant should be checked with a hydrometer for boiling and freezing temperature. This test indicates if the concentration of the antifreeze is sufficient for proper protection.
3. Using a voltmeter, insert the red (positive) probe into the coolant and touch the black (negative) lead to the radiator. A voltmeter reading of over 0.7 volts indicates that the antifreeze has become acidic and should be replaced. A high voltage also may indicate a combustion leak into the cooling system, causing the coolant to become an acid.
4. Pressure test the cooling system and look for leakage. Coolant leakage will often cause
   a. A grayish-white stain
   b. A rusty-color stain
   c. Dye stains from antifreeze (usually greenish)
5. Check for cool areas of the radiator indicating clogged sections.
6. Check operation and condition of the fan clutch, fan, and coolant pump drive belt.

NOTE: Check chapter 5 for further information on the operation of the cooling system and diagnosis of related problems. _____

The Paper Test

A soundly running engine should produce even and steady exhaust at the tail pipe. Using a piece of paper (even a dollar bill works) or a 3-inch by 5-inch card, hold it within 1 inch (2.5 centimeters) of the tail pipe with the engine running at idle. See Figure 6–2. The paper should blow out evenly without "puffing." If the paper is drawn *toward* the tail pipe at times, the valves in one or more cylinders could be burned. Other reasons why the paper might be sucked toward the tail pipe include the following:

1. The engine could be misfiring because of a lean condition that could occur normally when the engine is cold.
2. Pulsing of the paper toward the tail pipe could also be caused by a hole in the exhaust system. If exhaust escapes through a hole in the exhaust system, air could be drawn—in

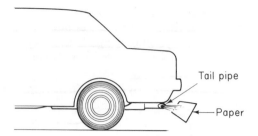

FIGURE 6–2 The paper test involves holding a piece of paper near the tail pipe of an idling engine. A good engine should produce even outward puffs of exhaust. If the paper is sucked in toward the tail pipe, a burned valve is a possibility.

■ TECH TIP ■

WHAT'S LEAKING?

The color of the leaks observed under a vehicle can help the technician determine and correct the cause. Some leaks, such as condensate (water) from the air-conditioning system, are normal, whereas a brake fluid leak is very dangerous. The following are colors of common leaks:

Sooty black	Engine oil
Yellow, green, blue	Antifreeze (coolant) or orange
Red	Automatic transmission fluid
Murky brown	Brake or power steering fluid or very neglected antifreeze (coolant)
Clear	Air-conditioning condensate (water) (normal)

FIGURE 6–3 Typical rocker cover (valve cover) gasket leak. Always check the <u>highest</u> and <u>most forward</u> parts of the engine that are wet when attempting to find a fluid leak.

the intervals between the exhaust puffs—from the tail pipe to the hole in the exhaust, causing the paper to be drawn toward the tail pipe.

Oil Leaks

Oil leaks can lead to severe engine damage if the resulting low oil level is not corrected. Besides causing an oily mess where the vehicle is parked, the oil leak can cause blue smoke to occur under the hood as leaking oil drips on the exhaust system. *Finding* the location of the oil leak can often be difficult. See Figures 6–3 and 6–4. To help find the source of oil leaks, follow these steps:

Step #1. Clean the engine or area around the suspected oil leak. Use a high-powered hot water spray to wash the engine. A coin-

operated car wash could also be used. Keep the engine running, and spray the entire engine and the engine compartment. Avoid letting the water come into direct contact with the air inlet and ignition distributor or ignition coil(s).

HINT: *If the engine starts to run rough or stalls when the engine gets wet, then the secondary ignition wires (spark plug wires) or distributor cap may be defective or have weak insulation. Be certain to wipe all wires and the distributor cap dry with a soft, dry cloth if the engine stalls.*

An alternative method is to spray a degreaser on the engine, then start and run the engine until warm. Engine heat

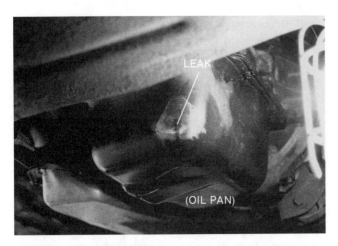

FIGURE 6–4   Blue oil smoke was caused by this hole in the oil pan. This photo is of a front wheel–drive vehicle on which the exhaust pipe wore a hole through the oil pan! It looks as if someone used a grinder on the pan, but this is just the way the technician found the pan after removing the exhaust pipe.

■ TECH TIP ■

THE FOOT POWDER SPRAY TRICK

The source of an oil or other fluid leak is often difficult to determine. A quick and easy method that works is the following. First, clean the entire area. This can best be done by using a commercially available degreaser to spray the entire area. Let it soak to loosen all accumulated oil and greasy dirt. Clean off the degreaser with a water hose. Let the area dry. Start the engine, and using spray foot powder or other aerosol powder product, spray the entire area. The leak will turn the white powder dark. The exact location of any leak can be quickly located.

helps the degreaser penetrate the grease and dirt. Use a water hose to rinse off the engine and engine compartment.

Step #2.   If the oil leak is not visible or oil seems to be coming from "everywhere," use a white talcum powder. The leaking oil will show as a dark area on the white powder. See the tech tip The Foot Powder Spray Trick.

Step #3.   Fluorescent dye can be added to the engine oil. Add about ½ oz (15 cc) of dye per 5 quarts of engine oil. Start the engine and allow it to run about 10 minutes to

FIGURE 6–5   Pushrod worn through a rocker arm.

thoroughly mix the dye throughout the engine. A black light can then be shown around every suspected oil leak location. The black light will easily show any and every oil leak location.

ENGINE NOISE DIAGNOSIS

An engine knocking noise is often difficult to diagnose. Several items that can cause a deep engine knock include the following:

- **Valves clicking** because of lack of oil to the lifters. This noise is most noticeable at idle when the oil pressure is the lowest. See Figure 6–5.
- **Torque converter** attaching bolts or nuts loose on the drive (flex) plate. This noise is most noticeable at idle or when there is no load on the engine.
- **Cracked drive (flex) plate.** The noise of a cracked drive (flex) plate is often mistaken for a rod or main bearing noise. See Figures 6–6 and 6–7.
- **Loose or defective drive belts.** If an accessory drive belt is loose or defective, the flopping noise often sounds similar to a bearing knock.
- **Piston pin knock.** This knocking noise is usually not affected by load on the cylinder. If the clearance is too great, a *double knock* noise is heard when the engine idles. If all cylinders are grounded out one at a time and the noise does not change, a defective piston pin could be the cause.
- **Piston slap.** A piston slap is usually caused by an undersize or improperly shaped piston or oversize cylinder bore. A piston slap is most noticeable when the engine is cold and tends to decrease or stop making noise as the piston expands during engine operation.

FIGURE 6-6   Typical drive (flex) plate as used on the principal end of an engine using an automatic transmission.

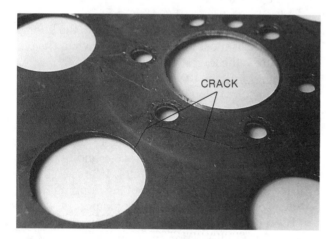

FIGURE 6-7   Cracked drive (flex) plate. The noise this plate made was similar to a rod bearing knocking noise.

■ **Timing chain noise.** An excessively loose timing chain can cause a severe knocking noise when the chain hits the timing chain cover. This noise can often sound like a rod bearing knock.

■ **Heat riser noise.** A loose (worn) or defective heat riser valve in the exhaust can make a knocking

noise similar to a bearing noise. Even a vacuum-controlled heat riser (also called an **early fuel evaporation** (EFE) valve) can make a knocking noise, especially under load, as the result of slight vacuum variations applied to the actuator diaphragm. To eliminate the heat riser as a possible cause, remove the vacuum hose to the actuator or retain the thermostatic valve with a wire or other suitable means.

■ **Rod bearing noise.** The noise from a defective rod bearing is usually load sensitive and changes in intensity as the load on the engine increases and decreases. A rod bearing failure can often be detected by grounding out the spark plugs a cylinder at a time. If the knocking noise decreases or is eliminated when a particular cylinder is grounded,

Typical noise		Possible causes
Clicking noise—like the clicking of a ballpoint pen	1.	Loose spark plug
	2.	Loose accessory mount (for air-conditioning compressor, alternator, power steering pump, etc.)
	3.	Loose rocker arm
	4.	Worn rocker arm pedestal
	5.	Fuel pump (broken mechanical fuel pump return spring)
	6.	Worn camshaft
	7.	Exhaust leak
	8.	Ping (detonation)
Clacking noise—like tapping on metal	1.	Worn piston pin
	2.	Broken piston
	3.	Excessive valve clearance
	4.	Timing chain hitting cover
Knock—like knocking on a door	1.	Rod bearing(s)
	2.	Main bearing(s)
	3.	Thrust bearing(s)
	4.	Loose torque converter
	5.	Cracked flex plate (drive plate)
Rattle—like a baby rattle	1.	Manifold heat control valve
	2.	Broken harmonic balancer
	3.	Loose accessory mount
	4.	Loose accessory drive belt or tensioner
Clatter—like rolling marbles	1.	Rod bearings
	2.	Piston pin
	3.	Loose timing chain
Whine—like an electric motor running	1.	Alternator bearing
	2.	Drive belt
	3.	Power steering
	4.	Belt noise (accessory or timing)
Clunk—like a door closing	1.	Engine mount
	2.	Drive axle shaft U-joint or constant velocity (CV) joint

FIGURE 6–8 Typical worn serpentine accessory drive belt. A defective or worn belt can cause a variety of noises, including squealing and severe knocking, similar to a main bearing knock if glazed or loose.

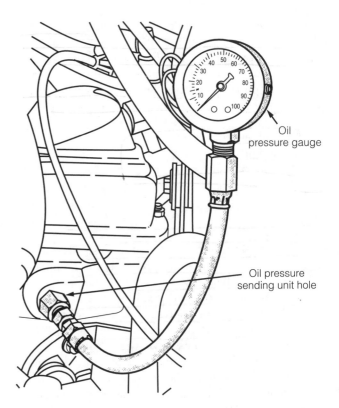

Oil pressure gauge

Oil pressure sending unit hole

FIGURE 6–9 To measure engine oil pressure, remove the oil pressure sealing (sender) unit usually located near the oil filter. Screw the pressure gauge into the oil pressure sending unit hole.

■ TECH TIP ■

ENGINE NOISE AND COST

A light ticking noise often heard at half engine speed and associated with valve train noise is a less serious problem than many deep-sounding knocking noises. Generally, the deeper the sound of the engine noise, the deeper the owner will have to go into his or her wallet to pay for repairs. A light "tick tick tick," though often not cheap, is usually far less expensive than a deep "knock knock knock" from the engine.

This observation is helpful when writing an estimate for an engine repair. You can always tell the vehicle owner that if the ticking becomes a knocking sound, the owner should be prepared to bring more money.

then the grounded cylinder is the one from which the noise is originating.

■ **Main bearing knock.** A main bearing knock often cannot be isolated to a particular cylinder. The sound can vary in intensity and may disappear at times depending on engine load. See Figure 6–8.

Regardless of the type of loud knocking noise, after the external causes of the knocking noise have been eliminated, the engine should be disassembled and carefully inspected to determine the exact cause.

OIL PRESSURE TESTING

Proper oil pressure is very important for the operation of any engine. *Low oil pressure can cause engine wear, and engine wear can cause low oil pressure.*

If main and rod bearings are worn, oil pressure is reduced because of leakage of the oil around the bearings. See chapter 16 for details on the oil pump and the lubrication system. Oil pressure testing is usually performed with the following steps:

Step #1. Operate the engine until normal operating temperature is achieved.

Step #2. With the engine off, remove the oil pressure sending unit or sender, usually located near the oil filter. Thread an oil pressure gauge into the threaded hole. See Figure 6–9.

> **HINT:** *An oil pressure gauge can be made from another gauge, such as an old air-conditioning gauge no longer used for air-conditioning work, and a flexible brake hose. The threads are often the same as those used for the oil pressure sending unit.*

Step #3. Start the engine and observe the gauge. Record the oil pressure at idle and at 2500 RPM.

Most vehicle manufacturers recommend a minimum oil pressure of 10 psi per 1000 RPM. Therefore, at 2500 RPM, the oil pressure should be at least 25 psi. Always compare your test results with the manufacturer's recommended oil pressure. Besides engine bearing wear, other possible causes for low oil pressure include

- Low oil level
- Diluted oil
- Stuck oil pressure relief valve

OIL ANALYSIS

Most large fleets and transit operations use oil analysis data as part of their normal preventive maintenance program. Oil analysis involves getting a sample of the engine's crankcase oil and sending it to a local or regional laboratory for analysis. The results can show mechanical engine problems before there is any other indication. Many engines have been "saved" by oil analysis. The engine can be removed and disassembled to correct faults found by the oil analysis before serious and expensive engine damage occurs. Some truck and bus companies use oil analysis not only to spot trouble early, but also to determine the maximum acceptable oil drain interval. To find a laboratory to perform oil analysis, look in the telephone yellow pages under "laboratories" or "testing laboratories" in larger cities.

GETTING THE SAMPLE

For the most accurate test results, the oil sample should be from a *warm* engine. The recommended procedure is to begin to drain the oil in the usual way by removing the drain plug. To prevent getting residue from the bottom of the oil pan, allow oil to drain for several seconds before placing the sample container into the oil stream. An alternate method is to siphon oil from the crankcase from the oil filler tube or crankcase vent passages. A 4-ounce (120–cubic centimeter) sample should be large enough for the testing laboratory.

STUDYING THE RESULTS

When the oil sample results are returned from the testing laboratory, they must be studied carefully to determine if any corrective action needs to be performed on the engine, or if the results are normal given the engine's hours, miles, and conditions of operation. Although some laboratories explain the test results, many laboratories do *not* interpret the test results for you. Most testing laboratories want the following information included with the sample to help them and you determine the results:

■ **TECH TIP** ■

USE THE KISS TEST METHOD

Engine testing is done to find the cause of an engine problem. All the simple things should be tested first. Just remember KISS—"keep it simple, stupid." A loose alternator belt or loose bolts on a torque converter can sound just like a lifter or rod bearing. A loose spark plug can make the engine perform as if it had a burned valve. Some simple items that can cause serious problems include the following:

Oil Burning

- Low oil level.
- Oil dilution caused by a leaking fuel pump (leaks gasoline and thins the oil).
- Clogged PCV valve or system, causing blowby and oil to be blown into the air cleaner.
- Dirty oil that has not been changed for a long time. Change the oil and drive for about 1000 miles (1600 kilometers) and change the oil and filter again.

Noises

- Loose torque-to-flex plate bolts (or nuts), causing a loud knocking noise.

    HINT: *Most of the time this problem will cause noise only at idle; the noise tends to disappear during driving or when the engine is under load.*

- A defective fuel pump , which may cause a ticking, lifter-type noise (may not affect pump operation if only the lever return spring is broken). Use a stethoscope to isolate the noise.
- A loose and/or defective drive belt, which may cause a rod or main bearing knocking noise. A loose or broken mount for the alternator, power steering pump, or air-conditioning compressor can also cause a knocking noise.

1. Total miles (kilometers) on the vehicle
2. Miles since the last oil change (oil life miles)
3. Engine description (gasoline, diesel, etc.)
4. Viscosity of oil originally

Following are the items that are measured during a typical oil sample test and a brief explanation of the meaning of the results.

Viscosity Increase

If viscosity is higher (thicker) than the original grade, this usually means that oxidation of the oil has occurred. Excessive oxidation can be caused by the following:

- Overheating due to weak cooling system function.
- Aeration (air mixed into the oil) due to oil being stirred up by moving engine parts. This commonly occurs if the oil level is below recommended level.
- Presence of small metal particles, which normally come from engine wear. These small metal particles act as a catalyst that speeds up the chemical reaction between oxygen and the engine oil, causing the oil to thicken.

Other products of oxidation include sludge, gum, varnish, lacquer, carbon deposits, and acidic compounds. Maximum allowable viscosity is generally considered to be 30% thicker than the original. If thickening is greater than 30%, careful inspection should be made of the engine cooling system. Corrective action should be performed as necessary, and the engine oil and filter should be replaced. The engine and vehicle use should be carefully monitored to ensure that severe oxidation does not reoccur.

Viscosity Decrease

Most testing laboratories consider a decrease in viscosity (oil becoming thinner) to be the result of fuel dilution. A maximum allowable fuel dilution of 3% of the volume is generally accepted. Fuel dilution results in thin oil and an increase in engine wear rates. A high level of fuel dilution may be due to

- Short driving cycles (especially during cold weather)
- A defective thermostat (stuck open), which could prevent the engine from reaching normal operating temperatures
- A defective choke (carburetor) or coolant temperature sensor
- A clogged exhaust gas passage under the intake (inlet) manifold
- A defective heat riser or control unit affecting intake (inlet) air temperature
- A defective carburetor float or power circuit, or a defective injector nozzle
- A clogged air filter or closed air inlet

Moisture

The contamination of engine oil by moisture (water) can result in poor lubrication and sludge formation. Normal readings are considered to be less than 0.05%. Readings higher than 2% are considered to be excessive by most testing laboratories.

A high level of moisture in the engine oil can be due to

- A leaking head gasket
- A cracked block
- A cracked head
- A clogged PCV valve and/or hoses
- An inoperative crankcase breather
- Short driving cycles
- Extended oil change intervals

Antifreeze

Engine oil contaminated with antifreeze (ethylene glycol) can congeal. If the oil congeals, it is too thick to flow through the engine and lubricate properly. Possible causes of antifreeze in engine oil include

- A cracked cylinder head
- A leaking head gasket
- A cracked block
- Sabotage

Iron (Fe)

Iron (chemical symbol Fe) is a major wear metal. Almost every oil sample will contain some iron, measured in parts per million (PPM), as the result of normal wear.

- Normal iron content: 50 to 250 PPM
- Abnormal iron content: 250 to 350 PPM
- Excessive iron content: over 350 PPM

Iron in the oil can come from wear and rusting of

- Rocker arms or pivot shaft
- Cylinders or cylinder sleeve
- Camshaft
- Valve guides
- Timing gear and/or chain
- Crankshaft
- Rings
- Oil pump
- Lifters
- Fuel pump rocker and/or fulcrum

Aluminum (Al)

Aluminum is also a wear metal and is also measured in parts per million (PPM).

- Normal aluminum content: 5 to 25 PPM
- Abnormal aluminum content: 30 PPM
- Excessive aluminum content: over 40 PPM

Aluminum can originate from

- Pistons
- Rod and/or main bearings

- Camshaft bearings
- Fuel pump

Copper (Cu)

Copper is another wear metal measured in parts per million (PPM).

- Normal copper content: 5 to 25 PPM
- Abnormal copper content: 100 PPM
- Excessive copper content: over 300 PPM

Copper can originate from

- Bearings
- Bushings (such as distributor, fuel pump, or oil pump)

Tin (Sn)

Tin may be found in the oil. It is another wear metal measured in parts per million (PPM).

- Normal tin content: 0 to 1 PPM
- Abnormal tin content: 5 to 10 PPM
- Excessive tin content: over 15 PPM

Tin can originate from

- Piston coating
- Bearings

The usual source of tin is the piston coating commonly plated on aluminum pistons. But tin can also come from bearings.

Chrome (Cr)

The oil may contain chrome wear metal. It is measured in parts per million (PPM) and originates almost exclusively from chrome piston rings. Some engines do not use chrome rings, and therefore no chrome should be found in the oil sample of these engines. Most heavy-duty diesel engines use chrome rings, and the amount of chrome found in the oil sample indicates ring wear.

- Normal chrome content: 5 to 25 PPM
- Abnormal chrome content: 30 PPM
- Excessive chrome content: 40 PPM

Silicon (Si)

Silicon is basically dirt or sand. Silicon is the most common substance on earth. More than one-fourth of the earth's crust is silicon. The word *silicone* is often confused with *silicon*. (*Silicone* is a term used to describe a large number of compounds wherein silicon replaces carbon in an organic substance for increased stability and resistance to extremes in temperature. Therefore, silicones [with an *e* at the end of the word] can be oils, greases, resins, and synthetic rubber.)

- Normal silicon content: 5 to 25 PPM
- Abnormal silicon content: 30 PPM
- Excessive silicon content: 40 PPM

COMPRESSION TEST

Testing an engine for proper compression is one of the fundamental engine diagnostic tests that can be performed. For smooth engine operation, all cylinders must have equal compression. An engine can lose compression by leakage of air through one or more of only three routes:

- Intake or exhaust valve
- Piston rings (or piston, if there is a hole)
- Cylinder head gasket

For best results, the engine should be warmed to normal operating temperature before testing. An accurate compression test should be performed as follows:

Step #1. Remove all spark plugs. This allows the engine to be cranked to an even speed. Be sure to label all spark plug wires.

> ■ **CAUTION:** Disable the ignition system by disconnecting the primary leads from the ignition coil or module or by *grounding* the coil wire after removing it from the center of the distributor cap. Also disable the fuel-injection system to prevent the squirting of fuel into the cylinder. ■

Step #2. Block open the throttle and choke (if the vehicle is so equipped). This permits the maximum amount of air to be drawn into the engine. This step also ensures consistent compression test results.

Step #3. Thread a compression gauge into one spark plug hole and crank the engine. See Figure 6–10. Continue cranking the engine through *four* compression strokes. Each compression stroke makes a "puffing" sound.

> **HINT:** *Note the reading on the compression gauge after the first puff. This reading should be at least one-half of the final reading. For example, if the final, highest reading is 150 psi, then the reading after the first puff should be higher than 75 psi. A low first-puff reading indicates possible weak pistons.*

Step #4. Record the highest readings and compare the results. Most vehicle manufacturers specify the minimum compression reading and the maximum allowable variation among cylinders. Most manufactur-

FIGURE 6–10 Typical compression gauge being used to check the compression on a V-8 engine. For best results, all the spark plugs should be removed to ensure consistent cranking speed.

■ TECH TIP ■

THE HOSE TRICK

Installing spark plugs can be made easier by using a rubber hose on the end of the spark plug. The hose can be a vacuum hose, fuel line, or even an old spark plug wire end. See Figure 6–11. The hose makes it easy to start the threads of the spark plug into the cylinder head. After starting the threads, continue to thread the spark plug for several turns. Using the hose eliminates the chance of cross-threading the plug. This is especially important when installing spark plugs in aluminum cylinder heads.

ers specify a maximum difference of 20% between the highest reading and the lowest reading. For example:

If the high reading is	150 psi
Subtract 20%	−30 psi
Lowest allowable compression is	120 psi

HINT: *To make the math quick and easy, think of 10% of 150, which is 15 (move the decimal point to the left one place). Now double it: 15 × 2 = 30. This represents 20%.*

NOTE: During cranking, the oil pump cannot maintain normal oil pressure. Extended engine cranking such as that which occurs during a compression test can cause hydraulic lifters to collapse. When the en-

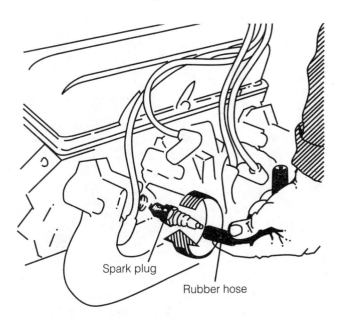

Spark plug

Rubber hose

FIGURE 6–11 Use a vacuum or fuel line hose over the spark plug to install it without danger of cross-threading the cylinder head.

gine starts, loud valve clicking noises may be heard. This should be considered normal after performing a compression test, and the noise should stop after the vehicle has been driven a short distance. _____

WET COMPRESSION TEST

If the reading of the compression test indicates low compression on one or more cylinders, add three squirts of oil to the cylinder and retest. This is called a **wet compression test,** when oil is used to help seal around the piston rings.

■ **CAUTION:** Do not use more oil than three squirts from a hand-operated oil squirt can. Too much oil can cause a hydrostatic lock, which can damage or break pistons or connecting rods or even crack a cylinder head. ■

Perform the compression test again and observe the results. If the first-puff readings greatly improve and the readings are a lot higher than without the oil, the cause of the low compression is worn or defective piston rings. If the compression readings increase only slightly (or not at all), then the cause of the low compression is usually defective valves. See Figure 6–12.

RUNNING COMPRESSION TEST

The compression test is commonly used to help determine engine condition. A compression test is usually performed with the engine cranking.

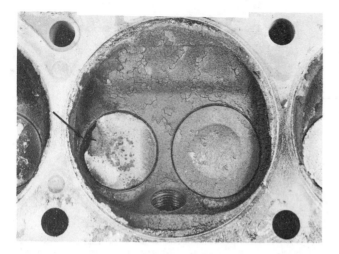

FIGURE 6–12 *Badly burned exhaust valve. A compression test could have detected a problem, and a cylinder leakage test (leak-down test) could have been used to determine the exact problem.*

What is the RPM of a cranking engine? An engine idles at about 600 to 900 RPM, and the starter motor obviously cannot crank the engine as fast as the engine idles. Most manufacturers' specifications require the engine to crank at 80 to 250 cranking RPM. Therefore, we are checking the compression of an engine at cranking speed to determine the condition of an engine that does not run at such low speeds.

But what should the compression of a running engine be? Some would think that the compression would be substantially higher, because the valve overlap of the cam is more effective at higher engine speeds and this would tend to increase the compression.

Actually, the compression pressure of a running engine is much *lower* than cranking compression pressure. This results from the volumetric efficiency. The engine is revolving faster, and therefore, there is less *time* for air to enter the combustion chamber. With less air to compress, the compression pressure is lower. Typically, the higher the engine RPM, the lower the running compression. For most engines, the value ranges are as follows:

- Compression during cranking: 125 to 160 psi
- Compression at idle: 60 to 90 psi
- Compression at 2000 RPM: 30 to 60 psi

As with cranking compression, the running compression of all cylinders should be equal. Therefore, a problem is not likely to be detected by single compression values, but by *variations* in running compression values among the cylinders. Broken valve springs, worn valve guides, bent pushrods, and worn cam lobes

are some of the items that would be indicated by a low running compression test reading on one or more cylinders.

PERFORMING A RUNNING COMPRESSION TEST

To perform a running compression test, remove just one spark plug at a time. With one spark plug removed from the engine, use a jumper wire to *ground* the spark plug wire to a good engine ground. This prevents possible ignition coil damage. Start the engine, push the pressure release on the gauge, and read the compression. Increase the engine speed to about 2000 RPM and push the pressure release on the gauge again. Read the gauge. Stop the engine, reattach the spark plug wire, and repeat the test for each of the remaining cylinders. Just like the cranking compression test, the running compression test can inform a technician of the *relative* compression of all the cylinders.

CYLINDER LEAKAGE TEST

One of the best tests that can be used to determine engine condition is the cylinder leakage test. This test involves injecting air under pressure into the cylinders one at a time. The amount and location of any escaping air helps the technician determine the condition of the engine. The air is put into the cylinder through a cylinder leakage gauge into the spark plug hole. See Figure 6–13.

Step #1. For best results, the engine should be at normal operating temperature (upper radiator hose hot and pressurized).

Step #2. The cylinder being tested must be at top dead center (TDC) of the compression stroke.

> **NOTE:** The greatest amount of wear occurs at the top of the cylinder because of the heat generated near the top of the cylinders. The piston ring flex also adds to the wear at the top of the cylinder.

Step #3. Calibrate the cylinder leakage unit as per manufacturer's instructions.

Step #4. Inject air into the cylinders one at a time, rotating the engine as necessitated by firing order to test each cylinder at TDC on the compression stroke.

Step #5. Evaluate the results:
Less than 10% leakage: good
Less than 20% leakage: acceptable
Less than 30% leakage: poor
More than 30% leakage: definite problem

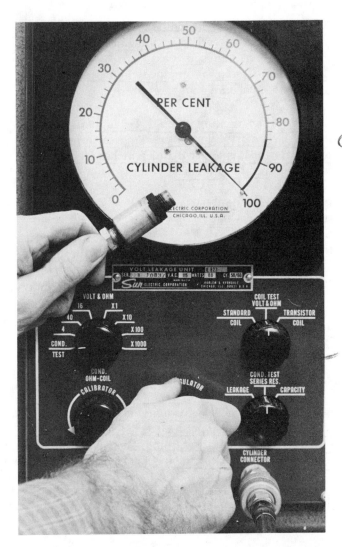

FIGURE 6–13 Typical cylinder leakage tester. The percentage of air escaping the cylinder is read on the gauge. An engine in good condition should not leak more than 20% of the air being forced into the cylinder.

HINT: *If leakage seems unacceptably high, repeat the test, being certain that the test is being performed correctly and that the cylinder being tested is at TDC on the compression stroke.*

Step #6. Check the source of air leakage.
   a. If air is heard escaping from the oil filler cap, the *piston rings* are worn or broken.
   b. If air is observed bubbling out of the radiator, there is a possible blown *head gasket* or cracked *cylinder head.*

   c. If air is heard coming from the carburetor or air inlet on fuel injection–equipped engines, there is a defective *intake valve(s).*
   d. If air is heard coming from the tail pipe, there is a defective *exhaust valve(s).*

CYLINDER POWER BALANCE TEST

Most large engine analyzers have a cylinder power balance feature. The purpose of a cylinder balance test is to determine if all cylinders are contributing power equally. It determines this by shorting out one cylinder at a time. If the engine speed (RPM) does not drop as much for one cylinder as for other cylinders of the same engine, then the shorted cylinder must be weaker than the other cylinders. For example:

Cylinder number	RPM drop when ignition is shorted
1	75
2	70
3	15
4	65
5	75
6	70

Cylinder #3 is the weak cylinder.

NOTE: Most automotive test equipment uses automatic means for testing for cylinder balance. Be certain to correctly identify the offending cylinder. Cylinder #3 as identified by the equipment may be the third cylinder in the firing order instead of the actual cylinder #3. ___

POWER BALANCE TEST PROCEDURE

When point-type ignition was used on all vehicles, the common method for determining which, if any, cylinder was weak was to remove a spark plug wire from one spark plug at a time while watching a tachometer and a vacuum gauge. This method is not recommended on any vehicle with any type of electronic ignition. If any of the spark plug wires are removed from a spark plug with the engine running, the ignition coil tries to supply increasing levels of voltage, attempting to jump the increasing gap as the plug wires are removed. This high voltage could easily track the ignition coil or damage the ignition module or both.

The acceptable method of canceling cylinders, which will work on all types of ignition systems, including distributorless, is to *ground* the secondary current for each cylinder. See Figure 6–14.

FIGURE 6–14 Using a vacuum hose and a test light to ground one cylinder at a time on a distributorless ignition system. This works on all types of ignition systems and provides a method for grounding out one cylinder at a time without fear of damaging any component.

The cylinder with the least RPM drop is the cylinder not producing its share of power.

VACUUM TESTING

Vacuum is pressure below atmospheric pressure and is measured in **inches** (or millimeters) of **mercury** (Hg). An engine in good mechanical condition will run with high manifold vacuum. Manifold vacuum is developed by the pistons as they move down on the intake stroke to draw the charge from the carburetor and intake manifold. Air to refill the manifold comes past the throttle plate into the manifold. Vacuum will increase anytime the engine turns faster or has better cylinder sealing while the throttle plate remains in a fixed position. Manifold vacuum will decrease when the engine turns more slowly or when the cylinders no longer do an efficient job of pumping.

Cranking Vacuum Test

Measuring the amount of manifold vacuum during cranking is a quick and easy test to determine if the piston rings and valves are properly sealing. (For accurate results, the engine should be warm and the throttle closed.)

Step #1. Disable the ignition.
Step #2. Connect the vacuum gauge to a manifold vacuum source.
Step #3. Crank the engine while observing the vacuum gauge.

Cranking vacuum should be higher than 2.5 inches of mercury. (Normal cranking vacuum is 3 to 6 inches Hg.) If it is lower than 2.5 inches Hg, then the following could be the cause:

- Too slow a cranking speed.
- Worn piston rings.
- Leaking valves.
- Excessive amounts of air bypassing the throttle plate. This could give a false low vacuum reading. Common sources include a throttle plate partially open or a high-performance camshaft with excessive overlap.

Idle Vacuum Test

An engine in proper condition should idle with a steady vacuum between 17 and 21 inches Hg. See Figure 6–15.

NOTE: Engine vacuum readings vary with altitude. A reduction of 1 inch Hg per 1000 feet (300 meters) of altitude should be subtracted from the expected values if testing a vehicle above 1000 feet (300 meters).

Low and Steady Vacuum

If the vacuum is lower than normal, yet the gauge reading is steady, the most common causes include

- Retarded ignition timing
- Retarded cam timing (check timing chain for excessive slack or timing belt for proper installation)

Fluctuating Vacuum

If the needle drops, then returns to a normal reading, then drops again and again returns, this indicates a sticking valve. A common cause of sticking valves is lack of lubrication of the valve stems.

HINT: *A common trick that some technicians use is to squirt some automatic transmission fluid (ATF) down the carburetor or into the air inlet of a warm engine. Often the idle quality improves and normal vacuum gauge readings are restored. The use of ATF does create excessive exhaust smoke for a short time, but it should not harm oxygen sensors or catalytic converters.*

If the vacuum gauge fluctuates above and below a center point, burned valves or weak valve springs may be indicated. If the fluctuation is slow and steady, unequal fuel mixture could be the cause.

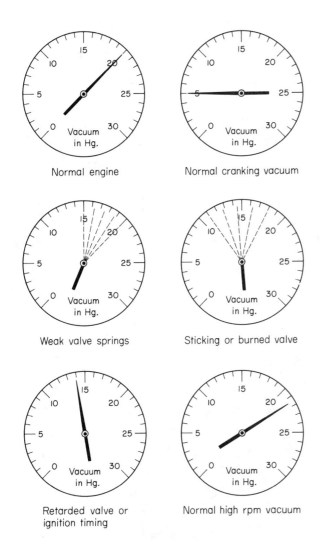

Normal engine   Normal cranking vacuum

Weak valve springs   Sticking or burned valve

Retarded valve or   Normal high rpm vacuum
ignition timing

FIGURE 6–15 Vacuum gauge as a diagnostic tool. Connect a vacuum gauge to a manifold vacuum source (a port that has vacuum at idle).

FIGURE 6–16 Notice all of the blowby gases escaping from the crankcase vent line. A clogged positive crankcase ventilation hose caused the fumes to back up into the intake.

ENGINE SMOKE DIAGNOSIS

Engine exhaust smoke color can indicate what engine problem might exist.

Typical exhaust smoke color	Possible causes
Blue	Blue exhaust indicates that the engine is burning oil. Oil is getting into the combustion chamber either past the piston rings or past the valve stem seals. Blue smoke only after start-up is usually due to defective valve stem seals.
Black	Black exhaust smoke is due to excessive fuel being burned in the combustion chamber. Typical causes include a defective or misadjusted

carburetor, leaking fuel injector, or excessive fuel pump pressure.

White (steam)   White smoke or steam from the exhaust is normal during cold weather and represents condensed steam. Remember, every engine creates about 1 gallon of water for each gallon of gasoline burned. If the steam from the exhaust is excessive, then water (coolant) is getting into the combustion chamber. Typical causes include a defective cylinder head gasket, a cracked cylinder head, or a cracked block in severe cases. See Figure 6–16.

EXHAUST RESTRICTION TEST

If the exhaust system is restricted, the engine will be low on power, yet smooth. Common causes of restricted exhaust include the following:

■ Clogged catalytic converter. Always check the ignition system for faults that could cause excessive amounts of unburned fuel to be exhausted. Excessive unburned fuel can overheat the catalytic converter and cause the beads or structure of the converter to fuse together, creating the restriction. A defective fuel delivery system could also cause excessive unburned fuel being dumped into the converter.

■ Clogged or restricted muffler. This can cause low power. Often a defective catalytic converter will shed particles that can clog a muffler. Broken internal baffles can also restrict exhaust flow.

■ Damaged or defective piping. This can reduce the power of any engine. Some exhaust pipe is constructed with double walls, and the inside pipe can collapse and form a restriction that is not visible on the outside of the exhaust pipe.

TESTING BACK PRESSURE WITH A VACUUM GAUGE

A vacuum gauge can be used to measure manifold vacuum at a high idle (2000 to 2500 RPM). If the exhaust system is restricted, pressure increases in the exhaust system. This pressure is called **back pressure.** Manifold vacuum will drop gradually if the engine is kept at a constant speed, if the exhaust is restricted.

The reason the vacuum will drop is that all of the exhaust leaving the engine at the higher engine speed cannot get through the restriction. After a short time (within 1 minute), the exhaust tends to "pile up" above the restriction and eventually remains in the cylinder of the engine at the end of the exhaust stroke. Therefore, at the beginning of the intake stroke, when the piston traveling downward should be lowering the pressure (raising the vacuum) in the intake manifold, the extra exhaust in the cylinder *lowers* the normal vacuum.

If the exhaust restriction is severe enough, the vehicle can become undriveable because cylinder filling cannot occur except at idle.

TESTING BACK PRESSURE WITH A PRESSURE GAUGE

Exhaust system back pressure can be measured directly by installing a pressure gauge into an exhaust opening. This can be accomplished in one of the following ways:

■ **With an oxygen sensor**—Remove the oxygen sensor and thread in an adapter to connect to a vacuum or pressure gauge.

NOTE: An adapter can be easily made by inserting a metal tube or pipe inside of an old discarded oxygen sensor. A short section of brake line works great. The pipe can be brazed to the oxygen sensor housing or it can be glued in with epoxy. An 18-millimeter compression gauge adapter can also be adapted to fit into the oxygen sensor opening. See Figure 6–17. _____

■ With the **exhaust gas recirculation (EGR) valve**—Remove the EGR valve and fabricate a plate as shown in Figure 6–18.

■ With the **air injection reaction (AIR) check valve**—Remove the check valve from the exhaust tubes leading down to the exhaust manifold. Use a rub-

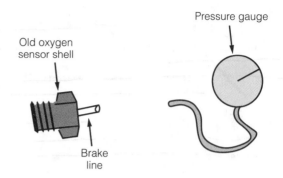

FIGURE 6–17   A back pressure tool can be easily made by attaching a short section of brake line to the shell of an old oxygen sensor. Braze or epoxy the tube to the shell.

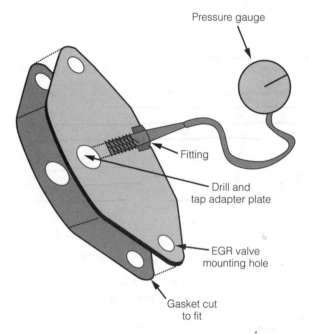

FIGURE 6–18   Back pressure can be measured directly by removing the exhaust gas recirculation valve and fabricating a steel plate with a fitting for the pressure gauge.

ber cone with a tube inside to seal against the exhaust tube. Connect the tube to a pressure gauge.

At idle the maximum back pressure should be less than 1.5 psi (10 kPa), and it should be less than 2.5 psi (15 kPa) at 2500 RPM.

TIMING CHAIN SLACK DIAGNOSIS

Engines with high mileage often have timing chains with slack that is excessive for proper operation. As the timing chain stretches, the cam retards in relation to the position

FIGURE 6–19 Checking ignition timing with a timing light. If the timing mark moves back and forth, suspect a worn timing chain or gears, or a distributor problem (if the vehicle is so equipped).

of the crankshaft and pistons. Because the camshaft operates the valves, this also causes the valves to open and close later in the stroke than they were designed to do. (This discussion does *not* involve engines equipped with timing *belts*.) This retarded or late closing of the intake valve and late closing of the exhaust valve tends to lower available power at low speeds. However, the retarded cam timing does tend to slightly improve high-engine speed performance. A typical comment from an owner of a vehicle with excessive timing chain stretch is that the engine performs best after "getting it going faster."

To determine the condition of a timing chain, follow this simple procedure:

Step #1. With the ignition off, rotate the engine by hand clockwise as viewed from the front or belt end (nonprincipal end) until the timing mark aligns with top dead center (TDC).

FIGURE 6–20 Excessive timing chain wear was observed on a Ford V-8 (over 10 degrees of slack). After replacing the timing chain, the real cause of the slack was finally discovered—a worn distributor gear.

NOTE: Do not turn the engine counterclockwise if turned past TDC! This will loosen the tension on the chain, and the results of the test will not be accurate. If the engine is accidentally turned beyond TDC, continue clockwise rotation until the timing mark once again lines up with TDC.

Step #2. Remove the distributor cap.
Step #3. Slowly rotate the engine counterclockwise as viewed from the front of the engine (nonprincipal end) while observing for any movement of the distributor rotor.
Step #4. Just as soon as the rotor starts to move, note the distance of the timing mark from TDC.

A distance of less than 5 degrees is normal and acceptable, especially for a high-mileage engine. A distance of 5 to 8 degrees is acceptable for a high-mileage engine, but not acceptable for a low-mileage engine. Very little change in the operation of the engine would be noticed if the timing chain were replaced. If the distance is over 8 degrees, the timing chain definitely requires replacement for proper engine operation and to prevent severe engine damage that could occur if the timing chain and/or gear should fail during engine operation. See Figures 6–19 and 6–20.

EXHAUST ANALYSIS AND COMBUSTION EFFICIENCY

A popular method of engine analysis involves the use of four-gas exhaust analysis equipment. See Figure 6–21. The four gases analyzed and their significance are the following.

FIGURE 6–21   A typical partial stream sample type of exhaust probe used to measure exhaust gases in parts per million (PPM) or percentage (%).

■ DIAGNOSTIC STORY ■

THE RIGHT NOISE— WRONG REPAIR

A technician diagnosed a tapping noise heard at idle on a small V-8 engine to be a noisy (defective) hydraulic lifter. The noise was heard in the cam-lifter area with a stethoscope at one-half engine speed. Because this was typical valve train noise, the technician removed the intake manifold and carefully inspected all valve train components. All of the hydraulic valve lifters looked and tested good and were replaced back in their original locations. The camshaft was carefully inspected. Finding no obvious problem, the technician reassembled the engine. After the engine was restarted, the noise was still present.

This time the technician really started listening everywhere for the noise. The noise was the loudest at the fuel pump. The fuel pump was replaced (it had a broken rocker arm return spring), and the noise was eliminated. The fuel pump operated off of the camshaft. The broken rocker arm return spring did not affect the operation of the fuel pump, but it did create noise that was transmitted through the engine along the camshaft.

Hydrocarbons

Hydrocarbons (HC) are unburned gasoline and are measured in parts per million (PPM). A correctly operating engine should burn (oxidize) almost all of the gasoline; therefore, very little unburned gasoline should be present in the exhaust. Acceptable levels of

HC are 50 PPM or less. High levels of HC could be due to excessive oil consumption caused by weak piston rings or worn valve guides. The most common cause of excessive HC emissions is a fault in the ignition system. Items that should be checked include

- Spark plugs
- Spark plug wires
- Distributor cap and rotor (if the vehicle is so equipped)
- Ignition timing
- Ignition coil

Carbon Monoxide

Carbon monoxide (CO) is unstable and will easily combine with any oxygen to form stable carbon dioxide (CO_2). The fact that CO combines with oxygen is the reason that CO is a poisonous gas (in the lungs, it combines with oxygen to form CO_2 and deprives the brain of oxygen). CO levels of a properly operating engine should be less than 0.5%. High levels of CO can be caused by clogged or restricted crankcase ventilation devices such as PCV valve, hose(s), and tubes. Other items that might cause excessive CO include

- Clogged air filter
- Incorrect idle speed
- Too-high fuel pump pressure
- Any other items that can cause a rich condition

Carbon Dioxide

Carbon dioxide (CO_2) is the result of oxygen in the engine combining with the carbon of the gasoline. An acceptable level of CO_2 is between 12% and 15%. A high reading indicates an efficiently operating engine. If the CO_2 level is low, the mixture may be either too rich or too lean.

Oxygen

The last of the four gases is oxygen (O_2). There is about 21% oxygen in the atmosphere, and most of this oxygen should be "used up" during the combustion process to oxidize all of the hydrogen and carbon (hydrocarbons) in the gasoline. Levels of O_2 should be very low (about 0.5%). High levels of O_2, especially at idle, could be due to an exhaust system leak.

NOTE: Adding 10% alcohol to gasoline provides additional oxygen to the fuel and will result in lower levels of CO and higher levels of O_2 in the exhaust. —

DIAGNOSING HEAD GASKET FAILURE

Several items can be used to help diagnose a head gasket failure:

- **Exhaust gas analyzer.** With the radiator cap removed, place the probe from the exhaust analyzer above the radiator filler neck. If the HC reading increases, the exhaust (unburned hydrocarbons) is getting into the coolant from the combustion chamber.
- **Chemical test.** A chemical tester using blue paper is also available. The paper turns yellow if combustion gases are present in the coolant.
- **Bubbles in the coolant.** Remove the coolant pump belt to prevent pump operation. Remove the radiator cap and start the engine. If bubbles appear in the coolant before it begins to boil, a defective head gasket or cracked cylinder head is indicated.
- **Excessive exhaust steam.** If excessive water or steam is observed coming from the tail pipe, this means that coolant is getting into the combustion chamber from a defective head gasket or a cracked head. If there is leakage between cylinders, the engine usually misfires and a power balancer test and/or compression test can be used to confirm the problem.

If any of the preceding indicators of head gasket failure occur, remove the cylinder head(s) and check all of the following:

1. Head gasket
2. Sealing surfaces—for warpage
3. Castings—for cracks

> **HINT:** *A leaking thermal vacuum valve can cause symptoms similar to those of a defective head gasket. Most thermal vacuum valves thread into a coolant passage, and they often leak only after they get hot.*

DASH WARNING LIGHTS

Most vehicles are equipped with several dash warning lights, often called "telltale" or "idiot" lights. These lights are often the only warning a driver receives that there may be engine problems. A summary of typical dash warning lights and their meanings follows.

Oil (Engine) Light

The red oil light indicates that the engine oil pressure is too low (usually lights when oil pressure is 3 to 7 psi (20 to 50 kPa). Normal oil pressure should be 10 to 60 psi (70 to 400 kPa), or 10 psi per 1000 engine RPM.

When this light comes on, the driver should shut off the engine immediately and check the oil level. If the oil level is okay, then there is a possible serious engine problem or a possible defective oil pressure sending (sender) unit. The automotive technician should always check the oil pressure using a known-to-be-good mechanical oil pressure gauge if low oil pressure is suspected.

> **NOTE:** Some automobile manufacturers combine the dash warning lights for oil pressure and coolant temperature into one light, usually labeled "**ENGINE**." Therefore, when the engine light comes on, the technician should check for possible coolant temperature and/or oil pressure problems.

Coolant Temperature Light

Most vehicles are equipped with a coolant temperature gauge or dash warning light. The warning light may be labeled "coolant," "hot," or "temperature." If the coolant temperature warning light comes on during driving, this usually indicates that the coolant temperature is above a safe level, or above about 250° F (120° C). Normal coolant temperature should be about 200° to 220° F (90° to 105° C).

If the coolant temperature light comes on during driving, the following steps should be followed to prevent possible engine damage:

1. Turn off the air conditioning and turn on the heater. The heater will help get rid of some of the heat in the cooling system.
2. Raise the engine speed in neutral or park to increase the circulation of coolant through the radiator.
3. If possible, turn the engine off and allow it to cool (this may take over an hour).
4. Do not continue driving with the coolant temperature light on (or the gauge reading in the red warning section or above 260° F), or serious engine damage may result.

> **NOTE:** If the engine does not feel or smell hot, it is possible that the problem is a faulty coolant temperature sensor or gauge.

Charge Light

The red charge warning light indicates that the charging system is not operating. The charge light may also be labeled "gen" or "alt" (alternator). Because most batteries are capable of supplying the electrical needs of the vehicle for a short time, it is not necessary to stop the engine if this warning light comes on. If, however, the charging system is not repaired or serviced, the engine will eventually cease running because the ignition system, which ignites the spark plugs, requires a certain level of voltage to operate (usually a minimum of 9 volts).

Computer Warning Light

Most vehicles with an engine control computer use dash warning lights to warn the driver that some computer sensor, actuator, or engine parameter is not within acceptable range.

The computer dash warning light called a malfunction indicator lamp (MIL) is usually orange in color and indicates a less than serious problem, whereas some computer warning lights may be red, indicating more serious engine problems. For example, some computer systems monitor oil pressure versus engine RPM, battery voltage, and coolant temperature. The computer warning lights might be labeled

Check Engine
Check Engine Soon
Check Engine Now
Power Loss
Power Limited

If an orange engine computer light comes on, continue driving and check for any stored trouble codes as per the vehicle manufacturer's procedures. If a *red* engine computer light comes on, it is best to stop the engine and check all vital engine systems before continuing operation. Follow the manufacturer's recommended procedures for determining the cause and corrective action required.

Emission Reminder Light

Many vehicles are equipped with an emission light notifying the driver that some emission-related service is required. Some manufacturers use a mechanical sign (flag) that covers a part of the odometer when the designated mileage occurs.

The need for an emission light depends upon the ability of the manufacturer to certify the engine's emission control systems. If corrective action is required to maintain the emission standards, then the driver must be notified at the appropriate mileage intervals. A service manual should be consulted whenever the emission indicator is encountered

1. To determine what corrective action should be taken to maintain acceptable emission levels
2. To determine the exact method to follow to reset the emission indicator

   NOTE: The emission light and the engine light are often confusing to drivers. Before attempting service work, make certain that the service is appropriate for the warning light. _____

SUMMARY

1. The first step in diagnosing engine condition is to perform a thorough visual inspection, including a check of oil and coolant levels and condition.
2. Oil leaks can be found by using a white powder or a fluorescent dye and a black light.

3. Many engine-related problems make a characteristic noise.
4. Oil analysis by a testing laboratory can reveal engine problems by measuring the amount of dissolved metals in the oil.
5. A compression test can be used to test the condition of valves and piston rings.
6. A cylinder leakage test fills the cylinder with compressed air, and the gauge indicates the percentage of leakage.
7. A cylinder balance test indicates whether or not all cylinders are working.
8. Testing engine vacuum is another procedure that can help the service technician determine engine condition.
9. If the timing chain has worn and stretched, the engine cannot produce normal power.
10. Exhaust analysis testing is another diagnostic tool that can tell the service technician whether or not the engine is performing correctly and efficiently.

REVIEW QUESTIONS

1. Describe four visual checks that should be performed on an engine if a mechanical malfunction is suspected.
2. List three simple items that could cause excessive oil consumption.
3. List three simple items that could cause engine noises.
4. Explain what could be wrong with an engine if the oil analysis report came back from a testing laboratory with the following information:

   Silicon: 35 PPM
   Tin: 1 PPM
   Aluminum: 31 PPM
   Copper: 57 PPM
   Chrome: 8 PPM
   Iron: 303 PPM
   Fuel dilution: none
   Antifreeze: none
   Moisture content: zero

5. Describe how to perform a compression test and how to determine what is wrong with an engine based on a compression test result.
6. Describe the cylinder leakage test.
7. Explain how a technician can safely ground out one cylinder at a time without damage to the electronics of the vehicle.
8. Describe how a vacuum gauge would indicate if the valves were sticking in their guides.
9. Describe the test procedure for determining if the exhaust system is restricted (clogged) using a vacuum gauge.

MULTIPLE-CHOICE QUESTIONS

1. Technician A says that the paper test could detect a burned valve. Technician B says that a grayish-white stain could be a coolant leak. Which technician is correct?
   a. A only
   b. B only
   c. Both A and B
   d. Neither A nor B

2. Two technicians are discussing oil leaks. Technician A says that an oil leak can be found using a fluorescent dye in the oil with a black light to check for leaks. Technician B says that a white spray powder can be used to locate oil leaks. Which technician is correct?
   a. A only
   b. B only
   c. Both A and B
   d. Neither A nor B

3. An increase in viscosity can be due to _____ .
   a. Wear metals in the oil
   b. Fuel dilution of the oil
   c. A clogged air filter
   d. All of the above

4. Antifreeze in the engine oil can cause _____ .
   a. The oil to become thinner (decrease viscosity)
   b. The oil to become thicker (increase viscosity)
   c. The oil to congeal
   d. Both b and c

5. A smoothly operating engine depends on _____ .
   a. High compression on most cylinders
   b. Equal compression between cylinders
   c. Cylinder compression levels above 100 psi (700 kPa) and within 70 psi (500 kPa) of each other
   d. Compression levels below 100 psi (700 kPa) on most cylinders.

6. A good reading for a cylinder leakage test would be _____ .
   a. Within 20% between cylinders
   b. All cylinders below 20% leakage
   c. All cylinders above 20% leakage
   d. All cylinders above 70% leakage and within 7% of each other

7. Technician A says that during a power balance test, the cylinder that causes the biggest RPM drop is the weak cylinder. Technician B says that if one spark plug wire is grounded out and the engine speed does not drop, a weak or dead cylinder is indicated. Which technician is correct?
   a. A only
   b. B only
   c. Both A and B
   d. Neither A nor B

8. *Cranking* vacuum should be _____ .
   a. 2.5 inches Hg or higher
   b. Over 25 inches Hg
   c. 17 to 21 inches Hg
   d. 6 to 16 inches Hg

9. Technician A says that a worn (stretched) timing chain and worn gears will cause the valve and ignition timing to be retarded. Technician B says that if the timing chain slack is over 8 degrees, the timing chain and gears should be replaced. Which technician is correct?
   a. A only
   b. B only
   c. Both A and B
   d. Neither A nor B

10. The low oil pressure warning light usually comes on _____ .
    a. Whenever an oil change is required
    b. Whenever oil pressure drops dangerously low (3 to 7 psi)
    c. Whenever the oil filter bypass valve opens
    d. Whenever the oil filter antidrain back valve opens

7

Engine Removal and Disassembly

OBJECTIVES

After studying Chapter 7, the reader will be able to

1. Describe how to remove an engine from a vehicle.
2. Explain the differences between a long block and a short block assembly.
3. Discuss how to remove cylinder heads without causing warpage.
4. List the steps necessary to remove a piston from a cylinder.
5. Explain how to remove a valve from a cylinder head.

The decision to repair an engine should be based on all the information about the engine that is available to the service technician. In some cases, the engine might not be worth repairing. It is the responsibility of the technician to discuss the advantages and disadvantages of the different repair options with the customer. The customer, who is paying for the repair, must make the final decision on the reconditioning procedure to be used. The decision will be based on the recommendation of the service technician.

COMPONENT REPAIR

Most customers want to spend the least amount of money, so they only have the faulty component repaired. If a part fails, it may only be the result of the faulty part. An example of this would be a failed timing sprocket and chain. The problem will be corrected when a new timing sprocket and chain are installed.

WHAT IS THE JULIAN DATE?

Often, engine designs or parts change during a production year. The point at which a change occurred is usually reported to technicians in service bulletins, service manuals, or parts books as a vehicle serial number or a certain Julian date. A Julian date is simply the number of the day of the year. For example, January 1 is the day 001 and December 31 is usually day 365. The Julian date is commonly used in industry. The Julian date is named for Julius Caesar, who first used a 365-day calendar, with 366 days every 4 years.

There are calendars available that have the day of the year listed to make usage of the Julian date easier.

On the other hand, a part may have failed because some other part was not working correctly. An example of this would be a rocker arm pivot that was badly scored because it did not get proper lubrication. Perhaps the lubrication was restricted by a faulty metering valve inside the hydraulic lifter. If only the rocker arm and pivot were replaced, the new rocker arm and pivot would soon fail because the lifter problem was not also repaired. Figure 7–1 shows a rocker arm and pivot from an engine on which this was done. The service technician should explain to the customer why the part failed and suggest different repairs that could be made to keep the part from failing again.

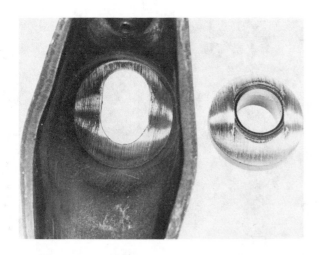

FIGURE 7-1 *Scoring of rocker arm and pivot caused by loss of lubrication. This problem is most commonly found on cylinders nearest the EGR valve. The extra heat of the exhaust passages in this area can overheat the oil, causing deposits that clog oil passages.*

VALVE JOB

Failure of a valve to seal on the seat is one of the most common cases of premature failure causing engine problems. When there is a leak between the valve and the seat, the combustion pressure is lowered. This will reduce both engine economy and power. The high-pressure combustion gases escaping between the leaking valve and seat will burn the valve face, and this, in turn, increases the leakage. The tops of the pistons are visible once the head is removed for a valve job. Their condition may indicate that the pistons should also be serviced.

Failure of a valve to seal on the seat can result from abnormal combustion, incorrect valve lash, valve stem deposits, abusive engine operation, and so on. Valve leakage is corrected by doing a **valve job.** This does not necessarily correct the malfunction that caused the valve to leak. Stopping valve leakage improves manifold vacuum. The greater manifold vacuum may draw the oil past worn piston rings and into the combustion chamber during the intake stroke, causing oil consumption to increase. See Figure 7-2.

MINOR OVERHAUL

In this discussion, engine overhaul includes both a ring and a valve job. New connecting rod bearings are usually installed during an overhaul. Sometimes, this type of reconditioning is called a **minor overhaul.** A minor

FIGURE 7-2 *An alternative to performing a valve job is to purchase remanufactured heads. The photo shows finished head assemblies as found on the showroom floor of a small engine remanufacturer. The top three numbers indicate engine size in cubic inches, and the bottom three numbers are the last three numbers of the casting number.*

overhaul can usually be done without removing the engine from the chassis. It does require removal of both the head and the oil pan. The overhaul is usually done when the engine lacks power, has poor fuel economy, uses an excessive amount of oil, produces visible tail pipe emissions, runs rough, or is hard to start. It is still only a *repair* procedure. Many worn parts remain in the engine. Other engine problems may be noticed after the oil pan is removed and the piston and rod assemblies are taken out. The customer should be informed about any other engine problem so that the service the engine requires can be authorized. In the high-performance industry, this procedure is called **freshening the engine.**

MAJOR OVERHAUL

A complete engine reconditioning job is called rebuilding. Sometimes, this type of reconditioning is called a **major overhaul.** To rebuild the engine, the engine must be removed from the chassis and be completely disassembled. All serviceable parts are reconditioned to either new or service standards. All bearings, gaskets, and seals are replaced. When the reconditioning is done properly, a rebuilt engine should operate as long as a new engine.

A special form of precision engine rebuilding is called **blueprinting.** Blueprinting is usually done to give the engine maximum performance. The clearances are all set near the maximum specifications and combustion chambers are adjusted to minimum and equal volumes. All servicing details are done with extreme care. The engine is carefully balanced. Blueprinting requires skilled and detailed labor and so is very expensive.

The vehicle is out of service while the engine is being rebuilt. This is inconvenient for some customers and very expensive for others. Because of the total cost, the customer might decide to replace the engine instead of having it rebuilt.

SHORT BLOCK

The quickest way to get a vehicle back in service is to exchange the faulty engine for a different one. In an older vehicle, the engine may be replaced with a used engine from a salvage yard. In some cases, only a reconditioned block, including the crankshaft, rods, and pistons, is used. This replacement assembly is called a **short block.** The original heads and valve train are reconditioned and used on the short block.

FITTED BLOCK

A **fitted block** is a reconditioned block with pistons only. The individual pistons are selected for proper clearance for each cylinder. A fitted block is generally not the preferred unit to purchase because the block does *not* contain the following components:

- Crankshaft and bearings
- Connecting rods and bearings
- Camshaft and bearings

LONG BLOCK

The replacement assembly is called a **long block** when the reconditioned assembly includes the heads and valve train. Many automotive machine shops maintain

FIGURE 7–3 Shipping area of a major regional engine remanufacturer. Note that each engine is bolted to a wooden pallet and covered in a plastic bag for shipment. Cores can be shipped back to the plant on the same wooden pallet.

a stock of short and long blocks of popular engines. Usually, the original engine parts, called a **core,** are exchanged for the reconditioned assembly. The core parts are reconditioned by the automotive machine shop and put back in stock for the next customer. See Figure 7–3.

REMANUFACTURED ENGINES

Some engines are **remanufactured.** The engine cores are completely disassembled, and each serviceable part is reconditioned with specialized machinery. Engines are then assembled on an engine assembly line similar to the original manufacturer's assembly line. The parts that are assembled together as an engine have not come out of the same engine. The remanufactured engine usually has new pistons, valves, and lifters, together with other parts that are normally replaced in a rebuilt engine. All clearances and fits in the remanufactured engine are the same as in a new engine. A remanufactured engine should give service as good as that of a new engine, and it will cost about half as much. Remanufactured engines usually carry a warranty. This means that they will be replaced if they fail during the period of the warranty. They may even cost less than a rebuilt engine because much of the reconditioning is done by specialized machines rather than by expensive skilled labor.

ENGINE REMOVAL

The engine exterior and the engine compartment should be cleaned before work is begun. A clean engine is easier to work on; and the cleaning not only helps to keep dirt out of the engine, but also minimizes accidental damage from slipping tools. The battery ground cable is disconnected to avoid the chance of sparks. An even better procedure is to remove the battery from the vehicle.

Working on the top of the engine is made easier if the hood is removed. With fender covers in place, the hood is loosened from the hinges. With a person on each side of the hood to support it, the hood is lifted off as the bolts that hold the hood are removed. The hood is usually stored on fender covers placed on the top of the vehicle, where it is least likely to be damaged.

The coolant is drained from the radiator and the engine block to minimize the chance of coolant getting into the cylinders when the head is removed. The exhaust manifold is disconnected. On some engines, it is easier to remove the exhaust pipe from the manifold. On others, it is easier to separate the exhaust manifold from the head and leave the manifold attached to the exhaust pipe. On V-type engines, the intake manifold must be removed before the heads can be taken off. In most cases, a number of wires, accessories, hoses, and tubing must be removed before the manifold head can be removed. If the engine is not familiar, it is a good practice to put tape on each of the items removed. The tape can be marked with the proper location of each item so that all items can be easily replaced during engine assembly.

All coolant hoses are removed, and the transmission oil cooler lines are disconnected from the radiator. The radiator mounting bolts are removed, and the radiator is lifted from the engine compartment. This gets the radiator out of the way so that it will not be damaged while you are working on the engine. This is a good time to have the radiator cleaned, while it is out of the chassis. If cleaning is not required, the radiator is placed where it will not be damaged as the overhaul

■ TECH TIP ■

A PICTURE IS WORTH A THOUSAND WORDS

Take pictures with a Polaroid camera or a video camera of the engine being serviced. These pictures will be worth their weight in gold when it comes time to reassemble or reinstall the engine. It is very difficult for anyone to remember the *exact* location of every bracket, wire, and hose. Referring back to the photos of the engine before work was started will help you restore the vehicle to like-new condition.

progresses. The vehicle trunk makes a good storage place for the radiator.

If the engine is air conditioned, the compressor can usually be separated from the engine, leaving all air-conditioning hoses securely connected to the compressor and lines. The compressor can be fastened to the side of the engine compartment, where it will not interfere with engine removal. It may also be necessary to loosen the air-conditioning condenser and fasten it aside. If it is necessary to disconnect the air-conditioning lines, use a refrigerant recovery system to prevent loss of refrigerant to the atmosphere.

All air-conditioning line openings should be securely plugged immediately after they are disconnected to keep dirt and moisture from the system. They should remain plugged until immediately prior to reassembly.

There are two ways to remove the engine. The engine can be lifted out of the chassis with the transmission/transaxle attached, or the transmission/transaxle can be separated from the engine and left in the chassis. The method to be used must be determined before the engine is removed from the vehicle.

Under the vehicle, the drive shaft (propeller shaft) or half shafts are removed and the exhaust pipes disconnected. In some installations, it may be necessary to loosen the steering linkage idler arm to give clearance. The transmission controls, speedometer cable, and clutch linkages are disconnected and tagged.

A sling, either a chain or lift cable, is attached to the manifold or head cap screws on top of the engine. A hoist is attached to the sling and snugged to take most of the weight. This leaves the engine resting on the mounts. (Most engines use three mounts, one on each side and one at the back of the transmission or at the front of the engine.) The rear cross-member is removed, and on rear wheel–drive vehicles, the transmission is lowered. The hoist is tightened to lift the engine. The engine will have to nose up as it is removed. The front of the engine must come almost straight up as the transmission slides from under the floor pan, as illustrated in Figure 7–4. The engine and transmission are hoisted free of the automobile, swung clear, and lowered on an open floor area.

NOTE: The engine is lowered and removed from underneath on some front-drive vehicles. See Figures 7–5 through 7–10.

ENGINE DISASSEMBLY

The following disassembly procedure applies primarily to pushrod engines. The procedure will have to be modified somewhat when working on overhead cam

FIGURE 7–4 An engine must be tipped as it is pulled from the chassis.

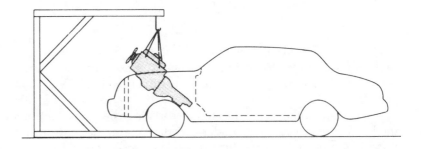

FIGURE 7–5 When removing just the engine from a front wheel–drive vehicle, the transaxle must be supported. Shown here is a typical fixture that can be used to hold the engine if the transaxle is removed or to hold the transaxle if the engine is removed.

FIGURE 7–6 This front wheel–drive engine was dropped out of the bottom of the vehicle along with the cradle (subframe) and transaxle as an assembly.

(a)

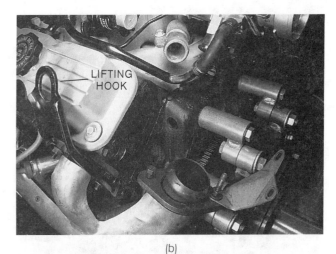

(b)

(c)

FIGURE 7–7 (a) Notice how this four-cylinder Ford engine is well balanced on the hoist. (b) Factory hook on rear (bell housing end) of the engine. (c) Factory hook on the front (accessory drive belt end) of the engine. These factory hooks are usually well placed for balance and ease of use because the factory uses these hooks while installing the engine in the vehicle. Time and labor are saved by not removing them after the engine is installed.

FIGURE 7–8 The transmission should be supported when the engine is removed. This engine was removed because all of the oil leaked out after the wrong oil filter was used during an oil change.

FIGURE 7–9 Look for bent, damaged, or broken parts as the engine is being removed from the vehicle. This broken engine mount could cause excessive engine movement and driveline stress.

FIGURE 7–10 Be certain not to damage these alignment dowel pins when removing or reinstalling a transmission. These dowel pins are critical for the proper alignment of the engine transmission assembly.

engines. Engines should be cold before disassembly to minimize the chance of warpage.

Removal of the rocker arm covers gives the first opportunity to see inside a part of the engine. See Figure 7–11. Make a good visual examination of this area to identify and determine the cause of any abnormal condition. Examine the rocker arms, valve springs, and valve tips for obvious defects.

Remove the manifold hold-down cap screws and nuts, and lift off the manifold. If the gaskets are stuck, a flat blade, such as that of a putty knife, can be worked alongside of the gaskets to loosen them. Care must be taken to avoid damaging the parting surface as the gasket is loosened. When the manifold and lifter valley cover are off of V-type engines, the technician has another opportunity to examine the interior of the engine. On some V-type engines, it is possible to see the condition of the cam at the bottom of the lifter valley.

With the manifold off of the V-type engine, note any obvious abnormal conditions, loosen the rocker arms, and remove the pushrods. The usual practice is to leave the lifters in place when doing only a valve job. The lifters can be removed at this time if they are causing the problem or if the engine valve train is to be serviced.

FIGURE 7–11 Typical deposits inside a rocker arm cover.

Remove the head cap screws and lift the head from the block deck. If the head gasket is stuck, carefully pry the head to loosen the gasket.

■ **CAUTION:** Aluminum cylinder heads often warp upward in the center of the head. Loosening the center head bolts first will tend to increase the warpage, especially if the head is being removed to replace a head gasket because of overheating. Always follow the torque

FIGURE 7–12   The top of the piston is completely gone on this engine. The parts were found in the oil pan.

FIGURE 7–13   Notice the badly burned exhaust valve.

table backward, starting with the highest-number bolt and working toward the lowest number. ∎

Special care should be taken to pry only on edges of the head that will not break. Parting surfaces should *not* be scratched. Scratched or burred surfaces will lead to leaks in the repaired engine.

The combustion chamber is exposed when the head is removed. The combustion chamber pocket in the head and the top of the piston should be given a thorough visual examination. The most obvious problem condition involves deposits or damage such as

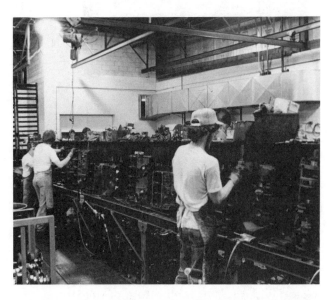

FIGURE 7–14   Engine disassembly on a conveyor line at a large regional engine remanufacturer. This remanufacturer can completely remanufacture about 200 engines a day.

those shown in Figures 7–12, 7–13, and 7–14. A normal combustion chamber is coated with a layer of hard, light-colored deposits. If the combustion chamber has been running too hot, the deposits will be very thin and white colored. Also see Figure 7–14.

CHECKING CYLINDER BORE

At this point, the cylinder taper and out-of-round of the cylinder bore should be checked just below the **ridge** and just above the piston when it is at the bottom of the stroke, as shown on the cutaway cylinder in Figures 7–15 and 7–16. These measurements will indicate how much cylinder wall work is required. If the cylinders are worn beyond the specified limits, they will have to be rebored to return them to a satisfactory condition.

Turn the engine upside down and remove the oil pan. This is the first opportunity to see the working parts in the bottom end of the engine. Deposits are again a good indication of the engine condition and the care it has had. Heavy sludge indicates infrequent oil changes. Hard carbon indicates overheating. The oil pump pickup screen should be checked to see how much plugging exists. The connecting rods and caps and main bearing caps should be checked to make sure that they are *numbered*. If not, they should be numbered with number stamps or a punch. The parts are marked so that they can be reassembled in exactly the same position. See Figures 7–17 and 7–18.

(a)

(b)

FIGURE 7–15 (a) When the head is first removed, the cylinder taper and out-of-round should be checked below the ridge and (b) above the piston when it is at the bottom of the stroke.

FIGURE 7–16 Most of the cylinder wear is on the top inch just below the cylinder ridge. This wear is due to the heat and combustion pressures that occur when the piston is near the top of the cylinder. (Courtesy of Dana Corporation.)

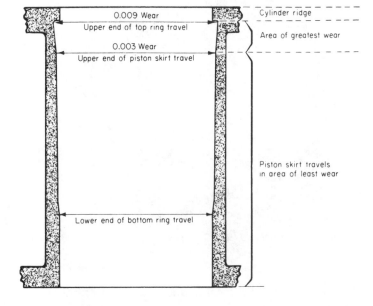

0.009 Wear
Upper end of top ring travel

0.003 Wear
Upper end of piston skirt travel

Lower end of bottom ring travel

Cylinder ridge

Area of greatest wear

Piston skirt travels in area of least wear

FIGURE 7–17 Notice the numbers on the connecting rods and main bearing caps.

118

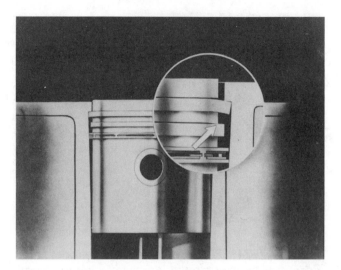

FIGURE 7–19 If the ridge at the top of a cylinder is not removed, the top piston ring could break the second piston ring land when the piston is pushed out of the cylinder during disassembly, or the second piston ring land could break when the engine is first run after reassembly with new rings. (Courtesy of Sealed Power.)

FIGURE 7–18 If the rods and mains are not marked, it is wise to use a punch to make identifying marks <u>before</u> disassembly of the engine.

REMOVING THE CYLINDER RIDGE

The ridge above the top ring must be removed before the piston and connecting rod assembly is removed. Cylinder wear leaves an upper ridge. Ridge removal is necessary to avoid catching a ring on the ridge and breaking the piston. Failure to remove the ridge is likely to cause the second piston ring land to break when the engine is run after reassembly with new rings, as pictured in Figure 7–19. The ridge is removed with a cutting tool that is fed into the metal ridge. A guide on the tool prevents accidental cutting below the ridge. The ridge reaming job should be done carefully with frequent checks of the work so that no more material than necessary is removed. One type of ridge reamer is shown in Figures 7–20 and 7–21.

PISTON REMOVAL

Rotate the engine until the piston that is to be removed is at top dead center (TDC). Remove connecting rod nuts from the rod so that the rod cap with its bearing half can be removed. Fit the rod bolts with protectors to keep the bolt threads from damaging the crankshaft journals, and remove the piston and rod assemblies.

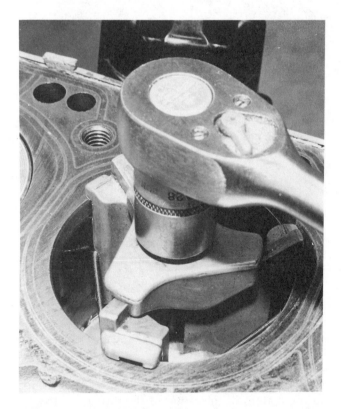

FIGURE 7–20 Ridge being removed with one type of <u>ridge reamer</u> before the piston assemblies are removed from the engine.

FIGURE 7–21 Ridge reamer and cylinder after ridge has been removed. Remanufacturers do not remove the cylinder ridge because all remanufactured engines are bored oversize and receive replacement pistons.

FIGURE 7–22 Normal piston thrust surface wear. This piston could be reconditioned to give further service.

PISTON CONDITION

Normal piston wear shows up as even wear on the thrust surfaces of the piston. The wear is from the top to the bottom in the center of the thrust surfaces, as shown in Figure 7–22. The top ring should be slightly loose in the groove. This type of piston can usually be reconditioned for additional useful service.

FIGURE 7–23 Piston burned as a result of detonation. The owner of this engine was operating the vehicle without mufflers and did not hear the engine-damaging spark knock. (The ignition was set too far advanced.)

Heat Damage

Holes in pistons, burned areas, severely damaged ring lands, and scoring are obviously abnormal conditions. The exact nature of the abnormal condition should be determined. This is necessary so that the cause can be corrected.

Combustion knock or detonation will burn the edge of the piston from the head down, in behind the rings, as pictured in Figure 7–23. This burning usually occurs at a point far from the spark plug, where the hot end gases rapidly release their heat energy during detonation. High temperature softens the piston, allowing combustion pressure to burn through, usually near the middle of the piston head, as shown in Figure 7–24. The piston metal will often show some spattering.

Another form of heat damage is scuffing, similar to that pictured in Figure 7–25. This happens when excess heat causes the piston to expand until it becomes tight in the cylinder bore. The lubricant is thinned from the heat and it is squeezed from the cylinder wall. This causes metal-to-metal contact. Excessive heat can come from a malfunctioning cooling system, as well as from abnormal combustion.

Piston rings may get hot spots on their face from a lack of lubrication, from high combustion temperatures, or from ineffective cooling systems. Metal from the ring hot spots will transfer to the cylinder wall, scuffing the ring and piston (Figure 7–26).

FIGURE 7–26   Piston ring scuffing caused by over-heating.

FIGURE 7–24   Hole burned through the head of a piston as a result of preignition.

FIGURE 7–27   Piston rings stuck in their grooves with hard carbon.

Corrosion Damage

Low operating temperatures will produce a corrosive mixture in the oil. Coolant leakage into the combustion chamber increases the rate of corrosion. Corrosion produces mottled gray pits on the aluminum piston. Low operating temperatures are caused by short-trip driving or by a faulty or missing cooling system thermostat.

Mechanical Damage

Piston damage can result from mechanical problems. Connecting rod misalignment and twist will show up as a diagonal thrust surface wear pattern across the piston skirt, which indicates that the piston is not operating straight in the cylinder (Figure 7–28).

FIGURE 7–25   Scuffed piston skirt caused by over-heating and lubrication breakdown.

Worn piston rings allow hot combustion gases to blow by the piston. The worn rings will also allow oil to come up from the crankcase to the combustion chamber. Hot combustion gases meet the oil in the area of the rings, where the heat will partially burn the oil. This produces hard carbon around the rings, causing them to stick in the grooves, as shown in Figure 7–27. If this is the only piston problem, it can be corrected by cleaning.

NOTE: If there is diagonal wear on the piston, the connecting rod *must* be reconditioned. See Chapter 14 for details.

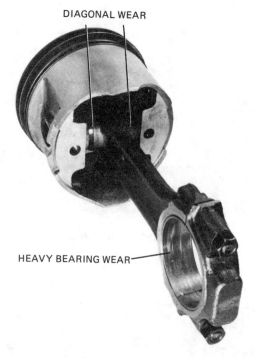

FIGURE 7-28   Angled piston skirt wear caused by a misaligned (twisted) connecting rod.

FIGURE 7-30   Cracked piston.

FIGURE 7-29   Piston damage when a pin lock ring came out.

This means that the rings are not running squarely on the walls, so they cannot seal properly.

Piston damage can come from the loss of a piston pin lock ring. The lock will come out if the lock grooves are damaged or if the lock ring is weak. It will also come out if the rod is bent so that a side load is placed on the piston pin, forcing it against the lock ring. The piston and possibly the cylinder will be badly damaged as the lock ring slides between them. A new piston will be required when this type of damage occurs, as shown in Figure 7-29.

Pistons can crack, usually on the skirt or near the piston pin boss. Cracks generally occur at high mileage, because of overloading or because the pistons were improperly designed. A typical piston skirt crack is shown in Figure 7-30.

Dirt entering the engine greatly increases the amount of wear. Dirt will scratch and wear the face of the piston rings and wear the side of the ring and groove. The side clearance of the top piston ring must not exceed 0.006 inches (0.15 millimeters). Dirt will come in with the air through a leaking air filter element or through an air leak. Dirt in the oil will cause abnormal wear on the piston skirts, the sides of the ring groove, and the oil ring. A badly worn piston ring and groove are shown in Figure 7-31. Worn piston rings must be replaced. Piston ring groove side wear is usually uneven. This causes the ring to hit only the high spots. The high spots cause high localized side loads on the ring when the ring is forced against the side of the groove. These loads may break the rings, which generally causes excessive piston land damage similar to that shown in Figure 7-32.

FIGURE 7–31   Badly worn piston ring and piston ring groove.

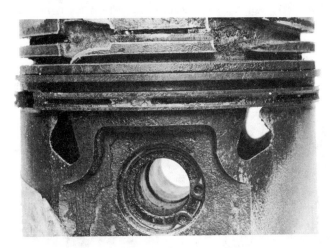

FIGURE 7–32   Piston lands damaged because of broken rings.

HARMONIC BALANCER REMOVAL

The next step in disassembly is to remove the coolant pump and the crankshaft **vibration damper** (also called a **harmonic balancer**). The bolt and washer that hold the damper are removed. The damper should be removed only with a threaded puller similar to the one in Figure 7–33. If a hook-type puller is used around the edge of the damper, it may pull the damper ring from the hub. If this happens, the damper assembly will have to be replaced with a new assembly. With the damper assembly off, the timing cover can be removed, exposing the timing gear or timing chain. Examine these parts for excessive wear and looseness. A worn timing chain on a high-mileage engine is shown in Figure 7–34. Bolted cam sprockets can be removed to free the timing chain. On some engines this will require removal of the crankshaft gear at the same time. Pressed-on gears and sprockets are removed from the

FIGURE 7–33   Puller being used to pull the vibration damper from the crankshaft.

shaft *only* if they are faulty. They are removed after the camshaft is removed from the block. It is necessary to remove the camshaft thrust plate retaining screws when they are used.

The camshaft can be removed at this time, or it can be removed after the crankshaft is out. It must be carefully eased from the engine to avoid damaging the cam bearings or cam lobes. This is done most easily with the front of the engine pointing up. Bearing surfaces are soft and scratch easily, and the cam lobes are hard and chip easily.

The main bearing caps should be checked for position markings before they are removed. They have been machined in place and will not fit perfectly in any other location. After marking, they can be removed to free the crankshaft. When the crankshaft is removed, the main bearing caps and bearings are reinstalled on the block to reduce the chance of damage to the caps.

CYLINDER HEAD DISASSEMBLY

After the heads are removed and placed on the bench, the valves are removed. A C-type valve spring compressor, similar to the one in Figure 7–35, is used to free the **valve locks** or **keepers.** The valve spring compressor is air powered in production shops where valve jobs are being done on a regular basis. Mechanical valve spring compressors are used where valve work is done only occasionally. After the valve lock is removed, the compressor is released to free the valve retainer and spring. See Figure 7–36. The spring assemblies are lifted from the head together with any spacers being used under the valve spring. Here again, the parts should be kept in order to aid in diagnosing the exact cause of any

FIGURE 7–34 Worn timing chain on a high-mileage engine. Notice that the timing chain could "jump a tooth" at the bottom of the smaller crankshaft gear where the chain is in contact with fewer teeth. Notice also that the technician placed all of the bolts back in the block after removal of the part. This procedure helps protect against lost or damaged bolts and nuts.

FIGURE 7–35 A valve spring compressor being used to remove the valve locks (keepers).

FIGURE 7–36 When using a valve spring compressor, it is best to use a magnet to help remove and hold the valve locks (keepers). When reinstalling, many technicians use grease to hold the locks (keepers) in place while releasing the spring pressure.

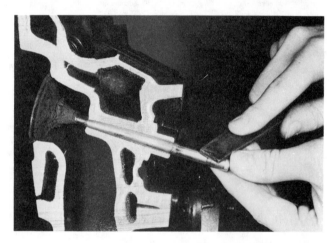

FIGURE 7–37 Always remove the burrs from around the valve lock grooves and tip before removing the valves from the head. The burrs could damage the guides if not removed. Spraying carburetor cleaner down between the valve and valve guide also helps in valve removal.

■ TECH TIP ■

HOLLANDER INTERCHANGE MANUAL

Most salvage businesses that deal with wrecked vehicles use a reference book entitled the *Hollander Interchange Manual*. In this yearly publication, every vehicle part is given a number. If a part or component, such as an engine or engine accessory, from one vehicle has the same Hollander number as that from another vehicle, then the parts are interchangeable. See Figure 7–38.

FIGURE 7–38 Hollander interchange manuals are available for both domestic and imported vehicles.

malfunction that shows up. The valve tip edge and lock area should be lightly filed or stoned, as shown in Figure 7–37, to remove any burrs *before* sliding the valve from the head. Burrs will scratch the valve guide.

When all valves are removed following the same procedure, the valve springs, retainers, locks, guides, and seats should be given another visual examination. Any obvious faults should be noted. Parts that are obviously not repairable should be marked and set aside for later reference and fault diagnosis. No further labor time should be spent on them. See Chapters 10 and 11 for valve and cylinder head service procedures.

SUMMARY

1. A repair, valve job, overhaul, and entire engine replacement are some of the solution options for an engine failure.
2. A short block is the block assembly with pistons and crankshaft. A long block also includes the cylinder head(s).

3. The factory lifting hooks should be used when hoisting an engine.
4. Cylinder heads should only be removed when the engine is cold. Also, always follow the torque table backward, starting with the highest-number head bolt and working toward the lowest number. This procedure helps prevent cylinder head warpage.
5. The ridge at the top of the cylinder should be removed before removing the piston(s) from the cylinder.
6. The connecting rod and main bearing caps should be marked before removing to ensure that they can be reinstalled in the exact same location when the engine is reassembled.
7. The tip of the valve stem should be filed before removing valves from the cylinder head to help prevent damage to the valve guide.

REVIEW QUESTIONS

1. Describe what a valve job includes.
2. Explain the differences between a minor and a major overhaul.
3. What does blueprinting an engine mean?
4. When should the factory-installed lifting hooks be used?
5. What is the purpose of the tapered dowel pins on the rear of most engine blocks?
6. Explain why the cylinder bore should be measured for taper and out-of-round before continuing with an engine disassembly.
7. State two reasons for the removal of the ridge at the top of the cylinder.
8. Explain why the burrs must be removed from valves before removing the valves from the cylinder head.

MULTIPLE-CHOICE QUESTIONS

1. A valve job involves _____ .
   a. Removing and replacing the cylinder head(s)
   b. Grinding the valve to prevent valve leakage
   c. Replacing any worn or damaged parts as needed
   d. All of the above
2. Blueprinting means _____ .
   a. The same as a minor overhaul
   b. The same as a major overhaul
   c. An overhaul with all parts equally matched
   d. Painting the engine blue after an overhaul

3. A long block can be made from a short block with the addition of _____ .
    a. Cylinder heads and valve train
    b. Intake and exhaust manifolds
    c. Oil pump, oil pan, and timing chain cover
    d. Fuel pump, carburetor, and air cleaner assembly

4. Lifting hooks are often installed at the factory because _____ .
    a. They make removing the engine easier for the technician
    b. They are used to install the engine at the factory
    c. They are part of the engine and should not be removed
    d. They make servicing the top of the engine easier for the technician

5. With the rocker cover (valve cover) removed, the technician can inspect all items *except* _____ .
    a. Combustion chamber deposits
    b. Rocker arms and valve spring
    c. Camshaft (overhead camshaft engine only)
    d. Valve stems and pushrods (overhead valve engines only)

6. After the oil pan (sump) is removed, the technician should inspect _____ .
    a. The oil pump and pickup screen
    b. To make certain that all rod and main bearings are numbered or marked
    c. The valve lifters (tappets) for wear
    d. Both a and b

7. The ridge at the top of the cylinder _____ .
    a. Is caused by wear at the top of the cylinder by the rings
    b. Represents a failure of the top piston ring to correctly seal against the cylinder wall
    c. Should not be removed before removing pistons except when reboring the cylinders
    d. Means that a crankshaft with an incorrect stroke was installed in the engine

8. Before the timing chain can be inspected and removed, the following component(s) must be removed _____ .
    a. Rocker cover (valve cover)
    b. Vibration damper
    c. Cylinder head(s)
    d. Intake manifold (V-type engines only)

9. Before the valves are removed from the cylinder head, what operations need to be completed?
    a. Remove valve locks (keepers)
    b. Remove cylinder head(s) from the engine
    c. Remove burrs from the stem of the valve(s)
    d. All of the above

10. Technician A says that a minor overhaul can often be done with the engine remaining in the vehicle. Technician B says that a core is required for most remanufactured engines. Which technician is correct?
    a. A only
    b. B only
    c. Both A and B
    d. Neither A nor B

Engine Cleaning, Crack Detection, and Repair

OBJECTIVES

After studying Chapter 8, the reader should be able to

1. List the types of engine cleaning methods.
2. Describe how to chemically clean parts.
3. Discuss how high temperatures can be used to clean engine parts.
4. List the various methods that can be used to check engine parts for cracks.
5. Describe crack repair procedures.

The purpose of any cleaning procedure is to restore like-new appearance. The soft plugs or core plugs will

■ TECH TIP ■

THE WAX TRICK

Before the engine block can be thoroughly cleaned, all oil gallery plugs must be removed. A popular trick of the trade involves heating the plug (not the surrounding metal) with an oxy-acetylene torch. The heat tends to expand the plug and make it tighter in the block. Do not overheat. See Figure 8–1.

As the plug is cooling, touch the plug with paraffin wax (beeswax or candle wax may be used). See Figure 8–2. The wax will be drawn down around the threads of the plug by capillary attraction as the plug cools and contracts. After being allowed to cool, the plug is easily removed.

have to be removed to thoroughly clean the cooling passages in the block and head. See the tech tip The Wax Trick.

MECHANICAL CLEANING

Mechanical cleaning involves scraping, brushing, and abrasive blasting. It should, therefore, be used very carefully on soft metals. Heavy deposits that remain after chemical cleaning will have to be removed by mechanical cleaning.

The most frequently used type of scraper is a **putty knife.** See Figure 8–3. The blade of the putty knife is pushed under the deposit to free it from the surface. The blade works best on flat surfaces such as gasket surfaces and the piston head. The broad blade of the putty knife prevents it from scratching the surface as it is used to clean the parts.

Wire brushes can be used on uneven surfaces. A hand wire brush can be used on the exterior of the block and on the head. A round wire brush used with a hand drill motor does a good job of cleaning the combustion chamber and parts of the head. A wire wheel can be used to clean the valves. See Figures 8–4 and 8–5.

■ **CAUTION:** Do not use a steel wire brush on aluminum parts! Steel is harder than aluminum and will remove some of the aluminum from the surface during cleaning. ■

CHEMICAL CLEANERS

Cleaning chemicals applied to the parts will mix with and dissolve the deposits. The chemicals loosen the deposits so that they can be brushed or rinsed from the

FIGURE 8–1   Heating oil gallery plugs on a small block Chevrolet V-8 block.

FIGURE 8–2   Applying the wax to the heated plug. Notice the wax vapors. This indicates that the plug is still slightly too hot. The wax needs to be liquid (not a vapor) to flow down around the threads of the plug.

FIGURE 8–3   Mechanical cleaning means using scrapers and similar tools to physically remove carbon and deposits.

FIGURE 8–4   Cleaning the combustion chamber with a rotary wire brush.

128

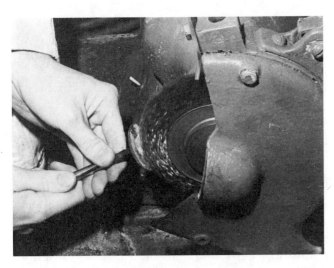

FIGURE 8–5   Cleaning carbon from a valve with a rotating wire wheel.

surface. A deposit is said to be **soluble** when it can be dissolved with a chemical or solvent.

Most chemical cleaners used for cleaning carbon-type deposits are a strong soap called a **caustic material.** A value called **pH,** measured on a scale from 1 to 14, is used to indicate the amount of chemical activity. The term *pH* is from the French *pouvoir hydrogine,* meaning hydrogen power. Pure water is neutral. On the pH scale, water is pH 7. Caustic materials have pH numbers from 8 through 14. The higher the number, the stronger the caustic action will be. **Acid materials** have pH numbers from 6 through 1. The lower the number, the stronger the acid action will be. Caustic materials and acid materials neutralize each other. This is what happens when baking soda (a caustic) is used to clean the outside of the battery (an acid surface). The caustic baking soda neutralizes any sulfuric acid that has been spilled or splashed on the outside of the battery.

■ **CAUTION:** Whenever working with chemicals, eye protection must be used. ■

SOLVENT-BASED CLEANING

Chemical cleaning can involve a spray washer or a soak in a cold or hot tank. The cleaning solution is usually solvent-based, with a medium pH rating of between 10 and 12. Most chemical solutions also contain silicates to protect the metal (aluminum) against corrosion. Strong caustics do an excellent job on cast-iron items but are often too corrosive for aluminum parts. Aluminum cleaners include mineral spirit solvents, as well as alkaline detergents.

■ **CAUTION:** When cleaning aluminum cylinder heads, blocks, or other engine components, be certain that the chemicals used are "aluminum safe." Many chemicals that are not aluminum safe may turn the aluminum metal black. Try to explain that to a customer! ■

WATER-BASED CHEMICAL CLEANING

Because of environmental concerns, most chemical cleaning is now performed using water-based solutions (called **aqueous based**). Most aqueous-based chemicals are silicate based and are mixed with water. Aqueous-based solutions can be sprayed or used in a tank for soaking parts. Aluminum heads and blocks usually require overnight soaking with the temperature of the solution kept at about 190° F (90° C). For best results, the cleaning solution should be agitated.

SPRAY WASHING

A spray washer directs streams of liquid through numerous high-pressure nozzles to dislodge dirt and grime on an engine surface. The force of the liquid hitting the surface, combined with the chemical action of the cleaning solution, produces a clean surface. Spray washing is typically performed in an enclosed washer (like a dishwasher), where parts are rotated on a washer turntable.

Spray washing is faster than soaking. A typical washer cycle is less than 30 minutes per load, compared to 8 or more hours for soaking. Most spray washers use an aqueous-based cleaning solution heated to 160° to 180° F (70° to 80° C) with foam suppressants. High-volume remanufacturers use industrial dishwashing machines to clean the disassembled engines' component parts. See Figure 8–6.

STEAM CLEANING

Steam cleaners are a special class of sprayers. Steam vapor is mixed with high-pressure water and sprayed on the parts. The heat of the steam and the propellant force of the high-pressure water combine to do the cleaning. Steam cleaning must be used with extreme care. Usually, a caustic cleaner is added to the steam and water to aid in the cleaning. This mixture is so active that it will damage and even remove paint, so painted surfaces must be protected from the spray. Engines are often steam cleaned before they are removed from the chassis.

FIGURE 8–6 Load of crankshafts being placed into a huge chemical cleaning system at a large engine remanufacturing plant.

FIGURE 8–7 Cylinder heads being cleaned in a pyrolytic oven. The term <u>pyrolytic</u> refers to the heating of organic compounds to very high temperatures. All that remains after cleaning is a fine dust. Most remanufacturers and rebuilders are using this type of equipment because of the absence of associated hazardous materials.

THERMAL CLEANING

Thermal cleaning uses heat to vaporize and char dirt into a dry, powdery ash. Thermal cleaning is best suited for cleaning cast iron, where temperatures as high as 800° F (425° C) are used, whereas aluminum should not be heated to over 600° F (315° C).

The major advantages of thermal cleaning include the following:

1. This process cleans inside as well as outside of the casting or part.
2. The waste generated is nonhazardous waste and is easy to dispose of.

However, the heat in the oven usually discolors the metal, leaving it looking dull.

A **pyrolytic** (high-temperature) oven cleans engine parts by decomposing dirt, grease, and gaskets with heat, in a manner similar to that of a self-cleaning oven. This method of engine part cleaning is becoming the most popular because there is no hazardous waste associated with it. Labor costs are also reduced because the operator does not need to be present during the actual cleaning operation. See Figure 8–7.

COLD TANK CLEANING

The cold soak tank is used to remove grease and carbon. The disassembled parts are placed in the tank so that they are *completely* covered with the chemical cleaning solution. After a soaking period, the parts

are removed and rinsed until the milky appearance of the emulsion is gone. The parts are then dried with compressed air. The clean, dry parts are usually given a very light coating of clean oil to prevent rusting. Carburetor cleaner, purchased with a basket in a bucket, is one of the most common types of cold soak agents in the automotive shop. Usually, the chemical will have water over its surface to prevent evaporation of the chemical. This water is called a **hydroseal.**

Parts washers are often used in place of the soaking tanks. The parts are moved back and forth through the cleaning solution, or the cleaning solution is pumped over the parts. This movement, called **agitation,** keeps fresh cleaning solution moving past the soil to help it loosen. The parts washer is usually equipped with a safety cover held open with a low-temperature **fusible link.** If a fire occurs, the fusible link will melt and the cover will drop closed to snuff the fire out.

HOT TANK CLEANING

The hot soak tank (Figure 8–8) is used for cleaning heavy organic deposits and rust from iron and steel parts. Caustic cleaning solution used in the hot soak tank is kept near 200° F (93° C) for rapid cleaning action. The solution must be inhibited when aluminum is to be cleaned. After the deposits have been loosened, the parts are removed from the tank and rinsed with hot water or steam cleaned. The hot parts will dry rapidly. They must be given a light coating of oil to prevent rusting.

FIGURE 8–9   Bead blasting a cylinder head.

FIGURE 8–8   Hot soak tank. (Courtesy of George Olcott Company)

HINT: *Fogging oil from a spray can does an excellent job of coating metal parts to keep them from rusting.*

VAPOR CLEANING

Vapor cleaning is popular in some automotive service shops. The parts to be cleaned are suspended in hot vapors above a perchloroethylene solution. The vapors of the solution loosen the soil from the metal so that it can be blown, wiped, or rinsed from the surface.

ULTRASONIC CLEANING

Ultrasonic cleaning is used to clean small parts that must be absolutely clean. Hydraulic lifters and diesel injectors are examples of these parts. The disassembled parts are placed in a tank of cleaning solution. The solution is vibrated at ultrasonic speeds to loosen all the soil from the parts. The soil goes into the solution or falls to the bottom of the tank.

VIBRATORY CLEANING

The vibratory method of cleaning is best suited for small parts. Parts are loaded into a vibrating bin with small odd-shaped ceramic or steel pieces, called **media,** with a cleaning solution of mineral spirits or water-based detergents. Detergents usually contain a lubricant additive to help the media pieces slide around more freely. The movement of the vibrating solution and the scrubbing action of the media do an excellent job of cleaning metal.

BLASTERS

Cleaning cast-iron or aluminum engine parts with solvents or heat usually requires another operation to achieve a uniform surface finish. Blasting the parts with steel, cast-iron, aluminum, or stainless steel shot, or glass beads is a simple way to achieve a matte or satin surface finish on the engine parts. See Figure 8–9. To keep the shot or beads from sticking, the parts must be dry without a trace of oil or grease prior to blasting. This means that blasting is the second cleaning method, after the part has been precleaned in a tank, spray washer, or oven.

Some blasting is done automatically in an airless shot blasting machine. Another method is to hard blast parts in a sealed cabinet.

■ **CAUTION:** Glass beads often remain in internal passages of engine parts, where they can come loose and travel through the cylinders when the engine is started. Among other places, these small, but destructive, beads can easily be trapped under the oil baffles of rocker covers, and in oil pans and piston ring grooves. To help prevent the glass beads from sticking, make sure that the parts being cleaned are free of grease and dirt and completely *dry.* ■

VISUAL INSPECTION

After the parts have been thoroughly cleaned, they should be reexamined for defects. A magnifying glass is helpful in finding these defects. Critical parts of a performance engine should be checked for cracks using specialized magnetic or penetration inspection equipment. Internal parts such as pistons, connecting rods, and crankshafts that have cracks should be replaced. Cracks in the block and heads can often be repaired. These repair procedures are described in a later section.

MAGNETIC CRACK INSPECTION

Checking for cracks using a magnetic field is commonly called **Magnafluxing,** which is a brand name. Cracks in engine blocks, cylinder heads, crankshafts, and other engine components are sometimes difficult to find during a normal visual inspection. This is the reason why all remanufacturers and most engine builders use a crack detection procedure on all critical engine parts.

Magnetic flux testing is the method most often used on steel and iron components. A metal engine part (such as a cast-iron cylinder head) is connected to a large electromagnet. Magnetic lines of force are easily conducted through the iron part. The magnetic lines of force are more concentrated on the edges of a crack. A fine iron powder can then be applied to the part being tested, and the powder will be attracted to the strong magnetic concentration around the crack. See Figures 8–10 through 8–13.

DYE PENETRANT TESTING

Dye penetrant testing is usually used on pistons and other parts constructed of aluminum or other nonmagnetic material. A dark red penetrating chemical is first sprayed on the component being tested. After cleaning, a white powder is sprayed over the test area. If a crack is present, the red dye will stain the white powder. Even though this method will also work on iron and steel (magnetic) parts, it is usually used only on nonmagnetic parts because magnetic methods do not work on these parts.

FLUORESCENT PENETRANT TESTING

Fluorescent penetrant requires a black light to be seen and can be used on iron, steel, or aluminum parts. This

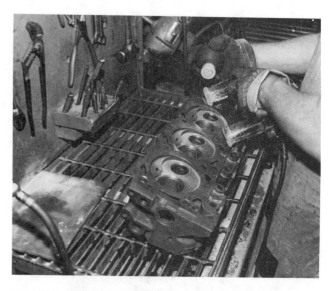

FIGURE 8–10 *Magnetic crack inspection being performed at a large engine remanufacturing plant.*

FIGURE 8–11 *The white iron powder tends to concentrate on the edges of cracks. This photo shows a crack through an exhaust seat of a cylinder head.*

method is commonly called **Zyglo,** which is a trademark of the Magnaflux Corporation. Any cracks show up as bright lines when viewed with a black light.

PRESSURE TESTING

Cylinder heads and blocks are often pressure tested with air and checked for leaks. All coolant passages are blocked with rubber plugs or gaskets, and compressed air is applied to the water jacket(s). The head or block is lowered into water. Air bubbles indicate a leak. For more accurate results, the water should be heated. The

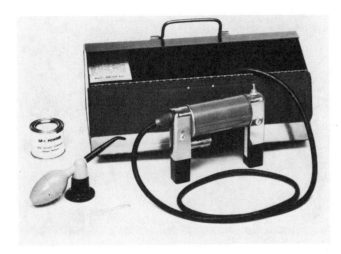

FIGURE 8–13 Magnetic crack inspection was used to find this cracked block.

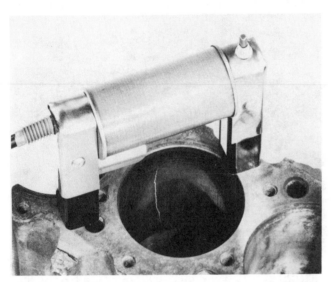

FIGURE 8–12 (a) Magnetic crack inspection equipment and (b) how a block crack in a cylinder looks after the fine iron powder is used. (Courtesy of George Olcott Company)

FIGURE 8–14 Pressure testing a Chevrolet V-8 block using hot water. Cylinder heads are also pressure tested using similar equipment. The hot water tends to expand the metal parts, and minor leaks are found more easily than if cold water were used to pressure test the component.

hot water expands the casting by about the same amount as in an operating engine.

An alternative method involves running heated water with a dye through the cylinder or block. Any leaks indicate a crack. See Figures 8–14 and 8–15.

CRACK REPAIR

Cracks in the engine block can cause coolant to flow into the oil or oil into the coolant. A cracked block can also cause coolant to leak externally from a crack that goes through to a coolant passage. Cracks in the head will allow coolant to leak into the engine, or they will allow combustion gases to leak into the coolant. Cracks across the valve seat cause hot spots on the valve. The

hot spots will burn the valve face. A head with a crack will either have to be replaced or have the crack repaired. Cracked heads are shown in Figures 8–16 through 8–18. Two methods of crack repair are commonly used: welding and plugging.

NOTE: A hole can be drilled at each end of the crack to keep it from extending further. This step is sometimes called **stop drilling.** Cracks that do not cross oil passages, bolt holes, or seal surfaces can sometimes be left unrepaired if stopped.

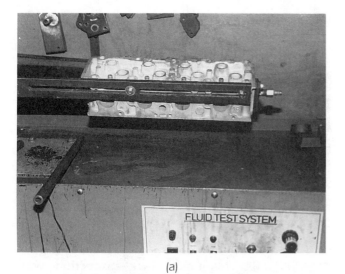

(a)

(b)

FIGURE 8–15 Aluminum cylinder head being checked for cracks in the coolant passages. (a) Head is being supported in preparation for testing. (b) Compressed air is put into the cylinder head while it is underwater, and the water is checked for bubbles from cracks in the casting.

CRACK WELDING CAST IRON

It takes a great deal of skill to weld cast iron. The cast iron does not puddle or flow as steel does when it is heated. Heavy cast parts, such as the head and block, conduct heat away from the weld so fast that it is difficult to get the part hot enough to melt the iron for welding. When it does melt, a crack will often develop next to the edge of the weld bead. Welding can be satisfactorily done when the entire cast part is heated red hot.

The head or block is placed on firebricks and supported in a level position so that the crack to be welded is on top. The casting is then heated until it becomes red hot. This may take several hours. The crack is

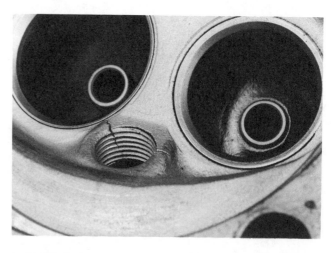

FIGURE 8–16   Crack through the spark plug hole.

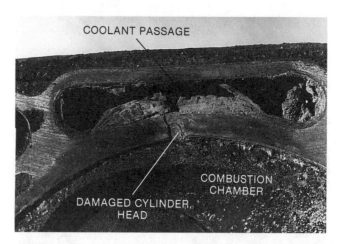

FIGURE 8–17   Damaged cylinder head between coolant passage (top) and combustion chamber (bottom).

welded after a hole is burned through the casting at each end of the crack to stop any additional cracking. Then the metal along the crack is melted out to leave a gap where the crack was. The gap is filled with the molten welding rod to make a bead above the surrounding metal and allowed to cool very slowly. The surface of the weld is smoothed after the casting has cooled.

CRACK WELDING ALUMINUM

Cracks in aluminum can be welded using a **Heli-arc** or similar welder that is specially designed to weld aluminum. See Figure 8–19. The crack should be cut or burned out before welding begins. The old valve seat insert should be removed if the crack is in or near the combustion chamber.

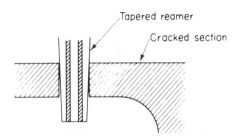

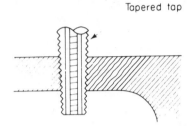

FIGURE 8–20   Reaming a hole for a tapered plug.

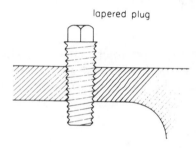

FIGURE 8–21   Tapping a tapered hole for a plug.

FIGURE 8–18   After cleaning and before machining operations are begun, carefully inspect for hidden cracks or other damage. Crack detection methods should <u>always</u> be used before restoring any engine casting such as cylinder heads.

FIGURE 8–22   Screwing a tapered plug in the hole.

FIGURE 8–19   This cylinder head is being repaired. Cracks were found in this Ford Escort cylinder head, and the material around the cracks has been cut out (note the missing exhaust valve seats). The failed area will be welded and remachined. After welding, the head will be stress relieved and straightened before final machining.

CRACK PLUGGING

In the process of crack plugging, the crack is closed using interlocking tapered plugs. The ends of the crack are center punched and drilled with the proper size of tap drill for the plugs. The hole is reamed with a tapered reamer (Figure 8–20). The hole is then tapped to give full threads (Figure 8–21). The plug is coated with sealer; then it is tightened into the hole (Figure 8–22). The plug is sawed about one-fourth of the way through; then it is broken off. The saw slot controls the breaking point (Figure 8–23). If the plug should break below the surface, it will have to be drilled out and a new plug installed. The plug should go to the full depth or thickness of the cast metal. After the first plug is installed on each end, a new hole is drilled with the tap drill so that it cuts into the edge of the first plug. This new hole is reamed and tapped, and a plug is inserted as before. The plug should fit about one-fourth of the way into the first plug to lock it into place (Figure 8–24). Interlocking plugs are placed along the entire crack, alternating slightly from side to side. The exposed ends of the plugs are peened over with a hammer to help secure them in place. The surface of the plugs is ground or filed down nearly to the gasket surface.

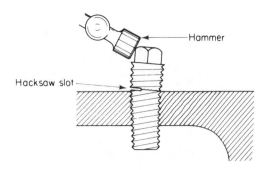

FIGURE 8–23   Cutting the plug with a hacksaw.

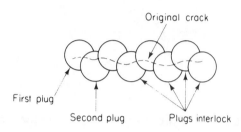

FIGURE 8–24   Interlocking plugs.

The plugs are ground down to the original surface in the combustion chamber and at the ports, using a hand grinder. The gasket surface of the head must be resurfaced after the crack has been repaired.

SUMMARY

1. Mechanical cleaning is used to remove deposits using scrapers or wire brushes.
2. Steel wire brushes should never be used to clean aluminum parts.
3. Most chemical cleaners are a strong soap called a caustic material.
4. Always use aluminum-safe chemicals when cleaning aluminum parts or components.
5. Thermal cleaning is done in a pyrolytic oven in temperatures as high as 800° F (425° C) to turn grease and dirt into harmless ash deposits.
6. Blasters use metal shot or glass beads to clean parts. All of the metal shot or glass beads must be cleaned from the part so as not to cause engine problems.
7. All parts should be checked for cracks using magnetic, dye penetrant, fluorescent penetrant, or pressure testing methods.
8. Cracks can be repaired by welding or by plugging.

REVIEW QUESTIONS

1. Describe five methods that could be used to clean engines or engine parts.
2. Explain magnetic crack inspection, dye penetrant testing, and fluorescent penetrant testing methods and where each can be used.
3. Explain why the use of blasters using metal shot or glass beads requires that the parts be cleaned before and after being blasted clean.

MULTIPLE-CHOICE QUESTIONS

1. A solvent is _____ .
   a. Pure water
   b. A type of bead used in bead blasting parts
   c. A chemical that can mix with and dissolve deposits
   d. A type of wire brush used to remove deposits
2. Cleaning chemicals are usually either a caustic material or an acid material. Which of the following statements is true?
   a. Both caustics and acids have a pH of 7 if rated according to distilled water.
   b. An acid is lower than 7 and a caustic is higher than 7 on the pH scale.
   c. An acid is higher than 7 and a caustic is lower than 7 on the pH scale.
   d. Pure water is a 1 and a strong acid is a 14 on the pH scale.
3. Many cleaning methods involve chemicals that are hazardous to use and expensive to dispose of after use. The least hazardous method is generally considered to be the _____ .
   a. Pyrolytic oven
   b. Hot vapor tank
   c. Hot soak tank
   d. Cold soak tank
4. Magnetic crack inspection _____ .
   a. Uses a red dye to detect cracks in aluminum
   b. Uses a black light to detect cracks in iron parts
   c. Uses a fine iron powder to detect cracks in iron parts
   d. Uses a magnet to remove cracks from iron parts
5. Technician A says that the fluorescent penetrant test method can be used to detect cracks in iron, steel, or aluminum parts. Technician B says that the dye penetrant test can only be used with aluminum parts. Which technician is correct?
   a. A only
   b. B only
   c. Both A and B
   d. Neither A nor B
6. Technician A says that engine parts should be cleaned before a thorough test can be done to detect cracks. Technician B says that pressure testing can be used to

find cracks in blocks or cylinder heads. Which technician is correct?

a. A only
b. B only
c. Both A and B
d. Neither A nor B

7. Cast-iron cylinder heads and blocks can be welded if cracked.

a. True
b. False

8. Aluminum cylinder heads and blocks can be welded if cracked.

a. True
b. False

9. Drilling a hole at each end of a crack _____ .

a. Stops the crack from getting larger
b. Allows room for the weld to expand
c. Allows the technician a method for determining how deep the crack goes into the cylinder head or block
d. Relieves stress in the cylinder head or block

10. Tapered pins used to repair cracks should be used _____ .

a. On cast-iron or aluminum blocks
b. Only on aluminum heads or blocks
c. Along with welding to repair a crack
d. Instead of welding on cast iron

9 Intake and Exhaust Manifolds

OBJECTIVES

After studying Chapter 9, the reader will be able to

1. Discuss the purpose and function of intake manifolds.
2. Explain the differences between carburetor manifolds and port injection manifolds.
3. Describe the operation of the exhaust gas recirculation system in the intake manifold.
4. List the materials used in exhaust manifolds and exhaust systems.
5. Discuss the operation of the heat riser and the need for manifold heating.

Smooth operation can only occur when each combustion chamber produces the same pressure as does every other chamber in the engine. For this to be achieved, each cylinder must receive a charge exactly like the charge going into the other cylinders in quality and quantity. The charges must have the same physical properties and the same air-fuel mixture.

Air coming into an engine will flow through the carburetor or injector throttle body. *All air entering any engine must be filtered.* See Figure 9–1.

NOTE: If an engine is operated without an air filter, the rate of engine wear is increased almost 10 times! —

CARBURETOR AND THROTTLE BODY INJECTION INTAKE MANIFOLDS

A carburetor and throttle body fuel injector force finely divided droplets of liquid fuel into the incoming air to form a combustible air-fuel mixture. See Figure 9–2 for

an example of a typical throttle body injection (TBI) unit. These droplets start to evaporate as soon as they leave the carburetor or throttle body injector nozzles. With a carburetor engine operating at its highest level of volumetric efficiency, about 60% of the fuel will evaporate by the time the intake charge reaches the combustion chamber. This means that there will be some liquid droplets in the charge as it flows through the manifold. *The droplets stay in the charge as long as the charge flows at high velocities.* At maximum horsepower, these velocities may reach 300 ft/sec. Separation of the droplets from the charge as it passes through the manifold occurs when the velocity drops below 50 ft/sec. Intake charge velocities at idle speeds are often below this value. When separation occurs—at low engine speeds—extra fuel must be supplied to the charge in order to have a combustible mixture reach the combustion chamber.

Manifold sizes represent a compromise. They must have a cross section large enough to allow sufficient charge flow for maximum power. The cross section must be small enough that the flow velocities of the charge will be high enough to keep the fuel droplets in suspension. This is required so that equal mixtures reach each cylinder. Manifold cross-sectional size is one of the reasons that engines designed especially for racing will not run at low engine speeds. Racing manifolds must be large enough to reach maximum horsepower. This size, however, allows the charge to move slowly, and the fuel will separate from the charge at low engine speeds. Fuel separation leads to poor accelerator response. Standard passenger vehicle engines are primarily designed for economy during light-load, partial-throttle operation. Their manifolds, therefore, have a much smaller cross-sectional area than do those of racing engines. This small size will help keep flow velocities of the charge high throughout the normal operating speed range of the engine.

In a four-stroke cycle, the inlet stroke is approximately one-fourth of the cycle. Four cylinders can, therefore, be attached to the same carburetor when the cylinders are timed so that each cylinder takes a different quarter of the 720-degree four-stroke cycle. This principle is also used in V-type automotive engines. In these engines, the intake manifold is divided into two sections or branches with runners on two levels. This style of intake manifold is said to have a **180-degree** or **dual plane** design. See Figures 9–3 and 9–4. Using this design, relatively long runners can be fit between the heads. Successively firing cylinders are fed alternately from the upper and lower runners, so the runner design must match the cylinder firing order. If the carburetor feeds all cylinders from one open plenum, it is said to have a **360-degree** or **single plane** design.

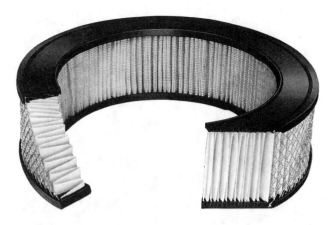

FIGURE 9–1 Typical replaceable pleated paper air filter element. Air filters should be changed regularly for proper engine operation and long life. Port fuel-injected engines often stall and run roughly with a partially clogged air filter. (Courtesy of AC Delco Division of GMC)

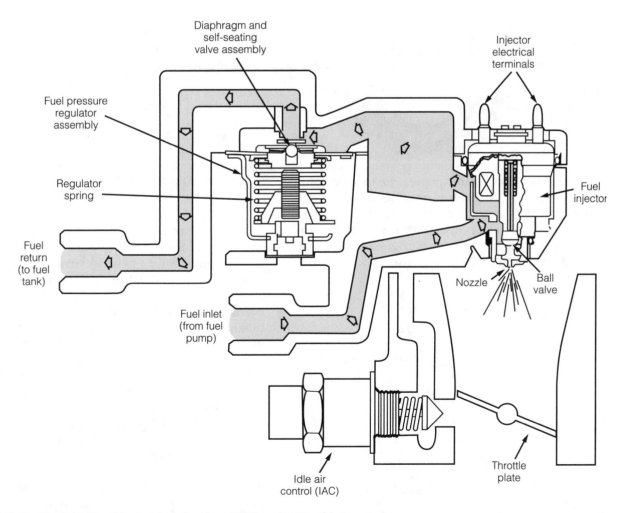

FIGURE 9–2 Typical throttle body injection (TBI) unit. The fuel and air mix before reaching the intake manifold.

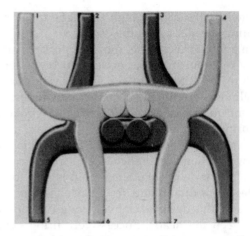

FIGURE 9–3 One side of a carburetor (or one injector of a dual throttle body fuel injector system) supplies fuel to one-half of the cylinders, which corresponds to every other cylinder in the firing order. (Courtesy of Ford Motor Company)

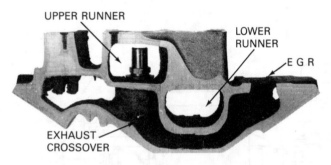

FIGURE 9–4 Most dual plane intake manifolds use runners on two levels to provide as equal a distance as possible between the throttle plate and intake valve of all cylinders. The two levels also result in smaller runners for higher mixture velocity and improved throttle response.

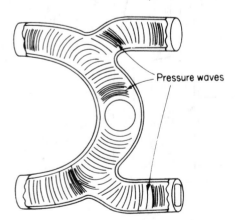

FIGURE 9–5 Effect of compression waves in a tuned intake manifold.

FIGURE 9–6 Primary barrels of the carburetor fit on the intake manifold bores near the center of the manifold.

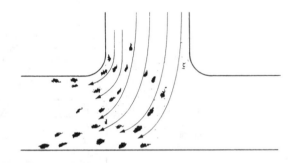

FIGURE 9–7 Heavy fuel droplets separate as they flow around an abrupt bend in an intake manifold.

In the tuned runners, the length is designed to take advantage of the natural pressure wave that occurs in a gas column. The pressure wave reaches the cylinder at the exact instant that the intake valve is open. This allows the charge to enter the cylinder with a supercharging or ram effect. The effect of intake manifold tuning is illustrated in Figure 9–5. On V-8 engines using four-barrel carburetors, the primary barrels are often placed approximately on the center of the runners to improve low-range and midrange performance. See Figure 9–6. The primary barrels of the carburetor are in use all of the time.

The way in which the charge flows through the intake manifold depends somewhat on the number of sharp runner bends, the smoothness of the runner's interior wall, and the runner's cross-sectional shape. Sharp bends tend to increase fuel separation. This is illustrated in Figure 9–7. The air, having less mass, is able to make turns much more quickly than the heavy fuel droplets. Rough interior runner surfaces add a

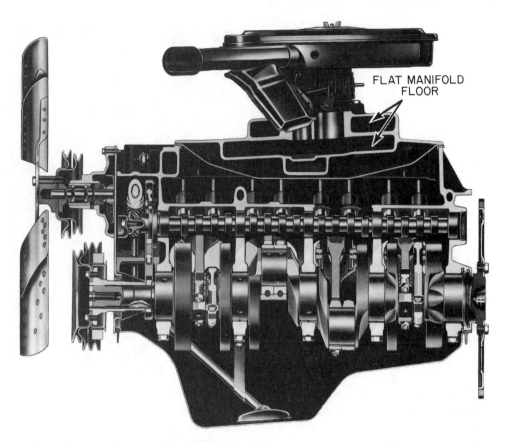

FLAT MANIFOLD
FLOOR

FIGURE 9–8 *Flat intake manifold floor. The flat floor prevents low spots where liquid fuel can collect. (Courtesy of Cadillac Motor Car Division, GMC)*

drag and turbulence to the charge. This can upset the charge distribution. A round runner has the greatest cross-sectional area for its wall surface area; however, a round section is not always the most desirable. Most engine manifold runner floors are flat. Any liquid fuel that drops out of the charge will spread in a thin layer over the manifold floor and rapidly evaporate. Manifolds are designed so that the manifold floor is level when the engine is mounted in the chassis. The flat manifold floor prevents low spots where liquid fuel can collect. This can be seen in Figure 9–8.

Main intake runners have cross-sectional areas of approximately 0.008 square inch per engine cubic inch of displacement. Branch runners have cross-sectional areas of approximately 0.006 square inch per CID. Ribs and guide vanes, such as those that can be seen in Figure 9–9, are often positioned in the floor of the manifold runners. They aid in equal distribution of the intake charge to the cylinders, even when some of the fuel remains in liquid form. It is just as important for the fuel to have equal distribution as it is for the air to have equal distribution.

OPEN AND CLOSED INTAKE MANIFOLDS

Two general intake manifold designs are used on modern V-type engines. The first type of manifold is an **open-type manifold.** Runners go through the open-type branches. Lifter valley covers are needed on engines using open-type manifolds. In some engines, the lifter valley covers are an extension of the intake manifold gasket. Figure 9–11 shows a typical open-type intake manifold.

The second type of intake manifold is a **closed-type manifold.** It is used on V-type engines as illustrated in Figure 9–12. This manifold has cast metal between the runners. It is used as a lifter valley cover as well as a manifold.

Closed-type manifolds on V-type engines have the exhaust crossover located just above the lifter valley, where engine oil could contact the hot surface. Hot exhaust in the crossover would heat the oil that lands on the surface of the crossover. This would cause oil oxidtion, called **coking.** Eventually, the coking would lead

FIGURE 9–9 Guide vanes in the floor of a typical intake manifold. These vanes or ribs help direct the air-fuel charge and to create turbulence in the manifold to help keep the fuel in the airstream. If the flow of the air-fuel mixture is allowed to slow, the heavier fuel tends to drop to the bottom of the manifold floor.

■ **TECH TIP** ■

EVERY OTHER CYLINDER

All engines of four or more cylinders fire and are furnished fuel according to firing order. The intake manifold on a V-type engine is designed so that each side of the carburetor or TBI unit supplies the air-fuel mixture to every other cylinder in the *firing order* for each barrel (venturi) of the carburetor or throttle body fuel-injection unit. It is easy to determine which cylinders are fed an air-fuel mixture from the same side of a carburetor or throttle body injector unit.

Step #1. Write out the cylinder numbers in their firing order: 1 6 5 4 3 2
Step #2. Mark every other cylinder in the firing order: 1 6 5 4 3 2

The marked cylinders share the same side of the carburetor, and the unmarked cylinders share the other side of the carburetor.

NOTE: Most V-6 engines are split so that the left bank of cylinders is on one runner and the right bank is on the other runner. Most V-8s have two cylinders on each side of the engine sharing a barrel with two cylinders of the opposite bank. See Figure 9–10.

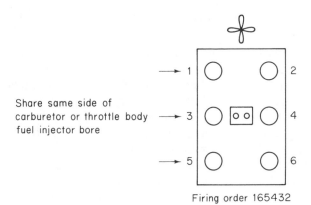

Share same side of carburetor or throttle body fuel injector bore →

1 ○   ○ 2

3 ○   □○○□   ○ 4

5 ○   ○ 6

Firing order 165432

FIGURE 9–10 Many V-6 engines that use a carburetor or a throttle body type of fuel injection use an intake manifold that is designed so that each side of the carburetor or TBI unit feeds fuel to every other cylinder in the firing order. This usually means that on a V-6, one entire side of the engine shares the same side of the carburetor. A vacuum leak on one side usually results in a very rough idle because of this design.

■ **TECH TIP** ■

THE GLUE AND ANTISEIZE COMPOUND TRICK

A common problem with using aluminum intake manifolds on a V-type cast-iron engine is that the gasket often fails. Aluminum expands at twice the rate of cast iron (0.0012 inch per 100° F for aluminum versus 0.0006 inch per 100° F for cast iron). As a result, when the engine gets warm, the intake manifold expands and tends to move upward, sliding over the surface of the cast-iron cylinder heads.

To help prevent premature intake manifold gasket failure, use a contact adhesive to glue the gasket to the cast-iron head. This helps hold the gasket in place for easier installation and prevents movement of the gasket against the cast iron. Then, before installing the aluminum intake manifold, coat the gasket and/or the sealing surface of the intake manifold with antiseize compound. This will allow movement without damage to the gasket.

to the need for frequent oil changes. Therefore, **shields** are put in engines to keep the oil from hitting these hot surfaces. A sheet-metal deflector may be fastened to the lifter valley side of the intake manifold to keep the

FIGURE 9–11 Open-type intake manifold on a V-type engine. The runners on this manifold are on a single plane.

FIGURE 9–12 Closed-type intake manifold on a V-type engine. Notice that the aluminum intake manifold extends over the cylinder heads and actually provides a rail for the valve covers. Sealing of this type of manifold is critical for proper operation and prevention of fluid and air leaks.

oil from the hot crossover. This is shown in the sectional view in Figure 9–13.

■ **CAUTION:** Be certain to remove and thoroughly clean under the heat shield. Trapped dirt and carbon can easily be dislodged when the engine is reassembled. This debris can do serious damage to new engine bearings and all other engine parts. ■

Some engines have a large single-piece manifold gasket to do the job of deflecting oil from the crossover (Figure 9–14).

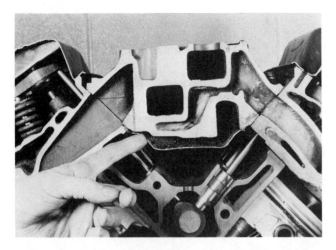

FIGURE 9–13 The finger points to a sheet-metal deflector oil shield fastened to the lifter valley side of the intake manifold. This shield protects the engine oil from the high temperature of the crossover exhaust passage through the manifold.

FIGURE 9–14 Single-piece intake manifold gasket that serves as an oil shield.

FIGURE 9–15 Typical carburetor air inlet preheat temperature regulator. If the preheat tube is defective or missing, serious cold-engine driveability problems occur. Most throttle body fuel-injection systems also use preheated air during the warm-up period. (Courtesy of Chevrolet Motor Division, GMC)

MANIFOLD HEAT

Heat is required in the manifold so that liquid fuel in the charge will evaporate as the charge travels from the carburetor to the combustion chamber. When heat is taken from the air in the intake charge by fuel evaporation, the charge by fuel evaporation temperature is lowered. Additional fuel will not evaporate from the cooled charge as rapidly as it would from a warm charge. Additional heat is supplied to the charge when it is needed. The added heat gives good fuel evaporation for smooth engine operation when the engine is cold. An intake charge temperature range of about 100° to 130° F (38° to 55° C) is necessary to give good fuel evaporation. In most current engines, heat is supplied to the intake manifold during low-temperature operation by a system known as a **thermostatic air cleaner (TAC).** Heat is picked up from around the exhaust manifold and routed to the air cleaner inlet. A thermostatically controlled bimetallic switch adjusts a **vacuum motor.** It controls the amount of heated air used. Parts of this system are shown in Figure 9–15. Another thermostatic valve, called a **heat riser,** directs exhaust gases against the intake manifold directly below the carburetor. On V-type engines, exhaust gas is routed through a passage called an exhaust **heat crossover.** Part of the exhaust gas is directed against the intake manifold directly under the throttle body. This can be seen in Figure 9–16.

NOTE: Port fuel-injected engines do not require an exhaust heat crossover because there is no fuel in the air flowing through the intake runner.

On some emission-controlled engines, the heat riser valve is operated by a vacuum diaphragm actua-

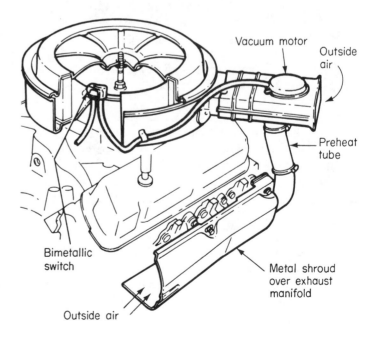

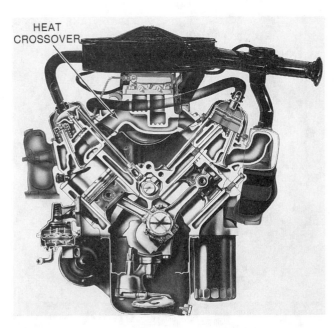

FIGURE 9–16 *Exhaust heat crossover on a V-type engine intake manifold. If this passage becomes clogged with carbon, the engine will perform poorly during the warm-up period and the choke will be prevented from opening on carburetor-equipped engines. (Courtesy of Chevrolet Motor Division, GMC)*

FIGURE 9–17 *Typical early fuel evaporation system. Manifold vacuum is applied to the actuator through a thermovacuum switch located in a cooling system passage near the thermostat. When the valve is closed, the exhaust is forced through the cylinder head, under the intake manifold, through the opposite cylinder head passage, and out through the left-side exhaust manifold.*

tor assembly controlled by a temperature-sensitive valve. This system is called **early fuel evaporation** (EFE). A typical EFE valve is shown in Figure 9–17.

When the engine gets fully warmed up, the heat riser valve directs the exhaust gas away from the intake manifold and crossover. The exhaust gas is sent directly out through the exhaust system.

Some engines use the coolant to supply heat to the charge mixture. Warm coolant is allowed to flow through a passage below the intake runners. Heat from the engine coolant is not available until the engine begins to warm up. Engine coolant is always used to provide intake manifold heat on an **inline engine** when the intake and exhaust manifolds are on opposite sides of the head. An example of these manifolds on a head is shown in Figure 9–18. Manifolds on V-type engines often contain a coolant passage. It connects the cooling system between the V heads. This passage provides a common cooling outlet for the engine cooling system at the thermostat.

CHOKE HEAT

The carburetor is designed with a choke to provide an excessively rich charge mixture for starting. Without the choke, there would not be enough of the

volatile part of the fuel to make a combustible mixture. There are two additional problems. First, the intake charge velocity is low during cranking, allowing the fuel to separate from the air. Second, no extra heat is available for fuel evaporation before the engine starts. Most chokes are automatic. They are closed by a temperature-sensing thermostatic spring. In some applications, heat is carried to the thermostatic spring through a tube from a heat chamber called a **stove**. The choke heat stove is often located in the exhaust manifold where it can pick up exhaust heat. An insulated tube carries warm air from the choke heat stove to the sensing spring on the carburetor. The intake manifold shown in Figure 9–19 has the choke heat stove. When it is in this location, the stove is heated by exhaust at the exhaust heat crossover in the intake manifold. Some applications

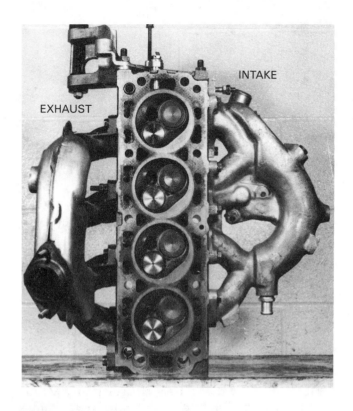

FIGURE 9–18 Head of an engine with the intake and exhaust manifolds on opposite sides of the head. This is called a cross-flow head.

EXHAUST

INTAKE

CHOKE SPRING AND VACUUM PISTON HOUSING

FAST IDLE CAM

UNLOADER TANG

CHOKE HEAT STOVE

FIGURE 9–19 A choke heat stove gets hot because exhaust gases flow through the intake manifold passage under the carburetor. The choke is heated by the drawing of filtered air through this heat stove and to the choke housing.

146

(a)

(b)

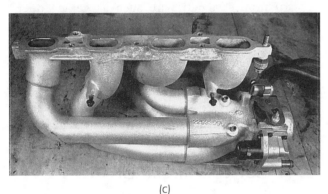

(c)

(d)

FIGURE 9–20 (a) Tuned intake manifold design as used on a port fuel-injected engine. The intake manifold can be designed with these long tubes to add low-speed torque because the only thing inside the manifold is air. (b) Four–valve head intake manifold showing two different-length intake runners. (c) Tuned intake runner for a port fuel-injected four-cylinder engine. (d) Tuned intake runners for a port fuel-injected V-6.

place the heat-sensing choke spring directly in the stove well. A link connects the choke spring with the carburetor choke plate.

PORT INJECTION INTAKE MANIFOLDS

The size and shape of port fuel-injected engine intake manifolds can be optimized because the only thing in the manifold is air. Therefore, the runner length and shape are designed for tuning only. There is no need to keep an air-fuel mixture homogenized throughout its trip from the carburetor or TBI unit to the intake valve.

- Long runners build low-RPM torque.
- Shorter runners provide maximum high-RPM power.

Some engines with four valve heads utilize a dual or variable intake runner design. At lower engine speeds, long intake runners provide low-speed torque. At higher engine speeds, shorter intake runners are opened by means of a computer-controlled valve to increase high-speed power. See Figure 9–20.

PLASTIC INTAKE MANIFOLDS

Most thermoplastic intake manifolds are molded from fiberglass-reinforced nylon. The plastic manifolds can be cast or injected molded. Some manifolds are molded in two parts and bonded together. Plastic intake manifolds are lighter than aluminum manifolds and can better insulate engine heat from the fuel injectors.

Plastic intake manifolds have smoother interior surfaces than do other types of manifolds, resulting in greater airflow. See Figures 9–21 and 9–22.

FIGURE 9–21 View from underneath of plastic intake manifold from a V-6 engine.

FIGURE 9–22 Plastic intake manifold airflow insert. These runners increase the velocity (speed) of the intake air to increase throttle response without creating resistance that could hurt horsepower at high engine speeds.

■ TECH TIP ■

THE ALUMINUM EPOXY TRICK

Often, aluminum intake manifolds are found to be corroded around the coolant passages. Rather than replacing the manifold, simply apply an 80% aluminum epoxy to fill the pitted area. Be sure that the area to be repaired is thoroughly cleaned, and mix the epoxy according to the manufacturer's instructions. The epoxy can be applied with a putty knife or other similar tool. After the epoxy has hardened, the area can be surfaced as usual. Epoxy can also be used to repair pitted coolant pumps.

■ TECH TIP ■

THE SNAKE TRICK

The EGR passages on many intake manifolds become clogged with carbon. This reduces the flow of exhaust and reduces the amount of exhaust gases in the cylinders. This can cause spark knock (detonation) and increase emissions of oxides of nitrogen (NO_X) (especially important in areas with enhanced exhaust emissions testing).

To quickly and easily remove carbon from exhaust passages, cut a length of about 1 foot (30 cm) from stranded wire such as garage door guide wire or from an old vehicle speedometer cable. Flare the end and place the end of the wire into the passage. Set the drill on reverse. Turn the drill on, and the wire will pull its way through the passage, cleaning the carbon as it goes, just like a snake in a drainpipe.

EXHAUST GAS RECIRCULATION

To reduce the emission of oxides of nitrogen (NO_X), engines have been equipped with **exhaust gas recirculation (EGR)** valves. From 1973 until very recently, they were used on almost all vehicles. Because of the efficiency of computer-controlled fuel injection, some newer engines do not require an EGR system to meet emission standards. Some engines use intake and exhaust valve overlap as a means of trapping some exhaust in the cylinder. The EGR valve opens at speeds above idle on a warm engine. When open, the valve allows a small portion of the exhaust gas to enter the intake manifold. Here, the exhaust gas mixes with and takes the place of some of the intake charge. This leaves less room for the intake charge to enter the combustion chamber. The recirculated exhaust gas does *not* enter into the combustion process. The result is a lower peak combustion temperature. As the combustion temperature is lowered, the production of oxides of nitrogen is also reduced.

The EGR system has some means of interconnecting the exhaust and intake manifolds. The interconnecting passage is controlled by the EGR valve. On V-type engines, the intake manifold crossover is used as a source of exhaust gas for the EGR system. A cast passage connects the exhaust crossover to the EGR valve. The gas is sent from the EGR valve to openings below the carburetor. On inline-type engines, an external tube is generally used to carry exhaust gas to the EGR valve. This tube is often designed to be long so that the

FIGURE 9–23 EGR tube used to supply and cool the exhaust gas to the EGR valve.

■ DIAGNOSTIC STORY ■

REVERSION PROBLEMS WITH A SATURN

A technician purchased a used two-cam, four-valve Saturn that had a restricted exhaust system. After the partially clogged catalytic converter was replaced, the engine had newfound power, but it had a slight hesitation problem during acceleration.

Further inspection revealed a thick black sludge buildup inside the intake manifold extending from the ports up to the throttle plate itself. After hours of cleaning, the engine ran perfectly again, but the technician was puzzled as to the cause of the excessively dirty intake manifold.

Remembering that the exhaust was partially restricted, the technician finally realized that exhaust gases take the path of least resistance and travel up into the intake manifold during valve overlap periods. The combination of hot exhaust gases and unburned fuel in the intake manifold had created the carbonized mess. This phenomenon is called **reversion.** Therefore, if heavy black carbon deposits are found in the intake manifold, carefully inspect and test the exhaust system for restriction.

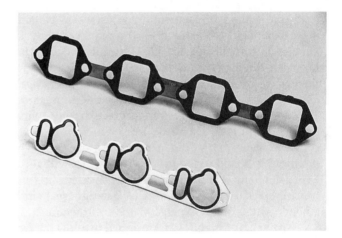

FIGURE 9–24 Intake manifold gaskets with synthetic rubber seals molded on a plastic or steel carrier. (Courtesy of Fel-Pro Incorporated)

INTAKE MANIFOLD GASKETS

Like heads, manifolds are torqued with high clamping loads. As a result, manifold gaskets used on older engines have the same types of construction and require the same fit and surface finish as do head gaskets.

Some older V-type engines use a large metal pan-type intake manifold gasket. It goes between the lifter valley and the bottom of the manifold. Its purpose is to keep oil from splashing on the bottom of the exhaust crossover in the manifold.

The latest intake manifold gasket designs have synthetic rubber O-ring types of beads molded on a plastic, fiber, or steel carrier. See Figure 9–24.

exhaust gas is cooled before it enters the EGR valve. Figure 9–23 shows a typical long EGR tube. The EGR valve is usually attached to an adapter between the carburetor and intake manifold. Here, it can release the exhaust gas directly into the intake manifold runner.

EXHAUST MANIFOLD DESIGN

The exhaust manifold is designed to collect high-temperature spent gases from the head exhaust ports. The hot gases are sent to an exhaust pipe, then to a catalytic converter, to the muffler, to a resonator, and on to the tail pipe, where they are vented to the atmosphere. This must be done with the least possible amount of restriction or back pressure while keeping the exhaust noise at a minimum.

Exhaust gas temperature will vary according to the power produced by the engine. The manifold must be designed to operate at both engine idle and continuous full power. Under full-power conditions, the exhaust manifold will become red-hot, causing a great deal of expansion.

NOTE: The temperature of an exhaust manifold can exceed 1500° F (815° C).

At idle, the exhaust manifold is just warm, causing little expansion. After casting, the manifold may be annealed. **Annealing** is a heat-treating process that takes out the brittle hardening of the casting to reduce the chance of cracking from the temperature changes. During vehicle operation, manifold temperatures usually do reach the high-temperature extremes. Most exhaust manifolds are made from cast iron to withstand extreme and rapid temperature changes. The manifold is bolted to the head in a way that will allow expansion and contraction. In some cases, hollow-headed bolts are used to maintain a gas-tight seal while still allowing normal expansion and contraction.

The exhaust manifold is designed to allow the free flow of exhaust gas. Some manifolds use internal cast-rib deflectors or dividers to guide the exhaust gases toward the outlet as smoothly as possible.

Severe bends have no measurable effect on the flow of exhaust gases as long as the required manifold cross section is maintained. Figure 9–25 shows two types of exhaust manifolds that fit inline engines.

Some exhaust manifolds are designed to go above the spark plug, whereas others are designed to go below. The spark plug and carefully routed ignition wires are usually shielded from the exhaust heat with sheet-metal deflectors. Typical deflectors can be seen in Figure 9–26.

Exhaust systems are especially designed for the engine-chassis combination. The exhaust system length, pipe size, and silencer are designed, where possible, to make use of the tuning effect of the gas column resonating within the exhaust system. Tuning occurs when the exhaust pulses from the cylinders are emptied into the manifold between the pulses of other cylinders. See Figure 9–27.

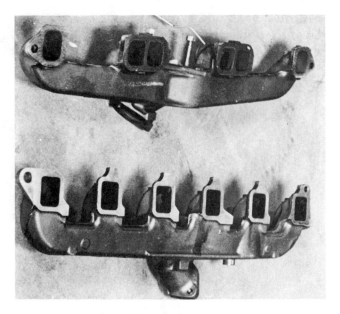

FIGURE 9–25 The top exhaust manifold has siamese runners. The bottom exhaust manifold has separate runners for each cylinder.

FIGURE 9–26 Example of heat deflector shields placed between the exhaust manifold and the spark plugs and plug wires. Even high temperature-resistant silicone jacket spark plug wires cannot withstand the high exhaust manifold temperatures.

Figure 9–28 compares an exhaust manifold used on a tuned exhaust system to a standard design.

EXHAUST MANIFOLD GASKETS

Exhaust heat will expand the manifold more than it will the head. It causes the exhaust manifold to slide on the sealing surface of the head. The heat also causes thermal stress. When the manifold is removed from the

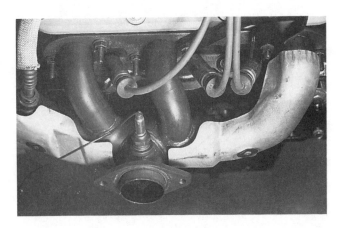

FIGURE 9–27 Original equipment (OE) type of tubular steel exhaust manifold.

engine for service, the stress is relieved and this may cause the manifold to warp slightly. Exhaust manifold gaskets are included in gasket sets to seal slightly warped exhaust manifolds. These gaskets *should* be used, even if the engine did not originally use exhaust manifold gaskets. When a perforated core exhaust manifold gasket has facing on one side only, put the facing side against the head and put the manifold against the perforated metal core. The manifold can slide on the metal of the gasket just as it slid on the sealing surface of the head.

Gaskets are used on new engines with tubing- or header-type exhaust manifolds. The gaskets often include heat shields to keep exhaust heat from the spark plugs and spark plug cables. They may have several layers of steel for high-temperature sealing. The layers are spot welded together. Some are embossed where special sealing is needed. See Figure 9–29. Many new engines do not use gaskets with cast exhaust manifolds. The flat surface of the new cast-iron exhaust manifold fits tightly against the flat surface of the new head.

HOW HEADERS WORK

On many engines, a welded steel tubing **header** is used instead of a cast-iron exhaust manifold. Use of the lightweight header allows a smooth, nearly ideal exhaust manifold design that will handle the large volume of exhaust gas produced when the engine is operating at high speeds.

Headers work in two ways:

1. Headers reduce exhaust system restriction. With a lower level of restriction, the exhaust can leave the engine more easily, requiring less power from the engine to push the exhaust out through the exhaust system.

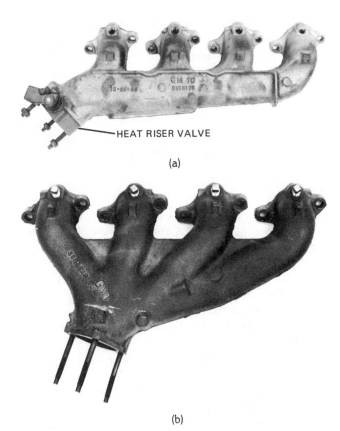

HEAT RISER VALVE

(a)

(b)

FIGURE 9–28 Cast exhaust manifold designs: (a) standard engine and (b) high-performance engine. Engine manufacturers now prefer to use tubular steel (header-type) exhaust manifolds because of lower weight.

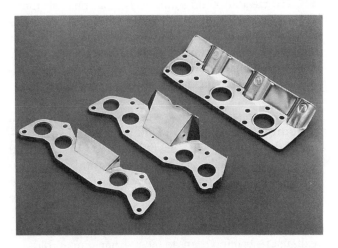

FIGURE 9–29 Exhaust manifold gaskets with heat shields to keep heat from the spark plug terminals. (Courtesy of Fel-Pro Incorporated)

2. Immediately after an exhaust pulse leaves an exhaust port, there is a lower pressure in the cylinder. **Tuned** headers are designed to combine individual exhaust pulses into one larger pulse, with a corresponding lower pressure behind the pulse. This low pressure is less than atmospheric pressure. This lower pressure actually helps to draw more air-fuel mixture into the cylinder.

This "reverse supercharging" works best at a certain level of engine RPM. This RPM level is based on primary tube and collector length. The longer the primary tube and collector, the lower the engine RPM level at which the header "works." Some headers use an adjustable collector. Use the shortest collector for high-RPM and the longest for lower-RPM benefits. Regardless of header design or lengths, the benefits only become measurable at higher engine speeds (generally over 3500 RPM, depending on engine design). See Figure 9–30.

For low- to medium-RPM power and torque:

1. The primary runner should be long (34 to 38 inches is typical long primary runner length).
2. The collector should also be long (12 to 15 inches is typical collector length for lower-engine speed torque and power).

For higher-RPM power and torque, the primary runner diameter should be increased and the length of tubes decreased. The collector can be shorter or made adjustable to tune in maximum torque at the desired engine speed.

NOTE: Header configuration is just one of many engine tuning factors that should be considered in the designing of an engine system. Other related factors include cam, cam timing, intake runner sizes, engine size, and compression. A change in one factor will usually influence the needs in all other areas. _____

Headers are working when the exhaust makes a **rapping** sound. With most headers used for street driving, the exhaust will generally start to rap at about 3500 RPM and will continue rapping until about 5000 RPM. At the higher RPM, the exhaust pulses are no longer able to reinforce each other; therefore, the reverse supercharging effect of the headers is reduced. However, the headers still provide a lower level of exhaust restriction than do most exhaust manifolds.

Because of the reduced exhaust back pressure, the EGR valve may not function correctly, resulting in spark knock, if header exhaust is added. Also, not all

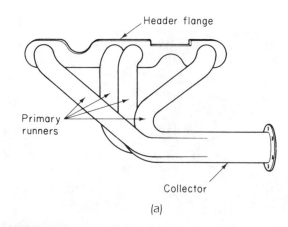

(a)

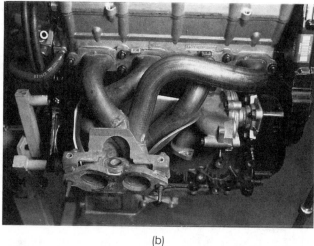

(b)

FIGURE 9–30   (a) Equal-length header exhaust manifold. (b) Factory tri-Y type of tubular exhaust manifold.

engine computers can compensate correctly for the changes in intake manifold pressure or the changed position of the oxygen sensor when headers are installed.

■ **CAUTION:** Federal, state, provincial, or local laws may prohibit the installing of header-type exhaust manifolds on vehicles operating on public streets and highways. ■

HEAT RISERS

A heat riser is used on carburetor-equipped engines and some throttle body fuel-injected engines. The purpose of the heat riser is to divert some exhaust to warm the intake manifold. The extra heat that this provides improves cold-engine driveability. If the heat riser were to become stuck in the open position (no heat to the intake manifold), the engine could idle roughly, stall, or hesitate during acceleration. If the heat riser

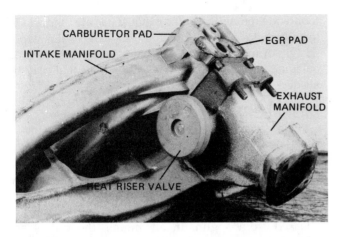

FIGURE 9–31 Heat riser at the junction of the intake and exhaust manifolds.

FIGURE 9–32 Typical catalytic converter. The small tube into the side of the converter comes from the air pump. The additional air from the air pump helps oxidize the exhaust into harmless H_2O (water) and CO_2 (carbon dioxide).

were to become stuck in the closed position (constant heat to the intake manifold), the engine would operate correctly when cold, but there could be spark knock (ping) or stalling when the engine was warm. On some inline engines, the intake manifold is attached to the exhaust manifold. The heat riser valve is located at this attachment point as shown in Figure 9–31. On V-type engines, the heat riser valve partially blocks one exhaust manifold exit, increasing the exhaust pressure in the exhaust manifold on that side of the engine. This forces the exhaust gases to flow through the intake manifold exhaust heat crossover passage to the opposite exhaust manifold.

CATALYTIC CONVERTERS

An exhaust pipe is connected to the manifold or header to carry the gases through a catalytic converter and then to the muffler or silencer. In single exhaust systems used on V-type engines, the exhaust pipe is designed to collect the exhaust gases from both manifolds using a Y-shaped design. Vehicles with dual exhaust systems have a complete exhaust system coming from each of the manifolds. In most cases, the exhaust pipe must be made of several parts in order for it to be assembled in the space available under the vehicle.

The catalytic converter is installed between the manifold and muffler to help reduce exhaust emissions. The converter has a heat-resistant metal housing. See Figure 9–32. A bed of catalyst-coated pellets or a catalyst-coated honeycomb grid is inside the housing. See Figures 9–33 and 9–34. As the exhaust gas passes through the catalyst, oxides of nitrogen (NO_X) are chemically reduced (nitrogen and oxygen separated) in the first section of the catalytic converter. In the second section of the catalytic converter, most of the hydrocarbons and carbon

FIGURE 9–33   Bead-type catalytic converter.

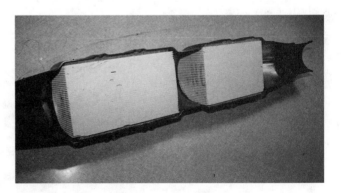

FIGURE 9–34   Cutaway of a three-way monolytic catalytic converter.

■ **TECH TIP** ■

CATALYTIC CONVERTERS ARE MURDERED

Catalytic converters start a chemical reaction but do not enter into the chemical reaction. Therefore, catalytic converters do not wear out and they do not die of old age. If a catalytic converter is found to be defective (nonfunctioning or clogged), look for the *root* cause. See Figure 9–35. Remember this:

"Catalytic converters do not commit suicide—they're murdered."

Items that should be checked when a defective catalytic converter is discovered include all components of the ignition and fuel systems. Excessive unburned fuel can cause the catalytic converter to overheat and fail.

FIGURE 9–35   Cutaway of defective (clogged) catalytic converter.

monoxide remaining in the exhaust gas are oxidized to form harmless carbon dioxide (CO_2) and water vapor (H_2O). An air-injection system or pulse air system is used on some engines to supply additional air that may be needed in the oxidation process.

MUFFLERS

When the exhaust valve opens, it rapidly releases high-pressure gas. This sends a strong air pressure wave through the atmosphere, which produces a sound we call an explosion. It is the same sound produced when the high-pressure gases from burned gunpowder are released from a gun. In an engine, the pulses are released one after another. The explosions come so fast that they blend together in a steady roar.

Sound is air vibration. When the vibrations are large, the sound is loud. The muffler catches the large bursts of high-pressure exhaust gas from the cylinder, smoothing out the pressure pulses and allowing them to be released at an even and constant rate. It does this through the use of perforated tubes within the muffler chamber. The smooth-flowing gases are released to the tail pipe. In this way, the muffler silences engine exhaust noise. Sometimes resonators are used in the exhaust system. They provide additional expansion space at critical points in the exhaust system to smooth out the exhaust gas flow. A cutaway muffler is pictured in Figure 9–36.

Most mufflers have a larger inlet diameter than outlet diameter. As the exhaust enters the muffler, it expands and cools. The cooler exhaust is more dense and occupies less volume. The diameter of the outlet of the muffler and the diameter of the tail pipe can be reduced with no decrease in efficiency.

The tail pipe carries the exhaust gases from the muffler to the air, away from the vehicle. In most cases, the tail pipe exit is at the rear of the vehicle, below the rear bumper. In some cases, the exhaust is released at the side of the vehicle, just ahead of or just behind the rear wheel.

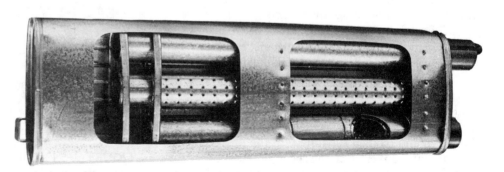

FIGURE 9–36   Muffler cut away to show the interior.

■ TECH TIP ■

THE CORRECT TOOLS SAVE TIME

When cast-iron exhaust manifolds are removed, the stresses built up in the manifolds often cause the manifolds to twist or bend. This distortion even occurs when the exhaust manifolds have been allowed to cool before removal. Attempting to reinstall distorted exhaust manifolds is often a time-consuming and frustrating exercise.

However, special spreading jacks can be used to force the manifold back into position so that the fasteners can be lined up with the cylinder head. See Figure 9–37.

(a)

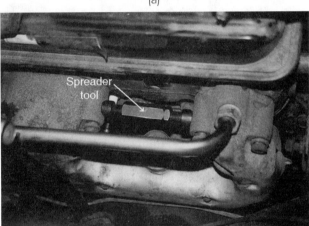

(b)

FIGURE 9–37   (a) Spreading (screw jack) tool. (b) The tool is installed between two runners of a Chevrolet exhaust manifold. The screw jack is turned until the bolt holes line up with the holes in the cylinder head.

The muffler and tail pipe are supported with brackets called **hangers.** The hangers are made of rubberized fabric with metal ends that hold the muffler and tail pipe in position so that they do not touch any metal part. This helps to isolate the exhaust noise from the rest of the vehicle.

SUMMARY

1. All air entering an engine must be filtered.
2. Engines that use carburetors or throttle body injection units are equipped with intake manifolds that keep the airflow speed through the manifold at 50 to 300 feet per second.
3. Intake manifolds are of either dual plane (180-degree) or single plane (360-degree) design.
4. Most intake manifolds have an EGR valve that regulates the amount of recirculated exhaust that enters the engine to reduce NO_X emissions.
5. Exhaust manifolds can be made from cast iron or stainless steel.
6. The exhaust system also contains a catalytic converter, exhaust pipes, and muffler. The entire exhaust system is supported by rubber hangers that isolate the noise and vibration of the exhaust from the rest of the vehicle.

REVIEW QUESTIONS

1. Why is it necessary to have intake charge velocities of about 50 feet per second?
2. Why can fuel-injected engines use larger (and longer) intake manifolds and still operate at low engine speed?
3. What is a tuned runner in an intake manifold?
4. Name three ways in which heat is added to the intake charge of a carburetor-equipped engine.
5. Why is it necessary to keep the engine oil off of the surface of the exhaust crossover passage in the intake manifold?
6. How does a muffler quiet exhaust noise?

MULTIPLE-CHOICE QUESTIONS

1. Intake charge velocity has to be _____ to prevent fuel droplet separation.
   a. 25 feet per second
   b. 50 feet per second
   c. 100 feet per second
   d. 300 feet per second

2. The intake manifold of a port fuel-injected engine _____ .
   a. Uses a dual heat riser
   b. Contains a leaner air-fuel mixture than does the intake manifold of a carburetor system
   c. Contains only fuel (gasoline)
   d. Contains only air

3. With a dual plane intake manifold, _____ .
   a. Successively firing cylinders are at different levels (sections) of the manifold
   b. All left-side cylinders receive air-fuel mixture from the left side of the carburetor or throttle body injection unit
   c. The intake runners are all of different lengths
   d. The manifold uses an exhaust passage

4. A heated air intake system is usually necessary for proper cold-engine driveability *except* _____ .
   a. On one- or two-barrel carburetor systems
   b. On four-barrel carburetor systems
   c. On port fuel-injection systems
   d. On throttle body fuel-injection systems

5. Another name for a heat riser type of valve that directs exhaust under the carburetor through a passage in the intake manifold is _____ .
   a. Heated air inlet system
   b. Early fuel evaporation valve
   c. Thermovacuum switch (valve)
   d. Exhaust gas recirculation valve

6. The purpose of the sheet-metal shield used on the lifter side of a V-type intake manifold is _____ .
   a. To protect the oil from burning on the exhaust crossover passage
   b. To protect the manifold from the hot engine oil
   c. To help keep the air-fuel charge cooler by keeping the hot engine oil off the bottom of the manifold
   d. To provide lubrication to the heat riser valve

7. Technician A says that a vacuum leak (air leak) on one cylinder of a V-type engine can affect another cylinder sharing the same intake manifold runner. Technician B says that some intake manifolds are designed to increase engine torque by providing a ram air effect. Which technician is correct?
   a. A only
   b. B only
   c. Both A and B
   d. Neither A nor B

8. Technician A says that header-type exhaust manifolds produce less back pressure than do most cast-iron exhaust manifolds. Technician B says that only cast-iron exhaust manifolds are used on production vehicles. Which technician is correct?
   a. A only
   b. B only
   c. Both A and B
   d. Neither A nor B

Cylinder Head and Guide Service

OBJECTIVES

After studying Chapter 10, the reader will be able to

1. Identify combustion chamber types.
2. Explain the operation of a stratified charge combustion chamber.
3. List the steps necessary to recondition a cylinder head.
4. Describe how to inspect and measure valve guides.
5. Discuss valve guide repair options.

Cylinder heads are the most frequently serviced engine components. The highest temperatures and pressures in the entire engine are located in the combustion chamber. Its valves must open and close thousands of times each time the engine is operated.

Combustion chambers of modern automotive overhead valve engines are of two basic types. One is the nonturbulent hemispherical chamber and the other is the turbulent wedge chamber.

HEMISPHERICAL COMBUSTION CHAMBER

In nonturbulent hemispherical combustion chambers, the charge is inducted through widely slanted valves. The charge is compressed and then ignited from a centrally located spark plug (Figures 10–1 and 10–2). The spark plug is as close as possible to all edges of the combustion chamber. Combustion radiates out from the spark plug, completely burning in the shortest possible time. This tends to reduce the formation of NO_X.

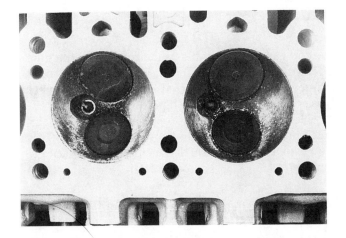

FIGURE 10–1 Hemispherical combustion chamber with a two-valve head.

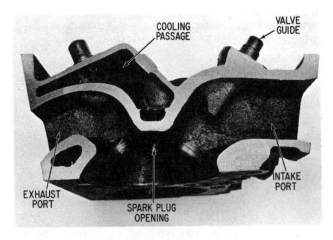

FIGURE 10–2 Sectional view of a hemispherical combustion chamber.

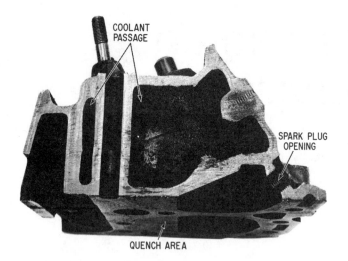

FIGURE 10–3 Sectional view of a wedge-shaped combustion chamber.

The end gases ahead of the flame front have little time to react, so knock is reduced. The rapidly burning charge in the hemispherical combustion chamber causes pressure to rise very rapidly.

Hemispherical combustion chambers are usually fulled machined to form the hemispherical shape. This is an expensive operation that increases the cost of the engine.

WEDGE COMBUSTION CHAMBER

The wedge-shaped combustion chamber is designed to produce smooth, uniform burning by controlling the rate of combustion. A sectional view of a wedge-shaped combustion chamber is shown in Figure 10–3. In wedge-shaped combustion chambers, the charge is inducted through parallel valves. As the piston nears the top of the compression stroke, it moves to a position that is close to a low or flat portion of the head. The gases are squeezed from between the piston and this head surface area. This area is called a **squish** or **quench area.** The gases squeezed from the squish area produce turbulence within the charge. *The turbulence thoroughly mixes the air and fuel in the charge.* The spark plug is positioned so as to be in the highly turbulent part of the charge. Ignition is followed by smooth and rapid burning of the turbulent charge. The combustion flame front radiates out from the spark plug. The end gases that would burn abnormally remain in the squish area. Here the end gases are cooled and they do not react, because this area is squeezed to be very thin, less than 0.100 inch (2.5 millimeters), when the piston is at the top center. The combustion chamber is designed to meet specific engine and fuel require-

FIGURE 10–4 Cutaway of a small-block Chevrolet engine showing the wedge-shaped combustion chamber.

ments. Turbulent combustion chambers usually remain as cast in the head, with no machining being done. See Figure 10–4.

SURFACE QUENCHING

Unburned hydrocarbon emission from engines needs to be reduced to levels as low as possible. The charge adjacent to the combustion chamber surface, which is from 0.002 to 0.020 inch (0.005 to 0.050 millimeter) thick, does not burn. The temperature of the combustion chamber surface is lower than the temperature required for combustion. This cools the part of the charge that is next to the surface to a temperature below its burning temperature. The combustion flame

FIGURE 10–5   *Chevrolet V-8 angled plug cylinder head. Note that the spring seats have been machined for larger-diameter valve springs and the screw-in type of rocker arm studs. The angled spark plug places the plug in a location more conducive to best combustion.*

goes out, and this leaves unburned hydrocarbons. These unburned hydrocarbons are expelled with the burned gases on the exhaust stroke. Combustion chamber surface quenching is one of the major causes of unburned hydrocarbons in the exhaust gas.

NOTE: This unburned gasoline (HC) is a major exhaust emission. The quench volume is reduced by operating the engine at normal operating temperatures. Therefore, a defective thermostat can cause excessive HC exhaust emissions as a result of the quenching of the air-fuel vapors on the colder than normal cylinder head or cylinder walls.

Combustion chambers having a low surface area for their volume, such as the hemispherical combustion chamber, produce low levels of unburned hydrocarbons. The wedge combustion chamber, which has a relatively high surface area-to-volume ratio, produces high levels of unburned hydrocarbons.

New designs use cast combustion chambers rather than expensive machined chambers. These chambers are called by names such as **polyspherical, hemiwedge, kidney-shaped,** and **pentroof.** All cylinder head designs try to place the spark plug in an ideal location for best combustion as shown in Figure 10–5.

STRATIFIED CHARGE COMBUSTION CHAMBER

The stratified engine gets its name from the layers or strata of different air-fuel mixtures that are formed within the swirling charge. Some of the layers have a rich air-fuel mixture, whereas others have a lean mixture. The overall stratified charge has a very lean air-fuel mixture.

A rich air-fuel mixture is easier to ignite with a spark plug than is a lean air-fuel mixture. For this reason, a rich charge surrounds the spark plug. When a

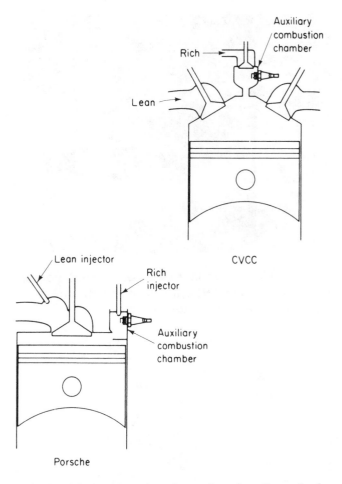

FIGURE 10–6   **Line drawings showing the principle of two stratified charge combustion chambers.**

hot flame develops in this rich charge after ignition, it puts both heat and pressure on the lean remaining charge. The lean part of the charge will then burn.

Two types of stratified charge designs have been used in production engines. One has a a carburetor and uses two combustion chambers, a main chamber and a prechamber. The other injects fuel into the swirling air near the end of the compression stroke. The spark plug is located near the injector, where it is surrounded by a rich fuel mixture.

See Figures 10–6 and 10–7.

MULTIPLE-VALVE COMBUSTION CHAMBER

The power that any engine produces is directly related to the amount of air-fuel mixture that is ignited in the cylinder. Increasing cylinder displacement is a common method of increasing engine power. Turbocharging and supercharging also increase engine power, but these increase engine cost as well.

FIGURE 10–7 Honda CVCC (compound vortex combustion chamber) cylinder head with one auxiliary valve partially removed.

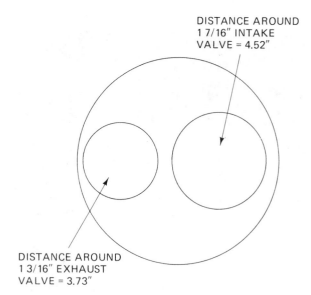

DISTANCE AROUND
1 7/16" INTAKE
VALVE = 4.52"

DISTANCE AROUND
1 3/16" EXHAUST
VALVE = 3.73"

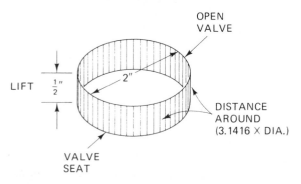

OPEN VALVE

LIFT ½"   2"

DISTANCE AROUND
(3.1416 × DIA.)

VALVE SEAT

OPENING AREA = DISTANCE × LIFT

FIGURE 10–8 Method for measuring the valve opening space.

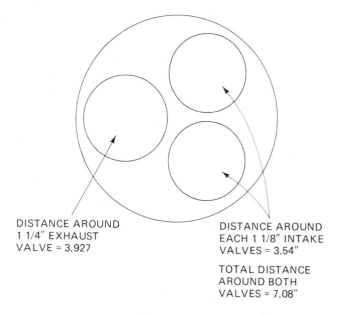

DISTANCE AROUND
1 1/4" EXHAUST
VALVE = 3.927

DISTANCE AROUND
EACH 1 1/8" INTAKE
VALVES = 3.54"

TOTAL DISTANCE
AROUND BOTH
VALVES = 7.08"

FIGURE 10–9 Comparing the valve opening areas between a two- and three-valve combustion chamber when the valves are open.

Adding more than two valves per cylinder permits more gas to flow into and out of the engine with greater velocity without excessive valve duration. **Valve duration** is the number of degrees by which the crankshaft rotates when the valve is off the valve seat. Increased valve duration increases valve overlap. The valve overlap occurs when both valves are off their seats at the end of the exhaust stroke and at the beginning of the intake stroke. At lower engine speeds, the gases can move back and forth between the open valves. Therefore, the greater valve duration hurts low-engine speed performance and driveability, but it allows for more air-fuel mixture to enter the engine for better high-speed power.

The maximum amount of gas moving through the opening area of a valve depends on the distance around the valve and the degree to which it lifts open.

See Figure 10–8. The normal opening lift is about 25% of the valve head diameter. For example, if the intake valve is 2.00 inches in diameter, the normal amount of lift off the seat (not cam lobe height) is 25% of 2.00 inches or ½ (0.500) inch. But the amount of air-fuel mixture that can enter a cylinder depends on the total area around the valve and not just the amount of lift. The distance around a valve is calculated by the equation $\pi \times D$ (3.1416 × Valve diameter). See Figure 10–9.

More total area under the valve is possible when two smaller valves are used rather than one larger

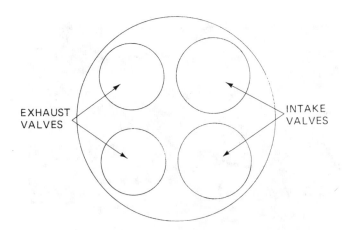

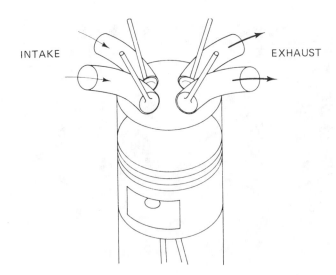

FIGURE 10–10 Typical four-valve head. The total area of opening of two small intake valves and two smaller exhaust valves is greater than the area of a two-valve head using much larger valves. The smaller valves also permit the use of smaller intake runners for better low-speed engine response.

FIGURE 10–12 Four valves in a hemispherical combustion chamber.

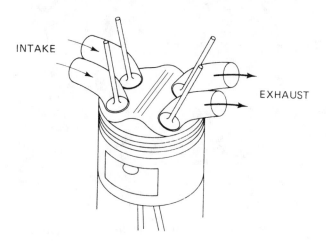

FIGURE 10–11 Four valves in a pentroof combustion chamber.

valve at the same valve lift. The smaller valves allow smooth low-speed operation (because of increased velocity of the mixture as it enters the cylinder as a result of smaller intake ports). Good high-speed performance is also possible because of the increased valve area and lighter-weight valves. See Figure 10–10.

When four valves are used, either the combustion chamber has a pentroof design, with each pair of valves in line (Figure 10–11), or it is hemispherical, with each valve on its own axis (Figure 10–12). Four valves on the pentroof design will be operated with dual overhead camshafts or with single overhead camshafts and rocker arms. Four valves in the hemispherical combustion chamber need a complex valve operating assembly,

usually from a single overhead camshaft. When four valves are used, it is possible to place the spark plug at the center of the combustion chamber. This is the best spark plug location for fast-burning combustion.

FOUR-VALVE HEAT

A four-valve cylinder head allows greater air and fuel flow than does a two-valve head of the same size. This additional air and fuel produces more heat and helps multivalve engines produce more power. However, the area around the exhaust valves often overheats, especially when the engine is operating at or near peak power levels. This heat buildup between the exhaust valves can cause the valves to burn or can cause softening and erosion of the area between the valve seats. All four valve heads should be carefully inspected for cracks or other cylinder head damage between the exhaust valves.

INTAKE AND EXHAUST PORTS

The part of the intake or exhaust system passage that is cast in the cylinder head is called a **port.** Ports lead from the manifolds to the valves. The most desirable port shape is not always possible because of space requirements in the head. Space is required for the head bolt bosses, valve guides, cooling passages, and pushrod openings. Inline engines may have both intake and exhaust ports located on the same side of the engine. Often, two cylinders share the same port because of the restricted space available. Shared ports are called **siamese ports.** See Figure 10–13. Each cylinder uses the port at a different time. Larger ports and better

FIGURE 10-13 Close-up view of a siamese exhaust port.

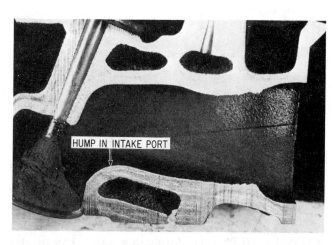

FIGURE 10-15 A hump in the intake port that actually increases the airflow capacity of the port.

FIGURE 10-14 Typical two-valve cross-flow cylinder head. The intake manifold is on the right side and the exhaust manifold is on the left side.

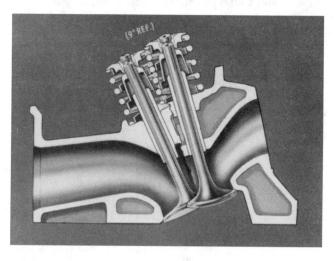

FIGURE 10-16 Cross-flow cylinder head having a long intake port on the left and a short exhaust port on the right. (Courtesy of Chevrolet Motor Division, GMC)

breathing are possible in engines that have the intake port on one side of the head and the exhaust port on the opposite side. This type of head is said to have a **cross-flow** head design. The cross-flow head shown in Figure 10-14 allows the valve to be located and angled so as to permit most efficient engine breathing. It also allows the spark plug to be placed near the center of the combustion chamber. All V-type engines have the cross-flow head design.

The flow of gases is often different than one might think. At times a restricting hump (Figure 10-15) within a port may actually increase the airflow capac-

ity of the port. It does this by redirecting the flow to an area of the port that is large enough to handle the flow. Modifications in the field, such as **porting** or **relieving,** would result in restricting the flow of such a carefully designed port.

The intake port in the head is relatively long, whereas the exhaust port is short. The long intake port wall is heated by coolant flowing through the head. The heat aids in vaporizing the fuel in the intake charge. The exhaust port is short so that the least amount of exhaust heat is transferred to the engine coolant. See Figure 10-16.

CYLINDER HEAD COOLANT PASSAGES

The engine is designed so that coolant will flow from the coolest portion of the engine to the warmest portion. The coolant pump takes the coolant from the radiator. The coolant is pumped into the block, where it is directed all around the cylinders. The coolant then flows upward through the gasket to the cooling passages cast into the cylinder head. The heated coolant is collected at a common point and returned to the radiator to be cooled and recycled.

NOTE: Reversed-flow cooling systems, such as that used on the Chevrolet LT1 V-8, send the coolant from the radiator to the cylinder heads first. This results in a cooler cylinder head and allows for more spark advance without engine-damaging detonation. _____

Typical coolant passages in a head are shown in Figure 10–17.

There are relatively large holes in the gasket surface of the head leading to the head cooling passages. The large holes are necessary to support the cooling passage core through these openings while the head is being cast. After casting, the core is broken up and removed through these same openings. Core support openings to the outside of the engine are closed with expansion plugs or soft plugs. These plugs are often mistakenly called freeze plugs. The openings between the head and the block are usually too large for the correct coolant flow. When the openings are too large, the head gasket performs an important coolant flow function. Special-size holes are made in the gasket. These holes correct the coolant flow rate at each opening. Therefore, it is important that the head gasket be installed correctly for proper engine cooling. A head gasket with special-size holes to cover the head openings is shown in Figure 10–18.

Carefully located openings, or deflectors, may be designed into the head. They direct the coolant toward a portion of the head where localized heat must be removed. Usually, this is in the area of the exhaust valve. Some of the deflectors are cast in the cooling passages.

LUBRICATING OVERHEAD VALVES

Lubricating oil is delivered to the overhead valve mechanism, either through the valve pushrods or through drilled passages in the head and block casting. There are special openings in the head gasket to allow the oil to pass between the block and head without

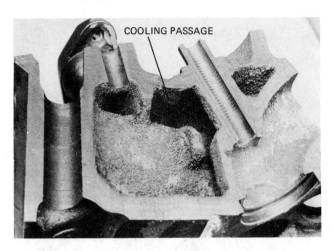

FIGURE 10–17 Coolant passages can be seen in this section of a cylinder head.

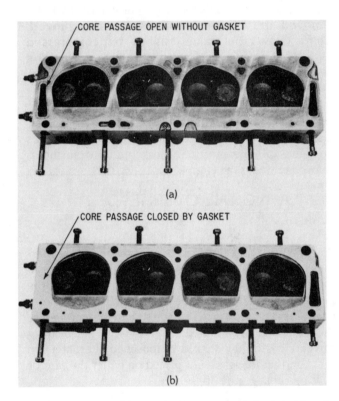

FIGURE 10–18 Coolant flow control. (a) Head core passages open without a gasket. (b) Gasket covering the left-hand core passage opening.

leaking. After the oil passes through the valve mechanisms, it returns to the oil pan through oil return passages. Some engines have drilled oil return holes, but most engines have large cast holes that allow the oil to return freely to the engine oil pan. The cast holes are large and do not easily become plugged.

FIGURE 10–19 *Before any camshaft can be removed, the followers or lifters must be removed. Notice how the valve has to be compressed slightly to remove the camshaft followers from the overhead camshaft engine.*

NOTE: Many aluminum cylinder heads have smaller than normal oil drain-back holes. If an engine has excessive oil consumption, check the oil drain holes before removing the engine.

REMOVING THE OVERHEAD CAMSHAFT

The overhead camshaft will have either one-piece bearings in a solid bearing support or split bearings and a bearing cap. When one-piece bearings are used, the valve springs will have to be compressed with a fixture or the finger follower will have to be removed before the camshaft can be pulled out endwise. When bearing caps are used, they should be loosened alternately so that bending loads are not placed on either the cam or bearing caps (Figure 10–19).

CYLINDER HEAD RECONDITIONING SEQUENCE

Although not all cylinder heads require all service operations, cylinder heads should be reconditioned using the following sequence:

1. Disassemble and thoroughly clean the heads. (See Chapter 7.)
2. Check for cracks and repair as necessary. (See Chapter 8.)

3. Check the surface that contacts the engine block and machine if necessary.
4. Check valve guides and replace or service as necessary.
5. Grind valves and reinstall them in the cylinder head with new valve stem seals. (See Chapter 11.)

CYLINDER HEAD RESURFACING

Remove the valves from the cylinder head as illustrated in Figures 10–20 and 10–21.

■ **CAUTION:** All valve train components that are to be reused must be kept together. As wear occurs, parts become worn together. Pushrods can be kept labeled if stuck through a cardboard box as shown in Figure 10–22. Be sure to keep the top part of the push rod at the top. Intake and exhaust valve springs may be different and must be kept with the correct valve. ■

A new engine is machined and assembled within a few hours after the heads and block are cast from melted iron. Newly cast parts have internal stresses within the metal. The stress results from the different thicknesses of the metal sections in the head. Forces from combustion in the engine, plus continued heating and cooling, gradually relieve these stresses. By the time the engine has accumulated 20,000 to 30,000 miles (32,000 to 48,000 kilometers), the stresses have been completely relieved. This is why some engine rebuilders prefer to work with used heads and blocks that are stress relieved. Used engines are often called **seasoned** because of the reduced stress and movement these components have as compared to new parts. The head will usually have some warpage when the engine is disassembled.

The engine should be cool (room temperature) before the cylinder heads are removed. As mentioned in chapter 7, the head bolts should be loosened in the reverse of the order used for tightening to avoid the possibility of warping. In other words, the head bolts should be loosened from the outside and you should work your way toward the center of the head. The surface must be thoroughly cleaned and inspected as follows:

Step #1. The surface is first scraped and then draw-filed (Figure 10–23) to remove any small burrs.
Step #2. The head should be checked in five planes as shown in Figures 10–24 and 10–25. Checking the cylinder head gasket surface in five planes checks the head for **warpage, distortion, bend,** and **twist.**

(a)

(b)

(c)

FIGURE 10–20 Removing valves from cylinder head. (a) A lead shot–filled plastic hammer is used to "break the taper" of the valve locks (keepers). (b) Instead of hitting the valve retainer, a socket can be used to spread the hammer-blow force. (c) Using a socket also prevents valve locks (keepers) from flying off if they should come loose.

(a)

(b)

FIGURE 10–21 (a) Using a spring compressor to compress the valve spring. Care should be used not to pinch fingers when removing (or installing) valve locks. (b) The valve locks can be easily removed if a magnet is placed near the valve while the valve spring is being compressed. Do not compress the valve spring any farther than is necessary to remove the locks.

FIGURE 10–22 Individual parts become worn together. Cardboard is a crude but effective material to use to keep all valve train parts together and labeled exactly as they came from the engine.

FIGURE 10–23 After scraping the gasket surface with a scraper, use a file and draw across the surface. When a file is drawn across the head sideways, little (if any) material is removed, but burrs and other surface imperfections are removed or highlighted.

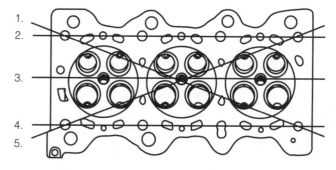

FIGURE 10–24 Cylinder heads should be checked in five planes for warpage, distortion, bend, or twist.

(a)

(b)

FIGURE 10–25 (a) Checking the head for warping. This head should not vary by over 0.002 inch in any 6-inch length and not by more than 0.004 inch overall. (Rule of thumb: no more than 0.001 inch per cylinder.) (b) Do not forget to check diagonally for twist. The same specifications apply. Always use a known-to-be-true straightedge.

These defects are determined by trying to slide a 0.004-inch (0.10-millimeter) feeler gauge under a straightedge held against the head surface.

NOTE: The cylinder head surface that mates with the top deck of the block is often called the **fire deck.**

The head should not vary by over 0.002 inch (0.05 millimeter) in any 6-inch (15-centimeter) length, or by more than 0.004 inch overall. Always check the manufacturer's recommended specifications.

NOTE: Always check the cylinder head thickness and specifications to be sure that material can be safely removed from the surface. Some manufacturers do not recommend *any* machining, but rather require cylinder head replacement if cylinder head surface flatness is not within specifications.

The head should also be resurfaced if there is any roughness caused by corrosion of the head gasket. This roughness can be felt on the head surface when you rub your fingernail across it. In precision engine rebuilding, *both* the head and the block deck are resurfaced as a standard practice.

RESURFACING METHODS

Two common resurfacing methods are used: milling and grinding. A **milling**-type of resurfacer uses metal-cutting tool bits fastened in a disk. The disk is the rotating work head of the mill. This can be seen in Figure 10–26. The surface **grinder** type uses a large-diameter abrasive wheel. Both types of resurfacing can be done with table-type surfacers and with precision-type surfacers. With a table-type surfacer, the head or block is passed over the cutting head that extends slightly above a worktable. The abrasive wheel is dressed before grinding begins. The wheel head is adjusted to just touch the surface. At this point, the feed is calibrated to zero. This is necessary so that the operator knows exactly the size of the cut being made. Light cuts are taken. The abrasive wheel cuts are limited to 0.005 inch (0.015 millimeter). The abrasive wheel surface should be wire brushed after each five passes, and the wheel should be redressed after grinding each 0.100 inch (2.50 millimeter). The mill-type cutting wheel can remove up to 0.030 inch (0.075 millimeter) on each pass. A special mill cutting tool or a dull grinding wheel is used when aluminum heads are being resurfaced.

NOTE: Resurfacing the cylinder head changes the compression ratio of the engine by about 1/10 point per 0.010 inches of removed material. For example, the compression ratio would be increased from 9.0:1 to 9.2:1 if 0.020 inches were removed from a typical cylinder head.

SURFACE FINISH

The surface finish of a reconditioned part is as important as the size of the part. Surface finish is measured in units called **microinches** (abbreviated μ in). The symbol in front of the inch abbreviation is the Greek letter mu. One microinch equals 0.000001 inch (0.025 micro-meter [μm]). The finish classification in microinches gives the distance between the highest peak and the deepest

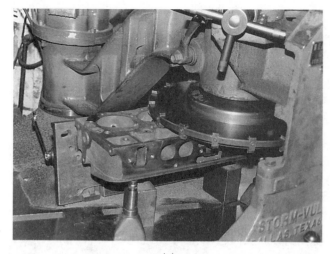

(a)

(b)

FIGURE 10–26 (a) Milling-type resurfacer machining the gasket surface of a cylinder head. (b) Grinder-type resurfacer.

valley. The usual method of expressing surface finish is by the **arithmetic average roughness height,** abbreviated **RA,** which is the average of the distance of all peaks and valleys from the mean (average) line. Surface finish is measured using a machine with a diamond stylus.

Another classification of surface finish, which is becoming obsolete, is called the **root mean square (RMS).** The RMS is a slightly higher number and can be obtained by multiplying RA × 1.11 = RMS.

Typical surface finish roughness recommendations for cast-iron and aluminum cylinder heads and blocks include the following:

Cast Iron

- Maximum: 110 RA (125 RMS) (Rough surfaces can limit gasket movement and conformity.)
- Minimum: 30 RA (33 RMS) (Smoother surfaces increase the tendency of the gasket to flow and *reduce* gasket sealing ability.)
- Recommended range: 60 to 100 RA (65 to 110 RMS)

Aluminum

- Maximum: 60 RA (65 RMS)
- Minimum: 30 RA (33 RMS)
- Recommended range: 50 to 60 RA (55 to 65 RMS)

The rougher the surface is, the higher the microinch finish measurement will be.

Typical preferred microinch finish standards for other engine components include the following:

- Crank and rod journal: 10 to 14 RA (12 to 15 RMS)
- Honed cylinder: 18 to 32 RA (20 to 35 RMS)
- Connecting rod big end: 45 to 72 RA (50 to 80 RMS)

CORRECTING INTAKE MANIFOLD ALIGNMENT

The intake manifold of a V-type engine may no longer fit correctly after the gasket surfaces of the heads are ground. The ports and the assembly bolt holes may no longer match. The intake manifold surface must be resurfaced to remove enough metal to rematch the ports and bolt holes. The amount of metal that must be removed depends on the angle between the head gasket surface and the intake manifold gasket surface. Figure 10–27 shows how this is calculated. Automotive machine shops doing head resurfacing have tables that

■ **TECH TIP** ■

THE POTATO CHIP PROBLEM

Most cylinder heads are warped or twisted in the shape of a typical potato chip (high at the ends and dipped in the center). After a cylinder head is ground, the surface *should* be perfectly flat. A common problem involves grinding the cylinder head in both directions while it is being held on the table that moves to the left and right. Most grinders are angled by about 4 degrees. The lower part of the stone should be the cutting edge. If grinding occurs along the angled part of the stone, too much heat is generated. This heat warps the head (or block) upward in the middle. The stone then removes this material, and the end result is a slight (about 0.0015-inch) depression in the center of the finished surface. To help prevent this from happening, always feed the grinder in the forward direction only (especially during removal of the last 0.003 inch of material).

(a)

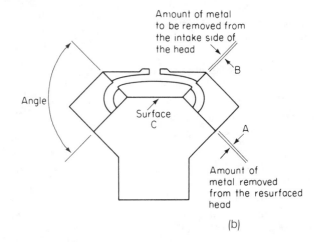

Angle	Amount to be removed from B
90°	A x 1.000
85°	A x 1.100
80°	A x 1.233
75°	A x 1.414
70°	A x 1.673
75°	A x 2.067
70°	A x 2.733
65°	A x 4.072

The amount removed from surface C is 1.4 x A

(b)

FIGURE 10–27   (a) Measuring the angle between the intake manifold and the head gasket surface. (b) The material that must be removed for a good manifold fit.

specify the exact amount of metal to be removed. It is usually necessary to remove some metal from both the front and the back gasket surface of closed-type intake manifolds used on V-type engines. This is necessary to provide a good gasket seal that will prevent oil leakage from the lifter valley.

■ **CAUTION:** Do not remove any more material than is necessary to restore a flat cylinder head–to–block surface. Some manufacturers limit *total* material that can be removed from block deck and cylinder head to 0.008 inch (0.2 millimeter). Removal of material from the cylinder head of an overhead camshaft engine shortens the distance between the camshaft and the crankshaft. This causes the valve timing to be *retarded* unless a special copper spacer shim is placed between the block deck and the gasket to restore proper crankshaft-to-camshaft centerline dimension. ■

ALUMINUM CYLINDER HEAD STRAIGHTENING

Aluminum expands at about twice the rate of cast iron when heated. Aluminum cylinder heads used on cast-iron blocks can warp and/or crack if they are overheated. The expanding cylinder head first hits the head bolts. Further expansion of the head causes the head to expand upward and bow in the center. If a warped (bowed) cylinder head is resurfaced, the stresses of expansion are still present, and if the cylinder head uses an overhead camshaft, further problems exist. With a D-shaped cylinder head (see Figure 10–28), the camshaft centerline bearing supports must also be restored. To restore the straightness of the cam bearing bore (sometimes called the **cam tunnel**) align boring and/or boring may be required.

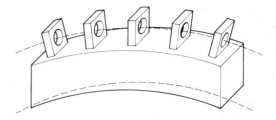

FIGURE 10–28 Warped overhead camshaft cylinder head. If the gasket surface is machined to be flat, the camshaft bearings will still not be in proper alignment. The solution is to straighten the cylinder head or align bore the cam tunnel because the head is actually D-shaped.

The best approach to use to restore a warped aluminum cylinder head (especially an overhead camshaft head) is to relieve the stress that has caused the warpage *and* to straighten the head before machining.

Step #1. Determine the amount of warpage with a straightedge and thickness (feeler) gauge. Cut shim stock (thin strips of metal) to one-half of the amount of the warpage. Place shims of this thickness under each end of the head.

Step #2. Tighten the center of the cylinder head down on a strong, flat base. A 2 inch–thick piece of steel that is 8 inches wide by 20 inches long makes a good support for the gasket surface of the cylinder head (use antiseize compound on the bolt thread to help in bolt removal).

Step #3. Place the head and base in an oven for 5 hours at 500° F (260° C). Turn the oven off and leave the assembly in the oven.

NOTE: If the temperature is too high, the valve seat inserts may fall out of the head! At 500° F, a typical valve seat will still be held into the aluminum head with a 0.002-inch interference fit based on calculations of thermal expansion of the aluminum head and steel insert.

Allow the head to cool in the oven for 4 or 5 hours to relieve any stress in the aluminum from the heating process. For best results, the cooling process should be allowed to occur overnight. Several cylinder heads can be "cooked" together, starting in the morning. After 5 hours of heat soak time, the oven should be turned off and the head allowed to cool.

If the cylinder head is still warped, the heating and cooling process can be repeated. After the head is straightened and the stress relieved, the gasket surface (fire deck) can be machined in the usual manner. To prevent possible camshaft bore misalignment problems, do not machine more than 0.010 to 0.015 inch (0.25 to 0.38 millimeter) from the head gasket surface.

■ TECH TIP ■

THE QUICK AND EASY DECARBONIZING TRICK

Carbon is a by-product of combustion. Carbon deposits accumulate in the combustion chamber and on the backsides of both intake and exhaust valves. These carbon deposits can build up on valves and valve guides, causing hesitation, rough idle, and even stalling problems. Carbon deposits can coat the combustion chamber and tops of pistons, causing an increase in compression and an increase in nitrogen (NO_X) emissions.

No chemical can dissolve carbon, but decarbonizing before the engine is disassembled can be as easy as the following:

Step #1. Pour a can of top engine cleaner into a large coffee can. Fill the top engine cleaner can with water and add that to the coffee can, creating a 50-50 mix of cleaner and water.

NOTE: The cleaner disperses and penetrates through the carbon, and the water in the mixture turns to steam in the combustion chamber to force the carbon off of internal engine parts.

Step #2. Start and run the engine until it reaches normal operating temperature. Connect one end of a length of $\frac{5}{32}$-inch ID vacuum hose to a manifold vacuum port close to the throttle plate and place the other end into the coffee can with the cleaner-water mixture.

Step #3. Operate the engine at a fast idle (2500 RPM) until all of the cleaner-water mixture is drawn into the engine. Stop the engine.

Step #4. Allow the cleaner to work for about 1 hour and then start the engine. Drive the vehicle aggressively to blow out the loosened carbon deposits. Repeat if necessary.

VALVE GUIDES

The valve guide supports the valve stem so that the valve face will remain perfectly centered or **concentric** with the valve seat. The valve guide is generally **integral** with the head casting for better heat transfer and for lower manufacturing costs. **Valve guide inserts** are always used where the valve stem and head materials are not compatible.

No matter how good the valves or seats are, they cannot operate properly if the valve guide is not accurate. In use, the valve operating mechanism pushes the valve tip sideways. This is the major cause of valve stem and guide wear. The valve normally rotates a little each time it is opened to keep wear even all around the stem. The valve guide, on the other hand, always has the wear in the same place. See Figure 10–29. This causes both the top and bottom ends of the guide to wear until the guide has an oval or egg shape. A guide must be reconditioned to match the valve that is to be used in that valve guide.

VALVE STEM-TO-GUIDE CLEARANCE

Engine manufacturers usually recommend the following valve stem-to-valve guide clearances:

- Intake valve: 0.001 to 0.003 inch (0.025 to 0.075 millimeter)
- Exhaust valve: 0.002 to 0.004 inch (0.05 to 0.10 millimeter)

Be sure to check the exact specifications for the engine being serviced. The exhaust valve clearance is greater than the intake valve clearance because the exhaust valve runs hotter and therefore expands more than the intake valve.

Excessive valve stem-to-guide clearance can cause excessive oil consumption. The intake valve guide is exposed to manifold vacuum that can draw oil from the top of the cylinder head down into the combustion chamber. In this situation, valves can also run hotter than usual because much of the heat in the valve is transferred to the cylinder head though the valve guide.

HINT: *A human hair is about 0.002 inch (0.05 millimeter) in diameter. Therefore, the typical clearance between a valve stem and the valve guide is only the thickness of a human hair.*

FIGURE 10–29   Scuffed valve guide.

■ TECH TIP ■

TIGHT IS NOT ALWAYS RIGHT

Many engine manufacturers specify a valve stem-to-valve guide clearance of 0.001 to 0.003 inch (0.025 to 0.076 millimeter). However, some vehicles, especially those equipped with aluminum cylinder heads, may specify a much greater clearance. For example, some Chrysler 2.2 liter and 2.5 liter engines have a specified valve stem-to-valve guide clearance of 0.003 to 0.005 inch (0.075 to 0.127 millimeter). This amount of clearance feels loose to those technicians accustomed to normal valve stem clearance specifications. While this large amount of clearance may seem excessive, remember that the valve stem increases in diameter as the engine warms up. Therefore, the *operating* clearance is smaller than the clearance measured at room temperature. Always double check the factory specifications before replacing a valve guide for excessive wear.

MEASURING VALVE GUIDES FOR WEAR

Valves should be measured for stem wear before valve guides are measured. The valve guide is measured in the middle with a small hole gauge. The gauge size is checked

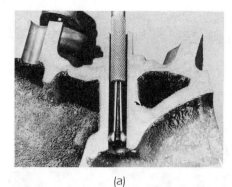
(a)

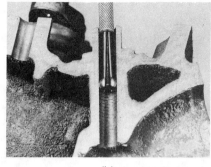
(b)

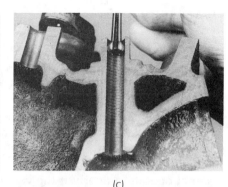
(c)

FIGURE 10–30   (a–c) A cutaway head is used to show how a small hole gauge is used to measure the taper and wear of a valve guide. (d) After it is adjusted to the valve guide size, the small hole gauge is measured with an outside micrometer.

(d)

with a micrometer. The guide is then checked at each end. This is shown using a cutaway valve guide in Figure 10–30. The expanded part of the ball should be placed crosswise to the engine where the greatest amount of valve guide wear exists. The dimension of the valve stem diameter is subtracted from the dimension of the valve guide diameter. If the clearance exceeds the specified clearance, the valve guide will have to be reconditioned.

Valve stem-to-guide clearance can also be checked using a dial indicator (gauge) to measure the amount of movement of the valve when lifted off the valve seat. See Figure 10–31.

OVERSIZE STEM VALVES

Most domestic automobile manufacturers that have integral valve guides in their engines recommend reaming worn valve guides and installing new valves with **oversize** stems. When a valve guide is worn, the valve stem is also likely to be worn. In this case, new

valves are required. If new valves are used, they can just as well have oversize stems as standard stems. Typically, available sizes include 0.003, 0.005, 0.015, and 0.030 inch oversize (often abbreviated **OS**). The valve guide is reamed or honed to the correct size to fit the oversize stem of the new valve. Figure 10–32 shows a reamer in a valve guide. The resulting clearance of the valve stem in the guide is the same as the original clearance. The oil clearance and the heat transfer properties of the original valve and guide are not changed when new valves with oversize stems are installed.

NOTE: Many remanufacturers of cylinder heads use oversize valve stems to simplify production. _____

VALVE GUIDE KNURLING

In the process known as valve guide knurling, a tool is rotated as it is driven into the guide. The tool *displaces* the metal to reduce the hole diameter of the guide.

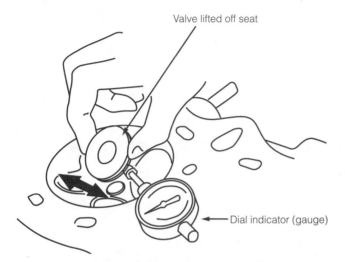

Valve lifted off seat

Dial indicator (gauge)

FIGURE 10–31 Measuring valve guide-to-stem clearance with a dial indicator while rocking the stem in the direction of normal thrust. The reading on the dial indicator should be compared to specifications because it does not give the guide-to-stem clearance directly. The valve is usually lifted to its maximum operating lift.

FIGURE 10–32 Reaming a valve guide to be oversize. This permits the use of new valves with oversize stem diameters. Many remanufacturers use this method to save the money and time involved in replacing or knurling valve guides and grinding old valves.

Knurling is ideally suited to engines with integral valve guides (guides that are part of the cylinder head and are nonremovable). It is recommended that knurling not be used to correct wear exceeding 0.006 inch (0.15 millimeter). In the displacing process, the knurling tool pushes a small tapered wheel or dull threading tool into the wall of the guide hole. This makes a groove in the wall of the guide without removing any metal, as pictured in Figures 10–33 and 10–34. The

■ TECH TIP ■

RIGHT SIDE UP

When replacing valve guides, it is important that the recommended procedures be followed. Most manufacturers specify that replaceable guides be driven from the combustion chamber side toward the rocker arm side. For example, big-block Chevrolet V-8 heads (396, 402, 427, and 454 cubic inches) have a 0.004-inch (0.05-millimeter) taper (small end toward the combustion chamber).

Other manufacturers, however, may recommend driving the old guide from the rocker arm side to prevent any carbon buildup on the guide from damaging the guide bore. Always consult the manufacturer's recommended procedures before attempting to replace a valve guide.

metal piles up along the edge of the groove just as dirt would pile up along the edge of a tire track as the tire rolled through soft dirt. (The dirt would be displaced from under the wheel to form a small ridge alongside the tire track.)

The knurling tool is driven by an electric drill through an speed reducer that shows the rotating speed of the knurling tool. The reamers that accompany the knurling set will ream just enough to provide the correct valve stem clearance for commercial reconditioning standards. The valve guides are honed to size in the precision shop when precise fits are desired. Clearances of knurled valve guides are usually one-half of the new valve guide clearances. Such small clearances can be used because knurling leaves so many small oil rings down the length of the guide for lubrication.

VALVE GUIDE REPLACEMENT

When an engine is designed with replaceable valve guides, their replacement is always recommended when the valve assembly is being reconditioned. The original valve guide height should be measured before the guide is removed so that the new guide can be properly positioned.

After the valve guide height is measured, the worn guide is pressed from the head with a properly fitting **driver.** Figure 10–35 shows how the driver is used to remove and replace valve guides. The driver has a stem to fit the guide opening and a shoulder that pushes on the end of the guide. If the guide has a flange, care should be taken to make sure that the guide is pushed out from the correct end, usually from the port side and

FIGURE 10–33 Knurling tool being used in a valve guide. After the knurling tool displaces the metal inside the guide, a reamer is run through the guide to produce a restored, serviceable valve guide.

FIGURE 10–34 Sectional view of a knurled valve guide.

FIGURE 10–35   Valve guide replacement procedure.

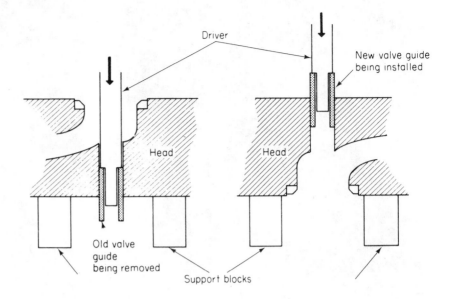

toward the rocker arm side. The new guide is pressed into the guide bore using the same driver. Make sure that the guide is pressed to the correct depth. After the guides are replaced, they are reamed or honed to proper inside diameter.

Replacement valve guides can also be installed to repair worn integral guides. Both **cast-iron** and **bronze** guides are available. See Figure 10–36. Three common valve guide sizes are as follows:

1. ⁵⁄₁₆ or 0.313 inch
2. ¹¹⁄₃₂ or 0.343 inch
3. ⅜ or 0.375 inch

VALVE GUIDE INSERTS

When the integral valve guide is badly worn, it can be reconditioned using an insert. This repair method is usually preferred in heavy-duty and high-speed engines. Two types of guide inserts are commonly used for guide repair: a thin-walled bronze alloy sleeve bushing and a spiral bronze alloy bushing. The thin-walled bronze sleeve bushings are also called **bronze guide liners.** The valve guide rebuilding kit used to install each of these bushings includes all of the reamers, installing sleeves, broaches, burnishing tools, and cutoff tools that are needed to install and properly size the bushings.

The valve guide must be bored to a large enough size to accept the thin-walled insert sleeve. The boring tool is held in alignment by a rugged fixture. One type is shown in Figure 10–37. Depending on the make of

the equipment, the boring fixture is aligned with the valve guide hole, the valve seat, or the head gasket surface. First, the boring fixture is properly aligned. The guide is then bored, making a hole somewhat smaller than the insert sleeve that will be used. The bored hole is reamed to make a precise, smooth hole that is still slightly smaller than the insert sleeve. The insert sleeve is installed with a press fit that holds it in the guide. The press fit also helps to maintain normal heat transfer from the valve to the head. The thin-walled insert sleeve is held in an installing sleeve. A driver is used to press the insert from the installing sleeve into the guide. A broach is then pressed through the insert sleeve to firmly seat it in the guide. The broach is designed to put a knurl in the guide to aid in lubrication. The insert sleeve is then trimmed to the valve guide length. Finally, the insert sleeve is reamed or honed to provide the required valve stem clearance. A very close clearance of 0.0005 inch (one-half of one thousandth of an inch) (0.013 millimeter) is usually used with the bronze thin-walled insert sleeve. See Figure 10–38.

SPIRAL BRONZE INSERT BUSHINGS

The spiral bronze alloy insert bushing is screwed into a thread that is put in the valve guide. The tap used to put cut threads in the valve guide has a long pilot ahead of the thread-cutting portion of the tap. This aids in restoring the original guide alignment. The long pilot is placed in the guide from the valve seat end. A power driver is attached to the end of the pilot that

(a)

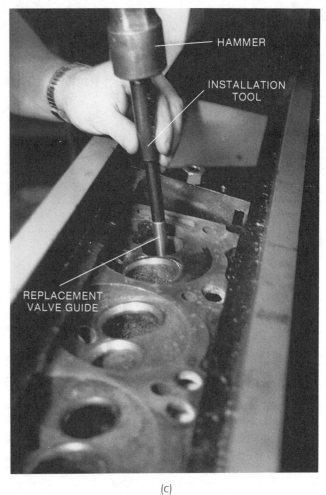

HAMMER

INSTALLATION
TOOL

REPLACEMENT
VALVE GUIDE

(c)

(b)

FIGURE 10–36 (a) Drilling out old valve guide in preparation for replacing the guide. (b) Reaming the hole after drilling. (c) Replacement guide being driven into the cylinder head.

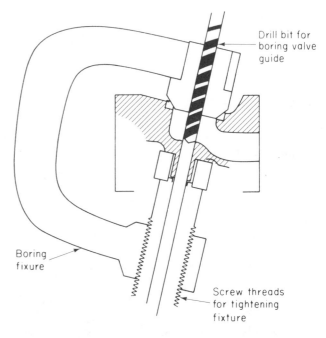

Drill bit for
boring valve
guide

Boring
fixture

Screw threads
for tightening
fixture

FIGURE 10–37 Type of fixture required to bore the valve guide to be oversize to accept a thin-walled insert sleeve.

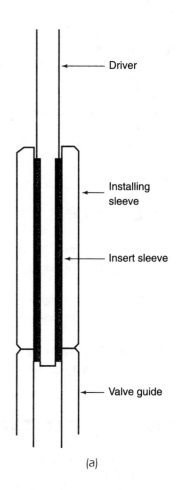

(b)

(c)

(d)

(a)

FIGURE 10–38 (a) The valve guide thin-walled insert being pushed into the valve guide from the installing sleeve. (b) Burnishing a thin-walled bronze liner. (c) Reaming a bronze guide liner (thin-walled bronze sleeve). (d) Finished installation. Bronze guides wear many times longer than cast-iron guides.

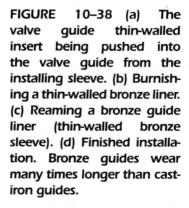

Driver

Installing sleeve

Insert sleeve

Valve guide

extends from the spring end of the valve guide. The threads are cut in the guide from the seat end toward the spring end as the power driver turns the tap, pulling it toward the driver. The tap is stopped before it comes out of the guide, and the power driver is removed. The thread is carefully completed by hand to avoid breaking either the end of the guide or the tap. An installed spiral bronze insert bushing can be seen in Figure 10–39.

The spiral bronze bushing is tightened on an inserting tool. This holds it securely in the wound-up position so that it can be screwed into the spring end of the guide. It is screwed in until the bottom of the bushing is flush with the seat end of the guide. The holding tool is removed, and the bushing material is trimmed to one coil *above* the spring end of the guide. The end of the bushing is temporarily secured with a plastic serrated bushing retainer and a worm gear clamp. This

FIGURE 10–39 Installed spiral bronze insert bushing.

holds the bushing in place as a broach is driven through the bushing to firmly seat it in the threads. The bushing is reamed or honed to size before the temporary bushing retainer is removed. The final step is to trim the end of the bushing with a special cutoff tool that is included in the bushing installation tool set. This type of spiral bronze bushing can be removed by using a pick to free the end of the bushing. It can then be stripped out and a new bushing inserted in the original threads in the guide hole. New threads do not have to be put in the guide. The spiral bushing design has natural spiral grooves to hold oil for lubrication. The valve stem clearances are the same as those used for knurling and for the thin-walled insert (about one-half of the standard recommended clearance).

SUMMARY

1. The most commonly used combustion chamber types include hemispherical, wedge, and pentroof.
2. Coolant and lubricating openings and passages are located throughout most cylinder heads.
3. Cylinder head reconditioning should start with cleaning and repairing, if needed, followed by resurfacing of valves and, finally, grinding of valves and seats.
4. Cylinder head resurfacing machines include grinders and milling machines.

5. Valve guides should be checked for wear using a ball gauge or a dial indicator. Typical valve stem-to-guide clearance is 0.001 to 0.003 inch for intake valves and 0.002 to 0.004 inch for exhaust valves.
6. Valve guide repair options include use of oversize stem valves, replacement valve guides, valve guide inserts, and knurling of the original valve guide.

REVIEW QUESTIONS

1. What forms the top and bottom of the combustion chamber?
2. What are the advantages of a hemispherical combustion chamber?
3. What are the advantages of a wedge combustion chamber?
4. What is meant by the term *cross-flow head?*
5. What is a siamese port?
6. Why are intake valves larger than exhaust valves?
7. What are the advantages of using four valves per cylinder?

MULTIPLE-CHOICE QUESTIONS

1. Hemispherical combustion chambers _____ .
   a. Create a turbulent air-fuel charge
   b. Always use four valves per cylinder
   c. Are nonturbulent
   d. Use inline (parallel) valves
2. For lowest hydrocarbon emissions, the following engine design feature is used: _____ .
   a. Low combustion chamber surface area–to–volume ratio
   b. High combustion chamber surface area–to–volume ratio
   c. Noncentrally mounted spark plug
   d. Increased (as much as possible) quench area
3. To help ensure proper engine cooling, the following cylinder head design features are used on most engines: _____ .
   a. Long exhaust ports and short intake ports
   b. Short exhaust ports and long intake ports
   c. Large exhaust crossover passages
   d. Coolant passages restricted by head gaskets
4. The gasket surface of a cylinder head, as measured with a straightedge, should have a maximum variation of _____ .
   a. 0.002 inch in any 6-inch length or 0.004 inch overall
   b. 0.001 inch in any 6-inch length or 0.004 inch overall
   c. 0.020 inch in any 10-inch length or 0.020 inch overall
   d. 0.004 inch in any 10-inch length or 0.008 inch overall

5. A warped aluminum cylinder head can be restored to useful service by _____ .
   a. Grinding the gasket surface and then align honing the camshaft bore
   b. Heating it in an oven at 500° F with shims under each end, allowing it to cool, and then machining it
   c. Heating the head to 500° F for 5 hours and cooling it rapidly before final machining
   d. Machining the gasket surface to one-half of the warped amount and then heating the head in an oven and allowing it to cool slowly

6. Most vehicle manufacturers recommend repairing integral guides using _____ .
   a. OS stem valves
   b. Knurling
   c. Replacement valve guides
   d. Valve guide inserts

7. Typical valve stem-to-valve guide clearance is_____ .
   a. 0.030 to 0.045 inch (0.8 to 0.10 millimeter)
   b. 0.015 to 0.020 inch (0.4 to 0.5 millimeter)
   c. 0.005 to 0.010 inch (0.13 to 0.25 millimeter)
   d. 0.001 to 0.004 inch (0.03 to 0.01 millimeter)

8. What other engine component may have to be machined if the cylinder heads are machined on a V-type engine?
   a. Exhaust manifolds
   b. Intake manifold
   c. Block deck
   d. Distributor mount (if the vehicle is so equipped)

9. Which operation should be performed first?
   a. Resurfacing the head
   b. Installing replacement guides

10. Which statement is true about surface finish?
    a. Cast-iron surfaces should be smoother than aluminum surfaces.
    b. The rougher the surface, the higher the microinch finish measurement.
    c. The smoother the surface, the higher the microinch finish measurement.
    d. A cylinder head should be a lot smoother than a crankshaft journal.

Valve and Seat Service

OBJECTIVES

After studying Chapter 11, the reader will be able to

1. Discuss various engine valve types and materials.
2. Describe how to test valve springs.
3. Explain the purpose, function, and operation of valve rotators.
4. List the steps necessary to reface a valve.
5. Describe how to grind valve seats.
6. Discuss how to measure and correct installed height and valve stem height.

Valves need to be reconditioned more often than any other engine part.

INTAKE AND EXHAUST VALVES

Automotive engine valves are of a **poppet valve** design. The valve is opened by means of a valve train that is operated by a cam. The cam is timed to the piston position and crankshaft cycle. The valve is closed by one or more springs.

Typical valves are shown in Figure 11–1. Intake valves control the inlet of cool, low-pressure induction charges. Exhaust valves handle hot, high-pressure exhaust gases. This means that exhaust valves are exposed to more severe operating conditions. They are, therefore, made from much higher-quality materials than the intake valves. This makes them more expensive.

The guide is centered over the **valve seat** so that the **valve face** and seat make a gas-tight fit. The face

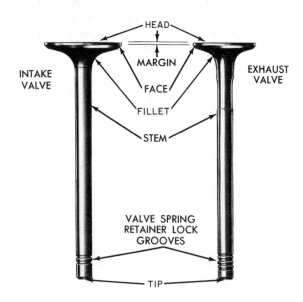

FIGURE 11–1 Identification of valve parts. (Courtesy of Chrysler Corporation)

and seat will have an angle of either 30 degrees or 45 degrees. These are the nominal angles. Actual service angles might be a degree or two different from these. Most engines use a nominal 45-degree valve and seat angle. A **valve spring** holds the valve against the seat. The valve **lock** (also called **keepers**) secures the spring **retainer** to the **stem** of the valve. For valve removal, it is necessary to compress the spring and remove the valve lock. Then the spring, valve seals, and valve can be removed from the head. A typical valve assembly is shown in Figures 11–2 and 11–3.

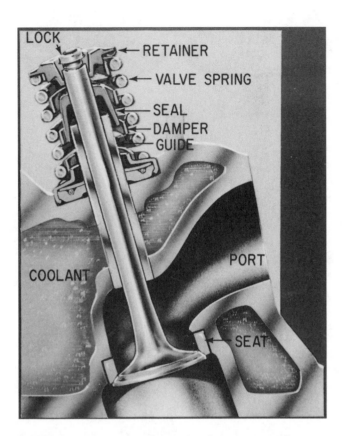

FIGURE 11–2 Identification of the parts of a typical valve assembly. (Courtesy of GMC)

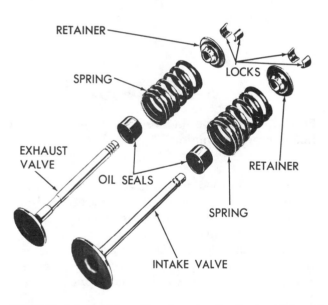

FIGURE 11–3 Identification and relationship of valve components. Note the different valve locks (keepers) used on the exhaust valve as compared to the intake valve. The oil seals shown are also called umbrella-type valve stem seals. (Courtesy of Chrysler Corporation)

■ **TECH TIP** ■

HOT ENGINE + COLD WEATHER = TROUBLE

Serious valve damage can occur if cold air reaches hot exhaust valves soon after the engine is turned off. An engine equipped with exhaust headers and/or straight-through mufflers can allow cold air a direct path to the hot exhaust valve. The exhaust valve can warp and/or crack as a result of rapid cooling. This can easily occur during cold, windy weather when the wind can blow cold outside air directly up the exhaust system. Using reverse-flow mufflers with tail pipes and a catalytic converter reduces the possibilities of this occurring.

VALVE SIZE RELATIONSHIPS

Extensive testing has shown that there is a normal relationship between the different dimensions of valves. Engines with cylinder bores that measure from 3 to 8 inches (80 to 200 millimeters) will have intake valves that measure approximately 45% of the bore size. The exhaust valve size is approximately 38% of the cylinder bore size. The intake valve must be larger than the exhaust valve to handle the same mass of gas. The larger intake valve controls low-velocity, low-density gases. The exhaust valve, on the other hand, controls high-velocity, high-pressure, denser gases. These gases can be handled by a smaller valve. Exhaust valve heads are, therefore, approximately 85% of the size of intake valve heads. For satisfactory operation, valve head diameter is nearly 115% of the valve port diameter. The valve must be large enough to close over the port. The extent to which the valve opens, called **valve lift**, is close to 25% of the valve diameter.

VALVE DESIGN

Poppet valve heads may be of various designs, from a **rigid valve** to an **elastic valve,** as shown in Figure 11–4. The rigid valve is strong, holds its shape, and conducts heat readily. It also causes less valve recession. Unfortunately, it is more likely to leak and burn than

FIGURE 11–4   Valve head types, from rigid (a) to elastic (d).

other valve head types. The elastic valve, on the other hand, is able to conform to valve seat shape. This allows it to seal easily, but it runs hot and the flexing to conform may cause it to break. A popular shape is one with a small cup in the top of the valve head. It offers a reasonable weight, good strength, and good heat transfer at a slight cost penalty. Elastic valve heads are more likely to be found on intake valves, and rigid, on exhaust valves.

VALVE MATERIALS

Alloys used in exhaust valve materials are largely of chromium for oxidation resistance, with small amounts of nickel, manganese, and nitrogen added. Heat-treating is used whenever it is necessary to produce special valve properties. Some exhaust valves are manufactured from two different materials when a one-piece design cannot meet the desired hardness and corrosion resistance specifications. The joint cannot be seen after valves have been used. The valve heads are made from special alloys that can operate at high temperatures, have physical strength, resist lead oxide corrosion, and have indentation resistance. These heads are welded to stems that have good wear resistance properties. Figure 11–5 shows an inertia welded valve before final machining. In severe applications, facing alloys such as stellite are welded to the valve face and valve tip. Stellite is an alloy of nickel, chromium, and tungsten and is nonmagnetic. The valve is aluminized where corrosion may be a problem. Aluminized valve facing reduces valve recession when unleaded gasoline is used. Aluminum oxide forms to separate the valve steel from the cast-iron seat to keep the face metal from sticking.

SODIUM-FILLED VALVES

Some heavy-duty applications use hollow stem exhaust valves that are partially filled with metallic sodium. An unfilled hollow valve stem is shown in

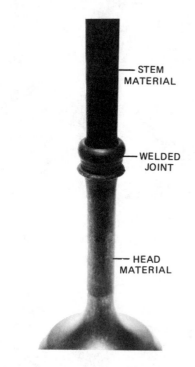

FIGURE 11–5   Inertia welded valve stem and head before machining.

Figure 11–6. The sodium in the valve becomes a liquid at operating temperatures. As it splashes back and forth in the valve stem, the sodium transfers heat from the valve head to the valve stem. The heat goes through the valve guide into the coolant. In general, a one-piece valve design using properly selected materials will provide satisfactory service for automotive engines.

VALVE SEATS

The valve face closes against a valve seat to seal the combustion chamber. The seat is generally formed as part of the cast-iron head of automotive engines. This is called an **integral seat.** The seats are usually induction hardened so that unleaded gasoline can be used.

FIGURE 11–6 Hollow valve stem. (Courtesy of Sealed Power Corporation)

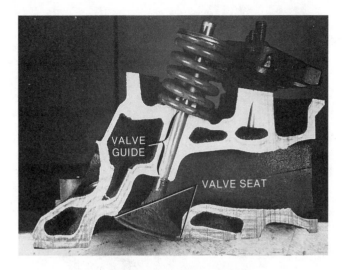

FIGURE 11–7 Sectional view of valve assembly showing integral valve seat and valve guide.

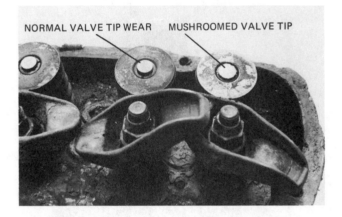

FIGURE 11–8 Mushroomed valve tip may indicate other valve train damage, such as excessive valve clearance (lash).

FIGURE 11–9 Badly burned exhaust valve.

This minimizes valve recession as the engine operates. Valve recession is the wearing away of the seat, so that the valve seats further into the head. Insert seats are used in applications for which corrosion and wear resistance are critical. Insert seats and guides are always required in aluminum heads. It should be noted that the exhaust valve seat runs as much as 180° F (100° C) *cooler* in aluminum heads than in cast-iron heads. Insert seats are also used as a salvage measure in the reconditioning of integral automotive engine valve seats that have been badly damaged. Typical integral valve seats and guides can be seen in Figure 11–7.

Valve seat distortion is a major cause of premature valve failure. Valve seat distortion may be temporary as the result of pressure and thermal stress or it may become permanent as the result of mechanical stress. Stress is a force put on a part that tries to change its shape.

VALVE INSPECTION

Careful inspection of the cylinder and valves can often reveal the root cause of failure. Excessive valve lash (clearance) can cause the top of the valve to be pounded until it becomes mushroomed as shown in Figure 11–8. Valve face burning (Figures 11–9 and 11–10) and valve face **guttering** (Figure 11–11) result from poor seating that allows the high-temperature

FIGURE 11–10   Valve face burning.

FIGURE 11–12   Typical intake valve seat wear. Also notice the excessive deposits on the valve. These deposits not only reduce the amount of air and fuel flow into the engine, but can also cause hesitation by absorbing fuel instead of allowing the fuel into the combustion chamber.

FIGURE 11–11   *Valve face guttering.*

FIGURE 11–13   Valve face peening.

and high-pressure combustion gases to leak between the valve and seat. Poor seating results from too small a valve lash, hard carbon deposits, valve stem deposits, excessive valve stem-to-guide clearances, or out-of-square valve guide and seat. A valve lash that is too small can result from improper valve lash adjustments on solid lifter engines. It can also result from misadjustments on a valve train using hydraulic lifters. The clearance will also be reduced as a result of valve head cupping or valve face and seat wear. Figure 11–12 shows typical intake valve and seat wear.

Hard carbon deposits are loosened from the combustion chamber. Sometimes, these flaking deposits stick between the valve face and seat to hold the valve

slightly off its seat. This reduces valve cooling through the seat and allows some of the combustion gases to escape. Continued pounding on hard carbon particles gives the valve face a **peened** appearance, pictured in Figure 11–13.

Fuel and oil on the hot valve will break down to become hard carbon and varnish deposits that build up on the valve stem. Heavy valve stem deposits are shown in Figure 11–14. These deposits cause the valve to stick in the guide so that the valve does not completely close on the seat and therefore cause the valve

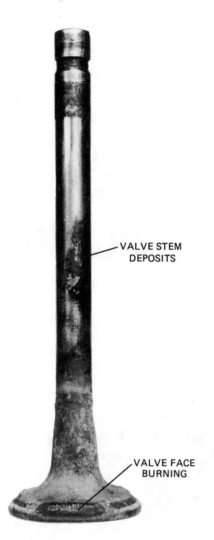

FIGURE 11–14 Valve stem with heavy deposits and valve face burning.

FIGURE 11–15 Intake valve with heavy deposits.

Excessive Temperatures

High valve temperature occurs when the valve does not seat properly; however, it can occur even when the valve is seating properly. Cooling system passages in the head may be partially blocked by faulty casting or by deposits built up from the coolant. A corroded head gasket will change the coolant flow. This can cause overheating when the coolant is allowed to flow to the wrong places. Extremely high temperatures are also produced by preignition and by detonation. These are forms of abnormal combustion. Both of these produce a very rapid increase in temperature that can cause uneven heating. The rapid increase in temperature will give a **thermal shock** to the valve. A thermal shock is a sudden change in temperature. The shock will often cause radial cracks in the valve. The cracks will allow the combustion gases to escape and gutter the valve face. A badly guttered valve face is shown in Figure 11–16. If the radial cracks intersect, a pie-shaped piece will break away from the valve head. A thermal shock can also result from rapid cycling of the engine from full throttle to closed throttle and back again. Valves with a hard metal facing have special problems. Excess heat causes the base metal to expand more than the hoop of the hard face metal. The hard face metal hoop is stressed until it cracks. The crack allows gases to gutter the base metal, as shown in Figure 11–17.

High engine speeds require high gas velocities. The high-velocity exhaust gases hit on the valve stem and tend to erode or wear away the metal mechanically. The gases are also corrosive, so the valve stem will tend to corrode. Corrosion removes the metal

face to burn. This is one of the most common causes of valve face burning.

If there is a large clearance between the valve stem and guide or faulty valve stem seals, too much oil will go down the stem. This will increase deposits, as shown on the intake valve in Figure 11–15. In addition, a large valve guide clearance will allow the valve to cock or lean sideways, especially with the effect of the rocker arm action. Continued cocking keeps the valve from seating properly and causes it to leak, burning the valve face.

Sometimes, the cylinder head will warp slightly warp as the head is tightened to the block deck during assembly. In other cases, heating and cooling will cause warpage. When head warpage causes valve guide and seat misalignment, the valve cannot seat properly and it will leak, burning the valve face.

FIGURE 11–16   Badly guttered valve face.

FIGURE 11–18   Necked valve stem.

FIGURE 11–17   Hoop stress cracks in a valve head.

FIGURE 11–19   Valve head broken from the stem.

chemically. The corrosion rate doubles for each 25° F (14° C) increase in temperature. Erosion and corrosion of the valve stem cause **necking** that weakens the stem and leads to breakage. Necking is shown in Figure 11–18.

Misaligned Valve Seats

When the valve-to-seat alignment is improper, the valve head must twist to seat each time the valve closes. If twisting or bending becomes excessive, it fatigues the stem, and the valve head will break from the stem. An example of this can be seen in Figure 11–19. The break appears as lines arching around a starting point. The head of the valve usually damages the piston when it gets trapped between the piston and the cylinder head.

High-Velocity Seating

High-velocity seating is indicated by excessive valve face wear, valve seat recession, and impact failure. It can be caused by excessive lash in mechanical lifters and by collapsed hydraulic lifters. Lash allows the valve to hit the seat without the effects of the cam ramp to ease the valve onto its seat. Excessive lash may also be caused by wear of parts, such as the cam, lifter base, pushrod ends, rocker arm pivot, and valve tip. Weak or broken valve springs allow the valves to float away from the cam lobes so that the valves are uncontrolled as they hit the seat. The normal tendency of hydraulic lifters is to pump up under valve float conditions, and this reduces valve impact damage.

Impact breakage may occur under the valve head or at the valve lock grooves. The break lines radiate from the starting point. Impact breakage may also cause the valve head to fall into the combustion cham-

FIGURE 11–20 Broken piston caused by a valve breaking from the stem.

FIGURE 11–21 Everything in the valve train has to be working correctly or an engine can be destroyed. The valve in this engine separated from the retainer at high engine speed, turned around in the cylinder, and punctured the piston.

ber. In most cases, it will ruin the piston before the engine can be stopped, as pictured in Figures 11–20 and 11–21.

High Mileage

Excessive wear of the valve stem (Figure 11–22), guide, face, and seat is the result of high mileage. The affected valves usually have a great buildup of deposits. The valves will, however, still be seating, and they will show no sign of cracking or burning.

When the valve stems do not have enough lubricant, they **scuff.** In scuffing, the valve stem temporar-

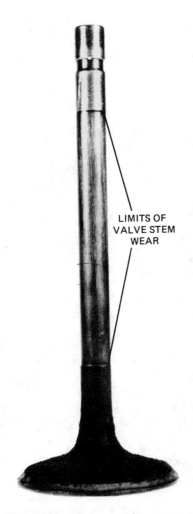

FIGURE 11–22 High-mileage valve stem wear.

ily welds to the guide when the valve is closed. The weld breaks as the valve is forced to open. Welded metal tears from the guide and sticks to the valve stem. An example of valve stem scuffing is shown in Figure 11–23. The metal knobs on the valve stem scratch the valve guide as it operates. This also scuffs the valve guide. In a short time, the valve will stick in the guide and not close. This will stop combustion in that cylinder. Both valve and valve guide will have to be replaced.

Often, valve tips become damaged. This damage can be seen before the valves are removed from the head. Some valve tip problems are caused by rapid rotation as the valve is being opened. This causes circles on the valve tip. Still other valves do not rotate at all. These valves wear in the direction of the rocker arm or finger follower movement. Examples of excessive valve tip wear can be seen in Figure 11–24.

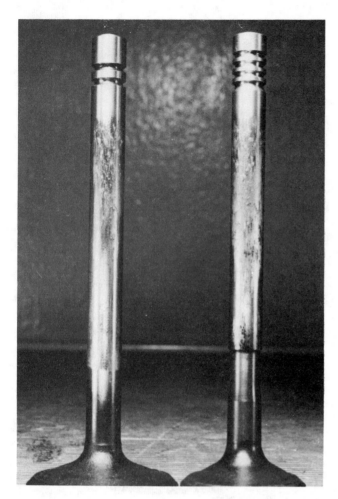

FIGURE 11–23   Valve stems scuffed as a result of loss of valve train lubrication.

FIGURE 11–24   Excessive valve tip wear.

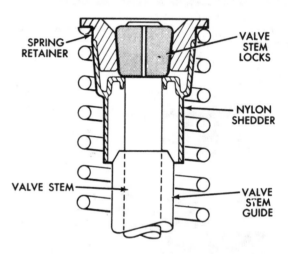

FIGURE 11–25   Parts of a valve lock and retainer assembly. (Courtesy of Cadillac Motor Car Division, GMC)

VALVE SPRINGS

A valve spring holds the valve against the seat when the valve is not being opened. One end of the valve spring is seated against the head. The other end of the spring is attached under compression to the valve stem through a valve spring retainer and a valve spring lock (keeper), as shown in Figure 11–25.

Valves usually have a single inexpensive valve spring. The springs are generally made of chromium vanadium alloy steel. When one spring cannot control the valve, other devices are added. Variable-rate springs add spring force when the valve is in its open position. This is accomplished by using closely spaced coils on the cylinder head end of the spring. The closely spaced coils also tend to dampen vibrations that may exist in an equally wound coil spring. The damper helps to reduce valve seat wear. Some valve springs use a flat coiled **damper** inside the spring. This eliminates spring surge and adds some valve spring tension.

The normal valve spring winds up as it is compressed. This causes a small but important turning motion as the valve closes on the seat. The turning motion helps to keep the wear even around the valve face. Figure 11–26 illustrates typical valve springs.

Multiple valve springs are used where large lifts are required and a single spring does not have enough strength to control the valve. Multiple valve springs generally have their coils wound in opposite directions. This is done to control valve spring surge and to prevent excessive valve rotation. **Valve spring surge** is the tendency of a valve spring to vibrate.

VALVE SPRING INSPECTION

Valve springs close the valves after they have been opened by the cam. They must close squarely to form a tight seal and to prevent valve stem and guide wear. It

FIGURE 11–26 Valve spring types (left to right): coil spring with equally spaced coils; spring with damper inside spring coil; closely spaced spring with a damper; taper wound coil spring.

FIGURE 11–28 Out-of-square valve spring. This spring should not be tested further, but should be replaced. A distorted valve spring exerts side loads on the valve, which often causes excessive valve guide wear.

FIGURE 11–27 Determining the squareness of a valve spring with a square on a flat surface. The spring should be replaced if more than ⅟₁₆ inch (1.6 millimeters) is measured between the top of the spring and the square.

is necessary, therefore, that the springs be square and have the proper amount of closing force. The valve springs are checked for squareness by rotating them on a flat surface with a square held against the side. They should be within ⅟₁₆ inch or 1.6 millimeters of being square. This is shown in Figure 11–27. Only the springs that are square should be checked to determine their compressed force. See Figure 11–28. Out-of-square springs will have to be replaced. The surge damper should be *removed* from the valve spring when the spring force is being checked. A valve spring scale is used to measure the valve spring force. One popular type, shown in Figure 11–29, measures the spring force directly. Another type uses a torque wrench on a lever system to measure the valve spring force. Valve springs are checked for the following:

1. Free height (without being compressed) (should be within ⅟₁₆ [0.060] inch)
2. Pressure with valve closed and height as per specifications
3. Pressure with valve open and height as per specifications

Most specifications allow for variations of plus or minus 10% from the published figures.

VALVE LOCKS

A valve lock is used on the end of the valve stem to retain the spring. Valve locks are also called valve keepers. The inside surface of the split lock uses a variety of grooves or beads. The design depends on the holding requirements. The outside of the split lock fits into a cone-shaped seat in the center of the valve spring retainer (see Figure 11–30).

One-piece valve spring retainers are forged from high-quality steel. They will hold their shape under the pounding they receive in operation.

VALVE ROTATORS

Some retainers have built-in devices called valve rotators. They cause the valve to rotate in a controlled manner as it is opened. The purposes and functions of valve rotators include the following:

FIGURE 11–29   One popular type of valve spring tester used to measure the compressed force of valve springs. Specifications usually include (1) free height (height without being compressed), (2) pressure at installed height with valve closed, and (3) pressure with valve open the maximum amount and height to specifications.

- Help prevent carbon buildup from forming
- Reduce hot spots on the valves by constantly turning them
- Help to even out the wear on the valve face and seat
- Improve valve guide lubrication

There are two types of valve rotators: free and positive.

- **Free rotators**—The rotators simply take the pressure off the valve to allow engine vibration to rotate the valve.
- **Positive rotators**—The opening of the valve forces the valve to rotate.

FIGURE 11–30   (a) Valve split lock types and (b) stem grooves.

One type of positive rotator uses small steel balls and slight ramps. Each ball moves down its ramp to turn the rotor sections as the valve opens. A second type uses a coil spring. The spring lies down as the valve opens. This action turns the rotator body in relation to the collar. Valve rotors are only used where it is

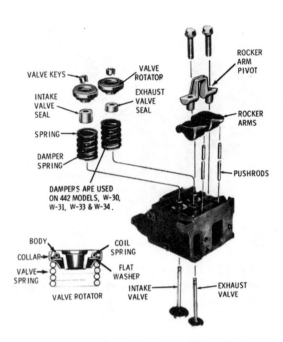

FIGURE 11–31   Parts of a valve assembly showing the location of the valve rotator. (Courtesy of Oldsmobile Division, GMC)

desirable to increase the valve service life because rotors cost more than plain retainers. See Figures 11–31 and 11–32.

VALVE RECONDITIONING PROCEDURE

Valve reconditioning is usually performed using the following sequence:

- *Step #1.* The valve stem is lightly ground and chamfered. This step helps to ensure that the valve will rest in the **collet** (holder of the valve stem during valve grinding) of the valve grinder correctly. This process is often called **truing** the value tip.
- *Step #2.* The face of the valve is ground using a valve grinder.
- *Step #3.* The valve seat is ground in the head. (The seat must be matched to the valve that will be used in that position.)
- *Step #4.* Installed height and valve stem height are checked and corrected as necessary.
- *Step #5.* After a thorough cleaning, the cylinder head should be assembled with new valve stem seals installed.

The rest of the chapter is devoted to valve face and seat reconditioning and cylinder head reassembly.

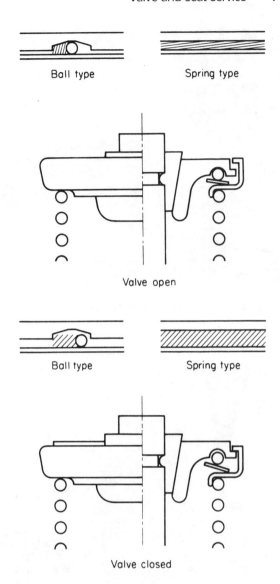

FIGURE 11–32   Types of valve rotator operation. Ball-type operation is on the left and spring-type operation is on the right.

VALVE FACE GRINDING

Each valve grinder operates somewhat differently. The operation manual that comes with the grinder should be followed for lubrication, adjustment, and specific operating procedures. The general procedures given in the following paragraphs apply to all valve grinding equipment.

■ **CAUTION:** Safety glasses should *always* be worn for valve and seat reconditioning work. During grinding operations, fine hot chips fly from the grinding stones. ■

FIGURE 11–33 Valve in a fixture to grind the valve tip.

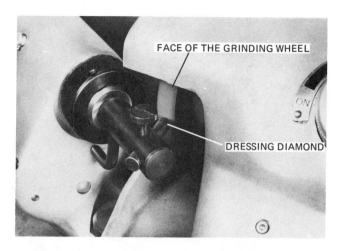

FIGURE 11–35 Dressing the face of the grinding wheel with a diamond dressing tool. This operation helps ensure a good-quality valve face finish.

FIGURE 11–34 Valve grinder set to the recommended angle to refinish a valve face. In this case, the angle is set to 44 degrees to provide a 1-degree interference angle between the valve face and the 45-degree valve seat angle.

FIGURE 11–36 Grinding the face of a valve. Note the use of cutting oil to lubricate and cool the grinding operation.

The face of the valve is ground on a **valve grinder.** Before starting with this, the tip of the valve should be lightly ground and chamfered. Many valve grinders use the end of the valve to center the valve while grinding. If the tip of the valve is not square with the stem, the face of the valve may be ground improperly. See Figure 11–33. After grinding the tip, set the grinder head at the **valve face angle** as specified by the vehicle manufacturer (Figure 11–34). The grinding stone is **dressed** with a special diamond tool to remove any roughness from the stone surface

(Figure 11–35). The valve stem is clamped in the work head as close to the fillet under the valve head as possible to prevent vibrations. The work head motor is turned on to rotate the valve. The wheel head motor is turned on to rotate the grinding wheel. The coolant flow is adjusted to flush the material away, but not so much that it splashes (Figure 11–36). The rotating grinding wheel is fed slowly to the rotating valve face. Light grinding is done as the valve is moved

(a)

(b)

FIGURE 11–37 (a) Finished valve face after grinding. Do not remove any more material than is necessary. (b) A valve that is bent. Notice how the grinding stone only removed material from about one-half of the valve face. This valve should be replaced.

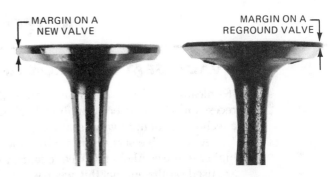

FIGURE 11–38 The difference in the margin on a new and a used valve head. The margin should be greater than 0.030 inch (0.8 millimeter) (about ½₂ inch or the thickness of an American dime). The thicker the margin is, the longer the valve will last.

FIGURE 11–39 Refacing a valve on a lathe using a special silicon carbide tool bit. The valve face is smoother than it would have been if the valve had been refaced with a stone.

back and forth across the grinding wheel face. The valve is never moved off the edge of the grinding wheel. It is ground only enough to clean the face (Figure 11–37). The margin of the exhaust valve should be over 0.030 inch (0.8 millimeter) when grinding is complete (Figure 11–38). To help visualize a 0.030-inch margin, note that this dimension is about ½₂ inch or the thickness of an American dime. Intake valves can usually perform satisfactorily with a margin less than 0.030 inch. Some vehicle manufacturers even allow intake valves to be used if they have at least a 0.005-inch margin. Always check the engine manufacturer's specifications for the cylinder being serviced. Aluminized valves will lose their corrosion resistance properties when ground. For satisfactory service, aluminized valves must be replaced if they require refacing.

Figure 11–39 shows the refacing of a valve using a lathe.

VALVE SEAT RECONDITIONING

The valve seats are reconditioned after the head has been resurfaced and the valve guides have been resized. The final valve seat width and position are checked with the valve that is to be used on the seat being reconditioned.

Valve seats will have a normal seat angle of either 45 degrees or 30 degrees. Narrow 45-degree valve seats will crush carbon deposits to prevent buildup of deposits on the seat. The valve will, therefore, close tightly on the seat. While the valve is closed on the seat, the valve heat will transfer to the seat and cylinder head. The 30-degree valve seat is more likely to burn

■ TECH TIP ■

VALVE SEAT RECESSION AND ENGINE PERFORMANCE

If unleaded fuel is used in an engine without hardened valve seats, valve seat recession is likely to occur in time. Without removing the cylinder heads, how can a technician identify valve seat recession?

As the valve seat wears up into the cylinder head, the valve itself also seats higher in the head. As this wear occurs, the valve lash *decreases*. If hydraulic lifters are used on the engine, this wear will go undetected until the reduction in valve clearance finally removes all clearance (bottoms out) in the lifter. When this occurs, the valve does not seat fully, and compression, power, and fuel economy are drastically reduced. With the valve not closing completely, the valve cannot get rid of its heat and will burn or begin to melt. If the valve burns, the engine will miss and not idle smoothly.

If solid lifters are used on the engine, the decrease in valve clearance will first show up as a rough idle only when the engine is hot. As the valve seat recedes farther into the head, low power, rough idle, poor performance, and lower fuel economy will be noticed sooner than they would be if the engine were equipped with hydraulic lifters.

To summarize, refer to the following symptoms as valve seat recession occurs.

1. Valve lash (clearance) decreases (valves are *not* noisy).
2. The engine idles roughly when hot as a result of reduced valve clearance.
3. Missing occurs, and the engine exhibits low power and poor fuel economy, along with a rough idle, as the valve seat recedes farther into the head.
4. As valves burn, the engine continues to run poorly, the symptoms include difficulty in starting (hot and cold engine), backfiring, and low engine power.

HINT: *If valve lash is adjustable, valve burning can be prevented by adjusting the valve lash regularly. Remember, as the seat recedes, the valve itself recedes, which decreases the valve clearance. Many technicians do not think to adjust valves unless they are noisy. If, during the valve adjustment procedure, a* decrease *in valve lash is noticed, then valve seat recession could be occurring.*

than a 45-degree seat because some deposits can build up to keep the valve from seating properly. The 30-degree valve seat will, however, allow more gas flow than a 45-degree valve seat when both are opened to the same amount of lift. See Figure 11–40. This is especially true with valve lifts of less than ¼ inch (6 millimeters). The 30-degree valve seat is also less likely to have valve seat recession than is a 45-degree seat. Generally, when 30-degree valve seats are used, they are used on the cooler-operating intake valves rather than on hot exhaust valves.

The valve seats are only resurfaced enough to remove all pits and grooves and to correct any seat runout. As metal is removed from the seat, the seat is lowered into the head (Figure 11–41). This causes the valve to be located farther into the head when it is closed on the seat. The result of this is that the valve tip extends out farther from the valve guide. The valve being low in the head also tends to restrict the amount of valve opening. This will reduce the flow of gases through the opened valve. The reduced flow of gases, in turn, will reduce the maximum power the engine can produce.

Ideally, the valve face and valve seat should have exactly the same angle. This is impossible, especially on exhaust valves, because the valve head becomes much hotter than the seat and so the valve expands more than the seat. This expansion causes the hot valve to contact the seat in a different place on the valve than it did when it was cold.

FIGURE 11–40 Relationship of the valve seating angles to the opening size with same amount of valve lift. Note that the 30-degree valve angle results in more flow past the valve than is seen with a 45-degree valve.

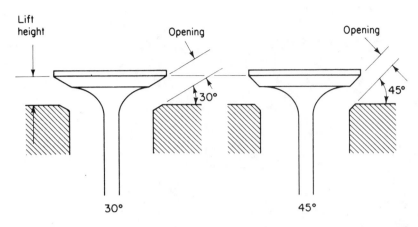

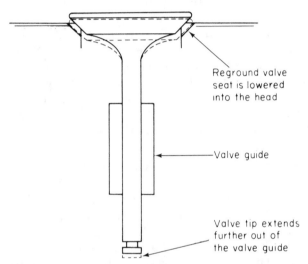

FIGURE 11–41 The valve seat is lowered into the cylinder head when ground. This lets the valve tip extend farther from the valve guide toward the rocker arm side of the cylinder head.

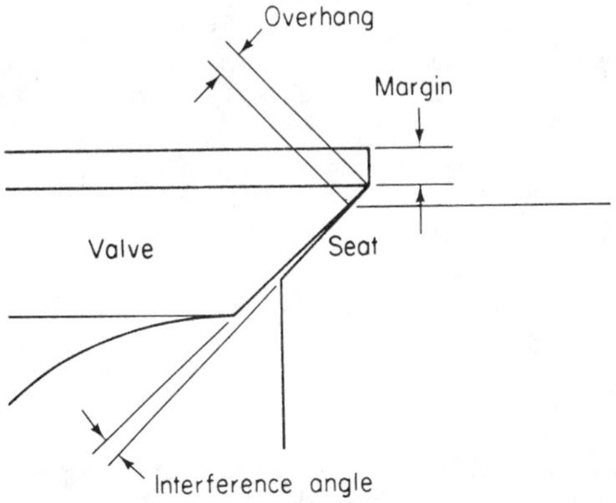

As a result of its shape, the valve does not expand evenly when heated. This uneven expansion also affects the way in which the hot valve contacts the seat. In valve and valve seat reconditioning, the valve is often ground with a face angle 1 degree less than the seat angle to compensate for the change in hot seating. This is illustrated in Figure 11–42. The angle between the valve face and seat is called an **interference angle.** It makes a positive seal at the combustion chamber edge of the seat when the engine is first started after a valve job. As the engine operates, the valve will peen itself on the seat. In a short time, it will make a matched seal. After a few thousand miles, the valve will have formed its own seat, as pictured in Figure 11–43.

The interference angle has another benefit. The valve and seat are reconditioned with different machines. Each machine must have its angle set before it is used for reconditioning. It is nearly impossible to

FIGURE 11–42 An interference angle gives the valve a tight-line seal at the combustion chamber edge of the seat.

set the exact same angles on both valve and seat reconditioning machines. Making an interference angle will ensure that any slight angle difference favors a tight seal at the combustion chamber edge of the valve seat when the valve servicing has been completed.

As the valve seats are resurfaced, their widths increase. The resurfaced seats must be narrowed to make the seat width correct and to position the seat properly on the valve face. The normal automotive seat is from ¹⁄₁₆ to ³⁄₃₂ inch (1.5 to 2.5 millimeters) wide. There should be at least ¹⁄₃₂ inch (0.8 millimeter) of the ground valve face extending above the seat. This is called **overhang.** The fit of a typical reconditioned valve and seat is shown in Figure 11–44. Some manufacturers recommend having the valve seat contact the middle of the valve face. In all cases, the valve seat width and the contact with the valve face should comply with the manufacturer's specifications.

For many years, most valve seats have been reconditioned with grinding wheels. Valve seat cutters are gradually becoming popular for reconditioning seats. The cutters will rapidly produce a good commercial-quality valve seat. See Figures 11–45 and 11–46.

FIGURE 11–43 Typical valve-to-seat fit after engine use.

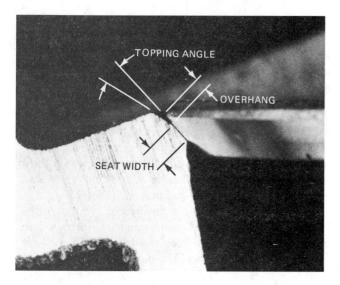

FIGURE 11–44 Fit of a typical reconditioned valve and seat.

VALVE GUIDE PILOTS

Valve seat reconditioning equipment uses a pilot in the valve guide to align the stone holder or cutter. Two types of pilots are used: tapered and expandable. Examples of these are pictured in Figure 11–47. **Tapered pilots** locate themselves in the least worn section of the guide. They are made in standard sizes and in oversize increments of

0.001 inch, usually up to 0.004 inch oversize. The largest pilot that will fit into the guide is used for valve seat reconditioning. This type of pilot restores the seat to be as close to the original position as possible when used with worn valve guides.

Two types of **expandable pilots** are used with seating equipment. One type expands in the center of the guide to fit like a tapered pilot. Another expands to contact the ends of the guide where there has been the greatest wear. The valve itself will align in the same way as the pilot.

NOTE: If the guide is not reconditioned, the valve will match the seat when an expandable pilot is used. ____

The pilot and guide should be thoroughly cleaned. A guide cleaner like the one shown in Figures 11–48 and 11–49 that is rotated by a drill motor does a good job of cleaning the guide. The pilot is placed in the guide to act as an aligned support or pilot for the seat reconditioning tools. An expandable pilot is shown in a cutaway valve guide in Figure 11–50.

VALVE SEAT GRINDING STONES

Three basic types of grinding stones are used. All are used dry. A **roughing stone** is used to rapidly remove large amounts of seat metal. This would be necessary on a badly pitted seat or when installing new valve seat inserts. The roughing stone is sometimes called a seat **forming stone**. After the seat forming stone is used, a **finishing stone** is used to put the proper finish on the seat. The finishing stone is also used to recondition cast-iron seats that are only slightly worn. **Hard seat stones** are used on hard stellite exhaust seat inserts.

NOTE: Stellite is a nonmagnetic hard alloy used for valve seats in heavy-duty applications. _____

The stone diameter and face angle must be correct. See Figure 11–51. The diameter of the stone must be larger than the valve head, but it must be small enough that it does not contact the edge of the combustion chamber. An oversize grinding stone is shown in Figure 11–52. The angle of the grinding surface of the stone must be correct for the seat. When an interference angle is used with reground valves, it is common practice to use a seat with the standard seat angle. The interference angle is ground on the valve face. In some cases, such as with an aluminized valve, the valve has the standard angle and the seat is ground to give the interference angle. The required seat angle must be determined *before* the seat grinding stone is dressed.

FIGURE 11–45 Seat cutter on the left and valve seat grinding stone on the right.

FIGURE 11–46 Seat cutter. <u>Never</u> rotate a seat cutter counterclockwise! The replaceable cutters will last a long time if treated with care, including avoiding excessive force and maintaining proper operating direction.

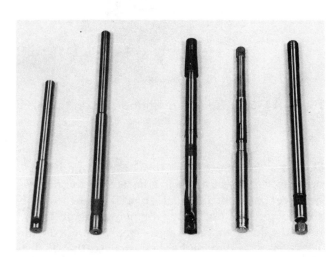

FIGURE 11–47 The two pilots on the left are of a solid tapered type. The three pilots on the right are adjustable (expandable) types.

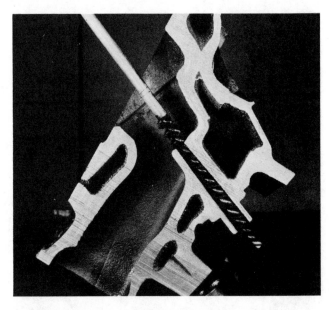

FIGURE 11–48 Sectioned head showing how a brush valve guide cleaner is used.

FIGURE 11–49 Using a valve guide brush with an electric drill. This cleaning of the valve guides is very important for proper valve seat reconditioning.

197

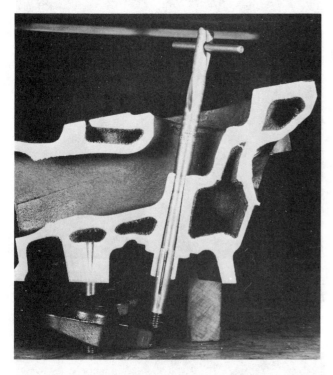

FIGURE 11–50   Expandable pilot shown in the valve guide of a sectioned head to illustrate how the pilot fits.

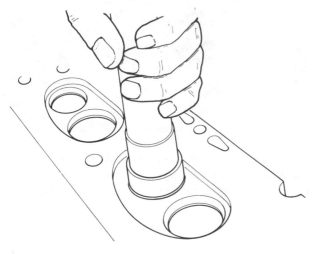

FIGURE 11–51   Properly fitting valve seat grinding stone.

DRESSING THE GRINDING STONE

The selected grinding stone is installed on the stone holder. A drop of oil is placed on the spindle of the dressing fixture, and the assembly is placed on the spindle. The dressing tool diamond (Figure 11–53) is

FIGURE 11–52   Valve seat grinding stone that is too large to use.

DIAMOND

HOLDER

FIGURE 11–53   Tip of a diamond dressing tool.

adjusted so that it extends ⅜ inch or less from its support. The valve seat angle is adjusted on the fixture. The driver for the seating tool is placed in the top of the stone holder. This assembly is shown in Figure 11–54. The holder and grinding stone assembly is rotated with the driver. The diamond is adjusted so that it just touches the stone face. The diamond dressing tool is moved slowly across the face of the spinning stone, taking a very light cut. Dressing the stone in this way will give it a clean, sharp cutting surface. It is necessary to redress the stone each time a stone is placed on a

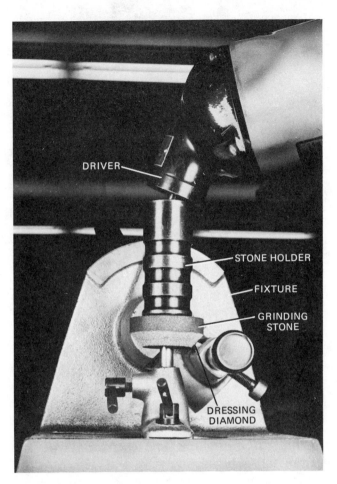

FIGURE 11–54 Typical assembly for dressing a valve seat grinding stone.

FIGURE 11–55 Dressing a valve seat grinding stone. Notice the grinding stone material being removed by the diamond-tip dressing tool.

and smooth across the entire surface, with no pits or roughness remaining (Figure 11–57).

Some of the induction hardness from the exhaust valve seat will sometimes extend over into the intake seat. It may be necessary to apply a slight pressure on the driver toward the hardened spot to form a concentric seat. The seat is checked with a dial gauge to make sure that it is concentric within 0.002 inch (0.05 millimeter) before the seat is finished (Figure 11–58).

NOTE: The dial gauge measurement of the valve seat is very important. The maximum acceptable variation is 0.002 inch. This reading gives the **total indicator runout (TIR)** of the valve seat.

Any remaining valve seats of the same size are completed before the stone is removed from the holder.

NARROWING THE VALVE SEAT

The valve seat becomes wider as it is ground. It is therefore necessary to narrow the seat so that it will contact the valve properly. The seat is **topped** with a grinding stone dressed to 15 degrees less than the seat angle. Topping lowers the top edge of the seat. The amount of topping required can best be checked by measuring the maximum valve face diameter using dividers (Figure 11–59). The dividers are then adjusted to a setting

holder, at the beginning of each valve job, and any time the stone is not cutting smoothly and cleanly while grinding valve seats. See Figure 11–55.

VALVE SEAT GRINDING

It is a good practice to clean each valve seat before grinding. This keeps the soil from filling the grinding stone. The pilot is then placed in the valve guide. A drop of oil is placed on the end of the pilot to lubricate the holder. The holder, with the dressed grinding stone, is placed over the pilot. The driver should be supported so that no driver weight is on the holder. This allows the stone abrasive and the metal chips to fly out from between the stone and seat to give fast, smooth grinding. Grinding is done in short bursts, allowing the seating stone to rotate for approximately ten turns. See Figure 11–56. The holder and stone should be lifted from the seat between each grinding burst to check the condition of the seat. The finished seat should be bright

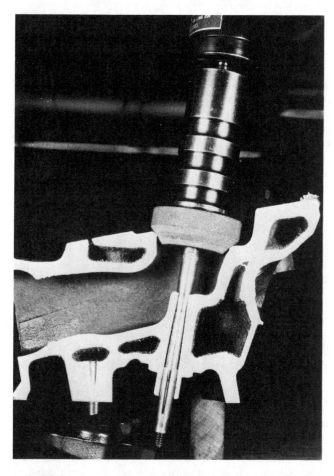

FIGURE 11–56 Typical setup for grinding a valve seat shown on a cutaway head.

FIGURE 11–58 Typical dial indicator type of micrometer for measuring valve seat concentricity.

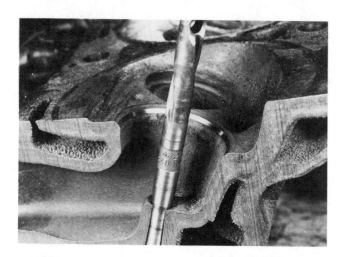

FIGURE 11–57 Finished valve seat shown on a cutaway head.

FIGURE 11–59 Measuring the maximum valve face diameter with dividers.

FIGURE 11–60 *Checking the maximum valve seat diameter with the dividers adjusted to be ¹⁄₁₆ inch less than the maximum valve face diameter.*

FIGURE 11–61 *Measuring the valve seat width.*

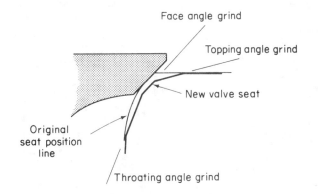

FIGURE 11–62 *Throating and topping angles used to adjust the new valve seat width and contact location on the valve face. Unless otherwise specified, the contact width should be ¹⁄₁₆ inch for intake valves and ³⁄₃₂ inch for exhaust valves.*

¹⁄₁₆ inch smaller to give the minimum valve face overhang. The seat is checked with the dividers (Figure 11–60), then topped with short grinding bursts, as required, to equal the diameter set on the dividers. The seat width is then measured (Figure 11–61). If it is too wide, the seat must be **throated** with a stone with a 60-degree angle. This removes metal from the port side of the seat, raising the lower edge of the seat. Throating is done with short grinding bursts until the correct seat width is achieved. Throating and topping angles are illustrated in Figure 11–62. Generally accepted seat widths are as follows:

- For intake valves: ¹⁄₁₆ inch or 0.0625 inch (about the thickness of a nickel) (1.5 millimeters)
- For exhaust valves: ³⁄₃₂ inch or 0.0938 inch (about the thickness of a dime and a nickel together) (2.4 millimeters)

The completed seat must be checked with the valve that is to be used on the seat. This can be done by marking across the valve face at four or five places with a felt-tip marker. The valve is then inserted in the guide so that the valve face contacts the seat. The valve is rotated 20 to 30 degrees and then removed. The location of the seat contact on the valve is observed where the felt-tip marking has been rubbed off from the valve. Valve seating can be seen in Figures 11–63 and 11–64. Valve seat grinding is complete when each of the valve seats has been properly ground, topped, and throated.

To summarize:

- Using a 30-degree topping stone (for a 45-degree seat) *lowers* the upper outer edge and narrows the seat.
- Using a 60-degree throating stone *raises* the lower inner edge and narrows the seat.
- Using a 45-degree stone *widens* the seat.

VALVE SEAT CUTTERS

Some automotive service technicians prefer to use valve seat cutters rather than valve seat grinders. See Figure 11–65. The valve seats can be reconditioned to commercial standards in much less time when using the cutters rather than the grinders. A number of cutting blades are secured at the correct seat angle in the cutting head of this valve seat reconditioning tool. The cutter angle usually includes the interference angle so that new valves with standard valve face angles can be used without grinding the new valve face. The cutters do not require dressing as stones do. The cutting head assembly is placed on a pilot in the same way that the grinding stone holder is used. The cutter is rotated by hand or by using a special speed reduction motor. Only metal chips are produced. The finished seat is checked for concentricity and fit against the valve face using the felt-tip marker method previously described.

FIGURE 11–63 On this cutaway head, the location of the valve seat is shown where the ink from the felt-tip pen has transferred from the seat to the valve face. Prussian blue can also be used instead of a felt-tip marker.

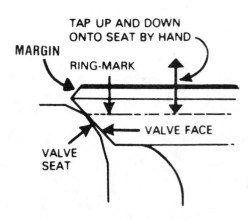

FIGURE 11–64 Relationship of a valve seat and face. (Courtesy of Neway)

FIGURE 11–65 Using a valve seat cutter to cut a three-angle seat. Some seat cutters can cut all three angles at the same time. (Courtesy of Neway)

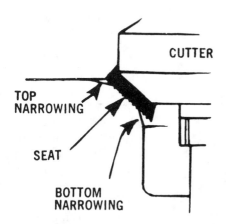

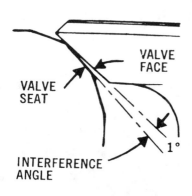

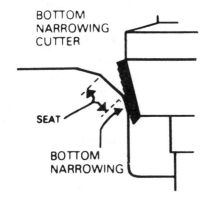

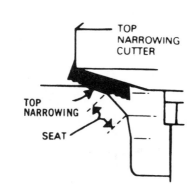

FIGURE 11–66 Testing for leakage past the valves by injecting compressed air into the combustion chamber through the spark plug hole. To prevent leakage at the head gasket surface, the cylinder head is placed on a foam rubber pad.

VALVE SEAT TESTING

After the valves have been refaced and the guides and valve seats have been resurfaced, the valves should be inspected for proper sealing and to make certain that the valve seat is concentric with the valve face. Several methods that are often used to check valve face-to-seat concentricity and valve seating include the following:

1. Vacuum testing can be done by applying vacuum to the intake and/or exhaust port using a tight rubber seal and a vacuum pump. A good valve face-to-seat seal is indicated by the maintaining of at least 28 inches Hg of vacuum. This method also tests for leakage around the valve guides. Put some engine oil around the guides; if vacuum increases, valve guides may have excessive clearance.
2. The ports or chamber can be filled with mineral spirits or some other suitable fluid. A good seal should not leak fluid for at least 45 seconds.
3. Valve seating can be checked by applying air pressure to the combustion chamber and checking for air leakage past the valve seat. See Figure 11–66.

VALVE SEAT REPLACEMENT

Valve seats need to be replaced if they are cracked or if they are burned or eroded too much to be reseated. A badly eroded valve seat is shown in Figure 11–67. It may not be possible to determine whether a valve seat needs to be replaced before an attempt is made to recondition the valve seat. Valve seat replacement is accomplished by using a pilot in the valve guide. This means that the valve guide must be reconditioned

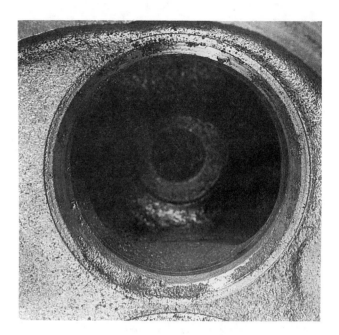

FIGURE 11–67   Badly eroded valve seat.

■ TECH TIP ■

THE MIG WELDER SEAT REMOVAL TRICK

A quick and easy method to remove insert valve seats is to use a microwire inert gas (MIG) welder. After the valve has been removed, use the MIG welder and lay a welding bead around the seat area of the insert. As the weld cools, it shrinks and allows the insert to be easily removed from the cylinder head.

before the seat can be replaced. Damaged **insert valve seats** are removed and the old seat counter bore is cleaned up to accept a new oversize seat insert. Damaged integral valve seats must be counter bored to make a place for the new insert seat.

The old insert seat is removed by one of several methods. A small **pry bar** can be used to snap the seat from the counter bore. It is sometimes easier to do this if the old seat is drilled to weaken it. Be careful not to drill into the head material. Sometimes, an expandable hook-type puller is used to remove the seat insert. See Tech Tip "The MIG welder seat removal trick." The seat counter bore must be cleaned before the new, oversize seat is installed. The replacement inserts have a 0.002- to 0.003-inch (0.05- to 0.07-millimeter) interference fit in the counter bore. The counter bores are cleaned and properly sized, using the same equipment described in the following paragraph for installing replacement seats in place of faulty integral valve seats.

Cracked or badly burned integral valve seats can often be replaced to salvage the head. All head cracks are repaired *before* the old integral seat is removed. The replacement seat is selected first. It must have the correct inside and outside diameters and it must have the correct thickness. Manufacturers of replacement valve seats supply tables that specify the proper seat insert to be used. If an insert is being replaced, the new insert must be of the same type of material as the original insert, or better. Insert exhaust valve seats operate at temperatures that are 100° to 150° F (56° to 83° C) hotter than those of integral seats up to 900° F (480° C). Upgraded valve and valve seat materials are required to give the same service life as that of the original seats. Removable valve seats are available in **cast iron, stainless steel, nickel cobalt,** or **powdered metal (PM).**

A counter bore cutting tool is selected that will cut the correct diameter for the outside of the insert. See the chart in Figure 11–70(b) for the recommended interference fit for cast iron (the diameter of the bore is smaller than the outside diameter of the seat insert). The cutting tool is positioned securely in the tool holder so that it will cut the counter bore at the correct diameter. The tool holder is attached to the size of pilot that fits the valve guide. The tool holder feed mechanism is screwed together so that it has enough threads to properly feed the cutter into the head. This assembly is placed in the valve guide so that the cutting tool rests on the seat that is to be removed. The supporting fixture, with the swivel head loosened, is placed over the tool holder. It is clamped to the cylinder head in a way that will put no loads on the tool holder. The fixture swivel is then clamped in place.

The new insert is placed between the support fixture and the stop ring. The stop ring is adjusted against the new insert so that cutting will stop when the counter bore reaches the depth of the new insert. See Figure 11–68. The boring tool is turned by hand or with a reduction gear motor drive. It cuts until the stop ring reaches the fixture. See Figure 11–69. The support fixture and the tool holder are removed. The pilot and the correct size of adapter are placed on the driving tool. Ideally, the seats should be cooled with dry ice to cause them to shrink. Each insert should be left in the dry ice until it is to be installed. This will allow it to be installed with little chance of metal being sheared from the counter bore. Sheared chips could become jammed under the insert, keeping it from seating properly. The chilled seat is placed on the counter bore. The driver with a pilot is then quickly placed in the valve guide so that the seat will be driven squarely into the counter bore. The driver is hit with a heavy hammer to seat the

FIGURE 11–68 *Adjusting the cutting tool stop ring with the new valve insert as a guide.*

FIGURE 11–69 *Seat cutting tool boring out the old eroded valve seat.*

FIGURE 11–70 (a) Seating the new chilled insert in the counter bore by hitting the driver with a heavy hammer. (b) Interference fit for valve inserts (hard cast or wrought inserts).

(a)

(b)

Outside diameter (in.)	Insert depth (in.)	Interference fit (in.)
0 – 1	$0 - \frac{1}{4}$	0.001 – 0.003
1 – 2	$\frac{1}{4} - \frac{3}{8}$	0.002 – 0.004
2 – 3	$\frac{3}{8} - \frac{9}{16}$	0.003 – 0.005
3 – 4	$\frac{9}{16} - 1$	0.004 – 0.006

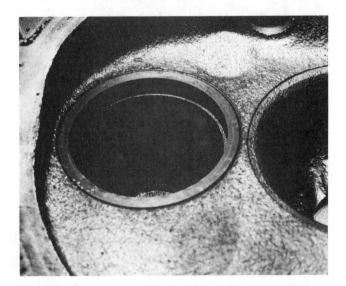

FIGURE 11–71 *Fully installed valve seat insert.*

insert, as shown in Figure 11–70. Heavy blows are used to start the insert, and lighter blows are used as the seat reaches the bottom of the counter bore. It serves no purpose to hit the driver after the insert is seated in the

bottom of the counter bore. The installed valve seat insert is peened in place by running a peening tool around the metal on the outside of the seat. The peened metal is slightly displaced over the edge of the insert to help hold it in place. A fully installed seat insert is shown in Figure 11–71. Seats are formed on the replacement inserts using the same procedures described for reconditioning valve seats.

VALVE STEM HEIGHT

Valve stem height is a different measurement from installed height. See Figure 11–72. Valve stem height is important to maintain for all engines, but especially for overhead camshaft engines. When the valve seat and the valve face are ground, the valve stem extends deeper into the combustion chamber and extends higher or further into the cylinder head.

The valve is put in the head, and the length of the tip is measured. The tip is ground to shorten the valve stem length to compensate for the valve face and seat grinding. The valve will not close if the valve tip extends too far from the valve guide on engines that have hydraulic lifters and nonadjustable rocker arms.

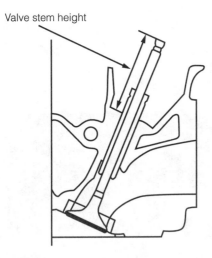

FIGURE 11–72 *Valve stem height is measured from the spring seat to the tip of the valve after the valve seat and valve face have been refinished. If the valve stem height is too high, up to 0.020 inch can be ground from the tips of most valves.*

■ TECH TIP ■

USE THE RECOMMENDED SPECIFICATIONS

A technician replaced valve seat inserts in an aluminum cylinder head. The *factory* specification called for a 0.002-inch interference fit (the insert should be 0.002 inch larger in diameter than the seat pocket in the cylinder head). Shortly after the engine was started, the seat fell out, ruining the engine.

The technician should have used the interference fit specification supplied with the replacement seat insert. Interference fit specifications depend on the type of material used to make the insert. Some inserts for aluminum heads require as much as 0.007-inch interference fit. Always refer to the specification from the manufacturer of the valve inserts when replacing valve seats in aluminum cylinder heads.

If the valve is too long, the tip may be ground by as much as 0.020 inch (0.50 millimeter) to reduce its length. If more grinding is required, the valve must be replaced. If it is too short, the valve face or seat may be reground, within limits, to allow the valve to seat deeper. Where excessive valve face and seat grinding has been done, shims can be placed under the rocker shaft on some engines as a repair to provide correct

FIGURE 11–73 *Checking installed height with a steel rule. Measure from spring seat surface of cylinder head to bottom surface of valve spring retainer.*

hydraulic lifter plunger centering. These shims must have the required lubrication holes to allow oil to enter the shaft.

ASSEMBLING THE CYLINDER HEAD

The head, valves, and valve springs should be rinsed with a petroleum-based cleaning fluid and then dried with compressed air. Thoroughly clean the valve guides by flushing with engine oil and wiping. Any remaining grinding grit could destroy a new engine after only a few hours of operation.

CHECKING INSTALLED HEIGHT

When the valves and/or valve seats have been machined, the valve projects farther than before on the rocker arm side of the head. (The valve face is slightly recessed into the combustion chamber side of the head.) The valve spring tension is, therefore, reduced because the spring is not as compressed as it was originally. To restore original valve spring tension, special valve spring spacers or inserts are installed under the valve springs. These shims are usually called **valve spring inserts** (VSI). Valve spring inserts are generally available in three different thicknesses:

1. 0.015 inch (0.38 millimeter)—For balancing valve spring pressure
2. 0.030 inch (0.75 millimeter)—Generally used for new springs on cylinder heads that have had the valve seats ground and valves refaced
3. 0.060 inch (1.5 millimeters)—Necessary to bring assembled height to specifications; these thicker inserts may be required if the seats have been resurfaced more than one time

Step #1. To determine the exact thickness of insert to install, measure the valve spring height (as installed in the head). See Figure 11–73.

Step #2. If the installed height is greater than specifications, select the insert (shim) that brings the installed height to within specifications. See Figure 11–74.

VALVE STEM SEALS

Leakage past the valve guides is a major oil consumption problem in any overhead valve (or overhead cam) engine. A high vacuum exists in the intake port, as shown in Figure 11–75. Most engine manufacturers also use valve stem seals on the exhaust valve, because a weak vacuum in the exhaust port area can draw oil into the exhaust stream, as illustrated in Figure 11–76.

Valve stem seals are used on overhead valve engines to control the amount of oil used to lubricate the valve stem as it moves in the guide. The stem and guide will scuff if they do not have enough oil. Too much oil will cause excessive oil consumption and will cause heavy carbon deposits to build up on the spark plug nose and on the fillet of the valves.

Types of Valve Stem Seals

Two basic types of valve stem seals are used. The **umbrella valve stem seal** holds tightly on the valve stem and moves up and down with the valve. Any oil that spills off the rocker arms is deflected out over the valve guide, much as water is deflected over an umbrella (Figure 11–77). As a result, umbrella valve stem seals are often called **deflector valve stem seals.**

Positive valve stem seals hold tightly around the valve guide, and the valve stem moves through the

(a)

(b)

FIGURE 11–74 (a) Valve spring inserts (VSI) (also called shims) are installed between the cylinder head and valve spring to restore the valve to proper installed height. (b) The serrations of the valve spring insert should face toward the cylinder head. The purpose of the serrations is to allow air to flow between the insert and the head to help keep the spring cooler.

seal. The seal wipes the excess oil from the valve stem (Figure 11–78). The Chevrolet **O-ring type of valve stem seal** keeps oil from leaking between the valve stem and valve spring retainer. The oil is deflected over the retainer and shield (Figure 11–79). The assembly controls oil like an umbrella-type oil seal. Both types of valve stem seal allow only the correct amount of oil to reach the valve guide to lubricate the valve stem. The rest of the oil flows back to the oil pan.

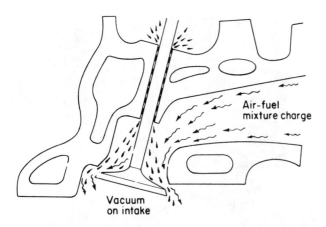

FIGURE 11–75 Engine vacuum can draw oil past the valve guides and into the combustion chamber. The use of valve stem seals limits the amount of oil that is drawn into the engine. If the seals are defective, excessive blue (oil) smoke is most often observed during engine start-up.

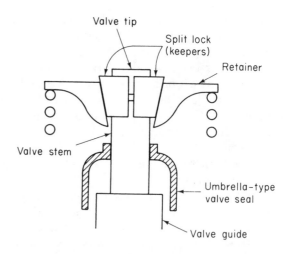

FIGURE 11–77 Location of umbrella-type valve stem oil seal. Note that the seal fits tightly on the valve stem and just covers the top of the valve guide.

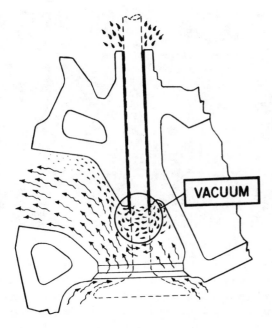

FIGURE 11–76 Engine oil can also be drawn past the exhaust valve guide because of a small vacuum created by the flow of exhaust gases. Any oil drawn past the guide would simply be forced out through the exhaust system and not enter the engine. Some engine manufacturers do not use valve stem seals on the exhaust valves. (Courtesy of Dana Corporation)

Valve Seal Materials

Valve stem seals are made from many different types of materials. They may be made from nylon or Teflon, but most valve stem seals are made from synthetic rubber. Three types of synthetic rubber are in common use:

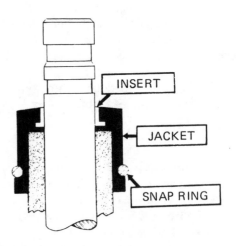

FIGURE 11–78 Positive-type valve stem oil seal. (Courtesy of Dana Corporation)

Nitrile (Nitril), polyacrylate, and Viton. Nitrile is the oldest valve stem seal material. It has a low cost and a low useful temperature. Engine temperatures have increased with increased emission controls and improved efficiencies. This made it necessary to use premium polyacrylate, even with its higher cost. In many cases, it is being retrofit to the older engines because it will last much longer than Nitrile. Diesel engines and engines used for racing, heavy trucks, and trailer towing, along with turbocharging, operate at still higher temperatures. These engines may require expensive Viton valve stem seals that operate at higher temperatures. See Figure 11–80.

It is interesting to note that an automotive service technician cannot tell the difference between these synthetic rubber valve stem seals if they have come

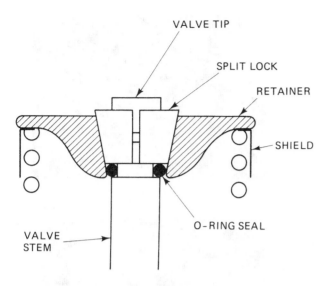

FIGURE 11–79 Chevrolet O-ring type of valve stem seal.

FIGURE 11–81 *The gaps between the halves of split locks (keepers) are necessary to ensure that the locks are properly seated in the grooves of the valve stem.*

FIGURE 11–80 *Poor-quality umbrella-type valve stem seal after several months of use. Note how heat has softened this seal and destroyed its sealing ability.*

out of the same mold for the same engine. Often suppliers that package gasket sets for sale at a low price will include low-temperature Nitrile, even when the engine needs higher-temperature polyacrylate. The technician assumes that the seals are made of the correct material. The seals fail soon after the engine is put back in operation. Your best chance of getting the correct valve stem seal material for an engine is to purchase gaskets and seals packaged by a major brand gasket company.

■ TECH TIP ■

DON'T FORGET TO INSPECT THE KEEPERS!

Valve locks or keepers are designed to retain the valve stem or keep it attached to the valve spring retainer under all operating conditions. The taper fit exerts the holding force. Before assembling the valves in the cylinder heads, place the split locks (keepers) in the groove(s) of the valve stem. There should be a slight gap between the keepers. If the keepers touch, they are not making full contact with the groove(s) of the valve stem. This could cause the keepers to release their grip on the valve at high engine speeds.

Using new valve keepers (split locks) is recommended, and every one should be inspected! Manufacturing flaws can create dimensions that are not to specifications, and a valve dropping at high engine speeds can result in destruction of the entire engine. See Figure 11–81.

INSTALLING THE VALVES

The cylinder head can be assembled after the head is thoroughly cleaned with soap and water to wash away any remaining grit and metal shavings from the valve grinding operation. Valves are assembled in the head, one at a time. The valve guide and stem are given a liberal coating of engine oil, and the valve is installed in its guide. Umbrella and positive valve stem seals are

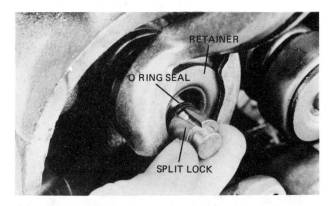

FIGURE 11–82 Proper installation of a typical Chevrolet O-ring valve stem seal and valve locks.

■ **TECH TIP** ■

DO NOT SIMPLY BOLT ON NEW CYLINDER HEADS

New assembled cylinder heads, whether aluminum or cast iron, are a popular engine buildup option. However, experience has shown that metal shavings and casting sand are often found inside the passages.

Before bolting on these "ready to install" heads, disassemble them and clean all passages. Often machine shavings are found under the valves. If this debris were to get into the engine, the results would be extreme wear or damage to the pistons, rings, block, and bearings. This cleaning may take several hours, but how much is your engine worth?

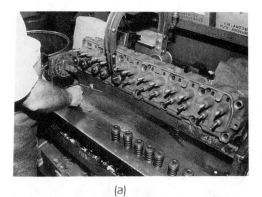

(a)

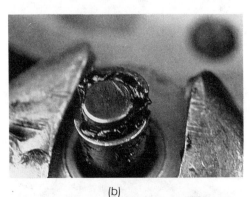

(b)

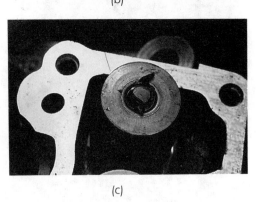

(c)

FIGURE 11–83 (a) Air-operated valve spring compressor being used to install valves. If the compressor compresses the valve spring too much, the O-ring valve stem seal may be knocked out of location when the compressor is released. (b) Putting grease on the split locks (keepers) helps to retain them when releasing pressure on the valve spring compressor to help prevent improper seating. (c) Valve after installation. Note the grease on the valve. The grease should be wiped off to prevent the possibility of certain greases clogging oil filters after the engine starts.

installed. Push umbrella seals down until they touch the valve guide. Use a plastic sleeve over the tip of the valve when installing positive seals. Make sure that the positive seal is fully seated on the valve guide and make sure that it is square. Hold the valve against the seat as the valve spring seat or insert, valve spring, valve seals, and retainer are placed over the valve stem. One end of the valve spring compressor pushes on the retainer to compress the spring. The O-ring type of valve stem seal is installed in the lower groove. The valve locks are installed while the valve spring is compressed. See Figure 11–82. Release the valve spring compressor slowly and carefully while making sure that the valve locks seat properly between the valve stem grooves and the retainer. Each valve is assembled in the same manner. See Figures 11–83 and 11–84. Attach the hose from a vacuum pump to the top of the assembled valve. *A vacuum will hold if the O-ring type of valve stem seal is correctly installed.*

FLOW TESTING CYLINDER HEADS

Many specialty engines are tested for the amount of air that can flow through the ports and valves of the engine. See Figure 11–85 for an example of combustion

FIGURE 11–84 *All valve springs should be checked for coil bind at maximum valve lift. The retainer can also hit the valve guide at high engine speeds if there is not sufficient clearance.*

COMBUSTION CHAMBER MACHINING

FIGURE 11–85 *Some technicians use standard automotive machine shop tools and equipment to machine the combustion chamber. This is often necessary if oversize valves are installed. (Courtesy of Chevrolet Motor Division, GMC)*

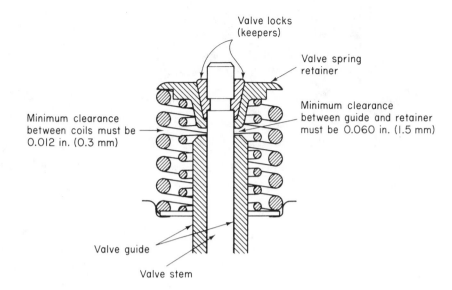

FIGURE 11–86 *Cylinder head setup for flow testing. Note the weak valve springs that are strong enough to keep the valves shut, yet weak enough to permit the flow bench operator to vary the intake valve opening amount.*

chamber machining to increase airflow. A flow bench is used to measure the amount of air (measured in cubic feet per minute [cfm]) that can flow through the valves at various valve openings.

After completion of the valve job and any port or combustion chamber work, weak valve springs are installed temporarily. See Figure 11–86. Modeling clay is then temporarily applied around the ports to improve flow characteristics around the port area

where the intake manifold would normally direct the flow into the port (see Figure 11–87).

Various thicknesses of metal spacers are placed between the cylinder head holding fixture and the valve stem. See Figure 11–88. Typical thicknesses used are 0.100 through 0.700 inch in 0.100-inch increments. The results are recorded on a work sheet. See Figure 11–89 and Figure 11–90.

CYLINDER HEAD FLOW VERSUS HORSEPOWER

Most comprehensive engine machine shops have the equipment to measure the airflow through cylinder head ports and valves. After the airflow through the open intake valve has been determined, a formula can be used to estimate horsepower. The following formula has proven to be a fairly accurate estimate of horsepower

FIGURE 11–87 Modeling clay is installed around the port to duplicate the flow improvement characteristics of an intake manifold.

0.100" THICK SPACER (OPENS VALVE OFF SEAT)

TEST VALVE SPRINGS

FIGURE 11–88 By varying the thickness of the metal spacers, the flow bench operator can measure the airflow through the intake and exhaust ports and valves at various valve lifts.

PRESSURE DROP ____28"____   NAME ____TEST INFO____

APPLICATION ____DART II IRON S.B/K.____

In = 2.055   Ex = 1.600

3 ANGLE   GRIND ONLY

VALVE LIFT (in.)

	CYL. #	COMMENTS		R 0.100		R 0.200		R 0.300		R 0.400		R 0.500		R 0.600		R 0.700
	IN		3	57.5	3	93.8	4	63.5	4	73.6	4	74.8	4	76.5	4	77.5
		CFM		88		144		189		219		223		228		231
	IN															
		CFM														
	IN															
		CFM														
A I R F L O W	IN															
		CFM														
	EX		2	60.5	3	58.5	3	70.0	3	76.0	3	80.2	3	82.0	3	83.2
		CFM		54		95		113		123		130		133		135
	EX															
		CFM														
	EX															
		CFM														
	EX															
		CFM														

FIGURE 11–89 Actual flow bench test work sheet. Note that the cylinder head was tested at up to 0.799 inch of lift!

212

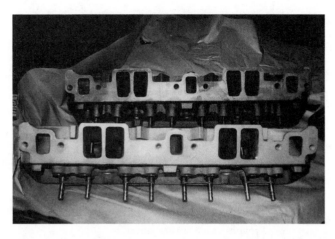

FIGURE 11–90 *The top cylinder head is stock and the bottom cylinder head has been ported using two different methods. The first inch from the gasket surface has been ground using a grinder to make the opening in the cylinder head match the intake manifold. The rest of the port between the valve and the gasket surfaces has been enlarged using acid. This acid treatment is a common "trick" used to increase the flow characteristics of a stock class cylinder head. The acid treatment gives the same rough cast-like surface as a completely stock cylinder head.*

when compared to dynamometer testing after the engine is built.

$$\text{Horsepower per cylinder} = \text{airflow at 28 inches of water} \times 0.598 \times 0.43$$

NOTE: The first part of the formula is used to convert airflow measurement from a basis of being tested at 28 inches of water to that of being tested at 20 inches of water.

For example, for a V-8 that measures 231 cfm of airflow at 28 inches of water:

$$\text{Horsepower} = 231 \times 0.598 = 138 \text{ cfm at 20 inches of water} \times 0.43$$
$$= 59.4 \text{ hp per cylinder} \times 8 = 475 \text{ hp}$$

■ **CAUTION:** Even though this formula has proven to be fairly accurate, there are too many variables in the design of any engine besides the airflow through the head for this formula to be accurate under all conditions. ■

SUMMARY

1. The exhaust valve is about 85% of the size of the intake valve.
2. Valve springs should be kept with the valve at the time of disassembly and tested for squareness and proper spring force.
3. Free and positive are two types of valve rotators.
4. Valve grinding should start with truing the valve tip; then the face should be refinished. A pilot is placed into the valve guide to position the stone or cutter correctly for resurfacing the valve seat.
5. The installed height should be checked and corrected with valve spring inserts if needed.
6. Valve stem height should be checked and the top of the valve ground if necessary.
7. After a thorough cleaning, the cylinder head should be assembled using new valve stem seals.

REVIEW QUESTIONS

1. Why is valve guide reconditioning the first cylinder head servicing operation?
2. When is the valve tip ground? How do you know how much to remove from the tip?
3. What is an interference angle between the valve and the seat?
4. Describe the difference between cutting and grinding valve seats.
5. How is a valve seat insert installed?
6. How is the correct valve spring insert (shim) selected and why are they used?

MULTIPLE-CHOICE QUESTIONS

1. In a normally operating engine, intake and exhaust valves are opened by a cam and closed by the _____.
   a. Rocker arms or cam follower
   b. Valve spring
   c. Lifters (tappets)
   d. Valve guide and/or pushrod
2. If an interference angle is machined on a valve or seat, this angle is usually _____.
   a. 1 degree
   b. 0.005 degree
   c. 1 to 3 degree
   d. 0.5 to 0.75 degree

3. Never remove more than _____ of material from the tip of a valve.
   a. 0.001 inch
   b. 0.002 inch
   c. 0.020 inch
   d. 0.050 inch

4. A valve should be discarded if the margin is less than _____ after refacing.
   a. 0.001 inch
   b. 0.006 inch
   c. 0.025 inch
   d. 0.060 inch

5. A valve seat should be concentric with the valve guide to a maximum TIR of _____.
   a. 0.006 inch
   b. 0.004 inch
   c. 0.002 inch
   d. 0.00015 inch

6. To lower and narrow a valve seat that has been cut at a 45-degree angle, use a cutter or stone of what angle?
   a. 60 degrees
   b. 45 degrees
   c. 30 degrees
   d. 15 degrees

7. Valve spring inserts (shims) are designed to _____.
   a. Increase installed height of the valve
   b. Decrease installed height of the valve
   c. Adjust the correct installed height
   d. Decrease valve spring pressure to compensate for decreased installed height

8. What is the proper relationship between intake and exhaust valve diameter?
   a. Intake valve size 85% of exhaust valve size
   b. Exhaust valve size 85% of intake valve size
   c. Exhaust valve size 38% of intake valve size
   d. Intake valve size 45% of exhaust valve size

9. Dampers (damper springs) are used inside some valve springs to _____.
   a. Prevent valve spring surge
   b. Keep the valve spring attached to the valve
   c. Decrease valve spring pressure
   d. Retain valve stem seals

10. Umbrella-type valve stem seals _____.
    a. Fit tightly onto the valve guide
    b. Fit on the valve face to prevent combustion leaks
    c. Fit tightly onto the valve stem
    d. Lock under the valve retainer

Camshaft and Valve Train Diagnosis and Service

OBJECTIVES

After studying Chapter 12, the reader will be able to

1. Describe how the camshaft and valve train function.
2. Discuss valve train noise and its causes.
3. Explain how to degree a camshaft.
4. Explain how a hydraulic lifter works.

The cam is driven by timing gears, chains, or belts located at the front of the engine. The gear or sprocket on the camshaft has twice as many teeth, or notches, as the one on the crankshaft. This results in two crankshaft turns for each turn of the camshaft. *The camshaft turns at one-half the crankshaft speed in all four stroke–cycle engines.*

CAMSHAFT FUNCTION

The camshaft's major function is to operate the valve train. Cam shape or **contour** is the major factor in determining the operating characteristics of the engine. The lobes on the camshaft open the valves against the pressure of the valve springs. The camshaft lobe changes rotary motion (camshaft) to linear motion (valves).

Cam lobe shape has more control over engine performance characteristics than does any other single engine part. Engines identical in every way except cam lobe shape may have completely different operating characteristics and performance. Two cam shapes for a small-block Chevrolet V-8 are shown in Figure 12–1.

The camshaft may also operate the following:

FIGURE 12–1 *Shape of two small-block Chevrolet V-8 cam lobes. A standard cam is on the left and a high-performance cam is on the right.*

- Mechanical fuel pump
- Oil pump
- Distributor

CAMSHAFT LOCATION

Pushrod engines have the cam located in the block. They are smaller and lighter than overhead cam engines. The camshaft is supported in the block by **camshaft bearings** and driven by the crankshaft with a gear or sprocket and chain drive.

CAMSHAFT PROBLEM DIAGNOSIS

The problem of a camshaft with a partially worn lobe is often difficult to diagnose. Sometimes a valve "tick tick tick" noise is heard if the cam lobe is worn. The ticking

■ TECH TIP ■

THE TUBE TRICK

Valve lifters are often difficult to remove because the ends of the lifters become mushroomed (enlarged) where they have contacted the camshaft. Varnish buildup can also prevent the lifters from being removed. Try this method:

Step #1. Raise the lifters upward, as far away from the camshaft as possible.

Step #2. Slide in a thin plastic or cardboard tube with slots in place of the camshaft. See Figure 12–2.

Step #3. Push the lifters downward into the tube. Use a long magnet to retrieve the lifters from the end of the tube.

This trick will work on almost every engine that has the camshaft in the block. If the tube is made from plastic, it has to be thin plastic to allow it to flex slightly. The length of the lifters is greater than the diameter of the cam bearings. Therefore, the lifter has to be pushed downward into the tube slightly to allow the lifter room to fall over into the tube.

FIGURE 12–2   Instead of prying old lifters up and out of the engine block, use a plastic (or cardboard) tube in place of the camshaft and push the lifters down. Then use a magnet to pull the old lifters out of the tube.

NOTE: Be sure to keep the pushrods and rocker arms together if they are to be reused. _____

Remove or lift up the lifters before carefully removing the camshaft. See the tech tip on the tube trick.

CAMSHAFT DESIGN

The camshaft is a one-piece casting with lobes, bearing journals, drive flanges, and accessory gear blanks. The accessory drive gear is finished with a gear cutter. The lobes and journals are ground to the proper shape. The remaining portion of the camshaft surface is not machined. See Figure 12–3.

On pushrod engines, camshaft bearing journals must be larger than the cam lobe so that the camshaft can be installed in the engine through the cam bearings. Some overhead cam engines have bearing caps on the cam bearings. These cams can have large cam lobes with small bearing journals. Cam bearings on some engines are progressively smaller from the front journal to the rear. Other engines use the same size of camshaft bearing on all the journals.

Most automotive camshafts used with flat or convex-faced lifters are made from hardened alloy cast iron. It resists wear and provides the required strength. The very hardness of the camshaft causes it to be susceptible to chipping as the result of edge loading or careless handling.

Cast-iron camshafts have about the same hardness throughout. If reground, they should be recoated with a phosphate coating.

noise can be intermittent, which makes it harder to determine the cause. If the engine has an overhead camshaft (OHC), it is usually relatively easy to remove the cam cover and make a visual inspection of all cam lobes and the rest of the valve train. In an overhead valve (OHV) engine, the camshaft is in the block, where easy visual inspection is not possible. However, camshaft lobe wear can be determined by simply removing the rocker cover(s). With the engine running, all the pushrods should be rotating. The small angle on the cam lobe and lifter offset causes the lifter and pushrod to rotate, except in the case of roller lifters. *If the pushrod is **not** rotating, the cam lobe (or lifter) is usually worn and both the camshaft and lifters should be replaced.*

CAMSHAFT REMOVAL

If the engine is of an overhead valve design, the camshaft is usually located in the block above the crankshaft. The timing chain and gears (if the vehicle is so equipped) should be removed after the timing chain (gear) cover is removed. Loosen the rocker arms (or rocker arm shaft) and remove the pushrods.

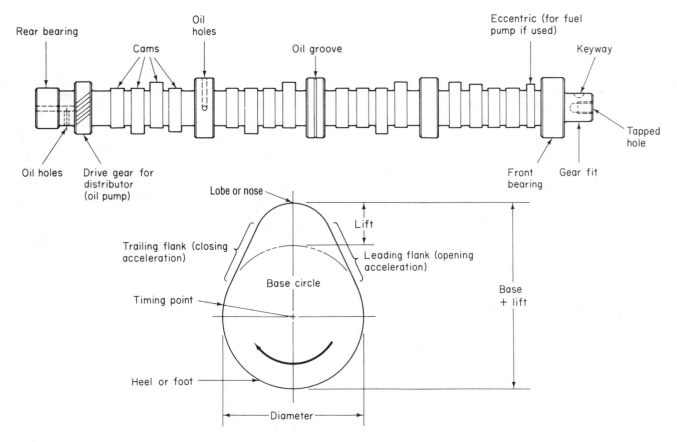

FIGURE 12–3 Cam and camshaft terms (nomenclature).

■ TECH TIP ■

HOT LIFTER IN 10 MINUTES?

A technician working in a new-vehicle dealership discovered a noisy (defective) valve lifter on a Chevrolet small-block V-8. Another technician questioned how long it would take to replace the lifter and was told, "Less than an hour"! (The factory flat rate was much longer than 1 hour.) Ten minutes later the repair technician handed the questioning technician a hot lifter that had been removed from the engine. The lifter was removed by the following steps:

1. The rocker cover was removed.
2. The rocker arm and pushrod for the affected valve were removed.
3. The distributor was removed.
4. A strong magnet was fed through the distributor opening into the valley area of the engine. (If the valve lifter is not mushroomed or does not have varnish deposits, the defective lifter can be lifted up and out of the engine; remember, the technician was working on a new vehicle.)
5. A replacement lifter was attached to the magnet and fed down the distributor hole and over the lifter bore.
6. The pushrod was used to help guide the lifter into the lifter bore.

After the lifter preload was adjusted and the rocker cover was replaced, the vehicle was returned to the customer in less than 1 hour.

Steel camshafts are usually SAE 4160 or 4180 steel and are usually induction hardened. Induction hardening involves heating the camshaft to cherry red in an electric field (heating occurs by electrical induction). The heated camshaft is then dropped into oil. The rapid cooling hardens the surface. Camshafts can also be hardened by using

- Liquid nitriding, which hardens to 0.001 to 0.0015 inch of thickness
- Gas nitriding, which hardens to 0.004 to 0.006 inch of thickness

Typical camshaft hardness should be 42 to 60 on the Rockwell "c" scale.

NOTE: Rockwell is a type of hardness test, and the *c* represents the scale used. The higher the number, the harder the surface. The abbreviation *Rc60*, therefore, indicates Rockwell hardness of 60 as measured on the c scale. ___

If this outer hardness wears off, the lobes of the camshaft are easily worn until they are almost completely rounded as shown in Figure 12–4. Also see Figures 12–5 and 12–6.

COMPOSITE CAMSHAFTS

A composite camshaft uses a lightweight tubular shaft with hardened steel lobes press-fitted over the shaft.

The actual production of these camshafts involves placing the lobes over the tube shaft in the correct position. Then a steel ball is drawn through the hollow steel tube, expanding the tube and securely locking the cam lobes in position. Defective or worn composite camshafts should be replaced.

CAMSHAFT LUBRICATION

Some engines transfer lubrication oil from the main oil gallery to the crankshaft around the camshaft journal or around the outside of the camshaft bearing. Cam bearing clearance is critical in these engines. If the clearance is too great, oil will leak out and the crankshaft bearings will not get enough oil. Other engines use drilled holes in the camshaft bearing journals to meter lubricating oil to the overhead rocker arm. Oil goes to the rocker arm each time the holes line up between the bearing oil gallery passage and the outlet passage to the rocker arm. Camshaft oil metering holes are shown in Figure 12–7. Also see Figures 12–8 and 12–9.

An eccentric cam lobe for the fuel pump is often cast as part of the camshaft. The fuel pump is operated by this eccentric with a long pump arm or pushrod. Some engines use a steel cup type of eccentric that is

FIGURE 12–4 Worn camshaft with two lobes worn to the point of being almost round.

FIGURE 12–5 Checking a camshaft for wear by measuring the lobe height with a micrometer.

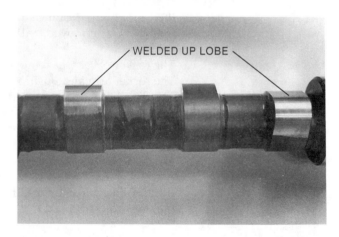

FIGURE 12–6 Worn camshaft that has been restored by welding the lobes and regrinding the original contour.

FIGURE 12–7 Hole through a camshaft bearing journal. The hole meters oil to a rocker shaft when it lines up with oil passages in the cam bearings.

FIGURE 12–8 Damaged camshaft bearing support. This overhead camshaft engine overheated because of an electric cooling fan circuit failure. The cylinder head warped upward in the center, causing a binding of the camshaft in the bearing.

bolted to the front of the cam drive gear. This allows a damaged fuel pump eccentric to be replaced without replacing an entire camshaft. Typical fuel pump eccentrics are identified on a number of camshafts pictured in Figure 12–10.

(a)

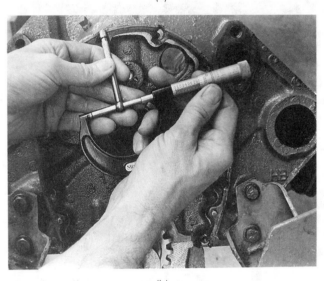

(b)

FIGURE 12–9 (a) A telescopic gauge being used to measure the inside diameter (ID) of a camshaft bearing. (b) An outside micrometer is used to measure the telescopic gauge.

CAMSHAFT DRIVES

The camshaft is driven by the crankshaft through gears, sprockets and chains, or sprockets and timing belts. Timing chains are not as wide as timing belts, so engines with timing chains can be shorter. Timing chains often have tensioners (dampers) pressing on the unloaded side of the chain. The tensioner pad is a Nylatron molding that is filled with molybdenum disulfide to give it low friction. The tensioner is held against the chain by either a spring or hydraulic oil pressure (Figure 12–11). The gears or sprockets are keyed to their shafts so that they can be installed in only one position. The gears and sprockets are then indexed together by marks on the gear teeth or chain

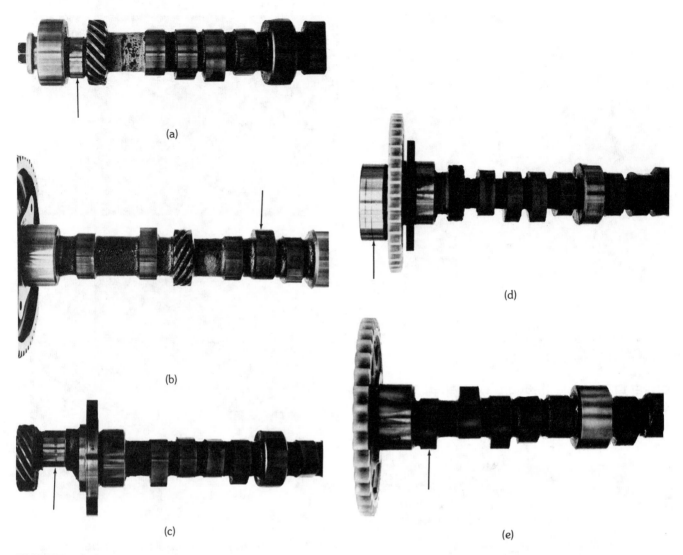

FIGURE 12–10   Typical fuel pump eccentric locations on camshafts used in pushrod engines.

links. When the crankshaft and camshaft timing marks are properly lined up, the cam lobes are indexed to the crankshaft throws of each cylinder so that the valves will open and close correctly in relation to the piston position. See Figure 12–12.

CAMSHAFT CHAIN DRIVES

The crankshaft gear or sprocket that drives the camshaft is usually made of sintered iron. When gears are used on the camshaft, the teeth must be made from a soft material to reduce noise. Usually, the whole gear is made of aluminum or fiber. When a chain and sprocket are used, the camshaft sprocket may be made of iron or it may have an aluminum hub with nylon teeth for noise reduction. Two types of timing chains are used.

1. **Silent chain type** (also known as a **flat-link** type, or **Morse** type for its original manufacturer). This type operates quietly but tends to stretch with use. See Figures 12–13 through 12–17.

   NOTE: When the timing chain stretches, the valve timing will be retarded and the engine will lack low-speed power. In some instances, the chain can wear through the timing chain cover and create an oil leak. See chapter 6 for on-the-vehicle timing chain stretch diagnosis.

2. **Roller chain type.** This type is noisier but operates with less friction and stretches less than the silent type of chain. See Figure 12–18.

(a)

(b)

PLASTIC
CHAIN GUIDES

HYDRAULIC
CHAIN TENSIONER

(c)

TENSIONER HELD
WITH A SPRING

TENSIONER HELD WITH
OIL PRESSURE

FIGURE 12–11 Timing chain tensioner.

PASSENGER CAR

TRUCK

FIGURE 12–12 Chain drive versus gear drive. With chain drive, the camshaft revolves in the same direction as the crankshaft. With this style of gear drive, the cam revolves in the opposite direction from the crankshaft. (Courtesy of Chevrolet Motor Division, GMC)

221

FIGURE 12-13 Two types of sprockets that can be used on the same engine. A cast-iron sprocket is on the left, and an aluminum nylon sprocket is on the right.

FIGURE 12-14 Close-up view of two types of timing chains. A silent chain is on the left, and a roller chain is on the right.

FIGURE 12-15 Excessively worn timing gear and chain.

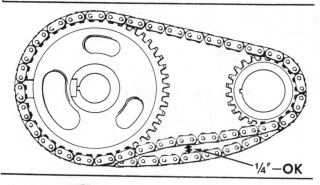

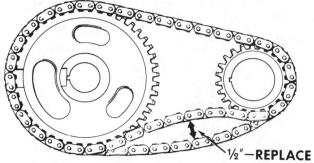

FIGURE 12-16 The industry standard for when to replace a timing chain and gears is when ½ inch (13 millimeters) or more of slack is measured in the chain. However, it is best to replace the timing chain and gear anytime the camshaft is replaced or the engine is disassembled for repair or overhaul. (Courtesy of Sealed Power Corporation)

FIGURE 12-17 Excessively worn timing chain guide. The metal guide finally broke into two pieces, making a lot of noise.

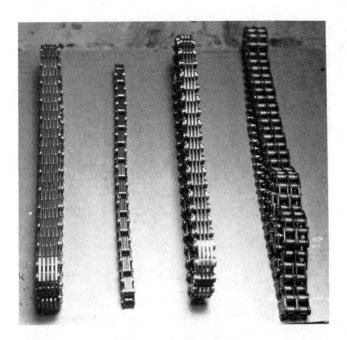

FIGURE 12–18 *Various styles of timing chains. The three chains on the left represent different styles of silent or flat-link chain. The roller chain on the right is much longer because it drives two overhead camshafts. Sound tests have determined that a silent (flat-link or Morse-style) chain is as much as 8 decibels quieter than a roller chain on the same engine.*

■ **TECH TIP** ■

CHECK THE CAMSHAFT AND THEN THE FUEL PUMP

Many mechanical fuel pumps operate off of a separate lobe on the camshaft. If this fuel pump lobe becomes worn, the stroke of the fuel pump is reduced and the amount of fuel being supplied to the engine is reduced. The engine may experience a lack of power or cut out and miss under load. The problem can also be intermittent, depending on other factors. A worn fuel pump cam lobe is often found on Ford 240– and 300–cubic inch inline six-cylinder engines. Some Ford Escort engines experience a worn fuel pump *pushrod* and behave similarly to an engine with a worn fuel pump cam lobe.

If a worn fuel pump cam lobe is suspected, perform a fuel pump capacity (volume) test. If the pump does not pump at least ½ pint in 15 seconds (1 pint in 30 seconds), then remove the pump and inspect for excessive cam lobe wear or fuel pump pushrod wear before replacing the fuel pump.

Some four-cam engines use a two-stage camshaft drive system:

> Primary: from crankshaft to camshaft
> Secondary: from one camshaft to another

See Figure 12–19.

CAMSHAFT BELT DRIVES

Many overhead camshaft engines use a timing belt rather than a chain. The belt is generally considered to be quieter, but it requires periodic replacement, usually every 60,000 miles (100,000 kilometers). Unless the engine is **freewheeling,** the piston can hit the valves if the belt breaks. See Figures 12–20 and 12–21.

CAMSHAFT TWISTING MOVEMENT

As the camshaft lobe pushes the lifter upward against the valve spring force, a backward twisting force is developed on the camshaft. After the lobe goes past its high point, the lifter moves down the backside of the lobe. This makes a forward twisting force (Figure 12–22). This action produces an alternating torsion force forward, then backward, at each cam lobe. This alternating torsion force is multiplied by the number of cam lobes on the shaft. The camshaft must have sufficient strength to minimize torsion twist. It must also be tough enough to minimize fatigue from the alternating torsion forces.

CAM CHUCKING

Cam chucking is the movement of the camshaft lengthwise in the engine during operation. Each camshaft must have some means to control the shaft end thrust. Two methods are in common usage. One method is to use a **thrust plate** between the camshaft drive gear or sprocket and a flange on the camshaft (Figures 12–23 and 12–24). This thrust plate is attached to the engine block with bolts. A second method is to use the thrust developed by the **oil pump turning effort** to hold the camshaft in the block (Figure 12–25). A flange on the back of the camshaft drive gear or sprocket rides against the front of the block. This keeps the camshaft from moving backward into the engine. In a few camshafts, a button, spring, or retainer that contacts the timing cover limits forward motion of the camshaft. See Figure 12–26.

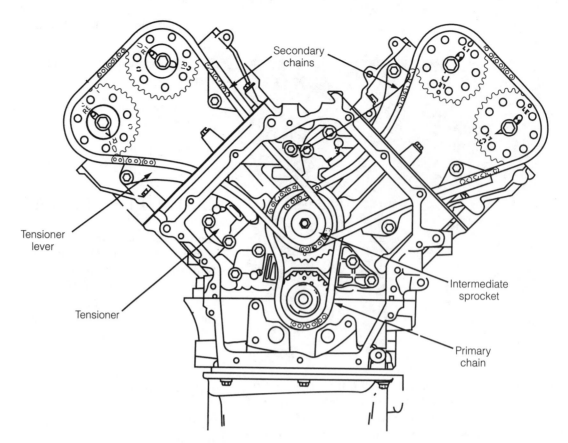

FIGURE 12–19 Typical dual overhead camshaft V-type engine that uses one primary timing chain and two secondary chains.

FIGURE 12–20 Worn timing belt. Notice the missing teeth. This belt broke at 88,000 miles because the owner failed to replace it at the recommended interval of 60,000 miles.

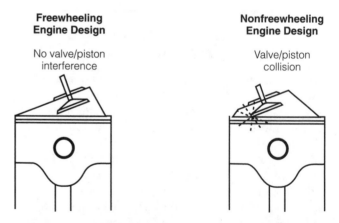

FIGURE 12–21 Many engines are designed as nonfreewheeling engines. If the timing belt (or chain) breaks, the piston still moves up and down in the cylinder while the valves remain stationary. With a freewheeling design, nothing is damaged, but in a nonfreewheeling engine, the valves are often bent.

224

(a)

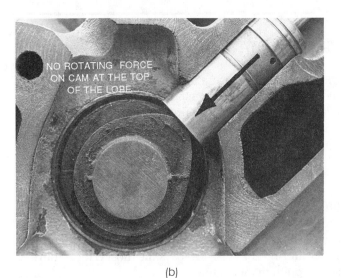

(b)

(c)

FIGURE 12–22 Lifter contact on the cam lobe. (a) The cam lobe is beginning to lift the lifter. (b) The lifter is fully raised. (c) The lifter is lowering.

FIGURE 12–23 Thrust plate controlling the camshaft end thrust on an overhead camshaft engine.

FIGURE 12–24 Typical thrust plate between the cam gear and a flange on the camshaft. Note the hole in the fiber composition gear to provide access to the thrust plate bolts.

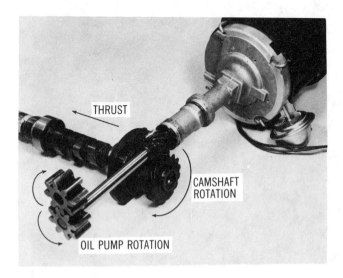

FIGURE 12–25 Oil pump turning effort produces end thrust on the camshaft.

FIGURE 12–26 Some engines use a spring-loaded button to help control cam chucking ("walking").

■ TECH TIP ■

ROLLER LIFTER CAM WEAR

After any engine equipped with roller lifters is run for a short time, it will wear a path on the camshaft. The path traveled by the roller over the cam causes the area to have a mirrorlike appearance. The area on both sides of this shiny path retains the dull finish of the original camshaft.

This wear pattern is often mistakenly assumed to be abnormal, and as a result, the camshaft and lifters are sometimes needlessly replaced. To avoid replacing good parts or not replacing worn parts, always carefully measure all engine parts.

LIFTER ROTATION

Most valve trains use a spherical lifter face, 50 to 80 inches (13 to 20 centimeters) in radius, that slides against the cam lobe. This produces a surface on the lifter face that is slightly convex, by about 0.002 inch. The lifter also contacts the lobe at a point that is slightly off center. This produces a small turning force on the lifter to cause some lifter rotation for even wear. In operation, there is a wide line of contact between the lifter and the high point of the cam lobe. These are the highest loads that are produced in an engine. The lifter contact on the top of the cam lobe can be seen in Figures 12–27 and 12–28. This surface is the most critical lubrication point in an engine.

CAMSHAFT LIFT

The **lift** of the cam is usually expressed in decimal inches and represents the distance that the valve is lifted off the valve seat. The higher the lift, the more air and fuel that can theoretically enter the engine. The more air and fuel burned in an engine, the greater the power potential of the engine. The amount of lift of a camshaft is often different for the intake and exhaust valves. If the specifications vary, the camshaft is called **asymmetrical.** If the lift is the same, the cam is called **symmetrical.** However, when the amount of lift increases, so do the forces on the camshaft and the rest of the valve train. Generally, a camshaft with a lift of over 0.500 inch (1.3 centimeters) is unsuitable for street operation except for use in engines that are over 400 cubic inches (6.0 liters).

The lift specifications at the valve face assume the use of the stock rocker arm ratio. If nonstock rocker arms with a higher ratio are installed (for example,

FIGURE 12–27   Typical lifter contact on the top of the cam lobe.

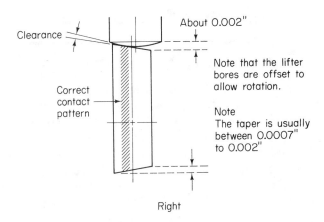

Most late model automotive cams are tapered to provide lifter rotation. The lifters have a spherical grind so that they do not ride on the edge of the cam lobe.
This contact spreads the load of the valve train against more of the lobe face.

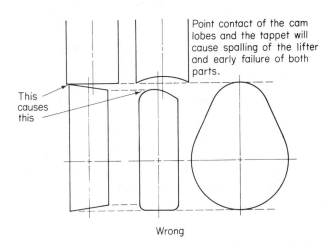

FIGURE 12–28   New lifters should always be used with a new camshaft. If worn lifters are used on a new camshaft, edge wear on the cam lobes will quickly wear the camshaft. (Courtesy of Sealed Power Corporation)

■ TECH TIP ■

BEST TO WARN THE CUSTOMER

A technician replaced a timing chain and gears on a Chevrolet V-8. The repair was accomplished correctly, yet after starting, the engine burned an excessive amount of oil. Before the timing chain replacement, oil consumption was minimal. The replacement timing chain restored proper operation of the engine and increased engine vacuum. Increased vacuum can draw oil from the crankcase past worn piston rings and through worn valve guides during the intake stroke. Similar increased oil consumption problems occur if a valve regrind is performed on a high-mileage engine with worn piston rings and/or cylinders.

To satisfy the owner of the vehicle, the technician had to disassemble and refinish the cylinders and replace the piston rings. Therefore, all technicians should warn customers that increased oil usage may result from almost any repair to a high-mileage engine.

1.6:1 rockers replacing the stock 1.5:1 rocker arms), the lift at the valve is increased. Also, because the rocker arm rotation covers a greater distance at the pivot of the rocker arm, the rocker arm can hit the edge of the valve retainer.

ROCKER ARMS

Rocker arms reverse the upward movement of the pushrod to produce a downward movement on the tip of the valve. Engine designers make good use of the rocker arm. It is designed to reduce the travel of the cam follower or lifter and pushrod while maintaining the required valve lift. This is done by using a rocker arm ratio of approximately 1.5:1, as shown in Figure 12–29. For a given amount of lift on the pushrod, the valve will open to 1.5 times the pushrod lift distance. This ratio allows the camshaft to be small, so the engine can be smaller. It also results in lower lobe-to-lifter rubbing speeds.

■ **CAUTION:** Using rocker arms with a higher ratio than stock can also cause the valve spring to compress too much and actually bind. Valve spring bind occurs

■ DIAGNOSTIC STORY ■

THE NOISY CAMSHAFT

The owner of an overhead cam four-cylinder engine complained of a noisy engine. After taking the vehicle to several technicians and getting high estimates to replace the camshaft and followers, the owner tried to find a less expensive solution. Finally, another technician replaced the serpentine drive belt on the front of the engine and "cured" the "camshaft" noise for a fraction of the previous estimates.

Remember, accessory drive belts can often make noises similar to valve or bad bearing types of noises. Many engines have been disassembled and/or overhauled because of a noise that was later determined to be from one of the following:

■ Loose or defective drive belt(s)
■ Loose torque converter–to–flex plate (drive plate) bolts (nuts)
■ Defective mechanical fuel pump

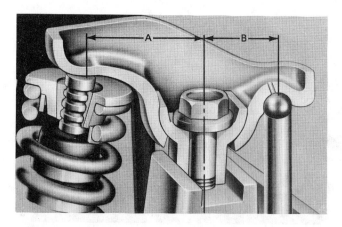

FIGURE 12–29 A 1.5:1 ratio rocker arm means that dimension A is 1.5 times the length of B. Therefore, if the pushrod is moved up 0.400 inch by the camshaft lobe, the valve will be pushed down (opened) 0.400 inch × 1.5, or 0.600 inch.

FIGURE 12–30 Typical cast rocker arm types.

when the valve spring is compressed to the point where there is no clearance at all in the spring. (It is completely compressed.) When coil bind occurs in a running engine, bent pushrods, broken rocker arms, or other valve train damage can result. ■

Rocker arms may be cast, forged, or stamped. Forged rocker arms are the strongest, but they require expensive manufacturing operations. Rocker arms may have bushings or bearings installed to reduce friction and increase durability. Cast rocker arms cost less to make and do not usually use bushings, but they do require several machining operations. They are not as strong as forged rocker arms but are satisfactory for passenger vehicle service. Typical cast rocker arms are shown in Figure 12–30.

Stamped rocker arms (Figure 12–31) are the least expensive type to manufacture. They are lightweight and very strong. Two general types are in use:

1. Those that operate on a ball or cylindrical pivot
2. Those that operate on a shaft

The ball and cylindrical pivot types are lubricated through hollow pushrods. The shaft type is lubricated through oil passages that travel from the block, through the head and into the shaft, and then to the rocker arms.

Overhead camshaft engines use several methods for opening the valves:

1. One type opens the valves directly with a **cam follower** or **bucket** (Figure 12–32).
2. The second type uses a **finger follower** that provides an opening ratio similar to that of a rocker arm (Figures 12–33 through 12–35). Finger followers open the valves by approximately 1½ times the cam lift. The pivot point of the finger follower may have a mechanical adjustment or it may have an automatic hydraulic adjustment.
3. A third type moves the rocker arm directly through a hydraulic lifter (Figure 12–36).

NOTE: Some newer engines have the hydraulic adjustment in the rocker arm.

FIGURE 12–31   Typical stamped rocker arm types.

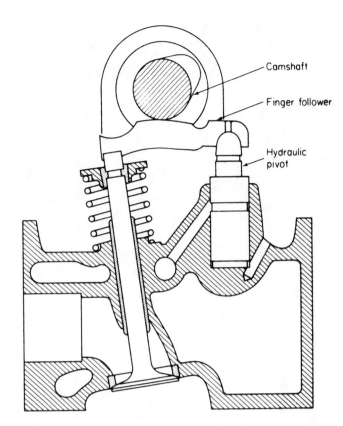

FIGURE 12–33   Overhead cam operating on a finger follower. A hydraulic pivot is on the right end of the finger follower. The finger follower operates the valve on the left.

FIGURE 12–32   Overhead cam operating directly on top of the bucket-type cam follower.

All engines have some method for keeping the rocker arm correctly positioned over the valve tip. Rocker arms are held in position on rocker shafts with springs and spacers. This can be seen in Figure 12–37. The rocker shaft keeps the rocker arms from twisting. Cylindrical pivots hold the rocker arms in position and keep it from twisting.

PUSHRODS

Pushrods are designed to be as light as possible and still maintain their strength. They may be either solid or hollow. If they are to be used as passages for oil to lubricate rocker arms, they *must* be hollow. Pushrods use a convex ball on the lower end that seats in the lifter. The rocker arm end is also a convex ball, unless there is an adjustment screw in the pushrod end of the rocker arm. In this case, the rocker arm end of the pushrod has a concave socket. It mates with the convex ball on the adjustment screw in the rocker arm. Pushrod end types are shown in Figure 12–38. Also see Figure 12–39.

PUSHROD LENGTH

The tolerance in the valve train allows for some machining of engine parts without the need to change pushrod length. However, if one or more of the following changes have been made to an engine, a different pushrod length may be necessary:

FIGURE 12–34 Roller-type rocker arm (finger follower) used with an overhead cam.

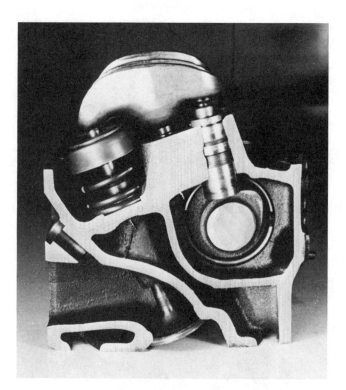

FIGURE 12–36 The overhead cam operates the rocker arm through a hydraulic lifter.

FIGURE 12–35 Finger follower held in place over the valve tip with a slot.

FIGURE 12–37 Convex rocker arm clearance adjustment ball fitting in a socket on the upper end of the pushrod.

- Block deck height machined
- Cylinder head deck height machined
- Camshaft base circle size reduced
- Valve length increased
- Lifter design changed

CAMSHAFT DURATION

The **duration of the camshaft** is the number of degrees of crankshaft rotation for which the valve is lifted off the seat. The specifications for duration can be different for the intake valves and the exhaust valves. If the durations of the intake and exhaust valves are different from each other, the cam is called asymmetrical. The specification for duration can be expressed by several different methods, which must be considered when comparing one cam to another. The three most commonly used methods are the following:

FIGURE 12-38   Types of pushrod ends.

ROCKER ARM SHAFTS CAN CAUSE STICKING VALVES

As oil oxidizes, it forms a varnish. Varnish buildup is particularly common on hot upper portions of the engine, such as rocker arm shafts. The varnish restricts clean oil from getting into and lubricating the rocker arms. The cam lobe can easily *force* the valves open, but the valve springs often do not exert enough force to fully close the valves. The result is an engine miss, which may be intermittent. Worn valve guides and/or weak valve springs can also cause occasional rough idle, uneven running, or missing.

HOLLOW PUSHROD DIRT

Many engine rebuilders and remanufacturers do not reuse old hollow pushrods. Dirt, carbon, and other debris are difficult to thoroughly clean from inside a hollow pushrod. When an engine is run with used pushrods, the trapped particles can be dislodged and ruin new bearings and other new engine parts.

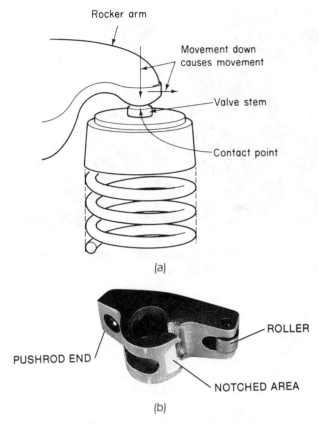

(a)

(b)

FIGURE 12-39   (a) As a rocker arm presses down on a valve, the rocker arm moves across the top of the valve stem. (b) High-performance rocker arms often use a roller tip to reduce friction, especially when using high-lift camshafts. This aluminum rocker arm was cracked as a result of coil spring bind. Note the machined notch on the spring side of the rocker arm for clearance when using larger-diameter valve springs.

1. **Duration of valve opening at zero lash** (clearance). If a hydraulic lifter is used, the lash is always zero. If a solid lifter is used, this method of expression refers to the duration of the opening of the valve *after* the specified clearance (lash) has been closed.

2. **Duration at 0.050-inch lifter (tappet) lift.** Because this specification method eliminates all valve lash clearances and compensates for lifter (tappet) styles, it is the preferred method to use when comparing one camshaft to another. Another method used to specify duration of some factory camshafts is to specify crankshaft duration at 0.010-inch lifter lift. The important point to remember is that the technician must be sure to use equivalent specification methods when comparing or selecting camshafts.

NOTE: Fractions of a degree are commonly expressed in units called minutes ('). **Sixty minutes equal 1 degree.** For example, 45' = ¾°, 30' = ½°, and 15' = ¼°.

FIGURE 12–40 Stamped plate held in place under the rocker pivot stud.

FIGURE 12–41 Hardened pushrods should be used in any engine that uses pushrod guides (plates). To determine if the pushrod is hardened, simply try to scratch the side of the pushrod with a pocketknife.

■ TECH TIP ■

THE SCRATCH TEST

All pushrods used with guide plates *must* be hardened on the sides and on the tips. To easily determine if a pushrod is hardened, simply use a sharp pocketknife to scrape the wall of the pushrod. A heat-treated pushrod will not scratch. See Figures 12–40 and 12–41.

3. **SAE camshaft specifications.** The valve timing and valve overlap are expressed in the number of degrees of crankshaft rotation for which the valves are off their seats. SAE's recommended practice is to measure all valve events at 0.006-inch (0.15-millimeter) valve lift. This method differs from the usual method used by vehicle or camshaft manufacturers. Whenever comparing valve timing events, be certain that the exact same methods are used on all camshafts being compared.

VALVE OVERLAP

Another camshaft specification is the number of degrees of overlap. **Camshaft overlap** is the number of degrees of crankshaft rotation between the exhaust and intake strokes for which both valves are off their seats.

■ A lower amount of overlap results in smoother idle and low–engine speed operation, but it also means that a lower amount of power is available at higher engine speeds.

■ A greater valve overlap causes rougher engine idle, with decreased power at low speeds, but it means that high-speed power is improved.

For example; A camshaft with 50 degrees (or less) of overlap may be used in an engine in which low-speed torque and smooth idle qualities are desired. Engines used with overdrive automatic transmissions benefit from the low-speed torque and fuel economy benefits of a small-overlap cam. A camshaft with 100 degrees of overlap is more suitable for use with a manual transmission, with which high-RPM power is desired. An engine equipped with a camshaft with over 100 degrees of overlap tends to idle roughly and exhibit poorer low–engine speed response and lowered fuel economy. See Figure 12–42.

The valve overlap is the number of degrees for which both valves are open near TDC. In the previous example, the intake valve starts to open at 19 degrees BTDC. The exhaust valve is also open during this upward movement of the piston on the exhaust stroke. The exhaust valve is open until 22 degrees ATDC.

To determine overlap, total the number of degrees for which the intake valve is open BTDC (19 degrees) and the number of degrees for which the exhaust valve is open ATDC (22 degrees).

$$\text{Valve overlap} = 19° + 22° = 41°$$

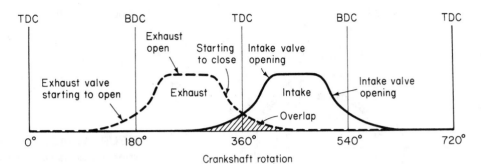

FIGURE 12–42 Graphic representation of a typical camshaft showing the relationship between the intake and exhaust valves.

LOBE CENTERS

Another camshaft specification that creates some confusion is the angle of the centerlines of the intake and exhaust lobes. This separation between the centerlines of the intake and exhaust lobes is called **lobe separation** or **lobe spread** and is measured in degrees. See Figure 12–43.

Two camshafts with identical lift and duration can vary greatly in operation because of variation in the angle between the lobe centerlines.

1. The smaller the angle between the lobe centerlines, the greater the amount of overlap. For example, 108 degrees is a narrower lobe center angle.
2. The larger the angle between the lobe centerlines, the less the amount of overlap. For example, 114 degrees is a wider lobe center angle.

NOTE: Some engines that are equipped with dual overhead camshafts and four valves per cylinder use a different camshaft profile for each of the intake and exhaust valves. For example, one intake valve for each cylinder could have a cam profile designed for maximum low-speed torque. The other intake valve for each cylinder could be designed for higher–engine speed power. This results in an engine that is able to produce a high torque over a broad engine speed range. ———

HOW TO DETERMINE LOBE CENTER ANGLE

To find the degree of separation between intake and exhaust lobes of a cam, use the following formula:

$$\frac{\text{Intake duration} + \text{Exhaust duration}}{4} - \frac{\text{Overlap}}{2} = \text{Number of degrees of separation}$$

See Figure 12–44 for a typical camshaft valve timing diagram.

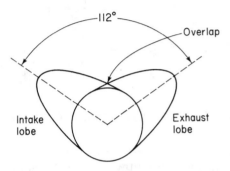

FIGURE 12–43 As the lobe center angle decreases, the overlap increases, with no other changes in the lobe profile lift and duration.

$$\text{Intake duration} = 15° + 59° + 180° = 254°$$
$$\text{Exhaust duration} = 59° + 15° + 180° = 254°$$
$$\text{Overlap} = 15° + 15° = 30°$$

The lobe separation angle can be determined by transferring the intake and exhaust duration and overlap into the formula as follows:

$$\frac{(254° + 254°)}{4} - \frac{30°}{2} = \frac{508°}{4} - \frac{30°}{2} = 127° - 15° = 112°$$

CAM TIMING SPECIFICATIONS

Cam timing specifications are stated in terms of the angle of the crankshaft in relation to top dead center (TDC) or bottom dead center (BDC) when the valves open and close.

INTAKE VALVE

The intake valves should open slightly before the piston reaches TDC and starts down on the intake stroke. This ensures that the valve is fully open when the piston travels downward on the intake stroke. The flow through a partially open valve (especially a valve ground at 45 degrees instead of 30 degrees) is greatly reduced as compared to that when the valve is in its fully open position. The intake valve closes after the piston reaches BDC because the air-fuel mixture has inertia, or the tendency of matter to remain in motion.

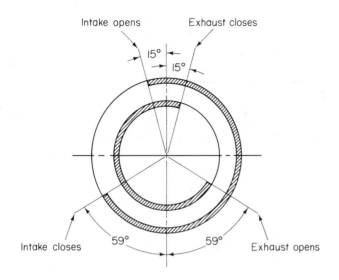

FIGURE 12–44 Typical cam timing diagram.

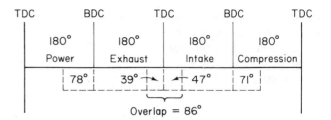

FIGURE 12–45 Typical high-performance camshaft specifications on a straight-line graph. Intake valve duration = 39° + 180° + 71° = 290°. Exhaust valve duration is 78° + 180° + 47° = 305°. Because intake and exhaust valve specifications are different, the camshaft grind is called asymmetrical.

Even after the piston stops traveling downward on the intake stroke and starts upward on the compression stroke, the inertia of the air-fuel mixture can still be used to draw in additional charge.

Typical intake valve specifications are to open at 19 degrees BTDC and close at 46 degrees after bottom dead center (ABDC).

EXHAUST VALVE

The exhaust valve opens while the piston is traveling down on the power stroke, before the piston starts up on the exhaust stroke. The exhaust valve's opening before the piston starts up on the exhaust stroke ensures that the combustion pressure is released and the exhaust valve is mostly open when the piston does start up. The exhaust valve does not close until after the piston has traveled past TDC and is starting down on the intake stroke. Because of inertia of the exhaust, some of the burned gases continue to flow out the exhaust valve after the piston is past TDC. This can leave a partial vacuum in the combustion chamber to start pulling in the fresh charge.

Typical exhaust valve specifications are to open at 49 degrees before bottom dead center (BBDC) and close at 22 degrees after top dead center (ATDC).

CAM TIMING CHART

During the four strokes of a four stroke–cycle gasoline engine, the crankshaft revolves 720 degrees (it makes two complete revolutions [2 × 360° = 720°]). Camshaft specifications are given in crankshaft degrees. In the example in Figure 12–45, the intake valve starts to open

at 39 degrees BTDC, remains open through the entire 180 degrees of the intake stroke, and does not close until 71 degrees ATDC. Therefore, the duration of the intake valve is 39 degrees plus 180 degrees plus 71 degrees, or 290 degrees.

The exhaust valve of the example camshaft opens at 78 degrees BBDC and closes at 47 degrees ATDC. When the exhaust valve specifications are added to the intake valve specifications in the diagram, the overlap period is easily observed. The overlap in the example is 39 degrees plus 47 degrees, or 86 degrees. The duration of the exhaust valve opening is 78 degrees plus 180 degrees plus 47 degrees, or 305 degrees. Because the specifications of this camshaft indicate close to and over 300 degrees of duration, this camshaft should only be used where power is more important than fuel economy.

The usual method of drawing a camshaft timing diagram is in a circle illustrating two revolutions (720 degrees) of the crankshaft. See Figure 12–46 for an example of a typical camshaft timing diagram for a camshaft with the same specifications as the one illustrated in Figure 12–45.

REGRINDING CAMSHAFTS

Worn camshafts can be restored to original lift and duration by one of two methods:

1. If the camshaft is not excessively worn (less than 0.030 inch), the lobes can be reground by decreasing the diameter of the base circle, restoring the original lift and duration. See Figure 12–47.
2. If the cam lobe wear is excessive, the lobes can be welded and reground back to their original specifications.

NOTE: According to major engine remanufacturers, only about 35% of camshafts can be reground. Therefore, about two-thirds of the camshafts received in engine cores are excessively worn and must be replaced. _____

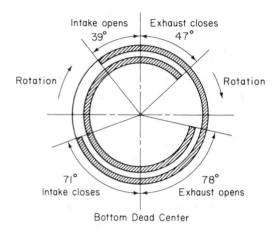

This valve timing diagram shows two revolutions (720°) of the crankshaft

FIGURE 12–46   Typical camshaft valve timing diagram with the same specifications as those shown in Figure 12–45.

INSTALLING THE CAMSHAFT

When the camshaft is installed, the lobes must be coated with a special lubricant containing molydisulfide. This special lube helps to ensure proper initial lubrication to the critical cam lobe sections of the camshaft. Many manufacturers recommend multiviscosity engine oil such as SAE 5W-30 or SAE 10W-30. Some camshaft manufacturers recommend using straight SAE 30 or SAE 40 engine oil and not a multiviscosity oil for the first oil fill. Some manufacturers also recommend the use of an antiwear additive such as zinc dithiophosphate (ZDP). The camshaft must be broken in by maintaining engine speed above 1500 RPM for the first 10 minutes of engine operation. If the engine speed is decreased to idle (about 600 RPM), the lifter (tappet) will be in contact with and exerting force *on* the lobe of the cam for a longer period of time than occurs at higher engine speeds. The pressure and volume of oil supplied to the camshaft area are also increased at the higher engine speeds. Therefore, to ensure long camshaft and lifter life, make certain that the engine will start quickly after reassembly to prevent long cranking periods and subsequent low engine speeds after a new camshaft and lifters have been installed. Whenever repairing an engine, follow these rules regarding camshaft and lifters:

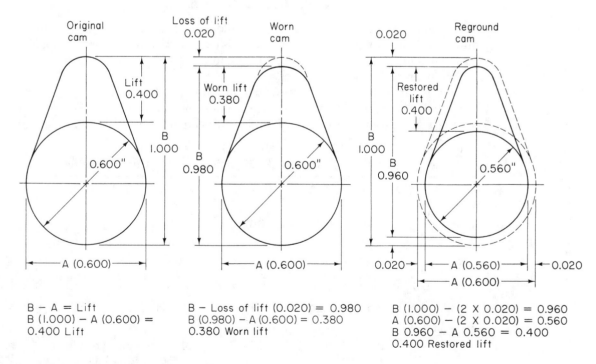

FIGURE 12–47   A worn camshaft lobe can be restored to its original lift by grinding the base circle smaller.

1. When installing a new camshaft, always install new valve lifters (tappets).
2. When installing new lifters, if the original cam is not excessively worn and if the pushrods all rotate with the original camshaft, the camshaft may be reused.

NOTE: Some manufacturers recommend that a new camshaft always be installed when replacing valve lifters. _____

---

3. *Never* use a hydraulic camshaft with solid lifters or hydraulic lifters with a solid lifter camshaft.
4. New lifters will be more compatible if the bottom part of the lifter that contacts the cam is polished with #600 grit sandpaper.

NOTE: Many molydisulfide greases can start to clog oil filters within 20 minutes after starting the engine. Most engine rebuilders recommend changing the oil and filter after ½ hour of running time. _____

DEGREEING THE CAMSHAFT

The purpose of degreeing the camshaft in the engine is to locate the valve action exactly as the camshaft manufacturers intended. The method most often recommended by camshaft manufacturers is the **intake lobe centerline method.** This method determines the exact centerline of the intake lobe and compares it to the specifications supplied with the replacement camshaft. On an overhead valve engine, the camshaft is usually degreed after the crankshaft, pistons, and camshaft are installed and before the cylinder heads are installed. To determine the centerline of the intake lobe, follow these steps using a degree wheel mounted on the crankshaft:

Step #1. *Locate the exact top dead center.* Install a degree wheel and bring the cylinder #1 piston close to TDC. Install a piston stop. (A piston stop is any object attached to the block that can act as a solid mechanical stop to prevent the piston from reaching the top of the cylinder.) Turn the engine clockwise until the piston *gently* hits the stop.

■ TECH TIP ■

TOO BIG = TOO BAD

A common mistake of beginning engine builders is to install a camshaft with too much duration for the size of the engine. This extended duration of valve opening results in a rough idle and low manifold vacuum, which causes carburetor metering problems and lack of low-speed power.

For example, a hydraulic cam with a duration greater than 225° at 0.050-inch lift for a 350–cubic inch engine will usually not be suitable for street driving. **Seat duration** is the number of degrees of crankshaft rotation that the valve is off the seat.

Common usage	Seat duration	Lift	Duration at 0.050 inch	Characteristics
Street	246°–254°	0.400	192°–199°	Smooth idle, power idle to 4500 RPM
Street	262°	0.432	207°	Broad power range, smooth idle, power idle to 4800 RPM
Street	266°	0.441	211°	Good idle for 350–cubic inch engines, power idle to 5200 RPM
Street— drag strip	272°	0.454	217°	Lope idle, power idle to 5500 RPM
Street— racetrack	290°	0.500	239°	Shaky idle, power idle to 5500–6500 RPM

■ **CAUTION:** Do not use the starter motor to rotate the engine. Use a special wrench on the flywheel or the front of the crankshaft. ■

Record the reading on the degree wheel, and then turn the engine in the opposite direction until it stops again and record that number. See Figure 12–48, indicating a reading of 30 degrees ATDC and 26 degrees BTDC. Add the two readings together and divide by 2 (30° + 26° = 56° ÷ 2 = 28°). Move the degree wheel until it is 28 degrees, and the engine has stopped rotating in either direction. Now TDC on the degree wheel is exactly at top dead center.

Step #2. Remove the piston stop and place a dial indicator on an intake valve lifter. To accurately locate the point of maximum lift (intake lobe centerline), rotate the engine until the lifter drops 0.050 inch on each side of the maximum lift point. Mark the degree wheel at these points on either side of the maximum lift point. Now count the degrees between these two points and mark the halfway point. This halfway point represents the **intake centerline.** This point is often located between 100 degrees and 110 degrees. See Figure 12–49.

Step #3. Now that both TDC and intake centerline have been marked, compare the actual intake centerline with the specification. For example, if the actual intake centerline is 106 degrees and the camshaft specification indicates 106 degrees, then the camshaft is installed **straight up.** See Figure 12–50. If the actual reading is 104 degrees, the camshaft is advanced by 2 degrees. If the actual reading is 108 degrees, the camshaft is retarded by 2 degrees.

If the measured values are different from specifications, special offset pins or keys are available to relocate the cam gear by the proper amount. Some manufacturers can provide adjustable cam timing sprockets for overhead cam engines.

Advanced Cam Timing

If the camshaft is slightly ahead of the crankshaft, the camshaft is called advanced. An advanced camshaft (maximum of 4 degrees) results in more low-speed torque with a slight decrease in high-speed power. Some aftermarket camshaft manufacturers design about a

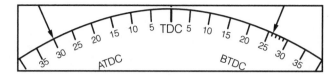

FIGURE 12–48 Degree wheel indicating where the piston stopped near top dead center. By splitting the difference between the two readings, the true TDC (28 degrees) can be located on the degree wheel.

FIGURE 12–49 The exact centerline of the cam intake lobe is being determined with a dial gauge and a degree wheel.

4-degree advance into their timing gears or camshaft. This permits the use of a camshaft with more lift and duration, yet still provides the smooth idle and low-speed responses of a milder camshaft.

Retarded Cam Timing

If the camshaft is slightly behind the crankshaft, the camshaft is called retarded. A retarded camshaft (maximum of 4 degrees) results in more high-speed power at the expense of low-speed torque.

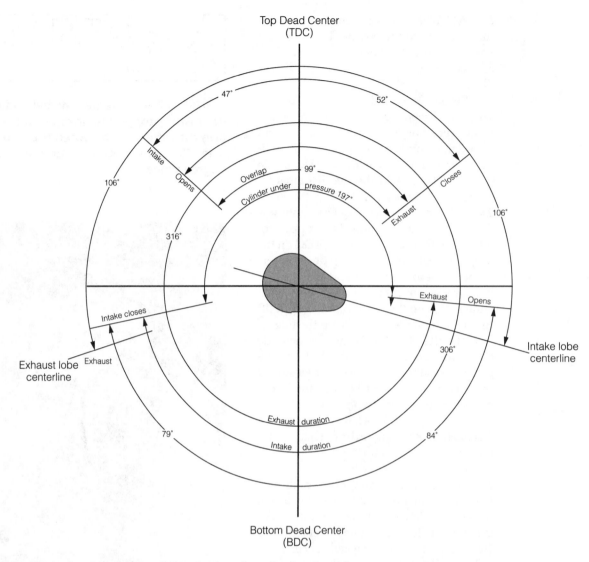

FIGURE 12–50 *Typical valve timing diagram showing the intake lobe centerline at 106 degrees ATDC.*

RECONDITIONED CAMSHAFTS

The production automotive camshaft is usually replaced if it has become worn beyond acceptable standards. Camshaft replacement may be less expensive than reconditioning. Camshafts with special grinds and heavy-duty camshafts are usually reconditioned. The cam bearing journals can be ground to a standard undersize in the same way in which crankshaft main bearing journals are ground. Worn cam lobes can also be ground to be undersize. When this is done, longer pushrods are required with hydraulic lifter valve trains to properly position the rocker arms. Engines with solid lifters can be adjusted to compensate for cam lobe grinding. An alternative means of reconditioning the cam lobes is to build them back up with weld or metal spray and then grind them to the original size and

shape. The lobe must be polished to obtain the proper microinch finish.

Most camshafts are coated at the factory with a polycrystalline structure chemical treatment. This coating is typically **manganese phosphate** and gives the camshaft a dull black appearance. The purpose of this treatment is to absorb and hold oil to help ensure lubrication during the break-in period. Under a microscope, this surface treatment looks like the surface of a golf ball.

CAMSHAFT STRAIGHTENING

Proper engine operation requires that the camshaft be straight to prevent binding in the cam bearings and to provide even valve opening for all cylinders. Place the camshaft on V blocks and place a dial gauge on the cam bearings. Maximum **total indicator runout (TIR)** should

■ TECH TIP ■

VALVE-TO-PISTON CLEARANCE VERSUS CAM TIMING

If the cam timing is *advanced* (relative to the crankshaft), the intake valve-to-piston clearance is *reduced*.

If the cam timing is *retarded*, the exhaust valve-to-piston clearance is *reduced*.

This is true because the intake valve lags behind the motion of the piston on the intake stroke, whereas the piston "chases" the exhaust valve on the exhaust stroke. See Figure 12–51.

FIGURE 12–51 Modeling clay was used to determine valve-to-piston clearance. Most manufacturers recommend a minimum of 0.070 inch (1.8 millimeters). The clay is cut with a knife and the thickness of the clay is measured to determine the static (engine not running) clearance. The clearance decreases as the speed of the engine increases because of valve timing variations and connecting rod stretch.

be 0.002 inch (0.05 millimeter). If the total indicated runout is excessive, use a blunt chisel and hammer and strike the camshaft on the high side. Camshaft regrinders often use an air-operated chisel to straighten camshafts before the final grinding of the bearing journals.

LIFTERS OR TAPPETS

Valve lifters or tappets follow the contour or shape of the camshaft lobe. This arrangement changes the cam motion to a reciprocating motion in the valve train. Most older-style lifters have a relatively flat surface that slides on the cam. See Figure 12–52. Some lifters, however, are designed with a roller to follow the cam contour. Roller lifters are used primarily in production engines to reduce valve train friction (by up to 8%). This friction reduction can increase fuel economy and help to offset the greater manufacturing cost. All roller lifters must use a retainer to prevent lifter rotation. The retainer ensures that the roller is kept in line with the cam. If the retainer broke, the roller lifter could turn, destroying both the lifter and the camshaft. See Figures 12–53 through 12–55.

Valve train clearance is also called **valve lash.** Valve train clearance must not be excessive, or it will cause noise or result in premature failure. Two methods are commonly used to make the necessary valve clearance adjustments. One involves a **solid valve lifter** with a mechanical adjustment, and the other involves a lifter with an automatic hydraulic adjustment built into the lifter body called a **hydraulic valve lifter.**

SOLID LIFTERS

Overhead valve engines with mechanical lifters have an adjustment screw at the pushrod end of the rocker arm or an adjustment nut at the ball pivot. Adjustable pushrods are available for some specific applications.

FIGURE 12–52 The bottom of a lifter should be convex and <u>not</u> concave, as is the bottom of this worn lifter. Using worn lifters with a new camshaft can cause excessive camshaft wear on the edges of the cam.

Valve trains using solid lifters must run with some clearance to ensure positive valve closure, regardless of the engine temperature. This clearance is matched by a gradual rise in the cam contour called a **ramp.** (Hydraulic lifter camshafts do not have this ramp.) The ramp will take up the clearance before the valve begins to open. The camshaft lobe also has a closing ramp to ensure quiet operation.

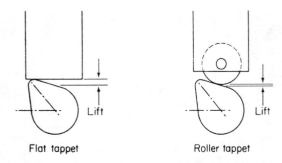

FIGURE 12-53 Note the difference in the amount of lift for a flat lifter (tappet) versus a roller lifter at the same cam angle. <u>Never</u> use a camshaft designed for roller tappets with flat tappets, or roller tappets on a camshaft designed for flat tappets.

FIGURE 12-55 All roller lifters (tappets) must be prevented from rotating during engine operation. Note the stamped steel retainers used to hold guide plates on this V-6 engine.

HYDRAULIC LIFTERS

A hydraulic lifter consists primarily of a hollow cylinder body enclosing a closely fit hollow plunger, a check valve, and a pushrod cup. Lifters that feed oil up through the pushrod have a metering disk or restrictor valve located under the pushrod cup. Engine oil under pressure is fed through an engine passage to the exterior lifter body. An undercut portion allows the oil under pressure to surround the lifter body. Oil under pressure goes through holes in the undercut section into the center of the plunger. From there, it goes down through the check valve to a clearance space between the bottom of the plunger and the interior bottom of the lifter body. It fills this space with oil at engine pressure. Slight leakage allowance is designed into the lifter so that the air can bleed out and the lifter can leak down if it should become overfilled. The operating principle of a hydraulic lifter is shown in Figures 12–57 and 12–58.

The pushrod fits into a cup in the top, open end of the lifter plunger. Holes in the pushrod cup, pushrod end, and hollow pushrod allow oil to transfer from the lifter piston center, past a metering disk or restrictor valve, and up through the pushrod to the rocker arm. Oil leaving the rocker arm lubricates the rocker arm assembly.

As the cam starts to push the lifter against the valve train, the oil below the lifter plunger is squeezed and tries to return to the lifter plunger center. A lifter check valve, either ball or disk type, traps the oil below the lifter plunger. This hydraulically locks the operating length of the lifter. The hydraulic lifter then opens the engine valve as would a solid lifter. When the lifter returns to the base circle of the cam, engine oil pressure

FIGURE 12-54 Typical roller lifters (tappets). Note how the two lifters are mechanically connected to prevent lifter rotation. If a roller lifter rotated, it would be quickly destroyed by the camshaft.

A lifter is solid in the sense that it transfers motion directly from the cam to the pushrod or valve. Its physical construction is that of a lightweight cylinder, either hollow or with a small-diameter center section and full-diameter ends. In some types that transfer oil through the pushrod, the external appearance is the same as for hydraulic lifters. See Figure 12–56.

FIGURE 12–56 *Typical solid valve lifters. The external appearance of the two lifters on the right is the same as that of a hydraulic lifter. The lifter on the far right is disassembled to show the internal parts required to control oil flow to the pushrod.*

again works to replace any oil that may have leaked out of the lifter.

The hydraulic lifter's job is to take up all clearance in the valve train. Occasionally, engines are run at excessive speeds. This tends to throw the valve open, causing **valve float.** During valve float, clearance exists in the valve train. The hydraulic lifter will take up this clearance as it is designed to do. When this occurs, it will keep the valve from closing on the seat. This is called **pump-up.** Pump-up will not occur when the engine is operated in the speed range for which it is designed.

Many overhead camshaft engines use a hydraulic lifter. See Figures 12–59 through 12–61 for examples of various styles and types of hydraulic lifters used on overhead camshaft engines.

LIFTER PRELOAD

Lifter preload is actually the distance between the pushrod seat inside the lifter and the snap ring of the lifter when the lifter is resting on the base circle (or heel) of the cam and the valve is closed. This distance should be about 0.020 to 0.045 inch. On engines with adjustable rocker arms, this distance or preload is determined by turning the rocker arm adjusting nut one-quarter to one full turn after zero lash (clearance) is determined. Tightening this adjusting nut further can cause the pushrod to bottom in the lifter. If the engine is rotated with the pushrod bottomed out, bent valves or bent or damaged pushrods, rocker arms, or rocker arm studs can result.

Engines that have been rebuilt or repaired and that do not use adjustable rocker arms are particularly at risk for damage. If any of the following operations have been preformed, lifter preload *must* be determined:

- Regrinding the camshaft (reduces base circle dimensions)
- Milling or resurfacing cylinder heads
- Milling or resurfacing block deck

- Grinding valves and/or facing valve stems
- Changing to a head gasket thinner or thicker than the original

Most lifters can accept a total variation in the entire valve train of about 0.080 to 0.180 inch. To determine lifter preload, rotate the engine until the valve being tested is resting on the base circle of the cam. For example, with the valve cover off and rotating the engine in the normal operating direction, watch the exhaust valve start to open. This means that the intake valve for that cylinder is resting on the base circle (heel) of the cam. Apply pressure down on the lifter. Wait several minutes for the lifter to bleed down. Measure the distance between rocker arm and valve stem. If the proper clearance is not obtained (generally between 0.020 and 0.045 inch), the following may need to be done to get the proper clearance:

1. Install longer or shorter pushrods. Manufacturers produce pushrods in various lengths. Some are available in lengths up to 0.100 inch longer or shorter than stock.
2. Install adjustable pushrods or rocker arms if possible.
3. Shim or grind rocker stands or shafts.

The following is a **rule of thumb:** Shim rocker arm supports to three-fifths of the measurement removed from the cylinder head (1.5:1 rocker ratio). For example, if 0.030 inch is removed from a cylinder head, shim the rocker arm to 0.030 inch times ⅗, or 0.018 inch.

DETERMINING LIFTER PRELOAD

The process of adjusting valves that use hydraulic valve lifters involves making certain that the lifter has the specified preload. A properly adjusted valve train should position the lifter in the center of its travel dimension.

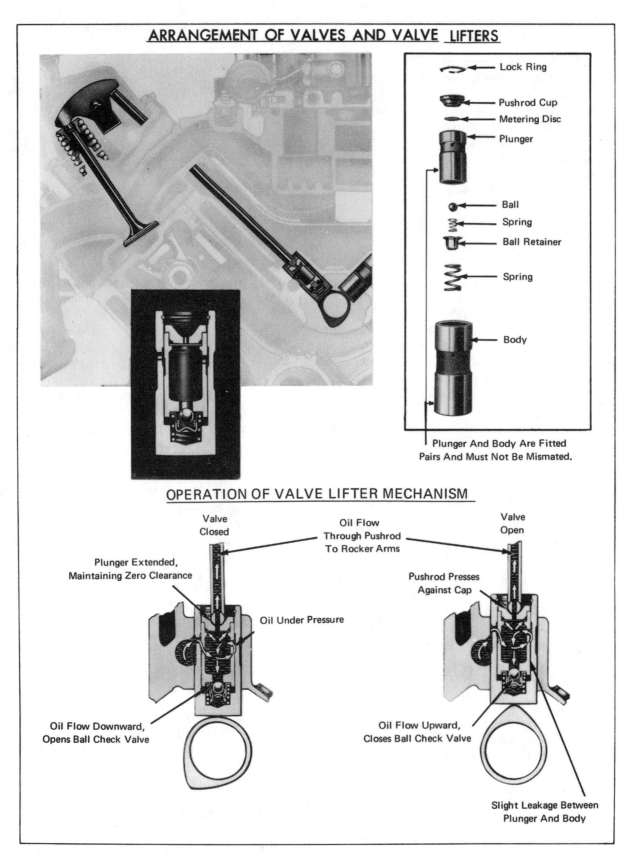

FIGURE 12–57 Operating principle of hydraulic lifters. (Courtesy of Cadillac Motor Car Division, GMC)

FIGURE 12–58 *Parts of two styles of hydraulic valve lifter (tappet).*

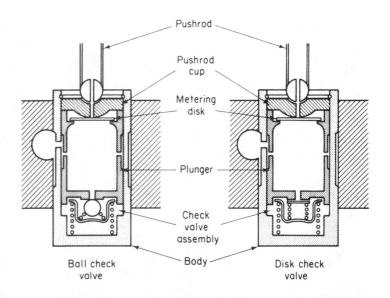

Pushrod

Pushrod cup

Metering disk

Plunger

Check valve assembly

Body

Ball check valve

Disk check valve

HYDRAULIC LIFTER

VALVE SPRING AND RETAINER

FOLLOWER

(a)

(b)

FIGURE 12–59 (a) Typical overhead camshaft four-cylinder engine using hydraulic lifters and followers. (b) Same engine with one follower and one lifter removed.

HYDRAULIC LIFTERS

FIGURE 12–60 This four-cylinder overhead cam engine uses rocker arms that are moved upward by the hydraulic lifters. The camshaft is in the cylinder head under the lifters.

243

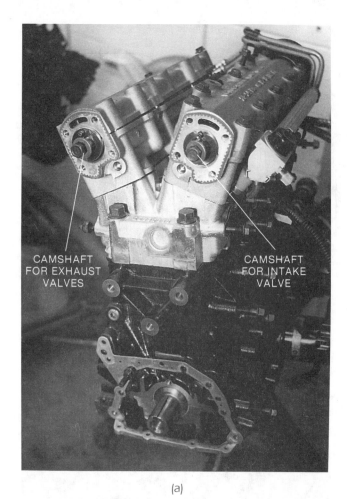

CAMSHAFT
FOR EXHAUST
VALVES

CAMSHAFT
FOR INTAKE
VALVE

(a)

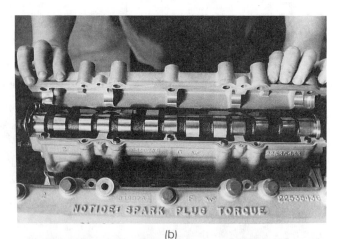

(b)

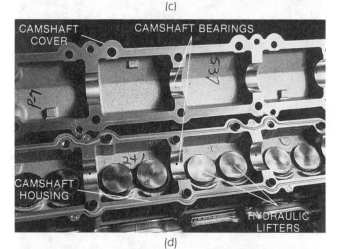

NOTICE! SPARK PLUG TORQUE
21-24 Nm OR 15-18 LBS FT

(c)

FIGURE 12–61 (a) A dual overhead camshaft inline four-cylinder engine. This engine has a cast-iron block with aluminum cylinder head and cam support housings (covers). (b) Removing the top of the camshaft housing shows that the camshaft bearings are a machined segment of the cover. (c) Removing the bottom section of the camshaft housing reveals the valves. The hydraulic lifters are still in the housing being removed. (d) With the camshaft removed, the tops of the hydraulic lifters are visible. (e) Camshaft housing showing one hydraulic lifter removed.

CAMSHAFT
COVER

CAMSHAFT BEARINGS

CAMSHAFT
HOUSING

HYDRAULIC
LIFTERS

(d)

(e)

244

The procedure for a valve train with *adjustable* rocker arms is as follows:

1. Rotate the engine clockwise as viewed from the nonprincipal or belt end (normal direction of rotation) until the exhaust lifter starts to move up.
2. Adjust the intake valve to zero lash (no preload) and then one-half turn more.
3. Rotate the engine until the intake valve is almost completely closed. Adjust the exhaust valve to zero lash and then one-half turn more.
4. Continue with this procedure for each cylinder until all the valves are correctly adjusted.

If the valve train uses *nonadjustable* rocker arms, the lifter preload must still be determined. The lifter preload *must* be measured if any or all of the following procedures have been performed on the engine:

- Head(s) milled
- Block decked
- Valves ground
- Any other machining operation that could change the valve train measurement

Shorter (or longer) replacement pushrods may be required to produce the correct lifter preload. Some engine manufacturers recommend using thin metal shims under the rocker arm supports if needed.

■ **CAUTION:** If shims are used under the rocker arm supports, be sure that the shim has the required oil holes. ■

DETERMINING PROPER LIFTER TRAVEL

To determine if shimming or use of replacement pushrods of different lengths is required, use the following procedure:

1. With the valve cover removed, rotate the engine until the valve lifter being tested is resting on the base circle of the camshaft.
2. Depress the pushrod into the lifter with steady pressure. This should cause the lifter to bleed down until the pushrod bottoms out in the lifter bore.
3. Measure clearance (lash) between the rocker arm tip and the stem of the valve. This measurement varies according to manufacturer and engine design, but it usually ranges from

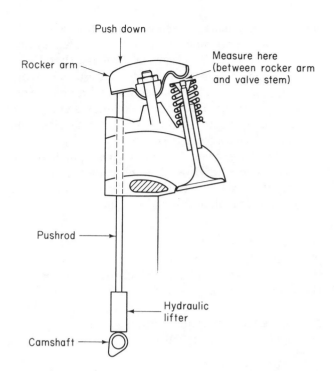

FIGURE 12–62 Procedure for determining proper lifter travel.

0.020 to 0.080 inch. See Figure 12–62. Always consult exact manufacturer's specifications before taking any corrective measures.

If the measurement is not within acceptable range, select the proper-length pushrods to achieve the proper lifter travel dimension and preload.

NOTE: Some engines use several different pushrod lengths depending on exact build date! Block casting numbers may be the same, but the engines may require different internal parts. Check with the manufacturer's specifications in the factory service manual for proper interchangeable parts.

VALVE NOISE DIAGNOSIS

Valve lifters are often noisy, especially at engine start-up. When the engine is off, some valves are open. The valve spring pressure forces the inner plunger to leak down (oil is forced out of the lifter). Therefore, many vehicle manufacturers consider valve ticking at one-half engine speed after start-up to be normal, especially if the engine is quiet after 10 to 30 seconds. Be sure that the engine is equipped with the correct oil filter, and that the filter has an internal check valve. If in doubt, use an original equipment oil filter. If all of the valves are noisy, check the level of the oil. If the oil level is low, the oil may have been **aerated** (air mixed with the oil) which would prevent proper operation of the hydraulic lifter. Low oil pressure can also cause all valves to be noisy. The oil level being too high can also cause noisy valve lifters. The connecting rods create foam as they rotate through the oil. This foam can travel through the oiling systems to the lifters. The foam in the lifters prevents normal operation and allows the valves to make noise.

If the valves are abnormally noisy, remove the rocker arm cover and use a stethoscope to determine which valves or valve train parts may be causing the noise. Check for all of the following items:

■ Worn camshaft lobe
■ Dirty, stuck, or worn lifters
■ Worn rocker arm (if the vehicle is so equipped)
■ Worn or bent pushrods (if the vehicle is so equipped)
■ Broken or weak valve springs
■ Sticking or warped valves

MECHANICAL LIFTER SERVICE

Mechanical lifters, like hydraulic lifters, should be replaced if the camshaft is replaced. If the lifters are to be reused, they *must* be kept in order and reinstalled in the exact positions in which they were originally used in the engine. All lifters should be cleaned and carefully inspected. If the base of the lifter is dished (concave), the lifter should be replaced.

NOTE: Regrinding of valve lifter bases is generally not recommended because the hardened areas of the lifter can be ground through.

As with any lifter, new or used, the bore clearance should be checked.

HYDRAULIC LIFTER SERVICE

Hydraulic lifter service begins with a thorough visual inspection. Compare the lifter wear to the corresponding lobe on the camshaft. *All lifters should be replaced during a major engine overhaul or a camshaft replacement.*

Vehicle manufacturers usually recommend that, because of their high cost, hydraulic roller lifters be checked for wear, disassembled, and cleaned rather than being replaced. Any other hydraulic lifter that is to be reused should also be disassembled and cleaned using the following steps:

Step #1. Select a clean work area and tray for the disassembled parts. See Figure 12–63.
Step #2. Disassemble the lifters and keep all parts in order.
Step #3. Clean all parts and reassemble. Always use a lintless cloth because lint can affect lifter operation.
Step #4. Test leak-down rate using a leak-down tester and special-viscosity fluid. See Figure 12–64.
  a. Measure the time required for the fluid to pass between the inner and outer body of the lifter.
  b. The time it takes for the lifter to collapse under a given weight should be longer than 10 seconds and less than 90 seconds.
  c. Check the service manual for the exact leak-down time for your vehicle. The average time for leak-down is 20 to 40 seconds.

HYDRAULIC VALVE LIFTER INSTALLATION

Most vehicle manufacturers recommend installing lifters *without* filling or pumping the lifter full of oil. If the lifter is filled with oil during engine start-up, the lifter may not be able to bleed down quickly enough and the valves may be kept open. Not only will the engine not operate correctly with the valves held open, but the piston could hit the open valves, causing serious engine damage. Most manufacturers usually specify that the lifter be lubricated. Roller hydraulic lifters can be lubricated with engine oil, whereas flat lifters require that engine assembly lube or extreme pressure (EP) grease be applied to the base.

BLEEDING HYDRAULIC LIFTERS

Air trapped inside a hydraulic valve lifter can be easily bled by simply operating the engine at a fast idle (2500 RPM). Normal oil flow through the lifters will allow all of the air inside the lifter to be bled out.

NOTE: Some engines, such as the many Nissan overhead camshaft engines, *must* have the air removed from the lifter before installation. This is accomplished by submerging the lifter in a container of engine oil and using a straightened paper clip to depress the oil passage check ball.

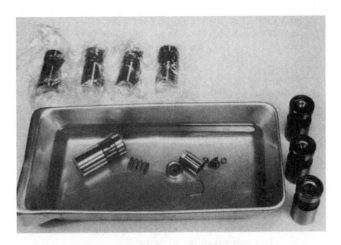

FIGURE 12–63 Cleaning a disassembled hydraulic lifter (tappet) in clean petroleum solvent. After cleaning and reassembly, all hydraulic lifters should be checked for proper leak-down rate using a special fluid and tester.

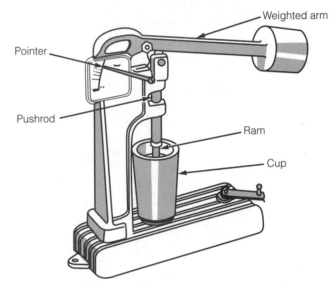

FIGURE 12–64 Typical hydraulic lifter leak-down tester.

Consult a service manual if in doubt about the bleeding procedure for the vehicle being serviced.

SUMMARY

1. The camshaft rotates at one-half the crankshaft speed.
2. The pushrods should be rotating while the engine is running if the camshaft and lifters are okay.
3. On overhead valve engines, the camshaft is usually placed in the block above the crankshaft. The lobes of the camshaft are usually lubricated by splash lubrication.
4. Silent chains are quieter than roller chains but tend to stretch with use.
5. Cam chucking is the movement of the camshaft lengthwise in the engine during operation.
6. The lift of a cam is usually expressed in decimal inches and represents the distance that the valve is lifted off the valve seat.
7. In many engines, camshaft lift is transferred to the tip of the valve stem to open the valve by the use of a rocker arm or follower.
8. Pushrods transfer camshaft motion upward from the camshaft to the rocker arm.
9. Camshaft duration is the number of degrees of crankshaft rotation that the valve is lifted off the seat.
10. Valve overlap is the number of crankshaft degrees both valves are open.
11. Camshafts should be installed according to the manufacturer's recommended procedures. Flat lifter camshafts should be thoroughly lubricated with extreme pressure lubricant.
12. If a new camshaft is installed, new lifters should also be installed.

REVIEW QUESTIONS

1. What puts thrust loads on a camshaft?
2. When is steel used as the camshaft material?
3. Explain why the lift and duration and lobe center dimension determine the power characteristics of the engine.
4. Explain lobe centerline.
5. List the various coatings that can be used on camshafts to harden and protect against wear.
6. Describe the operation of a hydraulic lifter.
7. Describe how to determine if the hydraulic lifter preload is correct.

MULTIPLE-CHOICE QUESTIONS

1. The camshaft makes _____ for every revolution of the crankshaft.
   a. One-quarter revolution
   b. One-half revolution
   c. One revolution
   d. Two revolutions

2. Valve lifters rotate during operation because of the _____ of the camshaft.
   a. Taper of the lobe
   b. Thrust plate
   c. Chain tensioner
   d. Bearings

3. If lift and duration remain constant and the lobe center angle decreases,_____ .
   a. The valve overlap decreases
   b. The effective lift increases
   c. The effective duration increases
   d. The valve overlap increases

4. If a camshaft is reground, _____ .
   a. The base circle is reduced
   b. The original lift is maintained
   c. The original duration is maintained
   d. All of the above

5. If the cam timing is advanced from the stock setting, _____ .
   a. The intake valve–to–piston clearance is increased
   b. The intake valve–to–piston clearance is reduced
   c. The exhaust valve–to–piston clearance is reduced
   d. Both a and c
   e. All of the above

6. Typical lifter preload is _____ .
   a. 0.001 to 0.003 inch
   b. 0.005 to 0.010 inch
   c. 0.020 to 0.045 inch
   d. 0.080 to 0.180 inch

7. A DOHC V-6 has how many camshafts?
   a. 4
   b. 3
   c. 2
   d. 1

8. The intake valve opens at 39 degrees BTDC and closes at 71 degrees ABDC. The exhaust valve opens at 78 degrees BBDC and closes at 47 degrees ATDC.
   a. Intake valve duration is 110 degrees
   b. Exhaust valve duration is 125 degrees
   c. Overlap is 86 degrees
   d. Both a and b

9. Hydraulic valve lifters can make a ticking noise when the engine is running if _____ .
   a. The valve lash is too close
   b. The valve lash is too loose
   c. The lobe centerlines are over 110 degrees
   d. Both a and c

10. Most camshafts are coated with _____ at the factory to add wear resistance.
   a. SAE 80W-90 gear lube
   b. SAE 5W-30 engine oil
   c. A phosphate coating
   d. Beeswax or candle wax

13

Engine Block Design and Service

OBJECTIVES

After studying Chapter 13, the reader will be able to

1. Describe the types of engine blocks and how they are manufactured.
2. List the machining operations required on most engine blocks.
3. Explain how the surface finish is achieved inside a cylinder bore.
4. List the steps necessary to prepare an engine block for assembly.

The engine block, which is the supporting structure for the entire engine, is made from gray cast iron or from cast- or die-cast aluminum alloy. The gray color is a result of the 3% of carbon in the form of graphite in the cast iron. The liquid cast iron is poured into a mold. The carbon in the cast iron allows for easy machining, often without coolant. The graphite in the cast iron also has lubricating properties. Newer blocks use thinner walls to reduce weight. Cast iron is strong for its weight and usually is magnetic. All other engine parts are mounted on or in the block. This large casting supports the crankshaft and camshaft and holds all the parts in alignment. Blocks are often of the **monoblock** design, which means that the cylinder, water jacket, main bearing supports **(saddles)**, and oil passages are all cast as one structure for strength and quietness. Large-diameter holes in the block casting form the cylinders to guide the pistons. The cylinder holes are called bores because they are made by a machining process called boring. Combustion pressure loads are carried from the head to the crankshaft bearings through the block structure. The block has

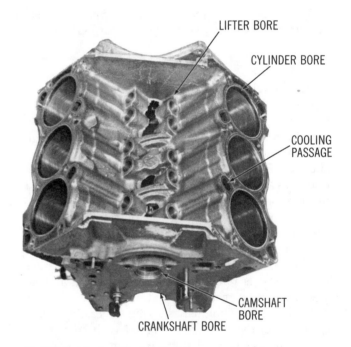

FIGURE 13–1 Typical V-type engine block.

webs, walls, and drilled passages to contain the coolant and lubricating oil and to keep them separated from each other. See Figure 13–1. Mounting pads or **lugs** on the block transfer the engine torque reaction to the vehicle frame through attached engine mounts. A large mounting surface at the rear of the engine block is used for fastening a bell housing or transmission.

The cylinder head(s) attach to the block. The attaching joints are sealed so that they do not leak. Gaskets are used in the joints to take up differences that are created by machining irregularities and that result from different pressures and temperatures.

249

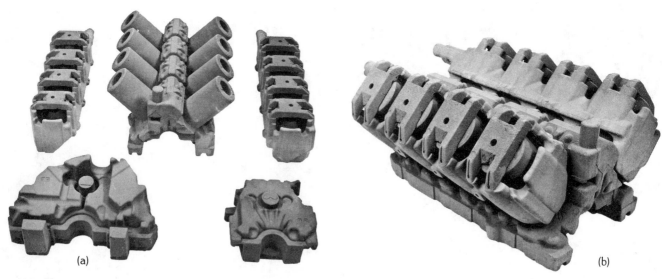

FIGURE 13–2   Casting cores. (a) Separate cores. (b) Assembled cores. (Courtesy of Central Foundry Division, GMC)

BLOCK MANUFACTURING

Cast-iron cylinder block casting technology continues to be improved. The trend is to make blocks with larger cores, using fewer individual pieces. Oil-sand cores, shown in Figure 13–2, are forms that shape the internal openings and passages in the engine block. Before casting, the cores are supported within a core box. The core box also has a liner to shape the outside of the block. Special alloy cast iron is poured into the box. It flows between the cores and the core box liner. As the cast iron cools, the core breaks up. When the cast iron has hardened, it is removed from the core box, and the pieces of sand core are removed through the openings in the block by vigorously shaking the casting. These openings in the block are plugged with **core plugs.** Core plugs are also called **freeze plugs** or **frost plugs.** Although the name infers that the plugs would be pushed outward if the coolant in the passages were to freeze, seldom do they work in this way.

One way to keep the engine weight as low as possible is to make the block with minimum wall thickness. The cast iron used with thin-wall casting techniques has higher nickel content and is harder than the cast iron previously used. Engine designers have used foundry techniques to make engines lightweight by making the cast-iron block walls and bulkheads only as heavy as necessary to support their required loads. They have omitted as much material as possible from the lifter gallery area. They have even designed small oil filters so that the attachment point size could be reduced.

CASTING NUMBERS

Whenever an engine part such as a block is cast, a number is put into the mold to identify the casting. These casting numbers can be used to check dimensions such as the cubic inch displacement and other information such as year of manufacture. Sometimes changes are made to the mold, yet the casting number is not changed. Most of the time the casting number is the best piece of identifying information that the service technician can use.

BLOCK MACHINING

After cooling and thorough cleaning, the block casting goes to the machining line. The top, bottom, and end surfaces are cleaned and semifinished with a **broach.** A broach is a large slab with a number of cutting teeth. Each tooth cuts a little more than the preceding tooth. It is somewhat like a large, coarse, contoured file. One pass of the broach will smooth both cylinder decks and the lifter valley cover rail. A second pass will smooth the upper main bearing bores and the oil pan rail. The ends of the block may be finished with a third broach. Some of these surfaces are completed with the broach operation; others need to be finished with a mill, a final broach, or a boring operation. Broaching leaves straight lines across the surface, whereas milling leaves curved lines.

The cylinders are bored and honed in a number of operations until they have the required size and finish. Figure 13–3 shows a part of a block production line. A slight notch or **scallop** is cut into the edge of the cylin-

FIGURE 13–3 One section of an engine production line. (Courtesy of Greenlee Brothers and Company)

der on some engines using very large valves (Figure 13–4). All drilling and thread tapping is accomplished on the block line.

ALUMINUM BLOCKS

Aluminum is used for some cylinder blocks and is non-magnetic and light in weight. Aluminum blocks may have one of several different types of cylinder walls:

- Cast-aluminum blocks may have steel cylinder liners (Saturn, Northstar, and Ford modular V-8s and V-6s). The cast-iron cylinder sleeves are either cast into the aluminum block during manufacturing or pressed into the aluminum block. These sleeves are not in contact with the coolant passages and are called **dry cylinder sleeves**. See Figure 13–5.
- Another aluminum block design has the block die cast from silicon-aluminum alloy with no cylinder liners. Pistons with zinc–copper–hard iron coatings are used in these aluminum bores (Chevrolet Vega and Porsche 944 engines). See Figure 13–6.
- Some engines have die-cast aluminum blocks with replaceable cast-iron cylinder sleeves. The sleeves are sealed at the block deck and at their base. Coolant flows around the cylinder sleeve, so this type of sleeve is called a **wet cylinder sleeve** (Cadillac 4.1, 4.5, and 4.9 liter V-8 engines).

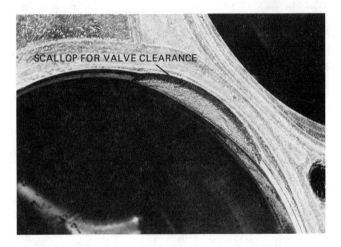

SCALLOP FOR VALVE CLEARANCE

FIGURE 13–4 Scallop on the upper edge of the cylinder for valve clearance.

Cast-iron main bearing caps are used with aluminum blocks. This is necessary to give the required strength.

BLOCK CONDITION

Block faults occur in the cylinder wall, cooling system, and shaft bore alignment, and as broken parts. All of the other engine parts depend on the block for support, alignment, and operating climate.

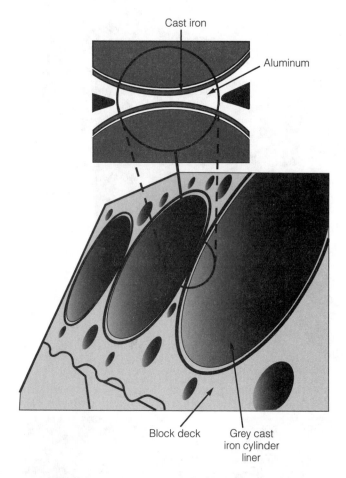

FIGURE 13–5   Cast-iron cylinder liners can either be cast or press-fit into an aluminum block.

FIGURE 13–6   Four-cylinder block die cast from silicon-aluminum alloy with no cylinder liners. Several manufacturers use this method to produce strong yet lightweight engine blocks. (Courtesy of Chevrolet Motor Division, GMC)

Cylinder wall wear of the type shown in Figure 13–7 is one of the most noticeable abnormal block conditions. Cylinder walls, in normal use, have a smooth glaze from smoothing effects of the piston and rings during operation.

Sometimes the connecting rod is allowed to strike the bottom edge of the cylinder as the piston and rod assembly are removed or installed. This will nick the bottom edge of the cylinder and raise sharp points. If these points are not removed, they will scratch the piston skirt of the reconditioned engine. See Chapter 8 for details on block cleaning and crack detection.

LOWER ENGINE BLOCK DESIGN

The engine block consists primarily of the cylinders with a web or bulkhead to support the crankshaft and head attachments. The rest of the block consists of a water jacket, a lifter chamber, and mounting flanges. In

FIGURE 13–7   Cylinder wall scored as the result of a broken piston ring.

most engine designs, each main bearing bulkhead supports both a cam bearing and a main bearing. The bulkhead is well ribbed to support and distribute loads applied to it. This gives the block structural rigidity and beam stiffness throughout its useful life.

FIGURE 13–8 *Typical shallow skirt block with the oil pan rail surface close to the crankshaft centerline. The block pictured here is upside down on a workbench.*

FIGURE 13–9 *Typical deep skirt block with the oil pan rail surface that extends well below the crankshaft centerline. The block pictured here is upside down on a workbench.*

■ TECH TIP ■

THE MOST FORWARD

Cylinder #1 is usually the cylinder that is most forward in the engine block. Most forward means closest to the accessory drive belts. This is helpful to remember when attempting to find cylinder #1, especially with transversely mounted V-type engines. This rule works for all current production engines. The exceptions include Pontiac-built V-8s and some Cadillac V-8s, neither of which are currently in production.

Two types of lower block designs are in use. A block of the first design type will be called a **shallow skirt block.** The shallow skirt block is the smaller and lighter of the two engine block types (Figure 13–8). It has the least amount of cast iron and this makes it a small, compact, lightweight block. Covers, such as the oil pan and timing cover, are largely lightweight aluminum die castings or sheet-steel stampings. The base of this block is close to the crankshaft centerline. This block base is called the **oil pan rail.**

The second type of block will be called a **deep skirt block.** In this type of block, the deep skirt extends the oil pan rail well below the crankshaft centerline. The deep skirt block improves the stiffness of the entire engine (Figure 13–9). When used on a V-type engine, it is often called a **Y block.** It provides a wider surface on

which to attach the bell housing. This greater rigidity ensures smooth, quiet engine operation and durability. The deep skirt must be wide enough to clear the connecting rods as they swing through the block, and therefore, a large oil capacity is provided with its use.

THE BLOCK DECK

The cylinder head is fastened to the top surface of the block. This surface is called the **block deck.** The deck has a smooth surface to seal *against* the head gasket. Bolt holes are positioned around the cylinders to form an even holding pattern. Four, five, or six head bolts are used around each cylinder in automobile engines. These bolt holes go into reinforced areas within the block that carry the combustion pressure load to the main bearing bulkheads. Additional holes in the block are used to transfer coolant and oil. See Figure 13–10.

CYLINDER SKIRTS

The cylinders may be of a **skirtless** design, flush with the interior top of the crankcase (Figure 13–11), or they may have a skirt that extends into the crankcase (Figure 13–12). **Extended skirt** cylinders are used on engines with short connecting rods. In these engines, the pistons move very close to the crankshaft. The cylinder skirt must go as low as possible to support the piston when it is at the lowest point in its stroke. This can be seen in Figure 13–13. The extended cylinder skirt allows the engine to be designed with a low overall engine height, because the engine has a small block size for its displacement.

FIGURE 13-10   Head bolt holes and coolant passages are easily identified after removing the cylinder head(s).

FIGURE 13-12   Cylinder skirt that extends below the interior top of the crankcase.

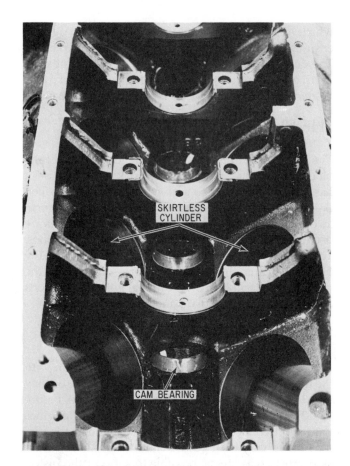

FIGURE 13-11   Skirtless cylinder that is flush with the interior of the top of the crankcase.

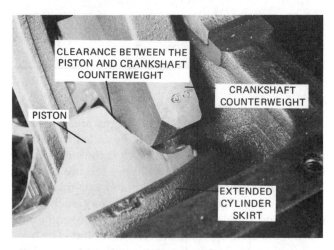

FIGURE 13-13   The piston comes very close to the crankshaft counterweight when it is at the bottom of the stroke on an engine that has a short connecting rod.

FIGURE 13–14 Coolant passages surrounding the cylinders.

FIGURE 13–15 Typical oil hole drilling in the main bearing web.

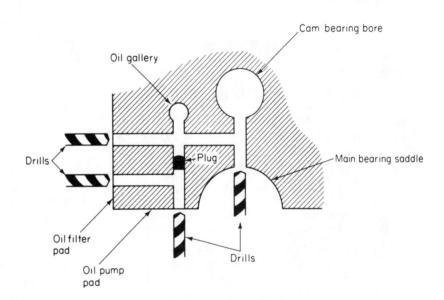

COOLING PASSAGES

Cylinders are surrounded by cooling passages. These coolant passages around the cylinders are often called the **cooling jacket** (Figure 13–14). In most skirtless cylinder designs, the cooling passages extend nearly to the bottom of the cylinder. In extended skirt cylinder designs, the cooling passages are limited to the upper portion of the cylinder.

LUBRICATING PASSAGES

An engine block has many oil holes that carry lubricating oil to the required locations. During manufacture, all of the oil holes are drilled from outside the block. Oil pas-

sages are rarely cast in engine blocks. When a curved passage is needed, intersecting drilled holes are used. In some engines, plugs are placed in the oil holes to direct oil to another point before it comes back to the original hole, on the opposite side of the plug. Typical oil hole drilling is illustrated in Figure 13–15. After oil holes are drilled, the unneeded open ends may be capped by pipe plugs, steel balls, or cup-type soft plugs. End plugs in the oil passages are a source of possible oil leakage in operating engines.

MAIN BEARING CAPS

The main bearing caps are cast separately from the block. They are machined and then installed on the block for a final bore finishing operation. With caps installed, the

FIGURE 13–16 Small-block Chevrolet blocks on an assembly line at a small regional remanufacturing plant. Note the left-hand dipstick hole and a pad cast for a right-hand dipstick.

■ TECH TIP ■

WHAT DOES LHD MEAN?

LHD means **left-hand dipstick.** This abbreviation is commonly used by rebuilders and remanufacturers in their literature in describing Chevrolet small-block V-8 engines. Before about 1980, most small-block Chevrolet V-8s used an oil dipstick pad on the left side (driver's side) of the engine block. Starting in about 1980, when oxygen sensors were first used on this engine, the dipstick was relocated to the right side of the block.

Therefore, to be assured of ordering or delivering the correct engine, knowing the dipstick location is critical. An LHD block cannot be used with the exhaust manifold setup that includes the oxygen sensor without major refitting or the installing of a different style of oil pan that includes a provision for an oil dipstick. Engine blocks with the dipstick pad cast on the right side are, therefore, coded as right-hand dipstick (RHD) engines.

NOTE: Some blocks cast around the year 1980 are cast with both right- and left-hand oil dipstick pads, but only one is drilled for the dipstick tube. See Figure 13–16.

FIGURE 13–17 Standard two-bolt main bearing cap.

cause they are individually finished in place. Main bearing caps may have cast numbers indicating their position on the block. If not, they should be marked.

Standard production engines usually use two bolts to hold the main bearing cap in place (Figure 13–17). Heavy-duty and high-performance engines often use additional main bearing support bolts. Many smaller high-speed engines use a cast-iron **girdle** or main bearing support. The four-bolt main cap can be of a cross-bolted design in a deep skirt block or of a parallel-bolted design in a shallow skirt block (Figure 13–18). Remember that the expansion force of the combustion chamber gases will try to push the head off the top and the crankshaft off the bottom of the block. The engine is held together with the head bolts and main bearing cap bolts screwed into bolt bosses and ribs in the block. The **bosses** are enlarged areas of the block that surround the openings. The extra bolts on the main bearing cap help to support the crankshaft when there are high combustion pressures and mechanical loads, especially during high–engine speed operation.

ENGINE BLOCK SERVICE

The engine block is the foundation of the engine. All parts of the block must be of the correct size and they must be aligned. The parts must also have the proper

main bearing bores and cam bearing bores are machined to the correct size and alignment. On some engines, these bores are honed to a very fine finish and exact size. Main bearing caps are *not* interchangeable or reversible, be-

FIGURE 13–18 Four-bolt main bearing caps: (top) cross-bolted design (Courtesy of Chrysler Corporation) and (bottom) parallel-bolted design.

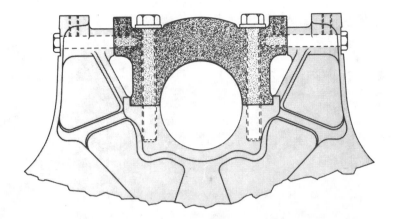

finishes if the engine is to function dependably for a normal service life. **Blueprinting** is the reconditioning of all the critical surfaces and dimensions so that the block is actually like new.

After a thorough cleaning, the block should be inspected for cracks or other flaws before machine work begins. If the block is in serviceable condition, the block should be prepared in the following sequence:

Operation #1. Align boring or honing main bearing saddles and caps.
Operation #2. Machining the block deck surface parallel to the crankshaft
Operation #3. Cylinder boring and honing

MAIN BEARING BORE ALIGNMENT

The main bearing journals of a straight crankshaft are in alignment. If the main bearing bores in the block are not in alignment, the crankshaft will bend as it rotates. This will lead to premature bearing failure and it could lead

to a broken crankshaft. The original stress in the block casting is gradually relieved as the block is used. Some slight warpage may occur as the stress is relieved. In addition, the continued pounding caused by combustion will usually cause some stretch in the main bearing caps. See Figures 13–19 through 13–22. Realigning and resizing the main bearing bores in the block is a procedure called **align boring** or **align honing.**

A number of different types of equipment are used to align the main bearing bores in the block. Some are simple fixtures that clamp on the block, whereas others place the block in a large production align boring or align honing machine. The align boring tool is a cutting tool, similar to a lathe tool. Honing uses a stone instead of a cutting tool and produces a finer finish than does align boring. It provides precise control of the main bearing bore size.

The same general steps are followed in align boring, regardless of the type of equipment used.

Step #1. First, a small amount of metal is removed from the main bearing cap parting surfaces.

FIGURE 13–19   Checking alignment of main bearing saddles with a straightedge and a thickness (feeler) gauge.

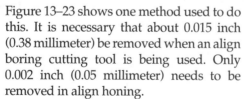

FIGURE 13–20   Saddle repair kits as used by major remanufacturers of industrial and commercial engines. These extra-thick bearing shells are used to compensate for the oversize boring of the block saddle area.

FIGURE 13–21   To prevent the need for scraping an engine block, the saddle of this automotive engine has been brazed. This restored the saddle height to be the same as that of the others.

FIGURE 13–22   After the saddle area was brazed, this block was remachined to original stock dimensions. Even though this procedure is generally not recommended, it may be used to save an expensive engine block.

Figure 13–23 shows one method used to do this. It is necessary that about 0.015 inch (0.38 millimeter) be removed when an align boring cutting tool is being used. Only 0.002 inch (0.05 millimeter) needs to be removed in align honing.

Step #2.   The resurfaced main bearing caps are torqued in place on the block.

Step #3.   The main bearing bores are checked to determine exactly where metal must be removed to align the bores. The align boring tool is adjusted at each main bearing bore to cut the correct diameter. A typical align boring fixture is shown in Figure 13–24.

NOTE: One dimension that is critical in all engines is the spacing between the cam bearing centerline and the crankshaft centerline. This must be maintained to have the proper cam drive gear mesh or the proper timing chain tension. If this dimension is not correct, it will lead to faulty timing and to premature failure of the cam drive. See Figure 13–25. _____

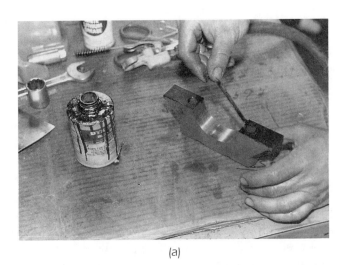
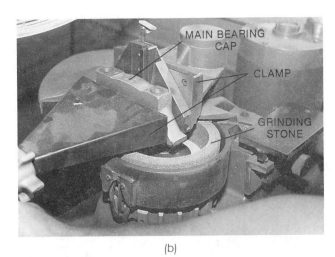

(a)   (b)

FIGURE 13–23 **(a) In preparation for align honing, the main bearing caps are coated with machinist bluing dye. Because less than 0.001 inch is to be removed from the bearing cap, the machinist wants to be certain that the material is removed equally. (b) One type of fixture used to remove a small amount of metal from a bearing cap.**

FIGURE 13–24 Align boring the main bearing bores of a large industrial engine.

Step #4. The align hone fits through all the main bearing bores at the same time. The align hone is stroked back and forth through the bearing bores to properly size them, as shown in Figure 13–26. It takes individual instruction and practice to develop a touch and the skill necessary to properly align main bearing bores in the block.

Step #5. The block and oil passages must be thoroughly cleaned after align boring to remove all abrasives and metal chips. The machined surfaces are coated with oil to prevent rusting until the block is finally cleaned for assembly. The aligned main bearing bores should be in exact alignment.

MACHINING THE DECK SURFACE OF THE BLOCK

An engine should have the same combustion chamber size in each cylinder. For this to occur, each piston must come up an equal distance from the block deck. The connecting rods are attached to the rod bearing journals of the crankshaft. Pistons are attached to the connecting rods. As the crankshaft rotates, the pistons come to the top of the stroke. When all parts are sized equally, all the pistons will come up to the same level. This can only happen if the block deck is parallel to the main bearing bores. See Figures 13–27 through 13–29.

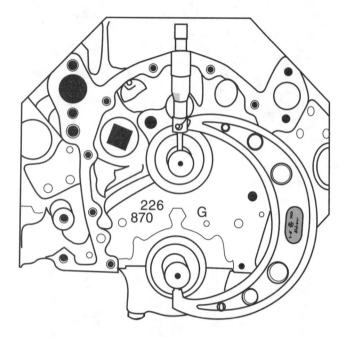

FIGURE 13–25 *Special setup to measure the centerline distance between the crankshaft and camshaft. During align boring, material is removed from the saddle area of the block, placing the crankshaft closer to the camshaft.*

The block deck must be resurfaced in a surfacing machine that can control the amount of metal removal when it is necessary to match the size of the combustion chambers. This procedure is called **decking the block.** The block is set up on a bar located in the main bearing saddles, or set up on the oil pan rails of the block. The bar is parallel to the direction of cutting head movement. The block is leveled sideways, and then the deck is resurfaced in the same manner as the head is resurfaced. Figure 13–30 shows a block deck being resurfaced by grinding. Also see Figure 13–31. The surface finish should be 60 to 100 RA (65 to 110 RMS) for cast iron and 50 to 60 RA (55 to 65 RMS) for aluminum block decks to be assured of a proper head gasket surface. See chapter 10 for additional information on surface finish.

CYLINDER BORING

Cylinders should be measured across the engine (perpendicular to the crankshaft), where the greatest wear occurs. Most wear will be found just below the ridge, and the least amount of wear will occur below the lowest ring travel. Most cylinders are serviceable if they are no more than 0.003 inch (0.076 millimeter) out-of-round, if they have no more than 0.005 inch (0.127 millimeter) taper, and if they have no deep scratches in the cylinder wall. Cylinder walls in this condition can be expected to have a normal service life when they are resurfaced. See Figure 13–32. The most effective way to correct excessive cylinder out of round, taper, or scoring is to **rebore** the cylinder. The rebored cylinder requires the use of a

FIGURE 13–26 *Align honing the main bearing bores.*

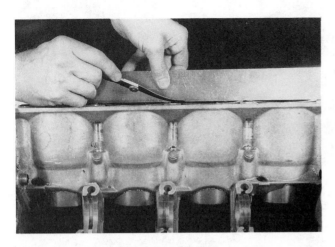

FIGURE 13-27 Check the level of the deck of a block with a straightedge. A good-quality straightedge should be accurate to 0.0002 inch (0.2 or two-tenths of a thousandth of an inch).

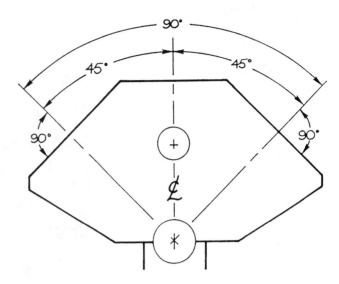

FIGURE 13-29 Machining a V-8 block helps to ensure that the deck surfaces are exactly 90 degrees from each other and that the block is square.

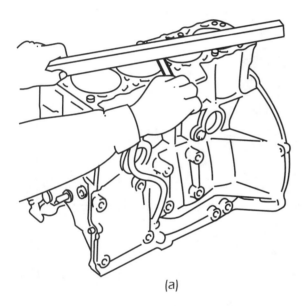

(a)

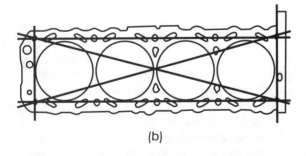

(b)

FIGURE 13-28 (a) Checking the flatness of the block deck surface using a straightedge and a feeler (thickness) gauge. (b) To be sure that the top of the block is flat, check the block in six places as shown.

new, oversize piston. Oversize pistons usually have the same weight as the original pistons, so a single cylinder on a multicylinder engine can be rebored without upsetting the quality of the engine balance.

The maximum bore oversize is determined by two things: the cylinder wall thickness and the size of the available oversize pistons. Before boring the block, make certain that the block is identified correctly (see Figure 13–33). If in doubt as to the amount of overbore that is possible without causing structural weakness, an **ultrasonic** test should be performed on the block to determine the thickness of the cylinder walls (see Figure 13–34). All cylinders should be tested. Variation in cylinder wall thickness occurs because of core shifting (moving) during the casting of the block. For best results, cylinders should be rebored to the smallest size possible.

HINT: *An easy way to calculate oversize (OS) piston size is to determine the amount of taper, double it, and add 0.010 inch (Taper × 2 + 0.010 in = OS piston). Common oversize measurements include 0.020 inch, 0.030 inch, 0.040 inch, and 0.060 inch. Use caution when boring for an oversize measurement larger than 0.030 inch.*

The pistons that will be used *must* always be in hand *before* the cylinders are rebored. The cylinders are then bored and honed to match the size of the pistons.

The cylinder must be perpendicular to the crankshaft for normal bearing and piston life. If the block deck has been aligned with the crankshaft, it can be used to align the cylinders. Portable cylinder boring bars are clamped to the block deck. Heavy-duty pro-

FIGURE 13–30 Block deck
being resurfaced with a
grinder.

FIGURE 13–31 Typical abrasive grit stones. A fine
grit stone is on the left and a coarse grit stone is
on the right.

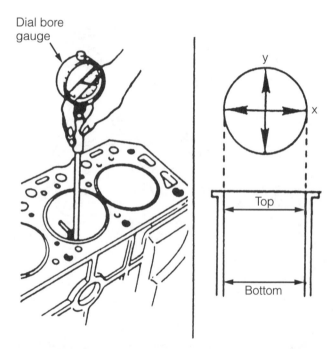

FIGURE 13–32 Checking the cylinder using a dial
bore gauge. First, measure the top of the cylinder
at 90 degrees from the crankshaft centerline. This
is the "X" diameter. Then, measure the diameter at
the top of the cylinder in line with the crankshaft.
This is the "Y" diameter. Subtracting the Y dimension from the X dimension will give the amount by
which the cylinder is out-of-round. Measure the
cylinder diameter at 90 degrees from the crankshaft centerline at the bottom of the cylinder.
Subtract this measurement from the X diameter to
calculate cylinder taper.

FIGURE 13–33 Typical block identification numbers stamped on the front section of a block deck. Rubbing chalk into the numbers and then wiping off the excess from the surface helps to make the numbers easier to read.

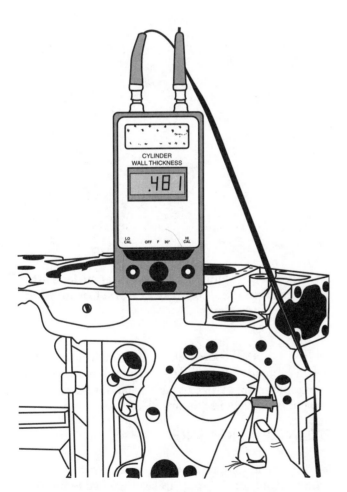

FIGURE 13–34 Ultrasonic testing can be used to determine the thickness of the cylinder walls. In this example, the thickness of the cast iron is 0.481 inch.

■ TECH TIP ■

ALWAYS USE TORQUE PLATES

Torque plates are thick metal plates that are bolted to the cylinder block to duplicate the forces on the block that occur when the cylinder head is installed. Even though not all machine shops use torque plates during the boring operation, the use of torque plates during the final dimensional honing operation is very beneficial. Without torque plates, cylinders can become out-of-round (up to 0.003 inch) and distorted when the cylinder heads are installed and torqued down. Even though the use of torque plates does not eliminate all distortion, their use helps to ensure a truer cylinder dimension.

duction boring machines support the block on the main bearing bores.

Main bearing caps should be torqued in place when cylinders are being rebored. In precision boring, a torque plate is also bolted on in place of the cylinder head while boring cylinders. See the tech tip Always Use Torque Plates. In this way, distortion is kept to a minimum. The general procedure used for reboring cylinders is to set the boring bar up so that it is perpendicular to the crankshaft. It must be located over the center of the cylinder. The cylinder center is found by installing centering pins in the bar. The bar is lowered so that the centering pins are located near the bottom of the cylinder, where the least wear has occurred. This locates the boring bar over the original cylinder center. Once the boring bar is centered, the boring machine is clamped in place to hold it securely. This will allow the cylinder to be rebored on the original centerline, regardless of the amount of cylinder wear. See Figures 13–35 and 13–36. A sharp, properly ground cutting tool is installed and adjusted to the desired dimension. Rough cuts remove a great deal of metal on each pass of the cutting tool. The surface of a rough cut is pictured in Figure 13–37. The rough cut is followed by a fine cut that produces a much smoother and more accurate finish, as shown in Figure 13–38. Different-shaped tool bits are used for rough and finish boring. The cutting tools are resharpened before each cylinder is bored to accurately control the bore diameter and the surface finish. The last cut is made to produce a diameter that is at least 0.002 inch (0.05 millimeter) smaller than the required diameter. The cylinder wall is then finished by honing. Honing produces the required cylinder diameter and surface finish. Each cylinder is

FIGURE 13–35 Production cylinder boring machine set up to begin boring a cylinder of a small-block Chevrolet V-8 engine.

FIGURE 13–36 Four-cylinder automotive engine being bored two cylinders at a time at a large engine remanufacturing plant. Note that the block is being indexed off of the side rails instead of from the saddles. Oil pan side rails, saddles, and the block deck should all be parallel surfaces.

FIGURE 13–37 Finish of the cylinder surface after a rough cut has been made. (Courtesy of Dana Corporation)

FIGURE 13–38 Finish of the cylinder surface after a fine cut is made. (Courtesy of Dana Corporation)

honed to give the correct clearance for the piston that is to operate in that cylinder.

SLEEVING THE CYLINDER

Sometimes, cylinders have a gouge so deep that it will not clean up when the cylinder is rebored to the maximum size. This could happen if the piston pin moved endways and rubbed on the cylinder wall. Cylinder blocks with deep gouges can be salvaged by **sleeving** the cylinder. This is done by boring the cylinder to a dimension that is greatly oversize to almost match the outside diameter of the cylinder sleeve. The sleeve is pressed into the rebored block; then the center of the sleeve is bored to the diameter required by the piston. The cylinder can be sized to use a standard-size piston when it is sleeved. See Figure 13–39.

CYLINDER HONING

It is important to have the proper surface finish on the cylinder wall for the rings to seat against. Some ring manufacturers recommend breaking the hard surface glaze on the cylinder wall with a hone before installing new piston rings. When honing is not required, no time

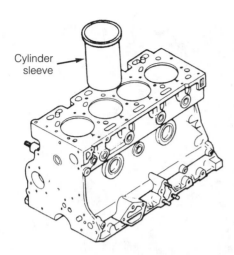

Cylinder sleeve

FIGURE 13–39 A sleeve can be used to save a block that is excessively worn. First, the cylinder is bored to be slightly (about 0.003 inch) smaller than the outside diameter of the sleeve, and then the block is heated (to about 200°F) and the sleeve cooled in ice. The sleeve is then pressed into the block to form a new cylinder wall surface.

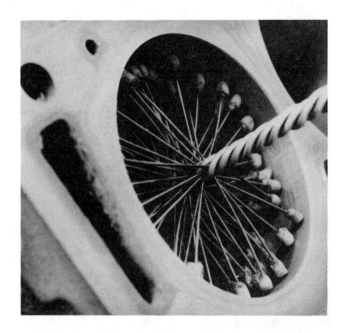

FIGURE 13–41 Brush (ball) type of deglazing hone in position for honing a cylinder.

FIGURE 13–40 Cutaway showing a spring-loaded deglazing hone in position for honing.

FIGURE 13–42 Cutaway engine shown with a sizing hone in position for honing.

is needed for honing or for cleanup. This reduces the reconditioning cost for the engine.

The cylinder wall should be honed to straighten the cylinder when the wall is wavy or scuffed. If honing is being done with the crankshaft remaining in the block, the crankshaft should be protected to keep honing chips from getting on the shaft.

Two types of hones are used for cylinder service. A **deglazing hone** removes the hard surface glaze remaining in the cylinder. It is a flexible hone that follows the shape of the cylinder wall, even when the wall is wavy. It cannot be used to straighten the cylinder. A spring-loaded deglazing hone is shown in Figure

13–40. A brush-type (ball-type) deglazing hone is shown in Figure 13–41. A **sizing hone** can be used to straighten the cylinder. Its honing stones are held in a rigid fixture with an expanding mechanism to control the size of the hone. The sizing hone can be used to straighten the cylinder taper by honing the lower cylinder diameter more than the upper diameter. As it rotates, the sizing hone only cuts the high spots so that cylinder out-of-round is also reduced. The cylinder wall surface finish is about the same when the cylinder is refinished with either type of hone. See Figures 13–42 through 13–44.

FIGURE 13–43 Chevrolet small-block V-8 being honed after boring. Note that the main bearing caps are installed and torqued during both the boring and the honing operations to help prevent block distortion.

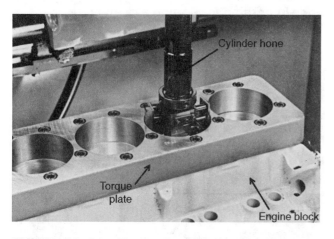

FIGURE 13–44 Honing a cylinder with a torque plate installed. The torque plate is bolted to the block and torqued so that it simulates the forces that act on the block when the cylinder head is installed. Therefore, the cylinder is machined to be true and straight when it is operating with the cylinder heads attached.

The hone is stroked up and down in the cylinder as the hone rotates. This produces a **crosshatch finish** on the cylinder wall. A typical honed cylinder is pictured in Figure 13–45. The angle of the crosshatch should be between 20 degrees and 60 degrees. Higher angles are produced when the hone is stroked more rapidly in the cylinder. The roughness of the finish is more important than the crosshatch. A coarse stone with a grit size of 70 is used for removing metal. A #150 grit hone is used to provide normal cylinder finish. If a polished cylinder wall is desired, stones with #280 grit are used in the hone.

FIGURE 13–45 Typical finished honed cylinder. Note the crosshatch pattern necessary to ensure proper lubrication and wear in the piston rings.

■ TECH TIP ■

BORE TO SIZE, HONE FOR CLEARANCE

Many engine rebuilders and remanufacturers bore the cylinders to the exact size of the oversize pistons that are to be used. After the block is bored to a standard oversize measurement, the cylinder is honed. The rigid hone stones, along with an experienced operator, can increase the bore size by 0.001 to 0.003 inch (1 to 3 thousandths of an inch) for the typical clearance needed between the piston and the cylinder walls.

For example:

Actual piston diameter = 4.0280 in
Bore diameter = 4.0280 in
Diameter after honing = 4.0300 in
Amount removed by honing = 0.002 in

NOTE: The minimum amount recommended to be removed by honing is 0.002 inch to remove the fractured metal in the cylinder wall caused by boring.

The size of the abrasive particles in the grinding and honing stones controls the surface finish. The size of the abrasive is called the **grit size.** The abrasive is sifted through a screen mesh to sort out the grit size. A coarse-mesh screen has few wires in each square inch, so large pieces can fall through. A fine-mesh screen has many wires in each square inch so that only small pieces can fall through. The screen is used to separate the different grit sizes. The grit size is the number of wires in each square inch of the mesh. A low-numbered grit has large pieces of abrasive material; a high-numbered grit has small pieces of abrasive material. The higher the grit number being used, the smoother the surface finish will be. A given grit size will produce the same finish as long as the cutting pressure is constant. With the same grit size, light cutting pressure produces fine finishes, and heavy cutting pressure produces rough finishes.

CYLINDER SURFACE FINISH

The surface finish should match the surface required for the type of piston rings to be used. See Chapter 14 for details on piston rings. Typical grit and surface finish standards include the following:

- Chrome—#180 grit (25 to 35 microinches)
- Cast iron—#200 grit (20 to 30 microinches)
- Moly—#220 grit (18 to 25 microinches)

Honing oil is wiped or flowed in the cylinders and on the honing stones. The hone is placed in the cylinder. Before the drive motor is turned on, the hone is moved up and down in the cylinder to get the feel of the stroke length needed. The end of the hone should just break out of the cylinder bore on each end. The hone must *not* be pulled from the top of the cylinder while it is rotating. Also, it must not be pushed so low in the cylinder that it hits the main bearing web or crankshaft. The sizing hone is adjusted to give a solid drag at the lower end of the stroke. The hone drive motor is turned on and stroking begins immediately. Stroking continues until the sound of the drag is reduced. The hone drive motor is turned off while still stroking. Stroking is stopped as the rotation of the hone stops. After rotation stops, the hone is collapsed and removed from the cylinder. The cylinder is examined to check the bore size and finish of the wall. If more honing is needed, the cylinder is again coated with honing oil and the cylinder is honed again. The finished cylinder should be within 0.0005 inch (0.013 millimeter) on both out-of-round and taper measurements. After honing, the top edge of the cylinder is given a slight chamfer to allow the rings to enter the cylinder during assembly. See Figure 13–46.

PLATEAU HONING

Plateau honing is a two-step machining operation that reduces cylinder and piston ring wear. The first step involves a rough stone that cuts a crosshatch pattern

FIGURE 13–46 **The operator is using a tapered sandpaper cone to chamfer the sharp edges at the top of the cylinders after boring, honing, and decking of the block. This operation is necessary to prevent damage to piston rings during installation of pistons. All bolt holes should also be countersunk at a 45-degree angle to prevent the head bolts from pulling threads during assembly.**

on the cylinder walls 0.0025 to 0.0030 inch (2½ to 3 thousandths of an inch) (0.06 to 0.07 millimeter) deep. A second honing operation uses a relatively soft stone to remove the sharp tops of the grooves left by the first, rough hone. See Figure 13–47. The smooth, final hone provides grooves in which engine oil can stay to lubricate piston rings.

It is not unusual to remove the cylinder head of an engine with over 100,000 miles (160,000 kilometers) and observe the hone marks still on the cylinder walls. Wet and dry sleeves are also plateau honed in some engines.

CYLINDER CLEANING

Cleaning the honed cylinder wall is an important part of the honing process. If any grit remains on the cylinder wall, it will rapidly wear the piston rings. This wear will cause premature failure of the reconditioning job. Degreasing and decarbonizing procedures will only remove the honing oil. They will *not* remove the abrasive. The *best* way to clean the honed cylinders is to scrub the cylinder wall with a brush using a mixture of *soap or detergent and water*. The block is scrubbed until it is absolutely clean. This can be determined by wiping the cylinder wall with a clean cloth. The cloth will pick up no soil when the cylinder wall is clean.

The cylinder walls can be cleaned with oil when the crankshaft has not been removed. Cleaning with oil takes more time and uses a great many more shop towels than does scrubbing. When oil cleaning, the honed

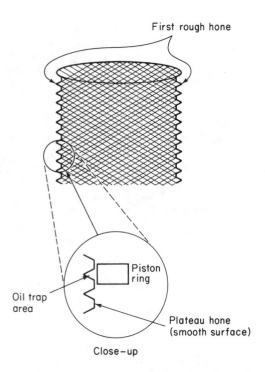

FIGURE 13–47 Plateau honing involves honing the cylinder with a coarse stone and then using a finer hone to flatten off the sharp peaks left from the coarse stone (forming a plateau).

cylinder wall is given a heavy coat of engine oil. This oil is wiped off. Some of the honing grit will come off with the oil. The procedure of coating the wall with oil and then wiping is repeated until the shop towel picks up no more soil. It will be necessary to put oil on each cylinder wall a dozen or more times to get the cylinder wall clean. The clean cylinder wall should be given a final coat of oil to protect it from rust until the block is recleaned for assembly.

BLOCK DETAILING

Before the engine block can be assembled, a final detailed cleaning should be performed.

1. All tapped holes should be chamfered and cleaned with the correct size of tap to remove any dirt and burrs. See Figure 13–48.
2. All oil passages (galleries) should be cleaned by running a long bottle-type brush through all holes in the block.
3. Coat the newly cleaned block with fogging oil to prevent rust. Cover the block with a large plastic bag to keep out dirt until it is time to assemble the engine.

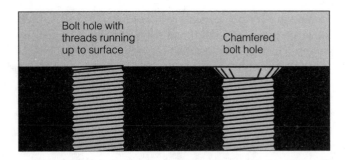

FIGURE 13–48 All bolt holes should be chamfered at the top to prevent the attaching bolts from pulling threads at the top surface.

SUMMARY

1. Engine blocks are either cast iron or aluminum.
2. Cores are used inside a mold to form water jackets and cylinder bores. After the cast iron has cooled, the block is shaken, which breaks up the cores so that they fall out of openings in the side of the block. Core plugs are used to fill the holes.
3. Aluminum blocks usually use cast-iron cylinder liners. Some engines use cylinder sleeves that are in contact with the coolant and are called wet cylinder sleeves.
4. The block deck is the surface to which the cylinder head attaches. This surface must be flat and true for proper engine operation.
5. Main bearing caps should be installed and torqued to specification before any machining is performed on the block.
6. The first machining operation is align boring or honing, followed by machining the block deck surface, followed by cylinder boring and honing.
7. The cylinder should be bored to the same size as the pistons diameter and then honed to the amount of cylinder bore–to–piston clearance specified.
8. All bolt holes should be chamfered and cleaned with a tap.

REVIEW QUESTIONS

1. How is cylinder #1 determined by looking at the block of a V-type engine?
2. Explain the difference between a shallow skirt and a deep skirt on a V block.

3. Explain why core plugs are called core plugs.
4. What is a broach and where is it used in the manufacturing process?
5. Describe the difference between a two-bolt and a four-bolt main engine block.
6. What is the difference between align boring and align honing?
7. What does decking the block mean?
8. Explain what microinch RA (RMS) finish means.
9. What is the difference between deglazing and honing a cylinder?
10. What is the best method to use to clean an engine block after honing?

MULTIPLE-CHOICE QUESTIONS

1. Cylinder #1 is generally _____.
   a. The most forward cylinder (closest to the accessory drive belt[s])
   b. The first one in the firing order
   c. The cylinder farthest from the principal end
   d. All of the above

2. A shallow skirt block _____.
   a. Has the oil pan rail below the centerline of the crankshaft
   b. Has the oil pan rail above the centerline of the crankshaft
   c. Has the oil pan rail close to the centerline of the crankshaft
   d. Has a more shallow oil pan (sump) than other engine types

3. The block deck is the _____.
   a. Bottom (pan rail) of the block
   b. Top surface of the block
   c. Valley surface of a V-type engine
   d. Area where the engine mounts are attached to the block

4. A broach is _____.
   a. A type of boring machine
   b. A type of casting technique
   c. A machining process that uses a large slab with a number of cutting teeth
   d. A type of honing machine used on production engines only

5. Which engine block machining process should be done first when reconditioning?
   a. Cylinder boring
   b. Decking the block
   c. Honing the cylinders
   d. Align boring (honing)

6. The standard measurement for surface finish is the microinch roughness average (RA). Which of the following is correct?
   a. The rougher the surface, the higher the microinch finish measurement.
   b. The smoother the surface, the higher the microinch finish measurement.
   c. The rougher the surface, the lower the microinch finish measurement.
   d. Both b and c.

7. Sleeving a cylinder means _____.
   a. Plating the inner walls of the cylinder with a different metal, such as nickel
   b. Boring the cylinder to be oversize and installing a cast-iron sleeve to restore the cylinder to the original diameter
   c. Boring the cylinder to be 0.020 to 0.060 inch oversize to accept oversize pistons
   d. Using a hone to finish the cylinder after boring

8. For honing a cylinder for moly piston rings, a _____ grit hone should be used.
   a. #150
   b. #180
   c. #220
   d. #280

9. After decking, boring, and honing an engine block, what other metal-removing operation should be performed?
   a. Align honing the main bearing caps and saddles
   b. Chamfering the cylinder bores and bolt holes
   c. Broaching the timing chain cover surface
   d. Filing the oil pan rails flat

10. The minimum amount of material that is recommended to be removed from the cylinder after boring is _____.
    a. 0.010 inch
    b. 0.008 inch
    c. 0.002 inch
    d. 0.001 inch

14 Pistons, Rings, and Connecting Rods

OBJECTIVES

After studying Chapter 14, the reader will be able to

1. Describe the purpose and function of pistons, rings, and connecting rods.
2. Explain how pistons and rods are constructed and what to look for during an inspection.
3. Discuss connecting rod reconditioning procedures.
4. Explain how piston rings operate and how to install them on a piston.

All engine power is developed by burning fuel in the presence of air in the combustion chamber. Heat from the combustion causes the burned gas to increase in pressure. The force of this pressure is converted into useful work through the piston, connecting rod, and crankshaft.

PURPOSE AND FUNCTION OF PISTONS, RINGS, AND CONNECTING RODS

The **piston** forms a movable bottom to the combustion chamber. It is attached to the connecting rod with a **piston pin** or **wrist pin**. The piston pin is allowed to have a rocking movement because of a swivel joint at the piston end of the connecting rod. The connecting rod is connected to a part of the crankshaft called a **crank throw**, **crankpin**, or **connecting rod bearing journal**. This provides another swivel joint. The center of the crank throw is the amount by which the large end of the connecting rod is offset from the crankshaft main bearing centerline. This dimension of the crankshaft determines the stroke of the engine.

NOTE: The stroke is the distance from the center of the main bearing journal to the center of the connecting rod journal times 2.

The earliest crankshafts were assembled with a metal rod or pin to which the connecting rod was attached. The term *crankpin* is carried over from this. The crankpin has been smoothed to operate with the connecting rod bearing, and so the surface is called the *bearing journal*.

Piston rings seal the small space between the piston and cylinder wall, keeping the pressure above the piston. When the pressure builds up in the combustion chamber, it pushes on the piston. The piston, in turn, pushes on the piston pin and upper end of the connecting rod. The lower end of the connecting rod pushes on the crank throw. This provides the force to turn the crankshaft. The turning force of the crankshaft turns the drive wheels through a drivetrain. *This turning force is torque.*

As the crankshaft turns, it develops inertia. *Inertia is the force that causes the crankshaft to continue rotating.* This action will bring the piston back to its original position, where it will be ready for the next power stroke. While the engine is running, the combustion cycle keeps repeating as the piston reciprocates (moves up and down) and the crankshaft rotates. These motions put mechanical forces on the engine parts. The combustion heat and mechanical forces are major considerations in the design of the parts.

PISTON AND ROD REMOVAL

It is necessary to remove the head and oil pan before the piston and rod assembly can be removed from the block. The head removal procedure was discussed in Chapter 7. The oil should be drained before the pan is removed.

FIGURE 14–1   Punch marks on connecting rod and rod cap to identify their location in the engine.

FIGURE 14–2   A piston skirt that was scored by a burr raised by hitting the bottom of the cylinder skirt with the connecting rod as it was being removed.

Step #1. The rod and caps should be checked for markings that identify their location. *If the rod and caps are not marked, they should be marked before disassembly.* If number stamps are not available, punch marks, as shown in Figure 14–1, can be used.

Step #2. The crankshaft is turned until the piston is at the bottom of its stroke. This places the connecting rod nuts or cap screws where they are easily accessible. They are removed, and the rod cap is taken off. This may require light tapping on the connecting rod bolts with a soft-faced hammer.

Step #3. Protectors should be placed over the rod bolt threads to protect the threads and the surface of the crankshaft journal. The piston and rod assembly is pushed out, care being taken to avoid hitting the bottom edge of the cylinder with the rod.

NOTE: If the cylinder is hit, it will raise a burr. If the burr is not removed, it will score the piston after the engine is reassembled and run, as shown in Figure 14–2.

The rod caps should be reattached to the rod after the assembly has been removed from the cylinder. The rod caps are not interchangeable between rods. The assembly must be handled carefully. Neither the piston nor the rod should be clamped in a vise. Careless clamping will cause them to warp or even crack. They should be placed on a parts stand so that they do not strike each other. The aluminum piston can be easily scratched or nicked.

NOTE: See Chapter 7 for ridge reaming procedures to be used before removing pistons from a high-mileage engine.

The rings are carefully removed from the piston to avoid damage to either the piston or the ring. The best way to remove them is to use a piston ring expanding tool.

PISTON DESIGN

When the engine is running, the piston starts at the top of the cylinder. As it moves downward, it accelerates until it reaches a maximum velocity slightly before it is halfway down. The piston comes to a stop at the bottom of the cylinder at 180 degrees of crankshaft rotation. During the next 180 degrees of crankshaft rotation, the piston moves upward. It accelerates to reach a maximum velocity slightly above the halfway point and then comes to a stop at the top of the stroke. Thus, the piston starts, accelerates, and stops twice in each crankshaft revolution. This reciprocating action of the

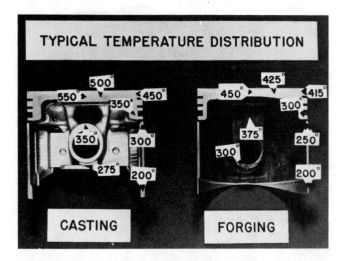

FIGURE 14–3 *Differences in temperature within pistons operated under the same conditions. (Courtesy of TRW)*

FIGURE 14–4 *The piston is very close to the crankshaft counterweight when the piston is at the bottom of the stroke. The piston has a slipper skirt when the connecting rod is short, as shown here.*

piston produces large **inertia forces.** Inertia is the force that causes a part that is stopped to stay stopped or a part that is in motion to stay in motion. The lighter the piston can be made, the less will be the inertia force that is developed. Less inertia will allow higher engine operating speeds. For this reason, pistons are made to be as light as possible while still having the strength that is needed.

The piston operates with its head exposed to the hot combustion gases, whereas the skirt contacts the relatively cool cylinder wall. This results in a temperature difference of about 275° F (147° C) between the top and bottom of the piston. The temperature difference between cast and forged pistons is shown in Figure 14–3.

Aluminum alloy has proven to be the best material from which to make pistons. It is lightweight and it provides adequate strength. Good design has been able to provide sufficient engine displacement with a small external engine size. This is done by keeping the height of the piston to a bare minimum and bringing it close to the crankshaft at the bottom of the stroke, as shown in Figure 14–4. This piston must still have enough strength to support combustion pressure and reciprocating loads. It must also have enough piston skirt to guide it straight in the bore. In addition, the piston must have heat expansion control for quiet, long-life operation. Finally, it holds the piston rings perpendicular to the cylinder wall so that they can seal properly.

A typical piston in an engine at 4000 RPM accelerates from 0 to 60 miles per hour (97 kilometers per hour) in about 0.004 seconds (4 milliseconds) as it descends about halfway down the cylinder.

PISTON HEADS

Because the piston head forms a portion of the combustion chamber, its shape is very important to the combustion process. Generally, low-cost, low-performance engines have **flat-top** pistons. Some of these flat-top pistons come so close to the cylinder head that **recesses** are cut in the piston top for valve clearance. Pistons used in high-powered engines may have raised domes or **pop-ups** on the piston heads. These are used to increase the compression ratio. Pistons used in other engines may be provided with a depression or a **dish.** The varying depths of the dish provide different compression ratios required by different engine models. A number of piston head shapes are shown in Figure 14–5.

Recesses machined or cast into the tops of the pistons for valve clearance are commonly called **eyebrows.**

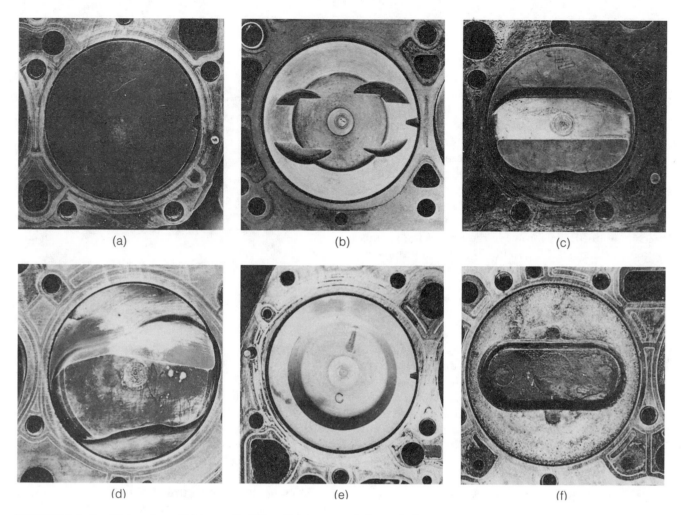

(a)

(b)

(c)

(d)

(e)

(f)

FIGURE 14–5 *Piston head shapes: (a) flat, (b) recessed, (c and d) pop-up, and (e and f) dished.*

■ TECH TIP ■

PISTON WEIGHT IS IMPORTANT!

All pistons in an engine should weigh the same to help ensure a balanced engine. Piston weight becomes a factor whenever changing pistons. Most aluminum pistons range in weight from 10 to 30 ounces (280 to 850 grams) (1 oz = 28.35 grams). *A typical paper clip weighs one gram.* If the cylinder has been bored, larger replacement pistons are obviously required. If the replacement pistons weigh more, this puts additional inertia loads on the rod bearings. Therefore, to help prevent rod bearing failure on an overhauled engine, the replacement pistons should not weigh more than the original pistons.

■ **CAUTION:** Some less expensive replacement pistons are a great deal heavier than the stock pistons, even in the stock bore size. ■

For the same reason, if one piston is being replaced, all pistons should be replaced or at least checked and corrected to ensure the same weight.

These recesses are also called **valve reliefs** or **valve pockets.** The depth of the eyebrows has a major effect on the compression ratio and is necessary to provide clearance for the valves if the timing belt of an overhead camshaft engine should break. Without the deep eyebrows, the pistons can hit the valves near TDC if the valves are not operating (closing) because of nonrotation of the camshaft. If an engine is designed not to have the pistons hitting the valves, the engine is called **freewheeling.** For example, the Ford Escort engine was changed in the mid-1980s to a freewheeling design by machining deeper eyebrows in the tops of the pistons. Before this change, if the timing belt broke, serious engine damage resulted, because the pistons would still move up and down a few times while the valves did not change position. When the pistons hit the valves, the pistons could be cracked, which in turn could crack the block, besides damaging the rods and bending valves.

The piston head must have enough strength to support combustion pressures. Ribs are often used on the underside of the head to maintain strength while at the same time reducing material to lighten the piston. These ribs are also used as cooling fins to transfer some of the piston heat to the engine oil. Typical ribs on the underside of the piston can be seen in Figure 14–6.

PISTON RING GROOVES

Piston ring **grooves** are located between the piston head and skirt (Figure 14–7). The width of the grooves, the width of the **lands** between the ring grooves, and the number of rings are major factors in determining minimum piston height. The outside diameter of the lands is about 0.020 to 0.040 inch (0.5 to 1.0 millimeters) smaller than the **skirt** diameter. See Figure 14–8. Some pistons for heavy-duty engines have oil ring grooves located on the piston skirt below the piston pin. Most engines use two compression rings and one oil control ring. They are all located above the piston pin.

NOTE: Some engines, such as the Honda high–fuel economy engine, use pistons with two rings: one compression ring and one oil ring. _____

Cylinder sealing is possible because of accurate machining and fitting procedures.

The piston ring groove must be deep enough to prevent the ring from hitting the base of the groove when the ring is pressed in so that it is flat with the land face. This is called **back spacing.** This groove depth becomes critical for some piston ring expander designs. These expanders wedge between the back of

FIGURE 14–6   Ribs on the underside of the piston.

the ring and the base of the groove. The sides of the groove must be square and flat so that the side of the piston ring will seal on the side of the groove. Oil ring grooves are vented in the base so that oil scraped from the cylinder wall can flow through the vents to the crankcase. This venting is done through drilled holes or slots, as shown in Figure 14–9.

PISTON EXPANSION

Piston expansion was a minor problem in old engines with cast-iron pistons. Owners of these engines would usually accept piston slap noise that resulted from large piston–to–cylinder wall clearances on cold engines, because the slap noise would usually stop when the engine warmed up. Some means of piston expansion control was required, however, as owners began to demand quiet engine operation.

PISTON SLOTS

Piston expansion was first controlled through a **slot** on the minor thrust surface of the piston skirts. These pistons were fitted in the cylinder with very little piston-to-cylinder clearance. The piston skirt would expand into the slot as the piston was heated during operation. The most popular slot types were the **U slot** and the **T slot.** The U slot design had two slots on the piston skirt that were connected near the top of the piston skirt, forming an inverted U shape. The T slot design had one slot down the piston skirt and a cross slot at the upper edge of the piston skirt to form the T shape. This method of expansion control carried over into the early aluminum pistons.

FIGURE 14–7 Names of piston parts.

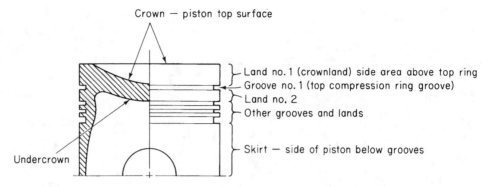

FIGURE 14–8 Piston skirt cam shape. (Courtesy of Chevrolet Motor Division, GMC)

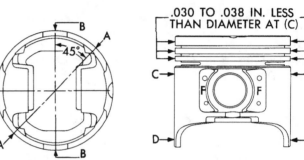

THE ELLIPTICAL SHAPE OF THE PISTON SKIRT SHOULD BE .010 TO .012 IN. LESS AT DIAMETER (A) THAN ACROSS THE THRUST FACES AT DIAMETER (B). MEASUREMENT IS MADE 1/8 IN. BELOW LOWER RING GROOVE

DIAMETERS AT (C) AND (D) CAN BE EQUAL OR DIAMETER AT (D) CAN BE .0015 IN. GREATER THAN (C)

CAM GROUND PISTONS

Aluminum pistons expand approximately twice as much as do cast-iron pistons with the same increase in temperature. With this much expansion, the expansion slot that was required made the pistons too weak. A better method of expansion control was devised using a **cam ground** piston skirt. With this design, the piston thrust surfaces closely fit the cylinder, and the piston pin boss diameter is fitted loosely. As the cam ground piston is heated, it expands along the piston pin so that it becomes nearly round at its normal operating temperatures. A cam ground piston skirt is illustrated in Figure 14–10.

PISTON HEAD SIZE

The lowest part of the piston skirt is at the greatest distance from the combustion chamber. It does not run as hot, so it expands less than the upper part. This allows the lower part of the piston skirt to be made larger than the upper part as measured across the thrust surface. The lower part of the skirt will have a close, cold fit in

the cylinder for quiet operation and a satisfactory piston service life. When the piston gets hot, the upper part will expand the most, so the piston skirt is straight. It then matches the cylinder wall. See Figure 14–11.

Most pistons have horizontal separation **slots** that act as **heat dams**. These slots reduce heat transfer from the hot piston head to the lower skirt. This, in turn, keeps the skirt temperature lower so that there will be less skirt expansion. Because the slot is placed in the oil ring groove, it can be used for oil drain-back as well as for expansion control. Some engines are built with a slot below the piston pin. This isolates the lower skirt from piston pin boss deflections caused by stress that occurs on the power stroke. The lower skirt can better maintain its size. These heat dam slots can be seen in Figures 14–12 and 14–13.

PISTON STRUT INSERTS

A major development in expansion control occurred when the piston aluminum was cast around two stiff steel **struts**. The struts are not chemically bonded to the

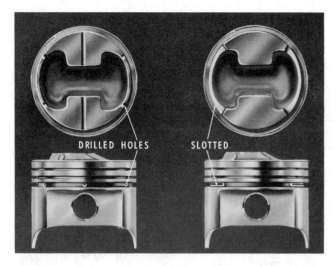

FIGURE 14–9 Oil ring groove venting using drilled holes and slots. (Courtesy of Chevrolet Motor Division, GMC)

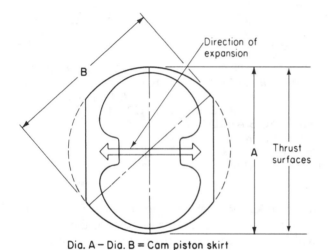

FIGURE 14–10 Piston cam shape. The largest diameter is across the thrust surfaces and perpendicular to the piston pin (lettered A).

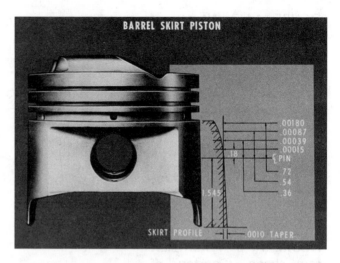

FIGURE 14–11 Design of a barrel-shaped piston skirt. (Courtesy of Chevrolet Motor Division, GMC)

FIGURE 14–12 Cast heat dam slots just below the oil ring grooves.

aluminum, nor do they add any strength to the piston. There is only a mechanical bond between the steel and aluminum. The bimetallic action of this strut in the aluminum forces the piston to bow outward along the piston pin. This keeps the piston skirt thrust surfaces from expanding more than the cast-iron cylinder in which the piston operates. Pistons with steel strut inserts allow good piston–to–cylinder wall clearance at normal temperatures. At the same time, they allow the cold operating clearance to be as small as 0.0005 inch (half a thousandth of an inch) (0.0127 millimeter). This small clearance will prevent cold piston slap and noise.

A typical piston expansion control strut is visible in Figures 14–14 and 14–15.

Heavy-duty pistons are cylindrical castings with ring grooves at the top, using a **trunk-type** skirt. The piston shown in figure 14–13 has a trunk-type skirt. With newer engines, the number and thickness of the piston rings have decreased and the cast-aluminum piston skirt has been reduced to a minimum by using an open-type **slipper skirt**. Examples of the slipper skirt piston are shown in Figures 14–12 and 14–15.

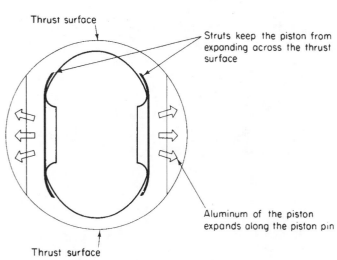

FIGURE 14–14 Action of the steel strut to help control expansion of the piston as it gets hot.

FIGURE 14–13 Sawed heat dam slot in the bottom of the oil ring groove and a cast slot below the piston pin.

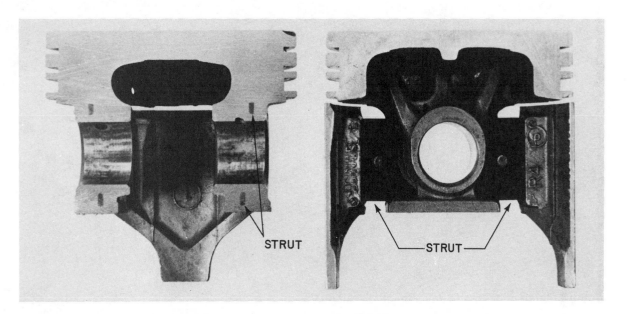

FIGURE 14–15 Two sectional views of a piston showing the expansion control strut.

HYPEREUTECTIC PISTONS

A standard cast-aluminum piston contains about 9% to 12% silicon and is called a eutectic piston. To add strength, the silicon content is increased to about 16%, and the resulting piston is called a **hypereutectic** piston. Other advantages of a hypereutectic piston are its 25% weight reduction and lower expansion rate. The disadvantage of hypereutectic pistons is their higher cost, because they are more difficult to cast and machine.

Hypereutectic pistons are commonly used in the aftermarket and as original equipment in many turbocharged and supercharged engines.

GRAIN FLOW

TOWER CONSTRUCTION

FIGURE 14–16 Grain flow lines can be seen in this forged aluminum piston with a trunk skirt.

FIGURE 14–17 Piston from a dual overhead camshaft engine with four valves per cylinder. This high-revving engine (redline at 7500 RPM) uses a short skirt piston and thin, low-friction piston rings.

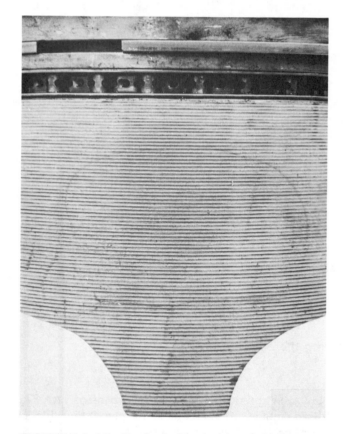

FIGURE 14–18 Typical piston skirt surfaces in common use.

278

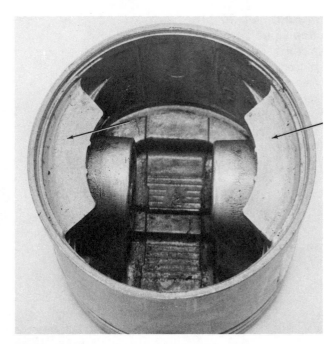

FIGURE 14–19   Typical location of pads used to balance pistons.

FORGED PISTONS

High-performance engines need pistons with added strength. They use impact-extruded forged pistons whose design falls between that of the two extremes of heavy-duty and automotive pistons. Figure 14–16 shows a forged aluminum piston with a trunk skirt, and Figure 14–17 shows a newer-design, lightweight aluminum piston.

PISTON SKIRT FINISH

For maximum life, the piston skirt surface finish is important. Turned grooves or waves 0.0005 inch (0.0125 millimeter) deep on the surface of some piston skirts produce a finish that will carry oil for lubrication. Other piston skirts are relatively smooth. Figure 14–18 shows typical surfaces of piston skirts. A thin tin-plated surface (approximately 0.00005 inch or 0.00125 millimeter thick) is also used on some aluminum pistons to help reduce scuffing and scoring during occasional periods of minimum lubrication. The piston skirt normally rides on a film of lubricating oil. Anytime the oil film is lacking, metal-to-metal contact will occur, and this starts piston scuffing.

Whenever two moving metallic parts lose lubrication between them, scuffing is likely to occur. **Scuffing** is the process by which the metals weld themselves together and then break loose. Welding can occur between the piston or piston rings and the cylinder walls when the piston stops at top dead center. As the piston starts back down from TDC, this weld breaks.

The rough surface that results wears ridges in the cylinder wall and on the piston ring or the piston itself.

Scuffing can be caused by a lack of lubrication and/or by detonation, which causes higher temperatures and pressures in the combustion chamber.

Scuffing often occurs when a faulty cooling system causes the engine to overheat. Overheating causes the oil to thin, and the heat overexpands the piston. Piston scuffing leads to poor oil control, short piston life, roughened cylinder bores, and scuffed rings.

PISTON BALANCE

Pistons are provided with **enlarged pads** or **skirt flanges** (Figure 14–19) that are used for controlling piston weight. Material is removed from the surface of these pads by the manufacturer as the last machining operation to bring the piston within the correct weight tolerances.

PISTON SERVICE

When engine servicing equipment is not available, the repairable piston and rod assemblies are taken to the automotive machine shop for reconditioning. See Figures 14–20 through 14–23. As a standard practice, the pistons are removed from the rods. After cleaning, the skirts of the used pistons should be resized, and a spacer is placed in the top of the upper ring grooves.

As the piston goes rapidly up and down in the cylinder, it tosses the rings to the top and to the bottom of the ring grooves. The pounding of each ring in its groove grad-

FIGURE 14–20 The first step to be performed if the pistons are not being replaced is to thoroughly clean them, starting with scraping off encrusted deposits. Chemical or ultrasonic cleaning may also be necessary.

FIGURE 14–21 Ring groove cleaner being used to remove carbon from the bottom of the piston ring grooves. Care must be used to prevent enlarging the grooves by scraping away any aluminum.

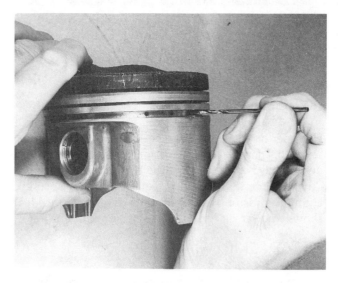

FIGURE 14–22 Complete piston cleaning includes cleaning the oil groove vent holes.

ually increases the piston ring side clearance. Material is worn from both the ring and the groove. The greater the side clearance is, the faster the wear becomes.

The upper ring groove can be reconditioned on industrial engines when the groove has worn by more than 0.005 inch (0.125 millimeter). To correct the ring groove clearance, the top ring groove is machined to be 0.025 inch (0.625 millimeter) wider than the standard groove. One type of tool used for this is pictured in Figure 14–24. A steel ring groove spacer is placed above the new piston ring in the reconditioned ring groove to return the ring side clearance to the standard dimension, as shown in Figure 14–25.

KNURLING PISTON SKIRTS

Automotive engine pistons are of aluminum slipper skirt design. In operation, the piston supports heavy side loads during the power stroke. This gradually causes a slight collapse of the piston skirt. The aluminum piston skirt also wears away. Piston skirt collapse and wear, in time, will allow the piston to rock slightly as it moves up and down in the cylinder. This slight rocking action also rocks the piston rings so that they keep changing their contact face against the cylinder wall. New piston rings cannot form a good moving seal if they are not held perpendicular to the cylinder. The best reconditioning procedure is to replace the pis-

FIGURE 14–23 Measuring a piston ring groove. Even the grooves of new replacement pistons should be measured to ensure that the proper-size piston rings are used.

FIGURE 14–24 One type of piston ring groove reconditioner.

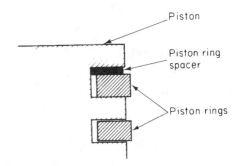

FIGURE 14–25 Ring groove spacer placed above the new upper ring in the reconditioned ring groove.

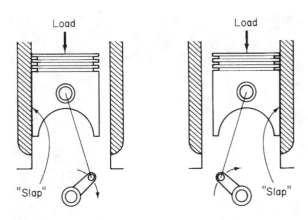

FIGURE 14–26 Excessive piston–to–cylinder wall clearance can cause piston slap noise, especially when the engine is cold.

ton with a new piston. It is necessary to resize the skirts of pistons when they are to be reused so that the pistons will not rock as they operate in slightly worn cylinders. See Figure 14–26.

Pistons used in industrial engines are resized by knurling to expand their skirts. Knurling interrupts the surface of the piston skirt, displacing the metal outward between the teeth of the knurling tool, as shown in Figure 14–27. This effectively increases the diameter of the piston skirt. The amount by which the skirt diameter is increased is controlled by the pressure put on the knurling tool by the service technician. In addition to increasing the piston skirt diameter, the knurled surface carries lubricating oil to help maintain the thin oil film that is required between the piston and cylinder. It is common practice to fit knurled pistons to clearances that are one-half the size of those specified for piston skirts that are not knurled.

Fitting of the piston must be done *after* the cylinder wall has been reconditioned. Knurling the piston cannot correct for excessive cylinder taper. New pistons will have to be installed in rebored cylinders.

PISTON PINS

Piston pins are used to attach the piston to the connecting rod. Piston pins are also known as **gudgeon pins** (a British term). The piston pin transfers the force produced by combustion chamber pressures and piston inertia to the connecting rod. The piston pin is made from high-quality steel in the shape of a tube to make it both strong and light. Sometimes, the interior hole of the piston pin is tapered, large at the ends and small in the middle of the pin. This gives the pin strength that is proportional to the location of the load placed on it. A

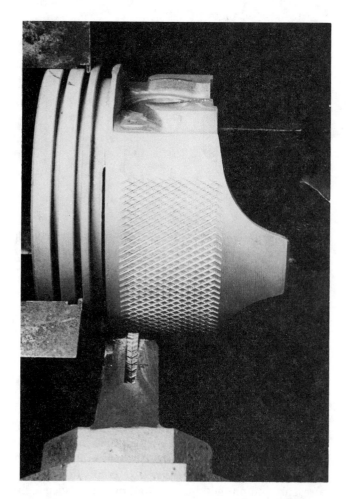

FIGURE 14–27   Knurling to resize the piston skirt.

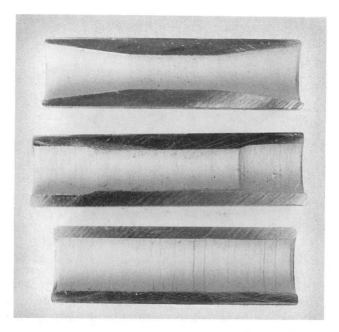

FIGURE 14–28   Cross-sectioned piston pins. Notice that the top two are taper bored to provide greater thickness (and strength) where the loads are highest.

double-taper hole such as this is more expensive to manufacture, so it is used only where its weight advantage merits the extra cost. See Figure 14–28.

PISTON PIN OFFSET

The piston pin holes are not centered in the piston. They are located toward the **major thrust surface,** approximately 0.062 inch (1.57 millimeters) from the piston centerline, as shown in Figure 14–29.

NOTE: The major thrust side is the side of the cylinder to which the rod points during the power stroke.

Pin offset is designed to reduce piston slap and the noise that can result as the large end of the connecting rod crosses over top dead center.

The minor thrust side of the piston head has a greater area than does the major side. This is caused by the pin offset. As the piston moves up in the cylinder on the compression stroke, it is riding against the minor thrust surface. When compression pressure

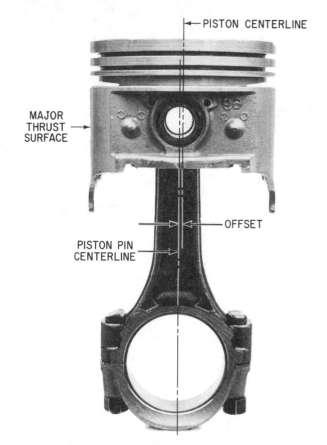

FIGURE 14–29   Piston pin is offset toward the major thrust surface.

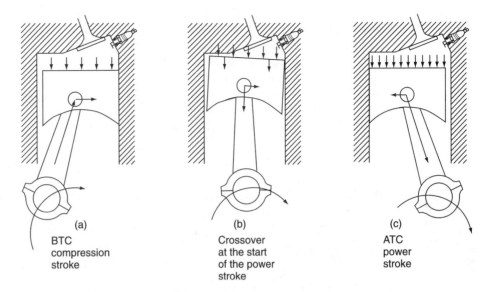

FIGURE 14–30 *Effect of piston pin offset as it controls piston slap.*

becomes high enough, the greater head area on the minor side causes the piston to cock slightly in the cylinder. This keeps the *top* of the minor thrust surface on the cylinder. It forces the *bottom* of the major thrust surface to contact the cylinder wall. As the piston approaches top center, both thrust surfaces are in contact with the cylinder wall. When the crankshaft crosses over top center, the force on the connecting rod moves the entire piston toward the major thrust surface. The lower portion of the major thrust surface has already been in contact with the cylinder wall. The rest of the piston skirt wipes into full contact just after the crossover point, thereby controlling piston slap. This action is illustrated in Figure 14–30.

Offsetting the piston toward the minor thrust surface would provide a better mechanical advantage. It also would cause less piston-to-cylinder friction. For these reasons, the offset is often placed toward the minor thrust surface in racing engines. Noise and durability are not as important in racing engines as is maximum performance.

NOTE: Not all piston pins are offset. In fact, many engines operate without the offset to help reduce friction and improve power and fuel economy. ———

PISTON PIN FIT

The finish and size of piston pins are very closely controlled. Piston pins have a smooth mirrorlike finish. Their size is held to tenths of thousandths of an inch so that exact fits can be maintained. If the piston pin is loose in the piston or in the connecting rod, it will make a rattling sound while the engine is running. If the pis-

ton pin is too tight in the piston, it will restrict piston expansion along the pin diameter. This will lead to piston scuffing. Normal piston pin clearances range from 0.0005 to 0.0007 inch (0.0126 to 0.0180 millimeter).

PISTON PIN RETAINING METHODS

It is necessary to retain or hold piston pins so that they stay centered in the piston. If piston pins were not retained, they would move endwise and groove the cylinder wall. Piston pins are retained by one of three general methods. The piston pin may be **full floating**, with some type of stop located at each end. It may, alternatively, be **fastened to the connecting rod**. In a few engines, the pin is **fastened to the piston**.

Full-floating piston pins in automotive engines are retained by lock rings located in grooves in the piston pin hole at the ends of the piston pin (Figures 14–31 through 14–33). Some engines use aluminum or plastic plugs in both ends of the piston pin. These plugs will touch the cylinder wall without scoring, to hold the piston pin centered in the piston.

Piston pins have been retained in connecting rods by a clamp bolt located in the piston end of the connecting rod. The piston pin used in the clamp has an undercut through which the edge of the clamp bolt fits. The clamp bolt locates the pin in the piston center and clamps the rod around the pin to hold it securely. The modern method of retaining the piston pin in the connecting rod is to make the connecting rod hole slightly smaller than the piston pin. The pin is installed by heating the rod to expand the hole or by pressing the pin into the rod. This retaining method will securely hold the pin. See Figure 14–34. This press or shrink fit is called an **interference fit.** Care must be taken to have the correct hole sizes, and the pin must be centered in the connecting rod. The interference fit method is the least expensive to use. It is, therefore, used in the majority of engines.

On automobile engines, the piston is free to move on the piston pin. On some heavy-duty engines, a cap screw on one side of the piston boss enters a hole or contacts a flat on the piston pin to retain the pin. The cap screw is placed on only one side of the piston. In this way, clamping does not interfere with the normal piston expansion that takes place along the pin.

PISTON PIN SERVICE

Piston pins do not normally become loose enough to cause a knock or tapping sound until the engine has very high mileage. The noise that a loose piston pin makes is a **double knock.** The knock is twice as fast as would be expected because the double knock occurs when the piston stops at the top and is starting downward again. The piston pin is more likely to produce a knock after the piston skirt has been resized and new piston rings installed. For this reason, automotive machine shops may install **oversize piston pins** when reconditioning piston and rod assemblies. The majority of domestic automobile manufacturers do not supply oversize piston pins through their parts departments. The manufacturers recommend replacing the used pistons with new pistons when the clearance between the pin and piston becomes excessive (over 0.001 inch or 0.025 millimeter). The new pistons have prefitted piston pins. This allows the connecting rod to be used without the small eye of the rod being resized. Once the connecting rod eye is honed to be oversize, an oversize piston pin must be used, and such piston pins are available in the parts replacement market. Installing an oversize piston pin in a used piston and rod will help the engine to run quietly for a reasonable length of time.

Both the piston and the small eye of the connecting rod are honed with precision equipment that can

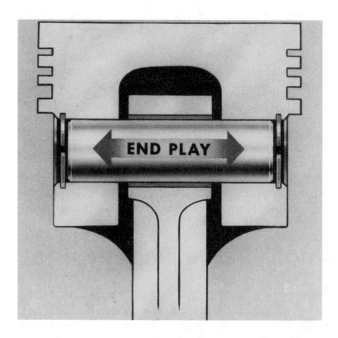

FIGURE 14–31 *Full-floating piston pin retained by a lock ring on each end of the piston pin.*

FIGURE 14–32 Piston pin lock ring.

FIGURE 14–33 Piston pin lock ring.

FIGURE 14–35 Honing a piston to fit an oversize piston pin.

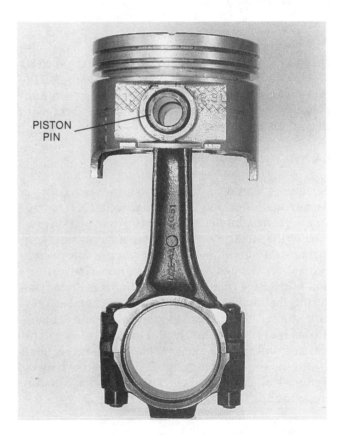

FIGURE 14–34 Interference fit type of piston pin.

PISTON
PIN

■ DIAGNOSTIC STORY ■

BIG PROBLEM, NO NOISE

Sometimes the piston pin can "walk" off the center of the piston and score the cylinder wall. This scoring is often not noticed because this type of wear does not create noise. Because the piston pin is below the piston rings, little combustion pressure is lost past the rings until the groove worn by the piston pin has worn the piston rings.

Troubleshooting the exact cause of the increased oil consumption is difficult because the damage done to the oil control rings by the groove usually affects only one cylinder.

Often, compression tests indicate good compression because the cylinder seals, especially at the top. More than one technician has been surprised to see the cylinder gouged by a piston pin when the cylinder head has been removed for service. In such a case, the cost of the engine repair immediately increases far beyond that of normal cylinder head service.

control the hole surface finish and the hole size, within 0.0001 inch (one tenth of one thousandth of an inch!) (0.0025 millimeter), either larger or smaller than the diameter of the piston pin. The piston pin hole in the piston is sized to give a clearance of 0.0002 to 0.0005 inch (0.0006 to 0.0012 millimeter). A typical pin hone is shown in Figure 14–35. When both the size

and the finish of the piston pin hole in the piston are correct, the piston pin will slide through the piston by means of its own weight when the piston is at room temperature. The small eye of the connecting rod is fitted with a **press** or interference fit. In this type of fit, the hole is honed to be 0.0008 to 0.0016 inch (0.002 to

FIGURE 14–36 One type of precision gauge required to check the size of the hole while it is being honed for an oversize piston pin.

0.004 millimeter) *smaller* than the diameter of the piston pin. This provides the correct press or interference fit. A precision measuring gauge of the type shown in Figure 14–36 is needed to measure the honed hole. When required, the large end of the connecting rod should also be resized before the piston is installed on the rod. (This is discussed in a later section.) Depending on the type of shop equipment used, the connecting rod may be aligned before assembly with the piston or after.

PISTON RINGS

Piston rings serve two major functions in engines. They form a sliding combustion chamber seal that prevents the high-pressure combustion gases from leaking past the piston. They also keep engine oil from getting into the combustion chamber. In addition, the rings transfer some of the piston heat to the cylinder wall, where it is removed from the engine through the cooling system.

Piston rings are classified into two types: **compression rings,** located toward the top of the piston, and **oil contorl rings,** located below the compression rings. The first piston rings were made with a simple rectangular cross section. This cross section was modified with tapers, chamfers, counter bores, slots, rails,

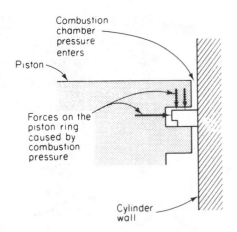

FIGURE 14–37 Combustion pressure forces the top piston ring downward and outward against the cylinder wall.

and expanders. Piston ring materials have also changed from plain cast iron to materials such as pearlitic and nodular iron, as well as steel. **Ductile iron** is also used as a piston ring material in some automotive engines. Piston rings may be *faced* with **chromium** or **molybdenum.**

COMPRESSION RINGS

A compression ring is designed to form a seal between the moving piston and the cylinder wall. This is necessary to get maximum power from the combustion pressure. At the same time, the compression ring must keep friction at a minimum. This is made possible by providing only enough static or built-in mechanical tension to hold the ring in contact with the cylinder wall during the intake stroke. Combustion chamber pressure during the compression, power, and exhaust strokes is applied to the top and back of the ring. This pressure will add the force on the ring that is required to seal the combustion chamber during these strokes. Figure 14–37 illustrates how the combustion chamber pressure adds force to the ring.

PISTON RING FORCES

The mechanical static tension of the ring results from the ring shape, material characteristics, and expanders used. Rings are manufactured so that they have a cam shape in their free state. When the piston ring is compressed to the cylinder size, it becomes round and develops the required static tension. Additional piston ring control causes the ring to twist toward the chamfers and counter bores when it is compressed to the size of the cylinder (Figure 14–38). Twist is used to provide

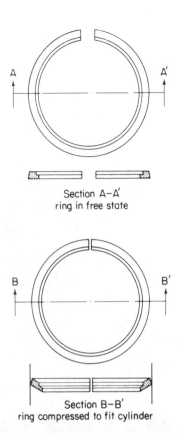

Section A–A'
ring in free state

Section B–B'
ring compressed to fit cylinder

FIGURE 14–38 A piston ring counter bore causes the ring to twist when it is compressed to fit the cylinder.

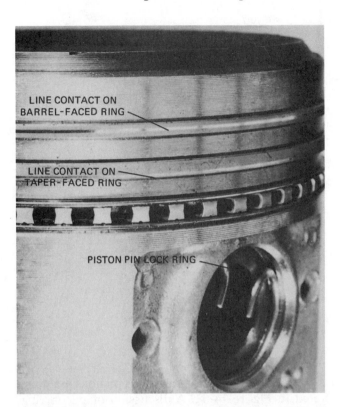

LINE CONTACT ON BARREL-FACED RING

LINE CONTACT ON TAPER-FACED RING

PISTON PIN LOCK RING

FIGURE 14–39 The piston rings are slightly used, so only the line contact shows. The upper, barrel-faced ring has line contact in the center. The second, taper-faced ring has line contact along the lower edge of the ring.

line contact sealing on the cylinder wall and in the piston ring groove. The line contact can be seen on the slightly used rings pictured in Figure 14–39. Line contact provides a relatively high unit pressure for sealing. At the same time, it allows low total ring force against the cylinder. This results in low ring friction. Pressure in the combustion chamber acts on the top piston ring. The pressure forces the ring to flatten on the bottom side of the piston ring groove. This action seals the ring-to-piston joint. The ring groove must have a flat and square side for this seal. Pressure behind the ring will also force it against the cylinder wall to seal the ring–to–cylinder wall contact surface. This action produces a **dynamic sealing force** that makes an effective moving combustion chamber seal.

RING GAP

The piston **ring gap** will allow some leakage past the top compression ring. This leakage is useful in providing pressure on the second ring to develop a dynamic sealing force. The amount of piston ring gap is critical. Too much gap will allow excessive **blowby**. Blowby is the leakage of combustion gases past the rings. Blowby will blow oil from the cylinder wall. This oil loss is followed by piston ring scuffing. Too little gap, on the other hand, will allow the piston ring ends to butt when the engine is hot. Ring end butting increases the mechanical force against the cylinder wall, causing excessive wear and possible engine failure.

A butt-type piston ring gap is the most common type used in automotive engines. Some low-speed industrial engines and some diesel engines use a more expensive tapered or seal-cut ring gap. These gaps are necessary to reduce losses of the high-pressure combustion gases. At low speeds, the gases have more time to leak through the gap. Typical ring gaps are illustrated in Figure 14–40.

PISTON RING CROSS SECTIONS

As engine speeds have increased, inertia forces on the piston rings have also increased. As a result, engine manufacturers have found it desirable to reduce inertia forces on the rings by reducing their weight. This has been done by narrowing the piston ring from ¼ inch (6 millimeters) to as little as ¹⁄₁₆ inch (1.6 millimeters).

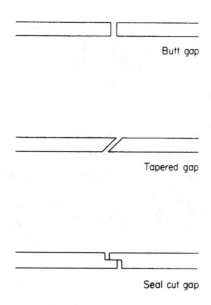

FIGURE 14–40   Typical ring gaps.

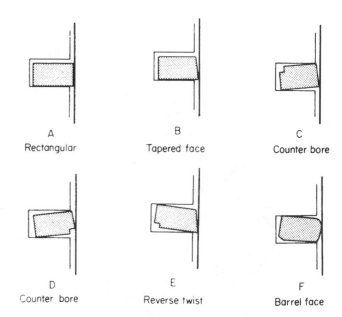

FIGURE 14–41   Typical compression ring cross sections.

Typical compression ring cross sections are illustrated in Figure 14–41. A discussion of piston ring cross sections must start with their original rectangular shape. This was first modified with a **taper face** that would contact the cylinder wall at the lower edge of the piston ring. When either a chamfer or counter bore relief is made on the *upper inside* corner of the piston ring, the ring cross section is unbalanced. This will cause the ring to twist in the groove in a positive direction. **Positive twist** will give the same wall contact as the taper-faced ring. It will also provide a line contact seal on the bottom side of the groove. Sometimes, twist and a taper face are used on the same compression ring.

Some second rings are notched on the *outer lower* corner. This, too, provides a positive ring twist. The sharp lower outer corner becomes a scraper that helps in oil control, but this type of ring has less compression control than do the preceding types.

By chamfering the ring's *lower inner* corner, a **reverse twist** is produced. This seals the lower outer section of the ring and piston ring groove, thus improving oil control. Reverse twist rings require a greater taper face or barrel face to maintain the desired ring face–to–cylinder wall contact.

Some rings replace the outer ring taper with a barrel face. The barrel is 0.0003 inch per 0.100 inch (0.0076 millimeter per 0.254 millimeter) of piston ring width. Barrel faces are found on rectangular rings as well as on torsionally twisted rings. See Figure 14–42 for an example of how piston ring twist during engine operation can wear the ring groove of the piston, as well as the face of the ring.

FIGURE 14–42   Cross-sectional view showing piston ring groove wear. (Courtesy of Dana Corporation)

CHROMIUM PISTON RINGS

A chromium facing on cast-iron rings greatly increases piston ring life, especially where abrasive materials are present in the air. During manufacture, the chromium-plated ring is slightly chamfered at the outer corners. About 0.0004 inch (0.010 millimeter) of chrome is then plated on the ring face. Chromium-faced rings are prelapped or honed before they are

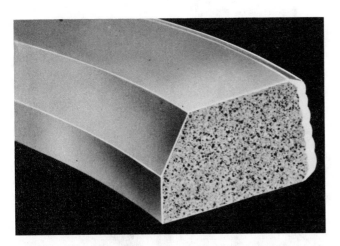

FIGURE 14–43 Chromium facing can be seen on the right side of the sectional view of the piston ring. (Courtesy of Sealed Power Corporation)

FIGURE 14–44 Molybdenum facing can be seen on the right side of the sectional view of the piston ring. (Courtesy of Sealed Power Corporation)

packaged and shipped to the customer. The finished chromium facing is shown in a sectional view in Figure 14–43.

MOLYBDENUM PISTON RINGS

Early in the 1960s, molybdenum piston ring faces were introduced. These rings proved to have good service life, especially under scuffing conditions. The plasma method is a spray method used to deposit molybdenum on cast iron to produce a long-wearing and low-friction piston ring. The plasma method involves an electric arc plasma (ionized gas) that generates an extremely high temperature to melt the molybdenum and spray-deposit a molten powder of it onto a piston ring. Therefore, **plasma rings** are molybdenum (moly) rings that have the moly coating applied by the plasma method. Most molybdenum-faced piston rings have a groove that is 0.004 to 0.008 inch (0.1 to 0.2 millimeter) deep cut into the ring face. This groove is filled with molybdenum, using a metallic (or plasma) spray method, so that there is a cast-iron edge above and below the molybdenum. This edge may be chamfered in some applications. A sectional view of a molybdenum-faced ring is shown in Figure 14–44.

Molybdenum-faced piston rings will survive under high-temperature and scuffing conditions better than chromium-faced rings. Under abrasive wear conditions, chromium-faced rings will have a better service life. There is little measurable difference between these two facing materials with respect to blowby, oil control, break-in, and horsepower. Piston rings with either of these two types of facings are far better than plain cast-iron rings with phosphorus coatings. A molybdenum-faced ring, when

used, will be found in the top groove, and a plain cast-iron or chromium-faced ring will be found in the second groove.

MOLY-CHROME-CARBIDE RINGS

Rings with moly-chrome-carbide coating are also used in some original equipment (OE) and replacement applications. The coating has properties that include the hardness of the chrome and carbide combined with the heat resistance of molybdenum. Ceramic-coated rings are also being used where additional heat resistance is needed, such as in some heavy-duty, turbocharged, or supercharged engines.

OIL CONTROL RINGS

The first rings to be called oil rings were tapered rings. The lower scraping edge removed a large part of the oil from the cylinder wall on the downstroke of the piston. In the next development, the oil rings were vented by slots machined through the ring. This allowed oil to return through the ring and openings in the piston. This machining, as shown in Figure 14–45, produced two scraping edges that performed better than the single edge. Figure 14–46 shows how the scraping action of the oil control ring can be used to lubricate the piston pin. Steel spring expanders were placed in the ring groove behind the ring to improve static radial tension. They forced the ring to conform to the cylinder wall. Many expander designs are used. One type of expander (Figure 14–47) acts as a spring between the ring groove base and the ring. The action of another type of expander (Figure 14–48) results from radial force when the two ends of the expander butt together. This creates static tension as the ring is forced into the piston ring groove by the cylinder.

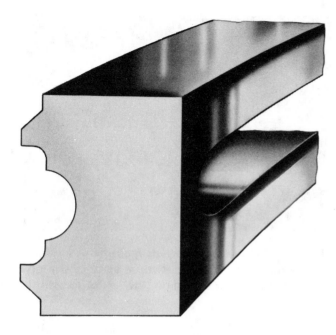

FIGURE 14–45   Cast-iron oil ring with a machined slot for oil venting. (Courtesy of Dana Corporation)

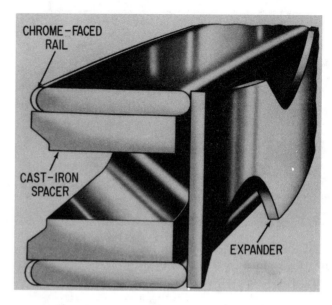

FIGURE 14–47   Oil ring with a cast-iron spacer, two chrome-faced rails, and an expander. (Courtesy of Dana Corporation)

FIGURE 14–46   The oil scraped from the cylinder walls by the oil control rings is directed to lubricate the piston pin in this design.

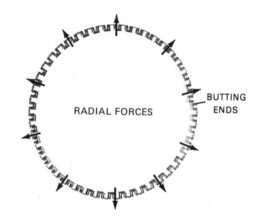

FIGURE 14–48   Oil ring expander type that provides radial force as it is compressed with the ends butting together.

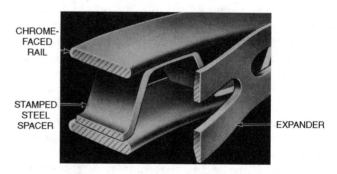

FIGURE 14–49   Oil ring with a stamped steel spacer, two chrome-faced rails, and an expander. (Courtesy of Sealed Power Corporation)

As oil ring requirements became greater, cast iron was no longer satisfactory. Steel **rails** with chromium or other types of facings replaced the cast-iron scraping edges. The rails are backed with **expanders** and separated with a **spacer.** This can be seen in Figure 14–49.

Some expander designs provide the spacing function as well as the expansion function. An oil ring with this type of construction is lightweight, having a desirable low level of inertia. It is well ventilated, so the oil can easily flow through it to the crankcase. It

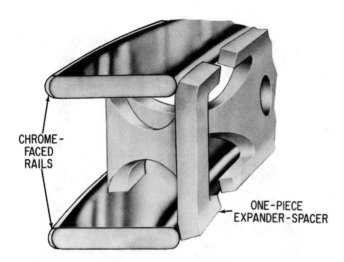

FIGURE 14–50 Oil ring with a one-piece expander-spacer and two chrome-faced rails. (Courtesy of Dana Corporation)

FIGURE 14–51 On the left is an oil ring having an expander-spacer and two chrome-faced rails. On the right is an oil ring having one chrome-faced rail and a combination expander-spacer-rail.

provides excellent oil control and it has a long service life. This type of oil ring is shown in Figure 14–50.

The latest design is a two-piece oil ring. One complex piece is an expander-spacer-rail. The other is a single rail. Two- and three-piece oil rings arc compared in Figure 14–51.

CONNECTING RODS

The connecting rod transfers the force and reciprocating motion of the piston to the crankshaft. The small end of the connecting rod reciprocates with the piston.

FIGURE 14–52 Rough casting for a connecting rod.

The large end rotates with the crankpin. These dynamic motions make it desirable to keep the connecting rod as light as possible while still having a rigid beam section. Use of lightweight rods also reduces the total connecting rod material cost.

Connecting rods are manufactured by casting, forging, and powdered (sintered) metal processes.

FORGED CONNECTING RODS

Forged connecting rods have been used for years. They are always used in high-performance engines. They are generally used in heavy-duty engines.

CAST CONNECTING RODS

Casting materials and processes have been improved so that they are used in most vehicle engines with high production standards. The cost of cast rods is lower than that of forged rods, both in the initial casting and in the machining. A typical rough connecting rod casting is shown in Figure 14–52. Generally, the forging method produces lighter-weight and stronger, but more expensive connecting rods.

POWDERED METAL CONNECTING RODS

Some production engines, such as the General Motors Northstar, switched from forged to powdered metal (PM) rods, which proved to be stronger. Each of the rods is blended into a tapered I beam section. The large split ring form for the crankshaft end is machined *after* the cap is assembled on the rod.

NOTE: Most powdered (sintered) metal connecting rods are broken at the parting end of the big end of the connecting rod. This rough broken surface helps ensure a perfect match when the pieces are bolted together. _

The hole will be a perfect circle. Therefore, the rod caps must not be interchanged. Assembly bolt holes are

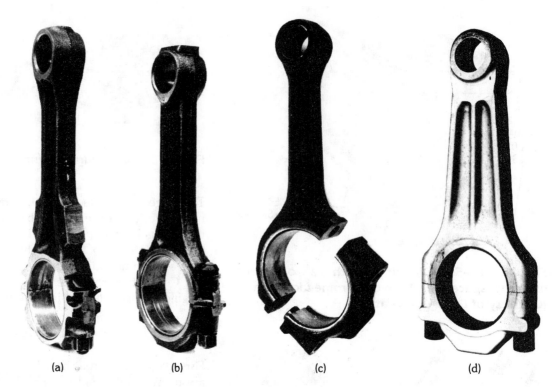

FIGURE 14–53   Connecting rod types. (a) Cast iron; note the thin parting line. (b) Forged steel; note the wide parting line. (c) Cap separated at an angle on a forged rod. (d) Forged aluminum racing rod.

closely reamed in both the cap and connecting rod to ensure alignment. The connecting rod bolts have **piloting surfaces** that closely fit these reamed holes. The connecting rod bolt heads are formed so that they have two or three sides that hold against the rod bolt bosses. The fourth side is left off so that there is enough cylinder skirt clearance as the crankshaft turns. Some connecting rod bolt heads are made on an angle to give this clearance. See Figure 14–53 for various types and shapes of connecting rods.

In some engines, offset connecting rods provide the most economical distribution of main bearing space and crankshaft cheek clearance. Some V-6 engines have the connecting rods offset by approximately 0.100 inch (2.54 millimeters). An example of this is pictured in Figure 14–54.

Connecting rods are made with balancing bosses so that their weight can be adjusted to specifications. Some have balancing bosses only on the rod cap. Others have a balancing boss above the piston as well. Some manufacturers put balancing bosses on the side of the rod, near the center of gravity of the connecting rod. Typical balancing bosses can be seen in Figure 14–55. Balancing is done on automatic balancing machines as the final machining operation before the rod is installed in an engine.

Most connecting rods have a **spit hole** that bleeds some of the oil from the connecting rod journal. Typical examples are shown in Figure 14–56. The hole may be drilled or it may be a chamfer on the cap parting surface. On inline engines, oil is thrown up from the spit hole into the cylinder in which the rod is located. On V-type engines, it is thrown into a cylinder in the opposite bank. The oil that is spit from the rod is aimed so that it will splash into the interior of the piston. This helps to lubricate the piston pin. Occasionally, adequate piston pin and cylinder wall lubrication is obtained without a spit hole. A hole similar to the spit holes may be used. It is called a **bleed hole.** Its only purpose is to control the oil flow through the bearing. Some heavy-duty engine connecting rods are drilled lengthwise. Oil flows through the drilled passage from the crankpin to the piston pin. This drilling is an expensive process and is used only where the spit hole method will not supply enough piston pin lubrication. See Figures 14–57 through 14–59 for additional connecting rod information.

ROD TWIST

During connecting rod reconditioning, the rod should be checked for twist. In other words, the hole at the small end and the hole at the big end of the connect-

FIGURE 14–54 On the left side is a piston and connecting rod from a V-6 engine. Note the full skirt piston and offset connecting rod. On the right is a piston and connecting rod from another V-6 that does not require an offset rod because the cylinder bores line up with the crankshaft throws directly. Note also the use of a lighter-weight piston.

FIGURE 14–55 **Typical locations of balancing bosses on connecting rods.**

ing rod should be parallel. No more than 0.002 inch (0.05 millimeter) of twist is acceptable. If measured rod twist is excessive, some specialty shops can remove the twist by bending the rod cold. Both cast and forged rods can be straightened. However, many engine builders replace the connecting rod if it is twisted. See Figure 14–60.

CONNECTING ROD SERVICE

As an engine operates, the forces go through the large end of the connecting rod. This causes the crankshaft end opening of the rod (eye) to gradually deform. The large eye of the connecting rod is resized during precision engine service.

Step #1. The parting surfaces of the rod and cap are smoothed to remove all high spots before resizing. A couple of thousandths

of an inch of metal is removed from the rod cap parting surface. This is done using the same grinder that is used to remove a slight amount of metal from the parting surface of main bearing caps. The amount removed from the rod and rod cap only reduces the bore size by 0.003 to 0.006 inch (0.08 to 0.15 millimeter).

NOTE: Powdered metal connecting rods cannot be reconditioned using this method. Most manufacturers recommend replacing worn powdered metal connecting rods.

Step #2. The cap is installed on the rod, and the nuts or cap screws are properly torqued. The hole is then bored or honed to be perfectly round and of the size and finish required to give the correct connecting rod bearing crush. Figure 14–61 shows the setup for resizing the rod on a typical hone used in engine reconditioning.

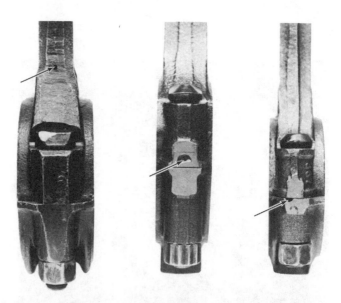

FIGURE 14–56 Connecting rod spit and bleed holes.

FIGURE 14–57 Assortment of connecting rods at a large engine remanufacturing facility. All of the connecting rods of the same engine are wired together to help ensure that the engine will be balanced when it is reinstalled with replacement pistons.

FIGURE 14–58 This connecting rod is stamped with the number 6, indicating a specified weight, and it is to be matched with a piston that is also stamped with a number indicating its weight. The factory service manual <u>must</u> be used when changing pistons and/or connecting rods to be assured of a balanced engine.

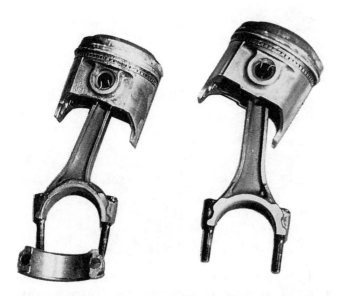

ANGLE WEAR ON
THE PISTON SKIRT

EDGE WEAR ON
THE BEARING

FIGURE 14–59 Not all defective connecting rods are as easy to visually check as the rod on the left. An incorrect oil filter caused a serious oil leak and this engine damage. The connecting rod and piston on the right came from the same engine, yet look undamaged.

FIGURE 14–60 Signs of connecting rod misalignment.

FIGURE 14–61 Resizing the big end of the connecting rod with a hone. To help ensure a more accurate and straighter job, hone two connecting rods at a time.

Even though material is being removed at the big end of the rod, the compression ratio is changed very little. The inside of the bore at the big end should have a 60- to 90-microinch finish for proper bearing contact and heat transfer.

ROD ALIGNMENT

The connecting rod must not be bent or twisted if it is to operate properly. A bent or twisted connecting rod will cause premature rod bearing and piston skirt

FIGURE 14–62 One type of fixture used to check the alignment of the piston and rod assembly.

FIGURE 14–63 Selection of reconditioned rods at a small engine remanufacturing plant. Most rebuilders attempt to reuse all connecting rods from the engine and keep them together. Whenever a rod cannot be used, a replacement is selected from this supply.

failure. A misaligned connecting rod will *not* hold the rings perpendicular to the cylinder wall, so the rings cannot function correctly. The first sign of misalignment is a wear pattern on the piston skirt and rod bearing that can be seen when the engine is disassembled. Rods can also be bent while they are being handled in the process of servicing. They should be checked as the last piston and rod reconditioning operation.

Rod alignment is checked on an alignment fixture. On some fixtures, the rod is aligned before it is connected to the piston. The piston and rod are assembled before using other types of alignment fixtures. One of these is illustrated in Figure 14–62. The rod can be straightened either by using lever bars or by using a special hydraulic press. After straightening, connecting rods should be stored vertically. See Figure 14–63.

PISTON AND ROD BALANCING

All pistons should be weighted. Carefully grind weight off of all but the lightest piston to match their weights.

All connecting rods should be weighted separately at both ends. Grind material from the balance pad area of each end to achieve equal weight for all rods matching the weight of the lightest rod.

■ TECH TIP ■

THE MIGHT-AS-WELLS

One of the hardest questions a technician or vehicle owner faces is, "How much work should be done to make a proper repair without incurring too much cost?" The technician wants to make a proper repair to prevent an early failure (and a customer comeback). The vehicle owner does not want to spend any more than is necessary for the repair service.

When the engine is disassembled, many small procedures, such as connecting rod reconditioning, are often left unperformed because of additional effort and cost. Connecting rod reconditioning is one of many operations considered important enough to be included in a proper engine repair or overhaul. Many engine rebuilders also recommend replacing all connecting rod bolts whenever the engine is disassembled. The major expense involves removing the engine from the vehicle; therefore, the technician "might as well" do a complete and thorough engine service job and convince the customer that the added expense of "doing it right" is the best money spent.

FIGURE 14–64 One type of precision gauge required to check the size of the hole while it is being honed for an oversize piston pin.

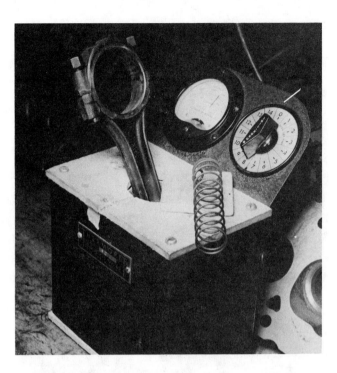

FIGURE 14–66 Heater being used to expand the piston pin eye of the connecting rod.

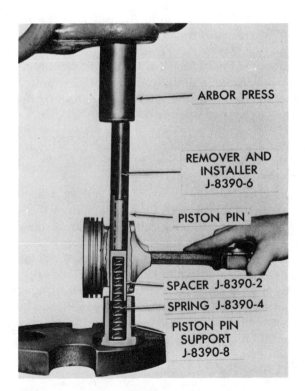

FIGURE 14–65 Typical fixture used to press a piston pin into a rod. (Courtesy of Cadillac Motor Car Division, GMC)

Labels in figure 14-65:
ARBOR PRESS
REMOVER AND INSTALLER J-8390-6
PISTON PIN
SPACER J-8390-2
SPRING J-8390-4
PISTON PIN SUPPORT J-8390-8

PISTON AND ROD ASSEMBLY

To assemble the piston and rod, the piston pin is put in one side of the piston. The small end of the connecting rod should be checked for proper size as shown in Figure 14–64. The piston and rod are placed on a press, using adapters and supports. This setup is shown in Figure 14–65. The pin is pressed into the rod until it is centered. The press-fit of the pin in the small eye of the rod will hold the pin securely in place during engine operation. This keeps it from sliding out and touching the cylinder wall. In precision engine shops, the small eye of the connecting rod is heated before the pin is installed. See Figures 14–66 and 14–67. This causes the rod eye to expand so that the pin can be pushed into place with little force. The pin must be rapidly pushed into the correct center position. There is only one chance to get it in the right place because the rod will quickly seize on the pin as the rod eye is cooled by the pin.

Full-floating piston pins operate in a bushing in the small eye of the connecting rod. The bushing can be replaced. The bushing and the piston are honed to the same diameter. This allows the piston pin to slide freely through both. The full-floating piston pin is held in place with a lock ring at each end of the piston pin. The lock ring expands into a small groove in the pin hole of the piston. The lock rings should always be replaced with new rings. These must be seated properly in the

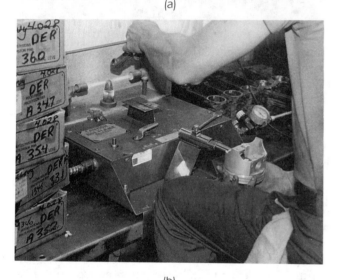

FIGURE 14–67 (a) Flame-type connecting rod heater. This is the type most often used by re-manufacturers because of the rapid heating. The rod should not be heated to more than 700° F (370° C). (If the rod turns blue, it is too hot.) (b) An operator removing the heated connecting rod and preparing to install it on the piston. Note the fixture used to hold the piston pin, and the dial indicator (gauge) used to ensure proper positioning.

ring groove. If the lock rings come out, the piston pin can ruin a piston and will usually cause heavy cylinder wall scoring as well.

Care must be taken to make sure that the pistons and rods are in the correct cylinder. They must face in the correct direction. There is usually a **notch** on the piston head

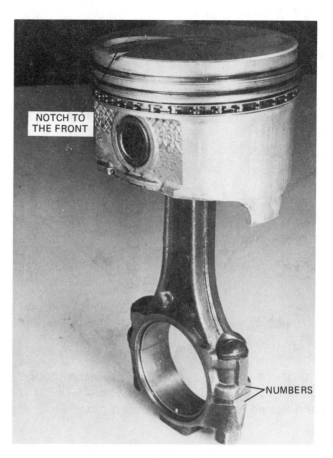

FIGURE 14–68 Position of the notch at the front of the piston, and the connecting rod numbers.

indicating the *front*. Using this will correctly position the piston pin offset toward the right side of the engine. The connecting rod **identification marks** on pushrod inline engines are normally placed on the camshaft side.

NOTE: The camshaft side of an inline OHV engine is also the oil filter side of most engines.

The notch and numbers on a piston and rod assembly can be seen in Figure 14–68. On V-type engines, the connecting rod cylinder identification marks are on the side of the rods that can be seen from the bottom of the engine when the piston and rod assemblies are installed in the engine. For assembly, the piston and rod are supported on an assembly fixture in a press. The piston pin is inserted in the piston and aligned with the rod hole. The service manual should be checked for any special piston and rod assembly instructions.

PISTON RING SERVICE

Each piston ring, one at a time, should be placed backward in the groove in which it is to be run. Its **side**

FIGURE 14–69 *The side clearance of the piston ring is checked with a thickness (feeler) gauge.*

FIGURE 14–71 *The ring gap is measured with a thickness (feeler) gauge.*

clearance in the groove should be checked with a feeler gauge, as shown in Figure 14–69. If a ring is tight at any spot, check for deposits or burrs in the ring groove. Each piston ring, one at a time, is then placed in the cylinder in which it is to operate.

NOTE: See chapter 13 for block preparation procedures that should be complete before the following operations are performed.

After the block and cylinder bores have been reconditioned, invert the piston and push each ring into the lower quarter of the cylinder (Figure 14–70); then measure the **ring gap** (Figure 14–71). It should be approximately 0.004 inch for each inch of bore diameter (0.004 millimeter for each centimeter of bore diameter). Leave the rings in the cylinder until they are to be installed on the piston. This will keep them from being mixed up or damaged.

The oil rings are installed first. The expander-spacer of the oil ring is placed in the lower ring groove.

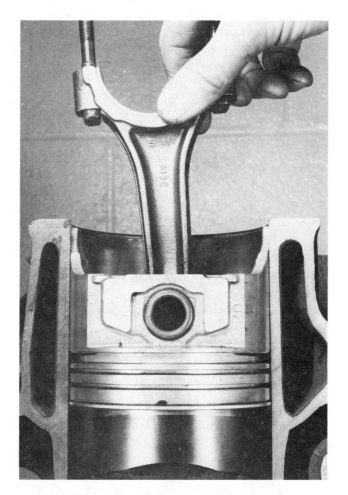

FIGURE 14–70 *A piston is used to push the ring squarely into the cylinder.*

FIGURE 14–72 One type of good-quality ring expander being used to install a piston ring.

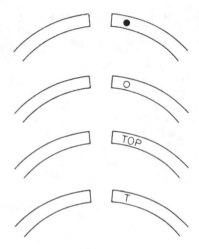

FIGURE 14–73 Identification marks used to indicate the side of the piston ring to be placed toward the head.

One oil ring rail is carefully placed above the expander-spacer by winding it into the groove. The other rail is placed below the expander-spacer. The ring should be rotated in the groove to make sure that the expander-spacer ends have not overlapped. If they have, the ring must be removed and reassembled correctly.

Installing the compression rings requires the use of a **piston ring expander tool** that will only open the ring gap enough to slip the ring on the piston. Figure 14–72 shows one of the best types of piston ring expanders in use for engine repair. Be careful to install the ring with the correct side up. The top of the compression ring is marked with a dot, the letter *T*, or the word *top* (Figure 14–73). After the rings are installed, they should be rotated in the groove to make sure that they move freely. The rings should be checked to make

sure that they will go fully into the groove so that the ring face is flush with the surface of the piston ring lands. Usually, the rings are placed on all of the pistons before any of the pistons are installed in the cylinders.

SUMMARY

1. The connecting rods should be marked before disassembly.
2. Pistons are cam ground so that when operating temperature is reached, the piston will have expanded enough across the piston pin area to become round.
3. Replacement pistons should weigh the same as the original pistons to maintain proper engine balance.
4. Some engines use an offset piston pin to help reduce piston slap when the engine is cold.
5. Piston rings usually include two compression rings at the top of the piston and an oil control ring below the compression rings.
6. If the ring end gap is excessive, blowby gases can travel past the rings and into the crankcase.
7. Many piston rings are made of coated cast iron to provide proper sealing.
8. If the connecting rod is twisted, diagonal wear will be noticed on the piston skirt.
9. Powdered metal connecting rods are usually broken at the big end parting line. Because of this rough junction, powdered metal connecting rods cannot be reconditioned— they must be replaced if damaged or worn.
10. The piston and the connecting rod must be correctly assembled according to identifying notches or marks.

REVIEW QUESTIONS

1. Describe the procedure for correctly removing the piston and rod assembly from the engine.
2. What methods are used to control piston heat expansion?
3. Why are some piston skirts tin plated?
4. Describe the effect of the piston pin offset as it controls piston slap.
5. Why is it important to keep the connecting rod cap with the rod on which it was originally used, and to install it in the correct way?
6. What causes the piston ring groove clearance to widen in service?
7. Describe how connecting rods are reconditioned.
8. How is the piston pin installed in the piston and rod assembly?

MULTIPLE-CHOICE QUESTIONS

1. Connecting rod caps should be marked (if they were not marked at the factory) before the piston and connecting rod assembly is removed from the engine _____.
   a. Because they are balanced together
   b. Because they are machined together
   c. To make certain that the heavier rod is matched to the heavier piston
   d. To make certain that the lighter rod is matched to the lighter piston

2. Many aluminum pistons skirts are plated with _____.
   a. Tin
   b. Lead
   c. Antimony
   d. Terneplate

3. A hypereutectic piston has _____.
   a. A higher weight than a eutectic piston
   b. A higher silicon content
   c. A higher tin content
   d. A higher nickel content

4. The purpose of casting steel struts into an aluminum piston is to _____.
   a. Provide increased strength
   b. Provide increased weight at the top part of the piston where it is needed for stability
   c. Provide increased heat transfer from the piston head to the piston pin
   d. Control thermal expansion

5. Full-floating piston pins are retained by _____.
   a. Lock rings
   b. A drilled hole with roll pin
   c. An interference fit between rod and piston pin
   d. An interference fit between piston and piston pin

6. When balancing pistons _____.
   a. Choose the heaviest and add weight to the others
   b. Choose the heaviest and grind weight off until it matches the *average* of all the others
   c. Choose the lightest and grind material from the other pistons until all pistons are of equal weight
   d. Balance the piston only after it is assembled with the connecting rod

7. A misaligned connecting rod causes what type of engine wear?
   a. Cylinder taper
   b. Barrel-shaped cylinders
   c. Ridge wear
   d. Angle wear on the piston skirt

8. Side clearance is a measure taken between the _____ and the _____.
   a. Piston (side skirt); cylinder wall
   b. Piston pin; piston pin retainer (clip)
   c. Piston ring; piston ring groove
   d. Compression ring; oil control ring

9. Piston ring gap should only be measured _____.
   a. After all cylinder work has been performed
   b. After installing the piston in the cylinder
   c. After installing the rings on the piston
   d. Both a and c

10. Piston damage is most likely to be caused by _____.
    a. Valves hitting the piston head
    b. Abnormal combustion
    c. Lugging the engine during operation
    d. High engine speeds that can break piston heads

15

■ ■ ■ ■ ■ ■

Crankshafts and Bearings

■ ■ ■

OBJECTIVES

After studying Chapter 15, the reader will be able to

1. Distinguish a cast crankshaft from a forged crankshaft.
2. Describe the purpose and function of a vibration damper.
3. Explain how crankshafts are reground and polished.
4. Discuss engine balance shafts and how they function.
5. Explain the purpose, function, and construction of engine bearings.

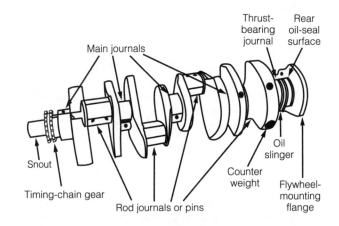

FIGURE 15–1 Typical crankshaft with main journals that support the crankshaft in the block. Rod journals are offset from the crankshaft centerline.

All the engine power is delivered through the crankshaft. The shaft must have the necessary shape and must be made from the proper materials to meet the power demands placed on it.

CRANKSHAFT PURPOSE AND FUNCTION

Power from expanding gases in the combustion chamber is delivered to the crankshaft through the piston, piston pin, and connecting rod. The connecting rods and their bearings are attached to a bearing journal on the crank throw. The crank throw is offset from the **crankshaft centerline.** The combustion force is applied to the crank throw after the crankshaft has moved past top center. This produces the turning effort or **torque,** which rotates the crankshaft. The crankshaft rotates on **main bearings.** These bearings are

split in half so that they can be assembled around the crankshaft main bearing journals.

The bearing **journal** is the surface of the crankshaft that operates on a bearing. Parts of a typical crankshaft are illustrated in Figure 15–1.

FORGED CRANKSHAFTS

Crankshafts used in high-production automotive engines may be either forged or cast. Forged crankshafts are stronger than the cast crankshaft, but they are more expensive. Forged crankshafts have a wide separation line where the flashings have been ground off. Cast crankshafts have a fine line where the mold parted. The flashing and parting lines can be used for identification.

Forged crankshafts are made from SAE 1045 or a similar type of steel. The crankshaft is formed from a hot

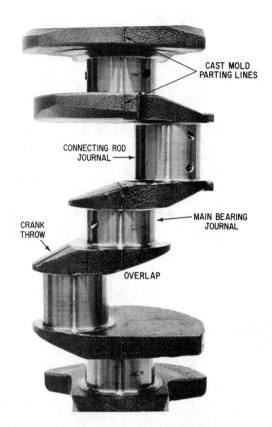

FIGURE 15–2 *Wide separation lines where the flashings have been removed from this forged crankshaft show that it has been twisted to index the crank throws.*

FIGURE 15–3 *Cast crankshaft showing the bearing journal overlap and a straight, narrow cast mold parting line.*

steel billet through the use of a series of forging dies. Each die changes the shape of the billet slightly. The crankshaft blank is finally formed with the last die. The blanks are then machined to finish the crankshaft. Forging makes a very dense, tough crankshaft with the metal's grain structure running parallel to the principal direction of stress. Figure 15–2 shows a typical forged crankshaft with wide separation lines where the flashings have been removed.

Two methods are used to forge crankshafts. One method is to forge the crankshaft in place. This is followed by straightening. The **forging in place** method is usually used with forged four- and six-cylinder crankshafts. A second method is to forge the crankshaft in a **single plane.** It is then twisted in the main bearing journal to index the throws at the desired angles. Throws are the offset part of the crankshaft. The amount of throw offset determines the piston stroke. The throw is one-half the stroke.

CAST CRANKSHAFTS

Casting materials and techniques have improved cast crankshaft quality so that cast crankshafts are used in most production automotive engines. Automotive

crankshafts may be cast in steel, nodular iron, or malleable iron. The major advantage of the casting process is that crankshaft material and machining costs are less than they are with forging. The reason for this is that the crankshaft can be made close to the required shape and size, including all complicated counterweights. The only machining required on a carefully designed cast crankshaft is the grinding of bearing journal surfaces and the finishing of front and rear drive ends. Metal grain structure in the cast crankshaft is uniform and random throughout. Because of this, the shaft is able to handle loads from all directions. Counterweights on cast crankshafts are slightly larger than counterweights on a forged crankshaft because the cast shaft metal is less dense and therefore somewhat lighter. The narrow mold parting surface lines can be seen on the cast crankshaft pictured in Figure 15–3.

SIX-CYLINDER ENGINE CRANKSHAFTS

The inline six-cylinder engine has six crank throws in three matched pairs. The throw is ground to make a crankpin. The smooth surface of the crankpin

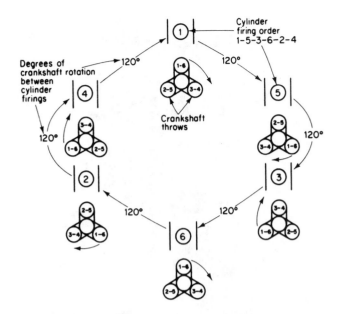

FIGURE 15–4   Crankshaft of an even-firing, inline, six-cylinder engine.

FIGURE 15–5   Cutaway of a V-type engine. Note the compact design.

is called the bearing journal. Each pair of throws on an inline six-cylinder engine is 120 degrees from the other pairs. This causes one pair of pistons to reach top center at each 120 degrees of crankshaft rotation. Pistons in cylinders #1 and #6, #2 and #5, and #3 and #4 move together as pairs. Each piston in a pair of pistons is 360 degrees out of phase with its mate in the 720 degree four-stroke cycle. This arrangement gives smooth, low-vibration operation. There are even power strokes, one at each 120 degrees of crankshaft rotation. This is illustrated in Figure 15–4. The crankshafts for these engines usually have one main bearing journal between each throw, making seven main bearings. Some have two throws between each main bearing, making four main bearings.

V-8 ENGINE CRANKSHAFTS

The V-8 engine has four inline cylinders in each of the two blocks that are placed at a 90-degree angle to each other. Each group of four inline cylinders is called a **bank.** The crankshaft for the V-8 engine has four throws. The connecting rods from two cylinders are connected to each throw, one from each bank. This can be seen in the cutaway V-type engine pictured in Figure 15–5. This arrangement results in a condition of being only minimally unbalanced. The V-8 engine crankshaft has two planes, so there is one throw every

90 degrees. A plane is a flat surface that cuts through the part. These planes could be seen if the crankshaft were cut lengthwise through the center of the main bearing and crankpin journals. Looking at the front of the crankshaft with the first throw at 360 degrees (up), the second throw is at 90 degrees (to the right), the third throw is at 270 degrees (to the left), and the fourth throw is at 180 degrees (down). There is one main bearing journal between each throw, so there are five main bearings in a V-8 engine. In operation with this arrangement, one piston reaches top center at each 90 degrees of crankshaft rotation so that the engine operates smoothly with even firing at each 90 degrees of crankshaft rotation. This can be seen in Figure 15–6.

FOUR-CYLINDER ENGINE CRANKSHAFTS

The crankshaft used on four-cylinder inline engines has four throws on a single plane. There is usually a main bearing journal between each throw, making it a five–main bearing crankshaft (Figure 15–7). Pistons move as pairs in this engine, too. Pistons in the #1 and #4 cylinders move together, and pistons #2 and #3 move together. Each piston in a pair is 360 degrees out of phase with the other piston in the 720 degree four-stroke cycle. With this arrangement, the four-cylinder inline engine fires one cylinder at each 180 degrees of crankshaft rotation. This is illustrated in Figure 15–8. A four-cylinder opposed engine and a 90 degree V-4 engine have crankshafts that look like that of the four-cylinder inline engine.

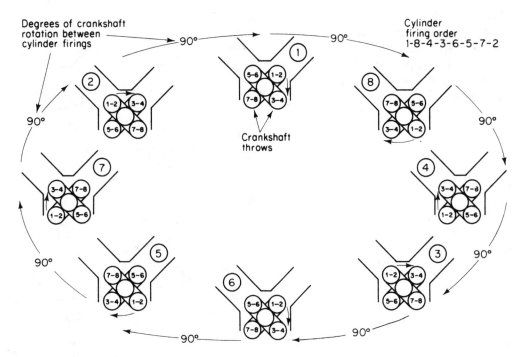

FIGURE 15–6   Crankshaft of an even-firing V-8 engine.

FIGURE 15–7   Five–main bearing crankshaft for an inline four-cylinder engine.

FIVE-CYLINDER ENGINE CRANKSHAFTS

The inline five-cylinder engine has a five-throw crankshaft with one throw at each 72 degrees. Six main bearings are used on this crankshaft. The piston in one cylinder reaches top center at each 144 degrees of crankshaft rotation. The throws are arranged to give a firing order of 1-2-4-5-3. Dynamic balancing has been one of the major problems with this engine design, yet the vibration has been satisfactorily dampened and isolated on both the Audi and Acura five-cylinder engines.

THREE-CYLINDER ENGINE CRANKSHAFTS

A three-cylinder engine uses a 120-degree three-throw crankshaft with four main bearings. This engine requires a balancing shaft that turns at crankshaft

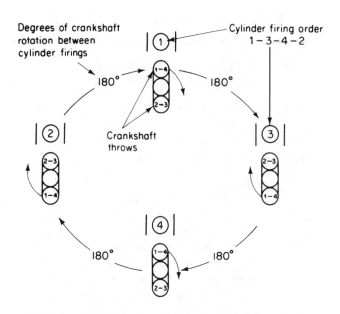

FIGURE 15–8   Crankshaft of an even-firing, inline, four-cylinder engine.

speed, but in the opposite direction, to reduce the vibration to an acceptable level.

ODD-FIRING 90-DEGREE V-6 ENGINE CRANKSHAFTS

In 1962, Buick introduced a V-6 engine with two banks of three cylinders each. The banks were placed at 90 de-

FIGURE 15–9 Odd firing pattern produced by a crankshaft with the crank throws 120 degrees apart operating in a 90-degree V-6 block.

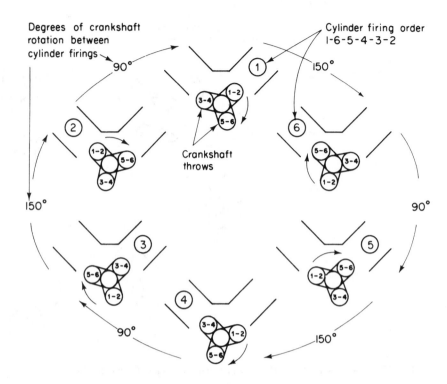

■ DIAGNOSTIC STORY ■

THE MYSTERIOUS ENGINE VIBRATION

A Buick-built 3.8-liter V-6 engine vibrated the whole car after a new short block had been installed. The technician who had installed the replacement engine did all of the following:

1. Checked the spark plugs
2. Checked the spark plug wires
3. Checked the distributor cap and rotor
4. Disconnected the torque converter from the flex plate (drive plate) to eliminate the possibility of a torque converter or automatic transmission pump problem
5. Removed all accessory drive belts one at a time

Yet the vibration still existed.

Another technician checked the engine mounts and found that the left (driver's side) engine mount was out of location, ripped, and cocked. The transmission mount was also defective. After the technician replaced both mounts and made certain that all mounts were properly set, the vibration was eliminated. The design and location of the engine mounts are critical to the elimination of vibration, especially on 90-degree V-6 engines.

grees to each other so that the engine could be machined on the V-8 production line. Essentially, this engine is a V-8 with one cylinder removed from each bank. The 90-degree V-6 engine uses a three-throw crankshaft with four main bearings. The throws are 120 degrees apart. As in typical V-type engines, each crank throw has two connecting rods attached, one from each bank. This V-6 engine design does not have even firing impulses because the pistons, connected to the 120-degree crankpins, do not reach top center at even intervals. The engine has a firing pattern of 150°-90°-150°-90°-150°-90°, as illustrated in Figure 15–9. This firing pattern produces unequal pulses that have to be isolated with engine mounts that have been carefully designed.

EVEN-FIRING 90-DEGREE V-6 ENGINE CRANKSHAFTS

The crank throws for the even-firing V-6 engine were split, making separate crankpins for each cylinder. The split throw can be seen in Figure 15–10. The crankpins were made 0.25 inch larger in diameter to give adequate strength. The four main bearings were kept. The crankpin journals were split; one was moved 30 degrees ahead. This angle between the crankpins on the crankshaft throws is called a **splay angle**. Figure 15–11 illustrates how the 30-degree splay angle allows even firing. A flange of 0.120 to 0.180 inch was left between the split crankpin journals. This provides a continuous fillet or edge for machining and grinding operations. It also provides a normal flange for the rod and bearing. This flange between the splayed crankpin journals is sometimes called a **flying web**. The even-firing 90-degree V-6 engine has a firing order of 1-6-5-4-3-2.

In 1978, Chevrolet introduced a 90-degree V-6 engine. This engine was adapted from the small-block Chevrolet V-8 by removing cylinders #3 and #6. The four–main bearing crankshaft of the 90-degree V-6 Chevrolet engine has an 18-degree splay angle between the adjacent crankpins. This design results in a firing pattern of 132°-108°-132°-108°-132°-108°. The firing pattern is illustrated in Figure 15–12. Some torque variation remains between power strokes, but the vibration is still 62% less than that of a 90-degree V-6 engine having only three crankpins.

60-DEGREE V-6 ENGINE CRANKSHAFTS

The 60-degree V-6 engine is similar to the even-firing 90-degree V-6 engine. The adjacent pairs of crankpins on the crankshaft used in the 60-degree V-6 engine have a splay angle of 60 degrees. This design allows even firing as shown in Figure 15–13. With this large 60-degree splay angle, the flange or flying web between the splayed crankpins is made heavier than on crankshafts with smaller splay angles. This is necessary to give strength to the crankshaft. The crankshaft of the 60-degree V-6 engine also uses four main bearings.

CRANKSHAFT OILING HOLES

The crankshaft is drilled, as shown in Figure 15–14 to allow oil from the main bearing oil groove to be directed to the connecting rod bearings. The oil on the

FIGURE 15–10 *Split crankpin journals splayed at 30 degrees used in an even-firing 90-degree V-6 block.*

FIGURE 15–11 **Even firing of a 90-degree V-6 engine using a crankshaft with 30-degree splayed crankpin journals.**

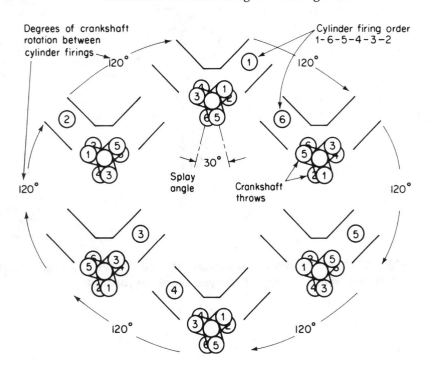

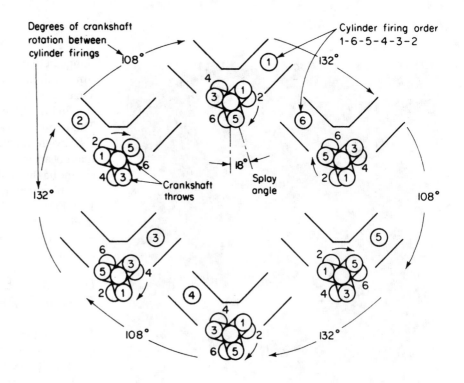

FIGURE 15–12 Firing pattern of a 90-degree V-6 engine using a crankshaft with 18-degree splayed crankpin journals.

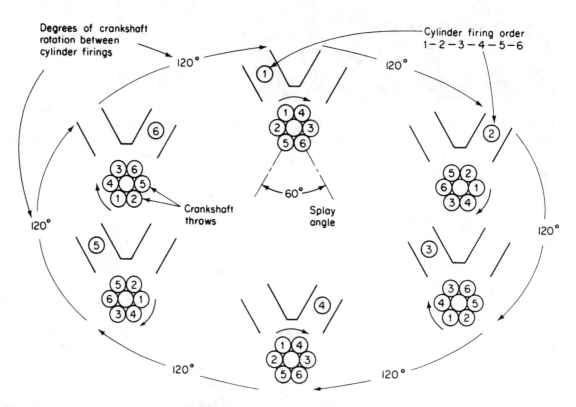

FIGURE 15–13 Even firing pattern of a 60-degree V-6 engine using a crankshaft with 60-degree splayed crankpin journals.

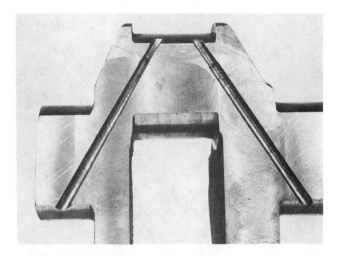

FIGURE 15–14 Crankshaft sawed in half, showing drilled oil passages between the main and rod bearing journals.

FIGURE 15–16 Balance hole drilled in a crankpin.

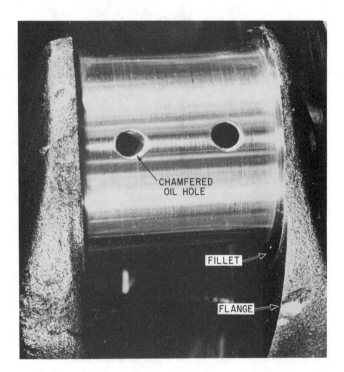

CHAMFERED
OIL HOLE

FILLET

FLANGE

FIGURE 15–15 Typical chamfered hole in a crankshaft bearing journal.

bearings forms a hydrodynamic oil film to support bearing loads. Some of the oil may be sprayed out through a spit or bleed hole in the connecting rod. The rest of the oil leaks from the edges of the bearing. It is thrown from the bearing against the inside surfaces of the engine. Some of the oil that is thrown from the

crankshaft bearings will land on the camshaft to lubricate the lobes. A part of the throw-off oil splashes on the cylinder wall to lubricate the piston and rings. Some large, heavy-duty engines have an oil passage drilled through the connecting rod to carry oil for lubricating the piston pin.

Stress tends to concentrate at oil holes drilled through the crankshaft journals. These holes are usually located where the crankshaft loads and stresses are the lowest. The oil holes lead the top center of the crankpin by approximately 80 degrees. Straight drilling eliminates places where dirt could become trapped. The edges of the oil holes are carefully chamfered to relieve as much stress concentration as possible. Chamfered oil holes are shown in Figure 15–15.

CRANKSHAFT LIGHTENING HOLES

Lightening holes in the crankpins do not reduce crankpin strength if the hole size is less than half of the crankpin diameter. Lightening holes will often increase crankshaft strength by relieving some of the natural stress in the crankshaft. The hole in the center of the crank throw is used for balancing, through control of the hole depth (Figure 15–16).

FIGURE 15–17   A crankshaft broken as a result of using the wrong torsional vibration damper.

CRANKSHAFT FORCES

Each time combustion occurs, the force deflects the crankshaft as it transfers torque to the output shaft. This deflection occurs in two ways, to bend the shaft sideways and to twist the shaft in torsion. The crankshaft must be rigid enough to keep the deflection forces to a minimum.

Crankshaft deflections are directly related to operating roughness of an engine. When back-and-forth deflections occur at the same vibrational **frequency** (number of vibrations per second) as that of another engine part, the parts will vibrate together. When this happens, the parts are said to **resonate.** These vibrations may become great enough to reach the audible level, producing a thumping sound. If this type of vibration continues, the part may fail. See Figure 15–17.

Harmful crankshaft twisting vibrations are dampened with a **torsional vibration damper.** It is also called a **harmonic balancer.** This damper or balancer usually consists of a cast-iron **inertia ring** mounted to a cast-iron **hub** with an **elastomer** sleeve.

HINT: *Push on the rubber (elastomer sleeve) of the vibration damper with your fingers or a pencil. If the rubber does not spring back, replace the damper.*

Two examples are shown in Figure 15–18. Elastomers are actually synthetic rubberlike materials. The inertia ring size is selected to control the amplitude of the crankshaft vibrations for each specific engine model. See Figures 15–19 and 15–20.

CRANKSHAFT BALANCE

Most crankshaft balancing is done during manufacture. Holes are drilled in the counterweight to lighten it to improve balance. Sometimes these holes are drilled after the

(a)

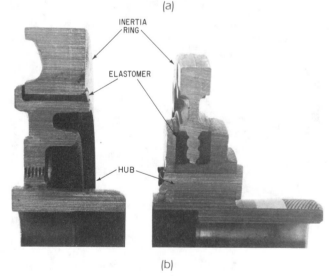

(b)

FIGURE 15–18   Crankshaft torsional dampers: (a) front view and (b) sectional view of two different types of dampers.

crankshaft is installed in the engine. Some manufacturers are able to control casting quality so closely that counterweight machining for balancing is not necessary. Engines with cast crankshafts usually have some external balancing. External balancing of these engines is accomplished by adding weights to the damper hub and to the flywheel

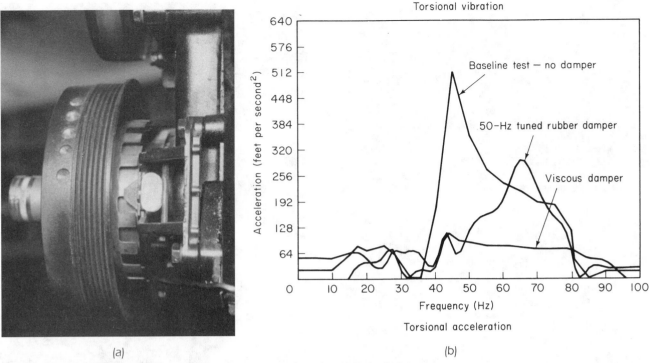

FIGURE 15–19   (a) Typical vibration damper showing where material has been drilled out to balance the assembly. (b) Graphic showing forces involved without a damper and with two styles of vibration dampers. A viscous damper is commonly used on heavy-duty diesel engines and racing engines.

FIGURE 15–20   A broken stock vibration damper used for racing. Extended high-RPM use finally caused the outer ring to separate from the rubber bond with the inner hub. When this occurred, severe vibration was felt throughout the entire race car.

or automatic transmission drive plate. Typical methods of adding balance weights are shown in Figure 15–21.

To reduce the counterweight size in the engine, some manufacturers will add weight to the vibration damper and flywheel. Engines balanced in this way are called **externally balanced,** whereas engines that have balanced crankshafts are called **internally balanced.** Crankshafts and vibration dampers cannot be interchanged because this will cause severe vibrations. For example, the 350–cubic inch Chevrolet V-8 is internally balanced, whereas the 400–cubic inch Chevrolet V-8 uses an externally balanced crankshaft. Chrysler engines also can be either internally balanced or externally balanced, depending on whether the crankshaft is cast or forged.

THRUST SURFACE

Automatic transmission pressure in the torque converter and clutch release forces tends to push the crankshaft toward the front of the engine. Thrust bearings in the engine will support thrust loads, as well as maintaining the crankshaft position. Smooth thrust bearing journal surfaces are ground on a small boss located on the crank-

(a)

(b)

FIGURE 15–21 (a) External balance weight added to the vibration damper. (b) Drive (flex) plate partially drilled to help balance the engine.

shaft cheek next to one of the main bearing journals (Figure 15–22). One main bearing has thrust bearing flanges that ride against these thrust bearings. Thrust bearings may be located on any one of the main bearing journals.

CRANKSHAFT INSPECTION

Shaft damage includes scored bearing journals, bends or warpage, and cracks. Damaged shafts must be reconditioned or replaced.

The crankshaft is one of the most highly stressed engine parts. *The stress increases by four times every time the engine speed doubles.* Any sign of a crack is a cause to

FIGURE 15–22   Thrust bearing located on one of the crankshaft main bearings.

reject the crankshaft. Most cracks can be seen during a close visual inspection. High-RPM racing crankshafts should be checked with Magnaflux, which will show up any very small cracks that would lead to failure.

Bearing journal scoring is one of the most common crankshaft defects. Scoring appears as scratches around the bearing journal surface. Generally, there is more scoring near the center of the bearing journal. This can be seen in Figure 15–23. Dirt and grit carried in the oil enter between the journal and bearing. If the particles are too large to get through the oil clearance between the journal and the bearing, they will partially embed in the bearing surface and scratch the journal. Dirt can also be left on the journal during assembly if the parts are not thoroughly cleaned.

Crankshaft journals can have nicks or pits in them. Nicks are caused by carelessness when the journal is bumped with another part while it is exposed or during assembly (Figure 15–24). Pits such as those pictured in Figure 15–25 are caused by corrosion.

Roughness and slight bends in journals can be corrected by grinding the journals on true centers. Forged shafts with excess bend should be straightened before grinding.

FIGURE 15–23 Scored connecting rod bearing journal.

FIGURE 15–25 The pitted part of the main bearing journal rides in the main bearing oil groove.

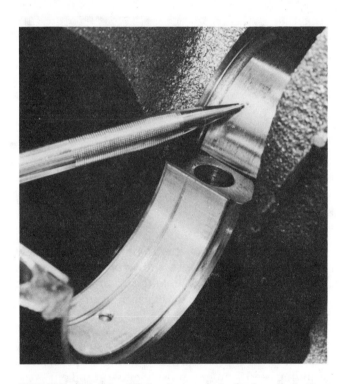

FIGURE 15–24 Nicked crankshaft journal that scratched the bearing.

FIGURE 15–26 Damaged connecting rod journal.

HINT: *If your fingernail catches on a groove when rubbed across a bearing journal, the journal is too rough to reuse and must be reground. Another test is to rub a copper penny across* the journal. If any copper remains on the crankshaft, it must be reground.

If the relatively inexpensive standard production crankshaft is damaged beyond grinding limits, it should be replaced. Excessive damage is pictured in Figure 15–26. More expensive racing crankshafts, or crankshafts that are to be modified, can have the journals built up by welding or by special metal spray techniques. They are then straightened and reground. This process

FIGURE 15–27 Connecting rod journal badly worn from lack of lubrication.

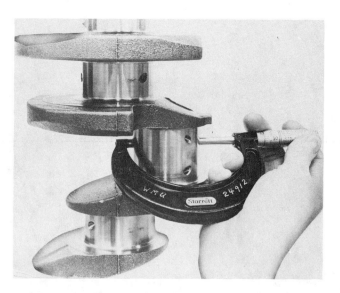

FIGURE 15–28 All journals of a crankshaft should be measured. Some crankshafts come from the factory with undersize journals on some or all of the main and/or rod bearings.

is expensive and, therefore, is done only when it is less costly than purchasing a new special crankshaft. The connecting rod journal shown in Figure 15–27 would have to be built up and reground to be used again.

CRANKSHAFT GRINDING

Crankshaft journals that have excessive out-of-round or excessive taper should be reground. The crankshaft will also have to be reground if the journals are badly scored. The journal will have to be ground if bearings are not available to compensate for wear of the journal. See Figures 15–28 and 15–29. Crankshafts may require straightening before grinding. The bearing journals of the used crankshaft should have less than 0.001 inch (0.025 millimeter) of out-of-round or taper from one end to the other.

Both crankshaft ends are placed in rotating heads on one style of crankshaft grinder. The main bearing journals are ground on the centerline of the crankshaft. The crankshaft is then offset in the two rotating heads just enough to make the crankshaft main bearing journal centerline rotate around the centerline of the crankpin. The crankshaft will then be rotating around the crankpin centerline. The journal on the crankpin is reground in this position. The crankshaft must be repositioned for each different crankpin center. Crankshafts are usually ground to be 0.010, 0.020, or 0.030 inch undersize.

FIGURE 15–29 This crankshaft will definitely require grinding because the wrong oil filter was installed. All of the oil leaked out, and the engine finally stopped because of lack of lubrication.

In another type of crankshaft grinder, the crankshaft always turns on the main bearing centerline. The grinding head is programmed to move in and out as the crankshaft turns to grind the crankpin bearing journals. The setup time is reduced when this type of grinder is used. Figure 15–30 shows a crankshaft being ground.

It takes a skilled machinist to operate a crankshaft grinder. The machinist must keep the grinding wheel properly dressed so that it will produce a smooth finish grind. The finished fillet must be of the same size

FIGURE 15–30   *Crankshaft being ground. Standard undersize measurements include 0.010, 0.020, and 0.030 inch.*

FIGURE 15–31   *All crankshafts should be polished after grinding. Both the crankshaft and the polishing cloth are being revolved.*

FIGURE 15–32   *After grinding and polishing, the crankshaft should be thoroughly cleaned. All oil passages should be cleaned with a brush. The operator shown here is using a solvent spray with a powered brush to clean the oil passages.*

FIGURE 15–33   *After the crankshaft is ground, the knurled part of the crankshaft that operates under a rope-type seal must be redone.*

and shape as the original fillet. The journal is polished, using a #320 grit polishing cloth and oil, to remove the fine metal "fuzz" remaining on the journal from grinding. This fuzz feels smooth when the shaft turns in the direction of the fuzz. When the fuzz is felt as the shaft turns in the opposite direction, it feels like a fine milling cutter. Polishing removes this fuzz. The crankshaft is rotated in its normal direction as the polishing cloth. This leaves a smooth shaft with the proper surface finish. *Most crankshaft grinders grind in the direction opposite of*

rotation and then polish in the same direction as rotation. See Figure 15–31. The oil hole chamfer in the journal should be smoothed so that no sharp edge remains to cut the bearing. Finally, the crankshaft oil passages are thoroughly cleaned. See Figures 15–32 through 15–34. The reground journals are coated with oil to keep them from rusting until they are to be cleaned for assembly.

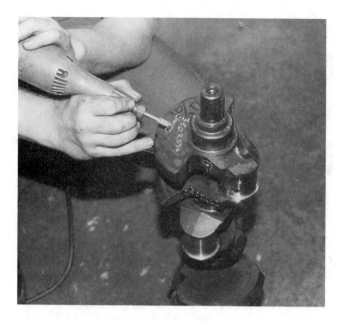

FIGURE 15–34 *This photo was taken at a small re-manufacturing company where every crankshaft is labeled using a rotary file. Most large remanufac-turers use a color code system to identify the type of crankshaft and the undersize measurement.*

WELDING A CRANKSHAFT

Sometimes it is desirable to salvage a crankshaft by building up a bearing journal and then grinding it to the original journal size. This is usually done by either electric arc welding or by use of a metal spray. Sometimes the journal is chrome plated. Chrome plat-ing makes an excellent bearing surface when the chrome is well bonded. If the bonding loosens, it will cause an immediate bearing failure.

BALANCING A CRANKSHAFT

It is desirable to balance an engine that is to be operated at high RPM levels. Balancing will also improve the durability of a low-speed engine. It is reported that 0.4 ounce (10 grams) of unbalance on a standard automo-tive crankshaft can cause an unbalance effect of 60 pounds at 6000 RPM.

When the crankshaft is balanced, **bob weights** are selected to equal the total weight of the piston and rod assembly. The bob weights are installed on the crank throws. Externally balanced crankshafts must also have the flywheel and damper installed. The balancer spins the crankshaft, usually at a low RPM level. The unbal-ance readout is similar to that of modern wheel bal-ancers. Counterweights that are too heavy are drilled

FIGURE 15–35 *Typical auxiliary shaft.*

to reduce their weight. Metal is welded to light coun-terweights to add the weight required for balance.

STRESS RELIEVING THE CRANKSHAFT

The greatest area of stress on a crankshaft is the fillet area. Stress relief is achieved by blasting the fillet area of the journals with #320 steel shot. This strengthens the fillet area and helps to prevent the development of cracks in this area. Gray duct tape is commonly used to cover the journal to prevent damage to the rest of the journal. Stress relief procedures are usually performed after the grinding and polishing of the crankshaft.

AUXILIARY SHAFTS

Pushrod engines operate all of the accessories from either the crankshaft or the camshaft. External engine accessories are driven by belts from a crankshaft pulley on the front of the engine. Inside the engine, the oil pump, fuel pump, and distributor are usually driven by the camshaft at one-half the crankshaft speed.

It is not so easy to drive the internal engine acces-sories with the camshaft on engines using overhead camshafts. These engines often use a small auxiliary shaft. Sometimes this shaft is called a **jack shaft.** It is driven by the timing belt or timing chain. Figure 15–35 shows a typical auxiliary shaft in the engine block.

BALANCE SHAFTS

Some engines use balance shafts to dampen normal engine vibrations. **Dampening** is reducing the vibra-tion to an acceptable level. A balance shaft turning at

FIGURE 15–36 Two counter-rotating balance shafts used to counterbalance the vibrations of a four-cylinder engine.

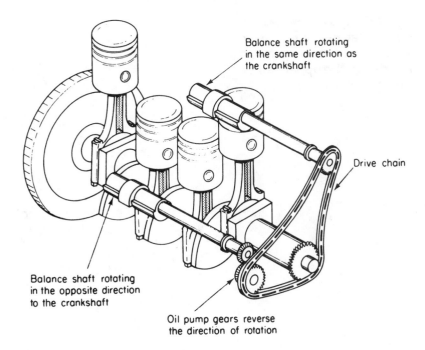

Balance shaft rotating in the same direction as the crankshaft

Drive chain

Balance shaft rotating in the opposite direction to the crankshaft

Oil pump gears reverse the direction of rotation

crankshaft speed but in the opposite direction is used on a three-cylinder inline engine. Weights on the ends of the balance shaft move in a direction opposite to the direction of the end piston. When the piston goes up, the weight goes down, and when the piston goes down, the weight goes up. This reduces the end-to-end rocking action on the three-cylinder inline engine.

Another type of balance shaft system is designed to counterbalance vibrations on a four-stroke, four-cylinder engine. Two shafts are used, and they turn at *twice* the engine speed. One of the shafts turns in the same direction as the crankshaft, and the other turns in the opposite direction. The oil pump gears are used to drive the reverse-turning shaft. Counterweights on the balance shafts are positioned to oppose the natural rolling action of the engine, as well as the secondary vibrations caused by the piston and rod movements. This design is shown in Figure 15–36.

Balance shafts are commonly found on the larger-displacement (over 2.0-liter) four-cylinder automotive engines. Mitsubishi introduced counterbalance shafts on four-cylinder engines in 1974. In 1988, both Ford and General Motors added a balance shaft to some of their 3.8-liter V-6 engines. The addition of balance shafts makes a big improvement in the smoothness of the engine. In V-6 engines, the improvement is most evident during idling and low-speed operation, whereas in the four-cylinder engines, balance shafts are especially helpful at higher engine speeds.

PRIMARY UNBALANCE

When the piston goes down in the cylinder, it tends to force the engine downward. When it goes up, it tends to force the engine upward. This causes a vertical shake in each direction on each crankshaft revolution. The piston moves farther and faster when the crankshaft is rotating in the upper half of the stroke than it does when the crankshaft is rotating in the lower half of the stroke, as shown in Figure 15–37. This greater imbalance when the crankshaft is in the upper half of the stroke is called **primary unbalance.** See Figure 15–38.

The counterweights could be sized large enough to balance the crankshaft, connecting rod, and piston. With this type of balance, the counterweight rotating upward would balance the piston going downward. The counterweight rotating downward would balance the piston going upward. As a result, there would be no vertical vibrating force or shake on the main bearings.

A counterweight this large would cause a side shake as great as the original up-and-down shaking caused by the primary unbalance, because there is no side-to-side weight to balance the crankshaft counterweight. See Figure 15–39. As a result, the crankshaft counterweight is made to be about half of the weight needed to balance the piston and connecting rod, so the counterweight does not balance all of the primary vertical shake. Some vertical and some horizontal primary shaking remains.

The movement of the reciprocating weight of the piston and upper connecting rod is affected by inertia.

FIGURE 15–37 *The piston moves farther and faster when the crankshaft is rotating in the upper half of the stroke.*

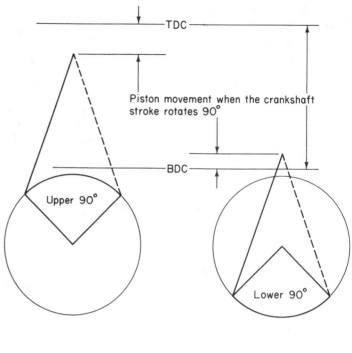

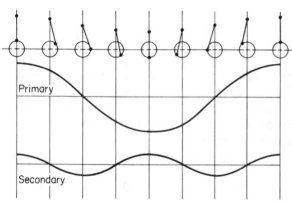

FIGURE 15–38 **Primary and secondary vibrations in relation to piston pin position.**

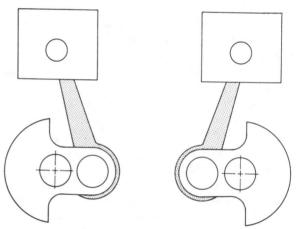

FIGURE 15–39 **Counterweight unbalance in the horizontal direction.**

Inertia is the force that tends to keep a body at rest when it is not moving and that causes it to continue its movement when it is in motion. It takes a force to overcome inertia to change the speed **(velocity)** of the body in motion. This force is **acceleration.** Positive acceleration increases the speed of movement and negative acceleration decreases the speed of movement.

Starting with the piston at top center, the piston must be accelerated from zero speed (at top center) to a maximum speed as the crankshaft nears 90 degrees. The acceleration force is greatest as the piston speed increases; then it decreases to zero as the maximum piston speed is reached. During the last half of the downstroke, the piston is slowed to a stop at bottom center by negative acceleration. Again, the negative acceleration force is maximum as the piston speed is reduced. Negative acceleration drops to zero as the piston stops at bottom center.

The piston is accelerated as it moves from bottom center until it reaches maximum speed, slightly over halfway up on the upward stroke. Acceleration increases and then drops to zero as the piston reaches its maximum speed at slightly more than halfway up the stroke. Negative acceleration slows the piston during the last half of the stroke. Negative acceleration drops to zero as the piston stops again at top center. The acceleration force changes twice on each stroke. The change in acceleration causes a secondary vibration at

FIGURE 15–40 In an inline four-cylinder engine, the pistons in the two middle cylinders move together and in the direction opposite to that of the two pistons on the end.

FIGURE 15–41 Typical balance shaft as installed in an inline four-cylinder engine.

twice the engine speed, and the secondary vibration rotates in a direction opposite to the crankshaft rotation.

In four-cylinder inline engines, the pistons in the two middle cylinders move upward as the pistons in the two end cylinders move downward. See Figure 15–40. This tends to balance the primary vertical unbalance. Horizontal primary unbalance remains. This, combined with secondary unbalance, causes engine vibration.

Shaking forces from the secondary unbalance in inline engines can be countered with two balance shafts rotating in opposite directions at twice the engine speed. Four-cylinder inline engines with balance shafts use two balance shafts in this way. An example is shown in Figure 15–41.

In 90-degree V-type engines, two connecting rods are fastened to the same crankpin on the crankshaft.

■ TECH TIP ■

THE KNOCK OF A FLEX PLATE

The source of a knocking noise in an engine is often difficult to determine without disassembling the engine. Generally, a deep engine knocking noise means that serious damage has occurred to the rods or main bearings and related parts. A flex plate (drive plate) is used on automatic transmission–equipped engines to drive the torque converter and provide a ring gear for the starter motor to crank the engine. Two common flex plate–related noises and their causes are as follows:

■ Torque converter attaching bolts or nuts can loosen (this is most common in four-cylinder engines, where vibration is more severe than six- or eight-cylinder engines). The torque converter can then pound on the holes of the flex plate, causing a loud knocking sound. However, if there is a load on the engine, as when the transmission is in drive or while driving under load, the sound should stop. At idle in park or neutral, the noise will be loudest, because the torque converter can float and will hit the sides of the holes in the flex plate.

■ If the flex plate is cracked, the resulting noise is very similar to a connecting rod or main bearing knock. The noise also seems to change at times, leading many technicians to believe that it involves a moving internal part that is lubricated, such as a rod or main bearing. The drive belts can also make a similar noise when they are loose, and belt-driven accessories can also produce similar noises.

Diagnosis should proceed as follows: During the diagnostic procedure, the technician should disconnect one drive belt at a time (if there is more than one) and then start the engine in an attempt to isolate the noise. Noises can be transmitted throughout the entire length of the engine through the crankshaft, making the source of the noise more difficult to isolate. If the flex plate is cracked, the noise is most noticeable when there is a change in engine speed or load. To help diagnose a cracked flex plate, raise engine speed to a high idle (1500 to 2000 RPM), then turn the ignition switch off. Before the engine stops, turn the ignition back on. If a knocking noise is heard when the engine restarts, the flex plate is cracked.

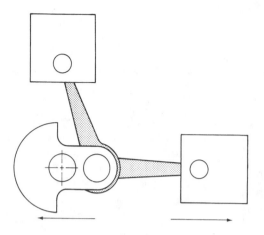

FIGURE 15–42   Balance of one crankpin on a V-type engine.

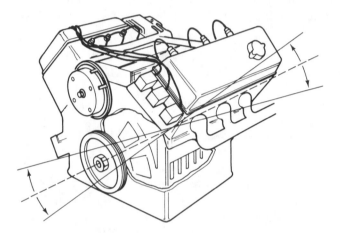

FIGURE 15–43   Direction of forces of a rolling couple.

(b)

(a)

(c)

FIGURE 15–44   (a) Balance shaft in a 90-degree V-6 engine. (b) The balance shaft is driven off of the camshaft gear at two times camshaft speed (this is the same as crankshaft speed). (c) A narrower than usual timing chain and sprocket are used to complete the installation.

The cylinders for the pistons on these connecting rods are at 90 degrees to each other. The crankshaft counterweight is large enough to fully balance one piston and connecting rod. Side shake caused by a fully balanced counterweight for one cylinder is offset by the piston and connecting rod in the second cylinder. What would have caused horizontal side shake on a single-cylinder engine becomes the balance weight for the paired cylinder. See Figure 15–42.

The crank throws on a V-6 engine do not balance each other from end to end, as the throws on a four-cylinder inline engine do. This causes a rolling action as the throws on each end of the crankshaft rotate. This is called **rolling couple** and is illustrated in Figure 15–43. The engine can be balanced so that the unbalanced rolling couple will move the engine vertically, horizontally, or at any angle in between; but some roll will be present. A **balance shaft** with a heavy unbalanced section is placed in the block above the camshaft. See Figure 15–44. It is driven at crankshaft speed. The movement of its unbalanced section is timed to oppose and minimize the unbalanced roll to make a smooth-running engine.

Any remaining vibration is usually absorbed by using soft engine mounts.

ENGINE BEARINGS

Engine bearings are the main supports for the major moving parts of any engine. The clearance between the bearings and the crankshaft is a major factor in maintaining the proper oil pressure throughout the entire engine. Most engines are designed to provide the maximum protection and lubrication to the engine bearings above all else.

Engine durability relies on bearing life. Bearing failure usually results in immediate engine failure.

Engine bearings are designed to support the operating loads of the engine and, with the lubricant, provide minimum friction. This must be achieved at all designed engine speeds. The bearings must be able to operate for long periods of time, even when small foreign particles are in the lubricant.

Most engine bearings are of the **plain** or **sleeve bearing** type. They need a constant flow of lubricating oil. Roller, ball, and needle bearings, which are called **antifriction bearings**, are used where only minimum lubrication is available.

Properly lubricated plain bearings cause no more friction than do the antifriction bearings. This results from the fact that the shaft is actually rolling on a film of oil. In automotive engines, the lubricating system supplies oil to each bearing during all the time that the engine runs. Only residual oil remaining from the last run will be on the bearing during engine start-up before the pressure builds up. This results in high friction and

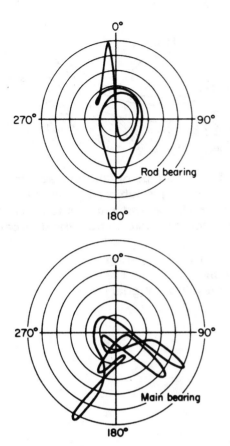

FIGURE 15–45 Typical rod and main bearing load diagrams. The circles on these polar diagrams indicate the amount of force on the bearing as it rotates.

wear. After the oil film forms, the metal-to-metal contact stops and friction drops, to stop bearing wear. Bearings and journals *only* wear when the parts come in contact with each other or when foreign particles are present.

Oil enters the bearing through the oil holes and grooves. It spreads into a smooth wedge-shaped oil film that supports the bearing load by the hydrodynamic action of the oil.

BEARING LOADS

It is important that the engine have large enough bearings that the bearing load is within the strength limits of the bearings. Bearing load capacity is calculated by dividing the bearing load in pounds by the projected area of the bearing. The projected area is the bearing length multiplied by the bearing diameter. The load on engine bearings is determined by developing a polar bearing load diagram that shows the amount and direction of the instantaneous bearing loads. Bearing load diagrams are shown in Figure 15–45.

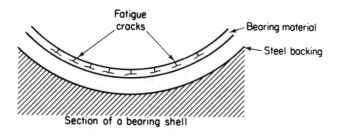

FIGURE 15–46 Shape of fatigue cracks in a bearing. If the bearing is subjected to continued high loads, the cracks expand and eventually cause the bearing material to flake off from the steel backing.

FIGURE 15–47 Bearing material missing from the shell as a result of fatigue.

FIGURE 15–48 Bearing material missing from the bearing as a result of fatigue failure.

The forces on the engine bearings vary with engine speed and load. On the intake stroke, the inertia force is opposed by the force of drawing in the air-fuel mixture. On the compression and power strokes, there is also an opposing force on the rod bearings. On the exhaust stroke, however, there is no opposing force to counteract the inertia force of the piston coming to a stop at TDC. The result is a higher force load on the *bottom* rod bearing due to inertia at TDC of the exhaust stroke. These forces tend to stretch the big end of the rod in the direction of rod movement.

1. As engine speed (RPM) increases, rod bearing loads decrease because of the balancing of inertia and opposing loads.
2. As engine speed (RPM) increases, the main bearing loads increase.

   NOTE: This helps explain why engine blocks with four-bolt main bearing supports are really only needed for high engine speed stability. —

3. Because the loads on bearings vary and affect both rod and main bearings, it is generally recommended that *all* engine bearings be replaced at one time.

BEARING FATIGUE

Bearings tend to flex or bend slightly under changing loads, This is especially noticeable in reciprocating engine bearings. Bearing metals, like other metals, tend to fatigue and break after being flexed or bent a number of times. Flexing starts fatigue, which shows up as fine cracks in the bearing surface. These cracks gradually deepen almost to the bond between the bearing metal and the backing metal. The cracks then cross over and intersect with each other, as illustrated in Figure 15–46. In time, this will allow a piece of bearing material to fall out. The length of time before fatigue will cause failure is called the **fatigue life** of the bearing. Bearings must have a long fatigue life for normal engine service. The harder the bearing material, the longer is its fatigue life. Soft bearings have a short fatigue life and low bearing load strength. They are generally low in cost and can only be used where the bearing requirements are low. See Figures 15–47 and 15–48.

BEARING CONFORMABILITY

The ability of bearing materials to creep or flow slightly to match shaft variations is called **conformability.** The bearing conforms to the shaft during the engine break-

FIGURE 15–49 Bearing wear caused by a mis-aligned journal. A bent connecting rod could also cause similar bearing wear.

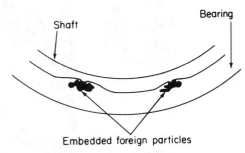

FIGURE 15–50 Bearing material covers foreign material as it embeds into the bearing.

in period. In modern automobile engines, there is little need for bearing conformability or break-in, because automatic processing has achieved machining tolerances that keep the shaft very close to the designed size. See Figure 15–49.

BEARING EMBEDABILITY

Engine manufacturers have designed engines to produce minimum crankcase deposits. This has been done by providing them with oil filters, air filters, and closed crankcase ventilation systems that minimize contaminants. Still, some foreign particles get into the bearings. The bearings must be capable of embedding these particles into the bearing surface so that they will not score the shaft. To fully embed the particle, the bearing material gradually works across the particle, completely covering it. The bearing property that allows it to do this is called **embedability.** Embedability is illustrated in Figures 15–50 and 15–51.

FIGURE 15–51 Foreign particles such as dirt embedded in the bearing material.

BEARING DAMAGE RESISTANCE

Under some operating conditions, the bearing will be temporarily overloaded. This will cause the oil film to break down, allowing the shaft metal to come in contact with the bearing metal. As the rotating crankshaft contacts the bearing high spots, the spots become hot from friction. The friction causes localized hot spots in the bearing material that seize or weld to the crankshaft. The crankshaft then breaks off particles of the bearing material and pulls the particles around with it, scratching or scoring the bearing surface. See Figures 15–52 and 15–53. Bearings have a characteristic called **score resistance**. It prevents the bearing materials from seizing to the shaft during oil film breakdown. This bearing characteristic is the result of the bearing material's relatively low melting temperature.

FIGURE 15–52   Bearing material starting to leave the steel backing.

(a)

(b)

FIGURE 15–53   Typical results of oil pressure loss: (a) extreme wear of the connecting rod journal, and (b) overheating finally leading to failure of the bearing.

Modern engine oils contain a small amount of chemical additives that add characteristics to the oil to satisfy special engine requirements. In time, under high engine temperatures and high bearing loads, the additives break down. They combine with the by-products of combustion and form acids in the oil. The bearings' ability to resist attack from these acids is called **corrosion resistance.** Corrosion can occur over the entire surface of the bearing. This will remove material and increase the oil clearance. It can also leach or eat into the bearing material, dissolving some of the bearing material alloys. Either type of corrosion will reduce bearing life.

BEARING MATERIALS

Three materials are used for automobile engine bearings: **babbitt, copper-lead alloy,** and **aluminum.** A layer of the bearing materials 0.010 to 0.020 inch (0.25 to 0.50 millimeter) thick is applied over a low carbon steel backing. The steel backing with a surface coating of bearing material formed as an engine bearing is called a bearing **shell.** The steel provides support needed for the shaft load. The bearing material meets the rest of the bearing operating requirements.

Babbitt is the oldest automotive bearing material. Babbitt is the name given to an excellent bearing mate-

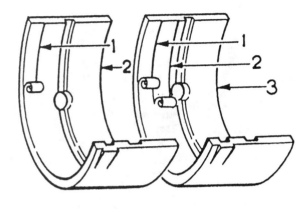

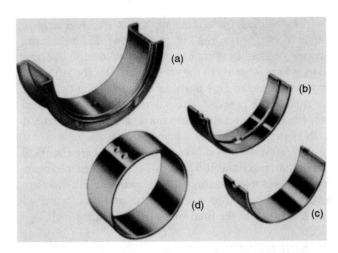

FIGURE 15–55 Typical bearing shell types found in modern engines. (Courtesy of Sealed Power Corporation)

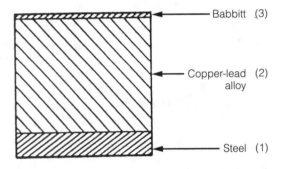

FIGURE 15–54 Typical two-layer and three-layer engine bearing insert showing the relative thickness of the various materials.

rial made originally from a combination of lead or tin and antimony. Isaac Babbitt (1799–1862) first formulated this material in 1839. Lead and tin are alloyed with small quantities of copper and antimony to give it the required strength. Babbitt is still used in applications in which material is required for soft shafts running under moderate loads and speeds. It will work with occasional borderline lubrication and oil starvation without failure.

Copper-lead alloy is a stronger and more expensive bearing material than babbitt. It is used for intermediate- and high-speed applications. Tin, in small quantities, is often alloyed with the copper lead bearings. This bearing material is most easily damaged by corrosion from acid accumulation in the engine oil. Corrosion results in bearing journal wear as the bearing is eroded by the acids.

Many of the copper-lead bearings have an **overlay** or third layer of metal. This overlay is usually of babbitt. Babbitt-overlayed bearings have high fatigue strength, good conformity, good embedability, and good corrosion resistance. The overplated bearing is a premium bearing. It is also the most expensive because the overplating layer, from 0.0005 to 0.001 inch (0.0125 to 0.025 millimeter) thick, is put on the bearing with an **electroplating** process. The layers of bearing material on a bearing shell are illustrated in Figure 15–54.

Aluminum was the last of the three materials to be used for automotive bearings. Automotive bearing aluminum has small quantities of tin and copper alloyed with it. This makes a stronger but more expensive bearing than either babbitt or copper-lead alloy.

Aluminum, with a small percentage of lead, is used for high-quality intermediate-strength bearings. Most of its bearing characteristics are equal to or better than those of babbitt and copper lead. Aluminum bearings are well suited to high-speed, high-load conditions.

Because of its expense, aluminum is often used along with bearings made from other bearing materials. For example, aluminum may be used for the highly loaded lower shell of the main bearing, with babbitt being used for the lightly loaded upper shell of the main bearing, on a single–main bearing journal.

BEARING MANUFACTURING

Modern automotive engines use **precision insert-type** bearing shells sometimes called **half-shell** bearings. The bearing is manufactured to very close tolerance so that it will fit correctly in each application. The bearing, therefore, must be made from precisely the correct materials under closely controlled manufacturing conditions. Figure 15–55 shows the typical bearing shell types found in modern engines.

Most of the precision insert bearing shells are manufactured in a continuous strip process. The low carbon steel backing is delivered to the bearing manufacturer in a roll. This steel must be within 0.001 inch (0.025 millimeter) of the thickness required. In processing, it is cleaned, flattened, and heated to the required bonding temperature.

The bearing material is applied to the steel strip in either of two ways, casting or sintering. In the casting process, melted bearing alloy is poured on the backing strip, where it bonds to the steel as it cools. The sintering process is similar. Fine particles of the bearing materials are mixed as a powder. The powdered bearing material is spread evenly on the continuous steel backing strip. It is then pressed and heated until it fuses together and bonds to the steel. Bonds of both processes are chemical rather than mechanical. The finished strip is cut into bearing blanks as it leaves this production line. The blanks are formed and coined to size in presses and then punched and machined to the final shape of the bearing shell.

BEARING SIZES

Bearings are usually available in standard (std) size, and in measurements 0.010, 0.020, and 0.030 inch *undersize*. Even though the bearing itself is thicker for use on a machined crankshaft, the bearing is referred to as undersize because the crankshaft journals are undersize. Factory bearings may be available in measurements 0.0005 or 0.001 inch undersize for precision fitting of a production crankshaft.

Before purchasing bearings, be sure to use a micrometer to measure *all* main and connecting rod journals.

BEARING CLEARANCE

The bearing-to-journal clearance may be from 0.0005 to 0.0025 inch (0.025 to 0.060 millimeter), depending on the engine. Doubling the journal clearance will allow more than *four* times as much oil to flow from the edges of the bearing. The oil clearance must be large enough to allow an oil film to build up, but small enough to prevent excess oil leakage, which would cause loss of oil pressure. A large amount of oil leakage at one of the bearings would starve other bearings farther along in the oil system. This would result in the failure of the oil-starved bearings.

BEARING SPREAD AND CRUSH

The bearing design also includes bearing **spread** and **crush.** They are illustrated in Figure 15–56. The bearing shell has a slightly larger arc than does the bearing housing. This difference is called bearing spread and it makes the shell 0.005 to 0.020 inch (0.125 to 0.500 millimeter) wider than the housing bore. A lip or **tang** locates the bearing endwise in the housing. The tang can be identified in Figure 15–57. Spread holds the bearing shell in the housing while the engine is being assem-

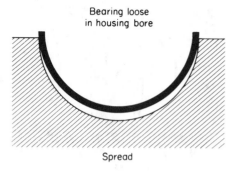
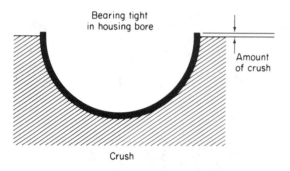

FIGURE 15–56   Bearing spread and crush.

FIGURE 15–57   Tang on a bearing used to properly locate the bearing during assembly.

bled. When the bearing is installed, each end of the bearing shell is slightly above the parting surface. When the bearing cap is tightened, the ends of the two bearing shells touch and are forced together. This force is called bearing crush. Crush holds the bearing in place and keeps the bearing from turning when the engine runs. Crush must exert a force of at least 12,000 psi (82,740 kPa) at 250° F (121° C) to hold the bearing securely in place. A stress of 40,000 psi (276,000 kPa) is considered maximum to avoid damaging the bearing or housing.

FIGURE 15–58 Spun bearing. The lower cap bearing has rotated under the upper rod bearing.

Bearing shells that do not have enough crush may rotate with the shaft. The result is called a **spun bearing,** as pictured in Figure 15–58.

Replacement bearings should be of a quality as good as or better than that of the original bearings. The replacement bearings must also have the same oil holes and grooves.

■ **CAUTION:** Some bearings may have oil holes in the top shell only. If these are incorrectly installed, no oil will flow to the connecting rods or main rods, which will result in instant engine failure. ■

Modified engines have more demanding bearing requirements and therefore usually require a higher-quality bearing to provide satisfactory service.

CAM BEARINGS

The camshaft in pushrod engines rotates in **sleeve** bearings that are pressed into bearing bores within the engine block. Overhead camshaft bearings may be either sleeve-type bushings called **full round** bearings or **split-type (half shell)** bearings, depending on the design of the bearing supports. In pushrod engines, the cam bearings are installed in the block. The best rule of thumb to follow is to replace the cam bearings whenever the main bearings are replaced. The replacement cam bearings must have the correct outside

```
SH 1090S
1-SH 1089   POSITION 1
2-SH 1090   POSITION 2&5
2-SH 1091   POSITION 3&4
```

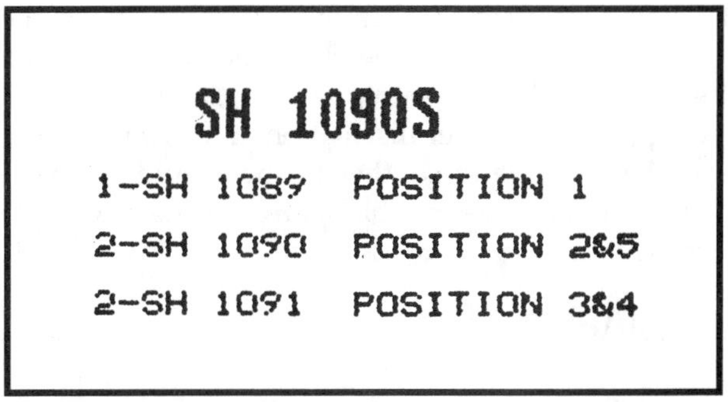

FIGURE 15–59 Typical cam bearing identification (instruction) sticker that accompanies replacement cam bearings. The cam bearing in position #1 is the front cam bearing. Proper cam bearing installation is critical to proper engine operation.

■ **TECH TIP** ■

COUNT YOUR BLESSINGS AND YOUR PAN BOLTS!

Replacing cam bearings can be relatively straightforward or can involve keeping count of the number of oil pan bolts! For example, Buick-built V-6s use different cam bearings depending on the number of bolts used to hold the oil pan to the block.

■ Fourteen bolts in the oil pan: The front bearing is special, but the rest of the bearings are the same.
■ Twenty bolts in the oil pan: Bearings #1 and #4 use two oil feed holes. Bearings #2 and #3 use single oil feed holes.

diameter to fit snugly in the cam bearing bores of the block. They must have the correct oil holes and be positioned correctly. Cam bearings must also have the proper inside diameter to fit the camshaft bearing journals. See Figure 15–59. See chapter 17 for block preparation procedures to be performed before installing camshaft bearings.

In many engines, each cam bearing is a different size. The largest is in the front and the smallest is in the rear. The cam bearing journal size must be checked and each bearing identified *before* assembly is begun. The location of each new cam bearing can be marked on the outside of the bearing with a felt-tip marker. This will help avoid mixing bearings. Marking in this way will not affect the bearing size or damage the bearing in any way. Cam bearings should be installed "dry" (not oiled). This prevents the cam bearing from moving (spinning) after installation. If the cam bearing were oiled, the rotation of the camshaft could cause the cam bearing to rotate and block oil holes that lubricate the camshaft.

SUMMARY

1. Forged crankshafts have a wide separation line.
2. Cast crankshafts have a narrow mold parting line.
3. Most crankshafts have counterweights that offset the weight and forces of the piston and connecting rod assembly.
4. Even-fire 90-degree V-6 engines require that the crankshaft be splayed to allow for even firing.
5. Lubrication to the main bearings is fed through the main oil gallery in the block. Oil for the rod bearings comes from holes in the crankshaft drilled between the main journal and the rod journal.
6. A vibration damper, also known as a harmonic balancer, is used to dampen harmful twisting vibrations of the crankshaft.
7. Most engines are internally balanced. This means that the crankshafts and vibration damper are both balanced. Other engines use the vibration damper to balance the crankshaft and are called externally balanced engines.
8. Most crankshafts can be reground to be 0.010, 0.020 or 0.030 inch undersize.
9. Crankshafts are ground in the direction opposite of rotation and polished in the same direction as rotation.
10. Most engine bearings are constructed with a steel shell for strength and are covered with a copper lead alloy. Many bearings also have a thin overlay of babbitt.
11. Bearings should have spread and crush to keep them from spinning when the crankshaft rotates.

REVIEW QUESTIONS

1. Describe the difference between a forged and a cast crankshaft.
2. How many degrees of crankshaft rotation are there between cylinder firings on an inline four-cylinder engine, an inline six-cylinder engine, and a V-8 engine?
3. Explain how and why crankshafts should be polished after grinding.
4. Explain the operation and use of auxiliary shafts.
5. Describe the use of balance shafts in an engine and explain how they help control engine vibration.
6. List four engine bearing properties.
7. Describe bearing crush and bearing spread.

MULTIPLE-CHOICE QUESTIONS

1. A forged crankshaft _____.
   a. Has a wide parting line
   b. Has a thin parting line
   c. Has a parting line in one plane
   d. Both b and c
2. A typical V-8 engine crankshaft has _____ main bearings.
   a. Three
   b. Four
   c. Five
   d. Seven
3. A four-cylinder engine fires one cylinder at every _____ degrees of crankshaft rotation.
   a. 270
   b. 180
   c. 120
   d. 90
4. A splayed crankshaft is a crankshaft that _____.
   a. Is externally balanced
   b. Is internally balanced
   c. Has offset main bearing journals
   d. Has offset rod journals
5. The thrust bearing surface is located on one of the main bearings to control thrust loads caused by _____.
   a. Lugging the engine
   b. Torque converter or clutch release forces
   c. Rapid deceleration forces
   d. Both a and c
6. If any crankshaft is ground, it must also be _____.
   a. Shot peened
   b. Chrome-plated
   c. Polished
   d. Externally balanced
7. If bearing-to-journal clearance is doubled, how much oil will flow?
   a. One-half as much
   b. The same amount, if the pressure is kept constant
   c. Double the amount
   d. Four times the amount
8. Typical journal-to-bearing clearance is _____.
   a. 0.00015 to 0.00018 inch
   b. 0.0005 to 0.0025 inch
   c. 0.150 to 0.250 inch
   d. 0.020 to 0.035 inch

9. A bearing shell has a slightly larger arc than the bearing housing. This difference is called _____.
   a. Bearing crush
   b. Bearing tang
   c. Bearing spread
   d. Bearing saddle

10. Bearing _____ occurs when a bearing shell is slightly above the parting surface of the bearing cap.
    a. Overlap
    b. Crush
    c. Cap lock
    d. Interference fit

16

Lubrication System Principles and Service

OBJECTIVES

After studying Chapter 16, the reader will be able to

1. Explain engine oil ratings.
2. Describe how an oil pump and engine lubrication work.
3. Discuss how and when to change the oil and filter.
4. Explain how to inspect an oil pump for wear.

Engine oil is the lifeblood of any engine. The purposes of engine oil include

1. *Lubricating* all moving parts to prevent wear
2. Helping to *cool* the engine
3. Helping to *seal* piston rings
4. *Cleaning,* and holding dirt in suspension in the oil until it can be drained from the engine
5. *Neutralizing* acids that are formed as the result of the combustion process
6. *Reducing* friction
7. *Preventing* rust and corrosion

LUBRICATION PRINCIPLES

Lubrication between two moving surfaces results from an oil film that separates the surfaces and supports the load. If oil were put on a flat surface and a heavy block were pushed across the surface, the block would slide more easily than if it were pushed across a dry surface. The reason for this is that a wedge-shaped oil film is built up between the moving block and the surface. This is illustrated in Figure 16–1.

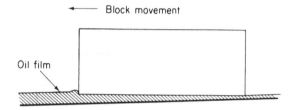

FIGURE 16–1 **Wedge-shaped oil film developed below a moving block.**

The force required to push the block across a surface depends on the weight of the block, how fast it moves, and the viscosity of the oil. Viscosity is the oil's thickness or resistance to flow.

The principle just described is that of **hydrodynamic lubrication.** The prefix *hydro-* refers to liquids, as in hydraulics, and *dynamic* refers to moving materials. Hydrodynamic lubrication occurs when a wedge-shaped film of lubricating oil develops between two surfaces that have relative motion between them. When this film becomes so thin that the surface high spots touch, it is called **boundary lubrication.**

The engine oil pressure system feeds a continuous supply of oil into the lightly loaded part of the bearing oil clearance. Hydrodynamic lubrication takes over as the shaft rotates in the bearing to produce a wedge-shaped hydrodynamic oil film that is curved around the bearing. This film supports the bearing and reduces the turning effort to a minimum when oil of the correct viscosity is used.

When the engine is not running, the crankshaft pushes much of the oil from around it as it settles to the bottom of the bearing. As the engine is cranked, the crankshaft tries to roll up the side of the bearing. If

330

Oil feed

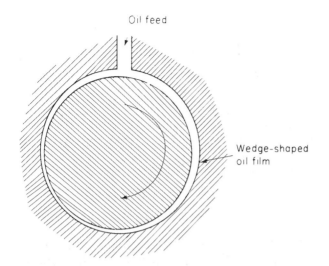

Wedge-shaped
oil film

FIGURE 16–2 Wedge-shaped oil film curved around a bearing journal.

some surface oil remains on the bearing, the shaft will slide back to the bottom of the bearing when it rolls onto this oil. Continued crankshaft rotation will cause this sequence of climbing and sliding back to repeat. This sequence continues until the oil pump supplies fresh oil to the bearing. The shaft continues to try to climb up the side of the bearing; however, it now grabs oil instead of the bearing surface. The rotation pulls oil around the shaft, forming a curved, wedge-shaped oil film that supports the crankshaft in the bearing as shown in Figure 16–2.

Most bearing wear occurs during the initial startup. Wear continues until a hydrodynamic film is established.

ENGINE LUBRICATION SYSTEMS

The primary function of the engine lubrication system is to maintain a positive and continuous oil supply to the bearings. Engine oil pressure must be high enough to get the oil to the bearings with enough force to cause the oil flow required for proper cooling. Normal engine oil pressure range is from 10 to 60 psi (200 to 400 kPa) (10 psi per 1000 engine RPM). On the other hand, hydrodynamic film pressures developed in the high-pressure areas of the engine bearings may be over 1000 psi (6900 kPa). The relatively low engine oil pressures, obviously, could not support these high bearing loads without hydrodynamic lubrication.

PROPERTIES OF ENGINE OIL

The most important engine oil property is its thickness or viscosity. As an oil cools, it thickens. As the oil heats, it gets thinner. Therefore, its viscosity changes with temperature. The oil must not be too thick at low temperatures to allow the engine to start. Thick low-temperature oil causes a very high coefficient of friction. If the coefficient of friction becomes too great, the cold engine will not have enough energy to carry the crankshaft over from one firing impulse to the next. When this happens, the engine will not start. There is a maximum oil viscosity that will keep an engine from starting when it is below a specified temperature. On the other end of the scale, with the engine hot, the oil thins (its viscosity lowers). If the viscosity of the oil becomes too low, boundary lubrication will occur and the coefficient of friction will increase. Engine oil viscosity must be between these two extremes. The oil must be thin enough to allow the engine to start when cold. It must be able to flow to the oil pickup and flow through the screen to the pump. It must still have enough body or viscosity to develop the correct hydrodynamic lubrication film when the engine reaches its normal operating temperature. An index of the change in viscosity between the cold and hot extremes is called the **viscosity index (VI)**. All oils with a high-viscosity index thin less with heat than do oils with a low-viscosity index.

Engine oils are sold with an SAE grade number (SAE standing for Society of Automotive Engineers). This grade number indicates the viscosity range into which the oil fits. Oils tested at 212° F (100° C) have a number with no letter following. For example, SAE 30 indicates that the oil has only been checked at 212° F (100° C). This oil's viscosity falls within the SAE 30 grade number range when the oil is hot. SAE 20W-20 indicates that the oil has been tested at both 0° F (−18° C) and 212° F (100° C). Its viscosity falls into the SAE 20W grade number range when the oil is cold and into the 20 grade number range when the oil is hot. An SAE 5W-30 multigrade oil is one that meets the SAE 5W viscosity specification when cooled to 0° F (−18° C) and meets the SAE 30 viscosity specification when tested at 212° F (100° C). Multigrade oils must have a higher viscosity index than do straight-grade oils.

Even though viscosity is the most important oil property, engine oil has other important properties. The lowest temperature at which oil will pour is called its **pour point.** Below this temperature, the oil will become plastic. A plastic will not produce hydrodynamic lubrication; therefore, the oil cannot be used below this temperature.

As oil is heated, the light, volatile parts of the oil boil off. When there are enough volatile vapors, they can be ignited with a small flame. The oil is at its **flash point** temperature when the vapors will ignite. The temperature at which the vapor continues to burn is called the **fire point.** Oil cannot function above the flash point temperature because its characteristics change at this temperature. The maximum useful temperature range of engine oil is between the pour point and flash point temperatures. The flash point test is also used to determine if used engine oil contains gasoline contaminants. Gasoline is more volatile than the engine oil, so the gasoline vapors will evaporate and burn at a much lower temperature than will the oil itself.

Engine oil must also resist oxidation. Oxidation is a form of oil breakdown that occurs as the oil combines with oxygen from the air. The engine oil must not bubble or foam, which would upset the hydrodynamic film. Neither the oil nor the additives in the oil should break down and form acids that would cause corrosion, scuffing, or rusting of engine parts. The additives help to disperse contaminants and hold them in suspension in the oil. The contaminants are drained with the oil to keep the engine clean.

The American Petroleum Institute (API), working with the engine manufacturers and oil companies, has established an engine oil performance classification. Oils are tested and rated in full-size multicylinder engines. The oil container is marked (usually printed) with the API classification of the oil. The API performance or service classification and SAE grade marking are the only information available to help determine which oil is satisfactory for use in an engine. See Figures 16–3 through 16–5 for typical API oil container "doughnuts."

There are three facts to know when changing oil:

1. Recommended SAE viscosity (thickness) for the temperature range that is anticipated before the next oil change
2. API quality rating as recommended by the engine or vehicle manufacturer
3. Recommended oil change interval (time or mileage)

VISCOSITY OF OIL (SAE RATING)

The word *viscosity* means resistance to flow. An oil with a high viscosity has a higher resistance to flow and is thicker than a lower-viscosity oil. A thick oil is not necessarily a good oil and a thin oil is not necessarily a bad oil. The viscosity is an important property, but it is not the only basis for the selection of the proper engine oil. Generally, the following items can be considered in the selection of an engine oil.

NOTE: The following items are to be used as a guide for selecting from various recommended viscosity ratings as specified by the engine or vehicle manufacturer.

FIGURE 16–3 American Petroleum Institute oil identification symbol doughnut for SAE 10W-30, SJ-rated engine oil.

FIGURE 16–4 API doughnut for SAE 5W-30, SH-CD engine oil. Note the "Energy Conserving II" rating.

FIGURE 16–5 API doughnut for SAE 20W-50, SH engine oil. Note the <u>lack</u> of the energy conserving label.

Thinner Oil

1. Improved cold-engine starting
2. Improved fuel economy

Thicker Oil

1. Improved protection at higher temperatures
2. Reduced fuel economy _____

OIL FORMULATION

Engine oils are manufactured in various viscosity grades. These different viscosity grades are formulated by using a viscosity index improver, which is a polymer designed to induce thickening of a thin base oil at higher temperatures. For example, a 10W-30 oil starts as an SAE 10W oil, and viscosity index improver polymers are added to bring the high-temperature viscosity up to SAE 30 standard. These polymers react with heat to restrict the rate of flow of the oil at higher temperatures.

The greater the amount of VI improver, the broader the viscosity range. For example, typical multiple-viscosity oils and the percentages of viscosity index improver that they use are as follows:

SAE 5W-30   7–8% VI
SAE 10W-30   6–8% VI
SAE 10W-40   12–15% VI
SAE 20W-50   6–8% VI

(Note that less VI improver is required for the SAE 20W-50 because the base oil stock starts out thicker than that of the other oils listed.)

Even though a 10W-40 oil will resist high-temperature thinning better than a 10W-30 oil, the increased amount of VI can contribute to some problems. As oil is used in an engine, it tends to thicken. This thickening occurs because of several factors:

- **Oxidation**—Engine oil is subjected to high temperatures and constant movement. Therefore, it can readily combine with oxygen in the air. When oil combines with oxygen, it becomes thicker.
- **Breakdown of polymer additives**—After 1000 to 2000 miles, the polymer additives can shear (break down) during use, which causes the oil to become thinner. This thinner oil tends to oxidize more readily than thicker oil. The increased oxidation causes the oil to thicken and form sludge. Some vehicle manufacturers do not recommend the use of SAE 10W-40 or 10W-50 or other wide–viscosity range oils because of possible VI additive problems and quality problems in some brands.

- **Catalytic metal action and combustion by-products**—Small metal particles that wear from engine parts act as a catalyst to increase the oxidation process. Copper is the most active of all wear metals and causes the most catalytic action. By-products of combustion, including moisture and acids, also contribute to engine oil thickening.

QUALITY OF OIL (API RATING)

Although it is generally difficult to purchase low-quality oil today, it is possible to select the incorrect grade for the intended application. The quality rating is established by test procedures set up by the *American Petroleum Institute (API)*, with the cooperation of the Society of Automotive Engineers.

In gasoline engine ratings, the letter *S* means *service*, but it can be remembered as being for use in *s*park ignition engines. The rating system is open-ended so that newer, improved ratings can be readily added as necessary (skipping the letter *I* to avoid confusion with the number 1).

SA   Straight mineral oil (no additives), not suitable for use in any engine
SB   Nondetergent oil with additives to control wear and oil oxidation
SC   Obsolete (1964)
SD   Obsolete (1968)
SE   Obsolete (1972)
SF   Obsolete (1980)
SG   Obsolete (1988)
SH   Highest rating from 1993–97
SJ   Highest rating starting in 1997

NOTE: Older-model vehicles can use the newer, higher-rated engine oil classifications where older, now obsolete ratings were specified. Newly overhauled antique cars or engines can also use the newer, improved oils, as long as the appropriate SAE viscosity grade is used for the anticipated temperature range. The new oils have all the protection of the older oils, plus additional protection. _____

Diesel classifications begin with the letter *C*, which stands for *commercial*, but which can also be remembered as being for use in *c*ompression ignition or diesel engines.

CA   Obsolete
CB   Obsolete
CC   Minimum rating for use in a diesel engine service
CD   Designed for certain naturally-aspirated, turbocharged, or supercharged diesel engines

CE   Designed for certain turbocharged or super charged heavy-duty diesel engine service

CF   For off-road indirect injected diesel engine service

CF-2   Two-stroke diesel engine service

CF-4   High-speed four-stroke cycle diesel engine service

CG-4   Severe duty high-speed four-stroke diesel engine service

ILSAC OIL RATING

The International Lubricant Standardization and Approval Committee (ILSAC) developed an oil rating that consolidates the SAE viscosity rating and the API quality rating. If an engine oil meets the standards, a "star burst" symbol is displayed on the front of the oil container. If the star burst is present, the vehicle owner and technician know that the oil is suitable for use in almost any gasoline engine. See Figure 16–6. The original GF-1 (gasoline fueled) rating was updated to GF-2 in 1997.

EUROPEAN OIL RATINGS

The organization known as Comite des Constructeurs d'Automobiles du Marche Commun (generally abbreviated CCMC) represents most of the Western European automobile and heavy-duty truck market. The organization's first oil ratings were issued in 1972. CCMC has been renamed Association des Constructeurs European d'Automobiles (ACEA). The organization uses different engines for testing than those used by API and SAE, and the requirements necessary to meet the ACEA standards are different, yet ACEA ratings generally correspond with most API ratings. ACEA standards tend to specify a minimum viscosity rating and certain volatility requirements not specified by API.

JAPANESE OIL RATINGS

The Japan Automobile Standards Organization (JASO) also publishes oil standards. The JASO tests use small Japanese engines, and their ratings require more stringent valve train wear standards than do other countries' oil ratings.

ENGINE OIL ADDITIVES

Additives are used in engine oils for three different reasons: (1) to replace some properties removed during refining, (2) to reinforce some of the oil's natural properties, and (3) to provide the oil with new properties it did not originally have. Oils from some petroleum oil fields require more and different additives than oils from other fields. Additives are usually classified according to the property they add to the oil.

Antioxidants reduce the high-temperature contaminants. They prevent the formation of varnish on the parts, reduce bearing corrosion, and minimize particle formation.

Corrosion preventives reduce acid formation that causes bearing corrosion.

Detergents and dispersants prevent low-temperature sludge binders from forming and keep the sludge-forming particles finely divided. The finely divided particles will stay in suspension in the oil to be removed from the engine as the oil is removed at the next drain period.

Extreme pressure and **antiwear additives** form a chemical film that prevents metal-to-metal seizure anytime boundary lubrication exists.

Viscosity index improvers are used to reduce viscosity change as the oil temperature changes.

Pour point depressants coat the wax crystals in the oil so that they will not stick together. The oil will then be able to flow at lower temperatures.

A number of other oil additives may be used to modify the oil to function better in the engine. These include rust preventives, metal deactivators, water repellents, emulsifiers, dyes, color stabilizers, odor control agents, and foam inhibitors.

Oil producers are careful to check the compatibility of the oil additives they use. A number of chemicals that will help each other can be used for each of the additive requirements. The balanced additives are called an **additive package**.

ENERGY CONSERVING ENGINE OILS

For an engine oil to be classified as energy conserving, the oil must be able to meet the specifications of an ASTM engine test VI standard. The oil being

FIGURE 16–6 The International Lubricant Standardization and Approval Committee (ILSAC) star burst symbol. If this symbol is on the front of the container of oil, then it is acceptable for use in almost any gasoline engine.

■ TECH TIP ■

DIRTY ENGINE OIL CAN CAUSE OIL BURNING

Service technicians have known for a long time that some of their customers never change the engine oil. Often these customers believe that because their engine uses oil and they add a new quart every week, they are doing the same thing as changing the oil. But dirty, oxidized engine oil can cause piston rings to stick and not seal the cylinder. Therefore, when the oil and filter are changed, the clean oil may free the piston rings, especially if the vehicle is driven on a long trip during which the oil is allowed to reach the normal operating temperature. An engine that is mechanically sound, but burning oil, may be "fixed" by simply changing the oil and filter.

tested must give a fuel economy increase of at least 1.5% as compared to a standard reference SAE 30 engine oil on which the same test has been performed. Oils that pass this test can be labeled as energy conserving on the API doughnut symbol on the oil container.

Energy Conserving II engine oils are formulated to improve fuel economy by 2.7% or more as compared to standard reference oil. Oils meeting this requirement can indicate "Energy Conserving II" on the lower portion of the API doughnut-shaped service symbol.

OIL BRAND COMPATIBILITY

Many technicians and vehicle owners have their favorite brand of engine oil. The choice is often made as a result of marketing and advertising, as well as word-of-mouth comments from friends, relatives, and technicians. If your brand of engine oil is not performing up to your expectations, then you may wish to change brands. For example, some owners experience lower oil pressure with a certain brand, than they do with other brands with the same SAE viscosity rating.

Most experts agree that regular oil changes are the most important regularly scheduled maintenance for an engine. It is also wise to check the oil level regularly and add oil when it is needed. According to SAE standard J-357, all engine oils must be compatible with all other brands of engine oil. Therefore, any brand of engine oil can be used as long as it meets the viscosity and API standards recommended by the vehicle manufacturer. Even though many people prefer a particular brand, be assured that, according to API and SAE, any *major* brand name engine oil can be used.

SYNTHETIC OIL

Synthetic engine oils have been available for years for military, commercial, and general public use. The term *synthetic* means that it is a manufactured product and not refined from a naturally occurring substance as engine oil (petroleum base) is refined from crude oil. Synthetic oil is processed from several different base stocks using several different methods. The categories of chemical compounds generally usable for synthetic engine oil include

1. Synthetic hydrocarbons (usually polyalphaolefins)
2. Organic esters (made by mixing an alcohol and an acid)
3. Polyglycols

Various brand names of synthetic engine oil may be made from any one or a compatible combination of these types of chemical compounds.

Some synthetic oils are mixed with petroleum base engine oils, but these must be labeled a *blend*.

The major advantage of using synthetic engine oil is in its ability to remain fluid at very low temperatures. This characteristic of synthetic oil makes it popular in colder climates where cold-engine cranking is important.

The major disadvantage is cost. The cost of synthetic engine oils can be four or five times the cost of petroleum base engine oils. The advantages and disadvantages are summarized as follows:

Advantages

1. Synthetic oils make cold weather starting easier.
2. Use of synthetics gives improved fuel economy, possibly as a result of lower internal engine friction.
3. Use of synthetics results in a cooler-operating engine because of lower internal engine friction.
4. The oil lasts longer because of its resistance to oxidation (vehicle manufacturers' recommendations for oil change intervals should still be followed).

Disadvantages

1. The cost of synthetics is four to five times the cost of petroleum oil.
2. Some synthetics cannot be used in certain engines without possible problems. See the oil manufacturer's instructions for the *exact* procedure to follow if converting to synthetic engine oil.
3. Because some synthetics are more fluid and my shrink gaskets and seals, some engines may leak oil when switched to synthetic oil from mineral oil.

OIL TEMPERATURE

Excessive temperatures, either too low or too high, are harmful to any engine. If the oil is too cold, the oil could be too thick to flow through and lubricate all engine parts. If the oil is too hot, the oil could become too thin to provide the film strength necessary to prevent metal-to-metal contact and wear. Estimated oil temperature can be determined with the following formula:

$$\frac{\text{Estimated oil}}{\text{temperature}} = \frac{\text{Oustside air}}{\text{temperature}} + 120°$$

For example

$$\frac{90° \text{ outside air}}{\text{temperature}} + 120° = \frac{210° \text{ estimated}}{\text{oil temperature}}$$

During hard acceleration (or high–power demand activities like trailer towing), the oil temperature will quickly increase. Oil temperature should not exceed 300° F (150° C).

OIL CHANGE INTERVALS

All vehicle and engine manufacturers recommend a maximum oil change interval. The recommended intervals are almost always expressed in terms of mileage or elapsed time (or hours of operation), whichever milestone is reached first.

Most vehicle manufacturers recommend an oil change interval of 7500 to 12,000 miles (12,000 to 19,000 kilometers) or 6 months. If, however, *any one* of the conditions in the following list exists, the oil change interval recommendation drops to a more reasonable 2000 to 3000 miles (3000 to 5000 kilometers)or 3 months. The important thing to remember is that these are recommended *maximum* intervals and they should be shortened substantially if any of the following operating conditions exists:

■ **TECH TIP** ■

FOLLOW THE HOLIDAYS

Vehicle owners frequently forget when they last changed the oil. This is particularly true of the person who owns or is responsible for several vehicles. A helpful method for remembering when the oil should be changed is to change the oil near the time of selected holidays that are about 3 months apart. For example, the following information may be helpful:

■ **Labor Day** (first Monday in September)—This holiday marks the traditional end of summer and an oil change at this time prepares the engine for the changing temperatures and moisture of the fall season.
■ **Christmas** (December 25)—An oil change near Christmas prepares the engine for very cold winter start-ups and short driving distances with generally long periods of idling, all of which are hard on engine oil.
■ **Easter** (in March or April)—This early spring date can vary from year to year, yet an oil change at this time prepares the engine for the moisture and changing temperatures of spring weather.
■ **Memorial Day** (May 30)—This holiday marks the traditional first day of summer. An oil change at this time prepares the engine for hot weather driving.

1. Operating in dusty areas
2. Towing a trailer
3. Short-trip driving, especially during cold weather (definition of a short trip varies among manufacturers, but it is usually defined as 4 to 15 miles (6 to 24 kilometers) each time the engine is started)
4. Operating in temperatures below freezing (32° F, 0° C)
5. Operating at idle speed for extended periods of time (such as normally occurs in police or taxi service)

Because most vehicles driven during cold weather are driven on short trips, most technicians and automotive experts recommend changing the oil every 2000 to 3000 miles or every 2 to 3 months, whichever occurs first.

OIL CHANGE PROCEDURE

The oil will drain more rapidly from a warm engine than from a cold one. In addition, the contaminants are more likely to be suspended in the oil immediately after running the engine. Position a drain pan under the drain plug; then remove the plug with care to avoid contact with hot oil.

■ **CAUTION:** Used engine oil has been determined to be harmful. Rubber gloves should be worn to protect the skin. If used engine oil gets on the skin, wash thoroughly with soap and water. ■

Allow the oil to drain freely so that the contaminants come out with the oil. It is not critically important to get every last drop of oil from the engine oil pan, because a quantity of used oil still remains in the engine oil passages and oil pump. While the engine oil is draining, the oil plug gasket should be examined. If appears to be damaged, it should be replaced.

NOTE: Honda recommends that the oil drain plug gasket be replaced at every oil change on many of their vehicles. The aluminum sealing gasket does not seal once it has been tightened. Always follow the vehicle manufacturer's recommendations.

When the oil stops running and starts to drip, reinstall and tighten the drain plug. Replace the oil filter if is to be done during this oil change. Refill the engine with the proper type, grade, and quantity of oil. Restart the engine and allow the engine to idle until it develops oil pressure; then check the engine for leaks, especially at the oil filter.

OIL FILTERS

The oil within the engine is pumped from the oil pan through the filter before it goes into the engine lubricating system passages. The filter is made from either closely packed cloth fibers or a porous paper. Large particles are trapped by the filter. Microscopic particles will flow through the filter pores. These particles are so small that they can flow through the bearing oil film and not touch the surfaces, so they do no damage.

Either the engine or the filter is provided with a **bypass** that will allow the oil to go around the filter element. The bypass allows the engine to be lubricated with dirty oil, rather than having no lubrication, if the filter becomes plugged. The oil also goes through the bypass when the oil is cold and thick. Most engine manufacturers recommend filter changes at every other oil change

FIGURE 16–7 *Typical internal bypass valve used inside an oil filter.*

period. Correct oil filter selection includes being certain to use a filter with an internal bypass when the engine is not equipped with one. See Figure 16–7.

NOTE: Many persons believe that oil filters will remove all dirt from the oil being circulated through the filtering material. Most oil filters will filter particles that are about 10 to 20 microns in size. A micron is a millionth of a meter or 0.000039 inch. Most dirt and carbon particles that turn engine oil black are less than a micron in size. In other words, it takes about 3,000,000 (3 million) of these carbon particles to cover a pin head. To help visualize how small a micron is, consider that a typical human hair is 60 microns in diameter. In fact, anything smaller than 40 microns is not visible to the human eye. The dispersants added to engine oil prevent dirt from adhering together to form sludge. It is the same dispersant additive that prevents dirt from being filtered or removed by other means. If an oil filter could filter particles down to 1 micron in size, it would be so restrictive that the engine would not receive sufficient oil through the filter for lubrication. Oil recycling companies use special chemicals to break down the dispersants, which permits the dirt in the oil to combine into larger units that can be filtered or processed out of the oil.

■ **TECH TIP** ■

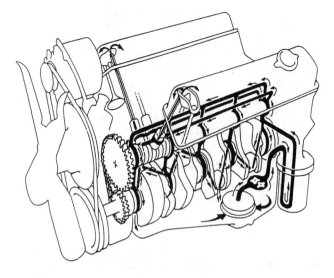

FIGURE 16–8 *Typical V-8 engine lubrication system. Oil is stored in the oil pan (sump) and drawn into the oil pump and through the oil filter and on through the oil passages (oil galleries).*

CHANGING OIL IN A TURBOCHARGED ENGINE

One of the most difficult jobs an engine oil has to do is to lubricate the extremely hot bearings of a turbocharger. After a turbocharger has been in operation, it is always wise to let the engine to idle for about 1 minute to allow the turbocharger to slow down before shutting off the engine. This allows the turbo to keep receiving oil from the engine while it is still revolving fast.

However, just as with any engine, the greatest amount of wear occurs during start-up, especially following an oil change when the oil has been drained from the engine. Some technicians fill the new oil filter with new oil prior to installation to help the engine receive oil as rapidly as possible after starting.

A number of vehicle manufacturers also suggest that turbo-equipped engines be "primed" before starting. This means that the engine should be rotated without ignition so that it does not start, to allow the oil pump to pump oil to the bearings of the turbocharger before the engine starts.

On older vehicles, it is a simple process to disconnect the ignition coil wire from the distributor cap and ground it to prevent coil damage. After the ignition has been disconnected in this manner, simply crank the engine for 15 seconds. Some manufacturers recommend repeating the 15 seconds of cranking after a 30-second period to allow the starter motor to cool.

Many of today's vehicles are equipped with electronic fuel-injection and direct-fire distributorless ignition systems. On these vehicles, it often requires a lot of time to disconnect either the ignition system or the fuel system to prevent the engine from starting.

There is one simple method that works on many fuel-injected vehicles. If the accelerator pedal is held down to the floor during cranking, the engine computer senses the throttle position and reduces the amount of fuel injected into the engine. This mode of operation is often called the **clear-flood mode,** and in it, the computer limits the fuel delivery to such an extent that the engine should not start.

Therefore, to prime most late-model turbocharged engines, simply depress the accelerator to the floor and crank for 15 seconds. To start the engine, simply return the accelerator pedal to the idle position and crank the engine.

OIL PUMPS

All production automobile engines have a full-pressure oil system. The pressure is maintained by an oil pump. The oil is forced into the lubrication system under pressure. A typical engine lubricating system is shown in Figure 16–8.

In most engines, the distributor drive gear meshes with a gear on the camshaft, as shown in Figure 16–9. The oil pump is driven from the end of the distributor shaft, often with a hexagon-shaped shaft. Some engines have a short shaft gear that meshes with the

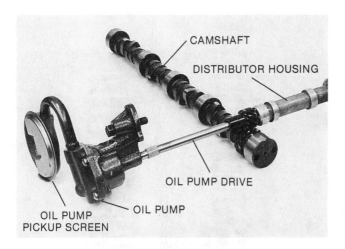

FIGURE 16-9 The oil pump is driven by an extension from the distributor drive gear on many engines.

FIGURE 16-11 Oil pump mounted in the front cover of the engine. The oil pump is driven by the crankshaft.

FIGURE 16-10 Separate gears drive the oil pump and distributor on this engine.

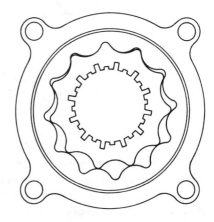

FIGURE 16-12 Geroter type of oil pump driven by the crankshaft.

cam gear to drive both the distributor and oil pump. Occasionally, an engine is built that uses separate gears on the distributor and on the oil pump. Both of these gears mate with the same cam gear. This can be seen in Figure 16-10. With these drive methods, the pump turns at one-half engine speed. In other engines, the oil pump is driven by the front of the crankshaft, in a stepup similar to that of an automatic transmission pump, so that it turns at the same speed as the crankshaft. Examples of a crankshaft-driven oil pump are shown in Figures 16-11 and 16-12.

Most automotive engines use one of two types of oil pumps: **gear** and **rotor** (Figure 16-13). All oil pumps are called **positive displacement pumps** and each rotation delivers the same volume of oil. This means that everything that enters must exit. The gear-type oil pump consists of two spur gears in a close-fitting housing. One gear is driven and the other idles. As the gear teeth come out of mesh, they tend to leave a space, which is filled by oil drawn through the pump inlet. When the pump is pumping, oil is carried around the *outside* of each gear in the space between the gear teeth and the housing as shown in Figure 16-14. As the teeth mesh in the center, oil is forced from the teeth into an oil passage, thus producing oil pressure. The rotor-type oil pump consists essentially of a special lobe-shaped gear meshing with the inside of a lobed rotor. The center lobed section is driven and

FIGURE 16–13 Rotor-type oil pump (trachoid design) on the left and gear-type oil pump on the right.

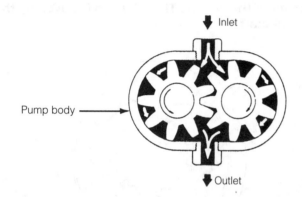

FIGURE 16–14 In a gear-type oil pump, the oil flows through the pump around the outside of each gear. This is an example of a positive displacement pump, wherein everything entering the pump must leave the pump.

the outer section idles. As the lobes separate, oil is drawn in just as it is drawn into gear-type pumps. As the pump rotates, it carries oil around and between the lobes. As the lobes mesh, they force the oil out from between them under pressure in the same manner as does the gear-type pump. The pump is sized so that it will maintain a pressure of at least 10 psi (70 kPa) in the oil gallery when the engine is hot and idling. Pressure will increase by about 10 psi for each 1000 RPM as the engine speed increases, because the engine-driven pump also rotates faster.

OIL PRESSURE REGULATION

In engines with a full-pressure lubricating system, maximum pressure is limited with a pressure **relief valve.** The relief valve (sometimes called the **pressure regulating valve**) is located at the outlet of the

FIGURE 16–15 Spring-loaded piston and ball-type oil pressure relief valve.

pump. The relief valve controls maximum pressure by bleeding off oil to the inlet side of the pump. See Figure 16–15. *The relief valve spring tension determines the maximum oil pressure.* If a pressure relief valve was not used, the engine oil pressure would continue to increase as the engine speed increased. Maximum pressure is usually limited to the lowest pressure that will deliver enough lubricating oil to all engine parts that need to be lubricated. *Three to 6 gallons per minute are required to lubricate the engine.* The oil pump is made so that it is large enough to provide pressure at low engine speeds and small enough that it will not **cavitate** at high speed. Cavitation occurs when the pump tries to pull oil faster than it can flow from the pan to the pickup. When it cannot get enough oil, it will pull air. This puts air pockets or cavities in the oil stream. A pump is cavitating when it is pulling air or vapors.

NOTE: This is the reason for sheet-metal covers over the pickup screen. Oil is trapped under the cover, which helps prevent the oil pump from drawing in air, especially during sudden stops or during rapid acceleration.

After the oil leaves the pump, it is delivered to the moving parts through drilled oil passages. It does not have to have any pressure after it reaches the parts that are to be lubricated. The oil film between

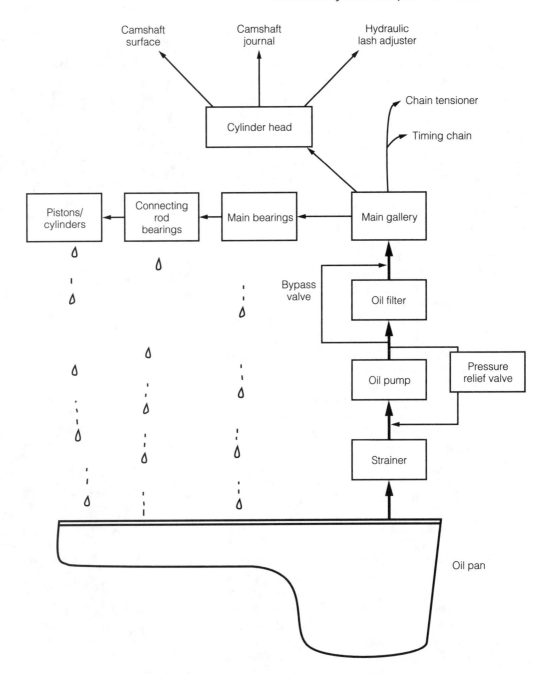

FIGURE 16–16   Oil flow through an engine starts at the oil pump pickup and eventually ends up with the oil dropping back into the oil pan.

the parts is developed and maintained by hydrodynamic lubrication. Excessive oil pressure requires more horsepower and provides no better lubrication than the minimum effective pressure. High oil pressure and the resulting high rates of oil flow may, in some cases, tend to erode engine bearings and lead to oil pump cavitation, and it uses more engine power. See Figure 16–16.

FACTORS AFFECTING OIL PRESSURE

Oil pressure can only be produced when the oil pump has a capacity larger than all the "leaks" in the engine. The leaks are the clearances at end points of the lubrication system. The end points are at the edges of bearings, the rocker arms, the connecting rod spit holes, and so on. These clearances are designed into the engine and are necessary for its proper operation. As the engine parts wear and clearance becomes greater, more oil will leak out. The oil pump **capacity** must be great enough to supply extra oil for these leaks. The capacity of the oil pump results from its size, rotating speed, and physical condition. If the pump is rotating slowly as the engine is idling, oil pump capacity is low. *If the leaks are greater than the pump capacity, engine oil pressure is low.* As the engine speeds up, the pump capacity increases and the pump tries to force more oil out of the leaks. This causes the pressure to rise until the pressure reaches the regulated maximum pressure.

The viscosity of the engine oil affects both the pump capacity and the oil leakage. Thin oil or oil of very low viscosity slips past the edges of the pump and flows freely from the leaks. Hot oil has a low viscosity, and therefore, a hot engine often has low oil pressure. Cold oil is more viscous (thicker) than hot oil. This results in higher pressures, even with the cold engine idling. High oil pressure occurs with a cold engine because the oil relief valve must open further to release excess oil than is necessary with a hot engine. This larger opening increases the spring compression force, and this, in turn, increases the oil pressure. Putting higher-viscosity oil in an engine will raise the engine oil pressure to the regulated setting of the relief valve at a lower engine speed. See chapter 6 for details on measuring oil pressure.

OIL PUMP CHECKS

The cover is removed to check the condition of the oil pump. The gears and housing are examined for scoring. If the gears and housing are heavily scored, the entire pump should be replaced. If they are lightly scored, the clearances in the pump should be measured. These clearances include the space between the gears and housing, the space between the teeth of the two gears, and the space between the side of the gear and the pump cover. Usually, a feeler gauge is used to make these measurements. Gauging plastic can be used to measure the space between the side of the gears and the cover. The oil pump should be replaced when excessive clearance or scoring is found. See Figure 16–17.

On most engines, the oil pump should be replaced as part of any engine work, especially if the cause for the repair is lack of lubrication.

NOTE: The oil pump is the "garbage pit" of the entire engine. Any and all debris is often forced through the gears and housing of an oil pump. _____

FIGURE 16–17   Badly worn oil pump, most likely caused by dirty or contaminated engine oil.

FIGURE   16–18   Gear-type   oil   pump   being checked for tooth clearance in the housing.

See Figures 16–18 and 16–19 for examples of oil pump clearance checks. Always refer to the manufacturer's specifications when checking the oil pump for wear. Typical oil pump clearances include the following:

1. End plate clearance: 0.0015 inch (0.04 millimeter)
2. Side (rotor) clearance: 0.012 inch (0.30 millimeter)

FIGURE 16–19 *Measuring the gear-to-cover clearance of an oil pump.*

3. Rotor tip clearance: 0.010 inch (0.25 millimeter)
4. Gear end play clearance: 0.004 inch (0.10 millimeter)

All parts should also be inspected closely for wear. Check the relief valve for scoring and check the condition of the spring. When installing the oil pump, coat the sealing surfaces with engine assembly lubricant. This lubricant helps draw oil from the oil pan on initial start-up.

OIL PASSAGES IN THE BLOCK

From the filter, oil goes through a drilled hole that intersects with a drilled main oil **gallery** or longitudinal header. This is a long hole drilled from the front of the block to the back. Inline engines use one oil gallery. V-type engines may use two or three galleries. One main gallery and two hydraulic valve lifter galleries used on a V-type engine can be seen in Figure 16–20. Passages drilled through the block bulkheads allow the oil to go from the main oil gallery to the main and cam bearings. In some engines, oil goes to the cam bearings first, and then to the main bearings.

It is important that the oil holes in the bearings match up with the drilled passages in the bearing saddles so that the bearing can be properly lubricated. Over a long period of use, bearings will wear. This wear causes excess clearance. The excess clearance will allow too much oil to leak from the side of the bearing. When this happens, there will be little or no oil left for bearings located farther downstream in the lubricating system. This is a major cause of bearing failure. If a new

bearing were installed in place of the oil-starved bearing, it, too, would fail unless the bearing having the excess clearance was also replaced.

VALVE TRAIN LUBRICATION

The oil gallery may intersect or have drilled passages to the valve lifter bores to lubricate the lifters. When hydraulic lifters are used, the oil pressure in the gallery keeps refilling them. On some engines, oil from the lifters goes up the center of a hollow pushrod to lubricate the pushrod ends, the rocker arm pivot, and the valve stem tip. In other engines, an oil passage is drilled from the gallery or from a cam bearing to the block deck, where it matches with a gasket hole and a hole drilled in the head to carry the oil to a rocker arm shaft. Some engines use an enlarged bolt hole to carry lubrication oil around the rocker shaft cap screw to the rocker arm shaft. This design is shown by a line drawing in Figure 16–21. Holes in the bottom of the rocker arm shaft allow lubrication of the rocker arm pivot. Mechanical loads on the valve train hold the rocker arm against the passage in the rocker arm shaft, as shown in Figure 16–22. This prevents excessive oil leakage from the rocker arm shaft. Often, holes are drilled in cast rocker arms to carry oil to the pushrod end and to the valve tip. Rocker arm assemblies need only a surface coating of oil, so the oil flow to the rocker assembly is minimized using restrictions or metered openings. The restriction or metering disk is in the lifter when the rocker assembly is lubricated through the pushrod. Cam journal holes that line up with oil passages are often used to meter oil to the rocker shafts.

Oil that seeps from the rocker assemblies is returned to the oil pan through drain holes. These oil drain holes are often placed so that the oil drains on the camshaft or on cam drive gears to lubricate them.

Some engines have a means of directing a positive oil flow to the cam drive gears or chain. This may be a nozzle or a chamfer on a bearing parting surface that allows oil to spray on the loaded portion of the cam drive mechanism.

OIL PANS

As the vehicle accelerates, brakes, or is turned rapidly, the oil tends to move around in the pan. Pan baffles and oil pan shapes are often used to keep the oil inlet under the oil at all times. As the crankshaft rotates, it acts like a fan and causes air within the crankcase to rotate with it. This can cause a strong draft on the oil, churning it so that air bubbles enter the oil. This causes oil foaming. Oil with air will not lubricate like liquid oil, so oil foaming can cause bearings to fail. A baffle or

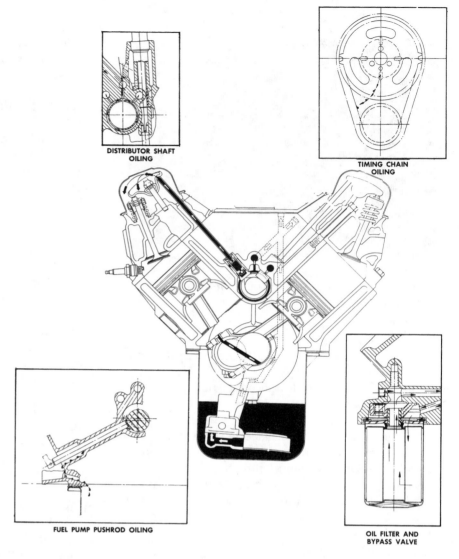

DISTRIBUTOR SHAFT OILING

TIMING CHAIN OILING

FUEL PUMP PUSHROD OILING

OIL FILTER AND BYPASS VALVE

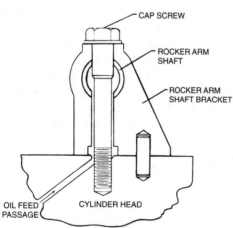

CAP SCREW

ROCKER ARM SHAFT

ROCKER ARM SHAFT BRACKET

OIL FEED PASSAGE

CYLINDER HEAD

FIGURE 16–21 Clearance around the rocker shaft bracket cap screw makes a passage for oil to get into the rocker shaft. (Courtesy of Dana Corporation)

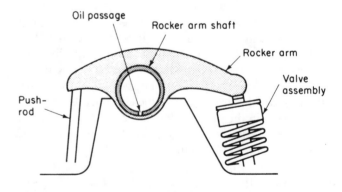

Oil passage

Rocker arm shaft

Rocker arm

Valve assembly

Push-rod

FIGURE 16–22 The rocker arm pivot is lubricated through the oil passage in the bottom of the rocker shaft. Other rocker arm styles are usually lubricated through a hollow pushrod.

FIGURE 16–23 Windage tray attached between the crankshaft and the oil pan.

windage tray is sometimes installed in engines to eliminate the oil churning problem. This may be an added part, as shown in Figure 16–23, or it may be a part of the oil pan. Windage trays have the good side effect of reducing the amount of air disturbed by the crankshaft, so that less power is drained from the engine at high crankshaft speeds.

OIL COOLERS

Oil temperature must also be controlled on many high-performance or turbocharged engines. See Figure 16–24 for an example of an engine oil cooler used on a production high-performance engine. A larger-capacity oil pan also helps to control oil temperature. Coolant flows through the oil cooler to help warm the oil when the engine is cold and cool the engine oil when the engine oil is hot. Oil temperature should be above 212° F (100° C) to boil off any accumulated moisture, but it should not exceed about 280° to 300° F (138° to 148° C).

POSITIVE CRANKCASE VENTILATION

All engines remove blowby gases with **positive crankcase ventilation (PCV)** systems. This system pulls the crankcase vapors into the intake manifold. The vapors are sent to the cylinders with the intake

FIGURE 16–24 Typical engine oil cooler. Engine oil is cooled by passing coolant from the radiator through the auxiliary housing. The oil filter screws to the cooler.

■ TECH TIP ■

CHECK THAT AIR CLEANER!

If oil is in the air cleaner, check the condition of the PCV valve and hoses.

■ TECH TIP ■

WHAT IS ACCEPTABLE OIL CONSUMPTION?

There are a number of opinions regarding what is acceptable oil consumption. Most vehicle owners do not want their engine to use *any* oil between oil changes even if they do not change it more often than every 7500 miles (12,000 kilometers)! Engineers have improved machining operations and piston ring designs to help eliminate oil consumption.

Many stationary or industrial engines are not driven on the road; therefore, they do not accumulate miles, yet they still may consume excessive oil.

A general rule for "acceptable" oil consumption is that it should be about 0.002 to 0.004 pounds per horsepower per hour. To figure, use the following:

$$\frac{1.82 \times \text{Quarts used}}{\text{Operating hp} \times \text{Total hours}} = \text{lb/hp/hr}$$

Therefore, oil consumption is based on the amount of work an engine performs. Although the formula may not be usable for vehicle engines used for daily transportation, it may be usable by the marine or industrial engine builder. Generally, oil consumption that is greater than 1 quart for every 600 miles (1000 kilometers per liter) is considered to be excessive with a motor vehicle.

charge to be burned in the combustion chamber. Under some operating conditions, the blowby gases are forced back through the inlet filter.

NOTE: A blocked or plugged PCV system is a major cause of high oil consumption, and contributes to many oil leaks. Before expensive engine repairs are attempted, check the condition of the PCV system. __

SUMMARY

1. Viscosity is the oil's thickness or resistance to flow.
2. Normal engine oil pump pressure ranges from 10 to 60 psi (200 to 400 kPa), or 10 psi per 1000 engine RPM.

3. Hydrodynamic oil pressure around engine bearings is usually over 1000 psi (6900 kPa).
4. Most vehicle manufacturers recommend use of SAE 5W-30 or SAE 10W-30 engine oil.
5. Most vehicle manufacturers recommend changing the engine oil every 6 months or every 7500 miles (12,000 kilometers), whichever comes first. Most experts recommend changing the engine oil every 3000 miles (5000 kilometers) or every 3 months to help ensure long engine life.
6. The oil pump is driven directly by the crankshaft or by a gear or shaft from the camshaft.

REVIEW QUESTIONS

1. What causes a wedge-shaped film to form in the oil?
2. What is hydrodynamic lubrication?
3. What is meant by the label "Energy Conserving"?
4. Explain why the oil filter is bypassed when the engine oil is cold and thick.
5. Explain why internal engine leakage affects oil pressure.
6. Explain the operation of the bypass valve located in the oil filter or oil filter adapter.
7. Describe how the oil flows from the oil pump, through the filter and main engine bearings, to the valve train.
8. What is the purpose of a windage tray?

MULTIPLE-CHOICE QUESTIONS

1. Normal oil pump pressure in an engine is _____.
   a. 3 to 7 pounds per square inch.
   b. 10 to 60 pounds per square inch
   c. 100 to 150 pounds per square inch
   d. 180 to 210 pounds per square inch
2. Oil change intervals as specified by the vehicle manufacturer _____.
   a. Are *maximum* time and mileage intervals
   b. Are *minimum* time and mileage intervals
   c. Only include miles driven between oil changes
   d. Generally only include time between oil changes
3. An SAE 10W-30 engine oil is _____.
   a. An SAE 10 oil with VI additives
   b. An SAE 20 oil with VI additives
   c. An SAE 30 oil with VI additives
   d. An SAE 30 oil with detergent additives
4. As engine oil is used in an engine _____.
   a. It becomes thinner as a result of chemical breakdown that occurs with age
   b. It becomes thicker because of oxidation, wear metals, and combustion by-products
   c. It becomes thicker because of temperature changes
   d. It becomes thinner because of oxidation, wear metals, and combustion by-products

5. Technician A says that the same brand name engine oil should be used throughout an engine's entire service life. Technician B says that any engine oil of the correct API and SAE rating can be used because all engine oils are compatible. Which technician is correct?
   a. A only
   b. B only
   c. Both A and B
   d. Neither A nor B

6. Technician A says that some vehicle manufacturers recommend diesel API grade and a gasoline grade for some engines. Technician B says that an oil with the specified API rating *and* SAE viscosity rating should be used in an engine. Which technician is correct?
   a. A only
   b. B only
   c. Both A and B
   d. Neither A nor B

7. Two technicians are discussing oil filters. Technician A says that the oil will remain perfectly clean if just the oil filter is changed regularly. Technician B says that oil filters cannot filter particles smaller than the human eye can see. Which technician is correct?
   a. A only
   b. B only
   c. Both A and B
   d. Neither A nor B

8. Turbocharged engines have special engine oil needs, including the following: _____
   a. Strict oil change intervals should be observed.
   b. Oil of the proper API and SAE ratings should be used.
   c. The turbocharger should be primed by cranking the engine before starting.
   d. All of the above.

9. A typical oil pump can pump how many gallons per minute?
   a. 3 to 6
   b. 6 to 10
   c. 10 to 60
   d. 50 to 100

10. In typical engine lubrication systems, what components are the last to receive oil and the first to suffer from a lack of oil or oil pressure?
    a. Main bearings
    b. Rod bearings
    c. Valve trains
    d. Oil filters

Engine Assembly

OBJECTIVES

After studying Chapter 17, the reader will be able to

1. List the steps for assembling an engine.
2. Describe how to measure bearing oil clearance using plastic gauging material.
3. Explain how to check for crankshaft end play and connecting rod side clearance.
4. Discuss how to fit pistons to individual cylinder bores.
5. Describe how to test for proper oil pressure before starting the engine.

All parts are attached to the engine block. The block, therefore, must be prepared before assembly can begin. The key to proper assembly of any engine is cleanliness. The work area must be clean, as well as the workbench space, to prevent dirt or other engine-damaging particles from being picked up and causing possible serious engine damage.

CLEANING OIL GALLERIES IN THE BLOCK

The block should have been cleaned prior to machining, and all oil gallery plugs should have been removed at that time. This would allow cleaning solvent to penetrate through the oil galleries and passages in the block.

■ **CAUTION:** Some blocks, like that of the small-block Chevrolet V-8, use a cup plug down inside an oil passage next to the distributor. Failure to remove this plug and clean this oil passage will cause the trapped dirt to flow with the new oil and ruin the newly installed bearings and crankshaft. Always check with a service manual or a knowledgeable engine rebuilder when cleaning oil passages. ■

Often the cleaning solution or the cleaning oven heat will not adequately clean out all of the varnish and debris in the small oil passages. Most experts suggest using long-handled oil gallery brushes commonly called "bottle brushes." These brushes usually are available in ¼-, ⅜-, and ⅝-inch diameters. Most experts recommend using the brushes by dipping them in solvent and running them through the oil galleries by hand.

BLOCK PREPARATION

All surfaces should also be checked for damage resulting from the machining processes. Other items that should be done before assembly begins include the following:

1. All threaded bolt holes should be chamfered.
2. All threaded holes should be cleaned with a tap.
3. Core plugs should be installed.
4. Oil gallery plugs should be installed using sealant on the threads. See Figure 17–1.

■ **CAUTION:** Avoid using Teflon tape on the threads of oil gallery plugs. The tape is often cut by the threads, and thin strips of the tape are then free to flow through the oil galleries where the tape can cause a clog, thereby limiting lubricating engine oil to important parts of the engine. ■

FIGURE 17–1 Oil passage (gallery) plug being installed with a T-handle wrench.

FIGURE 17–2 Installed convex-type soft plug.

INSTALLING CUPS AND PLUGS

Core holes left in the external block wall are machined and sealed with **soft core plugs** or **expansion plugs** (also called **freeze plugs** or **Welsh plugs**).

Soft plugs are of two designs. One type is a **convex type**. For its use, the core hole is counter bored with a shoulder. The counter bored hole is more expensive to machine than is a straight hole. The convex soft plug is placed in the counter bore, convex side out. It is driven in and upset with a fitted seating tool. This causes the edge of the soft plug to enlarge to hold it in place. Figure 17–2 shows an installed convex soft plug. A convex plug should be driven in until it reaches the counter bore of the core plug hole. The second, and the

FIGURE 17–3 Installed cup-type soft plug.

most common, type of hole plug is a **cup type.** This type of soft plug is fit into a smooth, straight hole. The outer edge of the cup is slightly bell mouthed. The bell mouth causes it to tighten when it is driven into the hole to the correct depth with a seating tool. An installed cup-type soft plug is shown in Figures 17–3 and 17–4. A cup plug is installed about 0.020 to 0.050 inch (0.5 to 1.3 millimeters) below the surface of the block, using sealant to prevent leaks.

CAUSES OF PREMATURE BEARING FAILURE

According to a major manufacturer of engine bearings, the major causes of premature (shortly after installation) bearing failure include the following:

Dirt (45%)
Misassembly (13%)
Misalignment (13%)
Lack of lubrication (11%)
Overloading or lugging (10%)
Corrosion (4%)
Other (4%)

Many cases of premature bearing failure may result from a combination of several of these items.

FIGURE 17–4   Cup plugs (also called expansion plugs or core plugs) being installed in cylinder heads before final assembly. Note the use of sealer on the plugs.

FIGURE 17–5   Cam bearing tool being used to remove a used cam bearing.

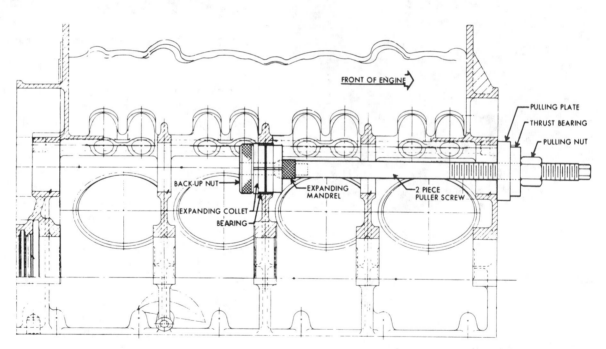

FIGURE 17–6   Screw-type puller being used to install a new cam bearing. (Courtesy of Buick Motor Division, GMC)

Therefore, to help prevent bearing failure, keep everything as clean as possible.

CAM BEARINGS

A cam bearing installing tool is required to insert the new cam bearing without damage to the bearing. A number of tool manufacturers design and sell cam bear-

ing installing tools. The feature they have in common is a shoulder on a bushing that fits inside the cam bearing, with a means of keeping the bearing aligned as it is installed. Figure 17–5 shows a camshaft bearing on the removing and installing tool. The bearing is placed on the bushing of the tool and rotated to properly align the oil hole. The bearing is then forced into the bearing bore of the block by either a pulling screw or a slide

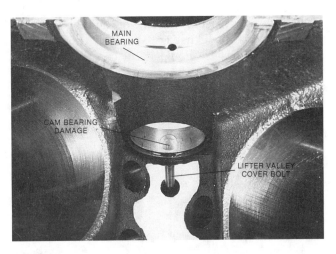

FIGURE 17–7   Cam bearing damaged by improper engine assembly.

FIGURE 17–8   Cam bearing that was driven in too far. The oil feed hole to the cam bearing was slightly covered.

hammer. A pulling screw type of tool is illustrated in Figure 17–6. The installed bearing must be checked to make sure that it has the correct depth and that the oil hole is indexed with the oil passage in the block. No additional service is required on cam bearings that have been properly installed. See Figures 17–7 and 17–8.

The opening at the back of the camshaft is closed with an expansion plug (Figure 17–9).

MEASURING MAIN BEARING CLEARANCE

The engine is assembled from the inside out. This method allows the technician to support the inner parts as they are assembled. Checks are made during assembly to ensure correct fits and proper assembly of the parts.

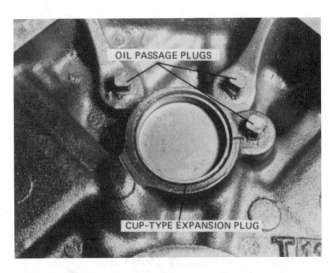

FIGURE 17–9   The opening in the back of the camshaft is closed with a cup-type expansion plug. Screw-type plugs are installed in the oil passages.

The main bearings are properly fit *before* the crankshaft is lubricated or turned. The oil clearance of both main and connecting rod bearings is set by selectively fitting the bearings. In this way, the oil clearance can be adjusted to within 0.0005 inch of the desired clearance.

■ **CAUTION:** Avoid touching bearings with bare hands. The oils on your fingers can start corrosion of the bearing materials. Always wear protective cloth or rubber gloves to avoid the possibility of damage to the bearing surface. ■

Standard bearings are available in measurements 0.001, 0.002, and 0.003 inch undersize to compensate for worn bearing journals. Bearings are also made in measurements 0.010, 0.020, and 0.030 inch undersize for use on reground journals. See Figure 17–10 for a typical main bearing design.

The crankshaft bearing journals should be measured with a micrometer to select the required bearing size. Remember that each of the main bearing caps will only fit one location and the caps must be positioned correctly. The correct-size bearings should be placed in the block and cap, making sure that the bearing tang locks into its slot. The upper main bearing has an oil feed hole. Carefully rest the clean crankshaft in the block on the upper main bearings. Lower it squarely, as shown in Figure 17–11, so that it does not damage the thrust bearing. Place a strip of *Plastigage* (gauging plastic) on each main bearing journal. Install the main bearing caps and tighten the bolts to specifications. Remove each cap and check the width of the *Plastigage* with the markings on the gauge envelope, as shown in Figure 17–12. This will indicate the oil clearance. If the shaft is out of round, the oil clearance should be checked at the point that has the *least* oil clearance.

CORRECTING BEARING CLEARANCE

The oil clearance can be reduced by 0.001 inch by replacing both bearing shells with bearing shells that 0.001 inch undersize. The clearance can be reduced by

"ONE TO THREE"

When engine technicians are talking about clearances and specifications, the unit of measure most often used is thousandths of an inch (0.001 inch). Therefore, a clearance expressed as "one to three" would actually be a clearance of 0.001 to 0.003 inch. The same applies to parts of a thousandth of an inch. For example, a specification of 0.0005 to 0.0015 inch would be spoken of as simply being "one-half to one and one-half." The unit of a thousandth of an inch is assumed, and this method of speaking reduces errors and misunderstandings.

HINT: *Most engine clearance specifications fall within 1 to 3 thousandths of an inch. The written specifications could be a misprint therefore if the specification does not fall within this general range, double-check the clearance value using a different source.*

0.0005 inch by replacing only one of the bearing shells with a bearing shell that is 0.001 inch smaller. This smaller bearing shell should be placed in the engine block side of the bearing (the upper shell). Oil clearance can be adjusted accurately using this procedure. Never mismatch the bearing shells by more than a 0.001 inch difference in size. Oil clearances normally run from 0.0005 to 0.002 inch.

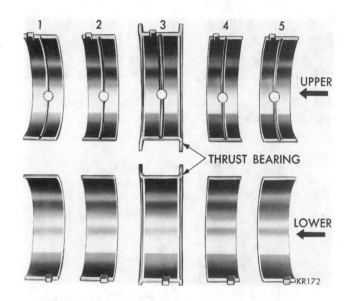

FIGURE 17–10 Typical main bearing set. Note that the upper halves are grooved for better oil flow and the lower halves are plain for better load support. This bearing set uses the center main bearing for thrust control. (Courtesy of Chrysler Corporation)

FIGURE 17–11 Crankshaft being carefully lowered into place.

The crankshaft is removed once the correct oil clearance has been established. The rear oil seal is installed in the block and cap; then the crankshaft journals are lubricated with assembly lubricant.

LIP SEAL INSTALLATION

Seals are always used at the front and rear of the crankshaft. Overhead cam engines may also have a seal at the front end of the camshaft and at the front end of an auxiliary accessory shaft. Either a lip seal or a rope seal is used in these locations. See Figures 17–13 and 17–14. The rear crankshaft oil seal is installed *after* the main bearings have been properly fit.

FIGURE 17–12 Checking the width of the plastic gauging strip to determine the oil clearance of the main bearing. An alternate method of determining oil clearance includes careful measurement of crankshaft journal and bearings.

FIGURE 17–13 Lip-type rear main bearing seal in place. The crankshaft is removed.

The lip seal may be molded in a steel case or it may be molded around a steel stiffener. The counter bore or guide that supports the seal must be thoroughly clean. In most cases, the back of the lip seal is dry when it is installed. Occasionally, a manufacturer will recommend the use of sealants behind the seal. An anaerobic sealer may be used to seal the mating surface of the rear main bearing cap on the block. The engine service manual should be consulted for specific sealing instructions. The lip of the seal should be well lubricated before the shaft and cap are installed.

ROPE SEAL INSTALLATION

Rope-type seals (braided fabric seals) are sometimes used as rear crankshaft oil seals. Some engines manufactured by Buick use rope-type seals at both the front and rear of the crankshaft. Rope-type oil seals must be compressed tightly into the groove so that no oil can leak behind them. With the crankshaft removed, the upper half of the rope seal is put in a clean groove and compressed by rolling a round object against it to force it tightly into the groove. A piece of pipe, a large socket, or even a hammer handle can be used for this, as shown in Figure 17–15. When the seal is fully seated in the groove, the ends that extend above the parting surface are cut to be flush with the surface using a sharp single-edge razor blade (Figure 17–16) or a sharp tool specially designed to cut the seal. The same procedures are used to install the lower half of the rope seal in the rear main bearing cap or seal retainer. The use of a small strip of anaerobic compound is often recommended to help seal the main bearing cap and block parting surface joint as the cap is installed.

The front rope-type oil seal packing is held in place with a retainer called a **shredder.** The old seal and

FIGURE 17–14 Rope-type rear main bearing seal in place, with the crankshaft removed.

shredder are driven from the timing cover case. The seal groove is cleaned, and a new rope-type seal packing is fitted in place with the ends of the seal at the top. The shredder is installed and staked in place. A staked shredder is pictured in Figure 17–17. Staking is done by upsetting the timing cover metal over the edge of the seal in several places around the seal. The rope seal packing is sized for the damper hub by rolling. The same techniques are used to seat the front seal as were used to seat the rear rope-type seal. Many front and/or rear seals are lip-type seals as shown in Figure 17–18.

ADDITIONAL SEALING LOCATIONS

Engines that have the oil pan rail extended below the crankshaft centerline have an additional rear seal requirement. The small gap between the side main

FIGURE 17–15 *Rolling a rope-type seal in a main bearing cap.*

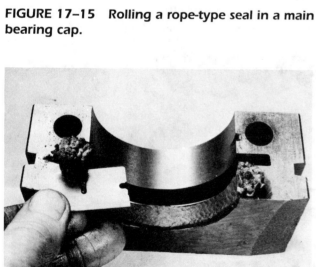

FIGURE 17–16 *Trimming the rope-type seal to length.*

bearing cap or seal retainer and the block must be sealed. There is no way to tighten the parts to close this space, so it must be filled with some type of a seal. Most of these spaces are sealed with a swelling-type seal strip. The sealing strip is put into a groove in the cap or retainer after the cap or retainer has been torqued in place. The sealing strip is first soaked for several minutes in petroleum solvent and then inserted in a groove, as shown in Figure 17–19. It may be necessary to use a blunt tool to firmly seat the sealing strip in the groove. The solvent and engine oil cause the sealing strip to swell in place to seal the gap. Sometimes, the seal will seep slightly when the engine is first run. The seepage will stop after a little use.

Formed-in-place gasket materials have found application as rear main bearing cap side seals. They are used in place of the expanding sealing strips. A special installing tool enables the service technician to squeeze room-temperature vulcanization (RTV) silicone into the gap until the space is full. The joint is properly sealed when the silicone cures.

INSTALLING THE CRANKSHAFT

The main bearing saddles, the caps, and the back of all the main bearing shells should be wiped clean; then the bearing shells can be put in place. It is important that each bearing tang line up with the slot in the bearing support. The bearing shells must have some spread to hold them in the bearing saddles and caps during assembly. The surface of the bearings is then given a thin coating of assembly lubricant to provide initial lubrication for engine start-up.

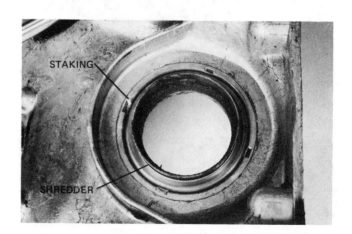

FIGURE 17–17 *The shredder is staked in place to hold the rope-type seal in a timing cover.*

NOTE: White grease is often used as assembly lubricant, especially by rebuilders and remanufacturers. —

The crankshaft with lubricant on the journals is carefully placed in the bearings to avoid damage to the thrust bearing surfaces. Figure 17–20 shows thrust surface damage resulting from careless assembly. The bearing caps are installed with their identification numbers correctly positioned. The caps were originally machined in place, so they can only fit correctly in their original position. The main bearing cap bolts are tightened finger tight, and the crankshaft is rotated. It should rotate freely.

THRUST BEARING CLEARANCE

Pry the crankshaft forward and rearward as shown in Figure 17–21. This will align the cap half of the thrust bearing with the block saddle half. The thickness (feeler) gauge will indicate the amount of thrust bearing clearance.

FIGURE 17–18 Lip seal with spring tension. This spring is called a garter spring.

FIGURE 17–19 Sealing strip being placed in the side groove of the main bearing cap.

Most engine specifications call for a range from 0.002 to 0.012 inch (0.02 to 0.3 millimeter). The crankshaft dial indicator gauge or a thickness (feeler) gauge can be used to determine the end thrust of the crankshaft (also called **crankshaft end play**).

If the clearance is too great, oversize main thrust bearings may be available for the engine. Semifinished bearings may have to be purchased and machined to size to restore proper tolerance.

TIGHTENING PROCEDURE FOR THE MAIN BEARING

Tighten the main bearing caps to the specified assembly torque, and in the specified sequence as shown in

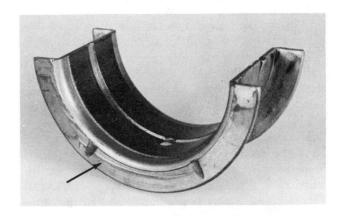

FIGURE 17–20 Damage to the thrust surfaces of the thrust bearing from careless assembly.

FIGURE 17–21 Checking crankshaft thrust bearing clearance with a thickness gauge. The technician in this photo has not yet installed the thrust bearing cap; this allows a better view of the actual movement and clearance as the crankshaft is pried back and forth.

Figure 17–22. Many manufacturers require that the crankshaft be pried forward or rearward during the main bearing tightening process. The shaft should turn *freely* after all of the main bearing cap bolts are fully torqued. It should never require over 5 pound-feet (6.75 Newton-meter [N-m]) of torque to rotate the crankshaft. An increase in the torque needed to rotate the crankshaft is often caused by a foreign particle that was not removed during cleanup. It may be on the bearing surface, on the crankshaft journal, or between the bearing and saddle.

TIMING DRIVES FOR PUSHROD ENGINES

On pushrod engines, the timing gears or chain and sprocket should be installed next. See Figures 17–23 and 17–24. The timing marks on the gears must line up when the gears are installed, as shown in Figure 17–25. The same is true of the sprockets, as shown in Figure 17–26. When used, the replaceable fuel pump eccentric is installed as the cam sprocket is fastened to the cam. The crankshaft should be rotated several times to see that the camshaft and timing gears or chain rotate freely. The timing mark alignment should be rechecked at this time. If the engine is equipped with a slinger ring, it should also be installed on the crankshaft, in front of the crankshaft gear. The slinger ring is positioned so that the outer edge faces away from the gear or sprocket, as shown in Figure 17–27.

It is assumed that the front oil seal is installed in the cover. The timing cover and gasket are placed over the timing gears and/or chain and sprockets. The attaching bolts are loosely installed to allow the damper hub to align with the cover as it fits in the seal. The damper is installed on the crankshaft. On some engines, it is a press-fit and on others it is held with a large center bolt. After the damper is secured, the attaching bolts on the timing cover can be tightened to the specified torque.

PISTON FITTING

After thorough block cleaning, the piston-to-cylinder clearance should be checked to make sure that the piston properly fits the cylinder in which it is to operate.

FIGURE 17–23 Before camshaft gears are installed on the camshaft, some gears must be heated. These gears are being warmed in <u>cooking oil</u>! The cooking oil heats the gears evenly so that they can be readily installed on the camshaft.

FIGURE 17–22 Measuring the crankshaft turning torque after each main bearing cap is properly tightened. An abnormal increase in torque indicates a problem that should be corrected before additional assembly.

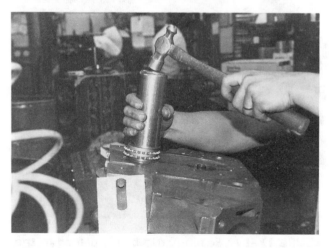

FIGURE 17–24 Installing a crankshaft gear.

The fit can be checked by determining the difference in the measured size of the piston and cylinder. Usually, a service technician will measure the piston-to-cylinder clearance with a strip thickness (feeler) gauge placed between the piston and the cylinder. The gauge thickness is the desired clearance measurement. Typical piston clearance range from about 0.0005 (½ thousandths of an inch to .0025 (2½ thousandths) of an inch (0.02 to 0.06 millimeter).

The cylinders and pistons, without rings, are wiped thoroughly clean to remove any excess protective lubricant and dust that may have accumulated on the surface. The strip thickness (feeler) gauge is placed in the cylinder along the thrust side. The piston is inserted in the cylinder upside down, with the piston thrust surface against the thickness (feeler) gauge. The piston is held in the cylinder with the connecting rod as the strip gauge is withdrawn. A moderate pull (from 5 to 10 pounds) on the gauge indicates that the clearance is the same as the gauge thickness. A light pull indicates that the clearance is greater than the gauge thickness, whereas a heavy pull indicates that the clearance is smaller than the gauge thickness. This measuring method is shown in Figure 17–28.

FIGURE 17–26 Timing marks on chain sprockets should be aligned to time the camshaft to the crankshaft.

FIGURE 17–25 Timing marks on both the cam gear (top) and the crankshaft gear (bottom) should align to time the camshaft to the crankshaft.

FIGURE 17–27 Typical slinger ring behind the front crankshaft oil seal.

All pistons should be tested in all cylinder bores. Even though all of the cylinders were honed to the exact same dimension and all pistons were machined to the same diameter, some variation in dimensions will occur. *Each piston should be selectively fitted to each cylinder.* This procedure helps to prevent mismatched assembled components and results in a better-performing and longer-lasting engine. By checking all cylinders, the technician is also assured that the machining of the block was done correctly.

When the clearance is too small, the size of the knurled piston can be reduced by lightly filing the knurled surface. The cylinder may have to be honed more to achieve the proper piston-to-cylinder clearance as illustrated in Figure 17–29. If the clearance is too great, the piston will have to be knurled more deeply (on a commercial engine) or it will have to be replaced with an oversize piston.

After the pistons have been fitted to each cylinder and the technician has ensured that no more machining of the block is necessary, the cam bearings and plugs should be installed.

RING END GAP

The bottom of the combustion chamber is sealed by the piston rings. They have to fit correctly in order to seal properly. Piston rings are checked both for side clearance and for gap, as discussed in chapter 14. Typical ring end gap measurements are about 0.004 inch per inch of cylinder bore as follows:

Piston diameter	Ring end gap
2 to 3 inches	0.007 to 0.018 inch
3 to 4 inches	0.010 to 0.020 inch
4 to 5 inches	0.013 to 0.023 inch

NOTE: If the gap is greater than recommended, some engine performance is lost. However, too small a gap will result in scuffing because of ring butting during operation, which forces the rings to scrape the cylinders.

If the ring gap is too large, the ring should be replaced with a ring having the next oversize diameter. If

FIGURE 17–28 Measuring the clearance between the piston and the cylinder wall with a strip thickness (feeler) gauge. There are no rings on the piston when this measurement is made.

the ring gap is too small, the ring should be removed and filed to make the gap larger. This is done by fastening a file in a vise. While both ends of the ring are held against the file, the ring is drawn along the file, as shown in Figure 17–30. In this way, metal is removed to increase the gap while the ring ends are kept parallel to maintain a square gap. The edges of the ring are stoned after filing to remove any sharp points that could scratch the piston or cylinder. The ring is frequently checked in the cylinder to bring the gap to the correct dimension. Install piston rings on pistons as per manufacturer's instructions. See Figures 17–31 and 17–32 for one method used by many engine and piston ring manufacturers.

INSTALLING PISTON AND ROD ASSEMBLIES

The cylinder is wiped with a lintless cleaning cloth. It is then given a liberal coating of clean engine oil. This oil is spread over the entire cylinder wall surface by hand.

The connecting rod bearings are prepared for assembly in the same way as are the main bearings. The piston is then inverted and sloshed around in clean petroleum-based cleaning fluid to remove all particles of dirt that may have gotten on it while the rings were being installed. The piston is air dried and then dipped in a bath of clean engine oil.

NOTE: Some overlapping (gapless) piston rings are installed dry, without oil. Some manufacturers recommend oiling only the oil control ring. Always check the piston ring instruction sheet for the exact procedure.

When the piston is lifted from the oil, it is held to drip for a few seconds. This allows the largest part of the oil to run out of the piston and ring grooves. The **piston ring compressor** is then put on the piston to hold the rings in their grooves. See Figures 17–33 and 17–34.

The bearing cap is removed from the rod, and protectors are placed over the rod bolts. The crankshaft is rotated so that the crankpin is at the *bottom* center. The upper rod bearing should be in the rod, and the piston should be turned so that the notch on the piston head is facing the front of the engine.

FIGURE 17–30   Method used to file the butt ends of a ring when the gap is too small.

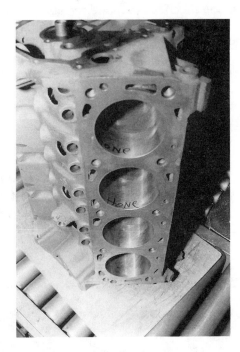

FIGURE 17–29   A V-8 block on an assembly line of an engine remanufacturer after it has been checked for piston-to-cylinder clearance. Note that the top two cylinders need some additional honing for proper clearance.

FIGURE 17–31   A good type of ring expander being used to install a piston ring.

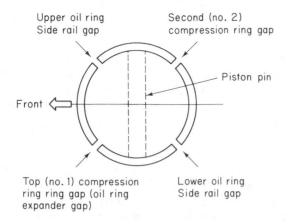

FIGURE 17-32 One method of piston ring installation. The location of ring gaps is shown here. Always follow the manufacturer's recommended method for the location of ring gaps and for ring gap spacing.

FIGURE 17-33 Dipping the piston, with rings installed into a container of engine oil is one method that can be used to ensure proper lubrication of pistons during installation in the engine cylinder. This method also ensures that the piston pin will be well lubricated.

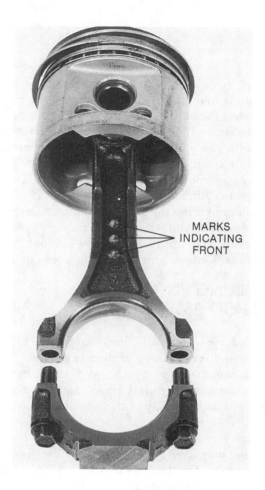

FIGURE 17-34 Before installing the pistons in a cylinder, double-check to make certain that the piston and rod assembly is facing in the correct direction. Most pistons have a V notch on the piston head to indicate the front of the engine. The marks on this connecting rod indicate the front.

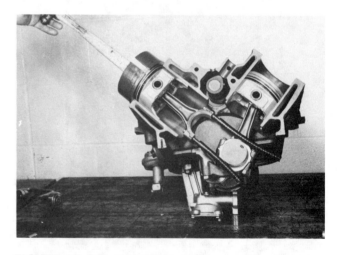

FIGURE 17-35 Installing a piston and rod assembly using a cast-iron ring compressor and placing short pieces of hose over the connecting rod bolts.

NOTE: If the piston does not have a notch or a "front" stamp on the piston, install the piston so that the valve reliefs end up being closest to the lifter valley on a V-type OHV engine. Also, be sure to install the piston in the correct bore and check to make sure that the larger valve relief aligns with the intake valve location. _____

The piston and rod assembly is placed in the cylinder through the block deck. The ring compressor must be kept tightly against the block deck as the piston is pushed into the cylinder. This procedure is illustrated on a cutaway V-type engine in Figure 17–35. The ring compressor holds the rings in their grooves so that they will enter the cylinder. Care should be taken to make sure that the rod or the bolts do not hit the cylinder wall or the crankpin journal. If they hit, they will cause a small nick. The nick will cause scoring. The piston is pushed into the cylinder until the rod bearing is fully seated on the journal. See Figures 17–36 through 17–38. The rod cap, with the bearing in place, is put on the rod. There are two methods that can be used to check for proper connecting rod clearance. Method #1 involves using Plastigage following the same procedure discussed for main bearing clearance. Using method #2 the retaining nuts or cap screws are installed and tightened only finger tight at this time. All of the piston assemblies should be installed before any of the connecting rod retaining nuts or cap screws are further tightened.

NOTE: Be certain to check for piston-to-crankshaft counterweight clearance. Most manufacturers specify a minimum 0.060 inch (1.5 millimeters). _____

TIGHTENING PROCEDURE FOR ROD BEARINGS

Check and record the torque required to rotate the crankshaft with all of the piston rings dragging on the cylinder walls. Next, the retaining nuts on one bearing should be torqued; then the torque required to rotate the crankshaft should be rechecked and recorded. Follow the same procedure on all of the rod bearings. If tightening any one of the rod bearing caps causes a large increase in the torque required to rotate the crankshaft, immediately stop the tightening process. Determine the cause of the increased rotating torque using the same method as was used on the main bearings. When all of the rod bearing retaining bolts are properly torqued, the total increase in the crankshaft turning torque should not be more than 5 pound-feet above the torque first recorded with the rod bearing retaining bolts finger tight.

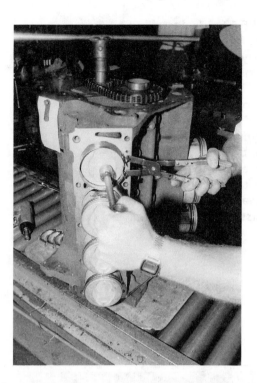

FIGURE 17–36 *Piston being installed in a cylinder on a production line of an engine remanufacturer. Crankshaft protectors have been installed on connecting rod bolts. Note the T handle on the crankshaft used to rotate the engine as pistons are installed.*

Rotate the crankshaft for several revolutions to make sure that the assembly is turning freely and that there are no tight spots. The bottom of the engine is then ready for final assembly.

ROTATING FORCE

Adjustment of the connecting rod oil clearance follows the same procedure that was used to adjust the oil clearance of the main bearings. The rotating torque of the crankshaft with all connecting rod cap bolts fully torqued should be as follows:

- Four-cylinder engine: 20 pound-feet maximum
- Six-cylinder engine: 25 pound-feet maximum
- Eight-cylinder engine: 30 pound-feet maximum

CONNECTING ROD SIDE CLEARANCE

The connecting rods should be checked to make sure that they still have the correct side clearance. This is measured by fitting the correct thickness of feeler

FIGURE 17–37 Installing a piston in a cylinder using a band-type ring compressor. The ring compressor should cover the area near the rings only. The lower part of the piston is already in the cylinder. If everything is well lubricated and the ring compressor is tight, one good tap with the handle of a hammer should install the piston in the cylinder.

FIGURE 17–38 Two commercially available connecting rod bolt protectors of different lengths. After the piston is installed, the protectors can be removed and the rod cap installed.

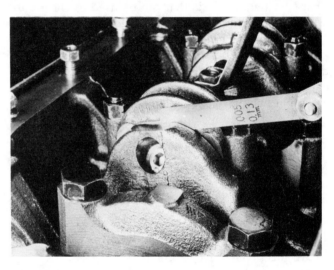

FIGURE 17–39 The connecting rod side clearance is measured with a thickness (feeler) gauge.

gauge between the connecting rod and the crankshaft cheek of the bearing journal (Figure 17–39). A dial gauge can also be set up to measure the connecting rod side clearance.

■ If the side clearance is too great, excessive amounts of oil may escape that can cause lower than normal oil pressure. To correct excessive clearance:

1. Weld and regrind or replace the crankshaft.
2. The connecting rods may be too thin or mismatched. Carefully measure all connecting rods and replace those that are too thin.

■ If the side clearance is too small, there may not be enough room for heat expansion. To correct a side clearance that is too small:

1. Regrind the crankshaft.
2. Replace the rods.

FIGURE 17–40 Fixture being used to hold bucket-type cam followers down as the camshaft is being slid endways into the cam bearings on an overhead cam engine.

INSTALLING THE CAMSHAFT FOR OVERHEAD CAM ENGINES

The camshaft is usually installed on overhead cam engines before the head is fastened to the block deck. Some engines have the camshaft located directly over the valves. The cam bearings on these engines can be either one piece or split. A fixture is required on one type of engine that has a one-piece cam bearing to hold the valves open as the cam is slid endways into the cam bearings. This is shown in Figure 17–40. The cam bearings and journals are lubricated before assembly. In other engine types, the camshaft bearings are split to allow the camshaft to be installed without the valves being depressed. The caps are tightened evenly to avoid bending the camshaft. The valve clearance or lash is checked with the overhead camshaft in place. Some bucket-type cam followers can be adjusted by turning a wedge-shaped screw with an internal hex wrench (Figure 17–41). Others have shims under a follower disk. One example of this type can be seen in Figure 17–42. On these, the camshaft is turned so that the follower is on the base circle of the cam. The clearance of each bucket follower can then be checked with a feeler gauge. The amount of clearance is recorded and compared to the specified clearance. The cam is then removed, and shims of the required thickness are put in the top of the bucket followers. If the clearances are within specifications, the cylinder head is ready to be installed.

The follower pivot should be put in place after the cam is installed on the finger follower type of overhead cam mechanism. Each valve spring is slightly depressed

FIGURE 17–41 Cam follower adjustment being made by turning a wedge-shaped screw with a hex (Allen) wrench.

■ DIAGNOSTIC STORY ■

THE NEW OIL PUMP THAT FAILED

A technician replaced the oil pump and screen on a V-8 with low oil pressure. After the repair, the oil pressure returned to normal for 2 weeks, but then the oil pressure light came on and the valve train started making noise. The vehicle owner returned to the service garage where the oil pump had been replaced. The technician removed the oil pan and pump. The screen was almost completely clogged with the RTV sealant that the technician had used to "seal" the oil pan gasket. The technician had failed to read the instructions that came with the oil pan gasket. Failure to follow directions and using too much of the wrong sealer cost the repair shop an expensive comeback repair.

to install the finger follower. This can be done with a special lever tool designed for this job, or it can be done using a common valve spring compressor and a flat plate across the combustion chamber. Mechanical pivots must be adjusted to provide the specific clearance or lash while the follower is on the base circle of the cam. Hydraulic pivots will automatically adjust to zero clearance.

FIGURE 17–42 Split-type cam bearings on an overhead cam engine using bucket-type cam followers. One bucket follower is removed to show the valve tip, retainer, and locks (keepers).

HEAD GASKETS

The head gasket is under the highest clamping loads. It must seal passages that carry coolant with antifreeze that is designed to penetrate a surface to pick up the heat. It is often required to seal a passage that carries hot oil with detergent and dispersant additives that are designed to soak into and capture any foreign materials. The most demanding job of the head gasket is to seal the combustion chamber. As a rule of thumb, about 75% of the head bolt clamping force is used to seal the combustion chamber. The remaining 25% seals the coolant and oil passages.

The gasket must seal when the temperature is as low as 40° below zero and as high as 400° F (204° C). The combustion pressures can get up to 1000 psi (6900 kPa) on gasoline engines and up to 2300 psi (16,000 kPa) on turbocharged diesel engines. Diesel engine head gaskets must seal almost 2½ times the pressure they are required to seal on gasoline engines. Diesel engines need a more complex head gasket to seal these very high combustion pressures.

Cylinder head bolts are tightened to a specified torque. This stretches the bolt. The combustion pressure tries to push the head upward and the piston downward on the power stroke. This puts additional stress on the head bolts, and it reduces the clamping load on the head gasket just when the greatest seal is needed. On a normally aspirated engine (without turbocharging), a partial vacuum on the intake stroke tries

to pull the head more tightly against the gasket. As the crankshaft rotates, the force on the head changes from pressure on the combustion stroke to vacuum on the intake stroke, then back to pressure. Modern engines have lightweight thin-wall castings. The castings are quite flexible, so that they move as the pressure in the combustion chamber changes from high pressure to vacuum. The gasket must be able to compress and recover fast enough to maintain a seal as the pressure in the combustion chamber changes back and forth between pressure and vacuum. As a result, the modern head gasket is made of a number of different materials assembled in a number of different ways for different models of engines.

Sandwich Head Gaskets

Older engines used a **sandwich** head gasket with metal facings and a soft asbestos fiber core. See Figure 17–43. The metal face required a relatively smooth sealing surface.

Perforated Steel Core Gaskets

Another older gasket design has a soft facing on the outside of a **perforated core.** See Figure 17–44. Both this gasket and the sandwich head gasket have thick, soft fibers. These fibers compress and relax after the engine is run. This reduces the resilience of the gasket, resulting in a lower clamping force or torque of the bolts and less sealability of the gasket. As a result, these gaskets must be *retorqued* after the engine is first run and cooled

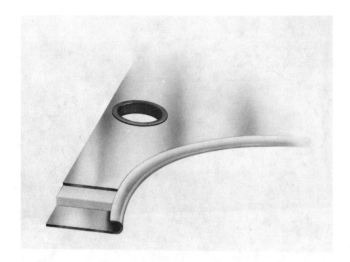

FIGURE 17–43 Sandwich-type head gasket. (Courtesy of Fel-Pro Incorporated)

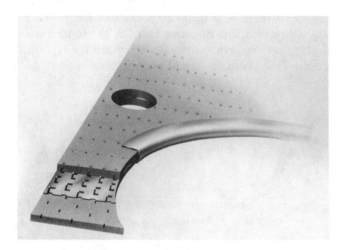

FIGURE 17–44 Perforated steel core head gasket. (Courtesy of Fel-Pro Incorporated)

back to room temperature following reassembly. They are retorqued again after 500 to 1000 miles (800 to 1600 kilometers) of operation. Retorquing is expensive to do on modern overhead valve or overhead cam engines because so much labor is needed to disassemble part of the engine to reach the head bolts. As a result, the gasket industry developed no-retorque gaskets.

Embossed Gaskets
The first no-retorque gasket was the **embossed steel shim** gasket (see Figure 17–45) made from steel from 0.015 to 0.021 inch (0.4 to 0.5 millimeter) thick.

The embossed beads are from 0.06 to 0.1 inch (1.5 to 2.5 millimeters) wide and from 0.007 to 0.03 inch (0.17 to 0.7 millimeter) high. Shim gaskets may be coated with aluminum or with a plastic to aid in seal-

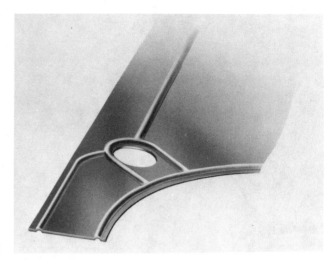

FIGURE 17–45 Embossed steel head gasket. (Courtesy of Fel-Pro Incorporated)

ing. They have no resilient fiber so they do not relax. Shim gaskets require smooth sealing surfaces because there are no fibers to conform to sealing surface roughness. Shim gaskets also require a flat sealing surface because the steel cannot compensate for slight warpage of the head and block deck. The steel shim gasket makes a good original equipment gasket when manufacturers use smooth, flat sealing surfaces. The shim gasket is *not* a good aftermarket gasket because used engines will usually have some warpage and often have rough sealing surfaces. Even if the warpage is removed by machining, often the resurfacing does not give a finish as smooth as the original finish.

Improved Perforated Steel Core Gaskets
Limitations of the no-retorque shim head gasket as an aftermarket gasket have been overcome by improving on the perforated steel core gasket. These gaskets are made with a much thinner, more dense facing material. For example, they might use aramid fibers with clay and synthetic bonders or **expanded graphite.** *Retorquing requirements depend on the density and thickness of the facing material.* The latest designs relax so little that they make good no-retorque head gaskets. A variation of this gasket design uses a **wire mesh core.** Another no-retorque design has rubber-fiber facings cemented to a **solid steel core** with an adhesive. See Figure 17–46. The thickness of the gasket is controlled by the thickness of the metal core. The thin, dense rubber-fiber facings relax very little, so retorquing is not required. The facing is thick enough to compensate for minor warpage and surface defects.

The fiber facing is protected around the combustion chamber with a metal **fire ring** or **armor.** See Figure 17–47.

FIGURE 17–46   Permatorque head gasket. (Courtesy of Fel-Pro Incorporated)

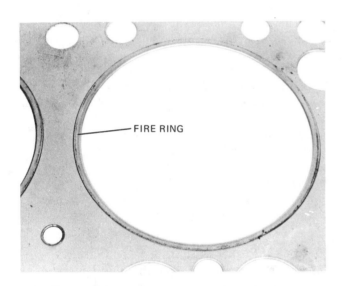

FIGURE 17–47   Head gasket with a fire ring.

FIRE RING

FIGURE 17–48   As a final check before installing a cylinder head, draw a file sideways across the head surface. Any burrs or nicks will be indicated by a bright spot. Because the file is being drawn lightly across the surface, no material is being removed except for small high spots.

FIGURE 17–49   Typical head gasket markings.

The metal also increases the gasket thickness around the cylinder so that it uses up to 75% of the clamping force and forms a tight combustion seal.

Multilayered Steel Gaskets

Multilayered steel (MLS) is being used from the factory on many newer engine designs such as the overhead camshaft Ford V-8s. The many layers of thin steel reduce bore and overhead camshaft distortion with less clamping force loss than previous designs. The use of multilayered steel gaskets also reduces the torque requirement and therefore reduces the stresses on the fasteners and engine block.

INSTALLING THE HEAD GASKET

The block deck and head surfaces should be rechecked for any handling nicks that could cause a gasket leak. All tapped holes should be cleaned with the correct-size bottoming tap to remove any dirt or burrs. See Figure 17–48. There are usually alignment pins or dowels at the front and rear of the block deck to position the gasket and head. Care should be taken to properly position any head gasket with markings (up, top, front, and so forth). See Figure 17–49. The gasket and head are placed on the block deck. All the head bolts are loosely installed. Very often, the head bolts have differ-

■ TECH TIP ■

WATCH OUT FOR WET AND DRY HOLES

Many engines, such as the small-block Chevrolet V-8, use head bolts that extend through the top deck of the block and end in a coolant passage. These bolt holes are called **wet holes**. Whenever head bolts that end up in the coolant passage are being installed, sealer must be used on the threads of the head bolt. Some engines have head bolts that are "wet," whereas others are "dry" because they end in solid cast-iron material. Dry hole bolts do not require sealant, but they still require some oil on the *threads* of the bolts for lubrication. Do not put oil into a dry hole because the bolt may bottom out in the oil. The liquid oil cannot compress, so the force of the bolt being tightened is transferred to the block by hydraulic force, which can crack the block.

ent lengths. Make sure that a bolt of the correct length is put into each location.

Put sealer on the threads of the assembly bolts that go into the cooling system. Put antiseize compound on bolts that hold the exhaust manifold. Lightly oil the threads of bolts that go into blind holes. See the tech tip Watch Out for Wet and Dry Holes.

NOTE: Most manufacturers recommend putting oil on the threads of bolts during reassembly. Lubricated threads will give as much as 50% more clamping force at the same bolt torque than threads that are tightened dry.

HEAD BOLT TORQUE SEQUENCE

The torque put on the bolts is used to control the clamping force. The clamping force is correct only when the threads are clean and properly lubricated. In general, the head bolts are tightened in a specified torque sequence in three steps. By tightening the head bolts in three steps, the head gasket has time to compress and conform to the block disk and cylinder head gasket surface. Follow that sequence and tighten the bolts to *one-third* the specified torque. Tighten them a second time

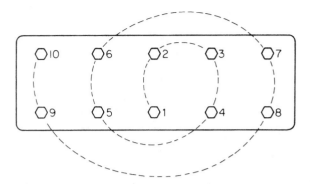

FIGURE 17–50 Typical cylinder head tightening sequence.

following the torque sequence to *two-thirds* the specified torque. Follow the sequence with a final tightening to the specified torque. See Figure 17–50.

TORQUE-TO-YIELD BOLTS

For years many diesel engines used a tightening procedure called the **torque-to-yield** or **torque-angle** method. It was first used on some bimetallic engines in the late 1970s. By the mid-1980s, it was being used on all the new engine designs. The purpose of the torque-to-yield procedure is to have a more constant clamping load from bolt to bolt. This aids in head gasket sealing performance and eliminates the need for retorquing. The torque-to-yield head bolts are made with a narrow section between the head and threads. As the bolts are tightened past their elastic limit, they yield and begin to stretch in this narrow section.

Torque-to-yield head bolts will not become any tighter once they reach this elastic limit, as you can see on the graph in Figure 17–51.

As a result, many engine manufacturers specify *new* head bolts each time the head is installed. If these bolts are reused, they are likely to break during assembly or fail prematurely as the engine runs. If there is any doubt about the head bolts, replace them.

Torque-to-yield bolts are tightened to a specific initial torque, from 18 to 50 pound-feet (25 to 68 Newton-meter [N-m]). The bolts are then tightened a specified number of degrees, following the tightening sequence. In some cases they are turned a specified number of degrees two or three times. The torque-to-yield method is also called the **torque-turn method** because it involves torquing the bolt and then turning it a specified number of degrees. Some specifications limit the maximum torque that can be applied to the bolt while the degree turn is being made. Torque tables in a service manual will show how much initial

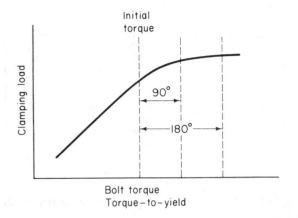

FIGURE 17–51 Due to variations in clamping force with turning force (torque) of head bolts, some engines are specifying the torque-to-yield procedure. The first step is to torque the bolts by an even amount called the initial torque. Final clamping load is achieved by turning the bolt a specified number of degrees. Bolt stretch provides the proper clamping force.

torque should be applied to the bolt and how many degrees the bolt should be rotated after torquing. See Figure 17–52.

TIMING DRIVES FOR OVERHEAD CAM ENGINES

With the head bolts properly torqued, the cam drive should be installed on overhead cam engines. This is done by aligning the timing marks of the crankshaft and camshaft drive sprockets with their respective timing marks. The location of these marks differs between engines, but the marks can be identified by looking carefully at the sprockets. The timing belt or chain must be tight on the left side of the engine. The crankshaft sprocket pulls the cam sprocket around from this side. It is on your right as you look at the front of the engine. This can be seen in Figure 17–53. The tightening idler may be on either or both sides of the timing belt or chain. After the camshaft drive is engaged, rotate the crankshaft through two full revolutions. On the first full revolution, you should see the exhaust valve almost close and the intake valve just starting to open when the *crankshaft* timing mark aligns. At the end of the second revolution, both valves should be closed, and all the timing marks should align on most engines. This is the position the crankshaft should have when cylinder #1 is to fire.

NOTE: Always check the manufacturer's recommended timing chain installation procedure.

Engines that use primary and secondary timing chains often require an exact detailed procedure for proper installation.

LIFTER AND PUSHROD INSTALLATION

The outside of the lifters and the lifter bores in the block should be cleaned and coated with assembly lubricant. The lifters are installed in the lifter bores and the pushrods put in place. There are different-length pushrods on some engines. Make sure that the pushrods are installed in the proper location. The rocker arms are then put in place, aligning with the valves and pushrods. Rocker arm shafts should have their retaining bolts tightened a little at a time, alternating between the retaining bolts. This keeps the shaft from bending as the rocker arm pushes some of the valves open.

HYDRAULIC LIFTERS

The retaining nut on some rocker arms mounted on studs can be tightened to a specified torque. The rocker arm will be adjusted correctly at this torque when the valve tip has the correct height. Other types of rocker arms require tightening the nut to a position that will center the hydraulic lifter. The general procedure for adjusting the hydraulic lifter types is to tighten the retaining nut to the point that all of the free lash is gone. The lifter plunger starts to move down after the lash is gone. From this point, the retaining nut is tightened by a specified amount, such as three-fourths of a turn or one and one-half turns.

HINT: *This method usually results in about three threads showing above the adjusting nut on a stock small-block Chevrolet V-8 equipped with flat-bottom hydraulic lifters.*

SOLID LIFTERS

The valve clearance or **lash** must be set on a solid lifter engine. This is required so that the valves can positively seat. Some service manuals give an adjustment sequence to follow to set the lash. If this is not available, then the following procedure can be used on all engines requiring valve lash adjustment. The valve lash is adjusted with the valves completely closed. The crankshaft is rotated in the normal direction until both valves of cylinder #1 are closed and the timing marks on the damper align with the top dead center indicator.

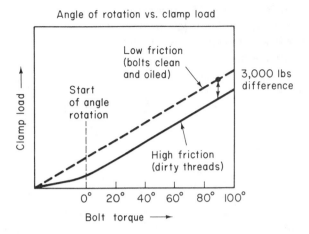

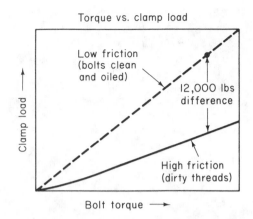

FIGURE 17–52 To ensure consistent clamp force (load), many manufacturers are recommending the torque-angle or torque-to-yield method of tightening head bolts. The torque-angle method specifies tightening fasteners to a low torque setting and then giving an additional angle of rotation. Notice that the difference in clamping force is much smaller than it would be if just a torque wrench with dirty threads were used.

FIGURE 17–53 *Timing belt that drives the cam and auxiliary shaft.*

Both valves are on the base circle of their cam lobes, so the valves are completely closed. If the valve lash given in the manual is specificly for an operating engine, the valve lash on a cold engine should initially be adjusted to be 0.002 inch (0.05 millimeter) *greater* than the operating valve lash specification. This cold valve lash adjustment will result in an operating valve lash very near the specified valve lash after the engine has been warmed. See Figure 17–54.

After the valve lash on cylinder #1 is set, the crankshaft is rotated in its normal direction of rotation to the next cylinder in the firing order. This is done by turning the crankshaft 90 degrees on eight-cylinder engines, 120 degrees on even-firing six-cylinder engines, and 180 degrees on four-cylinder engines. The valves on this next cylinder are adjusted in the same manner as were those on cylinder #1. This procedure is repeated on each cylinder *following the engine firing order* until all the valves have been adjusted. The service technician will usually go through the valve lash check a second time to make sure that the lash has been adjusted correctly.

The same valve lash adjustment sequence is used on overhead cam engines. Those engines with rocker arms or with adjustable finger follower pivots are adjusted in the same way as are pushrod engines with rocker arms. Engines with bucket cam followers have a different adjustment procedure. Some are adjusted by placing a shim with the correct thickness in the shim pocket. See Figure 17–55. Others are adjusted with a tapered adjusting screw.

FIGURE 17–54 Checking the valve lash (clearance) on an exhaust valve of an overhead camshaft engine.

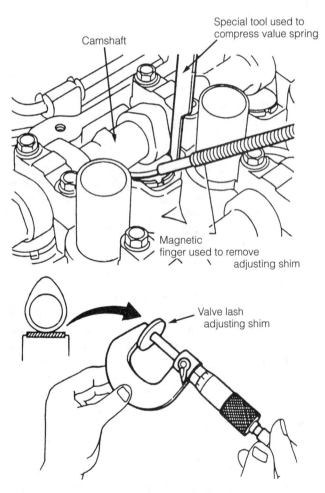

FIGURE 17–55 Some overhead camshaft engines use valve lash adjusting shims to adjust the valve lash. A special tool is usually required to compress the valve spring so that a magnet can remove the shim.

ASSEMBLY SEALANTS

RTV silicone is used by most technicians in sealing engines. **RTV,** or **room-temperature vulcanization** means that the silicone rubber material will cure at room temperature. It is not really the temperature that causes RTV silicone to cure, but the moisture in the air. RTV silicone cures to a tack-free state in about 45 minutes. It takes 24 hours to fully cure.

There are two types of RTV silicone:

1. The acetic acid type is volatile and causes corrosion. It should *not* be used in engine sealing. The vapors coming from the silicone go through the PCV system, through the intake system, and eventually out of the exhaust. This type of RTV will damage the oxygen sensor.
2. Amine-type silicone has low volatility and is the type that can be used for engine sealing without harming oxygen sensors.

RTV silicone is available in a number of different colors. The color identifies the special blend within a manufacturer's product line. Equal grades of silicone made by different manufacturers may have different colors. RTV silicone can be used in two ways in engine sealing:

1. It can be used as a gasket substitute between a stamped cover and a cast surface.
2. It is used to fill gaps or potential gaps. A joint between gaskets or between a gasket and a seal is a potential gap.

NOTE: RTV silicone should never be used around fuel because the fuel will cut right through it. Silicone should not be used as a sealer on gaskets. It will

FIGURE 17–56 Improperly sealed rocker cover (valve cover) gasket. Note the use of RTV silicone sealant on a cork-rubber gasket. The cover bolts were also overtightened, which deformed the metal cover around the bolt holes.

squeeze out to leave a bead inside and a bead outside the flange. The inside bead might fall into the engine, plugging passages and causing engine damage. The thin film still remaining on the gasket stays uncured, just as it would be in the original tube. The uncured silicone is likely to let the gasket or seal slip out of place. See Figure 17–56. ⎯⎯⎯⎯⎯⎯⎯⎯⎯⎯⎯⎯

Anaerobic sealers are sealers that cure in the absence of air. They are used as thread lockers (such as Loctite), and they are used to seal rigid machined joints between cast parts. Anaerobic sealers lose their sealing ability at temperatures above 300° F (149° C). On production lines, the curing process is speeded up by using ultraviolet light.

When the anaerobic sealer is used on threads, air does not get to it, so it hardens to form a seal to prevent the fastener from loosening. Teflon is added to some anaerobic sealers to seal fluids better. Anaerobic sealers can be used to seal machined surfaces without a gasket. The surfaces *must* be thoroughly clean to get a good seal. Special primers are recommended for use on the sealing surface to get a better bond with anaerobic sealers.

INSTALLING MANIFOLDS

The intake manifold gasket for a V-type engine may be a one-piece gasket or it may have several pieces. V-type engines with open-type manifolds have a cover over the lifter valley. The cover may be a separate part or it may be part of a one-piece intake manifold gasket.

Closed-type intake manifolds on V-type engines require gasket pieces at the front and rear of the intake manifold. Inline engines usually have a one-piece intake manifold gasket.

The intake manifold is put in place over the gaskets. Use a contact adhesive to hold the gasket and end seal if there is a chance they might slip out of place. Just before the manifold is installed, put a spot of RTV silicone on each of the four joints between the intake manifold gasket and end seals. The correct-length manifold bolts are installed. The bolts are tightened to the specified torque following the tightening sequence given in the applicable service manual.

Some exhaust manifolds do not use gaskets; others do. The gaskets and exhaust manifolds are installed. The exhaust manifold operates at very high temperatures, so there is usually some expansion and contraction movement in the manifold-to-head joint. It is very important to use attachment bolts, cap screws, and clamps of the correct type and length. They must be properly torqued to avoid both leakage and cracks.

NOTE: When the exhaust manifold gasket has facing on one side, put the facing toward the head and let the manifold rest against the metal side of the gasket. ⎯⎯

COVER GASKET MATERIALS

The gasket must be **impermeable** to the fluids it is designed to seal in or out. The gasket must *conform* to the shape of the surface, and it must be **resilient,** or elastic, to maintain the sealing force as it is compressed. Gaskets work best when they are compressed about 30%.

Cork Gaskets

Cork is the bark from a Mediterranean evergreen oak tree. It is made of very small, flexible, fourteen-sided, air-filled fiber cells, about 0.001 inch (0.025 millimeter) in size. The air-filled cells act like a pneumatic system. This gives resiliency to the cork gasket until the air leaks out. Because cork is mostly wood, it expands when it gets wet and shrinks when it dries. This causes cork gaskets to change in size when they are in storage and while they are installed in the engine. Oil gradually wicks through the organic binder of the cork, so a cork gasket often looks like it is leaking. Problems with cork gaskets led the gasket industry to develop cork cover gaskets using synthetic rubber as a binder for the cork. The synthetic rubber seals the cork grains so that they are not affected by changes in humidity, and it prevents oil wicking. These cork-rubber gaskets are easy to use, and they outlast the old cork gaskets. See Figure 17–57.

■ TECH TIP ■

THE RIGHT REPAIR, WRONG SEALANT

A technician replaced the rocker cover gasket on a four-cylinder engine. The technician used a popular brand of RTV silicone sealant, replacing the factory formed-in-place gasket material. The repair was completed quickly and correctly, and it did not leak.

Two weeks later, the owner returned, complaining of poor engine operation (stumbling, stalling, and poor fuel economy) and a "check engine" light coming on. The diagnostic procedure revealed a defective (contaminated) oxygen sensor. The technician had used the wrong type of RTV silicone. The fumes of the silicone sealant were drawn into the intake manifold through the positive crankcase ventilation system and burned in the cylinders. The by-products of this combustion formed silicon deposits on the oxygen sensor. To prevent oxygen sensor damage, always make certain to use a silicone product that states on the container that it is safe for use on newer vehicles and/or safe for oxygen sensors.

FIGURE 17–57   Left to right: cork-rubber, paper, composite, and synthetic rubber (elastomer) gaskets.

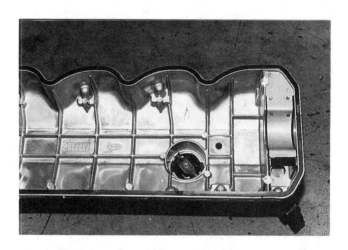

FIGURE 17–58   Typical cast-aluminum cam (valve) cover. Note the rubber gasket in the cast groove of the cover.

Fiber Gaskets

Some oil pans use fiber gaskets. Covers with higher clamping forces use gaskets with fibers that have greater density. For example, timing covers may have either fiber or paper gaskets.

Synthetic Rubber Gaskets

Molded, oil-resistant synthetic rubber is being used in more applications to seal covers. When it is compounded correctly, it forms a superior cover gasket. It operates at high temperatures for a longer period of time than does a cork-rubber cover gasket. See Figure 17–58.

Sealers

Sealers are nonhardening materials. Examples of sealer trade names include Form-A-Gasket 2, Pli-A-Seal, Tight Seal 2, Aviation Form-A-Gasket, Brush Tack, Copper Coat, Spray Tack, and High Tack. Sealers are always used to seal the threads of bolts that break into coolant passages. Sealers for sealing threads may include Teflon. Sealer is often recommended for use on shim-type head gaskets and intake manifold gaskets. These gaskets have a metal surface that does not conform to any small amounts of surface roughness on the

sealing surface. The sealer fills the surface variations between the gasket and the sealing surface.

Sealer may be used as a sealing aid on paper and fiber gaskets if the gasket needs help with sealing on a scratched, corroded, or rough surface finish. The sealer may be used on one side or on both sides of the gasket. Sealer should *never* be used on rubber or cork-rubber gaskets. Instead of holding the rubber gasket or seal, it will help the rubber to slip out of place because the sealer will never harden.

Antiseize Compounds

Antiseize compounds are used on fasteners in the engine that are subjected to high temperatures to prevent seizing galvanic action between dissimilar metals. These compounds minimize corrosion from moisture. Exhaust manifold bolts and nuts, oxygen sensors, and spark plugs, especially those that go into aluminum heads, are kept from seizing. The antiseize compound minimizes the chance of threads being pulled or breaking as the oxygen sensor or spark plug is removed.

HINTS FOR GASKET USAGE

Never reuse an old gasket. A used gasket or seal has already been compressed, has lost some of its resilience, and has taken a set. If a used gasket does reseal, it will not seal as well as a new gasket or seal.

A gasket should be checked to make sure it is the correct gasket. Also check the list on the outside of the gasket set to make sure that the set has all of the gaskets that may be needed *before* the package is opened.

An instruction sheet is included with most gaskets. It includes a review of the things the technician should do to prepare and install the gaskets to give the best chance of a good seal. The instruction sheet also includes special tips on how to seal spots that are difficult to seal or that require special care to seal on a particular engine.

INSTALLING TIMING COVERS

Most timing covers are installed with a gasket, but some use RTV sealer in place of the gasket. Cast covers use anaerobic compound as a gasket substitute. In either case, it is very important that any oil passages between the cover and the block be properly sealed. An air leak between the oil screen in the block and the inlet passage going to an oil pump in the timing cover will keep the oil pump from building up oil pressure. Air will be pulled into the pump, rather than oil being pulled from the oil pan. Leaks in the pressure passage from the oil pump will reduce the amount of oil available to the lubricating system. If the leak is external, it will show up on the outside of the engine. A bead of RTV silicone ⅛ to ³⁄₁₆ inch in diameter is put on the clean sealing surface (see Figure 17–59).

Encircle the bolt holes with the sealant. Install the cover before the silicone begins to cure so that the uncured silicone bonds to both surfaces. While installing the cover, do not touch the silicone bead; otherwise, the bead might be displaced, causing a leak. Carefully press the cover into place. Do not slide the cover after it is in place. Install the assembly bolts finger tight, and let the silicone cure for about 30 minutes, then torque the cover bolts.

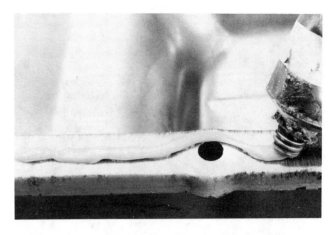

FIGURE 17–59   A ⅛- to ³⁄₁₆-inch (3- to 5-millimeters) bead of RTV silicone on a parting surface with silicone going around the bolt hole.

The gasket or sealant is put on the gasket surface of the timing cover. A light coat of assembly lubricant is wiped on the oil seal and damper hub for initial lubrication. The timing cover is put in place, and the assembly bolts are installed loosely until after the vibration damper has been installed. The hub of the vibration damper will properly position the timing cover by centering the front oil seal. The damper is placed on the crankshaft, making sure that the drive key is aligned with the slot in the hub. After the hub is on the crankshaft, the timing cover assembly bolts can be tightened to the specified torque.

INSTALLING THE VIBRATION DAMPER

Vibration dampers are seated in place by one of three methods. First, the damper hub of some engines is pulled into place using the hub attaching bolt. The second method uses a special installing tool that screws into the attaching bolt hole to pull the hub into place. The tool is removed and the attaching bolt installed and torqued. The last method is used on engines that have no attaching bolt. These hubs depend on a press-fit to hold the hub on the crankshaft. The hub is seated using a hammer and a special tube-type driver.

INSTALLING THE OIL PUMP

When an engine is rebuilt, the oil pump is replaced with a new pump. This ensures positive lubrication and long pump life.

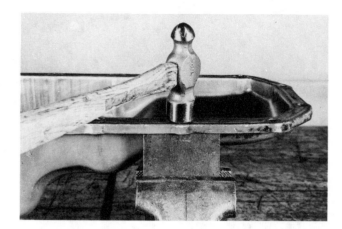

FIGURE 17–60 *Using a hammer to straighten the gasket rail surface before installing a new gasket. When the retaining bolts are tightened, some distortion of sheet-metal covers occurs. If the area around the bolt holes is not straightened, leaks can occur with the new gasket.*

The space between the oil pump gears is filled with assembly lubricant before the cover is put on the pump. This provides initial lubrication, and it primes the pump so that it will draw the oil from the pan when the lubrication system is first operated.

THE OIL PAN

The oil pan should be checked and straightened as necessary. See Figure 17–60. With the oil pump in place, the oil pan gaskets are properly positioned. A spot of RTV silicone is placed at each gasket joint just before the pan is installed. The oil pan is carefully placed over the gaskets. All of the oil pan bolts should be started into their holes before any are tightened. The bolts should be alternately snugged up; then they should be properly torqued.

INSTALLING THE COOLANT PUMP

A reconditioned, rebuilt, or new coolant pump should be used. Gaskets are fitted in place. The pump is secured with assembly bolts tightened to the correct torque.

A new thermostat is usually installed at this time. It is put in place, with care being taken to place the correct side of the thermostat toward the engine. The thermostat gasket is put in place. Sealers are used on the gasket where they are required. The thermostat housing is installed, and the retaining bolts are tightened to the proper torque.

■ TECH TIP ■

OIL PUMP PRECAUTIONS

The oil pump is the heart of any engine, and any failure of the oil circulation system often results in severe and major engine damage. To help prevent possible serious oil pump related failures, many engine builders recommend the following precautions:

1. Always be sure that the oil pump pickup tube (screen) is securely attached to the oil pump to prevent the pickup tube from vibrating out of the pump.
2. Use modeling clay to check pickup screen-to-oil pan clearance. For proper operation, there should be about ¼ inch (6 millimeters) between the oil pump pickup screen and the bottom of the oil pan.

ENGINE PAINTING

Painting an engine helps prevent rust and corrosion and makes the engine look new. See Figure 17–61.

Standard engine paints with original engine colors are usually available at the parts stores. Engine paints should be used rather than other types of paints. Engine paints are compounded to stay on the metal as the engine temperatures change. Normal engine fluids will not remove them. These paints are usually purchased in pressure cans so that they can be sprayed from the can directly onto the engine.

All parts that should not be painted must be covered before spray painting. This can be done with old parts, such as old spark plugs and old gaskets. This can also be done by taping paper over the areas to be covered. If the intake manifold of an inline engine is to be painted, it can be painted separately. Engine assembly can continue after the paint has dried.

CHECKING FOR PROPER OIL PRESSURE

With oil in the engine and the distributor out of the engine, oil pressure should be established before the engine is started. This can be done on most engines by rotating the oil pump by hand. This ensures that oil is delivered to all parts of the engine before the engine is started. A socket speed handle makes an ideal crank for turning the oil pump. A flat-blade adapter that fits the

FIGURE 17–61 Partially assembled engine being spray painted at an engine remanufacturing plant.

FIGURE 17–62 Drivers used to rotate oil pumps to prelubricate all parts of the engine before installing the distributor and starting the engine.

■ DIAGNOSTIC STORY ■

"OOPS"

After overhauling a big-block Ford V-8 engine, the technician used an electric drill to rotate the oil pump with a pressure gauge connected to the oil pressure sending unit hole. When the electric drill was turned on, oil pressure would start to increase (to about 10 psi), then drop to zero. Also, the oil was very aerated (full of air). Replacing the oil pump did not solve the problem. After hours of troubleshooting and disassembly, it was discovered that an oil gallery plug had been left out underneath the intake manifold. The oil pump was working correctly and pumped oil throughout the engine and out of the end of the unplugged oil gallery. It did not take long for the oil pan to empty; therefore, the oil pump began drawing in air that aerated the oil and the oil pressure dropped. Installing the gallery plug solved the problem. It was smart of the technician to check the oil pressure before starting the engine. This oversight of leaving out one gallery plug could have resulted in a ruined engine shortly after the engine was started.

NOTE: Many overhead camshaft engines use an oil passage check valve in the block near the deck. The purpose of this valve is to hold oil in the cylinder head around the camshaft and lifters when the engine is stopped. Failure to reinstall this check valve can cause the valve train to be noisy after engine start-up.

speed handle will operate on General Motors engines. The V-type Chrysler engine requires the use of the same flat-blade adapter, but it also requires an oil pump drive. One can be made by removing the gear from an old oil pump hex drive shaft. A ¼-inch drive socket can be used on Ford engines. Examples of these are pictured in Figure 17–62. Engines that do not drive the oil pump with the distributor will have to be cranked with the spark plugs removed to establish oil pressure. The load on the starter and battery is reduced with the spark plugs out so that the engine will have a higher cranking speed.

SETTING INITIAL IGNITION TIMING

After oil pressure is established, the distributor can be installed (if the engine is so equipped). Rotate the crankshaft in its normal direction of rotation until there is compression on cylinder #1. This can be done with the starter or by using a wrench on the damper bolt. The compression stroke can be determined by covering the opening of spark plug #1 with a finger as the crankshaft is rotated. Continue to rotate the crankshaft slowly as compression is felt, until the timing marks on the damper line up with the timing indicator on the timing cover. You will recall that at this crankshaft position, both valves are closed. With the timing marks aligned, the crankshaft is set at the point at which ignition *should* occur. Do not turn the crankshaft from this position until the distributor has been installed.

The angle of the distributor gear drive will cause the distributor rotor to turn a few degrees when installed. Before the distributor is installed, the shaft must be positioned to compensate for the gear angle. After installation, the rotor should be pointing to the #1 tower of the distributor cap, and if it is in the wrong position, the distributor will have to be lifted just enough to clear the gear teeth. The rotor is turned just enough to allow the distributor gear to mesh with the next drive gear tooth.

Sometimes, the distributor does not go all the way down into the engine because the end of the distributor shaft does not mesh with the oil pump drive. A simple method for getting the distributor shaft to line up with the oil pump drive is to crank the engine with the distributor installed as far as possible in the engine. As the engine is cranked, the rotating distributor shaft will line up with the oil pump drive, and then the distributor can be fully seated. The engine will have to be cranked through *two full revolutions* to correctly realign the timing marks on the compression stroke. With the distributor hold-down clamp loose, rotate the distributor housing slightly in the direction opposite to the direction of rotor rotation. On inductive pickup-type distributors, the tooth of the rotor and the timer core must line up. This distributor position is close enough to the basic timing position to start the engine. If the distributor hold-down clamp is slightly loose, the distributor housing can be adjusted to make the engine run smoothly after the engine has been started.

SUMMARY

1. All oil galleries must be thoroughly cleaned before engine assembly can begin.
2. All expansion cups and plugs should be installed with a sealer to prevent leaks. Avoid the use of Teflon tape on threaded plugs.
3. The cam bearings should be installed using a cam bearing installation tool.
4. Main bearings and rod bearings should be checked for proper oil clearance by precision measuring the crankshaft journals and inside diameter of bearings or by using plastic gauging material (plastigage).
5. The piston and rod assembly should be installed in the cylinder after being carefully fitted for each bore.
6. Connecting rod side clearance should be checked with a feeler (thickness) gauge.
7. Double-check the flatness of the block deck and cylinder head before installing the cylinder head.
8. Torque the cylinder head bolts according to the proper sequence and procedures.

9. Many cylinder heads use the torque-to-yield method, wherein the head bolts are tightened to a specified torque and then rotated a specified number of degrees.
10. The oil pressure should be tested before installation of the engine in the vehicle.

REVIEW QUESTIONS

1. Describe the procedure for fitting pistons to a cylinder.
2. Explain how main bearings should be checked and fitted to the crankshaft.
3. How is plastic gauging material (plastigage) used to determine oil clearance?
4. What is the procedure for checking thrust bearing clearance?
5. How should the connecting rod side clearance be measured and corrected?
6. How is the piston and connecting rod assembly installed in the engine?
7. What procedures should be followed for installing and torquing the cylinder head?
8. Describe the torque-to-yield head bolt tightening procedure.

MULTIPLE-CHOICE QUESTIONS

1. Typical piston-to-cylinder clearance is _____ .
   a. 0.001 to 0.003 inch
   b. 0.010 to 0.023 inch
   c. 0.100 to 0.150 inch
   d. 0.180 to 0.230 inch
2. If the gauging plastic strip is wide after the bearings are tightened, this indicates _____ .
   a. A large oil clearance
   b. An old, dried strip of plastic gauging material
   c. A small oil clearance
   d. A small side (thrust) clearance
3. The most common cause of premature bearing failure is _____ .
   a. Misassembly
   b. Dirt
   c. Lack of lubrication
   d. Overloading
4. Typical thrust bearing clearance is _____ .
   a. 0.001 to 0.003 inch
   b. 0.002 to 0.012 inch
   c. 0.025 to 0.035 inch
   d. 0.050 to 0.100 inch
5. Piston ring end gap can be *increased* by _____ .
   a. Filing the ring to make the gap larger
   b. Installing oversize rings
   c. Sleeving the cylinder
   d. Knurling the piston

6. The cylinder should be tightened (torqued) in what general sequence?
   a. The four outside bolts first, then from the center out
   b. From the outside bolts to the inside bolts
   c. From the inside bolts to the outside bolts
   d. Starting at the front of the engine and torquing bolts from front to rear

7. The torque-angle method involves _____ .
   a. Turning all bolts the same number of turns
   b. Torquing to specifications and loosening by a specified number of degrees
   c. Torquing to one-half specifications, then to three-quarter torque, then to full torque
   d. Turning bolts a specified number of degrees after initial torque

8. Turning the oil pump before starting the engine should be done _____ .
   a. To lubricate engine bearings
   b. To lubricate valve train components
   c. To supply oil to the camshaft
   d. All of the above

9. Most bolt torque specifications are for _____ .
   a. Clean threads only
   b. Clean and lubricated threads
   c. Dirty threads
   d. Dirty threads, but 50% can be added for clean threads

10. Cam bearings should be installed _____ .
    a. Dry
    b. Oiled
    c. With at least 0.010 inch of crush
    d. Both b and c

Engine Installation and Break-In

18

OBJECTIVES

After studying Chapter 18, the reader will be able to

1. List the steps necessary to install and start up a rebuilt engine.
2. Discuss the importance of torquing all bolts or fasteners that connect accessories to the engine block.
3. Describe what precautions must be taken to prevent damage to the engine when it is first started.
4. Explain how to break in a newly rebuilt engine.

FIGURE 18–1 Remanufactured engine being run on a stand. Note the small carburetor that is used for this test. Coolant is fed through the engine from passages attached with quick-disconnect fittings. No fuel pump or rocker arm (valve) cover gaskets are used, but the splashed-out oil flows under the grates on the floor and is used again.

The engine installation will have to be thoroughly checked to make sure that the engine is in proper condition to give the customer dependable operation for a long time.

All of the operating accessories have to be reinstalled on the engine. They have to be adjusted so that the engine will operate correctly. Some of the accessories can be checked as they are assembled, whereas others will have to be checked after the engine is running. See Figure 18–1.

MANUAL TRANSMISSION INSTALLATION

If the engine was removed with the transmission attached, the transmission should be reinstalled on the engine before other accessories are added. The flywheel is installed on the back of the crankshaft. Often, the attaching bolt holes are unevenly spaced so that the flywheel will fit in only one way to maintain engine bal-

ance. The pilot bearing or bushing in the rear of the crankshaft is usually replaced with a new one. This minimizes the possibility of premature failure of this part.

The clutch is installed next. Usually, a new clutch is used; at the least, a new clutch friction disk is installed. The clutch friction disk must be held in position using an alignment tool (sometimes called a *dummy shaft*) that is secured in the pilot bearing. This holds the disk in position while the pressure plate is being installed. Finally, the engine bell housing is put on the engine, if it was not installed before. The alignment of this type of bell housing is then checked. See Figure 18–2.

378

FIGURE 18–2 Bell housing alignment dowel pins are used to ensure proper alignment between the engine block and the transmission.

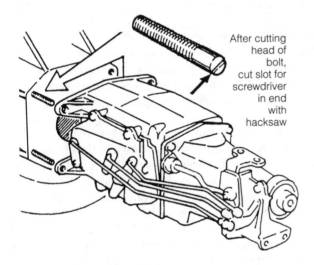

After cutting head of bolt, cut slot for screwdriver in end with hacksaw

FIGURE 18–3 Headless long bolts can be used to help install a transmission to the engine.

■ **TECH TIP** ■

THE HEADLESS BOLT TRICK

Sometimes parts do not seem to line up correctly. Try this tip the next time. Cut the head off of extra-long bolts that are of the same diameter and thread as those being used to retain the part, such as a transmission. See Figure 18–3. Use a hacksaw to cut a slot in the end of these guide bolts for a screwdriver slot. Install the guide bolts; then install the transmission. Use a straight-blade screwdriver to remove the guide bolts after securing the transmission with the retaining bolts.

■ **CAUTION:** Perfectly round cylinders can be distorted whenever another part of the engine is bolted and torqued to the engine block. For example, it has been determined that after the cylinders are machined, the rear cylinder bore can be distorted to be as much as 0.006 inch (0.15 millimeter) out of round after the bell housing is bolted onto the block! To help prevent this distortion, always apply the specified torque to all fasteners going into the engine block and tighten in the recommended sequence. ■

The clutch release yoke should be checked for free movement. Usually, the clutch release bearing is replaced, making sure that the new bearing is securely attached to the clutch release yoke. The transmission can then be installed.

The transmission clutch shaft must be guided straight into the clutch disk and pilot bearing. See the tech tip, The Headless Bolt Trick. The transmission clutch shaft is rotated, as required, to engage in the splines of the clutch disk. The assembly bolts are secured when the transmission fully mates with the bell housing.

■ **CAUTION:** Always adjust the clutch free-play *before* starting the engine to help prevent thrust bearing damage. ■

AUTOMATIC TRANSMISSION INSTALLATION

The drive plate is attached to the back of the crankshaft. Its assembly bolts are tightened to the specified torque. The bell housing is part of the transmission case on most automatic transmissions. Usually, the torque converter (Figure 18–4) will be installed on the transmission before the transmission is put on the engine. The torque converter should be rotated as it is pushed onto the transmission shafts until the splines of all the shafts are engaged in the torque converter. The torque converter is held against the transmission as the transmission is fitted on the back of the engine. The transmission mounting bolts are attached finger tight. The torque converter should be rotated to make sure that there is no binding. The bell housing is secured to the block; then the torque converter is fastened to the drive plate. The engine should be rotated. Any binding should be corrected before any further assembly is done.

STARTER

It is generally easier to install the starter before the engine is put in the chassis. The starter should be checked to make sure that the starter drive pinion does

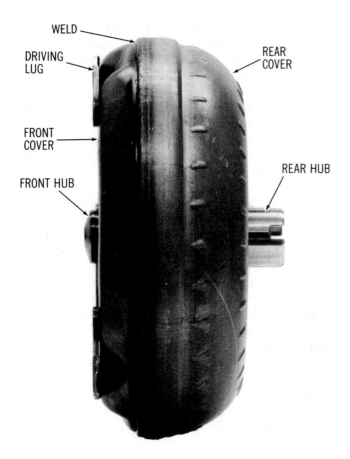

WELD

DRIVING LUG

REAR COVER

FRONT COVER

FRONT HUB

REAR HUB

FIGURE 18–4 Typical automatic transmission torque converter.

not bind on the ring gear. Shims can be installed between the starter mounting pad and the starter to adjust the pinion–to–ring gear clearance on the GM-type mounting. The starter mounting bolts are then tightened to the specified torque.

ACCESSORIES

All of the belt-driven engine accessories are mounted on the front of the engine. Some engines drive all of these accessories with one belt. Other engines use as many as four belts. The service manual or decal under the hood should be checked to determine the specific belt routing for the accessories used on the engine being built up. On some engines it is more convenient to install the front accessories before the engine is installed; on other engines, it is easier to put the engine in the chassis before installing the front accessories.

This is a good time to install the secondary ignition cables that connect the distributor cap to the spark plugs. The cables are threaded through their supports. The service manual should be checked for the proper routing. Cross fire can occur if the spark plug cables are routed incorrectly. The cables should not be either too long or too short. Long cables can contact and wear against parts of the engine, causing an electrical ground. Short cables will stretch and break, causing an electrical open. It may be desirable to install new spark plugs at this time because it is easy to reach them. Leave the spark plug out of cylinder #1 so that the compression stroke of this cylinder can be identified for setting the initial timing of the distributor if the distributor has not been installed.

ENGINE INSTALLATION

A sling, either a chain or lift cable, is attached to the manifold or head bolts on the top of the engine. A hoist is attached to the sling and snugged up to take the weight and to make sure that the engine is supported and balanced properly.

NOTE: Many engines for front wheel–drive vehicles are installed from underneath the vehicle. Often the entire drivetrain package is placed back in the vehicle while it is attached to the cradle. Always check the recommended procedure for the vehicle being serviced.

The engine must be tipped as it was during removal to let the transmission go into the engine compartment first. The transmission is worked under the floor pan on rear wheel–drive vehicles as the engine is lowered into the engine compartment. The front engine mounts are aligned; then the rear cross-member and rear engine mount are installed. The engine mount bolts are installed, and the nuts are torqued. Then the hoist is removed. Controls are connected to the transmission under the vehicle. This is also a good time to connect the electrical cables and wires to the starter. The exhaust system is then attached to the exhaust manifolds. If any of the steering linkage was previously disconnected, it can be reattached while work is being done under the vehicle. After the engine is in place, the front engine accessories can all be installed, if they were not installed before the engine was put in the chassis. The air-conditioning compressor is reattached to the engine, with care being taken to avoid damaging the air-conditioning hoses and lines.

COOLING SYSTEM

The radiator is installed and secured in place. This is followed by the cooling fan and shroud. The fan and new drive belts are installed and adjusted. New radiator hoses, including new heater hoses, should be installed. Coolant, a 50/50 mixture of antifreeze and

(a)

(b)

FIGURE 18–5 Most engine rebuilders install a temperature-sensitive device on the engine. These sensors are used by the rebuilders for warranty purposes to record any occurrence of engine overheating. (a) This small disk is glued to the engine block and will pop out if the engine overheats. (b) A sticker style. (Courtesy of the Automotive Engine Rebuilders Association)

water, is put in the cooling system after making sure that the radiator petcock is closed and the block drain plugs are in place. See Chapter 5 for proper procedure to follow to bleed trapped air from the cooling system. See Figure 18–5 for additional precautions.

FUEL AND EMISSION CONTROLS

The carburetor (if the vehicle is so equipped) should be installed with a new gasket. The fuel and vacuum hoses should be inspected carefully and replaced as required. The fuel-injection system (if the vehicle is so equipped) should be carefully inspected for damage while off the engine and then reinstalled, being certain to follow recommended procedures and torque settings. The fuel and air filters should be replaced. If the vacuum hoses and/or electrical wiring were not

marked, refer to the engine emission decal and service manual for the proper location and routing.

NOTE: The oxygen sensor should be replaced, especially if the engine had a blown head gasket or other problem that could have caused coolant to get on the sensor. Failure to replace the oxygen sensor(s) could cause the engine to operate too lean. ⎯⎯⎯⎯

ELECTRICAL SYSTEM

Connect all wiring to the starter and alternator as required. Connect the instrument wires to the electrical sending units on the engine. Double-check the condition and routing of all wiring, being certain that wires have not been pinched or broken, before installing a fully charged battery. Attach the positive cable first and then the ground cable. Check to make sure that the starter will crank the engine. Install and time the distributor; then connect the ignition cables to the spark plugs, again, being sure that they are routed according to the manufacturer's recommendations.

BREAK-IN ENGINE OIL

Many years ago, vehicle manufacturers used straight weight nondetergent engine oil as break-in oil. Today, the engine oil recommended for break-in (running in) is the same type of oil that is recommended for use in the engine. No special "break-in" oil is recommended or used by the factory in new vehicles. Good quality SAE 5W-30 or SAE 10W-30 engine oil is usually the specified viscosity recommended by most vehicle manufacturers.

ENGINE BREAK-IN

The engine oil and coolant levels are checked. Both oil and coolant should be brought up to the normal full level. The level of the oil in the manual transmission should be checked. If the automatic transmission has been drained, it must be filled with the proper type of ATF fluid before the engine is started. Additional ATF fluid will have to be added to bring the fluid level back up to the full mark after the engine has been run and the transmission has been shifted through all the gears.

The engine installation should be given one last inspection to see that everything has been put together correctly before the engine is started. If the engine overhaul and installation are done properly, the engine should crank and start on its own fully charged battery without the use of a fast charger or jumper battery. As soon as the engine starts and shows oil pressure, it should be brought up to a fast idle speed and *kept there*. This is necessary to make sure that the engine gets proper lubrication. The fast-running oil pump develops full pressure, and the fast-turning crankshaft throws plenty of oil on the cam and cylinder walls.

NOTE: In camshaft-in-block engines, the only lubrication sent to the contact point between the camshaft lobes and the lifters (tappets) is from the splash off of the crankshaft and connecting rods. At idle, engine oil does not splash enough for proper break-in lubrication of the camshaft.

Just as soon as you can tell that there are no serious leaks and the engine is running reasonably well, the vehicle should be driven to a road having minimum traffic. Here, the vehicle should be accelerated, full throttle, from 30 to 50 miles per hour (48 to 80 kilometers per hour). Then the throttle is fully closed while the vehicle is allowed to return to 30 miles per hour (48 kilometers per hour). This sequence is repeated 10 to 12 times. The acceleration sequence puts a high load on the piston rings to properly seat them against the cylinder walls. The piston rings are the only part of the modern engine that needs to be broken in. Good ring seating is indicated by a dry coating inside the tail pipe at the completion of the ring seating drive.

The vehicle is returned to the service area, where the basic ignition timing is set and the idle speed is properly adjusted if possible. The engine is again checked for visible fluid leaks. If the engine is dry, it is ready to be turned over to the customer.

The customer should be instructed to drive the vehicle in a normal fashion, neither babying it at slow speeds nor beating it at high speeds for the first 100 miles (160 kilometers). The oil and filter should be changed at 500 miles (800 kilometers) to remove any dirt that may have been trapped in the engine during assembly and to remove the material that has worn from the surfaces during the break-in period.

A well-designed engine that has been correctly reconditioned and assembled using the techniques described should give reliable service for many miles.

NORMAL OPERATING TEMPERATURE

Normal operating temperature is the temperature at which the upper radiator hose is hot and pressurized. Another standard method used to determine when normal operating temperature is reached is to observe the operation of the electric cooling fan, when the vehicle is so equipped. Many manufacturers define normal

operating temperature as being reached when the cooling fan has cycled on and off at least once after the engine has been started. Some vehicle manufacturers specify that the cooling fan should cycle twice. This method also helps assure the technician that the engine is not being overheated.

HOW TO WARM UP A COLD ENGINE

The greatest amount of engine wear occurs during start-up. The oil in a cold engine is thick, and it requires several seconds to reach all the moving parts of an engine. After the engine starts, the engine should *not* be raced, but rather allowed to idle at the normal fast idle speed as provided for by the choke fast-idle cam (on carburetor-equipped engines) or by the computer-controlled speed on fuel-injected engines. After the engine starts, allow the engine to idle until the oil pressure peaks. This will take from 15 seconds to about 1 full minute, depending on the outside temperature. *Do not allow the engine to idle for longer than 5 minutes.* Because an engine warms up faster under load, drive the vehicle in a normal manner until the engine is fully warm. Avoid full-throttle acceleration until the engine is completely up to normal operating temperature. This method of engine warm-up also warms the rest of the powertrain, including transmission and final drive component lubricants.

BREAK-IN PRECAUTIONS

Any engine overhaul represents many hours of work and a large financial investment. Precautions should be taken to protect the investment, including the following:

1. Never add cold water to the cooling system while the engine is running.
2. Never lug any engine. **Lugging** is increasing the throttle opening without increasing engine speed (RPM). Applying loads to an engine for *short periods* of time creates higher piston ring pressure against the cylinder walls and helps in the breaking-in process by helping to seat the rings.
3. Change oil and filter at 500 miles (800 kilometers) or after 20 hours of operation.
4. Remember that the proper air-fuel ratio is important to the proper operation and long life of any engine. Any air leak (vacuum leak) could cause engine-damaging detonation.
5. Be certain to use spark plugs for the proper heat range.

■ TECH TIP ■

CHECK FOR OIL LEAKS WITH THE ENGINE OFF

The owner of an older vehicle equipped with a V-6 engine complained to his technician that he smelled burning oil, but only *after* shutting off the engine. The technician found that the rocker cover gaskets were leaking. But why did the owner only notice the smell of hot oil when the engine was shut off? Because of the positive crankcase ventilation (PCV) system, engine vacuum tends to draw oil away from gasket surfaces. But when the engine stops, engine vacuum disappears and the oil remaining in the upper regions of the engine will tend to flow down and out through any opening. Therefore, a good technician should check an engine for oil leaks not only with the engine running, but also shortly after shut-down.

SUMMARY

1. Carefully install all accessories.
2. When installing the transmission and other components on the engine block, be sure to use a torque wrench and tighten all fasteners to factory specifications.
3. Always adjust the clutch free-play before starting the engine.
4. Temperature recording sensors should be installed on cylinder heads. This lets the rebuild technician know if the engine has been overheated.
5. A new oxygen sensor(s) should be installed to be assured that the engine operation will be within acceptable limits. If the oxygen sensor is defective, the engine may operate too lean. A lean-operating engine runs hotter than normal.
6. Change the engine oil after 500 miles (800 kilometers) or sooner, and use SAE 5W-30 or SAE 10W-30 engine oil.

REVIEW QUESTIONS

1. How are the clutch and bell housing installed?
2. What should be done to help prevent rear cylinder distortion when the bell housing is being installed on the engine?
3. Describe the engine break-in procedure.

MULTIPLE-CHOICE QUESTIONS

1. Every automotive engine should be filled with at least _____ quarts of engine oil before the engine is prelubricated or started.
   a. 2
   b. 3
   c. 4
   d. 5
2. If the bell housing is not properly torqued to the engine block, _____.
   a. The bell housing will distort
   b. The engine block will crack
   c. The rear cylinder can be distorted (become out of round)
   d. The crankshaft will crack
3. Break-in engine oil is _____.
   a. Of the same viscosity and grade as that specified for normal engine operation
   b. SAE 40
   c. SAE 30
   d. SAE 20W-50
4. Normal operating temperature is reached when _____.
   a. The radiator cap releases coolant into the overflow
   b. The upper radiator hose is hot and pressurized
   c. The electric cooling fan has cycled at least once (if the vehicle is so equipped)
   d. Both b and c
5. Lugging an engine means _____.
   a. Wide-open throttle in low gear above 25 miles per hour
   b. That engine speed does not increase when the throttle is opened wider
   c. Starting a cold engine and allowing it to idle for longer than 5 minutes
   d. Both b and c
6. Which computer sensor should be replaced if the engine had been found to have a defective head gasket or cracked head?
   a. Throttle position sensor
   b. Oxygen sensor
   c. Manifold absolute pressure sensor
   d. Engine coolant temperature sensor

■ ■ ■ ■ ■ ■ Answers to Even-Numbered Multiple-Choice Questions ■ ■ ■

CHAPTER 1

2. D 4. B 6. B 8. B 10. A

CHAPTER 2

2. D 4. A 6. B 8. B 10. B

CHAPTER 3

2. C 4. A 6. D 8. D 10. C

CHAPTER 4

2. C 4. C 6. A 8. B

CHAPTER 5

2. A 4. B 6. A 8. C

CHAPTER 6

2. C 4. C 6. B 8. A 10. B

CHAPTER 7

2. C 4. B 6. D 8. B 10. C

CHAPTER 8

2. B 4. C 6. C 8. A 10. D

CHAPTER 9

2. D 4. C 6. A 8. A

CHAPTER 10

2. A 4. A 6. A 8. B 10. B

CHAPTER 11

2. A 4. B 6. C 8. B 10. C

CHAPTER 12

2. A 4. D 6. C 8. C 10. C

CHAPTER 13

2. C 4. C 6. A 8. D 10. C

CHAPTER 14

2. A 4. A 6. C 8. A 10. B

CHAPTER 15

2. C 4. D 6. C 8. B 10. B

CHAPTER 16

2. A 4. B 6. C 8. D 10. C

CHAPTER 17

2. C 4. B 6. C 8. D 10. A

CHAPTER 18

2. C 4. D 6. B

Engine Repair Sample ASE Certification Test

1. Two technicians are discussing the markings on the heads of bolts (cap screws). Technician A says the higher the number of lines, the higher the strength of the bolt. Technician B says the higher the number on metric bolts, the higher the grade. Which technician is correct?
   a. A only
   b. B only
   c. Both A and B
   d. Neither A nor B

2. A metric bolt size of M8 means that _____.
   a. The bolt is 8 millimeters long
   b. The bolt is 8 millimeters in diameter
   c. The pitch (the distance between the crest of the threads) is 8 millimeters
   d. The bolt is 8 centimeters long

3. On a metric bolt sized M8 × 1.5, the 1.5 means that _____.
   a. The bolt is 1.5 millimeters in diameter
   b. The bolt is 1.5 centimeters long
   c. The bolt has 1.5 millimeters between the crest of the threads
   d. The bolt has a strength grade of 1.5

4. The diameter of the bolt is determined by the measurement across the _____.
   a. Flats of the head of the bolt
   b. Diameter of the threaded part of the bolt

5. Prevailing torque (lock) nuts should be replaced rather than reused after removal.
   a. True
   b. False

6. Technician A says that you should always pull a wrench toward you for safety. Technician B says that you should always push a wrench away from you for safety. Which technician is correct?
   a. A only
   b. B only
   c. Both A and B
   d. Neither A nor B

7. A DOHC V-6 has _____.
   a. One camshaft
   b. Two camshafts
   c. Three camshafts
   d. Four camshafts

8. If the bore of an engine is increased without any other changes except for the change to proper-size replacement pistons, the displacement will _____ and the compression rate will _____.
   a. Increase; increase
   b. Increase; decrease
   c. Decrease; increase
   d. Decrease; decrease

9. To increase the stroke of an engine, what part(s) must be changed?
   a. Crankshaft
   b. Connecting rods
   c. Crankshaft, connecting rods, and pistons
   d. Crankshaft and pistons

10. A battery is being tested. Technician A says that the surface charge should be removed before the battery is load tested. Technician B says that the battery should be loaded to two times the CCA rating of the battery for 15 seconds. Which technician is correct?
    a. A only
    b. B only
    c. Both A and B
    d. Neither A nor B

11. A fully charged 12-volt battery should measure _____.
    a. 12.6 volts
    b. 12.4 volts
    c. 12.2 volts
    d. 12.0 volts

12. A starter motor cranks the engine too slowly to start. Technician A says that the cause could be a weak or defective battery. Technician B says that the cause could be loose or corroded battery cable connections. Which technician is correct?

a. A only
b. B only
c. Both A and B
d. Neither A nor B

13. A technician is measuring the battery voltage while cranking the engine and observes 11.2 volts on the voltmeter. Technician A says that the starter may be defective. Technician B says that the correct specification is 9.6 volts during cranking; therefore, the starter, battery, or cables are defective. Which technician is correct?
   a. A only
   b. B only
   c. Both A and B
   d. Neither A nor B

14. The charging system voltage is found to be lower than specified by the vehicle manufacturer. Technician A says that a loose or defective drive belt could be the cause. Technician B says that a defective alternator could be the cause. Which technician is correct?
   a. A only
   b. B only
   c. Both A and B
   d. Neither A nor B

15. Battery voltage during cranking is below specifications. Technician A says that the engine may be the cause. Technician B says that the starter motor may be defective. Which technician is correct?
   a. A only
   b. B only
   c. Both A and B
   d. Neither A nor B

16. Two technicians are discussing distributorless (EI) ignition. Technician A says that the crankshaft sensor triggers the module. Technician B says that the module controls the primary circuit of the ignition coil. Which technician is correct?
   a. A only
   b. B only
   c. Both A and B
   d. Neither A nor B

17. An engine cranks but will not start. No spark is available at the end of a spark plug wire with a spark tester connected and the engine cranked. Technician A says that a defective pickup coil could be the cause. Technician B says that a defective ignition module could be the cause. Which technician is correct?
   a. A only
   b. B only
   c. Both A and B
   d. Neither A nor B

18. An engine miss is being diagnosed. One spark plug wire measured "OL" on a digital ohmmeter set to the K ohm scale. Technician A says that the spark plug should be replaced. Technician B says that the ignition coil should also be replaced. Which technician is correct?

a. A only
b. B only
c. Both A and B
d. Neither A nor B

19. Engine ping (spark knock or detonation) can be caused by _____.
   a. Advanced ignition timing
   b. Retarded ignition timing

20. Two technicians are discussing the diagnosis of a lack-of-power problem. Technician A says that a worn (stretched) timing chain could be the cause. Technician B says that retarded ignition timing could be the cause. Which technician is correct?
   a. A only
   b. B only
   c. Both A and B
   d. Neither A nor B

21. Technician A says that low fuel pressure can cause the engine to produce low power. Technician B says that all fuel pumps should be able to pump at least 2 pints (1 liter) per minute. Which technician is correct?
   a. A only
   b. B only
   c. Both A and B
   d. Neither A nor B

22. An intercooler is used on some turbocharged engines because _____.
   a. It lowers the temperature of the turbocharger
   b. It cools the air after it leaves the turbocharger
   c. It cools the lubricating oil for the turbocharger
   d. It helps to cool the engine coolant

23. An engine equipped with a turbocharger is burning oil (blue exhaust smoke all the time). Technician A says that a defective wastegate could be the cause. Technician B says that a plugged PCV system could be the cause. Which technician is correct?
   a. A only
   b. B only
   c. Both A and B
   d. Neither A nor B

24. An engine idles roughly and stalls occasionally. Technician A says that using fuel with too high an RVP level could be the cause. Technician B says that using winter-blend gasoline during warm weather could be the cause. Which technician is correct?
   a. A only
   b. B only
   c. Both A and B
   d. Neither A nor B

25. The octane rating posted on gasoline pumps represents _____.
   a. The research method
   b. The motor method
   c. The average of the research and motor methods
   d. The total (sum) of the RON and MON ratings

26. A vehicle runs terribly when the gasoline level in the tank is low. The engine runs okay when the fuel level in

the tank is above ⅛ tank. Technician A says that phase separation could be the cause. Technician B says that using a fuel with too much alcohol could be the cause. Which technician is correct?

a. A only
b. B only
c. Both A and B
d. Neither A nor B

27. A customer was concerned about using unleaded fuel in a vehicle designed for leaded gasoline. Technician A says that valve recession is likely to occur if unleaded fuel is used, even if the vehicle is driven only a few miles. Technician B says that an additive must be used to prevent serious and rapid engine damage from occurring. Which technician is correct?

a. A only
b. B only
c. Both A and B
d. Neither A nor B

28. During subfreezing weather, a vehicle equipped with a carburetor starts, runs for about 15 seconds, and then stops. The engine does not restart. Technician A says that gasoline freeze-up is a likely cause. Technician B says that the use of high-volatility gasoline could be the cause. Which technician is correct?

a. A only
b. B only
c. Both A and B
d. Neither A nor B

29. Technician A says that coolant flows through the engine passages and does not flow through the radiator until the thermostat opens. Technician B says that the temperature rating of the thermostat indicates the temperature of the coolant when the thermostat is opened fully. Which technician is correct?

a. A only
b. B only
c. Both A and B
d. Neither A nor B

30. Technician A says the higher the concentrations of antifreeze, the better. Technician B says that a 50/50 mix of antifreeze and water is the ratio recommended by most vehicle manufacturers. Which technician is correct?

a. A only
b. B only
c. Both A and B
d. Neither A nor B

31. Technician A says that if the thermostat is removed from the engine, the engine may overheat. Technician B says that coolant bypasses the thermostat when the thermostat is closed. Which technician is correct?

a. A only
b. B only
c. Both A and B
d. Neither A nor B

32. Technician A says that the radiator pressure cap is designed to raise the boiling point of the coolant. Technician B says that the radiator pressure cap helps prevent cavitation and, therefore, improves the efficiency of the coolant pump. Which technician is correct?

a. A only
b. B only
c. Both A and B
d. Neither A nor B

33. Technician A says that used antifreeze coolant is often considered to be hazardous waste. Technician B says that metals absorbed by the coolant when it is used in an engine are what makes antifreeze harmful. Which technician is correct?

a. A only
b. B only
c. Both A and B
d. Neither A nor B

34. Two technicians are discussing pressure testing the cooling system to check for leaks. Technician A says to pump up the system to 20 to 25 psi and watch for the pressure to drop. Technician B says that each component of the cooling system should be pressure checked individually by disconnecting it from the system. Which technician is correct?

a. A only
b. B only
c. Both A and B
d. Neither A nor B

35. A coolant pump has been replaced three times in 3 months. Technician A says that the drive belt(s) may be installed too tightly. Technician B says that a cooling fan may be bent or out of balance. Which technician is correct?

a. A only
b. B only
c. Both A and B
d. Neither A nor B

36. The "hot" light on the dash is being discussed by two technicians. Technician A says that the light comes on if the cooling system temperature is too high for safe operation of the engine. Technician B says that the light comes on whenever there is a decrease (drop) in cooling system pressure. Which technician is correct?

a. A only
b. B only
c. Both A and B
d. Neither A nor B

37. A compression test gave the following results:

Cylinder #1: 155
Cylinder #2: 140
Cylinder #3: 110
Cylinder #4: 105

Technician A says that a defective (burned) valve is the most likely cause. Technician B says that a leaking intake manifold gasket could be the cause. Which technician is correct?

a. A only
b. B only
c. Both A and B
d. Neither A nor B

38. An engine noise is being diagnosed. Technician A says that a double knock is likely to be due to a worn rod bearing. Technician B says that a knock only when the engine is cold is usually due to a worn piston pin. Which technician is correct?
    a. A only
    b. B only
    c. Both A and B
    d. Neither A nor B

39. Two technicians are discussing a compression test. Technician A says that the engine should be turned over with the pressure gauge installed for "three puffs." Technician B says that the maximum difference between the highest-reading cylinder and the lowest-reading cylinder should be 20%. Which technician is correct?
    a. A only
    b. B only
    c. Both A and B
    d. Neither A nor B

40. Technician A says that oil should be squirted into all of the cylinders before taking a compression test. Technician B says that if the compression greatly increases when some oil is squirted into the cylinders, it indicates defective or worn piston rings. Which technician is correct?
    a. A only
    b. B only
    c. Both A and B
    d. Neither A nor B

41. During a cylinder leakage (leak-down) test, air is noticed coming out of the oil filler opening. Technician A says that the oil filter may be clogged. Technician B says that the piston rings may be worn or defective. Which technician is correct?
    a. A only
    b. B only
    c. Both A and B
    d. Neither A nor B

42. A cylinder leakage (leak-down) test indicates 30% leakage, and air is heard coming out of the air inlet. Technician A says that this is a normal reading for a slightly worn engine. Technician B says that one or more intake valves are defective. Which technician is correct?
    a. A only
    b. B only
    c. Both A and B
    d. Neither A nor B

43. Two technicians are discussing a cylinder power balance test. Technician A says that the more the engine RPM drops, the weaker the cylinder. Technician B says that all cylinder RPM drops should be within 50 RPM of each other. Which technician is correct?
    a. A only
    b. B only
    c. Both A and B
    d. Neither A nor B

44. Technician A says that cranking vacuum should be the same as idle vacuum. Technician B says that a sticking valve is indicated by a floating vacuum gauge needle reading. Which technician is correct?
    a. A only
    b. B only
    c. Both A and B
    d. Neither A nor B

45. Technician A says that black exhaust smoke is an indication of too rich an air-fuel mixture. Technician B says that white smoke (steam) is an indication of coolant being burned in the engine. Which technician is correct?
    a. A only
    b. B only
    c. Both A and B
    d. Neither A nor B

46. Excessive exhaust system back pressure has been measured. Technician A says that the catalytic converter may be clogged. Technician B says that the muffler may be clogged. Which technician is correct?
    a. A only
    b. B only
    c. Both A and B
    d. Neither A nor B

47. A head gasket failure is being diagnosed. Technician A says that an exhaust analyzer can be used to check for HC when the tester probe is held above the radiator coolant. Technician B says that a chemical-coated paper that changes color in the presence of combustion gases can be used. Which technician is correct?
    a. A only
    b. B only
    c. Both A and B
    d. Neither A nor B

48. Two technicians are discussing disassembly of an engine. Technician A says that the engine can be disassembled in any order that is possible. Technician B says that cylinder heads and manifolds should have their attaching bolts loosened in the reverse order of the tightening sequence. Which technician is correct?
    a. A only
    b. B only
    c. Both A and B
    d. Neither A nor B

49. Technician A says that pistons should be removed from the crankshaft side of the cylinder when disassembling an engine to prevent possible piston or cylinder damage. Technician B says that the rod assembly should be marked before disassembly. Which technician is correct?
    a. A only
    b. B only
    c. Both A and B
    d. Neither A nor B

50. Before the valve is removed from the cylinder head, _____.
    a. The valve spring should be compressed and locks removed
    b. The valve tip edges should be filed
    c. The ridge should be removed
    d. Both a and b

51. A steel wire brush should be used to clean the gasket surface of an aluminum cylinder head.
    a. True
    b. False

52. A strong soap (caustic) used in cleaning engine parts has a _____ pH level.
    a. High
    b. Neutral
    c. Low

53. A matte or satin finish can be achieved using which method of cleaning?
    a. Ultrasonic
    b. Vibratory
    c. Blaster
    d. Pyrolytic oven

54. The heat shield was removed from the bottom of a V-8 intake manifold. Technician A says that the engine will run cooler. Technician B says that the oil may coke (harden) without the shield. Which technician is correct?
    a. A only
    b. B only
    c. Both A and B
    d. Neither A nor B

55. Technician A says that most engines equipped with a carburetor or throttle body injection unit use a heated intake manifold to help in vaporization. Technician B says that engines equipped with port fuel injection do not require that the manifold be heated. Which technician is correct?
    a. A only
    b. B only
    c. Both A and B
    d. Neither A nor B

56. Technician A says that the purpose of the exhaust gas recirculation system is to reburn the exhaust gases to reduce emissions. Technician B says that the exhaust in the EGR system helps prevent high combustion temperatures inside the combustion chamber. Which technician is correct?
    a. A only
    b. B only
    c. Both A and B
    d. Neither A nor B

57. Technician A says that catalytic converters should last the life of the vehicle unless damaged. Technician B says that catalytic converters wear out and should be replaced every 50,000 miles (80,000 kilometers). Which technician is correct?
    a. A only
    b. B only
    c. Both A and B
    d. Neither A nor B

58. Technician A says that all valve train parts that are to be reused should be kept together. Technician B says that intake valve springs may be of a different strength than exhaust valve springs. Which technician is correct?

    a. A only
    b. B only
    c. Both A and B
    d. Neither A nor B

59. A cast-iron cylinder head is checked for warpage using a straightedge and a feeler (thickness) gauge. The amount of warpage on a V-8 cylinder head was 0.002 inch (0.05 millimeter). Technician A says that the cylinder head should be resurfaced. Technician B says that the cylinder head should be replaced. Which technician is correct?
    a. A only
    b. B only
    c. Both A and B
    d. Neither A nor B

60. The higher the microinch finish, the _____ the surface.
    a. Rougher
    b. Smoother

61. Aluminum cylinder heads should be straightened before the head surface is machined.
    a. True
    b. False

62. The valve guide should be reconditioned or replaced *before* the valve seats are reconditioned.
    a. True
    b. False

63. Technician A says that a dial indicator (gauge) is often used to measure valve guide wear by measuring the amount by which the valve head is able to move in the guide. Technician B says that a ball gauge can be used to measure the valve guide. Which technician is correct?
    a. A only
    b. B only
    c. Both A and B
    d. Neither A nor B

64. Technician A says that a worn valve guide can be reamed and a valve with an oversize stem can be used. Technician B says that a worn valve guide must be replaced with a bronze insert to restore the cylinder head to useful service. Which technician is correct?
    a. A only
    b. B only
    c. Both A and B
    d. Neither A nor B

65. Technician A says that worn integral guides can be repaired by knurling. Technician B says that worn integral guides can be replaced. Which technician is correct?
    a. A only
    b. B only
    c. Both A and B
    d. Neither A nor B

66. Typical valve–to–valve guide clearance should be _____.
    a. 0.001 to 0.003 inch (0.025 to 0.076 millimeter)
    b. 0.010 to 0.030 inch (0.25 to 0.76 millimeter)
    c. 0.035 to 0.60 inch (0.89 to 1.52 millimeters)
    d. 0.100 to 0.350 inch (2.54 to 8.90 millimeters)

67. Technician A says that using a straight through exhaust system can cause valve problems, especially if the engine is operated in cold weather. Technician B says that Stellite is an alloy used in valves and valve seats that can be identified because it is nonmagnetic. Which technician is correct?
    a. A only
    b. B only
    c. Both A and B
    d. Neither A nor B

68. Technician A says that aluminum heads usually use integral valve seats. Technician B says that valve seats used in aluminum heads have to be replaced and cannot be resurfaced. Which technician is correct?
    a. A only
    b. B only
    c. Both A and B
    d. Neither A nor B

69. Before a valve spring is reused, it should be checked for _____.
    a. Squareness
    b. Free height
    c. Tension
    d. All of the above

70. Technician A says that the valve stem should be ground and chamfered before the valve face is ground. Technician B says that the valve face should be ground as close as possible to the limit of the margin, as specified by the engine manufacturer. Which technician is correct?
    a. A only
    b. B only
    c. Both A and B
    d. Neither A nor B

71. Many manufacturers recommend that valves be ground with an interference angle. This angle is the difference between the _____.
    a. Valve margin and valve face angles
    b. Valve face and valve seat angles
    c. Valve guide and valve face angles
    d. Valve head and margin angles

72. To narrow and lower a 45-degree valve seat, the technician should use a _____.
    a. 30-degree stone
    b. 45-degree stone
    c. 60-degree stone
    d. 75-degree stone

73. To widen a valve seat without lowering or raising its position, the technician should use a _____.
    a. 30-degree stone
    b. 45-degree stone
    c. 60-degree stone
    d. 75-degree stone

74. Valve stem height and installed height mean the same thing.
    a. True
    b. False

75. Valve spring inserts are used _____.
    a. Under the valve spring
    b. To restore proper installed height
    c. To restore proper spring tension after the valves and valve seats have been reconditioned
    d. All of the above

76. Technician A says that valve stem seals of the O-ring style are installed on top of the valve locks (keepers). Technician B says that a vacuum pump can be used to determine if the valve stem seal is correctly seated. Which technician is correct?
    a. A only
    b. B only
    c. Both A and B
    d. Neither A nor B

77. Two technicians are diagnosing a problem with an OHV V-8. The rocker covers have been removed and the engine is running. One pushrod is not rotating. Technician A says that the camshaft is worn and must be replaced. Technician B says that the lifter is worn and must be replaced. Which technician is correct?
    a. A only
    b. B only
    c. Both A and B
    d. Neither A nor B

78. A noisy valve train is being diagnosed. Technician A says that the rocker arm may be adjusted too tightly. Technician B says that the rocker arm may be adjusted too loosely or may be worn. Which technician is correct?
    a. A only
    b. B only
    c. Both A and B
    d. Neither A nor B

79. A cylinder is 0.002 inch out of round. Technician A says that the block should be bored and oversize pistons installed. Technician B says that oversize piston rings should be used. Which technician is correct?
    a. A only
    b. B only
    c. Both A and B
    d. Neither A nor B

80. After the engine block has been machined, the block should be cleaned with _____.
    a. A stiff brush with soap and water
    b. A clean rag and engine oil
    c. WD-40
    d. Spray solvent washer

81. Technician A says that piston rings should be installed with the dot or mark up (toward the cylinder head). Technician B says that the mark on the piston rings is used to identify the position (groove) in which the ring should be installed. Which technician is correct?
    a. A only
    b. B only
    c. Both A and B
    d. Neither A nor B

82. Two technicians are discussing piston ring gap. Technician A says that the ring should be checked in the same cylinder in which it is to be installed. Technician B says that the ends of the piston ring can be filed if the gap is too small. Which technician is correct?
   a. A only
   b. B only
   c. Both A and B
   d. Neither A nor B

83. Technician A says that connecting rod caps should be marked when the connecting rod is disassembled and then replaced in the exact same location and direction on the rod. Technician B says that each piston should be fit to each individual cylinder for best results. Which technician is correct?
   a. A only
   b. B only
   c. Both A and B
   d. Neither A nor B

84. Two technicians are discussing bearing clearance measurement. Technician A says that the main and rod bearing clearance should be measured with plastic gauging material. Technician B says that the engine crankshaft should be rotated for two complete revolutions when plastic gauging material is used between the crankshaft and the main or rod bearings. Which technician is correct?
   a. A only
   b. B only
   c. Both A and B
   d. Neither A nor B

85. When pistons are installed in the block, the notch on the piston should be facing _____.
   a. Toward the lifter side of the block
   b. Toward the front of the engine
   c. Toward the rear of the engine
   d. Away from the lifter side of the block

86. A bearing shell is being installed in a connecting rod. The end of the bearing is slightly above the parting line. Technician A says that this is normal. Technician B says that the bearing is too big. Which technician is correct?
   a. A only
   b. B only
   c. Both A and B
   d. Neither A nor B

87. Two technicians are discussing the cause of low oil pressure. Technician A says that a worn oil pump could be the cause. Technician B says that worn main or rod bearings could be the cause. Which technician is correct?
   a. A only
   b. B only
   c. Both A and B
   d. Neither A nor B

88. Oil is discovered inside the air cleaner assembly. Technician A says that the cause could be excessive blowby past the piston rings. Technician B says that the cause could be a clogged PCV valve, hose, or passage. Which technician is correct?
   a. A only
   b. B only
   c. Both A and B
   d. Neither A nor B

89. An engine uses an excessive amount of oil. Technician A says that clogged oil drain-back holes in the cylinder head could be the cause. Technician B says that worn piston rings could be the cause. Which technician is correct?
   a. A only
   b. B only
   c. Both A and B
   d. Neither A nor B

90. Two technicians are discussing torquing cylinder head bolts. Technician A says that many engine manufacturers recommend replacing the head bolts after use. Technician B says that many manufacturers recommend tightening the head bolts to a specific torque, then turning the bolts an additional number of degrees. Which technician is correct?
   a. A only
   b. B only
   c. Both A and B
   d. Neither A nor B

Cylinder Head Specialist Sample ASE Certification Test

1. An aluminum cylinder head is to be removed form an engine. Machinist A says that the head bolts should be loosened in a sequence starting at the center of the cylinder head and working toward the ends of the cylinder head. Machinist B says that the engine should be at room temperature before the cylinder head is removed. Which machinist is correct?
   a. A only
   b. B only
   c. Both A and B
   d. Neither A nor B

2. Machinist A says that all pushrods should be kept and arranged so that they can be replaced in their original locations when the engine is reassembled. Machinist B says that a rocker arm should be kept with the pushrod that it contacted. Which machinist is correct?
   a. A only
   b. B only
   c. Both A and B
   d. Neither A nor B

3. Machinist A says that a putty knife can be used to clean the gasket surface of cast-iron or aluminum cylinder heads. Machinist B says that a steel wire brush can be used to clean cast-iron and aluminum cylinder heads. Which machinist is correct?
   a. A only
   b. B only
   c. Both A and B
   d. Neither A nor B

4. Machinist A says that some chemicals can turn an aluminum cylinder head black. Machinist B says that an aqueous-based chemical cleaning method can be used to clean both cast-iron and aluminum cylinder heads. Which machinist is correct?
   a. A only
   b. B only
   c. Both A and B
   d. Neither A nor B

5. Machinist A says that thermal cleaning in a pyrolytic oven is best suited for cast-iron cylinder heads. Machinist B says that shot blasting or tumbling may also be necessary after a cylinder head is cleaned in an oven. Which machinist is correct?
   a. A only
   b. B only
   c. Both A and B
   d. Neither A nor B

6. Machinist A says that magnetic flux testing can be used to check for cracks in aluminum and cast-iron cylinder heads. Machinist B says that dye penetrant testing can be used to check for cracks in aluminum and cast-iron cylinder heads. Which machinist is correct?
   a. A only
   b. B only
   c. Both A and B
   d. Neither A nor B

7. Machinist A says that fluorescent penetrant testing can be used to check for cracks in aluminum and cast-iron cylinder heads. Machinist B says that pressure testing can be used to check for cracks in aluminum and cast-iron cylinder heads. Which machinist is correct?
   a. A only
   b. B only
   c. Both A and B
   d. Neither A nor B

8. Cracks in cylinder heads can be repaired by _____.
   a. Stop drilling
   b. Welding
   c. Plugging
   d. All of the above

9. Before a crack in cast-iron is welded, the cylinder head must first be _____.
   a. Pinned with cast-iron plugs
   b. Heated
   c. Brazed
   d. Machined

10. Machinist A says that aluminum cylinder heads can be welded to repair a crack. Machinist B says that the valve seat insert should be removed if the crack is near the combustion chamber. Which machinist is correct?
    a. A only
    b. B only
    c. Both A and B
    d. Neither A nor B

11. Machinist A says that tapered plugs can be used to repair a crack in a cast-iron cylinder head. Machinist B says that the tapered plugs should be coated in sealant and installed side by side with other plugs. Which machinist is correct?
    a. A only
    b. B only
    c. Both A and B
    d. Neither A nor B

12. A V-8 cylinder head has 0.001 inch (0.05 millimeter) of total warpage. Machinist A says that the cylinder head should be resurfaced. Machinist B says the cylinder head should also be checked for bend and twist. Which machinist is correct?
    a. A only
    b. B only
    c. Both A and B
    d. Neither A nor B

13. Cylinder head gasket surface finish is measured in what units?
    a. Millimeters
    b. Centimeters
    c. Microinches
    d. Nanometers

14. Machinist A says that the finish of a cast-iron cylinder head gasket surface should be between 60 and 100 units. Machinist B says that the finish of an aluminum cylinder head gasket surface should be between 50 and 60 units. Which machinist is correct?
    a. A only
    b. B only
    c. Both A and B
    d. Neither A nor B

15. Machinist A says that the valve timing will be *retarded* if material is removed from the head-to-block surface of the cylinder head of an overhead camshaft engine. Machinist B says that the valve timing will be *advanced* if material is removed from the cylinder head on an overhead valve type of engine. Which machinist is correct?
    a. A only
    b. B only
    c. Both A and B
    d. Neither A nor B

16. A V-type engine has had the head gasket surface refinished. What other machining operation should be performed?
    a. Machining the deck at least 0.008 inch to ensure a proper seal
    b. Machining the intake manifold
    c. Machining the exhaust manifolds
    d. All of the above

17. Two machinists are discussing stress relieving a warped aluminum cylinder head. Machinist A says that the head should be machined before stress relieving. Machinist B says that the head should be bolted to a thick slab of steel and placed in an oven to soak for 5 hours. Which machinist is correct?
    a. A only
    b. B only
    c. Both A and B
    d. Neither A nor B

18. A four-cylinder overhead camshaft engine cylinder head with integral cam bearings is being machined. Machinist A says that the camshaft centerline should be realigned by boring the camshaft journals. Machinist B says that the cylinder head should be straightened *before* the machining operation. Which machinist is correct?
    a. A only
    b. B only
    c. Both A and B
    d. Neither A nor B

19. Machinist A says that a loose valve seat should be staked. Machinist B says that the valve seat should be replaced. Which machinist is correct?
    a. A only
    b. B only
    c. Both A and B
    d. Neither A nor B

20. Machinist A says that a ball gauge and a micrometer can be used to determine valve guide clearance. Machinist B says that holding a dial indicator against the side of the valve while the valve is held in the open position is specified by some manufacturers as a method for checking valve guide wear. Which machinist is correct?
    a. A only
    b. B only
    c. Both A and B
    d. Neither A nor B

21. Typical valve guide clearance is _____.
    a. 0.003 to 0.008 inch (0.008 to 0.02 millimeter)
    b. 0.001 to 0.003 inch (0.025 to 0.076 millimeter)
    c. 0.005 to 0.008 inch (0.13 to 0.20 millimeter)
    d. 0.010 to 0.015 inch (0.25 to 0.38 millimeter)

22. Oversize stem valves are being installed in a cast-iron cylinder head with integral valve guides. Machinist A says that the old guide must be reamed. Machinist B says that the valve guide should be replaced. Which machinist is correct?
    a. A only
    b. B only
    c. Both A and B
    d. Neither A nor B

23. Two machinist are discussing knurling valve guides. Machinist A says that the valve guide should be reamed before the knurling operation. Machinist B says that the valve stem–to–valve guide clearance is usually one-half of the new guide clearance. Which machinist is correct?

a. A only
b. B only
c. Both A and B
d. Neither A nor B

24. Machinist A says that replacement guides are pressed into the cylinder head. Machinist B says that the replacement guide should be reamed or honed after installation. Which machinist is correct?
a. A only
b. B only
c. Both A and B
d. Neither A nor B

25. Machinist A says that a bronze thin-walled insert can be used to repair a worn valve guide. Machinist B says that a thin-walled insert is used with an oversize stem valve. Which machinist is correct?
a. A only
b. B only
c. Both A and B
d. Neither A nor B

26. Machinist A says that aluminized valves should not be machined. Machinist B says that the tip of the valve stem should be filed before the valve is removed from the cylinder head. Which machinist is correct?
a. A only
b. B only
c. Both A and B
d. Neither A nor B

27. Machinist A says that sodium-filled valves should not be ground. Machinist B says that sodium-filled valves require greater valve guide clearance than standard valves. Which machinist is correct?
a. A only
b. B only
c. Both A and B
d. Neither A nor B

28. Machinist A says that mushroomed valves should be replaced. Machinist B says that guttered valves should be replaced. Which machinist is correct?
a. A only
b. B only
c. Both A and B
d. Neither A nor B

29. Machinist A says that a dead-blow hammer should be used against the valve retainer before the valves are removed. Machinist B says that a valve spring should be compressed before the valve locks are removed. Which machinist is correct?
a. A only
b. B only
c. Both A and B
d. Neither A nor B

30. Valve springs should be tested for _____.
a. Free height
b. Squareness
c. Spring force
d. All of the above

31. Machinist A says that damper springs should be removed before checking for spring force. Machinist B says that the spring force should be checked at the spring's free height dimension. Which machinist is correct?
a. A only
b. B only
c. Both A and B
d. Neither A nor B

32. Machinist A says that the valve stem should be squared and chamfered *before* the valve face is ground. Machinist B says that the stem height determines how much of the valve stem should be ground. Which machinist is correct?
a. A only
b. B only
c. Both A and B
d. Neither A nor B

33. Machinist A says that a 60-degree stone can be used to widen a 45-degree seat. Machinist B says that a 30-degree stone can be used to raise a 45-degree seat. Which machinist is correct?
a. A only
b. B only
c. Both A and B
d. Neither A nor B

34. A 45-degree seat has been ground and is too wide. Machinist A says to grind the seat using a 45-degree stone. Machinist B says to use both a 30-degree and a 60-degree stone to narrow the seat. Which machinist is correct?
a. A only
b. B only
c. Both A and B
d. Neither A nor B

35. A valve has been ground and has less than the specified margin. Machinist A says to grind a 1-degree interference angle on the valve face. Machinist B says to compensate by grinding the valve seat 1 degree less than specified by the manufacturer. Which machinist is correct?
a. A only
b. B only
c. Both A and B
d. Neither A nor B

36. Machinist A says that valves should be ground until the margin is at the minimum allowable thickness according to the manufacturer's specification. Machinist B says that the thicker the margin left on a valve, the better. Which machinist is correct?
a. A only
b. B only
c. Both A and B
d. Neither A nor B

37. Machinist A says that a valve seat cutter should only be rotated clockwise. Machinist B says that a 60-degree cutter will raise and narrow a 45-degree valve seat. Which machinist is correct?
a. A only
b. B only
c. Both A and B
d. Neither A nor B

38. Machinist A says that a damaged or worn integral valve seat can be replaced with an insert valve seat. Machinist B says that a replacement valve seat insert should be welded in place. Which machinist is correct?
    a. A only
    b. B only
    c. Both A and B
    d. Neither A nor B

39. Machinist A says that valve stem height is the same as installed height. Machinist B says that installed height can be changed by grinding the tip of the valve stem. Which machinist is correct?
    a. A only
    b. B only
    c. Both A and B
    d. Neither A nor B

40. Machinist A says that the installation of valve stem seals of the O-ring type can be checked using a vacuum pump. Machinist B says that mineral spirits can be used in the combustion chamber to determine if the valve stem seals leak. Which machinist is correct?
    a. A only
    b. B only
    c. Both A and B
    d. Neither A nor B

Cylinder Block Specialist Sample ASE Certification Test

1. Machinist A says that all oil gallery plugs should be removed when the block is cleaned. Machinist B says that all core plugs should be removed before the block is cleaned. Which machinist is correct?
   a. A only
   b. B only
   c. Both A and B
   d. Neither A nor B

2. Machinist A says that aluminum blocks should only be cleaned using a blaster. Machinist B says that aluminum blocks can be cleaned in an oven. Which machinist is correct?
   a. A only
   b. B only
   c. Both A and B
   d. Neither A nor B

3. Before an engine block is machined, the machinist should first determine the minimum allowable _____.
   a. Bore center
   b. Block deck height
   c. Pan rail length
   d. Saddle depth

4. Machinist A says that the main bearing caps should be installed and torqued to specification before the block is align honed. Machinist B says that the main bearing caps should be installed and torqued to specification before the block is bored. Which machinist is correct?
   a. A only
   b. B only
   c. Both A and B
   d. Neither A nor B

5. Machinist A says that the block deck should be machined before align boring is done. Machinist B says that the block deck should be machined before the cylinders are bored. Which machinist is correct?
   a. A only
   b. B only
   c. Both A and B
   d. Neither A nor B

6. When align honing, about how much material should be removed from the main bearing caps?
   a. 0.002 inch (0.05 millimeter)
   b. 0.004 inch (0.10 millimeter)
   c. 0.008 inch (0.20 millimeter)
   d. 0.010 inch (0.25 millimeter)

7. The surface finish of a cast-iron block deck should be _____.
   a. 10 to 30 RA
   b. 30 to 60 RA
   c. 60 to 100 RA
   d. 100 to 120 RA

8. A cast-iron V-8 engine has two cylinders that are tapered 0.005 inch (0.13 millimeter). Machinist A says to hone all cylinders and use standard piston rings. Machinist B says to bore all cylinders to the same oversize measurement. Which machinist is correct?
   a. A only
   b. B only
   c. Both A and B
   d. Neither A nor B

9. A cast-iron V-8 block has one cylinder that is out of round by 0.005 inch (0.13 millimeter). The other cylinders are worn just to the point of being 0.003 inch out of round. Machinist A says to sleeve the one cylinder. Machinist B says to bore the one cylinder. Which machinist is correct?
   a. A only
   b. B only
   c. Both A and B
   d. Neither A nor B

10. Machinist A says that an engine should be bored to the largest possible size. Machinist B says that 0.005 inch (0.13 millimeter) should be left for honing after the cylinder is bored. Which machinist is correct?
    a. A only
    b. B only
    c. Both A and B
    d. Neither A nor B

11. Machinist A says that torque plates should be attached to the block deck when cylinders are being bored. Machinist B says that torque plates should be used when honing cylinders. Which machinist is correct?
    a. A only
    b. B only
    c. Both A and B
    d. Neither A nor B

12. Machinist A says that a sizing hone can be used to straighten a wavy cylinder. Machinist B says that a flexible hone should be used after the cylinder has been bored. Which machinist is correct?
    a. A only
    b. B only
    c. Both A and B
    d. Neither A nor B

13. Machinist A says that a hone stone with a high grit number produces a rougher surface than does a hone with a lower grit number. Machinist B says that the stone grit recommended for use with moly piston rings is 150. Which machinist is correct?
    a. A only
    b. B only
    c. Both A and B
    d. Neither A nor B

14. A finished honed cylinder should have a maximum out-of-round measurement and taper of _____.
    a. 0.0005 inch (0.013 millimeter
    b. 0.003 inch (0.096 millimeter)
    c. 0.005 inch (0.127 millimeter)
    d. 0.008 inch (0.20 millimeter)

15. After the block is machined, all bolt holes should be _____.
    a. Enlarged to the next size with a tap
    b. Chamfered
    c. Beveled
    d. Plugged

16. Machinist A says that the piston ring grooves should be machined before installing replacement piston rings. Machinist B says that pistons can be knurled to be used in worn cylinders. Which machinist is correct?
    a. A only
    b. B only
    c. Both A and B
    d. Neither A nor B

17. A full-floating piston pin should have about how much clearance?
    a. No clearance—should be press fit
    b. No clearance—should be interference fit
    c. 0.0005 inch (0.013 millimeter)
    d. 0.002 inch (0.05 millimeter)

18. Machinist A says that all connecting rods should be checked for twist. Machinist B says that forged connecting rods cannot be straightened if bent. Which machinist is correct?

    a. A only
    b. B only
    c. Both A and B
    d. Neither A nor B

19. Machinist A says that powdered metal connecting rods can be reconditioned using the same method as that used for standard cast rods. Machinist B says that all connecting rods of the same engine can be interchanged. Which machinist is correct?
    a. A only
    b. B only
    c. Both A and B
    d. Neither A nor B

20. When the big end of a connecting rod is resized, _____.
    a. The center-to-center dimension of the rod is lengthened slightly
    b. The center-to-center dimension of the rod is shortened slightly
    c. The diameter of the big end is reduced by about 0.003 inch (0.08 millimeter)
    d. The diameter of the big end is increased by about 0.003 inch (0.08 millimeter)

21. A connecting rod can be straightened by _____.
    a. Bending the rod while it is cold
    b. Placing the rod in a hydraulic press
    c. Heating the rod and twisting it to be straight using a special tool
    d. Machining the cheeks of the small end and large end of the rod to be parallel to each other

22. Machinist A says that the connecting rods should be balanced to ensure a smoothly operating engine. Machinist B says that material should be removed from the heaviest connecting rod so that its weight matches that of the lightest rod in the engine. Which machinist is correct?
    a. A only
    b. B only
    c. Both A and B
    d. Neither A nor B

23. A forged crankshaft can be identified by _____.
    a. Its heavy weight as compared to that of a cast crankshaft
    b. A thick parting line
    c. A thin parting line
    d. Its being harder than a cast crankshaft.

24. Machinist A says that if your fingernail catches when rubbed across a bearing journal, the journal must be reground. Machinist B says that both the main and the rod bearing journal should be ground by the same amount to maintain proper crankshaft balance. Which machinist is correct?
    a. A only
    b. B only
    c. Both A and B
    d. Neither A nor B

25. Machinist A says that the crankshaft should be ground in the direction opposite that of normal rotation of the crankshaft. Machinist B says that the crankshaft should be pol-

ished after grinding, in the same direction as that of normal crankshaft rotation. Which machinist is correct?
a. A only
b. B only
c. Both A and B
d. Neither A nor B

26. Machinist A says that undersize crankshaft journals can be welded up, then ground to size. Machinist B says that the fillet area of the crankshaft can be shot blasted to increase the crankshaft strength. Which machinist is correct?
a. A only
b. B only
c. Both A and B
d. Neither A nor B

27. Crankshafts should be polished using what grit of polishing cloth?
a. 150
b. 180
c. 220
d. 320

28. What is attached to the crankshaft while it is being spin tested for balance?
a. Bob weights
b. External balance weights
c. Internal balance weights
d. Pistons with connecting rods

29. An externally balanced crankshaft can be changed to an internally balanced crankshaft by replacing the vibration damper.
a. True
b. False

30. Machinist A says that grinding the crankshaft relieves the stresses in the crankshaft. Machinist B says that blasting the fillet area of the journals with #320 steel shot relieves the stress. Which machinist is correct?
a. A only
b. B only
c. Both A and B
d. Neither A nor B

31. The recommended microinch surface finish for crankshaft journals is _____.
a. 10 to 14 RA
b. 18 to 32 RA
c. 45 to 72 RA
d. 60 to 100 RA

32. The recommended microinch surface finish for the connecting rod big end is _____.
a. 10 to 14 RA
b. 18 to 32 RA
c. 45 to 72 RA
d. 60 to 100 RA

33. The recommended microinch surface finish for a honed cylinder is _____.
a. 10 to 14 RA
b. 18 to 32 RA
c. 45 to 72 RA
d. 60 to 100 RA

34. Machinist A says that the top of the cylinder bore should be chamfered after the cylinder is bored. Machinist B says that the bolt holes should be chamfered after the block has been decked. Which machinist is correct?
a. A only
b. B only
c. Both A and B
d. Neither A nor B

35. Machinist A says that the dowel pins should be removed from the block before the deck surface is machined. Machinist B says that plateau honing should be performed "dry" (without cooling lubricant). Which machinist is correct?
a. A only
b. B only
c. Both A and B
d. Neither A nor B

36. Machinist A says that all oil holes in the crankshaft should be cleaned with a brush and solvent after machining. Machinist B says that the rope seal area of the crankshaft should be knurled after the crankshaft journals have been machined. Which machinist is correct?
a. A only
b. B only
c. Both A and B
d. Neither A nor B

37. Machinist A says that lifter bores should be cleaned and honed if necessary. Machinist B says that some lifter bores may be machined to be oversize at the factory. Which machinist is correct?
a. A only
b. B only
c. Both A and B
d. Neither A nor B

38. Connecting rods should not be heated to above _____.
a. 250° F (120° C)
b. 450° F (230° C)
c. 650° F (340° C)
d. 850° F (450° C)

39. Machinist A says that a cracked block may be repaired using a cylinder sleeve if the crack is located in the cylinder wall. Machinist B says that all cylinders should be bored to the same size in the same engine. Which machinist is correct?
a. A only
b. B only
c. Both A and B
d. Neither A nor B

40. Machinist A says that the cylinder hone should be stopped before it is removed from the finished cylinder. Machinist B says that the ridge at the top of the cylinder should be removed after the cylinder is honed. Which machinist is correct?
a. A only
b. B only
c. Both A and B
d. Neither A nor B

Engine Assembly Specialist Sample ASE Certification Test

1. After an engine block has been machined, it should be cleaned using _____.
   a. WD-40 and a clean cloth
   b. A brush with soap and water
   c. Engine oil and a clean cloth
   d. Solvent spray and brake cleaner

2. Technician A says that oil gallery plugs have to be installed before core plugs are installed. Technician B says that the oil gallery passages should be cleaned after the block has been machined and before the gallery plugs are installed. Which technician is correct?
   a. A only
   b. B only
   c. Both A and B
   d. Neither A nor B

3. Technician A says that a bottoming tap should be used to clean all block threads before assembly of the engine begins. Technician B says that a taper tap should be used. Which technician is correct?
   a. A only
   b. B only
   c. Both A and B
   d. Neither A nor B

4. Technician A says that on a counter bore, convex plugs should be driven into the block until they stop. Technician B says that convex plugs should be installed with the convex side of the plug facing outward. Which technician is correct?
   a. A only
   b. B only
   c. Both A and B
   d. Neither A nor B

5. Technician A says that a cup-type plug should be installed flush with the block. Technician B says that a cup-type plug should be installed using sealant and pressed in to about 0.020 to 0.050 inch below the surface of the block. Which technician is correct?
   a. A only
   b. B only
   c. Both A and B
   d. Neither A nor B

6. Technician A says that dirt is the major cause of premature engine bearing failure. Technician B says that the main bearings should be installed and torqued to specification before the gallery plugs are installed. Which technician is correct?
   a. A only
   b. B only
   c. Both A and B
   d. Neither A nor B

7. A small-block Chevrolet V-8 engine is being assembled. Technician A says that the cam bearings should be installed before the crankshaft is installed. Technician B says that the oil gallery plugs must be installed before the cam bearings are installed. Which technician is correct?
   a. A only
   b. B only
   c. Both A and B
   d. Neither A nor B

8. Technician A says that cam bearing clearance must be determined and corrected if necessary, before the camshaft is installed on an OHV-type engine. Technician B says that camshaft bearing clearance can be checked using plastic gauging material. Which technician is correct?
   a. A only
   b. B only
   c. Both A and B
   d. Neither A nor B

9. Technician A says that the crankshaft should be carefully inspected and measured after it is received back from the machine shop. Technician B says that the block should be carefully inspected and measured after it is received back from the machine shop. Which technician is correct?

a. A only
b. B only
c. Both A and B
d. Neither A nor B

10. Technician A says that both sides of the main bearing shells should be lubricated before installation. Technician B says that fingerprints can cause corrosion damage to bearings where they are touched by bare hands. Which technician is correct?
a. A only
b. B only
c. Both A and B
d. Neither A nor B

11. Technician A says that the crankshaft should be rotated for two complete revolutions after installing plastic gauging material when measuring main bearing oil clearance. Technician B says that crankshaft end play can be measured with a dial indicator (gauge). Which technician is correct?
a. A only
b. B only
c. Both A and B
d. Neither A nor B

12. Technician A says that plastic gauging material can be used to check crankshaft end play. Technician B says that plastic gauging material can be used to measure connecting rod bearing oil clearance. Which technician is correct?
a. A only
b. B only
c. Both A and B
d. Neither A nor B

13. Typical engine bearing oil clearance is _____.
a. 0.001 to 0.003 inch (0.025 to 0.076 millimeter)
b. 0.010 to 0.030 inch (0.25 to 0.76 millimeter)
c. 0.020 to 0.040 inch (0.51 to 1.02 millimeters)
d. 0.060 to 0.080 inch (1.52 to 2.03 millimeters)

14. Technician A says that the rear main seal should be installed before checking for correct oil clearances. Technician B says that the main bearing caps must be torqued to specification when checking main bearing oil clearance using plastic gauging material. Which technician is correct?
a. A only
b. B only
c. Both A and B
d. Neither A nor B

15. Technician A says that the tang on the bearing shell should line up with the slot in the bearing support. Technician B says that the tang is installed opposite to the slot in some engines. Which technician is correct?
a. A only
b. B only
c. Both A and B
d. Neither A nor B

16. Technician A says that a feeler (thickness) gauge can be used to measure thrust bearing clearance. Technician B says that oversize main thrust bearings may be available for engines on which the thrust bearing clearance is too great. Which technician is correct?
a. A only
b. B only
c. Both A and B
d. Neither A nor B

17. Technician A says that the vibration damper should be driven onto the nose of the crankshaft. Technician B says that some vibration dampers simply slip on the crankshaft. Which technician is correct?
a. A only
b. B only
c. Both A and B
d. Neither A nor B

18. Technician A says that each piston should be selectively fitted to each cylinder. Technician B says that a strip feeler (thickness) gauge should be used to determine proper piston-to-cylinder clearance. Which technician is correct?
a. A only
b. B only
c. Both A and B
d. Neither A nor B

19. The clearance between the piston and the cylinder is too great. Technician A says that the piston could be knurled. Technician B says that the cylinder could be honed to provide the proper clearance. Which technician is correct?
a. A only
b. B only
c. Both A and B
d. Neither A nor B

20. Two technicians are discussing piston ring end gap. Technician A says that if the gap is too great, excessive blowby can occur. Technician B says that if the gap is too small, the ring could break. Which technician is correct?
a. A only
b. B only
c. Both A and B
d. Neither A nor B

21. Typical piston ring end gap is _____.
a. 0.001 to 0.003 inch
b. 0.100 to 0.300 inch
c. 0.004 inch per inch of bore diameter
d. 0.010 inch per inch of stroke length

22. Two technicians are discussing piston installation. Technician A says that the cylinder should be wiped with a lintless cloth and coated with a film of oil. Technician B says that the connecting rod bearing should be installed on the connecting rod before the piston is installed in the cylinder. Which technician is correct?
a. A only
b. B only
c. Both A and B
d. Neither A nor B

23. Technician A says that pistons should be installed with the notch on the top of the piston head facing the front of the engine. Technician B says that the valve reliefs should be closest to the lifter valley on V-type OHV engines. Which technician is correct?
    a. A only
    b. B only
    c. Both A and B
    d. Neither A nor B

24. Technician A says that the connecting rod can be installed on the piston pin facing in either direction. Technician B says that the piston pin should be lubricated before the piston-rod assembly is installed. Which technician is correct?
    a. A only
    b. B only
    c. Both A and B
    d. Neither A nor B

25. When an engine is being assembled, proper clearance should be maintained between the piston skirt and the crankshaft counterweight. Most manufacturers recommend a main clearance of _____.
    a. 0.010 inch (0.25 millimeter)
    b. 0.025 inch (0.64 millimeter)
    c. 0.040 inch (1.02 millimeters)
    d. 0.060 inch (1.52 millimeters)

26. Two technicians are discussing connecting rod side clearance. Technician A says that if the clearance is too great, the crankshaft may require replacement. Technician B says that excessive side clearance may decrease oil pressure when the engine is running. Which technician is correct?
    a. A only
    b. B only
    c. Both A and B
    d. Neither A nor B

27. Technician A says that connecting rod side clearance can be measured using plastic gauging material. Technician B says that connecting rod side clearance can be measured with a micrometer. Which technician is correct?
    a. A only
    b. B only
    c. Both A and B
    d. Neither A nor B

28. Technician A says that the crankshaft should be rotated after the pistons are installed. Technician B says that the turning torque should be measured after the pistons have been installed. Which technician is correct?
    a. A only
    b. B only
    c. Both A and B
    d. Neither A nor B

29. Two technicians are discussing assembling an engine that has had both the cylinder head and the block deck machined. Technician A says that a thicker head gasket or a shim gasket can be used to compensate for the machining. Technician B says that longer pushrods should be used. Which technician is correct?
    a. A only
    b. B only
    c. Both A and B
    d. Neither A nor B

30. Two technicians are discussing head gaskets. Technician A says that all head gaskets require that the head bolts be retorqued after the engine has been run. Technician B says that the torque specifications for head bolts are for dry (nonlubricated) threads. Which technician is correct?
    a. A only
    b. B only
    c. Both A and B
    d. Neither A nor B

31. Technician A says that sealer should be used on head bolts that go into the cooling system. Technician B says that oil should be squirted into "dry" bolt holes before head bolts are installed. Which technician is correct?
    a. A only
    b. B only
    c. Both A and B
    d. Neither A nor B

32. Two technicians are discussing the tightening procedure for cylinder head bolts. Technician A says that the specified torque should be applied to each bolt in the specified sequence. Technician B says that the head bolt tightening sequence should be repeated three times, increasing the amount of torque on the bolts each time and reaching the specified torque on the final (third) repetition. Which technician is correct?
    a. A only
    b. B only
    c. Both A and B
    d. Neither A nor B

33. Two technicians are discussing the torque-to-yield type of head bolts. Technician A says that many manufacturers specify the use of new head bolts when the engine is assembled. Technician B says that the bolt should be rotated a specified number of degrees after the bolt has been tightened to a torque specification. Which technician is correct?
    a. A only
    b. B only
    c. Both A and B
    d. Neither A nor B

34. A gear-driven camshaft becomes locked up and will not rotate after the thrust plate has been torqued to specifications. Technician A says that a spacer may be missing. Technician B says that the camshaft has not been timed correctly with the crankshaft. Which technician is correct?
    a. A only
    b. B only
    c. Both A and B
    d. Neither A nor B

35. Technician A says that all hydraulic valve lifters should be "pumped up" in a container of engine oil before installation. Technician B says that the bottom of flat lifters should be covered with extreme pressure–type lubricant before being installed. Which technician is correct?
   a. A only
   b B only
   c. Both A and B
   d. Neither A nor B

36. Technician A says that valve lash (clearance) should be adjusted after the engine is started. Technician B says that all hydraulic lifters are self-adjusting and do not require any adjustment. Which technician is correct?
   a. A only
   b. B only
   c. Both A and B
   d. Neither A nor B

37. A type of assembly sealant that is used to fill voids or potential openings and that cures in the presence of moisture is called _____.
   a. RTV silicone
   b. Anaerobic
   c. Antiseize
   d. Contact adhesive

38. A type of assembly sealant that is used between two machined surfaces and that cures in the absence of air is called _____.
   a. RTV silicone
   b. Anaerobic
   c. Antiseize
   d. Contact adhesive

39. Technician A says that the distance between the oil pickup screen and the bottom of the oil pan should be measured. Technician B says that the distance between the oil pickup screen and the bottom of the oil pan should be about 0.25 inch (6 millimeters). Which technician is correct?
   a. A only
   b. B only
   c. Both A and B
   d. Neither A nor B

40. Technician A says that the oil pump should be rotated to force oil through the engine before the engine is started. Technician B says that the engine should be started and kept running at a fast idle to help break in a flat lifter type of camshaft. Which technician is correct?
   a. A only
   b. B only
   c. Both A and B
   d. Neither A nor B

Index